707 c1
bT

GRIFFITH COLLEGE
DUBLIN

ITF

GRIFFITH COLLEGE
DUBLIN

OOS 131 AND

THE McGRAW-HILL INTERNATIONAL SERIES IN SOFTWARE ENGINEERING

Consulting Editor

Professor D. Ince
The Open University

Other titles in this series

Portable Modula-2 Programming	Woodman, Griffiths, Souter and Davies
SSADM: A Practical Approach	Ashworth and Goodland
Software Engineering: Analysis and Design	Easteal and Davies
Introduction to Compiling Techniques: A First Course Using ANSI C, LEX and YACC	Bennett
Rapid Information Systems Development	Bell and Wood-Harper
An Introduction to Program Design	Sargent
Object Oriented Databases: Applications in Software Engineering	Brown
SSADM Version 4: A Users Guide	Eva
Object Oriented Software Engineering with C^{++}	Ince
Expert Database Systems: A Gentle Introduction	Beynon-Davies

PRACTICAL FORMAL METHODS WITH VDM

Derek Andrews

and

Darrel Ince

McGRAW-HILL BOOK COMPANY

London · New York · St Louis · San Francisco · Auckland · Bogotá · Caracas
Hamburg · Lisbon · Madrid · Mexico · Milan · Montreal · New Delhi · Panama
Paris · San Juan · São Paulo · Singapore · Sydney · Tokyo · Toronto

Published by
McGRAW-HILL Book Company Europe
SHOPPENHANGERS ROAD · MAIDENHEAD · BERKSHIRE SL6 2QL · ENGLAND
TEL: 0628 23432   FAX: 0628 770224

British Library Cataloguing in Publication Data
Andrews, Derek
  Practical formal methods with VDM.
  1. Computer systems. Software development. Mathematical models
  I. Title   II. Ince, D. (Darrel)
  005.131
  ISBN 0-07-707214-6

Library of Congress Cataloging-in-Publication Data
Andrews, Derek.
  Practical formal methods with VDM/Derek Andrews and Darrel Ince.
    p. cm.
  Includes bibliographical references and index.
  ISBN 0-07-707214-6
  1. Computer software—Development.   I. Ince, D. (Darrel)
II. Title.
QA76.76.D47A52   1991   90–24725
005. 1—dc20   CIP

12345 CL 94321

Typeset by Derek Andrews

and printed and bound in Great Britain by Clays Ltd, St Ives plc

CONTENTS

Preface   xiv

1 Formal methods—an introduction   1
  1.1 Introduction   1
  1.2 Modern software development   2
  1.3 The problems with software development   4
  1.4 The use of mathematics   5
  1.5 Summary   9

2 Logic   10
  2.1 Introduction   10
  2.2 Predicates   10
  2.3 Quantifiers   14
  2.4 Proof   19
  2.5 Three-valued logic   23
  2.6 More about proof   28
  2.7 Summary   32

3 A language for specification   33
  3.1 Introduction   33
  3.2 The role of mathematics in software development   34
  3.3 Mathematical specification   35
  3.4 Summary   46

4 Sets   47
  4.1 Introduction   47
  4.2 Boolean set operators   48
  4.3 Specifying sets   50
  4.4 Set operators that deliver sets   52
  4.5 Some set-based specifications   53
    4.5.1 A system for checking chemical reactor names   53
    4.5.2 A simple library system   58
    4.5.3 The computer-based thesaurus   60
  4.6 Summary   66

5 Maps   **67**
  5.1 Introduction   67
  5.2 Maps   68
  5.3 Map operators   69
  5.4 Some examples of specifications involving maps   71
    5.4.1 Bag operations   71
    5.4.2 A system for administering a record library   73
    5.4.3 A simple filing subsystem   76
  5.5 Functions in VDM   79
  5.6 Summary   81

6 Sequences   **82**
  6.1 Introduction   82
  6.2 Sequence operators   83
  6.3 Some specifications involving sequences   86
  6.4 Summary   94

7 Abstract syntax   **95**
  7.1 Why abstract syntax?   95
  7.2 Composite objects   95
    7.2.1 The mu-operator   102
  7.3 Abstract syntax   103
  7.4 Summary   110

8 Data invariants   **111**
  8.1 Introduction   111
  8.2 Specifying data invariants   112
  8.3 Summary   117

9 Specifying systems   **118**
  9.1 Introduction   118
  9.2 The commands of VDM   119
    9.2.1 Operations   125
    9.2.2 Patterns and bindings   126
      Patterns   126
      Bindings   126
  9.3 Input and output   127
    9.3.1 Sequential files   128
      Input   129
      Output   130
      Opening files   130
      Closing files   131
      Testing for end of file   131
  9.4 The design problem   132
    9.4.1 Data flow design   132
      The data flow diagram   132
      The context diagram   135
      Levelling   135

	Building a data flow diagram for a system	135
	Guidelines for drawing data flow diagrams	138
	Other hints	138
9.5	The order of operations revisited	138
9.6	Summary	141

10 Large systems **143**

10.1	Introduction	143
10.2	A library system	143
10.2.1	The state for the library	148
10.2.2	The operations	151
10.3	Text patterns	155
10.3.1	The abstract syntax of patterns	156
10.3.2	The concrete syntax for patterns	160
10.4	Cash dispenser system	162
10.4.1	The design problem	163
10.4.2	Dispensing cash	165
10.4.3	Managing the customer details	175
10.4.4	Conclusions	179
10.5	Summary	181

11 From specifications to code **183**

11.1	Introduction	183
11.2	Satisfying specifications	183
11.3	Stepwise refinement	186
11.3.1	Adding the pre-condition to the post-condition	190
11.4	Program refinement	191
11.4.1	The assignment command	191
11.4.2	Setting variables	192
11.4.3	Command sequences—divide and conquer	194
11.4.4	The conditional command—case analysis	197
11.4.5	The while loop command—iteration	199
11.5	Integer multiplication	202
11.5.1	The problem	202
11.5.2	Getting started	202
11.5.3	The refinement strategy continued	204
11.5.4	The final step	205
11.6	The division problem revisited	208
11.7	An alternative approach	210
11.7.1	Some additional rules	214
11.8	Summary	215

12 Program development   **216**

12.1 The factorial problem   216

    12.1.1 The first solution   216

    12.1.2 A second solution   218

    12.1.3 A third solution   220

12.2 Finding guards and invariants   221

    12.2.1 Identifying the loop type incorrectly   224

12.3 Some refinement examples   225

    12.3.1 A second approach to multiplication   226

    12.3.2 Fast division   227

    12.3.3 A simple sort algorithm   232

        The first attempt   233

        The other approach   235

    12.3.4 A search problem   238

12.4 Postscript—avoiding logical constants   243

12.5 Summary   243

13 Data refinement   **245**

13.1 Introduction   245

13.2 The cash dispenser problem   245

    13.2.1 The problem   245

    13.2.2 The next step   260

    13.2.3 Now where?   261

13.3 A character stack   263

    13.3.1 The stack as an array   264

    13.3.2 The stack as a linked list   267

13.4 Modelling data   272

    13.4.1 Sets   272

    13.4.2 Sequences   273

    13.4.3 Mappings   273

13.5 Summary   273

14 A simple text editor   **274**

14.1 Introduction   274

14.2 An architecture for the editor   274

14.3 The buffer   277

14.4 The editor commands   278

    14.4.1 The abstract syntax   278

    14.4.2 When are commands valid?   281

14.5 The specification of the text editor   285

    14.5.1 The specification of the editing commands   287

14.6 The specification of the file commands   291

    14.6.1 The file store   291

        The file commands   292

        Auxiliary definitions   293

    14.6.2 A control structure for the editor   294

14.7 Some properties of the specification   298

14.8 Summary   300

15 The development of the editor   **302**
  15.1 Introduction   302
  15.2 The high-level design of a text editor   302
  15.3 The development of the editing commands   308
       15.3.1 The insert command   308
               The *read-and-mark-text* operation   310
               The *move-text* operation   313
               The code for the *execute-insert* operation   314
       15.3.2 The copy command   314
       15.3.3 The delete command   315
       15.3.4 The move command   316
       15.3.5 The current-line command   318
       15.3.6 The show command   319
       15.3.7 The display command   319
       15.3.8 The find command   320
       15.3.9 The substitute command   320
  15.4 The development of the file commands   323
       15.4.1 The edit command   324
       15.4.2 The write command   325
  15.5 The specification revisited   326
  15.6 Summary   326

16 The buffer abstract machine   **329**
  16.1 Introduction   329
  16.2 The data refinement   330
  16.3 The proofs   335
       16.3.1 The *block-copy* operation   335
               The domain rule   335
               The range rule   336
       16.3.2 The *add-line* operation   336
               The domain rule   336
               The range rule   337
       16.3.3 The *delete-end* operation   338
               The domain rule   338
               The range rule   338
       16.3.4 The *block-move* operation   338
               The domain rule   338
               The range rule   339
       16.3.5 The *init-buffer* operation   341
               The domain rule   341
               The range rule   341
  16.4 Implementing the operations   341
       16.4.1 The proofs   341
               The *block-copy* operation   341
               The *add-line* operation   344
               The *read-line* operation   345
               The *change-line* operation   345
               The *delete-end* operation   346

The *block-move* operation	351
The *init-buffer* operation	356
16.4.2 The final step	356
16.5 Summary	357
17 The user interface	**358**
17.1 Introduction	358
17.2 The concrete syntax of the commands	358
17.2.1 A simple approach brings problems	358
17.2.2 A first try	360
17.2.3 The concrete syntax	360
17.2.4 A better representation	362
17.3 Deriving the code for the command processor	362
17.3.1 From graph to code	367
17.3.2 Translating the command syntax	370
17.3.3 Tokens	376
17.4 The control of the editor	380
17.4.1 The final program	380
17.5 Behind the scenes	382
17.6 Summary	383
18 Further development of the editor	**384**
18.1 An enhancement: the undo command	384
18.2 Implementing the undo command	385
18.3 Proving the undo command	388
18.4 Summary	391
19 Postscript	**393**
19.1 Introduction	393
19.1.1 A calculus of correctness	394
19.2 The VDM-SL Standard	395
19.3 Further Reading	395
19.3.1 Logic, sets, map and sequences	395
19.3.2 Specifying systems	395
19.3.3 Developing specifications	396
19.3.4 From specifications to code	396
19.3.5 Data refinement	397
19.3.6 Examples	397
19.3.7 VDM	397
19.3.8 Formal methods	398
19.4 BIBLIOGRAPHY	398

A A summary of notation   **402**
  Types   402
    The basic types   402
    Type definitions   402
  Logic   404
    Propositional operators   404
    Quantifiers   404
    Equivalent expressions   404
  Sets   405
    Set expressions   405
    Set prefix operators   405
    Set infix operators   406
  Sequences   407
    Sequence expressions   407
    Sequence prefix operators   407
    Sequence infix operators   408
    Sequence application   408
  Maps   408
    Map expressions   409
    Map prefix and postfix operators   409
    Map infix operators   409
    Map application   410
  Records   411
    Record expressions   411

B Some auxiliary functions   **412**
  Sets   412
  Sequences   412
    Subsequences   413
    Locating elements in a sequence   413
    Operations for changing elements of a sequence 414
    Operations for constructing new sequences   414
    Additional operators   415

C An overview of the specification language   **416**
  A syntax for the specification language   416
    A specification document   416
    Definitions   416
      Type definitions   416
      State definition   417
      Value definitions   417
      Function definitions   418
      Operation definitions   418
    Statements   418
    Expressions   420
      Expression preambles   420
      Choice expressions   420
      Unary expressions   421

	Binary expressions	422
	Quantified expressions	422
	Iota expression	422
	Set expressions	423
	Sequence expressions	423
	Map expressions	423
	Tuple expression	423
	Record expressions	423
	Apply expressions	424
	Lambda expressions	424
	Is expressions	424
Undefined expression		424
Names and identifiers		424
State designators		424
Patterns		425
Bindings		425
Lexical specification		425
	General	425
	The character representation	425
	The symbol representation	427
Operator precedence		428
	The family of combinators	428
	The family of applicators	428
	The family of evaluators	428
	The family of relations	429
	The family of connectives	429
	The family of constructors	430
	Grouping	430
The type operators		430
Differences from Standard VDM-SL		430
The executable specification language		431
Notation		432
D Proof obligations		**433**
Satisfiability		433
Data refinement		433
	Domain rule	434
	Range rule	434

E Program refinement rules   **435**

Equivalent specification rule   435

The constant introduction rule   435

Assignment rules   436

The semicolon rules   436

    Following assignment   437

    Leading assignment   437

Selection rules   437

The iteration rule   438

The function body rule   439

The add variable rule   439

The expand frame rule   439

The contract frame rule   439

Index   **440**

PREFACE

Software developers face major problems. There is a sad history of projects delivering software that is late and does not meet user requirements. Moreover, those projects that do manage to produce software that meets user requirements tend to overspend on budgets in order to do so. There are a number of reasons for this—some of these reasons are managerial and some technical—and this book is an attempt to describe one solution to many of the technical problems.

A large number of the technical problems arise from the notations that are used for development. Typically, a developer might use natural language for system specification, a graphical notation for design and a programming language for implementation. Using such notations leads to two problems. First, they are ambiguous and, consequently, are open to misinterpretation. Second, they are non-homogeneous and difficult to validate. For example, it is very difficult to check that a graphical design correctly implements a natural language system specification. It should be noted, however, that a graphical notation is an excellent tool for 'sketching' designs, and is also a good tool to think with—properties that are exploited in this book.

The solution is to use mathematics as a development medium: a software system is specified using discrete mathematics, its design is expressed in the same mathematics and it is programmed using a programming language that has precise mathematical semantics. Validation is then carried out by mathematical proof.

The mathematics used in this book is discrete mathematics—predicate calculus and set theory—the type of mathematics taught in the first year of a computer science degree. The development technique that we use is called VDM, which stands for the Vienna Development Method, invented at the IBM Vienna Laboratories.

The material in this book has been regarded as difficult. We believe that this is a myth. In order to demonstrate that it is a myth we have tried to make this book as sympathetic to the reader as possible; we hope that it is so sympathetic that it will make an excellent self-study text.

There are a number of features of this book which we hope will appeal to the reader. First, there are a large number of worked examples which the reader can carry out, and then compare with our answers. Second, there are a number of case studies which show systems being developed mathematically. One of the weaknesses of current books on mathematical methods of software development is that large scale programs are not described; we hope that this book will go some way towards overcoming this weakness.

There are a number of prerequisites for this book. First, the reader should have some understanding of predicate calculus and set theory. Although we do revise these concepts in the first part of the book we feel the reader should be relatively comfortable with the mathematical symbolism involved in these branches of mathematics. Second, the reader should have a knowledge of one high-level programming language.

Because of these prerequisites we would expect that this book could be read with profit by second-year undergraduate students on computer science courses, and by staff working in the computer industry. We have deliberately designed the book such that it can be studied in a number of ways. The first eight chapters are a very gentle introduction to VDM specifications. This would make it suitable as a text to accompany a course which concentrates on VDM as a specification method. The final eleven chapters are more difficult and describe the VDM specification language as a medium for development. We would envisage that this material would be used in conjunction with the first eight chapters to back up a course on abstract data types and formal software development.

The book has been written to show VDM being used in a rigorous style, rather than in a formal style. This choice is deliberate as the authors feel that it is necessary to understand the ideas behind the use of mathematics in software development before the methods are applied with full formality. (D.C.I. in his book 'Fashioning the Baroque' described the formal methods camp as being divided into two—Roundheads and Cavaliers—this book has been written for the Cavaliers.)

Chapters 1–10 of this book cover formal specification together with the necessary mathematical background and would be suitable for a course covering specification only.

Chapters 11–19 cover the area of program development—data refinement and program refinement. The process of deriving correct code specification. It should be noted that the proof rules in Chapters 11 and 13 are particularly difficult, especially on the first reading, but it is well worth while to persevere with them and to look at their applications in Chapters 12–17. In the development chapters the cavalier attitudes seem to take on distinctly 'roundhead pretensions' and the proofs look particularly complicated and formal. However, this is not so. The proofs are, by formal software development standards, quite informal and in fact, after some practice, many steps can be left out since the proof to be done is usually straightforward and obvious. This book is interested in teaching the ideas of software development and concepts of proof and the sort of strategies and techniques which need to be used to develop correct programs. We are not interested in proving the absolute correctness of programs—only a convincing argument that they are probably correct. Absolute correctness by proof is tedious and best left to machines, but it should be remembered that to be able to 'drive' such machines the idea of what needs to be proved and strategies for deriving proofs must be understood, and that is what the latter part of this book is about.

We also make no excuses for leaving much of the development to the reader. The book is trying to describe an overall approach rather than do all of the work, in fact completing the development makes an excellent project—others are also suggested.

There are a number of people who we would wish to thank. D.C.I. would like to thank his wife, Stephanie, who provided much needed support during the development of this book. D.J.A. would like to thank his wife, Lucinda who provided support, and his two children who put up with him while writing the text. D.J.A. would also like to thank Cliff Jones who has provided advice, encouragement and support over a long period of time, Rick Thomas who has commented on various drafts of this book and the students of Leicester University who acted as guinea pigs on the courses that used the material of this book.

We would both like to thank Andrew Ware, Senior commissioning editor at McGraw-

Hill and Camilla Myers and Liz Nemecek, Production Editors, for their patience and support. Final thanks must be to Mario Wolczko and Brian Ritchie who provided the base LaTeX macros used in this book, to Andrew Tervorrow who provided OzTeX, an implementation of TeX on the Apple Macintosh which was used to typeset the book and to all the other programmers who ported TeX related software to the Apple Macintosh.

FORMAL METHODS—AN INTRODUCTION

AIMS

- To describe how current software projects are organized.
- To describe some of the problems that occur with current software development methods.
- To demonstrate how mathematics can be used as a system specification and design specification language.
- To demonstrate some of the advantages of mathematics over current software notations.

1.1 INTRODUCTION

Many companies face major problems in software development. These problems surface in a number of ways: development teams going over budget, systems being delivered too late and which do not meet user requirements. The major reason for this is the fact that software systems, compared with other artefacts such as bridges or televisions, are much more complex. The number of interconnections between modules in a software system makes the number of interconnections in the most complex piece of electronic equipment look minuscule.

Over the last thirty years researchers and industrial developers have attempted to conquer this complexity. There is a long history of advances which have caused increases in productivity. These advances have included high-level programming languages, time-shared operating systems, software tools, better notations for system design and new development techniques such as object-oriented design. However, even these techniques seem to have only caused small increases in productivity.

A graphic indication of the problems that still occur is shown in Fig. 1.1. This shows the fate of eight American software projects. The figures are staggering: only $0.1m worth of software was used, while $3.2m worth of software was never delivered. Admittedly, these figures are from a small number of projects taken from a notoriously difficult application area: real-time defence systems. However, similar but less extreme figures can be extracted from today's software projects. For example, a report by the British House of Commons Public Accounts Committee highlighted an overspend of £4b pounds in terms of project cost over-runs on an annual budget of £8.2b—with the major culprit being software.

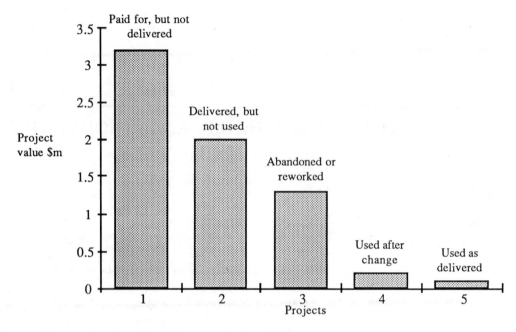

Figure 1.1   The fate of American software projects.

Before looking at the reasons why the tools and techniques we currently use have not affected our productivity it is worth describing, in a little detail, the way that we currently develop software.

1.2   MODERN SOFTWARE DEVELOPMENT

The modern software development project is normally split into a number of phases. These are: requirements analysis, system specification, system design, detailed design and programming. These phases are carried out in parallel with a series of tasks which check that the system under development is correct. These tasks are known collectively as *validation* and *verification*.

Requirements analysis is the process of discovering what a customer requires from a computer system. Requirements analysis is carried out using a number of means: interviewing customers and members of their staff, analysing questionnaires and examining the functions of a current manual or computerized system. The input to the requirements analysis process is a document known as the *statement of requirements*. This is usually written in natural language and varies in length from a single paragraph to a multi-volume work containing millions of words of text. A main feature of this document is that it will contain large numbers of errors, ambiguities and contradictions. This is to be expected—customers are not skilled in writing documentation.

The next stage of the development process is *system specification*. This is the process of writing down the characteristics of the system that is to be developed. These characteristics include *functions* and *constraints*. A function is a statement of what the system is to do: a constraint is some statement that constrains the performance of the system. An example of a function is the statement:

> When the *up* command is typed by the operator all radars that are functioning will be activated.

It tells the developer what a system is to do. Two examples of constraints are the statements:

> The response to all the commands must be less than 0.6 ms, even when the system is loaded at its peak.

> The system should fit into no more than 560K of main memory.

Normally, the system specification will also contain subsidiary information such as the training programme that is to be provided for the customer's staff. However, the main features of interest to the developer—and of course the customer—are the system functions and constraints. The main output from the system specification phase is a document called the system specification, a detailed account of the functions and constraints of a system with all the errors, ambiguities and contradictions in the statement of requirements removed.

The system specification is the main input document to *system design*. This is the process of defining the architecture of a system. This architecture is expressed in terms of chunks of software known either as modules, subroutines or procedures, depending on what programming languages are used. There are two reasons for this division into chunks. First, there will be actions which are required at many points in the software system. The natural way for this to be implemented would be as a subroutine called from many places in the system. The second reason for splitting a system into chunks is that in all software projects, apart from the most trivial, a number of programmers will be used and maximum use of these programmers' time is achieved by giving them tractable chunks of software to program. The major aim in system design is to produce an architecture that implements all the functions expressed in the system specification and at the same time respects the constraints expressed in that document.

The next phase of software development is *detailed design*. This is the process of defining the processing that occurs inside a particular module, procedure or subroutine. A number of notations have been designed for this. Flow charts were once a very popular notation for conveying detailed designs. However, these have virtually disappeared in favour of textual representations such as program design languages. A number of software developers omit the detailed design phase and progress directly to implementation.

The process of *implementation* involves the conversion of a detailed design—or system design, if detailed design is omitted—into executable program code. This is the easiest part of the software project; errors committed during this phase are much less serious than, say, an error committed during system specification which lies undetected until the end of the software project.

A set of activities that occur throughout the software project, which check that the system that is being developed is correct, are known collectively by the terms *validation* and *verification*. Validation checks that a system being developed meets user requirements. Verification checks that a task in the software project has been carried out correctly.

Probably the best known validation activities are *system testing* and *acceptance testing*. These are similar activities which check that the programmed software system meets user requirements by executing it with typical data. The major difference between system and acceptance testing is the fact that the former occurs within the developer's environment, with external devices such as nuclear reactors and avionics hardware being simulated by software; the latter is a test of the system within the environment in which it is intended to operate.

The best example of verification is *unit testing*: the process of checking a coded subroutine, module or procedure with test data. The aim of unit testing is to check that the programming process has been carried out correctly. The programmer develops a set of test data which checks the functionality of the coded module and ensures that this test data executes all the statements of the module and a high proportion of branches.

1.3 THE PROBLEMS WITH SOFTWARE DEVELOPMENT

Many of the problems in software development surface towards the end of the software project. Typical examples are:

1. The discovery, during integration testing, that the interfaces between individual chunks of the system are incompatible.
2. The discovery, during system testing, that major errors occur when normal test data is used: wrong data being displayed on a VDU, a VDU screen going blank in the middle of a transaction or wrong results being displayed.
3. An irate customer discovering during acceptance testing that many of the functions that are implemented in the final system have side-effects that interfere with the business and use of the system.

In order to examine why such events occur it is useful to focus in on the system specification. This document is the key document in the software project and a document that often exhibits many of the problems that bedevil software projects. The system specification is the key document on a project for a number of reasons. First, it is used by the designers in a project to develop the system design. Second, it is used by technical writers who develop user documentation. Third, it is used by quality assurance staff to produce the system and acceptance tests which check that a system meets user requirements.

Any problems in the system specification will surface in a number of ways: they will lead to a system design that does not meet user requirements, system and acceptance tests that check the wrong functions and constraints and a user manual that does not describe the system that has been developed.

The main medium currently used for system specifications is natural language, or in more advanced development environments graphical notations overlaid with natural language. Natural language is an excellent medium for poetry and novels, but has a number of disadvantages when used as a medium for describing a system precisely.

Part of the problem with natural language is educational; staff who enter computer companies usually come from a scientific and engineering environment where communicational skills tend to be de-emphasized in comparison with technical skills. Many analysts, designers and programmers have major problems with writing, evidenced by the loathing with which the documentation process is viewed by the large majority of staff. However, even if we conquer the problem of communicational skills—a prospect that is highly unlikely, considering the amount of resource that would be required—there still remains major problems with the medium of natural language itself.

The major problem is ambiguity. For example, consider the statement shown below, taken from a system specification:

> The operator name consists of the operator's name and password; the password consists of six digits. It should be displayed on the security VDU and deposited in the login file when an operator logs into the system.

In the extract above does the word 'it' refer to the password or the operator identity? Natural language also encourages the use of platitudes. It is a rare system specification that does not contain the phrase 'the system should be easy to use' or 'the system should be developed using well-understood principles'. Such platitudes often hide some functionality—for example, the phrase user-friendly might be a veiled reference to a WIMP interface or a help facility—however, it is the case that natural language encourages the expression of such platitudes, rather than the reality that lies below.

Another problem with natural language is that it is easy to write a system specification in which different levels of functionality are sprinkled together in the document. For example, a high-level description of a stock control system may be hidden by a large amount of details about its operations—including the format of screens and what keystrokes are required to carry out certain functions. While such detail is important it is really only needed later in a project, during system design, and should not hide the essential functions of a system.

A further problem with natural language as a specification medium is that it encourages the inclusion of implementation and design details. Such directives usually tell the developer to design a system in a particular way, or give details that are only important during the later implementation stages of a project. We have seen many specifications containing statements such as:

> The main file should have an indexed sequential organization.

> The system should contain modules that read in a data item from the main sensor, write a data item to the VDU screen and overwrite the customer database.

Such statements should be discouraged: they clutter up the system specification and overconstrain the developer in seeking solutions. Design and implementation directives often prevent the developer from seeking optimal designs.

The next section of this chapter contains a brief introduction to the use of mathematics in system development. If your mathematical knowledge is sparse or you feel a little shaky about mathematics it is worth skipping this section and reading the next three chapters which teach the mathematics in some detail. It might then be worth your while to return to this subsection.

1.4   THE USE OF MATHEMATICS

The aim of this section is to describe, in outline, how mathematics can be used as a specification notation during system specification and system design. In order to illustrate this a simple example is used: that of a symbol table for a compiler. Such a symbol table would hold program identifiers during the compilation process and is used to check the syntax of a program and generate object code. Let us assume, first, that no more than

MAXIDS identifiers will be held in the table and, second, that a number of operations on the symbol table have been identified. These operations are *initialize*, which sets up an empty symbol table; *insert*, which inserts a particular identifier into a symbol table; *delete*, which removes a particular identifier from a symbol table; and *check*, which checks that a particular identifier is in a symbol table.

In a mathematical specification the stored data is usually modelled by a mathematical structure. In this example the structure used is a set: a collection of objects that contains no duplicates. The set used in this example will be a set of identifiers. Notice that the set exactly captures the properties of the symbol table without any extraneous details being involved. The major property of a symbol table is that it contains identifiers where there are no duplicates. The set definition contains no extraneous details such as the storage medium on which the set is held or the organization of the symbol table—whether it is an array or a linked list.

The first mathematical extract that is required is a statement known as the *data invariant*. This states what must be true of the stored data in an application throughout the life of the application. In the case of the symbol table example the number of identifiers must never exceed *MAXIDS*. This is written as

$$\text{card } sym\text{-}table \leq MAXIDS$$

where card is the cardinality operator which gives the number of members currently in a set. The next stage is to define the operations. In the remainder of this book you will see, in greater detail, that operations such as *insert* and *delete* can be written in a mathematical system specification using a statement known as a *pre-condition* and a statement known as a *post-condition*.

A pre-condition states what must be true in order for an operation to be defined and a post-condition defines the result of the processing that an operation carried out. As an example of the use of these statements consider the *insert* operation. For this operation to be defined the identifier to be inserted must not be in the symbol table and there must be less than *MAXIDS* identifiers in the table. This can be written as

$$\text{pre } id \notin sym\text{-}table \wedge \text{card } sym\text{-}table < MAXIDS$$

where *id* is the identifier to be inserted and *sym-table* is the symbol table. The result of the *insert* operation will be defined by the post-condition.

$$\text{post } sym\text{-}table = \overleftarrow{sym\text{-}table} \cup \{id\}$$

This states that after the *insert* operation has been executed the symbol table is updated by forming the union of the previous value of the symbol table and a singleton set containing the program identifier to be inserted. The 'hook' symbol over an identifier is used to show the value of a variable before an operation is executed. The second argument to the union operator, *id*, is enclosed in curly brackets since the union operator requires sets as its operands. The specification of the *delete* operation in terms of pre- and post-conditions is shown below:

$$\text{pre } id \in sym\text{-}table$$

$$\text{post } sym\text{-}table = \overleftarrow{sym\text{-}table} - \{id\}$$

The pre-condition states that for the operation to be defined the program identifier must be contained in the symbol table. The post-condition states that after the operation has been completed the symbol table will be equal to the old value of the symbol table with the program identifier removed.

The specification of the *check* command is shown below. There is no pre-condition since it is defined no matter what state the symbol table is in. This is written as true. The result of the operation is a Boolean value denoted by r and is true if the program identifier is in the symbol table and false otherwise.

> pre true
>
> post $r \Leftrightarrow (id \in sym\text{-}table)$

Finally, the *initialize* command can be defined. The pre-condition is true and the post-condition is that an empty symbol table is created, i.e. an empty set is created:

> pre true
>
> post $sym\text{-}table = \{\,\}$

This, then, is a way of specifying a system: in terms of operations and pre- and post-conditions that affect the stored data of the system. This represents the top-level specification. It is also possible to use this form of specifications for design.

Assume that we are faced now with the process of design. This involves the system designer looking at the system specification, extracting out non-functional requirements, such as the response time and maximum amount of memory to be used, and defining an architecture that respects these constraints. Let us assume that this has been done and that the designer has fixed on an implementation that involves some form of ordered storage, for example using a linked list, and that the algorithm used for the table involves adjusting the position of an element that has just been looked up. The adjustment involves the movement of the element to the front of the list. This means that, on average, frequently accessed elements will be at the front of the list.

This arrangement is highly effective in terms of lookup time when a small number of elements in a symbol table are frequently accessed, and for relatively large tables makes a linear search a feasible proposition. An example of this occurring is shown in Fig. 1.2.

The top half of Fig. 1.2 shows the state of the list before the operation *check* occurs, while the bottom half shows the state of the list after the *check* operation has been carried out with the identifier 'F' as its argument. For the sake of simplicity the list is shown holding only single-letter identifiers.

The list can be represented by enumerating its elements between square brackets. Thus, the list shown in the top half of Fig. 1.2 can be written as

$$[\text{A}, \text{C}, \text{V}, \text{F}, \text{G}, \text{K}]$$

The data invariant for this new structure will be

> len $sym\text{-}tabler \leq MAXIDS \wedge$
>
> len $sym\text{-}tabler = $ card elems $sym\text{-}tabler$

where *sym-tabler* is the new representation of the symbol table. The first conjunct states that no more than $MAXIDS$ identifiers will be stored in the list. The second conjunct states that each element of the list will be unique. This conjunct uses the operator elems. This forms the set of all elements in the members of the list *sym-tabler*. This predicate will only be true if there all the elements of the list are unique. The pre- and post-conditions for the *insert* command are

> pre len $sym\text{-}tabler < MAXIDS \wedge id \notin$ elems $sym\text{-}tabler$

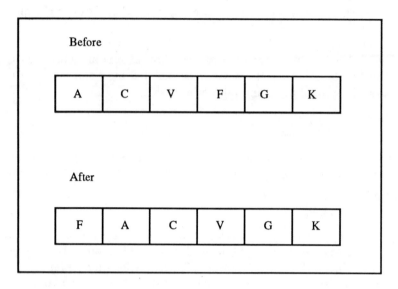

Figure 1.2   An example symbol table used for the *check*(F) operation.

and

$$\text{post } \textit{sym-tabler} = \overleftarrow{\textit{sym-tabler}} \ ^\frown [id]$$

The pre-condition is similar to that in the previous *insert* operation: it states that there must be room in the list for the identifier, denoted by *id*, that is to be inserted and is not already present. The post-condition is different. It uses the $^\frown$ operator that concatenates or joins together two lists. In the post-condition above it is used to specify that after the *insert* operation has been applied the new list will be the old list concatenated with a list that contains the single element *id*.

The specification of the new *delete* operation is a little more difficult. The pre-condition is that the element to be deleted occurs as an element in *sym-tabler*. This can be written as

$$\text{pre } id \in \text{elems } \textit{sym-tabler}$$

The post-condition can be written as:

$$\text{post } \exists i \in \{0\} \cup \text{inds } \textit{sym-tabler} \cdot$$
$$\textit{sym-tabler}(1, \dots, i) \ ^\frown$$
$$[id] \ ^\frown$$
$$\textit{sym-tabler}(i+1, \dots, \text{len } \textit{sym-tabler}) = \overleftarrow{\textit{sym-tabler}}$$

The post-condition states that there is a natural number i for which the old value of *sym-tabler* will be the new value of the *sym-tabler* up to the $(i-1)$th element concatenated with *id* and then concatenated with the new value of *sym-tabler* from the ith element to the last element. The expression $\textit{sym-tabler}(i, \dots, j)$ stands for the sub-sequence of elements starting at the ith element and finishing at the jth element. In fact, we could re-write this specification, using an auxiliary function (see Appendix B); the *del* function deletes the ith element of a list.

$$\text{post } \exists i \in \text{inds } \overset{\frown}{sym\text{-}tabler} \cdot del(\overset{\frown}{sym\text{-}tabler}, i) = sym\text{-}tabler \wedge$$

$$\overset{\frown}{sym\text{-}tabler}(i) = id$$

The specification of the new *check* command is shown below. The pre-condition is true. The post-condition is

$$\text{post } r \Leftrightarrow id \in \text{elems } \overset{\frown}{sym\text{-}tabler} \wedge$$

$$(\exists i \in \text{inds } \overset{\frown}{sym\text{-}tabler} \cdot \overset{\frown}{sym\text{-}tabler}(i) = id \wedge$$

$$sym\text{-}tabler = [id] \overset{\frown}{} del(\overset{\frown}{sym\text{-}tabler}, i)$$

$$\vee$$

$$id \notin \text{elems } \overset{\frown}{sym\text{-}tabler} \wedge$$

$$sym\text{-}tabler = \overset{\frown}{sym\text{-}tabler})$$

The first term defines the result of the operation: true if the identifier is in the symbol table, false otherwise. As before the identifier r denotes the boolean result of the operation. If the identifier is found in the original (initial) value of $sym\text{-}tabler$[1] then the predicate involving two conjuncts holds. The first of these just states that the list contains the element id which is being sought for, and remembers its position. The second conjunct states that the remainder of $sym\text{-}tabler$, after the first element, will be equal to the value of $sym\text{-}tabler$ before the operation, apart from the identifier we have found, which is moved to the front. This conjunct uses existential quantification to identify a value of i which gives the position of id in the input value of $sym\text{-}tabler$. The second pair of conjuncts holds if the identifier is not in the symbol table and in this case we do nothing.

There are many more details to be given about the use of discrete mathematics for the specification of systems; for example the exact syntax of pre-conditions, post-conditions and data invariants have not yet been outlined; neither have we discussed the validation process which checks that a design meets a system specification. Suffice it to say that the remainder of this book will discuss these topics in very much more detail.

What is important at this stage is for you to recognize that mathematics is an excellent medium for modelling an application. Modelling lies at the heart of any engineering discipline. It involves deriving a representation of an artefact in which unimportant detail is omitted. Mathematics enables the developer to omit much of this detail: platitudes, constraints, design directives and implementation directives.

1.5 SUMMARY

This chapter has described many of the deficiencies found in current system specification notations. It has attempted to convince you that mathematics offers a major hope of alleviating these deficiencies. The chapter has also sketched how mathematics can be used for system specifications: to document a data invariant which describes the constant properties of the stored data of a system and to document pre- and post-conditions of operations—a pre-condition being a condition that must be true for an operation to be executed and a post-condition being a condition that must hold after an operation is executed.

---

[1]Remember that the input (initial) value of an identifier is denoted by writing a hook over the identifier name: $\overset{\frown}{sym\text{-}tabler}$.

2

LOGIC

AIMS

- To describe how logic can be used to express the specification of a system.
- To describe the main facilities of the branch of logic known as predicate calculus.
- To demonstrate some simple rules of inference that can be used in formal methods of software development.
- To outline the relevance of three-valued logic to the particular development method described in this book.

2.1 INTRODUCTION

The previous chapter described a number of problems that affect software development. The key to the solution of these problems lies in the use of discrete mathematics which provides an exact basis for describing system specifications, system designs and, of course, program code. This chapter looks at the building block of discrete mathematics: logic or, to be more precise, that branch of logic known as predicate calculus. Subsequent subsections will describe the operators of predicate calculus and examine how simple proofs can be carried out within predicate calculus. Towards the end of the chapter the topic of three-valued logic will be examined. This is a form of logic that is particularly relevant to the development method that this book describes: VDM. However, before proceeding it is worth first answering the question: what is a predicate?

2.2 PREDICATES

A predicate is an expression that can be true or false and whose value is determined by the value of its constituents. Some examples of predicates are shown below:

$$x > 23$$
$$a + b \leq 4000$$
$$a = 34 \wedge b = 2000$$
$$a = i + u \wedge u = s^2$$

The first predicate is straightforward: all it says is that if x is greater than 23 then its value will be true, and false otherwise. The second predicate is slightly more complicated: it states that its value will be true if the sum of a and b is less than or equal to 4000, and false otherwise. The third predicate is a little more complicated: it involves the use of a logical operator ∧ which stands for *and*. The predicate states that it will be true if both *a* is equal to 34 and *b* is equal to 2000. We shall discuss the use of operators such as ∧ in a later part of this section.

The four examples above are predicates: they all have the value true or false and their value depends on the value of their constituents. For example, the value of the third predicate depends on the value of the variables denoted by the identifiers *a* and *b*.

During the discussion of logic in this chapter we shall assume that arithmetic expressions can be written in the way that you would write them in a programming language, but we will use some mathematical symbols that are available. For example, all the following are examples of valid arithmetic expressions:

$$(a + b/34 + s^3) \times 44 - w^5$$
$$sum \times opsum - 78$$
$$(azimuth - distance \times 80)^2$$
$$\sin(i + w)$$

Identifiers are (roughly) equivalent to programming language identifiers and the whole range of arithmetic operators will be used.

What will also be used will be predicate calculus operators such as ∧. These operators are either binary (take two arguments), or unary (take one argument). The first operator we shall describe is the one that has already been introduced, the *and* operator. Predicate calculus operators are defined in a special way in that they are defined by the values that they yield for different values of their arguments. This is displayed in a table-like structure known as a truth table. The truth table for the *and* operator is shown below:

	$A \wedge B$	B	
		true	false
A	true	true	false
	false	false	false

The truth table shows all the combinations of the variables A and B and the corresponding values of the expression $A \wedge B$. For example, it shows that if A is false and B is false then the corresponding value of $A \wedge B$ is false. The major point to notice about the table above is that the value of $A \wedge B$ is true *if and only if* the values of its operands, or as they are often called conjuncts, are themselves true.

Given such a truth table we can determine the values of predicate calculus expressions that contain the *and* operator. For example, the expression

$$a = 12 \wedge b > 34$$

is false if the value of *a* is 23 and the value of *b* is 78. The reason that it is false is that although *b* is greater than 34, *a* is certainly not equal to 12. Hence the first argument is false and the second argument is true, giving a false value to the whole expression. What then might be the value of the expression

$$a = 12 \wedge b > 34 \wedge sum = 12 \wedge prod > 34$$

if *a* is equal to (denotes the value) 12, *b* is equal to 234, *sum* is equal to 12 and *prod* is equal to 34. This expression contains three *and* operators, but, unfortunately, our truth table only contains one *and* operator. The way out of this dilemma is simple and that is to specify the rules of precedence that hold when the value of expressions are evaluated. When we evaluate arithmetic expressions we have rules of precedence which state, for example, that the arithmetic expression $a + b \times c$ is evaluated as $a + (b \times c)$ and not as $(a + b) \times c$ with the addition operator taking precedence over the multiplication operator.

The precedence rule for predicate calculus expressions which all contain the same operator is to evaluate them from left to right. Thus the expression above would be evaluated as

$$(((a = 12 \wedge b > 34) \wedge sum = 12) \wedge prod > 34)$$

where the innermost brackets would be evaluated first, this gives an order of evaluation as

$$((\text{true} \wedge sum = 12) \wedge prod > 34)$$
$$(\text{true} \wedge prod > 34)$$
$$\text{true} \wedge \text{false}$$
$$\text{false}$$

When you have had a lot of practice with the evaluation of predicate calculus expressions you will be able to short circuit such evaluations by spotting patterns which reduce the work considerably. For example, in the predicate calculus expression which we have evaluated above the fact that one of the arguments is false means that the final value of the expression is false.

There are a number of rules of precedence for predicate calculus expressions. However, they will be described later in this chapter—after more operators are described.

The next operator is the *or* operator. Its truth table is shown below

		B	
$A \vee B$		true	false
A	true	true	true
	false	true	false

It shows that the result of an expression involving two arguments is true if at least one of the arguments is true and false otherwise. The arguments of the *or* operator are known as *disjuncts*.

A unary operator which is frequently used in the predicate calculus is the *not* operator. This has the effect of reversing the value of its truth value. Its truth table is shown below:

A	$\neg A$
true	false
false	true

The last two operators are shown below. The first is the equivalence operator $\Leftrightarrow$ which has the value true when both its arguments have the same truth value. The other operator is the implication operator $\Rightarrow$. The truth table for the equivalence operator is

		B	
$A \Leftrightarrow B$		true	false
A	true	true	false
	false	false	true

and the truth table for the implication operator is

		B	
$A \Rightarrow B$		true	false
A	true	true	false
	false	true	true

The equivalence operator stands for the English phrase *if and only if*. For example, the expression

raining   ⇔   take umbrella

stands for *if and only if it is raining will I take an umbrella*; that is if I am seen with an umbrella (outside) then you can be sure that it is raining, and that if it is raining I will be seen with an umbrella.

The implication operator stands for *if . . . then*, thus the expression

raining   ⇒   take umbrella

means *if it is raining, then I will take an umbrella*. There is a subtle difference between this and the equivalence operator. The expression above means that if it is raining then I will be seen outside with an umbrella. However, if I am seen outside with an umbrella it does not mean that it is raining; for example, the sky could just be cloudy and I could be taking a wise precaution. The use of the equivalence operator would guarantee that if I had my umbrella outside then it would be raining.

There are a number of rules of precedence that determine the order in which predicate calculus expressions are evaluated. Already you have seen one example of these rules: that when a series of expressions are separated by *and* operators the evaluation is from left to right. This is but a special case of the first rule of precedence shown below. The rules are:

1. When a series of predicate calculus expressions are separated by the same binary operator the evaluation is from left to right.
2. When an expression contains brackets the expressions that contain the deepest brackets are evaluated first, followed by the next deepest bracketed expression and so on.
3. The precedence of operators is ⇔ , ⇒ , ∨, ∧, and ¬, with the equivalence operator having the lowest precedence and the negation operator having the highest precedence.

The precedence rules mean that an expression such as

$$a \lor b \land c \implies d \land e$$

would be evaluated in the order indicated by the bracketed version of the expression shown below:

$$(a \lor (b \land c)) \implies (d \land e)$$

First, the arguments of the ∨ operator are evaluated, this is followed by the expressions involving the ∧ operators and, finally, the expression involving the ⇒ operator.

Worked example 2.1 What is the order of evaluation of the following predicate. Write down your answer by enclosing the expression in brackets that indicate the order of evaluation.

$$\neg a \lor b \land c \implies d \lor r \iff s \lor e \land w \lor f \land k$$

SOLUTION

$$(((\neg a) \lor (b \land c)) \implies (d \lor r)) \iff ((s \lor (e \land w)) \lor (f \land k))$$

■

Given this method of evaluating expressions in the predicate calculus it is now very easy to calculate the value of a particular expression. For example, the expression

$$a \lor b \land c \Leftrightarrow k \land l$$

can be calculated given that a is equal to true, b is equal to false, c is equal to true, k is equal to false and l is equal to true. First, we determine the order of evaluation. This is shown below, with brackets denoting the order:

$$(a \lor (b \land c)) \Leftrightarrow (k \land l)$$
$$(a \lor (\text{false} \land \text{true})) \Leftrightarrow (k \land l)$$
$$(a \lor \text{false}) \Leftrightarrow (k \land l)$$
$$(\text{true} \lor \text{false}) \Leftrightarrow (k \land l)$$
$$\text{true} \Leftrightarrow (\text{false} \land \text{true})$$
$$\text{true} \Leftrightarrow \text{false}$$
$$\text{false}$$

First, the expressions enclosed by the innermost brackets are evaluated by looking up their value in a truth table, followed by the next innermost, and so on. Finally the whole expression is reduced to a particular truth value.

Exercise 2.1

1. If a is equal to 12, b is equal to 34, c is equal to 99 and d is equal to 1038 what are the values of the following expressions:

   (a) $a + b$

   (b) $a < b \land a = b$

   (c) $a \times b > c \lor a + c > d \lor \text{true}$

   (d) $(a = 12 \lor b < 23) \Leftrightarrow c = 4 \land d = 5 \land d = 44 \Leftrightarrow b < 34$

   (e) $a + b > 2 \Rightarrow c + d > 3 \Rightarrow a = 12$

   (f) a^2

2. By bracketing the following expressions show the order of evaluation. Assume that a, b, c, d and e are expressions that have either a true or false value.

   (a) $a \lor b \lor c \lor d \lor e$

   (b) $a \lor b \lor c \lor d \Rightarrow e$

   (c) $a \Rightarrow c \Leftrightarrow d \Rightarrow b \Rightarrow e \Leftrightarrow b \Rightarrow e \Leftrightarrow b \land c$

   (d) $a \Rightarrow \neg\neg\neg\neg b \Rightarrow c$

   (e) $a \land e \land c \land b \lor d \land e$

   (f) $(a \land b \Rightarrow c) \Leftrightarrow d \land e \lor a \Rightarrow c \land d$

2.3 QUANTIFIERS

The predicates that we have described so far in this book have not been totally adequate to describe realistic systems. The aim of this section is to describe a further facility in the predicate calculus which enables collections of objects to be described and reasoned about. In order to do this we first have to introduce a concept that is described in much more detail in Chapter 4: the set. For the purposes of this chapter we shall define a set as a collection of objects of which none is equal to another. One particular set that we will refer to a large number of times in this chapter is $\mathbb{N}$, the set of natural numbers starting at 0 and finishing at plus infinity. Another set is the set $\{a, \ldots, b\}$ which is the collection of integers starting at a and finishing at b and including both of these values. Thus, $\{3, \ldots, 9\}$ represents the seven consecutive integers starting at 3 and finishing at 9.

In order to reason about collections of objects such as N, two operators known as quantifiers are used. The first quantifier is known as the universal quantifier and it describes a predicate that must hold for all the items inside a collection of objects. The general form of the universal quantifier is

$$\forall t \in T \cdot predicate$$

where t is a variable that ranges over the set T and takes as its value each member of T, and predicate is a predicate that involves t and is true for every value of t selected from the set T. An example of such a predicate is shown below:

$$\forall n \in \{1, \ldots, 20\} \cdot n^2 < 10000$$

This states that for every value of n taken from the collection of consecutive integers starting at 1 and finishing at 20 each n, when squared, will be less than 10000.

Worked example 2.2 Write down the predicate that states that all the integers between 1 and 33 will be less than 200.

SOLUTION

$$\forall n \in \{1, \ldots, 33\} \cdot n < 200$$

∎

An important point to make is that the variable inside a quantified expression—known as a bound variable—can be of any form. For example, a correct answer to the preceding worked example would be

$$\forall p \in \{1, \ldots, 33\} \cdot p < 200$$

or

$$\forall var \in \{1, \ldots, 33\} \cdot var < 200$$

You can in fact put more than one variable into a quantified expression. For example, the predicate below states that for any two natural numbers x and y, if x is not equal to y then x is either greater than y or x is less than y.

$$\forall x, y \in \mathsf{N} \cdot x \neq y \Rightarrow x > y \lor x < y$$

Remember that the $\Rightarrow$ operator stands for 'if … then …'. The predicate above can then be read as: when we take any two natural numbers x and y from the collection of natural numbers, if x is not equal to y then it must be greater than or less than y.

Worked example 2.3 Write down the predicate that states that if any two natural numbers differ by one then the two numbers are not equal to each other.

SOLUTION

$$\forall x, y \in \mathsf{N} \cdot x = y + 1 \Rightarrow x \neq y$$

∎

It is important to realize the exact meaning of the universal quantifier. What is hidden under this facility is a series of conjuncts. For example, the predicate

$$\forall x \in \{1, \ldots, 5\} \cdot x < 10$$

stands for the predicate

$$1 < 10 \wedge 2 < 10 \wedge 3 < 10 \wedge 4 < 10 \wedge 5 < 10$$

What is hidden under a universal quantifier is a possible infinite chain of predicates separated by the *and* operator. As well as having a number of bound variables ranging over the same set it is also possible to have the bound variables ranging over a number of sets. In this book you will rarely find more than two such sets. An example of this is shown below:

$$\forall x \in \{1, \ldots, 5\}, y \in \{5, \ldots, 10\} \cdot x = y \implies x = 5$$

This states that if you take a number from the set of numbers from 1 to 5 and a number from the set of numbers ranging from 5 to 10 , and if the numbers are equal, then the number extracted from each set must be 5.

Worked example 2.4   Write down the predicate that states that if you take a number from the set $\{1, \ldots, 6\}$ and the set $\{3, \ldots, 1000\}$ then the sum of the numbers must lie between 4 and 1006.

SOLUTION

$$\forall x \in \{1, \ldots, 6\}, y \in \{3, \ldots, 1000\} \cdot 4 \leq x + y \wedge x + y \leq 1006$$

∎

It is important to point out at this stage that quantified expressions are predicates, and that just like predicates they can take true or false values. For example, it is quite permissible to write

$$\forall x \in \{1, \ldots, 5\} \cdot x > 10\,000$$

even though the predicate is false.

The second quantifier that we will describe in this section is the existential quantifier. This asserts that a predicate is true for *at least* one value in a collection—or set—of values. The existential quantifier is distinguished from the universal quantifier by the use of the symbol $\exists$. An example of its use is shown below:

$$\exists x \in \{1, \ldots, 5\} \cdot x < 3$$

What this predicates states is that there is at least one value of x contained in the collection of integers from 1 to 5 such that x is less than three. In fact there are two. An important point to make about the existential quantifier is that it asserts that a property holds for at least one item in a set. The form of a predicate involving the existential quantifier is exactly the same as that involving the universal quantifier.

Worked example 2.5   Write down the predicate that states that there is at least one natural number that lies between 3 and 8.

SOLUTION

$$\exists x \in \mathbf{N} \cdot 3 \leq x \wedge x \leq 8$$

∎

In the same way that the universal quantifiers can have their bound variables ranging over a number of sets the existential quantifier has this property too. For example, the predicate

$$\exists x, y \in \{1, \ldots, 10\} \cdot x + y = 19$$

states that in the set of consecutive natural numbers ranging from 1 to 10 there are at least two integers which, when added together, give 19. These would be 9 and 10.

Another example of this mixing of sets is shown below in the predicate

$$\exists x \in \{1, \ldots, 8\}, y \in \{10, \ldots, 100\} \cdot x \times y = 81$$

which is true since it describes the integers 3 and 27.

Worked example 2.6 Write down the predicate that states that there is at least one natural number in the set of consecutive integers starting at 1 and finishing at 100 and one natural number in the set of natural numbers starting at 200 and finishing at 500 which are equal.

SOLUTION

$$\exists i \in \{1, \ldots, 100\}, j \in \{200, \ldots, 500\} \cdot i = j$$

∎

As well as sets such as $\{1, \ldots, 100\}$ and $\mathbf{N}$, sets can be denoted by variable names. For example, the predicate

$$\exists x \in a \cdot x < 100$$

asserts that inside the set a, assumed to contain natural numbers, there is an element that is less than 100.

Worked example 2.7 Write down the predicate that states that there are no elements in the set ss of natural numbers that lie between 3 and 100.

SOLUTION

$$\forall i \in ss \cdot i \leq 3 \vee 100 < i$$

∎

So far we have shown how existential and universal quantifiers can be used by themselves. However, the full power of this facility can be obtained when they are combined together. For example, the statement that in the set a there is an element that is greater or equal to all the other elements in the set can be written as

$$\exists i \in a \cdot \forall j \in a \cdot i \geq j$$

This just states that there is an element i inside a which when compared with each of the elements of a will be greater or equal to them.

Worked example 2.8 Which of the following predicates are true and which are false for any finite set of numbers?

$$\exists i \in a \cdot \forall j \in a \cdot i \geq j$$
$$\exists i \in a \cdot \forall j \in a \cdot i > j$$

SOLUTION   The first predicate will be true since there will always be a member of a set of numbers that is greater than or equal to all the others: it is the maximum number. The second predicate is, however, false. The universally quantified part is applied to every element of a including i, and i can never be greater than itself.   ∎

Another example of the use of both universal quantifier and existential quantifiers is the translation of the statement there exists a particular number in a set, say a, that is a prime. This can be written as

$$\exists i \in a \cdot \forall j \in \mathbb{N} \cdot \neg \exists k \in \mathbb{N} \cdot j \times k = i$$

All this states is that there is an element i inside a that cannot be formed by multiplying one natural number by another natural number. Is this predicate correct? The answer is no.

Worked example 2.9 Why is the above predicate not correct? Can you modify it so that it becomes correct?

SOLUTION   The predicate is not correct because there is a natural number that when multiplied by another natural number will give i. That number is 1. The correct version of this predicate is

$$\exists i \in a \cdot \forall j \in \mathbb{N} \cdot \neg \exists k \in \mathbb{N} \cdot j \neq 1 \wedge k \neq 1 \Rightarrow j \times k = i$$

This precludes the use of 1 and states that there exists a natural number in a such that there is not a natural number k which when multiplied by any other natural number j will give i, provided that j is not 1 and k is not 1. This is rather a complicated way of saying that there is a prime in the set a. Later in this book we will give you some notational devices that enable this statement to be written more succinctly.   ∎

Exercise 2.2

1. Which of the following predicates are true and which are false?
   - (a) $\forall i \in \{33, \ldots, 100\} \cdot i < 3 \wedge 100 < i$
   - (b) $\forall i \in \mathbb{N} \cdot 10\,000 < i$
   - (c) $\exists i \in \mathbb{N} \cdot \exists j \in \{1, \ldots, 100\} \cdot i > j$
   - (d) $\exists i \in \{1, \ldots, 3\} \cdot \forall j \in \{1, \ldots, 100\} \cdot i > j$
   - (e) $\forall x, y \in \{1, \ldots, 100\} \cdot x \times y = -20$
   - (f) $\forall x \in \{1, \ldots, 4\}, y \in \{5, \ldots, 15\} \cdot x + y = 19 \Rightarrow x = 5 \wedge y = 14$
   - (g) $\forall x \in \{1, \ldots, 4\}, y \in \{5, \ldots, 15\} \cdot x + y = 19 \Rightarrow x = 4 \wedge y = 15$

2. Translate the following statements into the predicate calculus using universal and existential quantification.
   - (a) There is at least one natural number greater than 10.

(b) All the natural numbers are greater than 10.

(c) There are two numbers in the set of consecutive numbers from 5 to 90 that add up to 23.

(d) All pairs of natural numbers add up to 89.

(e) No number in the set of consecutive numbers starting from 19 to 23 is exactly divisible by 17.

(f) Each consecutive pair of natural numbers add up to an even number.

(g) The sum of the pairs of numbers in the set of consecutive number starting with 66 and finishing with 78 is always less than 200.

2.4   PROOF

The process of demonstrating that a certain predicate holds assuming that a number of other predicates is true is a vitally important process which forms part of a formal method of software development. It is used to demonstrate the consistency of a system specification, and also to show that a particular design meets its system specification. This section will informally examine the proof process. A predicate that is demonstrated to be true is known as a *theorem*.

When we carry out a proof we usually use the fact that certain predicates are true in order to demonstrate that another predicate is true. For example, in order to demonstrate that a theorem in geometry is true—a theorem being just a special type of predicate— we use some of the axioms that have been demonstrated earlier, for example that the angles of a triangle sum to $180°$. In order to carry out this proof a mechanism is needed that relates true predicates either to the predicate that we wish to prove true or to intermediate predicates that help us prove the final result. This mechanism is known as a *rule of inference*. In order to demonstrate what this is an example is in order. One rule of inference is shown below

$$\frac{P_1 \wedge \ldots \wedge P_n}{P_i}$$

A rule of inference states that if the predicate above the line is true then the predicate below the line is true. In the example above it states that if the predicate consisting of the n conjuncts is true then any conjunct P_i will be true, where i varies from 1 to n. This rule of inference follows directly from the truth table definition of the *and* operator, where a predicate containing only *ands* will only be true if all of its conjuncts are individually true. This rule is known as the *and*-elimination rule because the result at the bottom of the line does not contain an *and* operator.

Worked example 2.10   Fill in the top line of the rule of inference shown below

$$\frac{}{P_1 \vee \ldots \vee P_n}$$

SOLUTION   The rule of inference is

$$\frac{P_i}{P_1 \vee \ldots \vee P_n}$$

This states that if any predicate P_i is true then the predicate formed by or-ing all the predicates from P_1 to P_n is true, where i ranges from 1 to n. This again follows from the definition of the *or* operator where a predicate containing only *or* operators will be true if any of its arguments is true. This rule is known as the *or*-introduction rule since it introduces the *or* operator below the line.   ■

Some other rules of inference are shown below:

$$\frac{P_1, \ldots, P_n}{P_1 \wedge \ldots \wedge P_n}$$

This states that if all the predicates between P_1 and P_n are true then the conjunction of all the predicates is true. This rule is known as the *and*-introduction rule. There is also the *or*-elimination rule which has the form

$$\frac{P_1 \vee \ldots \vee P_n; P_1 \Rightarrow E; \ldots; P_n \Rightarrow E}{E}$$

This states that if the disjunction of all the predicates P_i is true and if every predicate implies the predicate E, then E will be true. The semicolons separate out the list of predicates. Three useful predicates involving implication and equivalence are shown below.

$$\frac{P_1 \Rightarrow P_2; P_2 \Rightarrow P_1}{P_1 \Leftrightarrow P_2}$$

$$\frac{P_1 \Leftrightarrow P_2}{P_1 \Rightarrow P_2; P_2 \Rightarrow P_1}$$

$$\frac{P_1 \Rightarrow P_2; P_1}{P_2}$$

The first rule is known as the *equivalence*-introduction rule. It states that if P_1 implies P_2 and P_2 implies P_1 then the predicates are equivalent to each other. The next rule is the dual of this *equivalence*-introduction rule, and is known as the *equivalence*-elimination rule. The final rule is known as the *implication*-elimination rule and just states that if P_1 implies P_2 and if P_1 is true then P_2 is true. These rules can be used in proofs to show that a particular predicate calculus expression is true. Two further rules are shown below. The first is known as the *implication*-transitivity rule, the second the *equivalence*-transitivity rule.

$$\frac{P_1 \Rightarrow P_2; P_2 \Rightarrow P_3}{P_1 \Rightarrow P_3}$$

$$\frac{P_1 \Leftrightarrow P_2; P_2 \Leftrightarrow P_3}{P_1 \Leftrightarrow P_3}$$

A number of laws of predicate calculus can be used in deriving proofs. These laws can be derived from first principles, but are presented here as basic laws whose truth is assumed. They are written in the form of equivalences which are true. For example, the law of double negation is written as $\neg\neg P_1 \Leftrightarrow P_1$ which states that whenever P_1 has the value true, $\neg\neg P_1$ will have the value true and vice versa, and that whenever P_1 has the value false then $\neg\neg P_1$ will have the value false and vice versa. (It should be noted that some of these rules are not valid in the Logic of Partial Functions—see below.)

Commutative laws

$$P_1 \lor P_2 \iff P_2 \lor P_1$$
$$P_1 \land P_2 \iff P_2 \land P_1$$
$$(P_1 \iff P_2) \iff (P_2 \iff P_1)$$

Associative laws

$$P_1 \lor (P_2 \lor P_3) \iff (P_1 \lor P_2) \lor P_3 \iff P_1 \lor P_2 \lor P_3$$
$$P_1 \land (P_2 \land P_3) \iff (P_1 \land P_2) \land P_3 \iff P_1 \land P_2 \land P_3$$

Distributive laws

$$P_1 \lor (P_2 \land P_3) \iff (P_1 \lor P_2) \land (P_1 \lor P_3)$$
$$P_1 \land (P_2 \lor P_3) \iff (P_1 \land P_2) \lor (P_1 \land P_3)$$

De Morgan's laws

$$\lnot (P_1 \land P_2) \iff \lnot P_1 \lor \lnot P_2$$
$$\lnot (P_1 \lor P_2) \iff \lnot P_1 \land \lnot P_2$$

The law of negation

$$\lnot \lnot P_1 \iff P_1$$

The law of the excluded middle

$$P_1 \lor \lnot P_1 \iff \text{true}$$

The law of contradiction

$$P_1 \land \lnot P_1 \iff \text{false}$$

The law of implication

$$P_1 \implies P_2 \iff \lnot P_1 \lor P_2$$

The law of equality

$$(P_1 \iff P_2) \iff (P_1 \implies P_2 \land P_2 \implies P_1)$$

Laws of *or* simplification

$$P_1 \lor P_1 \iff P_1$$
$$P_1 \lor \text{true} \iff \text{true}$$
$$P_1 \lor \text{false} \iff P_1$$
$$P_1 \lor (P_1 \land P_2) \iff P_1$$

Laws of *and* simplification

$$P_1 \land P_1 \iff P_1$$
$$P_1 \land \text{true} \iff P_1$$
$$P_1 \land \text{false} \iff \text{false}$$
$$P_1 \land (P_1 \lor P_2) \iff P_1$$

All the laws above can be written using the notation that we have used for rules of inference. For example, De Morgan's laws can be written as

$$\overline{\lnot (P_1 \land P_2) \iff \lnot P_1 \lor \lnot P_2}$$

$$\overline{\neg (P_1 \lor P_2) \iff \neg P_1 \land \neg P_2}$$

All this states is that the bottom line is true without any other predicate being true. The commutative and associative laws are straightforward; they are of the same form as arithmetic laws which state that $a + b$ is equivalent to $b + a$. Distributive laws are used for factoring predicate expressions. De Morgan's laws are laws which enable bracketed negated expressions to be expanded out. The law of negation just states that not not *anything* is equivalent to *anything*; thus if it is not not raining then it is raining. The law of the excluded middle essentially states that a predicate is either true or false. The law of contradiction states that a predicate cannot be both true and false. The laws of implication and equality are used to simplify expressions using the implication and equivalence operators. Finally the laws of *or* and *and* simplification are used to simplify predicates that contain *and* operators or *or* operators.

These laws can be employed in proofs by means of a rule of inference which we shall refer to as the equivalence rule of inference. It has the form:

$$\frac{P_1 ; P_1 \iff P_2}{P_2}$$

This just states that if two predicates are equivalent and one of the predicates is true then the other predicate has to be true.

Both rules of inference and the laws shown above are used in proofs. These proofs have the form that some predicate p is to be demonstrated to be true given the truth of a series of other predicates $a_1, \ldots, a_n$ known as premises. An example of this process is shown below where the truth of the predicate expression $r \lor (q \Rightarrow r)$ is established from the premises $p \land q$ and $p \Rightarrow r$. The steps in the proof are shown below:

1	$p \land q$	premise
2	$p \Rightarrow r$	premise
3	p	*and*-elimination 1
4	r	*implication*-elimination 2, 3
5	$r \lor (q \Rightarrow r)$	*or*-introduction 4

The first two lines are the premises which are assumed to be true. The third line uses the *and*-elimination rule to eliminate the and operator in line 1. This is shown by the reference to line 1 in the commentary to the right. Line 4 uses the *implication*-elimination rule of inference and the truth of the predicates on lines 2 and 3 to derive the fact that r is true. Finally, the fifth line shows that $r \lor (q \Rightarrow r)$ can be derived from the truth of r on line 4 and the *or*-introduction rule of inference. This rule states that if a predicate is true then any number of predicates can be *ored* with that predicate and the result is true; this is exactly what happens in line 5. The general form of such proofs is

line number   true predicate   commentary referring to rules
of inference, previous lines and laws

Another example of a proof is shown below—one that uses a number of the laws. It establishes the truth of p from the premises $p \lor q$ and $\neg q$:

1	$p \lor q$	premise
2	$\neg q$	premise
3	$\neg \neg (p \lor q)$	law of double negation, 1
4	$\neg (\neg p \land \neg q)$	De Morgan's law, 3
5	$\neg (\neg p \land \text{true})$	substitution 2, 4
6	$\neg (\neg p)$	law of *and*-simplification, 5
7	p	law of double negation 6

The third line is just an application of the law of double negation; the premise on line 1 is true and hence the double negation of this premise is true. Line 4 just applies one of the De Morgan's laws to the innermost negation. The fifth line shows that since line 2 is true it can be substituted by true in the true predicate in line 4. The predicate in line 5 is then simplified by means of the law of *and*-simplification. This gives the predicate p by the law of double negation.

What we have done in this section is to introduce the concept of proof as being a collection of true predicates which lead from a series of premises to a theorem by applying laws or rules of inference. We shall return to the notion of proof in more detail later in this chapter. However, before doing this it is worth digressing and looking at a complication when predicate calculus is used for developing computer programs.

2.5 THREE-VALUED LOGIC

There are two main reasons why formal methods should be used in system development. The first is that the task of writing a mathematical definition of a computer system is an excellent way of understanding it before starting to write the code. The exercise of writing a formal specification forces the architect of the system to have a better understanding of the problem about to be solved. The second reason is that if a mathematical specification of a computer system exists, then there is the possibility of developing the program and showing that the program does indeed satisfy the specification—a proof of the correctness of the program. The idea of this is that if the program satisfies the specification, which will be shown by proving some theorems about the program and the specification, it is in some sense correct.

VDM, the formal software development method that is taught in this book, provides a framework for development whereby a whole string of artefacts are built—by an artefact we mean a specification or a program. The first of these artefacts is the specification and the last is an executable program; the in-between artefacts could be either specifications or programs (or both). Each artefact is based on the previous one. If each artefact can be proved to be correct with respect to the one produced before, the author could argue that the final artefact, the program, is correct. The correctness of an artefact is something that we should be able to decide upon. This judgement should not be a value judgement, but should be reinforced with some sort of argument for the correctness.

The framework in which the correctness of any statement can be judged is the logic that we have described in this chapter. It is a tool mathematicians have been using to prove the correctness of statements for some 3000 years. The correctness of an artefact which is part of a development can be written down as a logical statement, and if the statement is true then the artefact is correct and if the statement is false the artefact is wrong.

However, computers introduce a problem into this development method, one which mathematicians can carefully avoid but, sadly, computer programmers cannot. It is a problem that crops up in disguise when writing programs. One of the artefacts whose correctness we are checking is a program, and, as is well known, computer programs can indefinitely loop—here we have the problem of an undefined mathematical expression (the program!).

Consider the following program which claims to provide the result of dividing a by b

```
q:= 0;
r:= a;
while ¬ (r < b) do
    r:= r − b;
    q:= q + 1
end
```

This program faithfully models the division process, and could even be said to model division by 0. If this program fragment is executed with a having a value of 4 and b having a value of 0 and we wait for the results, nothing will happen—the program will loop forever.

It could be argued that this type of program should not be written, but unfortunately it is, and a way of modelling this type of program is needed. It is also necessary to show that the programs we write do not belong to this class. Using this example as a guide, there is the possibility of defining an undefined mathematical expression as one that supplies no information—we are, in some sense, still waiting for the answer to appear. We do this by introducing an undefined value which, in some sense, could be said to contain no information—a sort of mathematical equivalent of the looping program.

The undefined expression problem can also occur in specifications. Consider the following logical expression:

$$x \neq 0 \implies (x/x) = 1$$

which states that if x is not equal to 0 then x divided by x is equal to 1. This should be true in all circumstances. It states an obvious property of integers (or even reals); it also seems a reasonable thing to write down. Unfortunately, if x is equal to 0, which is a valid value to associate with x, then the expression x/x is undefined and the logical expression becomes

$$\mathsf{false} \implies (\text{an undefined expression}) = 1$$

What we have is that false implies some undefined expression. There are two things that need to be done: undefined expressions need to be given a 'value' and the logical operators need to be extended to handle this new value. This new value, which can be thought of as being an undefined value, or better a value that contains no information, is usually written as:

$$\perp$$

and is referred to as 'bottom'. The idea of no information needs to be explained; the denotation 'true' conveys information about something being 'true', the denotation 'false' is supposed to convey information about the 'falsity' of something and the denotation '3' about the 'threeness' of something. The denotation '$\perp$' is supposed to convey absolutely no information whatsoever—just like a looping program, no useful knowledge is generated. This suggests the new 'bottom' value could be pictured as follows:

The lines joining true and false with bottom indicate that, in some sense, they contain more information than bottom.

This bottom value can also be added to the other sets of values that are used in specifications; for example bottom can be added to the natural numbers so that a meaning can be ascribed to the expression

$$x/0$$

This expression denotes bottom. How is this new value related to the other natural numbers?

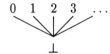

It contains less information than any of the natural numbers. In fact, any set D can be extended by the value that denotes no information, namely 'bottom'.Thus, the set $D = \{a, b, c, d, \ldots\}$ can be extended to

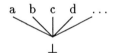

The question that is worth asking is: how can bottom be used with the logical operators that we have previously described? Before examining this question in more detail it is worth considering how the logical operators are used. Their main use is in the proof of correctness of statements and the concept of a mathematical proof depends heavily on the meaning of the operators such as the *and, or* and *implication* operators. Will the addition of a new value alter this dependency in a way that would force us to rethink our concept of a proof?

The following requirements of a logic system that allows for an undefined value can be written down:

1. The proof rules should, where possible, be consistent with classical logic. These rules have stood the test of time, have proved to be very successful and are well-understood.
2. Conjunction (*and*) and disjunction (*or*) should be commutative—otherwise we would need to change the way we think about proofs.
3. Most standard laws of logic should hold (we do not expect all of them to hold because of the new value, but the important ones should).
4. There should be a clear way of explaining the failure of those classical laws that do not carry over to the new logic.
5. Implication should behave as we would expect it to—again, it would be necessary to change the way we think about proofs if this was not true in the new logic; unfortunately there is a small problem with implication, see below.

The form of logic that contains this additional undefined value is called a logic of partial functions (LPF). How should the logical operators be extended to handle this new undefined value, equivalently, how should the truth tables be extended to handle this new value? The classical two-valued logic truth tables for *and* is as follows:

		B	
$A \land B$		true	false
A	true	true	false
	false	false	false

If the guidelines listed above are accepted, the corresponding truth table for the new LPF must agree with the truth table from classical logic for the values true and false. This gives a first approximation for the truth table for *and*:

		B		
$A \land B$		true	false	$\perp$
	true	true	false	?
A	false	false	false	?
	$\perp$	?	?	?

How should the '?' be filled in? They could be filled in by asking the question 'do we have enough information to provide an answer?' With this approach the result of

false $\land \perp$

should be false, because no matter what further information about the missing value is obtained, this will not change the ultimate result. What about

true $\land \perp$

Until more information is obtained, nothing can be said about the result; the answer is still unknown. Therefore the result of

true $\land \perp$

should be bottom. Finally,

$\perp \land \perp$

is equivalent to bottom. This sort of informal argument allows the table to be completed as follows:

		B		
$A \land B$		true	false	$\perp$
	true	true	false	$\perp$
A	false	false	false	false
	$\perp$	$\perp$	false	$\perp$

A similar approach can be used to develop the truth table for *or*. When we know both values the results should be as for classical logic. If one of the values is true and the other is undefined, we have enough information to deduce that the result is true. If one of the values is false and the other is undefined, we do not have enough information, so the result must be undefined. If both arguments are undefined, then the result is undefined. This gives us the following table for disjunction:

		B		
$A \lor B$		true	false	$\perp$
	true	true	true	true
A	false	true	false	$\perp$
	$\perp$	true	$\perp$	$\perp$

Worked example 2.11 Write down the truth table for the *not* operator.

SOLUTION The table for the *not* operator is shown below

A	$\neg A$
true	false
false	true
$\bot$	$\bot$

■

We can try to informally derive the truth table for $\Rightarrow$ and then compare it with the table we obtained from the law of implication that $A \Rightarrow B$ is equivalent to $\neg A \lor B$. The table for $\neg A \lor B$ is shown below:

	$\neg A \lor B$	B true	false	$\bot$
	true	true	false	$\bot$
A	false	true	true	true
	$\bot$	true	$\bot$	$\bot$

If we are given no information and we can show that the consequence of the implication is true, it seems that

$\bot \Rightarrow$ true

should be accepted as true. Correspondingly, if from no information we discover that the consequence of the implication is false, we have not really shown anything, we still have not got enough information and, therefore, we should deduce that

$\bot \Rightarrow$ false

is undefined. If we deduce no information from something which is true, we have learnt nothing so

true $\Rightarrow \bot$

should be undefined. From a false statement we can deduce anything including nothing at all, so

false $\Rightarrow \bot$

should be true. Finally, if we have no information and deduce nothing we have not learnt anything so

$\bot \Rightarrow \bot$

should be undefined. These definitions agree with the $\neg A \lor B$ interpretation. Consequently the truth table can be written as.

	$A \Rightarrow B$	B true	false	$\bot$
	true	true	false	$\bot$
A	false	true	true	true
	$\bot$	true	$\bot$	$\bot$

The truth table for $\Leftrightarrow$ can be deduced from the fact that it is equivalent to $(A \Rightarrow B) \land (B \Rightarrow A)$:

		B		
$A \Leftrightarrow B$		true	false	$\bot$
	true	true	false	$\bot$
A	false	false	true	$\bot$
	$\bot$	$\bot$	$\bot$	$\bot$

2.6   MORE ABOUT PROOF

The proof strategy that mathematicians use depends heavily on the definition of implication which we have extended with an undefined value. How will this change our strategy for doing proofs? Perhaps now is the time to consider exactly what a proof is.

Mathematicians tend to be rather cavalier about the way they present their proofs: usually they leave the most difficult proofs for their readers to do—usually the ones that are labelled as being trivial! As the correctness of computer software will be highly dependent on the correctness of the proofs, the proofs that we carry out should be given in more detail than is normally necessary in mathematics. The more care that is taken with a proof means a greater confidence in correctness for the final program that is based on that proof.

Ultimately proofs can be carried out in such detail that a machine could check their correctness, which would give an exceptionally high level of confidence in the correctness of the final program. The approach of this book to documenting a proof will be more detailed than that taken by mathematicians, but not as formally as might be necessary for safety-critical systems. We are interested in presenting how proofs are tackled and supplying sufficient detail that the proofs could be formalized if it was felt necessary.

Informally a proof is a convincing argument of the correctness of a statement. Consider the following equation, supposing that we want to prove that

$$1 + 2 + 3 + \ldots + n = n \times (n+1)/2$$

A proof by induction might proceed as follows:

Case 1. $n = 0$

l.h.s. $= 0 =$ r.h.s.

Case 2. Assume the theorem is true for n, we will prove it true for $n + 1$

1	$1 + 2 + 3 + \ldots + n + (n + 1) =$	
	$n \times (n+1)/2 + (n+1)$	assumption
2	l.h.s. $= (n^2 + n + 2 \times n + 2)/2$	rules of arithmetic, 1
3	l.h.s. $= (n^2 + 3 \times n + 2)/2$	rules of arithmetic, 2
4	l.h.s. $= (n + 1) \times (n + 2)/2$	rules of arithmetic, 3
5	l.h.s. $= (n + 1) \times ((n + 1) + 1)/2$	rules of arithmetic, 4

Thus the theorem is true for $n = 0$, and if it is true for n, then it is true for $n + 1$. Hence it is true for all natural numbers.

As can be seen from the simple example above, the tools that we use are mainly substitution and the properties of arithmetic operators such as commutativity, associativity, etc. In the above proof we have also used induction, something that can be taken on trust: assumed to be true or can be proved as a theorem having been derived from the properties of the natural numbers.

The strategy we should use is that we should not use any rule without proving it first. For example, in the proof above all the properties of arithmetic were assumed, since the approach of this book is rigorous rather than formal this is acceptable. If anything is assumed or there is some doubt about its correctness then it should be proved.

The idea behind the formalization of mathematics is to treat it as a game, and a proof will be a series of valid moves in the game. The starting positions in the game are the initial assumptions, or premises, written down as strings of symbols, and the allowed moves are defined by rules of inference or assumed laws, which describe transformations that can be made to the strings of symbols. Any valid positions in the game, i.e. intermediate strings of symbols that occur during the application of the inference rules, are theorems—true statements, some of which are interesting, some of which are not. If we wish to prove a theorem we must demonstrate that the string of symbols representing that theorem can be obtained by transforming a starting position (an existing theorem or axiom) to that string.

If we are to construct proofs, what moves are possible? If we have a proof of E assuming Γ then we would write

$$\Gamma \vdash E$$

where Γ is a series of expressions. For example, if we were trying to prove that the predicate a followed from the predicates b, c and d, then Γ would be b, c and d while E would be a. The expression above means that in all those worlds where the expressions in Γ are true, then E is also true. We would then use rules of inference and laws that allow us to manipulate and transform the expression(s) of Γ so that after one or more transformations we would obtain the expression E. We would then claim that we had a proof of E under the assumptions denoted by the expressions of Γ. If we were working rigorously, rather than formally, some of the steps might be skipped or carried out informally. If all the expressions in Γ are true—are premises or proved theorems—then we can add E to our set of proved theorems and it can be used in other proofs.

Our rules of inference are written in the following style:

$$\frac{\text{if we have something which matches this}}{\text{then it can be replaced by this}}$$

with suitable pattern matching and substitution; or equivalently

$$\frac{\text{if we have a proof of this}}{\text{then we have proved this}}$$

If something is always true and does not need any assumptions, what logicians call a tautology, this can be written as

$$\frac{}{\text{we have proved this}}$$

The result can be deduced from nothing. For example, the rule of inference

$$\frac{E_1 \wedge E_2}{E_1}$$

and the following expression

$$\vdash (A_1 \wedge A_2) \wedge A_3$$

would allow us to deduce

$$\vdash A_1 \wedge A_2$$

Notice that $A_1 \wedge A_2$ was pattern matched with the E_1 and A_3 with E_2 so the rule allows $A_1 \wedge A_2$ to be deduced.

Unfortunately the following rules do not hold in the logic of partial functions:

$$\frac{}{E_1 \vee \neg E_1}$$

which is the law of the excluded middle, and also

$$\frac{}{E \Rightarrow E}$$

More importantly, the following rule of inference does not hold:

$$\frac{E_1 \vdash E_2}{\vdash E_1 \Rightarrow E_2}$$

This has an effect on the way we do proofs. In classical logic if we have to prove something of the form

$$A \Rightarrow B$$

we are really being asked to prove

$$\vdash A \Rightarrow B$$

The approach taken is to assume A (is true) and show B (is true). An informal argument is that if A is false then $A \Rightarrow B$ is true anyway, and if A is true this can be used in the proof of B. What is really happening is that by assuming A and proving B we are carrying out the following proof:

$$A \vdash B$$

and the classical deduction rule above allows us to deduce

$$\vdash A \Rightarrow B$$

This rule does not hold in general in LPF! Luckily, however, if A is always defined, not equal to bottom, then in this case the rule is valid in LPF. Thus to show

$$\vdash A \Rightarrow B$$

we need to show that A is always defined and when it is true, then B is true. If we write

$$\delta(A)$$

for A is defined, i.e. the function δ returns true if A is defined and false if it is not, then the above can be written formally as

$$\frac{\delta(A); A \vdash B}{A \Rightarrow B}$$

The style of our proofs will be a series of terms linked together by justifications, terms being transformed from one form into another using that justification; so we will write

$$A$$

$$= \text{"justification of step"}$$

$$B$$

In this case the justification we use must work both ways, i.e. we can deduce A from B or B from A. If the justification only works in one way, i.e. we can only go from A to B, then we will write

A

$\Rightarrow$ "justification of step"

B

An example of the first case would be

$x + y - x$

$=$ "rules of addition"

y

and an example of the second case would be

$x > y$

$\Rightarrow$ "rules of arithmetic"

$x \geq y$

In this style, the last part of the proof on page 28 would be

Case 2. Assume the theorem is true for n, we will prove it true for $n + 1$

$1 + 2 + 3 + \ldots + n + (n + 1)$

$=$ "assumption"

$n \times (n + 1)/2 + (n + 1)$

$=$ "rule of arithmetic"

$(n^2 + n + 2 \times n + 2)/2$

$=$ "rules of arithmetic"

$(n^2 + 3 \times n + 2)/2$

$=$ "rules of arithmetic"

$(n + 1) \times (n + 2)/2$

$=$ "rules of arithmetic"

$(n + 1) \times ((n + 1) + 1)/2$

Most of the proofs we will use in this book are of the form

$\forall x \in X \cdot A \Rightarrow B$

and it will be necessary to show that this is a true statement, i.e. it is always true—it has the value **true**. This will usually be done by first assuming an arbitrary x and showing

$A \Rightarrow B$

is true. This is proved by assuming that A is true and using this assumption to prove B, i.e. using the assumption to show B is true. We also need to show that A can never be undefined. Therefore, for arbitrary x, by assuming A and deriving B and by showing that A can never be undefined we have effectively shown that

$\forall x \in X \cdot A \Rightarrow B$

is true.

2.7 SUMMARY

A specification language for software systems is much easier to use if we are allowed to write undefined terms in our predicates. The logic of partial functions allows us to interpret these expressions, and the proof rules used will allow proofs of statements of correctness. The proof rules we use are the ones that most mathematicians are familiar with, except that a certain amount of care must be taken with the undefined ('bottom') value. The style of proofs we will adopt is reasonably straightforward and easy to carry out. They can, if necessary, be translated into a more formal style, but for the purposes of learning how to apply formal methods this is unnecessary. It should be noted that formal proofs are very tedious to carry out and best done with machine aid—at least a proof editor which will allow proofs to be manipulated trivially on a computer screen. A better tool would be a theorem prover whose proof techniques are understood, and this tool would help us carry out the proofs.

3

A LANGUAGE FOR SPECIFICATION

AIMS

- To describe how mathematics can be used as a specification medium.
- To describe how a particular mathematical language based on the software development method VDM can be used to specify complex systems.
- To describe the role of proof in formal software development.

3.1   INTRODUCTION

In the first chapter of this book we described some of the weaknesses of conventional software development. Briefly, these were: inexactness, the fact that it is exceptionally difficult to write specification documents in natural language which would be interpreted in the same way by all those staff who need to process them; the inability of project documents to support the vital reasoning processes required during the analysis and design phases; and the fact that implementation details intrude during the early phases of software development.

The main aim of this chapter is to convince you that mathematics is an excellent medium for specification, and demonstrate how this works out in practice.

Mathematics possesses a number of properties that make it an excellent candidate for expressing functionality.

Exactness   When a mathematician writes a statement such as

$$a \times (b + c) = a \times b + a \times c$$

there is no possibility of any misunderstanding occurring. The mathematical part of a theorem or proof can be understood by anyone from any country.

No implementation bias   Let us assume that we wish to specify the operation of a program to add two numbers a and b to form a number c. This can be written mathematically as a specification

$$c = a + b$$

This specification states what happens when the program finishes, but does not state *how* it occurs. It could be implemented very simply by means of a single assignment statement in a high-level language, or it could be implemented in a more complicated way using an assembler language which carried out the process using bit-by-bit operations. The important point about using mathematics is that details do not intrude.

Ability to reason   Reasoning is a process that all mathematicians carry out. For example, when a mathematician demonstrates that if two sets of numbers are disjoint their intersection is the empty set, a series of proof rules and axioms are used to carry out this demonstration. As you will see later in this book, this type of reasoning can be carried out on large, complex functional specifications and is directly relevant to the systems analysis process. Reasoning is at the heart of any software project, for example an analyst on a real-time chemical plant monitoring project would start with a number of propositions such as *inlet valve is closed, outlet valve is closed* and *ambient temperature is high* and attempt to reason that the monitoring system is in a dangerous state. Mathematics is a good medium to support this reasoning.

Succinctness   A mathematical specification is short, compared, say, with an implementation. As an example of this consider the specification for a program which checks that an identifier *id* is contained in a symbol table *sym*. We shall assume that the symbol table is specified as a set. If the identifier is contained in the table a boolean *b* is set to true and set to false otherwise. This can be written as

$$b \iff id \in sym$$

where $\in$ is the set inclusion operator which yields true whenever *id* is contained in the set *sym* and false otherwise. Compared with an English description of the function, or the implementation itself, this is very short and, assuming facility with a mathematical notation, is easier to read.

3.2   THE ROLE OF MATHEMATICS IN SOFTWARE DEVELOPMENT

In this book we will describe how mathematics is used in software engineering and, in particular, how one particular notation and development method is employed in software development. The aim of this section is to place the mathematics in context, before looking at the main concepts behind what is known as *formal methods of software development*.

The first stage of the software development process is that of analysis. The analyst who carries out this process examines the statement of requirements produced by a customer, looks at any manual or existing computer systems and attempts to derive a system specification.

In terms of the formal method described in this book what emerges is a list of operations that are needed for the system, together with a description of the stored data which these operations access and modify. Typical operations for a stock control system might include those which:

1. Return the number of items currently in stock.
2. Return with the names of those items out of stock.

3. Deposit some delivered item of stock in a warehouse.
4. Notify the system that a new item is to be stocked.

Both operations and the stored data—as will be seen later in this chapter—can be specified using mathematics. Once the analyst has written a first version of this specification, an attempt is made to verify that it is correct. In order to do this he poses a number of questions to the customer which represent properties of the system to be implemented. Typical questions for a stock control system might be:

1. If an order for an item that is out of stock is received will this result in an error message being generated?
2. If new stock is received and the current location in the warehouse for that stock is full, then does the system allocate an empty storage location?

The answers that the customer gives to these questions are checked with the specification. If the specification agrees with these answers, then the specification is released; if not, the specification is modified. In checking the specification the analyst uses proof to check the answers.

Once a specification has been developed the next stage is to produce a design. This process consists of designing a database that is capable of supporting the operations identified during analysis, but, at the same time, satisfies response and memory requirements discovered during analysis.

The quality assurance activities that occur during this phase involve the designer checking that the design operations correctly implement the operations identified during analysis. This is carried out using mathematical proof.

The final stage is implementation. At this point in a software project, the developer will have identified the programming language to be used in the project. Implementation consists of transforming the database, specified during design, into the concrete data structures of the language used for implementation—data structures such as arrays, records and lists. The operations specified in design are also transformed into procedures or subroutines of the target language. Again, mathematical proof is used to check that the implementation is a correct reflection of the design.

In the description above, the use of mathematical proof as a quality assurance mechanism is stressed. However, as you will see later in this book, a high degree of assurance can be achieved by means of a less rigid strategy.

3.3   MATHEMATICAL SPECIFICATION

In order to describe the main concepts behind formal methods of software development it is worth using a simple and rather artificial example. Such an example does not show the power of using mathematics as a development medium—there will be plenty of these later in the book—however, it is of a sufficient size to highlight the concepts.

The example involves the specification of a program that adds two natural numbers together, the two numbers being less than 10. Let us assume that the numbers are called a and b with the result being c. Figure 3.1 shows a graphical way of describing the specification.

It shows only part of the specification, and describes a set that contains a pair of objects: the first object is a pair of natural numbers and the second object is a single natural number which is the result of adding the elements of the pair.

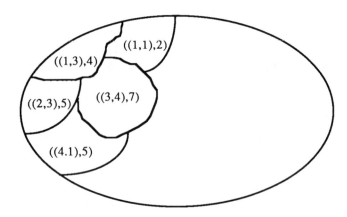

Figure 3.1   A graphical description of the action of a program.

If the figure was complete then we would have a specification for an addition program. However, this way of specifying a system—by means of enumerating all possibilities—has a major problem associated with it: it gives rise to potentially large or infinite specifications. However, a more succinct specification based on this idea is possible.

Fig. 3.1 shows a set, a special type of set known as a *relation*, which contains pairs. The elements of this relation can be described by means of what is called a *set comprehension*:

$$\{((a, b), c) \mid a, b, c \in \mathbb{N} \land a < 10 \land b < 10 \land c = a + b\}$$

This states that the program for adding two natural numbers less than 10 can be described by a set of pairs. The individual elements of the set are of the form $((a, b), c)$ where a, b and c are natural numbers and where a and b are less than 10 and c is the sum of a and b. The symbol $\mathbb{N}$ stands for the set of natural numbers: integers greater or equal to zero.

This rather artificial example personifies the essence of a mathematical specification of a system, even though we have talked about it as a program. First, there is stored data, in the example above this is the collection of variables a, b and c. This collection of stored data is known as a *state*. Next, there are also two conditions that define the action of the program. There is the condition $a < 10 \land b < 10$, which describes the range of data for which the operation is valid, and the condition $c = a + b$, which describes the result of the processing. The first condition is known as a *pre-condition*; the second condition is known as a *post-condition*.

The set comprehension shown above can be expressed a little more neatly using a notation originally known as *Meta-IV*.[1] This notation is the one associated with the technique known as the *Vienna Development Method* (VDM)—the development method which is used in this book.

---

[1] Now called *VDM-SL*: VDM—Specification Language

```
state Numbers of
      a : N
      b : N
      c : N
end

addnumbers
ext wr a : N
    wr b : N
    wr c : N
pre a < 10 ∧ b < 10
post c = ⃖a + ⃖b
```

The first four lines define the type of the stored data. This stored data is known as a *state* and its name is *Numbers*. It consists of three components a, b and c which are all natural numbers (indicated by $\mathbb{N}$). The remainder of the specification defines the operation *addnumbers*. The first line of this specification names the operation, and then specifies that the operation has no parameters and returns no result. We will see later in this chapter how parameters and results are defined in VDM.

The next line states that the operation will access all of the components of the state *Numbers*, each of which is of type $\mathbb{N}$. The keyword ext describes this, while the keyword wr states that the access to each of the components is write access; that is the named components of the state are written to and changed. The fourth line of the operation specification uses the keyword pre to describe the pre-condition, while the fifth line describes the post-condition using the keyword post.

There is a convention in the pre and post-conditions of operations that is peculiar to VDM and which need some explanation; it is the use of the 'hook' symbol $(\overleftarrow{id})$. This symbol is used to indicate the value of a state component before an operation is carried out. It is used only in the post-condition and not in the pre-condition where, by implication, the state, when referenced, is assumed to be the state just before the operation is executed.

The post-condition thus states that after the operation *addnumbers* is executed, the c component of the state after the operation is equal to the sum of the values of the a and b components of the state before the operation is executed. Note that nothing is said about the values of the components a and b after the operation has executed. If we wanted to specify that the values of these two components were unchanged, we could either write

$$\text{post } c = \overleftarrow{a} + \overleftarrow{b} \wedge a = \overleftarrow{a} \wedge b = \overleftarrow{b}$$

which requires that the final values of a and b should equal the initial values. Alternatively, we could mark these two components of the state as read-only:

```
addnumbers
ext rd a : N
    rd b : N
    wr c : N
pre a < 10 ∧ b < 10
post c = a + b
```

where *a* and *b* have been defined as read-only by the use of the keyword rd.

The final point to make about the specification is to note that keywords are displayed in sans serif type, while states and state components are written in italics; also, the name of an operation is written in italic.

This example has been simple. Another example, which brings out some more elements of the VDM notation, is shown below. It concerns the functional specification for a system that keeps track of the state of a series of reactors in a chemical plant. In such a plant the reactors are either operating or are shut down.

A number of operations are required for this system: one that closes down an operating reactor, one that starts up an already closed down reactor, one that returns with the number of reactors which are shut down, one that closes down all the reactors that are currently operating and one that checks that a particular reactor is closed down.

The state for the system is shown below:

values

ALL-REACTS: *Reactors*-set

types

Reactset = *Reactors*-set

Reactors = ...

state *Plant* of
    operating : *Reactset*
    shut-down : *Reactset*
inv *mk-Plant*(*operating*, *shut-down*) $\triangle$
    operating $\cap$ *shut-down* = { } $\wedge$
    operating $\cup$ *shut-down* = *ALL-REACTS*
init *mk-Plant*(*operating*, *shut-down*) $\triangle$
    operating = { } $\wedge$
    shut-down = *ALL-REACTS*
end

The second line defines a constant *ALL-REACTS*. The fourth line states that *Reactset* is defined to be a collection, or *set*, of reactors. The second and third lines of the state define a chemical plant which consists of two components: those reactors that are currently in service (*operating*) and those reactors that have been shut down (*shut-down*).

The inv part introduces a new concept, that of a *data invariant*. This is a condition which describes what must be true of a state *throughout* the execution of a system. Data invariants crop up time and time again in software development; some examples are shown below:

1. The master file will always be in ascending order of employee key.
2. The collection of orders will always contain remote orders and telephone orders.
3. The symbol table will always contain at least one identifier.
4. The line printer queue will never be empty.

The data invariant for the chemical plant is that a reactor will always either be shut down or operating, but never both, and that the collection of reactors in the system will be the combined collection of shutdown reactors and operating reactors. This is shown in the second and third lines of the data invariant which state that the intersection of the operating and shutdown sets is equal to the empty set, and the collection of all the reactors is the union of the operating reactors and the closed down reactors.

The data invariant for chemical plant can hence be read as

> The data invariant for the state *Plant* with components *operating* and *shut-down* is defined as the intersection of *operating* and *shut-down* being equal to the empty set, and the union of *operating* and *shut-down* being equal to all the reactors.

The final part of the description gives the initial value of the state. It specifies that the operating reactors will be the empty set and the shut down reactors will be all the available reactors (denoted by the constant *ALL-REACTS*).

Sometimes it is necessary to refer to the data invariant as a function delivering a boolean value defined in the following way (the integration of the invariant with the state should be thought of as a shorthand for the following style of definition).

$$inv\text{-}Plant : Plant \rightarrow \mathbb{B}$$

$$inv\text{-}Plant(mk\text{-}Plant(operating, shut\text{-}down)) \quad \triangleq$$
$$operating \cap shut\text{-}down = \{\,\} \land$$
$$operating \cup shutdown = ALL\text{-}REACTS$$

The symbol $\mathbb{B}$ stands for the set of all Boolean values. The argument in the function definition contains an alternative way of referring to the components of a state that involves a facility known as a *make function*. The make function is written as the prefix *mk-* followed by the object name and returns an object which has the type of the state; it has a series of parameters consisting of the components of the state, thus the instantiation of the make function

$$mk\text{-}Plant(op, shut)$$

produces a state that has components *op* and *shut*. When used in a defining position (a position where an identifier is to be bound to, or associated with a value) then values are to be assigned to the identifier components of the make function—this will be described in detail later in the book.

The final lines of the state definition define what the initial value of the state is. By convention this is written as a predicate that restricts the values that the component of the state may have so that the predicate is true. It states that the initial value of the state is formed by constructing a plant with two empty sets representing the functioning reactors, shut down reactors and a constant that defines the collection of all reactors.

The operations on the state can now be defined. The first operation closes down an already operating reactor. Its specification is shown below:

$$close\text{-}down\ (reac{:}\ Reactors)$$

ext wr $operating\ :\ Reactset$
$\quad\quad shut\text{-}down\quad :\ Reactset$

pre $reac \in operating$

post $operating = \overleftarrow{operating} - \{reac\} \land$
$\quad\quad shut\text{-}down = \overleftarrow{shut\text{-}down} \cup \{reac\}$

The first line states that the operation is called *close-down* and that, unlike the operations in the previous example, it has a parameter: *reac*, which is a reactor. The second and third lines state that the operation will change the set of operating reactors and the set of shutdown reactors. The fourth line states that the operation is only defined for reactors which are currently operating, the $\in$ being the set membership operator. The fifth and sixth lines state what happens after the operation has been executed: first, *reac* is removed from the set of operating reactors; second, *reac* is added to the set of shutdown reactors.

Notice that a decision has been made by the specifier that when a reactor has ceased operating it is added to the set of shutdown reactors, rather than just being removed from the set of operating reactors.

Worked example 3.1 Write down the specification of the operation which starts up a specified reactor. Use the specification of the *close-down* operation as a template.

SOLUTION

> $start\text{-}up\ (reac: Reactors)$
> ext **wr** $operating$: $Reactset$
> $shut\text{-}down$: $Reactset$
> **pre** $reac \in shut\text{-}down$
> **post** $operating = \overleftarrow{operating} \cup \{reac\} \wedge$
> $shut\text{-}down = \overleftarrow{shut\text{-}down} - \{reac\}$

∎

This *start-up* operation is the dual of the previous one. The specification of the operation which returns with the number of reactors that are shut down is

> $no\text{-}shut\text{-}down\ ()\ n: \mathbb{N}$
> ext **rd** $shut\text{-}down$: $Reactset$
> **pre** true
> **post** $n = $ card $shut\text{-}down$

This is a relatively simple specification. Three things are of note. First, the operation does not have any parameters, just a result which is the number of reactors that are closed down. Second, the state is only read from and is, therefore, not changed; this is indicated by the use of the rd keyword in the second line. Third, the pre-condition for the operation being carried out is true; this means that the operation will always be valid and that the pre-condition does not restrict the values of the state as in the *start-up* operation where the reactor to be started up must have been closed down.

The operation for the *close-down-all* operation is shown below. This closes down all the reactors that are currently operating.

> $close\text{-}down\text{-}all\ ()$
> ext **wr** $operating$: $Reactset$
> $shut\text{-}down$: $Reactset$
> **pre** card $operating \geq 1$

$$\text{post } operating = \{\,\} \wedge$$
$$shut\text{-}down = \overleftarrow{shut\text{-}down} \cup \overleftarrow{operating}$$

Here the operation has no parameters and no result. Its pre-condition states that for the operation to be valid there must be at least one reactor currently operating. The post-condition states that after the operation has been executed, the reactors that were currently operating are added to the collection of shutdown reactors. The final operation checks that a particular reactor is closed down.

$$check\text{-}closed \ (reac\text{:} \ Reactors) \ closed\text{:} \ \mathbf{B}$$

ext rd $shut\text{-}down$: $Reactset$

pre true

post $closed \ \Leftrightarrow \ reac \in shut\text{-}down$

The operation only requires access to $shut\text{-}down$, which is read. The pre-condition places no restrictions on the operation. The post-condition states that the result $closed$ is given the value true if $reac$ is in $shut\text{-}down$ and false otherwise (the symbol $\Leftrightarrow$ stands for logical equivalence).

Earlier in this chapter we stated that mathematical proof plays a major part in a formal method of software development. At that point in the book we stated that there was little we could do to illustrate this, the reason being that we had not described some of the mathematical facilities that are part of VDM. A small, and perhaps artificial, example of the role of proof, certainly during analysis, can now be given by looking at the operation $start\text{-}up$. This has the post-condition

$$operating = \overleftarrow{operating} \cup \{reac\} \wedge$$
$$shut\text{-}down = \overleftarrow{shut\text{-}down} - \{reac\}$$

A question that an analyst may ask during the specification phase is: when the startup command is executed, will the combined collection of reactors that are operating and shut down remain the same? Formal mathematical proof can now be used to demonstrate this. An informal proof is shown below.

The collection of operating and shutdown reactors before the operation is executed is

$$\overleftarrow{operating} \cup \overleftarrow{shut\text{-}down}$$

and we know from the pre-condition that $reac \in \overleftarrow{shut\text{-}down}$ (remember that the pre-condition describes values before the operation is executed, and in the post-condition hooked identifiers describe such values). The collection of operating and shut down reactors after the operation is executed is

$$operating \cup shut\text{-}down$$

Now, from the post-condition of the startup operation this is equal to

$$(\overleftarrow{operating} \cup \{reac\}) \cup (\overleftarrow{shut\text{-}down} - \{reac\})$$

which is equal to

$$\overleftarrow{operating} \cup \overleftarrow{shut\text{-}down} \cup \{reac\}$$

Now the pre-condition for $start\text{-}up$ requires that $reac \in shut\text{-}down$ which means that $reac \in \overleftarrow{shut\text{-}down}$ (the old value of $shut\text{-}down$), therefore

$$\overline{operating} \cup \overline{shut\text{-}down} \cup \{reac\} = \overline{operating} \cup \overline{shut\text{-}down}$$

which is the collection of reactors that are operating and shut down. Therefore, this combined collection remains unaffected by the operation.

Another proof involves checking that the data invariant component

$$operating \cap shut\text{-}down = \{\,\}$$

is unaffected by this operation. The proof of this involves a number of steps. First, the data invariant is assumed to hold for the state before the operation is executed, that is

$$\overline{operating} \cap \overline{shut\text{-}down} = \{\,\}$$

The question then to ask is: does the invariant hold after the operation. This means proving that

$$operating \cap shut\text{-}down = \{\,\}$$

From the post-condition we know that

$$operating = \overline{operating} \cup \{reac\}$$
$$shut\text{-}down = \overline{shut\text{-}down} - \{reac\}$$

Substituting for $operating$ and $shut\text{-}down$ in

$$operating \cap shut\text{-}down$$

gives

$$(\overline{operating} \cup \{reac\}) \cap (\overline{shut\text{-}down} - \{reac\})$$

This can be simplified to

$$(\overline{operating} \cap (\overline{shut\text{-}down} - \{reac\})) \cup (\{reac\} \cap (\overline{shut\text{-}down} - \{reac\}))$$

The second half of this expression $(\{reac\} \cap (\overline{shut\text{-}down} - \{reac\}))$ reduces to the empty set and hence the expression becomes

$$\overline{operating} \cap (\overline{shut\text{-}down} - \{reac\})$$

which is equal to

$$(\overline{operating} \cap \overline{shut\text{-}down}) - \{reac\}$$

Now since the data invariant holds before the operation we have

$$\overline{operating} \cap \overline{shut\text{-}down} = \{\,\}$$

Thus we have

$$\{\,\} - \{reac\}$$

which reduces to

$$\{\,\}$$

Hence, we have proved that

$$operating \cap shut\text{-}down = \{\,\}$$

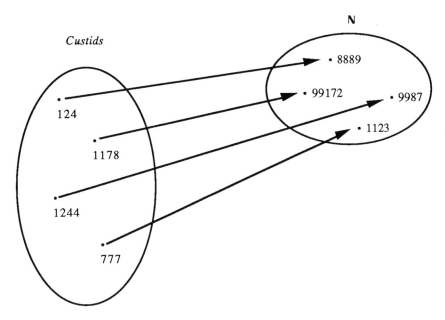

Figure 3.2 A function modelling a bank system.

which is the data invariant. Thus, we have shown that if the data invariant holds before the operation is executed, then it holds after the operation is executed.

To conclude this chapter a final example is given. It involves a simple, rather unrealistic, banking system, where each customer in the bank has one account and where a number of operations are required: to credit an account, to debit an account, to introduce a new customer into the bank system and to calculate the total amount of funds on deposit. We shall assume that no more than 1000 accounts are held in the bank. This system is modelled by means of a structure known as a *map*.

This is really a partial function: a set of ordered pairs, the first item in a pair being a customer identity with the second item in a pair being a balance of the account. A particular value of this state is

$$\{124 \mapsto 8889,$$
$$1178 \mapsto 99172,$$
$$1244 \mapsto 9987,$$
$$777 \mapsto 1123\}$$

This shows that the customer with the identity 124 has an account that contains 8889 pence (£88.89) and that customer 1244 has a balance of £99.87. This state can be shown graphically, as in Fig. 3.2, where the fact that there is a relationship between two sets is shown: there is a set of customer identities *Custids* which consists of natural numbers and a set of natural numbers which represent account balances in pence. The arrows in the diagram represent the connection. The left-hand side is known as the *domain* of the map while the right hand set is known as the *range* of the map.

The state of the bank system can now be specified:

types

$$Bank = Custids \xrightarrow{m} \mathbb{N}$$

state $Banking\text{-}system$ of
      $bk \ : \ Bank$
inv $mk\text{-}Banking\text{-}system(bk)$ $\triangleq$ card dom $bk \leq 1000$
init $mk\text{-}Banking\text{-}system(bk)$ $\triangleq$ $bk = \{\,\}$
end

The first line of the state says that the bank will be modelled by means of a map from *Custids* to the natural numbers. The invariant states that there will be no more than 1000 customers in the bank, i.e. there will be no more than 1000 elements in the domain of the map. The final line states that the initial value of the map will be an empty set.

Worked example 3.2 Write down the specification of the operation *newcustomer* which adds a new customer to the bank. Assume that this is achieved by means of the addition of a pair containing the customer name and a balance of zero to the map that represents the state. The specification will require the use of the dom operator which returns the set containing all the first items in each pair contained in a map.

SOLUTION

    $newcustomer \ (newcust\colon Custids)$
    ext wr $bk \ : \ Bank$
    pre $newcust \notin$ dom $bk \land$ card dom $bk < 1000$
    post $bk = \overleftarrow{bk} \cup \{newcust \mapsto 0\}$

                                                                         ■

This operation requires write access to the bank. The pre-condition states that the customer is not already in the bank and there are less than 1000 customers known to the bank; the post-condition states that the bank, after the operation is executed, is equal to the union of the bank before the operation unioned with a single pair which contains the new customer identity and a zero balance. The operation assumes that when a customer is introduced into the bank his account is set to zero pence.

The operation that credits an account is shown below, it has two parameters *cust*, the customer, and *amount*, the amount to be credited

    $credit \ (cust\colon Custids, amount\colon \mathbb{N})$
    ext wr $bk \ : \ Bank$
    pre $cust \in$ dom bk
    post $bk = \overleftarrow{bk} \dagger \{cust \mapsto (\overleftarrow{bk}(cust) + amount)\}$

The *credit* operation requires write access to the bank. The pre-condition states that the operation is defined if *cust*, the customer whose account is to be amended, is known to the bank system. The post-condition states that after the operation has been executed, the bank is equal to the old bank in which the entry for *cust* has been overwritten by a new pair $\{cust \mapsto \overleftarrow{bk}(cust) + amount\}$; the first element of this pair is the customer and the second element is the previous balance to which *amount* has been added. The term $\overleftarrow{bk}(cust)$ is called *mapping application*; it returns the pair in the range of $\overleftarrow{bk}$ that corresponds to the *cust*, i.e. the previous value of the account. The operator † carries out the overwriting.

The *debit* operation is similar to the *credit* operation. However, one point that should be made clear is that since the range of the bank map is the natural numbers, the model—which is of course, by necessity, simplistic—only envisages that an account will contain a non-negative amount of currency, i.e. no overdrafts are allowed. This is catered for in the pre-condition to *debit*:

> $debit$ $(cust: Custids, amount: \mathbb{N})$
>
> ext wr bk : $Bank$
>
> pre $cust \in \text{dom } bk \wedge amount \leq bk(cust)$
>
> post $bk = \overleftarrow{bk} \dagger \{cust \mapsto (\overleftarrow{bk}(cust) - amount)\}$

The pre-condition states that the operation *debit* is only defined if the customer has an account, and the amount in his or her account is such that the debit will not reduce it to an overdraft level. The post-condition states that the bank is updated by replacing the pair corresponding to *cust* with the pair that has *cust* as the first element and the amount formed by subtracting from the previous balance the amount *amount*.

The operation that calculates the total amount of funds in the bank is shown below; it introduces a new concept which makes operations more readable:

> $totalfunds$ () $tot: \mathbb{N}$
>
> ext rd bk : $Bank$
>
> pre true
>
> post $tot = sumof(bk)$
>
> $sumof : Bank \rightarrow \mathbb{N}$
>
> $sumof(sn)$ $\triangleq$ if $sn = \{\}$
> then 0
> else let $cust \in \text{dom } sn$ in
> $sn(cust) + sumof(\{cust\} \triangleleft sn)$

The operation specification is straightforward apart from the use of *sumof*. This is a call of a function that processes a map, and returns with a natural number that represents the sum of the elements in the range of the map.

The definition of the function *sumof* follows the definition of the operation. Its first line states that it takes a value of type *Bank* (which is a map) and returns a natural number. The second line starts the definition of the function, it states that if *sn* is the empty map then, obviously, the sum of the elements in the range of the map are zero. However, if this is not true the else part holds; it states that *cust* will be an (arbitrary) element of the domain of the map *sn*, and then that the sum will be the value associated with the element *cust* of the map plus the sum of the map from which *cust* has been removed by means of the operator ◁. This is an example of a recursive definition, and is similar to recursive procedures in any programming language.

The major reason for declaring *sumof* separately as a function is for readability. You will find that the pre- and post-conditions in the VDM notation will often be long and complicated. When they are it is a good tactic to separate them out and define them separately—an example of the divide and conquer paradigm.

This section has described how a system can be specified mathematically. In user terms the specification of an operation consists of a pre- and a post-condition. This can be looked upon as an exact statement of the contract between the customer and the developer. A post-condition for an operation states that the developer will deliver a system that, when the operation is executed, will result in the post-condition being true. It is important to stress that there is no guarantee what will happen if the pre-condition does not hold.

The following exercises will give you practice in thinking about VDM specifications. At this stage of the book we have not taught you the detailed syntax of VDM, so do not worry about getting this aspect of the specification incorrect.

Exercise 3.1

1. A system is intended to keep track of the names of staff in an advertising company. Three operations are required for the system: an operation that adds a name to the database of stored names, an operation that removes a name from the database of stored names and an operation that checks if a particular name is in the database. Write down the state and a specification of the operations. Do not write down the data invariant.
2. A system is intended to keep track of the programs currently executing in an operating system. There are three types of programs: those running, those suspended and those awaiting execution. No program can be of more than one type, for example a program cannot simultaneously be suspended and awaiting execution. Also, the collection of programs is known to the system as the current programs. Write down the data invariant.

3.4   SUMMARY

This chapter has been introductory in nature. What it has described is a mathematical language for describing systems. This language enables the developer to define the state, data invariant and operations that make up a system. The state is the stored data of the system, the data invariant is a condition that describes what must be true *throughout* the execution of the system and the operations are actions that examine and alter the state.

Each operation is characterized by a pre-condition and a post-condition. The pre-condition defines what must be true *before* an operation is executed for the action of the operation to be defined; the post-condition describes what is true *after* the operation is executed. This form of specification gives rise to a series of proof obligations which must be shown to be true by the developer in order to validate the system. The chapter described one such obligation—that an operation should not violate the data invariant.

4

SETS

AIMS

- To introduce the set as the building block of the Vienna Development Method.
- To describe operation specifications in more detail than in previous chapters.
- To describe a number of built-in set functions and operations.
- To illustrate the use of sets within simple VDM specifications.

4.1 INTRODUCTION

In the previous chapter we have outlined the structure of VDM specifications. In this chapter we will describe how the specifications are defined. To do this we will describe a basic building block of VDM: the set.

A set is a collection of objects that contains no duplicates. Thus the collection of natural numbers:

$$12, 122, 66, 67, 55, 2$$

is a set. In VDM a collection of objects that are a set are enclosed within curly brackets. Thus, the set of integers above would be represented by

$$\{12, 122, 66, 67, 55, 2\}$$

Sets can contain duplicate elements, but repeating an element has no meaning, the first occurrence is enough; also the order in which the elements are written doesn't matter, so the following sets are all equal:

$$\{1, 1, 2, 3\} = \{1, 2, 2, 3\} = \{2, 3, 1\} = \{1, 2, 3\}$$

This way of writing down a set defines it by enumerating its members. As you will see later in this chapter, there are better, more succinct ways of defining a set. VDM assumes the existence of a number of sets, $\mathbf{B}$, $\mathbf{N}$, $\mathbf{N}_1$, $\mathbf{Z}$, $\mathbf{Q}$ and $\mathbf{R}$:

$$\mathbf{B} = \{\mathsf{true}, \mathsf{false}\}$$
$$\mathbf{N} = \{0, 1, 2, \ldots\}$$
$$\mathbf{N}_1 = \{1, 2, \ldots\}$$
$$\mathbf{Z} = \{\ldots, -1, 0, 1, \ldots\}$$
$$\mathbf{Q} = \text{The rational numbers}$$
$$\mathbf{R} = \text{The real numbers}$$

The set **B** is known as the *Booleans*, the set **N** is known as the *natural numbers*, the set N_1 is the natural numbers apart from zero, the set **Z** is known as the *integers*, the set **Q** is known as the *rationals* and the set **R** is known as the *real numbers*. A set with no members is known as the empty set and is written as { }.

The elements of sets can be single objects, as with the elements of **Z**. They can also be sets of objects. For example, the set

$$\{\{1,2\},\{\},\{1,3\},\{1,5,6,7\}\}$$

contains elements which, themselves, are sets; it contains four elements.

Worked example 4.1 The set above does not seem to satisfy our definition of a set: that is a collection of objects none of which are equal to each other. For example, the set contains the element 1, three times. Can you explain this apparent contradiction?

SOLUTION There is no contradiction. The elements of the set are sets of natural numbers, not natural numbers. There are four of these elements, none of which are equal to each other. ■

4.2 BOOLEAN SET OPERATORS

A number of operators are defined on sets. We shall examine those that deliver Boolean results first.

The first we shall examine are the set membership operators $\notin$ and $\in$. The $\in$ operator checks if a particular element is contained in a set. It returns a true value if it is. Thus, all the following will deliver true:

$3 \in \{3, 12, 23, 24\}$
ARTHUR $\in \{$BEN, ARTHUR, WILLIAM$\}$
$22 \in \{22\}$
$45 \in$ **N**

Notice the third expression, which just states that 22 is contained in the singleton set which just contains the natural number 22.

The operator $\notin$ is the opposite of $\in$; it returns a value true if a particular element is not contained in a set, and false otherwise. Thus, all the following are true:

$2 \notin \{34, 23, 20908, 77\}$
DAVE $\notin \{$JIM, ROB, BILL$\}$
$-1 \notin$ **N**
RCT1 $\notin \{$RCT2, RCT5, RCT6, RCT17$\}$

It is important to point out that the set membership operators have as the left-hand operand a member of a set and as the right-hand operand a set itself.

Worked example 4.2 What is the value of the expression

$N \in Z$

SOLUTION The value is undefined. You may have been tempted to say that the value is true because the natural numbers can be found in the integers. However, remember that the set membership operators take an element of a set as their left-hand operand and a set as their right-hand operand. In the above expression the left-hand and right-hand operands are both sets. ■

Two other operators which return Boolean values are the set inclusion operators. These are $\subset$ and $\subseteq$. The first is the proper subset operator, the second the subset operator. They have two operands, both of which are sets. They check that a set is a subset, or a proper subset, of another set. A set A is a subset of another set B if all the elements of A are contained in B. The operator $\subseteq$ returns true if its left-hand operand is a subset of its right-hand operand, and false otherwise. Thus, the following are true:

$\{2\} \subseteq \{2, 3, 6, 7, 9\}$
$\{\text{ALF}\} \subseteq \{\text{ALF}, \text{GEOFF}, \text{BILL}\}$
$\{3\} \subseteq \{3\}$
$\{\text{RCT}1, \text{RCT}2\} \subseteq \{\text{RCT}1, \text{RCT}2, \text{RCT}3, \text{RCT}4\}$

A set A is a proper subset of another set B if A is a subset of B and not equal to B. The operator $\subset$ returns true if its left-hand operand is a proper subset of its right-hand operand, and false otherwise. Thus, all the following are true.

$\{3\} \subset \{34, 3\}$
$\{1, 2, 3, 4\} \subset \{1, 2, 3, 4, 5\}$
$\{\text{DAVE}\} \subset \{\text{DAVE}, \text{BILL}\}$
$\{\text{REACT}1\} \subset \{\text{RXQ}, \text{RX}3, \text{RX}4, \text{RX}5, \text{REACT}1\}$

An important point to notice about subsets is that the empty set is a subset of any set and proper subset of any non-empty set, thus all the following are true:

$\{\} \subseteq \{34, 3, 1234\}$
$\{\} \subseteq \{1, 2, 3, 4, 5\}$
$\{\} \subset \{\text{DAVE}, \text{BILL}, \text{JOE}\}$
$\{\} \subset \{\text{RXQ}, \text{RX}3, \text{RX}4, \text{RX}5, \text{REACT}1, \text{REACT}2\}$

Worked example 4.3 What is the result of the following expression?

$\mathbb{N} \subseteq \mathbb{Z} \wedge \mathbb{N} \subset \mathbb{Z}$

SOLUTION The result is the Boolean value true. Both the left-hand and right-hand side of the conjunct are true since the natural numbers are both a subset and a proper subset of the integers. ■

Exercise 4.1

1. What is the value of the following expressions?

   (a) $\{1\} \subseteq \mathbb{Z}$
   (b) $\{1, 2, 3\} \subseteq \{1, 2\}$
   (c) $\{\text{SPOOLER}\} \subseteq \{\text{SPOOLER}, \text{SYSADMIN}, \text{SCHEDULER}\}$
   (d) $3 \in \{3, 2, 4, 1000\}$
   (e) $\text{DAVE} \notin \{\text{DAVE}, \text{WILLIAM}, \text{ARTHUR}\}$

2. What is the value of the following expressions?

    (a) $\{1, 2, 3\} \subset \{1, 2\} \wedge \mathbb{Z} \subset \mathbb{N}$

    (b) $3 \in \{31, 2, 4, 1000\} \vee \mathbb{Z} \subset \mathbb{N}$

    (c) $\{\text{SPOOLER}\} \subseteq \{\text{SPOOLER}, \text{SYSADMIN}, \text{SCHEDULER}\} \wedge \mathbb{Z} \subset \mathbb{N}$

4.3   SPECIFYING SETS

At the beginning of this section we described how a set can be specified by means of an enumeration, whereby the elements are listed, separated by commas. For example,

$$\{1, 5, 66, 78, 1090\}$$

is an example of a five element set. This way of specifying a set suffers from a number of disadvantages. First, for sets with a large number of elements this is clearly impractical; for infinite sets, such as the even natural numbers it is impossible. Second, quoting elements of a set does not give the reader an idea of the properties of the members of the set; for example, the set

$$\{1, 2, 3, 5, 7\}$$

could represent the set of all odd natural numbers less than 9 or the set of all primes less than 9.

    The first way of specifying sets succinctly involves the specification of sets of integers. A set of consecutive integers can be specified by

$$\{integer_1, \ldots, integer_2\}$$

This represents the subset of integers

$$\{integer_1, integer_1 + 1, integer_1 + 2, \ldots, integer_2\}$$

Thus, the set

$$\{3, \ldots, 7\}$$

represents the set of five consecutive integers starting with 3 and finishing with 7.

    Worked example 4.4 What is the result of the expression

$$\{4, \ldots, 1\}$$

SOLUTION This represents the consecutive natural numbers starting at 4 and ascending to 1. However, there is no set of natural numbers that satisfies this expression, therefore it represents the empty set $\{\,\}$. ■

    A more general—and hence useful—form of specification is known as *set comprehension*. It has the form

$$\{\text{set membership} \mid \text{term}\}$$

Where *set membership* consists of an expression that relates a variable to a set and *term* is an expression that defines the form of the elements of the set. An example is shown below:

$$\{x \in \{1, 3, 5, 11\} \mid 4 < x\}$$

This contains the set membership expression $x \in \{1, 3, 5, 11\}$, which states that the elements of the set are formed by examining the values 1, 3, 5 and 11. The elements of the set all satisfy the predicate $4 < x$. This means that the set specified above is thus $\{5, 11\}$.

An example of a more complicated set comprehension is shown below, where *topmost* is the set $\{23, 12, 1, 22\}$.

$$\{x \in \mathbf{Z} \mid 15 < x \wedge x \in topmost\}$$

This represents the set whose elements are taken from the integers which are greater than or equal to 15 but which are also contained in the set *topmost*. This represents the set $\{22, 23\}$.

An important point to make at this stage is that it is irrelevant which variables are used in the set membership expression. For example the following set comprehensions all represent the same set:

$$\{x \in \{1, 3, 5, 11\} \mid 4 < x\}$$
$$\{y \in \{1, 3, 5, 11\} \mid 4 < y\}$$
$$\{anyvariable \in \{1, 3, 5, 11\} \mid 4 < anyvariable\}$$
$$\{gobbledegook \in \{1, 3, 5, 11\} \mid 4 < gobbledegook\}$$

Worked example 4.5 Write down a set comprehension expression for the set

$$\{1, \ldots, 100\}$$

SOLUTION The set will be the set of natural numbers whose elements are greater or equal to 1 and less than or equal to 100.

$$\{y \in \mathbf{N} \mid 1 \leq y \wedge y \leq 100\}$$

∎

A final way of specifying sets is to use the operator $\mathcal{F}$. When this is applied to a set it produces a set of all the finite subsets of its arguments. Thus, the result of the expression

$$\mathcal{F}\{1, 2\}$$

is

$$\{\{\,\}, \{1\}, \{2\}, \{1, 2\}\}$$

Exercise 4.2

1. What is the value of the following expressions?

   (a) $\{1, \ldots, 12\}$
   (b) $\{1, \ldots, 1\}$
   (c) $\{x \in \{2, 3, 4, 5\} \mid 2 < x\}$
   (d) $\{x \in \{2, 3, 4, 5\} \mid 22 < x\}$
   (e) $\{y \in \{2, 3, 4, 5\} \mid x^2 - 12 < 0\}$

2. Which of the following expressions are true?

   (a) $\{\,\} \in \mathcal{F}\mathbf{N}$
   (b) $\{x \in \{2, 3, 4, 5\} \mid 22 < x\} \in \mathcal{F}\{1, 2, 3\}$

(c) $\{1, \ldots, 13\} \subseteq \{2, \ldots, 23\}$
(d) $\mathcal{F}\{1, \ldots, 2\} = \mathcal{F}\{1, \ldots, 3\}$
(e) $\mathcal{F}\mathbf{B} = \{\{\text{true}\}, \{\text{false}\}, \{\text{true}, \text{false}\}\}$

4.4 SET OPERATORS THAT DELIVER SETS

This section describes some operators that give sets as results. The first two are $\cup$ and $\cap$. The first operator, *set union* operates on two sets; it returns the set that contains the collection of objects that occur in either of the operands. For example, the result of the expression

$\{\text{ARTHUR}, \text{WILLIAM}, \text{DAVE}\} \cup \{\text{DAVE}, \text{TOM}, \text{WILLIAM}\}$

is

$\{\text{ARTHUR}, \text{WILLIAM}, \text{DAVE}, \text{TOM}\}$

Notice that although DAVE and WILLIAM occur in both operands, they do not occur twice in the result. This is because since the result is a set, duplicates are meaningless, and not recommended. The second operator $\cap$, set intersection, returns the set of objects that are contained in both operands. Thus, the result of

$\{1, 2, 5, 8, 10, 34\} \cap \{1, 2, 6, 34\}$

is

$\{1, 2, 34\}$

Worked example 4.6 Write down, using set comprehension, an expression that defines the set intersection operator applied to two sets A and B which contain elements of type X.

SOLUTION The expression is

$\{x \in X \mid x \in A \land x \in B\}$

This defines the set of natural numbers that are contained in both A and B. ∎

The definition of the set union operator is similar to the solution to worked example 4.6:

$\{x \in X \mid x \in A \lor x \in B\}$

The set difference operator $-$, when applied to two set operands, produces the set that contains those elements in the left-hand operand that are not in the second operand. Thus, the result of the expression

$\{12, 33, 5, 66, 7\} - \{12, 33, 2, 8\}$

is

$\{5, 66, 7\}$

The definition of the set difference operator is

$\{x \in X \mid x \in A \land x \notin B\}$

The final set operators—those which give the most trouble of all—are the distributed intersection and distributed union operators. These are written as large versions of the set union and set intersection operators, thus, $\bigcup$ and $\bigcap$. The former is a unary operator which is applied to a set whose elements are themselves sets. It forms the union of all the sets inside the set to which the operator is applied. Thus,

$$\bigcup\{s_1, s_2, s_3, \dots, s_n\} = s_1 \cup s_2 \cup s_3 \dots \cup s_n$$

For example,

$$\bigcup\{\{1,2\}, \{3,4,5\}, \{1,3,6\}\} =$$
$$\{1,2\} \cup \{3,4,5\} \cup \{1,3,6\} =$$
$$\{1,2,3,4,5,6\}$$

The distributed intersection operator is very similar, except that it forms the intersection of all the sets that are elements of the set to which it is applied. Thus,

$$\bigcap\{s_1, s_2, s_3, \dots, s_n\} = s_1 \cap s_2 \cap s_3 \dots \cap s_n$$

For example,

$$\bigcap\{\{1,21\}, \{35,41,5\}, \{11,30,61\}\} =$$
$$\{1,21\} \cap \{35,41,5\} \cap \{11,30,61\} =$$
$$\{\}$$

since the sets inside the set that is the operand contain no common elements.

Exercise 4.3

1. What is the value of the following expressions?

   (a) $\bigcup\{\{\text{TIM}, \text{ARTHUR}\}, \{\text{LES}, \text{TIM}, \text{ROB}\}, \{\text{JOE}, \text{BILL}, \text{DAVE}\}\}$
   (b) $\bigcap\{\{1,2\}, \{1,5,6\}, \{3,6,8,9\}\}$
   (c) $\bigcap\{\{1,21\}, \{11,5,6\}, \{3,6,8,9\}\} \cup \bigcup\{\{1,7\}, \{12,23,21\}\}$

2. Which of the following expressions are true?

   (a) $\bigcap\{\{1,2\}, \{1,5,6\}, \{3,6,8,9\}\} = (\{2,3,1\} - \{2,3\})$
   (b) $\bigcap\{\{\}\} = \bigcup\{\{\}\}$
   (c) $\bigcup\{\{\}\} = \bigcap\{\{1,21\}, \{1,51,6\}, \{1,6,8,9\}\}$

3. Write down a set comprehension that describes

   (a) The set of even integers.
   (b) The set of odd integers greater than 44.
   (c) The set of reactors inside the set *react* which are also in the set *non-functioning*.

4.5   SOME SET-BASED SPECIFICATIONS

4.5.1   A system for checking chemical reactor names

The aim of this section is to describe a selection of VDM specifications for some simple systems. These systems only involve sets. A secondary aim of this section is to teach you how VDM specifications are structured. In order to describe the specification a further, simple operator is required. This is card, which returns the number of elements in a set. For example,

$$\text{card}\,\{1,3,5,6,77,88,101\} = 7$$

The first system is based on the informal statement of requirements.

> A system is to be developed which checks that the name of a chemical reactor typed in by a chemical plant operator is valid. A number of commands are to be implemented. The first checks that a specified reactor is a valid one. The second adds a specified reactor to the collection of valid reactors. The third removes a particular reactor from the collection of valid reactors. No more than N reactors will be on-line at any time.

This statement of requirements assumes that the part of the system described needs a set of reactors. The first line of the specification defines the state that is to be manipulated. The state, as you will remember from Chapter 3, is the database which is operated on by the defined operations. The state, in this case study, is a set of valid reactors. We choose a set because what is required is a collection of data representing valid reactors that contains no duplicates. The first line of the VDM specification will then be

> *Set-reactors* = *Reactor*-set

This specifies that the data type *Set-reactors* will be a set of reactors, i.e. each element of *Set-reactors* will be taken from the collection of all possible sets formed by permuting the elements of *Reactor*. This assumes that *Reactors* has already been defined, we shall assume that somewhere in our specification there will be such a definition. Assume that in this definition that *Reactor* only contained

> {REACT1, REACT2, REACT3}

Then

> *Reactor*-set

will be a type that defines the following values

> {{ },
> {REACT1}, {REACT2}, {REACT3},
> {REACT1, REACT2}, {REACT1, REACT3}, {REACT2, REACT3},
> {REACT1, REACT2, REACT3}}

This means that as the specified operations for the system will be executed the state will have one of the values that are the elements of the set of reactors. At the beginning of the operation the state might be { }; when REACT1 is added to the set of reactors then the state becomes {REACT1}; when a second reactor REACT2 is added then the state becomes {REACT1, REACT2}; if, say, REACT1 is removed from the state then it then becomes {REACT2}; and so on. Each value that the state attains is contained in the set of reactors.

The next line of a specification contains a condition which must be true for the state *throughout* the execution of the system it is describing. In the statement of requirements the only condition that holds is that the number of reactors which are on-line, and hence valid, will be no greater than N. This condition is written as

> card *rct* $\leq$ N

This just states that for a state *rct*, which, from our definition, is a set of reactors, the cardinality of *rct* will always be less than or equal to N. Notice how this statement, known as a *data invariant*, is introduced. The data invariant is a function that has the name '*inv*' followed by a hyphen and the name of the state that the invariant describes. The function then defines the invariant as described in Chapter 3. The specification has become:

types

$Set\text{-}reactors = Reactor\text{-}\mathsf{set}$

state $Reactor\text{-}system$ of
    rct : $Set\text{-}reactors$
inv $mk\text{-}Reactor\text{-}system(rct)$ $\triangleq$ card $rct \leq$N
init $mk\text{-}Reactor\text{-}system(rct)$ $\triangleq$ $rct = \{\,\}$
end

The last line of the above specification describes the initial value of the state. This defines the initial value of the state to be the empty set, i.e. when the system starts up the set of valid states will contain no reactors. The choice of what to call the initial state is up to the specifier; whatever is decided will always be interpreted as the initial value of the state described by the specification.

The next step is to define the operations that access the state. You will remember from Chapter 3 that the operations that access the state will have the form:

operation-name (arguments) result

ext read and write information

pre pre-condition

post post-condition

operation-name gives the name of the operation, **arguments** are the name of the arguments of the operation together with their types and *result* gives the name of the result together with its type. The read and write information specifies how the operation will affect elements of the state: whether it will be read from or written to. The pre-condition is a predicate which gives a condition that must be true for the operation to be guaranteed to function correctly; the post-condition is a description of the condition that must be true after the operation is executed.

In order to see how operations are defined let us consider the operations implied in the statement of requirements for the program that manipulates a set of valid reactors. There are three operations implied in the statement: first, an operation that checks that a reactor is contained in the set of valid reactors; second, an operation that adds a reactor to a valid set of reactors; and third, an operation that deletes a reactor from the set of valid reactors.

The first operation is shown below:

check-react (*reac*: *Reactor*) *in*: $\mathbb{B}$

ext rd *rct* : *Set-reactors*

pre true

post $in \Leftrightarrow reac \in rct$

The first line gives the name of the operation (*check-react*), the part in brackets states that the operation has one argument *reac* which is of type *Reactor*. The final part of this first line states that the operation has the result, denoted by the identifier *in*, which is a Boolean.

The second line states that the operation requires read access to the state component *rct* which is of type *Set-reactors*, and which represents *Reactor*-set. The fact that the operation only requires read access means that the data is only retrieved from the state: the state is not overwritten.

The third line, the pre-condition, is introduced by the keyword pre. The pre-condition states that the operation *check-react* is defined when the input satisfies the predicate true, i.e. it is always defined. The post-condition states that after *check-react* has been executed then the result of the operation, denoted by *in*, will be true if *reac* is contained in the state *rct* and false otherwise.

The operation that adds a reactor to the set of valid reactors *add-react* is shown below:

$$add\text{-}react \ (reac\text{:} Reactor)$$

ext wr $rct \ : \ Set\text{-}reactors$

pre $reac \notin rct \wedge$ card $rct < N$

post $rct = \overleftarrow{rct} \cup \{reac\}$

The first line gives the name of the operation and its argument, since the operation updates the state and does not return a value, there is no result specified on this line. The argument is a reactor called *reac*. The second line states that write access is required to the state. The pre-condition states that for the operation to be defined the reactor *reac* must not be contained in the state component *rct* and less than N reactors are on-line. The final line, which contains the post-condition, states that after the operation has finished the state after the operation *rct* is equal to the state before the operation $\overleftarrow{rct}$ to which the element *reac* has been added. Notice that in the final line, curly brackets are placed around the element *reac*. This is because the set union operator is defined only for set operands; *reac* is not a set, it is an element of a set. However, placing curly brackets around *reac* makes it a set.

Worked example 4.7 Write down the specification for an operation *remove-react* which removes a specified reactor from the state representing the collection of valid reactors.

SOLUTION The specification is

$$remove\text{-}react \ (reac\text{:} Reactor)$$

ext wr $rct \ : \ Set\text{-}reactors$

pre $reac \in rct$

post $rct = \overleftarrow{rct} - \{reac\}$

∎

The first line gives the name of the operation; there is no result and one argument *reac*: the reactor to be removed from the state. The second line states that write access is needed to the state. The pre-condition states that for the operation to be defined the reactor to be removed must be contained in the state. The final line, the post-condition, states that after the operation has been executed, the set of valid reactors after the operation has been executed will be equal to the set of valid reactors before the operation has been executed with the element denoted by *reac* removed.

The full specification, containing comments, is:

values

$N : \mathbb{N}$

types

$Set\text{-}reactors = Reactor\text{-}set$

$Reactor = \ldots$

state $Reactor\text{-}system$ of
  $rct\ :\ Set\text{-}reactors$
inv $mk\text{-}Reactor\text{-}system(rct) \quad \triangle \quad$ card $reacts \leq N$
init $mk\text{-}Reactor\text{-}system(rct) \quad \triangle \quad reacts = \{\,\}$
end

operations

check-react checks that a reactor *reac* is contained in the collection of valid reactors.

  check-react (*reac*: *Reactor*) *in*: **B**
  ext rd $rct\ :\ Set\text{-}reactors$
  pre *true*
  post $in \quad \Leftrightarrow \quad reac \in rct$

The operation *add-react* adds a reactor *reac* to the collection of valid reactors.

  add-react (*reac*: *Reactor*)
  ext wr $rct\ :\ Set\text{-}reactors$
  pre $reac \notin rct \wedge$ card $rct < N$
  post $rct = \overleftarrow{rct} \cup \{reac\}$

The operation *remove-react* removes the reactor *reac* from the collection of valid reactors.

  remove-react (*reac*: *Reactor*)
  ext wr $rct\ :\ Set\text{-}reactor$
  pre $reac \in rct$
  post $rct = \overleftarrow{rct} - \{reac\}$

The major thing to notice about this specification is that each operation is accompanied by an English language narrative. You may find this strange, especially if you remembered our strictures about natural language earlier in this book. However, what is important is that the narrative is not the main medium for specification, as in the documents that we criticized in Chapter 1. It is a subsidiary medium which supports the main medium: discrete mathematics. It acts very much like the comments in a programming language.

Before examining the next example it is worth recapping the steps that we have carried out.

1. Read the statement of requirements.
2. Derive the state, based on the properties of the stored data.
3. Ask what condition(s) must be true throughout the execution of the system described by the statement of requirements. Specify the condition(s) as a data invariant.
4. Specify the initial value of the state.

5. From a reading of the statement of requirements, identify the operations required for the system to be developed. Each operations may require arguments, possibly a result, a definition of any read/write access to the state and pre- and post-conditions.

4.5.2 A simple library system

The next specification is based on the following informal statement of requirements.

A system is to be built which administers the books in a library. Books are borrowed by the clients of the library from the shelves.

Books will either be borrowed, lent to a client or missing. A system is to be developed which enables a library assistant to carry out the tasks listed below.

- Register a book being borrowed.
- Register a book being returned.
- Register a book that is missing.
- Register a book being no longer missing.
- Display the number of books currently borrowed.
- Adds a book to the library system.

This statement of requirements is rather artificial; it does not include details of clients who borrow books, the maximum number of books borrowed, the date of borrowing and the date of return of books, etc. At this stage in this book we have not described the type of facilities that enable such a realistic specification to be defined. Consequently, we shall concentrate on the properties outlined in the statement of requirements above.

In this example we shall concentrate on the operations. We shall assume a state made up of three sets: the set of borrowed books, the set of books on the shelves and the set of books that is currently missing. We shall assume that *Book-id* has been defined elsewhere.

types

$Books = Book\text{-}id\text{-}\mathsf{set}$

state *Library* **of**
$$shelf\text{-}books\ :\ Books$$
$$missing\text{-}books\ :\ Books$$
$$borrowed\text{-}books\ :\ Books$$
inv $mk\text{-}Library(sb, mb, bb)\ \triangleq\ is\text{-}disj(\{sb, mb, bb\})$
end

The first operation is one that registers a book being borrowed. This will be the operation *borrow-book*:

$borrow\text{-}book\ (bk: Book\text{-}id)$
ext wr $shelf\text{-}books, borrowed\text{-}books\ :\ Books$
pre $bk \in shelf\text{-}books$
post $shelf\text{-}books = \overleftarrow{shelf\text{-}books} - \{bk\}\ \wedge$
$$borrowed\text{-}books = \overleftarrow{borrowed\text{-}books} \cup \{bk\}$$

The first line just states that the operation is called *borrow-book* and that it has one argument *bk*. The next line states that write access is required to the set of borrowed books and the set of books on the library shelves. The pre-condition on the third line states that for the operation to be defined the book that is to be borrowed must be on the shelves of the library, that is, it must be contained in *shelf-books*. The final lines state that the effect of the operation is first to remove *bk* from *shelf-books* and then to place it into *borrowed-books*.

Worked example 4.8 Specify the operation corresponding to the return of a book. Assume that the name of the operation is *return-book*.

SOLUTION

> *return-book* (*bk*: *Book-id*)
>
> ext wr *shelf-books*, *borrowed-books* : *Books*
>
> pre *bk* $\in$ *borrowed-books*
>
> post *shelf-books* = $\overleftarrow{shelf\text{-}books}$ $\cup$ {*bk*} $\wedge$
>   *borrowed-books* = $\overleftarrow{borrowed\text{-}books}$ − {*bk*}

The operation is very similar to *borrow-book*, except that the book that has been returned has been removed from *borrowed-books* and added to *shelf-books*. ∎

The operations that register the fact that a book is missing and that a book is no longer missing are:

> *missing-book* (*bk*: *Book-id*)
>
> ext wr *shelf-books*, *missing-books* : *Books*
>
> pre *bk* $\in$ *shelf-books*
>
> post *shelf-books* = $\overleftarrow{shelf\text{-}books}$ − {*bk*} $\wedge$
>   *missing-books* = $\overleftarrow{missing\text{-}books}$ $\cup$ {*bk*}

> *not-missing-book* (*bk*: *Book-id*)
>
> ext wr *shelf-books*, *missing-books* : *Books*
>
> pre *bk* $\in$ *missing-books*
>
> post *shelf-books* = $\overleftarrow{shelf\text{-}books}$ $\cup$ {*bk*} $\wedge$
>   *missing-books* = $\overleftarrow{missing\text{-}books}$ − {*bk*}

Worked example 4.9 Write down the specification for the final two operations: *no-of-borrowed* and *add-book*.

SOLUTION The specifications for the operations are shown below.

> *no-of-borrowed* () *no-borrowed*: $\mathbb{N}$
>
> ext rd *borrowed-books* : *Books*
>
> pre *true*
>
> post *no-borrowed* = card *borrowed-books*

$add\text{-}book\ (bk\text{:}\ Book\text{-}id)$

ext **wr** $shelf\text{-}books$ $\qquad\qquad\qquad$: $Books$
$\quad$ **rd** $missing\text{-}books, borrowed\text{-}books$: $Books$

pre $bk \notin shelf\text{-}books \cup missing\text{-}books \cup borrowed\text{-}books$

post $shelf\text{-}books = \overleftarrow{shelf\text{-}books} \cup \{bk\}$

The first operation has no argument and one result. The result is *no-borrowed*: the number of books borrowed by users of the library. The pre-condition is true since the operation will be defined for all values of the state. The post-condition just states that when the operation has been completed the argument of the operation will be equal to the cardinality of the set *borrowed-books*, i.e. the number of books borrowed. The second operation *add-book* is relatively straightforward. The operation has one argument which is bk, the book to be added to the library. The operation requires write access to *shelf-books* and the pre-condition states that for the operation to be defined the book to be added bk must not already be a book that is either borrowed, missing or on the shelves of the library. The post-condition states that after the operation has been completed the book is added to those on the shelves. ■

4.5.3   The computer-based thesaurus

A thesaurus is a collection of words that are partitioned into sets. Each set consists of words that have the same meaning. For example, the collection of words

$\qquad$ bloc, faction, cabal, camp, caucus, coalition, junta, lobby, sector

all have the same meaning: a collection of individuals organized to place pressure on another individual or group of individuals. A thesaurus is a valuable aid to writers as it enables them not to repeat themselves and to pick words that may differ only slightly in semantics. Thesauri are now published by all the main publishers of dictionaries, and a number are now becoming computerized. This small case-study involves operations required to maintain and access a computer-based thesaurus.

> A program is required which maintains and accesses a file containing a thesaurus. This program should enable the user to use four commands. The first command adds a particular word to the thesaurus. To use this command the user types in a word that is already in the thesaurus and a new word that has the same meaning. The effect of the command is to add the new word to the file. The second command removes a word from the thesaurus. To use this command the user provides this word and the effect of the command is to remove it from the file. The third command returns the words that have the same meaning as a particular word. The user types in the word and the program returns those words in the file that have the same meaning. The fourth command just returns the number of words that have the same meaning as a particular word. The user types in the word and the program returns the number of similar words.

At this stage it is worth recapping the steps that are needed to develop the specification.

1. Read the statement of requirements.
2. Derive the state based on the properties of the stored data.

3. Ask what condition(s) must be true throughout the execution of the system described by the statement of requirements. Specify the condition(s) as a data invariant.

4. Specify the initial value of the state.

5. From a reading of the statement of requirements, identify the operations required for the system to be developed. Each operation may require arguments, possibly a result, a definition of any read/write access to the state and pre- and post-conditions.

The first step is to *read the statement of requirements*. We shall assume you have done this. The next step is to *derive the state based on the properties of the stored data*. In order to do this it might be worth examining some possible ways of organizing the data.

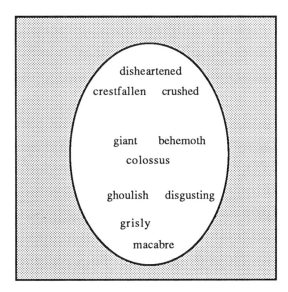

Figure 4.1   An incorrect way of modelling a thesaurus.

One way of organizing the thesaurus is shown in Fig. 4.1. It shows the file being modelled as a set of words. The thesaurus shown in the figure is small for simplicity sake, and contains only data on three sets of similar meaning words: *disheartened, crestfallen* and *crushed; giant, behemoth* and *colossus;* and *ghoulish, disgusting, grisly* and *macabre*. It is obvious from this that a simple set is inadequate since there is no information about which words are associated together. A better way of organizing the thesaurus is shown in Fig. 4.2.

Here the thesaurus is modelled by a set whose individual items are sets of words. The type of the thesaurus will then be

> *Thesaurus* = (*Word*-set)-set

and the state is

> state *Thesaurus-system* of
>   *th* : *Thesaurus*
> end

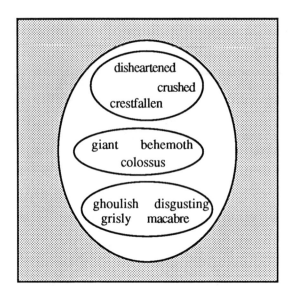

Figure 4.2   An improved way of modelling a thesaurus.

where *Word* has been defined previously. The next step is to define the data invariant, the condition describing the state, which must be true throughout the execution of the system that uses the state.

> **Worked example 4.10** What is true throughout the use of the thesaurus? Do not worry about writing the condition using mathematics, express it in English. Assume that we do not have the complication of words that are spelt the same having two different meanings, for example *rib* meaning a bone and *rib* to make fun of.
>
> SOLUTION The condition that is true is that the individual members of the thesaurus—which you will remember are sets themselves—do not have any common members; that is, a word in the thesaurus will not be a member of more than one collection of similar meaning words. ∎

How might the answer to the previous worked example be specified? One possible solution is

> state *Thesaurus-system* of
>   *th* : *Thesaurus*
> inv *mk-Thesaurus-system*(*th*) $\triangleq$ $\bigcap th = \{\,\}$
> end

Here the invariant states that the distributed intersection of the sets which are contained in the thesaurus is the empty set. This looks seductively correct. Is it? The answer is no. A simple example will show that it is not. Consider one possible value of the state shown below:

$\{\{\text{OLD}, \text{AGED}\},$
$\quad \{\text{NEW}, \text{PRISTINE}\},$
$\quad \{\text{HUGE}, \text{MAMMOTH}, \text{COLOSSUS}, \text{PRISTINE}\}\}$

Here the word *pristine* occurs in two of the members of the set. Yet, when the distributed intersection is applied the empty set is returned. Try it out for yourself; you will find that no matter what order you apply the distributed intersection, the empty set always emerges.

Another attempt is called for. In order to construct the correct data invariant let us try expressing it in English:

> If we take any two sets in the collection of sets in the thesaurus their intersection will be the empty set.

This looks much better. It certainly works when it is applied to the simple example above. In mathematical terms it can be written as

> state *Thesaurus-system* of
> $\quad$ *th* : *Thesaurus*
> inv *mk-Thesaurus-system*(*th*) $\quad \triangle \quad \forall x, y \in \textit{th} \cdot x \cap y = \{\,\}$
> end

Worked example 4.11 Does the following expression adequately describe the property of the thesaurus?

> state *Thesaurus-system* of
> $\quad$ *th* : *Thesaurus*
> inv *mk-Thesaurus-system*(*th*) $\quad \triangle \quad \forall x, y \in \textit{th} \cdot x \cap y = \{\,\}$
> end

SOLUTION Not quite. You will remember from Chapter 2 that when a quantifier is used in a predicate it ranges over all the elements of the set that are specified. Thus, x and y can also refer to the same set and the intersection of two equal sets will not be the empty set, unless, of course the two sets were both empty. The predicate would need to be modified to read:

> state *Thesaurus-system* of
> $\quad$ *th* : *Thesaurus*
> inv *mk-Thesaurus-system*(*th*) $\quad \triangle \quad \forall x, y \in \textit{th} \cdot x \neq y \Rightarrow x \cap y = \{\,\}$
> end

which states that for any two sets contained in *th*, if they are not the same set then their intersection will be the empty set. ∎

The next step is to *specify the initial value of the state*. This is relatively straightforward, the initial value will be the empty set

> init *mk-Thesaurus-system*(*th*) $\quad \triangle \quad \textit{th} = \{\,\}$

The last step is *from a reading of the statement of requirements identify any operations required for the system to be developed. Each operation requires arguments, possibly a result, a definition of read/write access to the state and the pre- and post-conditions.*

There will be four operations. The first adds a word to the thesaurus, the second removes a word from the thesaurus, the third finds all the similar words to a particular word and the fourth finds the number of similar words to a particular word. We shall assume that the names of these operations are *add-word*, *remove-word*, *find-words* and *count-words*.

The first of these operations is shown below:

> *add-word* (*wrdmean, wrdadd*: *Word*)
>
> **ext wr** *th* : *Thesaurus*
>
> **pre** *wrdmean* $\in \bigcup th \land$
>   *wrdadd* $\notin \bigcup th$
>
> **post let** *inset* = $\{x \in Word \mid \exists y \in \overleftarrow{th} \cdot wrdmean \in y \land x \in y\}$ **in**
>   *th* = $(\overleftarrow{th} - \{inset\}) \cup \{inset \cup \{wrdadd\}\}$

The first line gives the name of the operation and specifies that there are two arguments, both of which are words. The first argument *wrdmean* is the word that means the same as the word to be inserted. The second argument is *wrdadd* which is the word to be inserted.

The second line specifies that since the state is going to be altered write access is required. The pre-condition states that for the operation to be defined *wrdmean* must be contained in the combined collection of words in the thesaurus and the word added *wrdadded* must not be in the combined collection of words in the thesaurus. The post-condition is a little more complicated. It makes use of the set

$$\{x \in Word \mid \exists y \in \overleftarrow{th} \cdot wrdmean \in y \land x \in y\}$$

which is the set of similar words in the thesaurus to *wrdmean*. It uses the let facility in VDM to state that in the post condition the set *inset* stands for this set. The let facility is very similar to a local declaration in a programming language; it associates an identifier with an expression which is usually so complicated that to write it over and over again in a pre-condition or a post-condition would make them unreadable.

The post-condition states that the state *th* after the operation will equal the state before the operation minus the set of similar words to *wrdmean* unioned with the set of similar words to *wrdmean* but with *wrdadd* added. In this way we specify the addition of *wrdadd* to the thesaurus.

Worked example 4.12   Write down the specification for the operation *remove-word*. You will find that the let facility of VDM will come in handy.

SOLUTION   The specification is shown below:

> *remove-word* (*rmword*: *Word*)
>
> **ext wr** *th* : *Thesaurus*
>
> **pre** *rmword* $\in \bigcup th$
>
> **post let** *inset* = $\{x \in Word \mid \exists y \in \overleftarrow{th} \cdot rmword \in y \land x \in y\}$ **in**
>   *th* = $(\overleftarrow{th} - \{inset\}) \cup \{inset - \{rmword\}\}$

The first two lines are straightforward. The third line, the pre-condition, states that the word to be removed must be in the thesaurus; the fourth and fifth lines, the post-condition, state that the thesaurus, after the operation has been executed, is equal to the thesaurus before the operation minus the set containing *rmword* unioned with the set containing *rmword*, but with *rmword* removed. ∎

Worked example 4.13 Write down the specification for the operation *find-words*.

SOLUTION The specification is

> *find-words* (*wrd*: *Word*) *simwords*: *Word*-set
>
> ext rd *th* : *Thesaurus*
>
> pre *wrd* $\in \bigcup th$
>
> post *simwords* $= \{x \in Word \mid \exists y \in th \cdot wrd \in y \wedge x \in y\} - \{wrd\}$

The first line shows that the operation has one argument *wrd*, the word that is to be looked up in the thesaurus, and one argument *simwords*, the collection of words similar to *wrd* in the thesaurus. The second line states that only read access is required to the thesaurus since the operation is one that queries it. The third line is the pre-condition; it states that the word to be looked up must be contained in the thesaurus. The fourth line states that the argument to the operation *simwords* will be the set of similar words minus the word *wrd*. ∎

The final operation is shown below. It is straightforward and we provide no explanation.

> *count-words* (*wrd*: *Word*) *numwords*: $\mathbb{N}$
>
> ext rd *th* : *Thesaurus*
>
> pre *wrd* $\in \bigcup th$
>
> post *numwords* $=$ card $\{x \in Word \mid \exists y \in th \cdot wrd \in y \wedge x \in y\} - 1$

Worked example 4.14 What if the specification of *count-words* had been written as

> *count-words* (*wrd*: *Words*) *numwords*: $\mathbb{N}$
>
> ext wr *th* : *Thesaurus*
>
> pre *wrd* $\in \bigcup th$
>
> post *numwords* $=$ card $\{x \in Word \mid \exists y \in \overleftarrow{th} \cdot wrd \in y \wedge x \in y\} - 1 \wedge$
>
> $\quad th = \overleftarrow{th}$

i.e., with *th* being replaced by $\overleftarrow{th}$. Would this still be a correct specification?

SOLUTION Yes, because the last line of the post-condition states that the state *th* is unchanged by the operation. This means that $\overleftarrow{th} = th$ and they can be used interchangeably. ∎

Before finishing with this example it is worth stating that there are better ways of modelling a thesaurus. However, we have yet to meet the facilities that allow us to do this.

Exercise 4.4

1. A computer system is to be developed which keeps track of the members of a series of software project teams. A team contains no more than 10 members. How would you use sets to model this situation? Write down the state, the data invariant, the initial value of the state and the specification of two operations *remove* and *move*. The *remove* operation removes all the members from a particular team, it has one

parameter which is the name of one of the members of the team to be removed. The *move* operation moves a particular member of a team to another team. This operation has two parameters: the name of the person to be moved and a name of one of the members of the team to which the person is to be added.

2. A compiler keeps a symbol table of all the program identifiers that it currently is able to recognize. This table can be modelled by means of a set. There will be no more than 100 identifiers in the table. Write down the state, the data invariant and the initial value of the state for the specification of the symbol table. Also write down the specification of two operations *join* and *sift*. The *join* operation takes two symbol tables which have no symbols in common, and merges them to form a single symbol table. The *sift* operation takes a symbol table and removes those symbols greater than eight characters long. Assume that a function *lesseq-eight* has already been written which returns true if a symbol is less than or equal to eight characters in length, and false otherwise.

4.6   SUMMARY

This chapter has described the basic building block of VDM: the set. It has described the main property of sets: the fact that a set does not contain duplicate elements and how to specify sets. A number of operators, such as card and ∪ have been described and some simple specifications involving sets have been developed. This chapter has also provided further examples of how a VDM specification is structured in terms of a state, a data invariant, an initial value of a state and a series of operations. Each operation is specified in terms of its effect on the state, a pre-condition and a post-condition. After finishing this chapter you should be familiar with the structure of such specifications and be able to write down specifications of a similar complexity to those presented in this chapter.

5

MAPS

AIMS

- To describe how maps are specified and used in VDM.
- To show how certain applications can be modelled using maps.
- To describe a number of small case studies using maps.
- To describe the form and structure of functions in VDM.
- To provide you with further practice in the use of make functions.

5.1 INTRODUCTION

In the previous chapter we described sets: collections of objects where duplication was not allowed. This chapter extends the previous one, in that a special type of set is described: *the map*, which has a property that enables it to be frequently used for modelling computer systems. In order to examine the properties of this particular mathematical structure consider the following excerpts from a system specification.

Each account holder at the bank is only allocated one current account.

In the monitoring system each monitoring instrument is attached to a single point on one of the reactors.

Each customer has a single address.

An item stored in the warehouse will be contained in one bin.

The important thing to notice about these excerpts is that they define objects that relate the members of two sets. In the first example the two sets are account holders and current accounts; in the second example the sets are monitoring instruments and reactors; in the third example the sets are customers and addresses; finally, the fourth example relates items to bins.

Worked example 5.1 Can you spot any other feature that the four examples have in common?

SOLUTION The major feature is that each item from one set (account holders, monitoring instruments, customers, items) is associated with only one item in the second set. ∎

The solution to the previous worked example gives the essential property of the objects which this chapter will describe. They are known as maps and contain information that relates single items in one set to single items in another set.

5.2 MAPS

An example of a map is shown in Fig. 5.1.

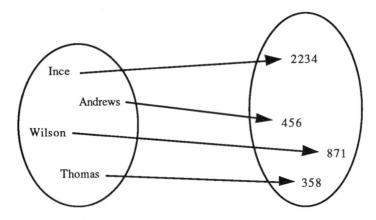

Figure 5.1 An example of a map.

Here, the map models the relationship between the customers in a bank and the account numbers of the accounts for each customer. For example, the account number of Andrews is 456. Also notice that the arrows show the important property of a map: that one item in the leftmost set is associated with only one item in the rightmost set. In VDM the set shown in Fig. 5.1 is represented as:

$$\{\text{WILSON} \mapsto 871, \text{THOMAS} \mapsto 358, \text{ANDREWS} \mapsto 456, \text{INCE} \mapsto 2234\}$$

Here, like sets, the order of the elements is immaterial. The collection of elements that lie to the left of the arrows is known as the *domain* of the map, while the collection of elements that lie to the right of each arrow is known as the *range* of the map. Each element of the map is known as a *maplet*. Thus, the map above contains four maplets, and the domain of the map is

$$\{\text{WILSON}, \text{THOMAS}, \text{ANDREWS}, \text{INCE}\}$$

while the range is

$$\{871, 358, 456, 2234\}$$

Maps are declared by writing

$$T = D \xrightarrow{m} R$$

What this says is that the type T will take values from all the possible maps that can be constructed and that have their domain a subset of D and their range a subset of R. Thus,

$$Bank\text{-}sys = \{100, \ldots, 600\} \xrightarrow{m} Account\text{-}holders$$

where *account-holders* is the set $\{\text{TIMMS}, \text{DAVIS}, \text{ROBERTS}\}$. Possible values that a value of type *Bank-sys* might have are shown below:

{ }
{100 ↦ Timms}
{102 ↦ Davis, 555 ↦ Roberts}
{102 ↦ Davis, 305 ↦ Roberts}
{111 ↦ Davis, 115 ↦ Roberts, 346 ↦ Timms}

In the same way that sets can be specified maps can be specified. For example, the constructive specification

$$\{i \mapsto \text{Dick} \mid i \in \{1, 2\}\}$$

defines the map

$$\{1 \mapsto \text{Dick}, 2 \mapsto \text{Dick}\}$$

Worked example 5.2 Earlier we described how a simple banking system which relates an account to a customer can be modelled using a map. In a more realistic system each customer would be allowed to own more than one account. Can you model this using a map? If so, how would you do it?

SOLUTION It is possible. Instead of relating an account holder to a single account you can relate the account holder to a set of accounts. This can be specified as

$$Bank\text{-}sys = \{100, \dots, 600\} \xrightarrow{m} Account\text{-}holders\text{-set}$$

∎

Exercise 5.1

1. How would you model an application that is intended to keep track of the cost of products in a retails sales system?
2. A system is intended to keep track of the components that a particular domestic electronics product consists of. How would you model such a system?
3. A system is intended to keep details of the files on a computer system where there are a number of users. How would you model this system using a map?

5.3 MAP OPERATORS

There are a number of operators that can be applied to maps. The first two are the dom and rng operators. The first extracts the domain from a map, while the second extracts the range. For example,

dom {1 ↦ Davis, 5 ↦ Roberts, 6 ↦ Timms} = {1, 5, 6}
rng {1 ↦ Davis, 5 ↦ Roberts, 6 ↦ Timms} = {Davis, Roberts, Timms}
rng {1 ↦ Davis, 5 ↦ Davis, 6 ↦ Davis} = {Davis}

Notice that the operand in the last example is still a map, although each of the second elements in the map are the same. Remember that the definition of a map is that each element of the domain is only associated with *one* element of the range.

The application of a map to a value in its domain will give the corresponding value in the range. For example, if the map *acc* is

{1000 ↦ Timkins, 1005 ↦ Roberts, 1002 ↦ Cobert}

then $acc(1000)$ is equal to TIMKINS.

Worked example 5.3 Is the following identity always true for any map mp?

card dom mp = card rng mp

SOLUTION This is false. As a counter-example consider the map

$\{1000 \mapsto \text{ROBERTS}, 1005 \mapsto \text{ROBERTS}, 1002 \mapsto \text{WILKINS}\}$

Here the cardinality of the domain of the map is 3, the domain of the map is the set $\{1000, 1005, 1002\}$ which has a cardinality of 3, while the cardinality of the range, $\{\text{WILKINS}, \text{ROBERTS}\}$, is 2. ∎

The map overwrite operator † gives a map that contains all the maplets in its second operand, together with those maplets from the first operand whose first elements are not in the domain of the second operand. Thus,

$\{1000 \mapsto \text{TIMKINS}, 1005 \mapsto \text{ROBERTS}, 1002 \mapsto \text{COBERT}\} \dagger \{1005 \mapsto \text{TIMMS}\}$

is equal to

$\{1000 \mapsto \text{TIMKINS}, 1005 \mapsto \text{TIMMS}, 1002 \mapsto \text{COBERT}\}$

Two further operators are the map restriction and map deletion operators. The map restriction operator ◁ has two operands: the first operand is a set, while the second operand is a map. It forms the map which is constructed by extracting those maplets that have their first element equal to a member of the set. Thus, the following are true:

$\{100, 10\} \lhd \{100 \mapsto \text{TIM}, 10 \mapsto \text{ROB}, 12 \mapsto \text{DAVE}\} = \{100 \mapsto \text{TIM}, 10 \mapsto \text{ROB}\}$
$\{13\} \lhd \{100 \mapsto \text{TIM}, 10 \mapsto \text{ROB}, 12 \mapsto \text{DAVE}\} = \{\ \}$

The map deletion operator ◁ has two operands. The first operand is a set and the second operand is a map. This operator forms the map which is constructed by selecting those maplets in the second operand whose first element is not contained in the first operand. Thus, the following is true

$\{100, 10\} \ntriangleleft \{100 \mapsto \text{TIM}, 10 \mapsto \text{ROB}, 12 \mapsto \text{DAVE}\} = \{12 \mapsto \text{DAVE}\}$
$\{100, 10, 12\} \ntriangleleft \{100 \mapsto \text{TIM}, 10 \mapsto \text{ROB}, 12 \mapsto \text{DAVE}\} = \{\ \}$

Worked example 5.4 In a warehouse application the fact that a supplier manufactures certain parts is modelled by the map *supdbase*.

$Supplier = Supplier\text{-}names \xrightarrow{m} Products\text{-set}$

Assume that

$supdbase \in Supplier$

and that a product can be supplied by more than one supplier. Using the operators which we have described in this chapter write down:

1. The products supplied by Jones.
2. The number of products supplied by Williams.
3. Those products not supplied by Timms.

SOLUTION

1. *supdbase*(JONES)
2. card *supdbase*(WILLIAMS)
3. $\bigcup$ rng *supdbase* − *supdbase*(TIMMS)

The first two solutions are relatively straightforward; they just involve the application of the map to each supplier. The third answer is a little more difficult. It involves finding all the products that are supplied and then subtracting from this the products supplied by TIMMS. ∎

Exercise 5.2

1. What is the value of the following expressions?

    (a) dom {100 ↦ TIM, 10 ↦ ROB, 12 ↦ DAVE}
    (b) rng {100 ↦ TIM, 10 ↦ ROB, 12 ↦ DAVE}
    (c) {1000 ↦ 3, 1005 ↦ 4, 1002 ↦ 1} † {1002 ↦ 6}
    (d) {1008 ↦ 3, 1065 ↦ 4, 1112 ↦ 1} † {1111 ↦ 6}
    (e) {128} ◁ {100 ↦ TIM, 10 ↦ ROB, 12 ↦ DAVE}

2. If the map *price* relates cars to their price, the set *BL* contains the cars made by British Leyland and *Fiat* the cars made by Fiat. Write down the following descriptions using the map facilities and set facilities described in this chapter and Chapter 4.

    (a) No car is made by both British Leyland and Fiat.
    (b) The price of the Montego 1.3L (a car made by British Leyland).
    (c) The prices of Fiat cars.
    (d) The number of Fiat cars that have a price between £6000 and £7000.
    (e) The map formed by changing the price of the Montego 1.3L to £5500.

3. If the map *accounts* relates the name of account holders to the set of accounts that they own and the map *balance* relates account names to their balance, write down VDM expressions that:

    (a) Deliver the set of names of account holders who have at least one account that is overdrawn.
    (b) Deliver the number of overdrawn accounts.
    (c) Deliver the number of accounts owned by Wilkinson.
    (d) Deliver the total balance of all the accounts owned by Roberts.
    (e) Deliver the set of account holders who only own one account.

5.4 SOME EXAMPLES OF SPECIFICATIONS INVOLVING MAPS

5.4.1 Bag operations

A set is a collection of objects with the restriction that duplicates are not allowed. In some applications there will be circumstances where this restriction will need to be relaxed. A set where this restriction does not occur is known as a *bag*. Assume that we wish to model a bag that contains natural numbers. How can we do this?

Worked example 5.5 How can maps be used to represent bags of natural numbers? (Hint: it will require the built-in VDM set $\mathbb{N}_1$ which is the set of natural numbers excluding zero.)

SOLUTION What is required is a map from the natural numbers to $\mathbb{N}_1$, where the domain of the map represents the numbers in the bag and the range of the map represents the total number of numbers in the bag. Thus, the bag containing three occurrences of the number 5, two occurrences of the number 9 and ten occurrences of the number 559 can be represented as

$$\{5 \mapsto 3, 9 \mapsto 2, 559 \mapsto 10\}$$

∎

Let us assume that a number of operations are required: an operation that increases the occurrence of a number in a bag by one, inserts a new number into a bag, finds the number of occurrences of a number in a bag and decreases the occurrence of a number in a bag by one. First, the state needs to be defined, along with the data invariant and the initial value of the state. Happily there are no conditions that restrict the bag so there is no need for a data invariant. The definition of the state and the initial state is shown below:

$$Bagsnat = \mathbb{N} \xrightarrow{m} \mathbb{N}_1$$

state Bag of
    bg : $Bagsnat$
init $mk\text{-}Bag(bg)$ $\triangleq$ $bg = \{\}$
end

The specification of the operation that returns with the number of occurrences of a number n in a bag is shown below

$bag\text{-}count$ $(n:\mathbb{N})$ $num:\mathbb{N}$

ext rd bg : $Bagsnat$

pre true

post $num = count(bg, n)$

This operation is fairly straightforward, apart from the post-condition. This uses a function $count$ which returns with the number of occurrences of the second parameter in the bag that is the first parameter. A function is used in this example because the act of extracting the number of a particular item in the bag will be used a number of times in the specification. The definition of the function is shown below

$count$: $Bagsnat \times \mathbb{N} \to \mathbb{N}$

$count(b, i)$ $\triangleq$ if $i \in$ dom b
                then $b(i)$
                else 0

Later in this chapter we shall describe functions in VDM in a little more detail. However, at this stage it is worth outlining the structure of the function $count$. The first line gives the name of the function, $count$, followed by the type of the parameters $\mathbb{N}$ and $Bagsnat$ to the left of the arrow symbol; the result of the function is written on the right hand side of the arrow The second line defines the action of $count$ it states that if i is in the domain of the bag b, then the number of occurrences of i in the bag is given by applying the function b to i. However, if i is not in the domain then this means that there are zero occurrences of i in the bag, and hence zero is returned.

The operation that increases the number of occurrence of a natural number n in the bag is shown below

$inc\text{-}bag\ (n{:}\mathbb{N})$

ext wr $bg\ :\ Bagsnat$

pre $true$

post $bg = \overleftarrow{bg} \dagger \{n \mapsto count(\overleftarrow{bg}, n) + 1\}$

The only tricky part of this operation is the post-condition. What it says is that after the operation has been executed, the bag bg will be modified by overwriting the entry corresponding to number n by the maplet formed from n and the number formed by incrementing the old number of occurrences of n by one.

Worked example 5.6 Specify the *dec-bag* operation which decreases the occurrence of the natural number n in the bag.

SOLUTION

$dec\text{-}bag\ (n{:}\mathbb{N})$

ext wr $bg\ :\ Bagsnat$

pre $n \in \text{dom}\ bg$

post $\overleftarrow{bg}(n) > 1 \wedge bg = \overleftarrow{bg} \dagger \{n \mapsto count(\overleftarrow{bg}, n) - 1\}$
$\quad\quad \vee$
$\overleftarrow{bg}(n) = 1 \wedge bg = \{n\} \triangleleft \overleftarrow{bg}$

∎

The final operation is *ins-bag* which inserts a new number n into the bag bg.

$ins\text{-}bag\ (n{:}\mathbb{N})$

ext wr $bg\ :\ Bagsnat$

pre $n \notin \text{dom}\ bg$

post $bg = \overleftarrow{bg} \cup \{n \mapsto 1\}$

5.4.2 A system for administering a record library

Part of a system for administering a record library keeps track of customers who have borrowed records. A customer can borrow up to five records and the record library has space for 10 000 records. A number of operations are required: an operation that corresponds to a customer borrowing a record, an operation which corresponds to a customer returning a record and an operation which corresponds to the owner of the record library checking which records are currently missing. We will concentrate on these functions solely and not worry about the part of the specification that deals with overdue loans.

The first part of the system to be specified is the state. This is shown below

types

$Recstock = Record\text{-set}$

$Borrowings = Customer \xrightarrow{m} Record\text{-set}$

state *Library* of
   recs : *Recstock*
   loans : *Borrowings*
end

The second and third lines define the data types *Recstock* and *Borrowings*. The fourth to seventh lines define the data type *Library* which will be a composite type that has two components: *recs* which is of type *Recstock* and *loans* which is of type *Borrowings*; *recs* represents the stock of records in the library while *loans* contains details of who currently has borrowed what records.

We shall assume that all the customers of the record library can be found in the domain of loans, and that if a customer has not borrowed any records the particular maplet will map the customer to the empty set. You may remember that the definition on these two lines is very much like declaring a record type in a programming language such as Pascal.

The data invariant is relatively simple: all it should say is that each customer should have borrowed no more than five records, the library will contain no more than 10 000 records, that any record on loan will be known to the library and that no two customers will have borrowed the same record.

Worked example 5.7 Write down the data invariant; assume that it starts with

$$inv\text{-}Library(mk\text{-}Library(recs, loans)) \quad \triangleq$$

where *recs* and *loans* are the components of the library representing the set of records and the loans. Remember the make function constructs an instance of a library with the components *recs* and *loans*.

SOLUTION

$$inv\text{-}Library((mk\text{-}Library(recs, loans)) \quad \triangleq$$
   $\text{card } recs \leq 10\,000 \land$
   $\forall i \in \text{dom } loans \cdot \text{card } loans(i) \leq 5 \land$
   $\bigcup \text{rng } loans \subseteq recs \land$
   $\forall c_1, c_2 \in \text{dom } loans \cdot c_1 \neq c_2 \implies loans(c_1) \cap loans(c_2) = \{\,\}$

The first conjunct states that there will be no more than 10 000 records in the library, the second conjunct states that each customer will be allowed to borrow no more than five records, the third conjunct states that the records on loan will be a proper subset of the records in stock and the fourth conjunct states that no two borrowers will have borrowed the same record. ∎

The full specification of the state, including its initial value (*TOTALSTOCK* is a constant that defines the inital stock of records), is shown below:

values

$TOTALSTOCK : Recstock$

types

$Recstock = Record\text{-set}$

$Borrowings = Customer \xrightarrow{m} Record\text{-set}$

state $Library$ of
      $recs$: $Recstock$
     $loans$: $Borrowings$
inv $mk\text{-}Library(recs, loans)$ $\triangleq$
   card $recs \le 10\,000 \wedge$
   $\forall i \in \text{dom } loans \cdot \text{card } loans(i) \le 5 \wedge$
   $\bigcup \text{rng } loans \subseteq recs \wedge$
   $\forall c_1, c_2 \in \text{dom } loans \cdot c_1 \ne c_2 \Rightarrow loans(c_1) \cap loans(c_2) = \{\,\}$
init $mk\text{-}Library(recs, loans)$ $\triangleq$
   $loans = \{\,\} \wedge recs = TOTALSTOCK$
end

The first operation is *borrow*, which records the fact that a customer c has borrowed a particular record r.

   $borrow\ (c\text{: } Customer, r\text{: } Record)$
   ext rd $recs$: $Recstock$
      wr $loans$: $Borrowings$
   pre $c \in \text{dom } loans \wedge$
      card $loans(c) < 5 \wedge$
      $r \notin \bigcup \text{rng } loans \wedge$
      $r \in recs$

   post $loans = \overleftarrow{loans} \dagger \{c \mapsto \overleftarrow{loans}(c) \cup \{r\}\}$

The first three lines are straightforward. The pre-condition states that for the operation to be executed properly then the customer must be in the *loans* component of the state *Library*, the customer must have borrowed less than five records and the record to be borrowed has not been borrowed by another member of the library.

    The post-condition states that after the *borrow* operation has been executed the maplet corresponding to the customer c is updated by unioning it with the singleton set which contains the record that has been borrowed.

Worked example 5.8 Write down the specification of an operation *return* which results in the return of a record to the record library.

SOLUTION

   $return\ (c\text{: } Customer, r\text{: } Record)$
   ext rd $recs$: $Recstock$
      wr $loans$: $Borrowings$
   pre $c \in \text{dom } recs \wedge r \in loans(c)$

   post $loans = \overleftarrow{loans} \dagger \{c \mapsto \overleftarrow{loans}(c) - \{r\}\}$

■

The specification is straightforward as it represents the opposite of the *return* operation. The only slightly difficult part is the pre-condition. All it states is that, for the operation to be successful, the customer who returns a record is recognized by the system and that he or she has actually borrowed the record that has been returned. The set expression *loans*(*c*) returns the complete set of all records borrowed by the customer *c*.

Exercise 5.3

1. Define an operation to add a new record to the library.
2. Define an operation to delete a record from the library—the record should not be out on loan.
3. Define an operation to add a new customer.
4. Define an operation to remove a customer—the customer should not have any records on loan.

5.4.3   A simple filing subsystem

A filing subsystem is part of an operating system that supervises the organization of files on the computer upon which the operating system is installed. We shall assume that in the file subsystem we are considering a user can own any number of files that occupy a number of blocks of storage, but that a user can only own files that occupy up to *UPP-BLOCKS* of storage. Another, more artificial assumption that we shall make is that duplicate file names are not allowed; i.e. a user may not pick another file name that is the same as a file name selected by another user. We shall also assume that there will be a collection of blocks of storage which are currently unused; i.e. no file uses these blocks.

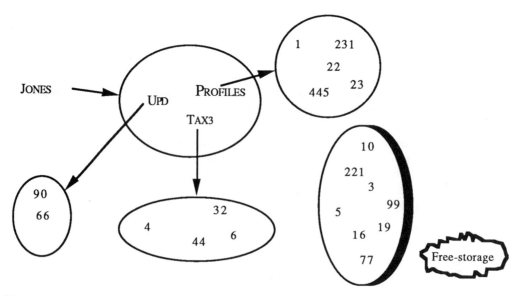

Figure 5.2   An instance of the state of the filing system.

A snapshot of the files of one user Jones is shown in Fig. 5.2. The figure shows that the user Jones owns three files: UPD, TAX3 and PROFILES, and that each of these files occupies a number of blocks, for example TAX3 occupies blocks 4, 44, 6 of storage. Also shown in the figure is the free store that contains those blocks that are not used by any files.

The state for this application will model the association between users and files by means of a map; it will also model the association between files and the blocks that they use—again, by means of a map. The collection of free blocks will be modelled by a set:

values

$MAX\text{-}BLOCKS$:$\mathbb{N}$

$UPP\text{-}BLOCKS$:$\mathbb{N}$

types

$Block = \{1, \ldots, MAX\text{-}BLOCKS\}$

$Blocks = Block\text{-set}$

$Directory = User \xrightarrow{m} File\text{-name-set}$

$File\text{-to-blocks} = File\text{-name} \xrightarrow{m} Blocks$

$User = \ldots$

$File\text{-name} = \ldots$

state $Filing\text{-system}$ of
$\qquad free\ :\ Blocks$
$\qquad owned\ :\ Directory$
$\qquad occupied\ :\ File\text{-to-blocks}$
end

where $MAX\text{-}BLOCKS$ is assumed to be some constant whose value is to be defined. The definition of $Filing\text{-system}$ states that it will have three components: the free blocks, the map that models the ownership of files and the map that models the relation between files and the blocks that they occupy. Note that in the above specification the keyword values introduces any constants used by the specification. The types $User$ and $File\text{-name}$ are left undefined and will be defined later in the development; the only requirement is that the two sets defined by these types are disjoint. (The ... convention will be used to denote those types that will be defined later in the development, and a requirement will always be made of any types (sets) that are left undefined and unless otherwise stated, they all must be mutually disjoint.)

Worked example 5.9 Write down in English the data invariant that describes the filing system.

SOLUTION There are a number of components to this invariant:

- The total number of blocks that a user has associated with his or her files is no larger than $UPP\text{-}BLOCKS$.
- A file does not share blocks with another file.

- A file does not contain a block that is in free storage.
- Duplicate file names are not used.
- A file that is known to the system will be marked as occupying some blocks, including a total of zero blocks.

This information will need to be recorded in the invariant. ■

The data invariant can be expressed as the following predicate, where each conjunct of the predicate, taken in order, corresponds to the bullet points in the answer to the previous worked example:

$$inv\text{-}Filing\text{-}system(mk\text{-}Filing\text{-}system(free, ow, occ)) \quad \triangle$$
$$\forall us \in \text{dom } ow \cdot \text{card}\left(\bigcup\{occ(fn) \mid fn \in ow(us)\}\right) \leq UPP\text{-}BLOCKS \wedge$$
$$\forall f_1, f_2 \in \text{rng } ow \cdot f_1 \neq f_2 \Rightarrow occ(f_1) \cap occ(f_2) = \{\} \wedge$$
$$\forall us \in \text{dom } ow \cdot \forall file \in ow(us) \cdot occ(file) \cap free = \{\} \wedge$$
$$\forall us_0, us_1 \in \text{dom } ow \cdot us_0 \neq us_1 \Rightarrow ow(us_0) \cap ow(us_1) \neq \{\} \wedge$$
$$\bigcup \text{rng } ow = \text{dom } occ$$

Let us assume that three operations are required for the system: an operation that creates a file for a particular user and adds it to the system, an operation that deletes a file owned by a particular user and an operation that counts up the number of blocks currently used by a particular user. The specification of the first operation is shown below:

$$create\text{-}file\ (fn: File\text{-}name, us: User)$$

ext wr $owned$: $Directory$
$\quad\quad occupied$: $File\text{-}to\text{-}blocks$

pre $us \in \text{dom } owned \wedge$
$\quad \text{card}\left(\bigcup\{occupied(fn) \mid fn \in owned(us)\}\right) < UPP\text{-}BLOCKS \wedge$
$\quad fn \notin \bigcup \text{rng } owned$

post $owned = \overleftarrow{owned} \cup \{us \mapsto fn\} \wedge$
$\quad\quad occupied = \overleftarrow{occupied} \cup \{fn \mapsto \{\}\}$

The operation is only properly defined if the user is known to the system, that no other user has a file called fn, the user does not already possess a file called fn and the user owns less than $UPP\text{-}BLOCKS$. The effect of the operation is to keep the number of free blocks unchanged, to update the ownership details of the subsystem with a file owned by user us and to update the details of blocks owned by files by adding a maplet that shows a new file is created with no blocks.

The operation that deletes a file owned by a particular user is shown below:

$$delete\text{-}file\ (fn: File\text{-}name, us: User)$$

ext wr $free$: $Blocks$
$\quad\quad owned$: $Directory$
$\quad\quad occupied$: $File\text{-}to\text{-}blocks$

pre $us \in \text{dom } owned \wedge$
$\quad fn \in owned(us)$

$$\text{post } owned = \overleftarrow{owned} \dagger \{us \mapsto (\overleftarrow{owned}(us) - \{fn\})\} \wedge$$
$$free = \overleftarrow{free} \cup occupied(fn) \wedge$$
$$occupied = \{fn\} \triangleleft \overleftarrow{occupied}$$

The final operation specification is shown below. It involves the use of the function *countup*.

> *count-files* (*us*: *User*) *block-count*: N
>
> ext rd *occupied* : *File-to-blocks*
>   *owned*   : *Directory*
>
> pre *us* $\in$ dom *owned*
>
> post *block-count* = card $(\bigcup\{occupied(fn) \mid fn \in owned(us)\})$

The specification is very simple: all it states is that the operation requires read access, that the user is known to the system and that after the operation has been executed *block-count* will denote a count of the blocks owned by files that are associated with user *us*.

5.5 FUNCTIONS IN VDM

Specifying functions in VDM is relatively easy, the general form of a function definition is:

> function name : argument types $\longrightarrow$ result type
>
> function name(arguments) $\triangleq$ function definition

As an example consider the function *addstwo*, which takes two natural numbers as arguments and delivers their sum:

> *addstwo* : $\mathsf{N} \times \mathsf{N} \to \mathsf{N}$
>
> *addstwo*(a, b) $\triangleq$ $a + b$

The first line states that the function takes a pair of natural numbers and delivers a single natural number. The second line states that the function takes two natural numbers a and b and produces their arithmetic sum. Another example of a function is shown below. It returns with the number of elements in a set of natural numbers greater than 10:

> $gr10$: N-set $\to \mathsf{N}$
>
> $gr10(s)$ $\triangleq$ card $\{el \in s \mid el > 10\}$

Worked example 5.10 Write down the definition of a function that takes two parameters, a set of natural numbers and a natural number, and delivers the number of times exact multiples of the second parameter occur in the first parameter.

SOLUTION

> *findmulto* : N-set $\times \mathsf{N} \to \mathsf{N}$
>
> *findmulto*(S, b) $\triangleq$ card $\{el \in S \mid \exists n \in \mathsf{N}_1 \cdot el = n \times b\}$

■

Functions can be defined recursively. For example, a definition of a recursive function *sumset* is shown below. It has one argument; which is a set of natural numbers, and it returns with the sum of the natural numbers in the set:

$$sumset : \mathbb{N}\text{-set} \rightarrow \mathbb{N}$$

$$sumset(S) \quad \triangle \quad \text{if } S = \{\,\}$$
$$\text{then } 0$$
$$\text{else let } i \in S \text{ in}$$
$$i + sumset(S - \{i\})$$

The first line is straightforward. All it does is to define the arguments and result of the function. The definition of the function is a little more difficult. It states that if the set S is empty, then the function will return zero; otherwise, it will return the sum of an element i in S together with the total of the elements in S with i removed.

Now, with this toolkit we can make the previous invariant more readable. The invariant can be defined as

$$inv\text{-}Filing\text{-}system(mk\text{-}Filing\text{-}system(free, ow, occ)) \quad \triangle$$
$$\forall us \in \text{dom } ow \cdot user\text{-}owns(us, ow, occ) \leq \text{UPP-BLOCKS} \land$$
$$no\text{-}shared\text{-}blocks(ow, occ) \land$$
$$consistent\text{-}free\text{-}storage(free, ow, occ) \land$$
$$no\text{-}duplicate\text{-}names(ow) \land$$
$$\bigcup \text{rng } ow = \text{dom } occ$$

The invariant has been rewritten using a number of auxiliary functions, and the definition of these functions are given below.

$$user\text{-}owns : User \times Directory \times File\text{-}to\text{-}blocks \rightarrow \mathbb{N}$$

$$user\text{-}owns(us, ow, occ) \quad \triangle \quad \text{card}\left(\bigcup\{occ(fn) \mid fn \in ow(us)\}\right)$$

This function returns the total number of blocks that a user has associated with his files.

$$no\text{-}shared\text{-}blocks : Directory \times File\text{-}to\text{-}blocks \rightarrow \mathbb{B}$$

$$no\text{-}shared\text{-}blocks(ow, occ) \quad \triangle$$
$$\forall f_1, f_2 \in \text{rng } ow \cdot f_1 \neq f_2 \Rightarrow occ(f_1) \cap occ(f_2) = \{\,\}$$

Check that a file does not share blocks with another file.

$$consistent\text{-}free\text{-}storage : Blocks \times Directory \times File\text{-}to\text{-}blocks \rightarrow \mathbb{B}$$

$$consistent\text{-}free\text{-}storage(free, ow, occ) \quad \triangle$$
$$\forall us \in \text{dom } ow \cdot \forall file \in ow(us) \cdot occ(file) \cap free = \{\,\}$$

Check that a file does not contain a block that is in free storage.

$$no\text{-}duplicate\text{-}names : Directory \rightarrow \mathbb{B}$$

$$no\text{-}duplicate\text{-}names(ow) \quad \triangle$$
$$\forall us_0, us_1 \in \text{dom } ow \cdot us_0 \neq us_1 \Rightarrow ow(us_0) \cap ow(us_1) \neq \{\,\}$$

Check that no duplicate names are allowed.

5.6 SUMMARY

This chapter has described the use of maps and sets as the building block of VDM. It has shown how practical specifications can be built up using states that can be modelled using maps. Also, it has described the uses and definitions of functions in VDM. Such functions play an important part in ensuring the readability of a VDM specification, in that they are used to replace convoluted parts of text which may be repeated a number of times in a VDM specification.

6

SEQUENCES

AIMS

- To introduce the sequence as a basic facility of VDM.
- To introduce a number of sequence operations and functions.
- To illustrate the use of sequences within simple VDM specifications.

6.1 INTRODUCTION

What is a sequence? In order to answer this question it is worth looking at extracts from some informal statements of requirements:

> When the sales clerk types the ADD command the order that has been placed is added to a queue of orders that are waiting to be satisfied.

> Incoming planes are queued in the order in which they arrive within the local airspace of the airport.

> The scheduler of the operating system will pick the next program to be executed from the list of current programs. These will be stored in order of current priority.

These three examples—one taken from a commercial data processing system, one taken from a real-time air-traffic control system and one taken from a computer operating system—include examples of sequences. The sequence, as you will see in this chapter, is an all pervading object which occurs in every branch of software development.

A sequence is, in effect, a collection of items which are ordered in a particular way. In the first example above the items are purchase orders, and seem to be stored in the order in which they arrive; in the second example above the items are planes and, again, seem to be stored in the order in which they arrive; finally, in the third example the items are programs, and are stored in an order determined by their priority. This, then, is the essence of sequences: a collection of items where ordering is of paramount importance. This means, of course, that sequences are rather different from sets which are just collections of objects with no ordering properties.

First, how are sequences represented? Their representation is similar to that of sets. The sequence of programs SYS, PR1, TAXCALC and PR2 is represented by enclosing them in square brackets and separating them by commas. Thus

[SYS, PR1, TAXCALC, PR2]

represents the sequence with SYS being the first element of the sequence, PR1 the second element, etc. The important point to make about this representation is that the ordering of elements inside the square brackets is important, since ordering is a property of sequences. Because of this property, the sequence above is not equal to the sequence

[SYS, PR2, TAXCALC, PR1]

where, if the objects formed a set, they would be equal.

Another property of sequences that sets do not share is that duplicates are allowed and are meaningful. For example, the sequence

[PR1, PR2, PR1, TAXCALC, UPD1, PR1]

is a valid sequence while

{PR1, PR2, PR1, TAXCALC, UPD1, PR1}

though a valid set is meaningless because of the duplication of elements. The empty sequence is written as [], just as the empty set is written as { }.

Collections of sequences are formed by means of the generator *. This generates a type of all the possible sequences taken from some set of objects. Thus, if the set staff was equal to

{JONES, WILSON, ROBERTS}

then *staff** would be all the finite sequences that could be constructed from the elements of the set *staff*.

Worked example 6.1 How many sequences would be generated by *staff**?

SOLUTION The number is infinite. The reason is that sequences can contain duplicate values. Consequently, sequences such as

[JONES, JONES, JONES, JONES, JONES, JONES, JONES, JONES]

would occur as well as sequences with infinitely large numbers of occurrences of JONES. ■

6.2 SEQUENCE OPERATORS

There are a number of operators that can be applied to sequences. The first is the len operator. This gives the length of the sequence: the number of items contained in the sequence. Thus, all the following statements are true:

len [] = 0
len [1, 2, 4] = 3
len [ARTHUR] = 1
len [BILL, TOM, DAVE, ROB] = 4

A common operation required for sequences is to extract the head, or first element, of the sequence. This is the function of the hd operation. Thus, all the following statements are true:

hd [DAVE] = DAVE
hd [ROB, DAVE, SIMON] = ROB
hd [1, 2, 5, 7, 89] = 1
hd [TOM, TOM, TOM, TOM, TOM] = TOM

An important point to make about hd is that the result of the operation is undefined if the operand is the empty sequence. A similar operation to hd is tl. This returns the remainder, or tail, of a sequence after the head has been removed. Thus, both of the following statements are true:

tl [DAVE] = []
tl [TAX1, UPD, PR2] = [UPD, PR2]

An important point to make about the first example involving tl is that when its operand is a sequence containing one element the tail of that sequence is the empty sequence.

Two other important operators are the inds operator and elems operator. The inds operator, when applied to a sequence, returns the set $\{1, \ldots, n\}$, where n is the number of elements in the sequence. The elems operator, when applied to a sequence, returns the set that consists of the elements of the sequence. Thus, the following statements are all true:

inds [d] = $\{1, \ldots, 1\}$ = $\{1\}$
inds [a, b, c] = $\{1, \ldots, 3\}$
elems [ART, WILL, TOM] = $\{$ART, WILL, TOM$\}$
elems [] = $\{\}$
inds s = $\{1, \ldots, \text{len } s\}$

Worked example 6.2 Which of the following expressions are true? Here s is any sequence of objects; what the objects are is irrelevant for the purpose of this worked example:

card (inds s) = card (elems s)
1 $\in$ inds s

SOLUTION Both are false. The first expression is true only as long as the elements of s are not duplicated. For example, if s was $[a, b, c, d, d, d]$ then the left-hand side of the expression would be card $\{1, \ldots, 6\}$ which is 6, while the right-hand side would be card $\{a, b, c, d\}$ which would be 4. The second expression is only true if s was a non-empty sequence, since if s was empty then inds s would be the empty set and 1 would not be contained in it. ∎

All the operators that we have described so far have extracted something from a sequence. The next operator $\frown$ joins two sequences together. It forms the *concatenation* of two sequences. Thus, the following statements are all true:

$[1, 2, 3] \frown [2, 3, 4] = [1, 2, 3, 2, 3, 4]$
$[1] \frown [] = [1]$
$[\text{ALF}] \frown [\text{BILL}, \text{TOM}] = [\text{ALF}, \text{BILL}, \text{TOM}]$
$[] \frown [] = []$

The formal definition of the concatenation operator is

$$s_1 \; ^\frown \; s_2 = s$$
$$\Leftrightarrow \; \mathsf{len}\,(s_1 \; ^\frown \; s_2) = \mathsf{len}\,s \; \wedge$$
$$\forall i \in \mathsf{inds}\,s_1 \cdot s_1(i) = s(i) \; \wedge$$
$$\forall i \in \mathsf{inds}\,s_2 \cdot s_2(i) = s(\mathsf{len}\,s_1 + i)$$

Here the first conjunct states that the concatenation of s_1 and s_2 is equal to s provided that their lengths are equal, the remaining conjuncts state that the sequence formed by concatenating s_1 and s_2 is the sequence that is the same in its first $\mathsf{len}\,s_1$ positions as s_1 and is the same in the remaining $\mathsf{len}\,s_2$ positions as s_2. Note that $s(i)$ gives the ith element of the sequence s.

The equality operator $=$ returns true if the sequences have a one-to-one correspondence between elements and the elements are in the same order. Thus, the following statements are all true:

$$[\,] = [\,]$$
$$[1, 2] = [1, 2]$$
$$[\textsc{alf}, \textsc{tom}, \textsc{rob}] = [\textsc{alf}, \textsc{tom}, \textsc{rob}]$$
$$[\textsc{pr}1] = [\textsc{pr}1]$$

Worked example 6.3 Formally define equality between two sequences s_1 and s_2.

SOLUTION The definition is shown below. The two sequences are equal if their lengths are the same and every element of the first sequence is contained in the second sequence in a corresponding position:

$$s_1 = s_2 \; \Leftrightarrow \; \mathsf{len}\,s_1 = \mathsf{len}\,s_2 \wedge \forall i \in \mathsf{inds}\,s_1 \cdot s_1(i) = s_2(i)$$

∎

As well as sequence equality, VDM defines inequality $\neq$. Thus, the following statements are true:

$$[\,] \neq [a, b]$$
$$[\textsc{a}, \textsc{b}] \neq [\textsc{b}, \textsc{a}]$$
$$[1] \neq [1, 2, 3]$$
$$[\textsc{alf}, \textsc{jim}, \textsc{rob}, \textsc{arthur}] \neq [\textsc{jim}]$$

The $(\_, \ldots, \_)$ operator is a useful one, and is often used in VDM specifications. It extracts a subsequence from a sequence. For example, it would be used to extract the subsequence represented by the third to fifth elements of a sequence. The operator has three arguments: two integers and a sequence. The first integer is the first index within the sequence argument of the subsequence; the second integer is the final index within the sequence argument of the subsequence. Thus, if you wished to extract the subsequence in positions 2 to 8 of the sequence s_1 then you would write

$$s_1(2, \ldots, 8)$$

Given the subsequence extraction operator the following statements are true:

$$[1, 2, 4, 5](1, \ldots, 3) = [1, 2, 4]$$
$$[1, 2, 8, 9, 29](3, \ldots, 5) = [8, 9, 29]$$
$$[1, 4, 6, 7, 9](1, \ldots, 1) = [1]$$
$$[1, 5, 8, 89](3, \ldots, 2) = [\,]$$

Note that the fourth example, where the subsequence is defined by a first position that is less than the second position, gives the empty sequence.

Exercise 6.1

1. What is the value of the following expressions:

    (a) len []
    (b) len [1, 2, 3] + len [3]
    (c) [hd [a, b]] ⌢ [hd [c, d]]
    (d) tl [1, 2, 3, 4, 5] ⌢ [hd [1, 2, 2]]
    (e) tl ([1, 2]) ⌢ [1, 2]

2. Write down, using the VDM facilities described in this chapter, the following English language statements:

    (a) The length of the sequence s is less than 14.
    (b) The first three elements of the sequence p are a subset of the set $\{2, 4, 6, 8\}$.
    (c) The middle element of the sequence s, which contains 9 elements, is always less than 421.
    (d) The final element of the sequence s_3 is greater than 405.
    (e) The length of the sequence formed by concatenating the sequences s_2 and s_4 is greater than 15.
    (f) The element ALF will never be found in the sequence s.
    (g) The sequence *prior* will always contain a subset of the first five elements of the sequence *totalpr*.

6.3   SOME SPECIFICATIONS INVOLVING SEQUENCES

The aim of this section is to describe some simple specifications that involve the use of sequences. The first specification involves some operations on a *stack*, a data structure also known as a *first-in-first-out* store. When elements are inserted on a stack they are placed at the front of the stack, and when elements are removed from a stack they are removed from the front. Some sequence insertions and removals are shown in Fig. 6.1, which shows the state of a stack of integers after each operation.

   Here items are added at the front of the stack, and when an item is removed it is taken from the front of the stack.

   In this example we shall assume that the stack will contain objects of type *Message*, where *Message* has somehow been defined earlier. The definition of the stack will then be

> state *Message-stack* of
>   *st* : *Message**
> end

We shall also assume that the stack will contain no more than 50 items.

Worked example 6.4   Write down the data invariant which expresses the fact that the stack contains no more than 50 items

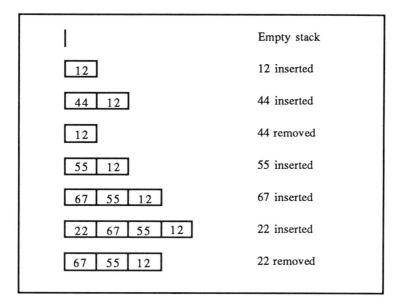

Figure 6.1   The operation of a stack.

SOLUTION The definition is shown below. All it states is that the length of the sequence representing the stack is always less than or equal to 50.

$inv\text{-}Message\text{-}stack : Message^* \rightarrow \mathbf{B}$

$inv\text{-}Message\text{-}stack(mstack) \quad \triangleq \quad \text{len } mstack \leq 50$

■

The initial state will be the empty stack, therefore this can be written as

init $mk\text{-}Message\text{-}stack(st) \quad \triangleq \quad st = [\,]$

The next part of the specification concerns the operations that are required. We shall assume that there are four: *pop*, *push*, *leng* and *popn*. The first operation takes the top element off the stack; the second operation adds an element to the stack; the third operation returns with the number of items currently on a stack; and, finally, the fourth operation removes the first n items from the stack.

The specification of *pop* is shown below:

pop () *rem*: *Message*

ext wr st : $Message^*$

pre $st \neq [\,]$

post $\overleftarrow{st} = [rem] ^\frown st$

The pre-condition simply states that for *pop* to be defined then the stack must not be empty. The post-condition states that after the operation has occurred the new stack will be equal to the old stack with the element at the top of the stack removed.

Worked example 6.5 Write down the specification of the *push* operation.

SOLUTION The specification is shown below.

> *push* (*rem*: *Message*)
>
> ext wr *st* : *Message**
>
> pre true
>
> post $st = [rem] \frown \overleftarrow{st}$

■

The operation *leng* is trivial; it is shown below.

> *leng* () *no*: $\mathbb{N}$
>
> ext rd *st* : *Message**
>
> pre true
>
> post $no = \text{len } st$

Worked example 6.6 Write down the specification of the *popn* operation which takes the first *n* items from the stack. Assume that the heading of the operation is

> $popn(n: \mathbb{N}) msset: Message\text{-set}$

where *n* is the number of items to be extracted from the stack and *msset* is the destination of the items.

SOLUTION The specification is shown below.

> *popn* (n: $\mathbb{N}$) *msset*: *Message*-set
>
> ext wr *st* : *Message**
>
> pre $\text{len } st \geq n$
>
> post $msset = \text{elems } \overleftarrow{st}(1, \ldots, n) \wedge$
> $\overleftarrow{st} = \overleftarrow{st}(1, \ldots, n) \frown st$

■

It is worth reinforcing the lessons learnt in developing the specification for the stack by developing another specification, this time for a related object: the queue. The difference between a stack and a queue is that when an object is added it is placed at the end of the queue, rather than, as in the stack, being added to the front. When an object is removed from a queue it is taken, like the stack, from the front.

Given this description a specification incorporating a number of operations can be developed. We shall assume that three operations need to be specified: *addq*, *removeq* and *numinq*. The first operation adds an item to a queue, the second removes an item from a queue and the third operation gives the number of items in the queue. We shall also assume that the queue will contain no more than 200 items and that it is defined by

```
state Mess-queue of
     mq : Messages*
inv ...
init ...
end
```

Worked example 6.7 Write down the initial state and the data invariant for the queue example.

SOLUTION The initial state and the data invariant are shown below:

```
state Mess-queue of
     mq : Message*
inv mk-Mess-queue(mq)   △   len mq ≤ 200
init mk-Mess-queue(mq)  △   mq = []
end
```

    ■

The specifications for *removeq* and *numinq* are shown below:

removeq () *om*: *Message*
ext wr *mq* : *Message**
pre *mq* ≠ []
post $\overleftarrow{mq}$ = [*om*] $\frown$ *mq*

numinq () *no*: $\mathbb{N}$
ext rd *mq* : *Message**
pre true
post *no* = len *mq*

Worked example 6.8 Write down the specification for the *addq* operation.

SOLUTION The specification is shown below:

addq (*nm*: *Message*)
ext wr *mq* : *Message**
pre true
post *mq* = $\overleftarrow{mq}$ $\frown$ [*nm*]

    ■

Worked example 6.9 Assume that we have a queue of natural numbers defined as

    Numqueue = $\mathbb{N}$*

with a data invariant that states that there will always be less than 10 entries in the queue and that no entry is duplicated. How would you specify the data invariant?

SOLUTION

$$inv\text{-}Numqueue : Numqueue \rightarrow \mathbb{B}$$

$$inv\text{-}Numqueue(nqueue) \quad \triangle$$
$$\text{card } nqueue < 10 \,\wedge$$
$$\forall i, j \in \text{inds } nqueue \cdot i \neq j \; \Rightarrow \; nqueue(i) \neq nqueue(j)$$

The first conjunct is straightforward; the second conjunct says that if we examine any two elements in the queue, assuming that they are not the same element, then their contents will not be the same. ■

The third and final example of a queue specification involves a slightly more complex example. It involves the specification of a piece of operating system software which allocates and de-allocates blocks of backing storage memory used for files. During the operation of a computing system users will be continually creating and deleting files: when a file is created the operating system requires a number of free blocks of storage to create the file, the number of blocks depending on the size of the file to be created; when a file is deleted the blocks making up the file need to be marked as being free for any new files.

The stored data that the operating system uses to keep track of allocated blocks can be modelled by a queue and two sets. Each queue element will consist of a set of blocks which have been released by a file. The first set will contain all the blocks which are free, the second set will contain all the blocks currently used by files. An example of this state is shown in Fig. 6.2.

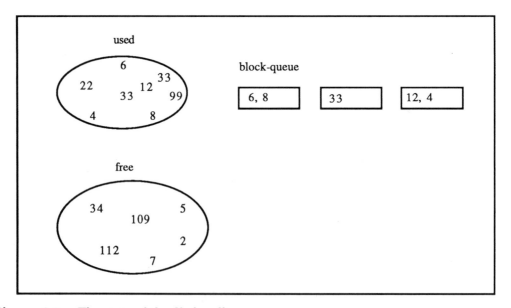

Figure 6.2   The state of the file handler.

The blocks that are free, ready to be allocated to a file, are contained in the set *Free*; the blocks that are currently used by files are contained in the set *Used*. The blocks to be returned are held in the queue *Block-queue*, with each element containing blocks that have been returned from one file; for example the first element in Fig. 6.2 contains blocks 6 and 8. When the head of the queue is removed the state shown in Fig. 6.2 will be that shown in Fig. 6.3.

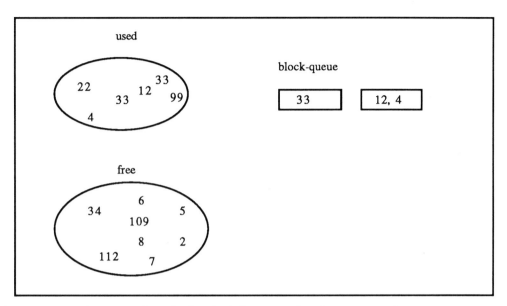

Figure 6.3   The state after the head of the queue has been removed.

The elements that were contained in the head of the queue are removed from the queue; they are also are removed from the used set and added to the free set. Now that we have an intuitive feel for the problem a specification for a number of operations is required.

Assume there are four operations that are required. The first, *bqremove*, removes an element from the queue of blocks, as shown in Figure 6.3. The second, *bqadd*, adds an element to the queue of blocks. The third operation, *bqenough*, given a request for a number of blocks, checks whether there are enough free blocks to satisfy the request. Finally, the operation *bqinitialize* takes a set of blocks and initializes the state so that this set of blocks is unused. The types used, the system and the state can be described as:

types

Used-blocks = *Block*-set

Free-blocks = *Block*-set

Block-queue = *Block*-set*

state *Store-manager* of
      used : *Used-blocks*
      free : *Free-blocks*
   queue : *Block-queue*
end

We shall assume that blocks has been defined previously. The data invariant for this problem is quite tricky.

> **Worked example 6.10** Write down, in English, the properties of the state shown in Fig. 6.2 which must be true throughout the execution of the block handler subsystem.

SOLUTION There are three properties

- The sets *used* and *free* will not contain any common elements. This is a consequence of the fact that a block cannot simultaneously be free and used in a file.
- Each set contained in every element of *queue* must be a subset of *used*. This is a consequence of the fact that *queue* will contain block numbers of blocks that are currently in use.
- No block will be contained in more than one element of *queue*. This is a consequence of the fact that blocks are not shared in files.

■

The mathematical facilities for defining such a complex data invariant will be described in a later chapter and so we will leave the exact form of this data invariant until then. Let us concentrate on the operations. The first, *bqremove*, removes the head of block-queue and places its contents into the set *free*. The specification of the operation is shown below:

$$bqremove\ ()$$

ext wr *used* : *Used-blocks*
    free   : *Free-blocks*
    queue   : *Block-queue*

pre len *queue* > 0

post $\overleftarrow{queue} = [\text{hd } \overleftarrow{queue}] \frown queue\ \wedge$
    $used = \overleftarrow{used} - \text{hd } \overleftarrow{queue}\ \wedge$
    $free = \overleftarrow{free} \cup \text{hd } \overleftarrow{queue}$

The post-condition contains three conjuncts. The first conjunct states that after the operation is executed the queue of blocks will have its first element removed; the second conjunct states that the used blocks will have the head of the queue removed; and the third conjunct states that the set of free blocks will have the head of the queue added to it.

> **Worked example 6.11** Write down the specification of the operation *bqadd* which adds a set of blocks to the block queue.

SOLUTION The specification is shown below

$$bqadd\ (blks\text{: } Block\text{-set})$$

ext rd *used* : *Used-blocks*
    wr *queue* : *Block-queue*

pre *blks* $\subseteq$ *used*

post $queue = \overleftarrow{queue} \curvearrowright [blks]$

■

The specification for the operations *bqenough* and *bqinitialize* are shown below:.

$bqenough\ (no:\mathbb{N})\ available: B$

ext rd *free* : *Free-blocks*

pre true

post $available \Leftrightarrow \textsf{card}\ free \geq no$

$bqinitialize\ (blks: Block\text{-set})$

ext wr *free* : *Free-blocks*
    used   : *Used-blocks*
    queue : *Block-queue*

pre true

post $free = blks\ \wedge$
    $used = \{\ \}\ \wedge$
    $queue = []$

These are both fairly simple specifications. The pre-condition of *bqenough* is true; the post-condition is true only if there are more blocks in *free* than the number required. The pre-condition of *bqinitialize* is true, and the post-condition simply states that when the operation is executed the set of free blocks becomes the set *blks* of blocks provided; the set of used blocks is the empty set and the queue is the empty queue.

Exercise 6.2

1. A computer system is to be developed that will process a queue of customer numbers. This queue will have no more than 200 entries and, although a customer number will occur a number of times in the queue, they are not allowed to occur more than five times. Write down the data invariant. Assume that the customer numbers belong to the set *cust-numbers*.

2. A computer system is to be developed that will process a queue of block numbers, with each block number describing a location in a file. There will be no more than 100 entries in the queue and no adjacent queue element will contain the same block number. Write down the data invariant. Assume that the blocks are taken from the set *blocks*.

3. In an air traffic control system the names of aeroplanes are held in a queue. A flight will only occur once in a queue. Write down the data invariant and the specification of two operations: *add* and *remove*. The first operation adds a particular flight at the *i*th position in the queue, while the second operation removes the *i*th element in the queue. Assume that flights belong to the set *flights*.

4. In a transaction processing system transaction numbers are held in a queue, with each element of the queue containing a set of transaction numbers. Each element of the queue will contain no more than six transaction numbers, no transaction number will appear in more than three queue elements and the queue will contain no more than 200 elements. Write down the data invariant and the specification of an operation *rem3* that removes all the items from the queue containing more than three transaction numbers. Assume that transaction numbers are taken from the set *trnum*.

5. A queue contains natural numbers. The numbers will be in ascending order and will contain duplicates. Write down the data invariant and also the specification of an operation *remove*, which removes all the elements that are duplicated. Therefore if, for example, the queue contained

$$[1, 2, 3, 6, 7, 7, 7, 19, 89, 90, 90, 102, 104, 104]$$

then the operation would transform it to

$$[1, 2, 3, 6, 7, 19, 89, 90, 102, 104]$$

6.4 SUMMARY

This chapter of the book has described how sequences—collections of objects where ordering is important—are defined. Also, it has described a number of operations that remove elements from a sequence and form new sequences. Finally, the chapter has described a number of specifications that involve various important manifestations of sequences.

ABSTRACT SYNTAX

AIMS

- To describe the facilities of the specification language for describing composite objects.
- To describe the facilities of the specification language for assembling objects into complex systems.
- To describe the abstract syntax of the specification language.
- To show how abstract syntax is employed in specifications.

7.1 WHY ABSTRACT SYNTAX?

So far, in this book, the specification examples have all involved simple objects, for example they have involved objects such as words and reactors. Because of this the examples have been rather artificial: the objects that computer programs normally manipulate tend to consist of a number of components. For example, a bank account consists of an account number, the name of the account holder, the current balance of the account, the overdraft limit of the account and the address of the account holder. The notation that we have described so far cannot cater for this degree of complexity; however some simple extensions allow us to define objects that have an unlimited complexity. The main tool is the composite object.

7.2 COMPOSITE OBJECTS

When writing a specification it is frequently necessary to represent objects which can be thought of in two ways. First, as a complete entity in its own right and second, with components. A familiar example of this is a date; most of the time a date would be thought of as being one single object with operations defined on it such as *tomorrow*, *yesterday*, *add-interval*, and *compute-interval*.

$$tomorrow: Date \rightarrow Date$$
$$yesterday: Date \rightarrow Date$$
$$add\text{-}interval: Date \times \mathbb{Z} \rightarrow Date$$
$$compute\text{-}interval: Date \times Date \rightarrow \mathbb{Z}$$

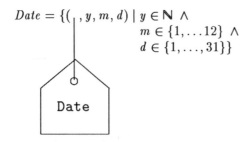

$$Date = \{(\;,y,m,d) \mid y \in \mathbf{N} \land$$
$$m \in \{1,\ldots 12\} \land$$
$$d \in \{1,\ldots,31\}\}$$

Figure 7.1   A way of representing the set *Date*.

Relationships between these operations can be written down, for any date *d*:

$$tomorrow(yesterday(d)) = d$$
$$yesterday(tomorrow(d)) = d$$
$$compute\text{-}interval(add\text{-}interval(d,n),d) = n$$

To define such an operation it may be necessary to work with a date in terms of the components from which it is made up. How can these two views of a date be represented in the specification language? To represent a date there is a *make function* for building a date out of its components and some means of decomposing a date into its components. It will be assumed, for simplicity, that only the dates of this century (assumed to end in 1999) are to be represented.

To construct a date a make function is used. It takes as its arguments the components of a composite object and forms the object itself. The make function is designated by prefixing the name of the composite type with the characters *mk-*; thus the *mk-Date* function is used to take three numbers and construct a date from them:

$$mk\text{-}Date\colon \{0,\ldots,99\} \times \{1,\ldots,12\} \times \{1,\ldots,31\} \to Date$$

Selectors are used to take a date apart, these could be *year*, *month*, and *day*. The selectors are written like the field selectors of Pascal or Modula-2, and work in the obvious way:

$$mk\text{-}Date(85,9,24).day = 24$$
$$mk\text{-}Date(85,9,24).month = 9$$
$$mk\text{-}Date(85,9,24).year = 85$$
$$\text{if } s \in Date \text{ then } mk\text{-}Date(s.year, s.month, s.day) = s$$

The make function and selectors are, in some sense, inverses of each other, one to build and three to destroy. But what does the set of dates look like? It could be represented as a triple, the first component being the year, the second the month and the third the day, but this is not quite enough. In fact a date would be represented by a list of four values. The first one being a label or flag saying this object is a date—the element is of type date followed by the three integers representing the year, month and day. The concept is illustrated in Fig. 7.1.

Of course, there is no need to go to such an extreme as drawing in a little flag each time: it is possible just to use the make function itself as the flag, and therefore the set *Date* could be written:

$$Date = \{mk\text{-}Date(x,y,z) \mid x \in \ldots\}$$

Though this would do as a way of defining the set date, it does not explain where the (name of the) selectors come from. For example, the selector *year* is defined as follows:

$mk\text{-}Date(x, y, z).year = x$

The specification language has a way of bringing all of these ideas together. A date will be defined as a composite object, in a similar way to the record (or structure) concept found in many programming languages. Using a notation which is similar to the record constructor of Pascal the definition of a date can be written:

$$
\begin{array}{lll}
Date = \text{compose } Date \text{ of} \\
\quad year & : & \{0, \dots, 99\} \\
\quad month & : & \{1, \dots, 12\} \\
\quad day & : & \{1, \dots, 31\} \\
\text{end}
\end{array}
$$

The selector functions are defined in the compose construct, and the name for the type, in this case *Date*, is also defined there. Note that is not necessary to give a name to the set which is the same as its type, the set could just as easily have been given the name *Date-values*.

$$
\begin{array}{lll}
Date\text{-}values = \text{compose } Date \text{ of} \\
\quad year & : & \{0, \dots, 99\} \\
\quad month & : & \{1, \dots, 12\} \\
\quad day & : & \{1, \dots, 31\} \\
\text{end}
\end{array}
$$

It is common practice to give a set a name that is the same as its type. This occurs so frequently that the first version of the definition of a date can be written:

$$
\begin{array}{lll}
Date \ :: & year & : \{0, \dots, 99\} \\
& month & : \{1, \dots, 12\} \\
& day & : \{1, \dots, 31\}
\end{array}
$$

This is still not quite right, the set *Date* is still a little too large; it allows the 31 November 1991 and of course, the 29 February 1983, both of which are invalid. A predicate could be used to restrict the elements in the date set. This predicate, is in fact, a type invariant since any operations on dates would need to preserve it.

$inv\text{-}Date : Date\text{-}values \rightarrow \mathbb{B}$

$inv\text{-}Date(dt) \quad \triangleq$
 let $mk\text{-}Date\text{-}values(y, m, d) = dt$ in
 $(m \in \{1, 3, 5, 7, 8, 10, 12\} \wedge d \in \{1, \dots, 31\}) \vee$
 $(m \in \{4, 6, 9, 11\} \wedge d \in \{1, \dots, 30\}) \vee$
 $(m = 2 \wedge \neg \, is\text{-}leap\text{-}year(y) \wedge d \in \{1, \dots, 28\}) \vee$
 $(m = 2 \wedge is\text{-}leap\text{-}year(y) \wedge d \in \{1, \dots, 29\})$

The two definitions could be put together in the following way to give a better definition of *Date*.

$Date = \{x \in Date\text{-}values \mid inv\text{-}Date(x)\}$

This can also be put together so the invariant applies to the composite object:

$$
\begin{array}{lll}
Date \ :: & year & : \{0, \dots, 99\} \\
& month & : \{1, \dots, 12\} \\
& day & : \{1, \dots, 31\}
\end{array}
$$

$$\text{inv}\,(mk\text{-}Date(year, month, day)) \quad \triangleq$$
$$(month \in \{1, 3, 5, 7, 8, 10, 12\} \land day \in \{1, \ldots, 31\}) \lor$$
$$(month \in \{4, 6, 9, 11\} \land day \in \{1, \ldots, 30\}) \lor$$
$$(month = 2 \land \neg\,is\text{-}leap\text{-}year(y) \land d \in \{1, \ldots, 28\}) \lor$$
$$(m = 2 \land is\text{-}leap\text{-}year(y) \land d \in \{1, \ldots, 29\})$$

In order to illustrate the notation further, consider the description shown below of items in a stock control system:

$$
\begin{array}{rll}
Item & :: & part\text{-}name & : & Name\text{-}\text{set} \\
& & stock\text{-}no & : & \mathbb{N} \\
& & reorder\text{-}level & : & \{0, \ldots, 100\} \\
& & current\text{-}level & : & \{0, \ldots, 10000\}
\end{array}
$$

This describes items that consist of a part name taken from a set of names (names having been defined somewhere else), a stock number used for identification, a reorder level which, when stock falls below the number, is used for reordering and a current level of stock. This last item is declared on the assumption that there will never be more than ten thousand items in stock. Such definitions can be incorporated into specifications along with the other facilities that we have discussed before. For example, the declarations for a system for keeping track of flights for an airline is shown below. The type *Flight-number* will be defined later in the development.

types

$Cities = \{\text{PARIS}, \text{ROME}, \text{LONDON}, \text{FRANKFURT}\}$

$$
\begin{array}{rll}
Time & :: & hrs & : & \{0, \ldots, 23\} \\
& & mins & : & \{0, \ldots, 59\}
\end{array}
$$

$Aircraft\text{-}type = \{\text{BOEING}\,727, \text{BOEING}\,737, \text{AIRBUS}\,320, \text{BOEING}\,747\}$

$Flight\text{-}number = \ldots$

$$
\begin{array}{rll}
Flight & :: & aircraft\text{-}name & : & Aircraft\text{-}type \\
& & destination & : & Cities \\
& & leave\text{-}time & : & Time \\
& & arrive\text{-}time & : & Time
\end{array}
$$

state *Flight-database* **of**
$$flights\ :\ Flight\text{-}number \xrightarrow{m} Flight$$
end

The declarations describe how a database of flight information will be organized around a map that relates flight numbers to flight details. These flight details are defined by the composite object *Flight* that contains the type of the aircraft allocated to the flight, the destination of the flight, the time the flight departs and the time that the flight arrives at its destination. In order to define *Time* a composite object is defined that has two components that match the hours and the minutes of the time.

Worked example 7.1 Why could the time not be defined as

$$Time = \{0, \ldots, 2359\}$$

where a time of the form $hh{:}mm$ is represented by the value $hh \times 100 + mm$.

SOLUTION The reason is that this would allow invalid values of time such as 2288. A data invariant could be written which eliminated these values. However, it is a much simpler process to use a composite data type. ∎

Worked example 7.2 A system program used in an operating system keeps track of the programs currently in the main memory of the computer. Each program is given a unique identifier. The system program requires data on the size of the program, and its location in main memory. Write down the definitions that would be used in a formal specification. Assume that the maximum length of a program is $MAXL$ bytes and the largest addressable memory unit will be location $LIMIT$.

SOLUTION The definition is shown below:

types

$Mem\text{-}location = \{1, \ldots, LIMIT\}$

$Prog\text{-}id = \ldots$

$Prog\text{-}length = \{1, \ldots, MAXL\}$

$Program = Prog\text{-}id \xrightarrow{m} Prog\text{-}detail$

$Prog\text{-}detail ::\quad length\ :\ Prog\text{-}length$
$\qquad\qquad\qquad location\ :\ Mem\text{-}location$

state $Program\text{-}database$ of
$\qquad progs\ :\ Program$
end

An alternative would be

types

$Prog\text{-}id = \ldots$

$Prog\text{-}detail ::\quad length\ :\ \{1, \ldots, MAXL\}$
$\qquad\qquad\qquad location\ :\ \{1, \ldots, LIMIT\}$

state $Program\text{-}database$ of
$\qquad progs\ :\ Prog\text{-}id \xrightarrow{m} Prog\text{-}detail$
end

Whichever version you choose is often a matter of taste. However, if you are going to write operation specifications that directly refer to the type such as $Prog\text{-}length$ then the first version is the obvious one. A good way of choosing between various solutions is to select the one which is easiest to read—too many type names sometimes makes things more complicated than they really are. ∎

Given this method of specifying composite objects how can they be referred to in a specification? There are a number of ways. Conceptually, the simplest is to use selectors. A selector, when applied to an object that has a composite type, returns with the component of that object corresponding to the selector. Each component is associated with a selector and the selector name is the name of the component. Thus, the type specification

$$Tem \quad :: \quad \begin{array}{rcl} part\text{-}name & : & Name \\ stock\text{-}no & : & \mathbb{N} \\ reorder\text{-}level & : & \{0, \dots, 100\} \\ current\text{-}level & : & \{0, \dots, 10000\} \end{array}$$

would be associated with the selectors *part-name*, *stock-no*, *reorder-level* and *current-level*. Each of these selectors when applied to an object of type *Tem* will return the value of the component corresponding to the selector. For example, if a specification referred to a variable *lorder* and the specifier wanted to say that the reorder level will be less than the current level then this would be written as:

$$lorder.reorder\text{-}level < lorder.current\text{-}level$$

Here the selector *reorder-level* extracts out the reorder level from *lorder* and the selector *current-level* extracts out the current level from lorder.

The make function can be used to construct a value of this type:

$$mk\text{-}Tem(\text{WIDGET}, 3001, 100, 145)$$

It forms the composite value (object) which has its *part-name* component equal to WIDGET, its *stock-no* component equal to 3001, its *reorder-level* component equal to 100 and its *current-level* component equal to 145. By using a make function the components of a composite object can be named and, hence, be employed in a specification. As an example consider the composite object *Room-details* that is used in a meetings booking system. This is defined below:

$$Room\text{-}range = \{1, \dots, 200\}$$

$$Room\text{-}details \quad :: \quad \begin{array}{rcl} max\text{-}size & : & Room\text{-}range \\ current\text{-}size & : & Room\text{-}range \end{array}$$

where *max-size* represents the largest number of occupants in a room, and *current-size* represents the current number of occupants in the room. A predicate that we might write could check whether the number of current occupants is greater than the maximum number of occupants allowed. Using a make function, this can be written as

$$is\text{-}room\text{-}full : Room\text{-}details \rightarrow \mathbb{B}$$

$$is\text{-}room\text{-}full(mk\text{-}Room\text{-}details(m, c)) \quad \triangleq \quad c > m$$

alternatively we could write

$$is\text{-}room\text{-}full : Room\text{-}details \rightarrow \mathbb{B}$$

$$is\text{-}room\text{-}full(rd) \quad \triangleq$$
$$\quad \text{let } mk\text{-}Room\text{-}details(m, c) = rd \text{ in}$$
$$\quad c > m$$

or even

$$is\text{-}room\text{-}full : Room\text{-}details \rightarrow \mathbb{B}$$

$$is\text{-}room\text{-}full(rd) \quad \triangleq \quad rd.current\text{-}size > rd.max\text{-}size$$

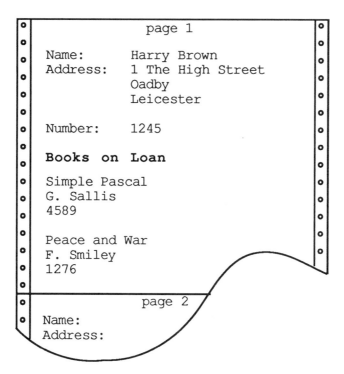

Figure 7.2   An example listing from a library system.

It is worth looking at the first two versions of *is-room-full* in some detail as the idea used—to break a composite object into its components—crops up time and time again in specifications. The function requires as an argument an object of type *Room-detail*. This is pattern matched by the make function, which denotes an object of the requisite type but with components *c* and *m*. These components, once they are named by the obvious pattern matching, can then be referred to elsewhere.

In general the choice between using a make function or in using selectors really depends on how many of the components of a composite object are going to be referred to. If the majority are to be referred to, then use a make function; however, if a few are to be referred to, then selectors would be the mechanism to be employed.

Worked example 7.3   The computer system that manages the local lending library has a program that produces the following (example) output that lists its customers and the books they have out on loan. An example listing is shown in Fig. 7.2. Write down an abstract description of this listing.

SOLUTION

$Overdue\text{-}list = Entry\text{-}\text{set}$

$$Entry :: \quad name \ : \ Name$$
$$addr \ : \ Address$$
$$user \ : \ Userid$$
$$on\text{-}loan \ : \ Book\text{-}info\text{-}\text{set}$$

$$Book\text{-}info :: \quad title : Title$$
$$author : Name$$
$$num : Bookid$$

Notice that we have documented only the information content of the listing, the formatting information has been ignored—this is implementation detail. If we wanted to specify the order in which the customers occurred in the listing (by name for example) and the order in which the books were listed (by title for example) we could add some data type invariants that documented this fact.

$$Listing = Entry^*$$
$$\text{inv } (l) \quad \triangle \quad is\text{-}ordered\text{-}by\text{-}custs(l)$$

$$Entry :: \quad name : Name$$
$$addr : Address$$
$$user : Userid$$
$$on\text{-}loan : Book\text{-}info^*$$
$$\text{inv } (mk\text{-}Entry(\text{-},\text{-},\text{-}, on\text{-}loan)) \quad \triangle \quad is\text{-}ordered\text{-}books(on\text{-}loan)$$

The definitions of *is-ordered-by-custs* and *is-ordered-books* have been left. ■

7.2.1 The mu-operator

Sometimes it is useful to be able to change the component of a composite object. One way of doing this is to use the *record modifier* operator, also called the μ-operator; if a new value of the composite object C defined below was required with a component changed, then the notation allows the new value to be created from the old.

$$C :: sel_1 : Set_1$$
$$sel_2 : Set_2$$
$$sel_3 : Set_3$$

If $c \in C$ and $c = mk\text{-}C(x, y, z)$ then

$$\mu(c, sel_1 \mapsto d) = mk\text{-}C(d, y, z)$$
$$\mu(c, sel_2 \mapsto a) = mk\text{-}C(x, a, z)$$
$$\mu(c, sel_1 \mapsto s) = mk\text{-}C(x, y, s)$$

The general form of the μ-operator is

$$\mu(\text{expression denoting a record}, \text{selector name} \mapsto \text{new value})$$

The selector name, together with the associated new value can be repeated, so

$$\mu(c, sel_1 \mapsto d, sel_3 \mapsto s) = mk\text{-}C(d, y, s)$$

would denote a new object with new values for the first and third components.

Exercise 7.1

1. A system is to record information about vehicles passing a particular point on a road. The system is capable of detecting the type of vehicle, its registration number and the time at which the vehicle passed the point. Write down suitable types and a state for recording this information.
2. Write an abstract syntax that describes the 'information contents' of a book, working down through parts, chapters, sections, paragraphs, ... etc.

3. Write down a state suitable for recording information about the customers of the local library and information about the books they borrow.
4. The state of a system can convey its essential properties. Illustrate this by defining the state for each of the following file systems:

   (a) a single-level file system in which files are referred to directly by their name;
   (b) a file system in which directories may be nested (i.e. a directory entry may be linked to a file, or to another directory);
   (c) a file system similar to (b) above, but with the additional property that a file may be known by different names.

7.3 ABSTRACT SYNTAX

Now we can address the problem of how sets, sequences, maps and composite objects are to be put together to describe large systems. Most of the notation has already been used with some explanation, relying on the reader's intuition to provide the correct understanding. One of the aims of the specification language is to provide familiar concepts using a reasonably straightforward syntax, so that a guess at the meaning is likely to be correct.

For example, suppose we want to build a system to model a bank and its customers. As customers can share accounts we cannot keep the account information in with customer information (database designers would also prefer to keep the two concepts separate).

types

$$Customers = Customer\text{-}no \xrightarrow{m} Details$$

$$Current\text{-}accounts = Current\text{-}acc\text{-}no \xrightarrow{m} \dots$$

$$Savings\text{-}accounts = Savings\text{-}acc\text{-}no \xrightarrow{m} \dots$$

$$Customer\text{-}no = \mathsf{Token}_1$$

$$Current\text{-}acc\text{-}no = \mathsf{Token}_2$$

$$Savings\text{-}acc\text{-}no = \mathsf{Token}_3$$

$$Details = \dots$$

state *Banking-system* **of**
    cust : *Customers*
    cur : *Current-accounts*
    save : *Savings-accounts*
end

The type identifier Token denotes an infinite set of names, or tokens, that can be compared for equality. If more than one of these types (sets) are needed, we can write Token_1, Token_2, etc.; note that these sets are all assumed to be mutually disjoint. The exact denotation for a token value is not defined. Typically a token would be implemented as a number or a character string.

But what information goes into *Details*? Possible information that needs to be recorded about a customer are their name, address, how much money they have in their current account, providing they have an account of course, their sex, and the account numbers of any saving accounts if they have any. So a first attempt at the details is as follows

$$Details \ :: \quad \begin{aligned} name \ &: \ Name \\ gender \ &: \ Sex \\ age \ &: \ \mathbb{N} \\ current \ &: \ Current\text{-}acc\text{-}no \\ saving \ &: \ Savings\text{-}acc\text{-}no\text{-}\text{set} \end{aligned}$$

If we look at this first attempt there are more details that need to be added. Customers must be either male or female. We only need to recall information about a current account if the customer actually has a current account; if they do not then this field needs to be left empty. Note that every person with an account is a bank customer, (but not necessarily the other way around, for example a customer may only have lodged his/her will at the bank). In the age field we would like to store a natural number or perhaps, for those customers that do not want the bank to know their age, some sort of flag to say 'over 18', i.e. legally an adult. We choose for the moment to leave the exact format of a name until a later time—now is too early to consider such details. Is there any way in which we can record these facts in the composite object?

We are leaving the exact form of the type *Name* undefined for the moment, and this can be recorded thus:

$$Name = \ldots$$

The type *Sex* could be written explicitly as follows:

$$Sex = \{\text{Male}, \text{Female}\}$$

The two identifiers Male and Female have been introduced; they are values which denote the idea of being female, or male in the same sort of way as the denotation '4' (or 'IV') denotes the idea of 'four-ness'. To introduce a constant that denotes some value, an identifier in small capitals is used. (When sketching by hand, underscore can be used to mark constants that denote themselves.) The idea is similar to that of enumerated types in Pascal or Modula-2. A constant models some constant attribute of the real world (such as being male or female). We will introduce a special version of the union operator that is used only in defining types:

$$Sex = \{\text{Male}\} \mid \{\text{Female}\}$$

remember, this is just another way of writing

$$Sex = \{\text{Male}\} \cup \{\text{Female}\}$$

It seems a little wasteful of notation to have the braces, could we not just write

$$Sex = \text{Male} \mid \text{Female}$$

The '$\mid$' operator is used only in type definitions and is a binary operator defined between set types and singleton constants. In the above, Male and Female can only be constants, so in the above there is no ambiguity. A convention will be adopted that the set braces can be left off around singleton identifier constants if there is no possibility of ambiguity—we can usually tell from the context whether we mean CON-ID or {CON-ID}.

We can also use this idea to deal with the problem of age. A set could be defined that allows the age of a person to be given either as a natural number, their age in years, or expressed as being 'over 18'.

$$Age = \mathbb{N} \mid \text{ADULT}$$

This means that the set *Age* contains all the natural numbers and the value ADULT, which models the concept of being over 18. We can see what set of values is described by the type *Age* by 'expanding' the type definition.

$$\begin{aligned} Age &= \mathbb{N} \mid \text{ADULT} \\ &= \mathbb{N} \mid \{\text{ADULT}\} \\ &= \mathbb{N} \cup \{\text{ADULT}\} \\ &= \{x \mid x \in \mathbb{N} \vee x = \text{ADULT}\} \end{aligned}$$

In the above derivation, line 2 removes the ambiguity, line 3 writes $\cup$ in place of the type operator |, and line 4 expands the definition of the *union* operator.

The next problem to resolve is how to represent a missing value in a component. Some customers do not have current accounts, so they do not need a component in their details to store the current account number. This could be expressed by just leaving out the relevant information from their details.

$$mk\text{-}Details(\text{McDONALD}, \text{FEMALE}, 18, \{\,\})$$

The above represents an eighteen year old female customer with no current account and no savings accounts. There is a problem with leaving values out: first it is difficult to tell if a value has been forgotten or has been left out because it is not needed; second, if there are several optional components, how do we tell which one has been left out? The solution is to use the 'this page has deliberately been left blank' solution. We write something which means (literally) nothing. The special identifier nil is used to denote a missing value, so a customer with no current or savings bank accounts would be written as

$$mk\text{-}Details(\text{McDONALD}, \text{FEMALE}, 18, \text{nil}, \{\,\})$$

That a value is optional is recorded by placing square brackets around the corresponding type descriptor in question, so our *Details* composite object can be written as follows, where the fact that a current account has been recorded as an optional value. The fact that a customer may have no saving accounts can be modelled by using the empty set as a component value.

$$\begin{aligned} Details \ :: \quad name \ &: \ Name \\ gender \ &: \ Sex \\ age \ &: \ Age \\ current \ &: \ [Current\text{-}acc\text{-}no] \\ saving \ &: \ Savings\text{-}acc\text{-}no\text{-}\text{set} \end{aligned}$$

The 'optional' brackets around *Current-acc-no* are an abbreviation for

$$Current\text{-}acc\text{-}no \mid \text{nil}$$

and this is what we adopt as a definition of square brackets. So writing a type as

$$[Current\text{-}acc\text{-}no]$$

means

$$Current\text{-}acc\text{-}no \cup \{\text{nil}\}$$

where a nil value means 'may not be present'.

There is one other piece of notation used in the definition of *Details* above. The definition could have been written as follows:

$$
\begin{array}{rl}
Details :: & name \ : \ Name \\
& gender \ : \ Sex \\
& age \ : \ Age \\
& current \ : \ Current\text{-}acc \\
& saving \ : \ Savings\text{-}accs
\end{array}
$$

Here the sets *Current-acc* and *Savings-accs* have been introduced by defining

$$
Current\text{-}acc = [Current\text{-}acc\text{-}no]
$$

$$
Savings\text{-}acc = Savings\text{-}acc\text{-}no\text{-set}
$$

all that has happened is to introduce a name for the type

$$
Current\text{-}acc\text{-}no \mid \text{nil}
$$

the equals symbol just introduces another name for a type.

The next step is to model the accounts themselves. Suppose the rules for bank accounts are as follows:

> The bank stores a record of all transactions against a current account. There is no limit on overdrafts. There are four styles of savings account, these are normal, high interest, special children's account and long term. There are different interest rates on normal savings accounts and children's savings accounts. High interest accounts only pay interest if there has been no transactions against the account for thirty days. Long term accounts need to be kept for a fixed number of years. The bank does not need to record information about transactions against savings accounts, but these accounts cannot be in deficit.

This suggests the following types to describe accounts.

$$
\begin{array}{rl}
Current :: & total \ : \ Amount \\
& status \ : \ (\text{CR} \mid \text{DB}) \\
& trans \ : \ Transactions
\end{array}
$$

$$
Transactions = Transaction^*
$$

$$
\begin{array}{rl}
Transaction :: & date \ : \ Date \\
& amount \ : \ Amount \\
& type \ : \ (\text{CR} \mid \text{DB})
\end{array}
$$

A current account records the total amount of money that a customer has, together with a list of transactions against the account.

$$
Savings = Child \mid Saving \mid High \mid Term
$$

$$
Child :: total \ : \ Amount
$$

$$
Saving :: total \ : \ Amount
$$

$$
\begin{array}{rl}
High :: & total \ : \ Amount \\
& date \ : \ Date
\end{array}
$$

$$
\begin{array}{rl}
Term :: & total \ : \ Amount \\
& length \ : \ Years
\end{array}
$$

A savings account can be one of the four account types. The type descriptions are obvious; but note that the values in a child's saving account are the same as the values of a term saving account—the composite object flag is used to distinguish between the two.

Finally we can put everything together to obtain the state and types for our bank.

types

$Customers = Customer\text{-}no \xrightarrow{m} Details$

$Current\text{-}accounts = Current\text{-}acc\text{-}no \xrightarrow{m} Current$

$Savings\text{-}accounts = Savings\text{-}acc\text{-}no \xrightarrow{m} Savings$

$Customer\text{-}no = \mathsf{Token}_1$

$Current\text{-}acc\text{-}no = \mathsf{Token}_2$

$Savings\text{-}acc\text{-}no = \mathsf{Token}_3$

$Details ::$
$\quad\quad name : Name$
$\quad\quad gender : Sex$
$\quad\quad age : Age$
$\quad\quad current : Current\text{-}acc$
$\quad\quad saving : Savings\text{-}accs$

$Name = \ldots$

$Sex = \text{MALE} \mid \text{FEMALE}$

$Age = \mathbb{N} \mid \text{ADULT}$

$Current\text{-}acc = [Current\text{-}acc\text{-}no]$

$Savings\text{-}accs = Savings\text{-}acc\text{-}no\text{-set}$

$Current ::$
$\quad\quad total : Amount$
$\quad\quad status : (\text{CR} \mid \text{DB})$
$\quad\quad trans : Transactions$

$Transactions = Transaction^*$

$Transaction ::$
$\quad\quad date : Date$
$\quad\quad amount : Amount$
$\quad\quad type : (\text{CR} \mid \text{DB})$

$Savings = Child \mid Saving \mid High \mid Term$

$Child :: total : Amount$

$Saving :: total : Amount$

$High ::$
$\quad\quad total : Amount$
$\quad\quad date : Date$

$$Term \ :: \quad total \ : \ Amount$$
$$length \ : \ Years$$

$$Amount = \ldots$$

$$Date = \ldots$$

$$Years = \ldots$$

state *Banking-system* of
     cust : *Customers*
     curr : *Current-accounts*
     save : *Savings-accounts*
end

Before finishing this chapter it is worth describing a facility of the VDM language that often crops up with composite objects. Often you will find that there is a need to model recursive data types, where a component of a data type contains a reference to the data type. These recursive data types usually turn up during design where the underlying data is expressed as a linked list, a tree or some other data type which has a component that refers to itself. An example of this is shown below:

$$List \ :: \ next \ : \ [List]$$
$$item \ : \ Data$$

Here a composite type *List* is defined as having two components: a component *item* of type *Data* which holds some information and a component *next* which contains a *List*. The square brackets indicate that not only could *next* contain a list but it could also contain the special item nil, the denotation for nothing; roughly equivalent to a null pointer in C or Pascal. Clearly, the definition above is one of a simple linked list.

Exercise 7.2

1. Using the following definition of a tree

$$Tree = \mathsf{N} \mid Node$$

$$Node \ :: \quad left \ : \ Tree$$
$$right \ : \ Tree$$

define a function

$$max\text{-}tree: Tree \rightarrow \mathsf{N}$$

which returns the largest element of the tree, and a function

$$sum\text{-}tree: Tree \rightarrow \mathsf{N}$$

which returns the sum of the elements in the tree.

2. Using the following definition of a tree

$$Tree = [\mathsf{N} \mid Node]$$

$$Node \ :: \quad left \ : \ Tree$$
$$right \ : \ Tree$$

define a predicate

$$test\text{-}trees: Tree \times Tree \rightarrow \mathsf{B}$$

which is satisfied if the leaves of the two trees have the same values in the same order; the structure of the trees should have no effect on the result.

3. An expression can be represented as a tree using the following abstract syntax:

$Expr = Value \mid Binary\text{-}expr \mid Monadic\text{-}expr$

$Value = \mathbb{N}$

$Binary\text{-}expr :: \quad left \; : \; Expr$
$\qquad\qquad\qquad op \; : \; Binary\text{-}op$
$\qquad\qquad right \; : \; Expr$

$Binary\text{-}op = \text{ADD} \mid \text{SUB} \mid \text{MULT} \mid \text{DIV}$

$Monadic\text{-}expr :: \qquad op \; : \; Monadic\text{-}op$
$\qquad\qquad\qquad operand \; : \; Expr$

$Monadic\text{-}op = \text{PLUS} \mid \text{MINUS}$

Define a function *eval* which evaluates an abstract representation of an expression

$eval: Expr \rightarrow \mathbb{Z}$

4. It is possible to represent the tree form of an expression in a linear representation which would conform to the following abstract syntax:

$Polish\text{-}expr = Token^*$

$Token = Value \mid Operator$

$Operator = Binary\text{-}op \mid Monadic\text{-}op$

The linear representation is called forward Polish and takes the form of an operator followed by its two operands if the operator is dyadic, or an operator followed by its operand if the operator is monadic. For example the expression

$$(8 + 5) \times (-11 - 3)$$

would be represented as

$$[\text{MULT}, \text{ADD}, 8, 5, \text{SUB}, \text{MINUS}, 11, 3]$$

Write an operation that takes the abstract representation of an expression (*Expr*) and translates it into the equivalent forward Polish form.

$trans: Expr \rightarrow Polish\text{-}expr$

Assume the definitions of *Expr*, *Value*, *Binary-op* and *Monadic-op*, as given above.

5. Specify a system to manage a collection of books owned by a library. The following operations should be provided:

(a) add a new book;
(b) return a book that had been borrowed;
(c) delete a book;
(d) borrow a book;
(e) determine if a book is borrowed;
(f) list all books by a given author;
(g) list all books whose title contains a certain word.

The system should be able to handle authors who write several books and books which share a title, but have different authors.

7.4 SUMMARY

All these constructors can be used to build large, complex, sets; these sets can be used to represent the real world, thus we are able to model any particular system. It is all important to structure the state in a reasonable fashion using the equals sign to rename types. It is possible to write the state as a single enormous equation but this tends to make it somewhat unreadable. The state can be written as a series of equations or definitions structured in such a way that the various components of the system can easily be seen. A state written in this way bears a resemblance to the definition of programming languages using BNF (Backus-Naur Form), i.e. syntax, and in fact it is following the model of BNF that calls for various notations or conventions to be used here—vertical bar in BNF means roughly the same as vertical bar in the abstract syntax notation.

One further point, the reader might be wondering about the difference between a set and a type. A set is a collection of values, a type is the name of a set which is a collection of values. It does no harm (most of the time) to mix these concepts up and regard a type as the set it denotes—something this book does all the time.

There is still one question to be asked, are these constructors and operators sufficient to build any set? The answer to this question is yes.

DATA INVARIANTS

AIMS

- To describe the role of data invariants in formal software development.
- To describe how data invariants are a reflection of the intrusion of the real world into specifications.

8.1 INTRODUCTION

Real data very rarely fits nice mathematical statements about that data. As a simple example, consider the specification of a symbol table. One way to define this data would be to specify it as a set. In many ways this is a good choice: a set models the situation of the symbol table where each item contained in that table is unique. However, reality often intrudes, in terms of conditions that must hold for a particular application. For example, one condition that often imposes itself on stored data is a size limitation. In terms of the symbol table a specification may insist on an upper limit on the number of items contained in the table. Limitations of a data type that must hold during the execution of a system are known as *data invariants*. They are predicates that must be true throughout the execution of the system.

Another example of a data type where real-life intrudes is a queue of files awaiting printing by a line printer in an operating system. A way of specifying such a queue is by means of a sequence of files. Two possible intrusions from reality which would form part of the data invariant are some restriction on size, say, some upper limit on the number of items in the queue, and a limitation on the ordering of the items in the queue; for example, the order may be in terms of some priority or in terms of the size of the files that are to be printed.

Worked example 8.1 The following is a natural language description of a banking system. What is the data invariant? Express it in natural language.

> The banking system is to maintain the accounts of a number of customers of the bank. Given the average size of such accounts we envisage that the maximum number of accounts will be 20 000. The main function of the system is to update the balance of each account belonging to a customer, no customer owning more than five accounts. A customer is allowed an overdraft but this should never be more than £5 000.

SOLUTION The data invariant will be the conjunction of the following four conditions:

- No more than five accounts are to be assigned to a customer.
- Each customer will be given account numbers that are unique and, therefore, will not be shared by other customers.
- The maximum number of allowable accounts will be 20 000.
- That an overdraft will be no more than £5 000.

■

8.2   SPECIFYING DATA INVARIANTS

Now that we have briefly outlined the concept of a data invariant the next question that comes naturally to mind is: how should such a condition be specified? In order to illustrate this it is necessary to return to the symbol table example. Let us assume that the symbol table contains names that are sequences of characters, that no name of more than 12 characters will be allowed in the symbol table and that each item in the table will start with an alphabetic character. The types and state for such a table can be defined as:

```
types

Name = Char*

state Symbol-table of
        syms : Name-set
inv ...
end
```

where *Char* is some defined type which is the set of allowable characters that symbol table entries can be comprised of. The data invariant for this data type consists of three conditions which need to be conjoined:

1. That no more than 50 entries are allowed in the symbol table.
2. That entries containing more than 12 characters will not be contained in the symbol table.
3. That each entry in the symbol table will start with a lower-case alphabetic character.

The mathematical definition of this data invariant is shown below:

```
types

Name = Char*

state Symbol-table of
    syms : Name-set
inv mk-Symbol-table(syms)   △
    card syms ≤ 50 ∧
    ∀c ∈ syms ·
        len c ≤ 12 ∧ ('a' ≤ hd c ∧ hd c ≤ 'z')
end
```

The first two lines define the state. The data invariant is introduced by means of the keyword inv and will be a function from the types of the components of the state to the set of Boolean values, namely a predicate.

In this example it consists of two outermost conjuncts: the first conjunct defines the maximum number of elements in a symbol table and the second conjunct, which itself is composed of two further conjuncts, asserts that each sequence of characters in the symbol table will have a length no greater than 12 characters and will start with an alphabetic character. Here we have assumed, of course, that the character set *char* will have an ordering on the characters 'a' < 'b' < 'c' ... 'y' < 'z' and that these characters are represented consecutively in the character set.

In order to reinforce this idea the second data invariant which describes the banking example is now presented. Remember that the conditions which must be true throughout the execution of the banking system are:

1. No more than five accounts are to be assigned to a customer.
2. Each customer will be given account numbers that are unique and, therefore, not shared by other customers.
3. The maximum number of allowable accounts will be 20 000.
4. An overdraft will be no more than £5000.

The state and data invariant are shown below:

> **types**
>
> $Accounts = Customer\text{-}no \xrightarrow{m} Account\text{-}detail$
>
> $Account\text{-}detail = Account\text{-}no \xrightarrow{m} Balance$
>
> $Balance = \mathbb{Z}$
>
> **state** $Banking\text{-}system$ **of**
> $accs$: $Accounts$
> **inv** $mk\text{-}Banking\text{-}system(accs)$ $\triangle$
> $\forall cust \in \text{dom } accs \cdot \text{card dom } accs(cust) \leq 5 \wedge$
> $\forall cusn_1, cusn_2 \in \text{dom } accs \cdot$
> $cusn_1 \neq cusn_2 \Rightarrow \text{dom } accs(cusn_1) \cap \text{dom } accs(cusn_2) = \{\,\} \wedge$
>   **let** $all\text{-}accounts = \text{merge rng } accs$ **in**
> $\text{card dom } all\text{-}accounts \leq 20\,000 \wedge$
> $\forall det \in \text{dom } all\text{-}accounts \cdot all\text{-}accounts(det) \geq -5\,000$
>   **end**

The first two conjuncts are straightforward and describe the limitation on the number of accounts that each customer holds and the total number of accounts in the system. The third and fourth conjuncts are a little more difficult. The third conjunct states that each function associated with a particular customer will only contain account balances greater than the overdraft limit of £5000. The fourth conjunct states that there will be no common elements in any of the domains of the functions used to model the association between an account number and the balance in an account.

Worked example 8.2 A computer operating system keeps track of a series of processes that are ready to be executed by a physical processor. Such processes are activated as being ready for execution during the running of the operating system. The processes are identified by a process number and a priority between 1 and 5. The algorithm used for allocating a process to a processor takes the process with the highest priority. If two processes share this same highest priority then the process that was made ready at the earliest time is selected for execution. Write down a state and a data invariant that describes this situation.

SOLUTION A state must be devised that reflects this situation. Since there is a natural ordering among processes a sequence can be used. The conditions that must always be true for this state would be:

- There should not be any duplicate processes in the sequence.
- The queue will be ordered on process priority and the time at which the process was made available for possible execution.

The formal specification of the state is shown below:

types

$$Process\text{-}detail :: \quad name \ : \ Sname$$
$$priority \ : \ \{1, \dots, 5\}$$
$$date \ : \ Date$$

state $Queue$ **of**
$\qquad queue \ : \ Process\text{-}detail^*$
end

where $Sname$ is the data type chosen to hold the names of processes and $Date$ is the data type containing the calendar time. The specification of the data invariant is shown below:

state $Queue$ **of**
$\qquad queue \ : \ Process\text{-}detail^*$
inv $mk\text{-}Queue(queue) \quad \triangleq$
$\qquad \forall i, j \in \text{dom } queue \cdot i \neq j \ \Rightarrow \ queue(i).name \neq queue(j).name \ \land$
$\qquad \forall i, j \in \text{dom } queue \cdot i < j \ \Rightarrow \ great\text{-}order(queue(i), queue(j))$
end

where the function $great\text{-}order$ takes two $process\text{-}details$ and returns true if they are ordered according to the rule given in the worked example. A definition of this function is shown below

$$great\text{-}order : Process\text{-}detail \times Process\text{-}detail \rightarrow \mathbb{B}$$

$$great\text{-}order(a, b) \quad \triangleq$$
$$a.priority > b.priority$$
$$\lor$$
$$(a.priority = b.priority \land a.date < b.date)$$

∎

These then are data invariants: conditions that must be true throughout the execution of a system. An important point to be made about such predicates is that the data invariant of a design for a particular specification will almost invariably be more complex than the data invariant for the specification. As an example consider the example of the symbol table presented earlier in this section. The specification for this is:

$Name = Char^*$

state $Symbol$-$table$ of
    $syms$: $Name$-set
inv mk-$Symbol$-$table(syms)$ $\triangle$
    card $syms \leq 50 \wedge$
    $\forall c \in syms \cdot$
        len $c \leq 12 \wedge$ ('a' $\leq$ hd $c \wedge$ hd $c \leq$ 'z')
end

Let us assume that we decide to design the system in terms of a sequence of names, and that this sequence is to be kept in order according to the number of times that each name has been looked up. Such an ordering ensures that a linear search, for example, would be a more efficient proposition than it would normally be; thus, in this case, the state will become:

types

$Name = Char^*$

$Name$-$detail$ :: nm : $Name$
              acc : $\mathbb{N}$

state $Symbol$-$table$ of
    $syms$: $Name$-$detail^*$
inv mk-$Symbol$-$table(syms)$ $\triangle$
    card $syms \leq 50 \wedge$
    $\forall i \in$ inds $syms \cdot$
        len $syms(i).nm \leq 12 \wedge$
        ('a' $\leq$ hd $(syms(i).nm) \wedge$ hd $(syms(i).nm) \leq$ 'z') $\wedge$
    $\forall i, j \in$ inds $syms \cdot i < j \Rightarrow syms(i).acc \geq syms(j).acc$
end

The added complexity comes from the fact that some extra information has been added which speeds up retrieval operations that have resulted in the data invariant containing more complex references to items, together with an extra conjunct that reflects the ordering inherent in the stored data.

So far in this book we have ignored the topic of validation. However, this chapter gives us the first good opportunity to demonstrate how some validation can be carried out on a formal specification. You will remember that the data invariant is a condition that must be true *throughout* the life of a system and that operations cannot violate the data invariant.

A first check that the specifier has to perform on a specification is that any operation defined in the specification does not violate the data invariant, i.e. does not make it become false. Normally this check can be carried out informally but, occasionally, it will be necessary to resort to mathematical proof.

In order to illustrate how validation would be carried out let us reconsider the specification of a list of product identifiers in a stock control system. In such a system stock-control clerks will be telephoned by customers asking whether a particular item is currently in stock and whether there are enough in stock of that item to satisfy a particular order. The functional specification for such a system can be based on a state that is a map. Let us also assume that the company for whom this system has been built will never stock more than 1000 items.

The state and the data invariant can be formally specified as:

types

$$Warehouse = Product\text{-}name \xrightarrow{m} \mathbb{N}$$

state $Warehouse\text{-}system$ **of**
$\quad whs\ :\ Warehouse$
inv $mk\text{-}Warehouse\text{-}system(whs) \quad \triangleq$
$\quad \forall it \in \text{dom } whs \cdot whs(it) \leq 1000$
end

Let us assume that there are two operations, *addtostock*, which adds a specified quantity of a product to the stocks held in the warehouse, and *enquire*, which checks whether a customer order can be satisfied. The first operation has a quantity delivered and a product name as parameters, while the second operation has a product name together with the number of items required by the customer.

The operations are shown below:

$addtostock\ (pname: Product\text{-}name, number: \mathbb{N})$

ext wr $whs\ :\ Warehouse$

pre $pname \in \text{dom } whs\ \wedge$
$\quad whs(pname) + number \leq 1000$

post $pname = \overleftarrow{pname} \dagger \{pname \mapsto \overleftarrow{whs}(pname) + number\}$

$enquire\ (pname: Product\text{-}name, number\text{-}ordered: \mathbb{N})\ available: \mathbb{B}$

ext rd $whs\ :\ Warehouse$

pre $pname \in \text{dom } whs$

post $available \Leftrightarrow number\text{-}ordered \leq whs(pname)$

The second operation, *enquire*, only has read access to the state. This means that the state, after the operation, will be the same as before the operation. The general rule is, then, that any operation that just consults the state, and hence has read access, does not need to be checked for violating the data invariant.

The operation *addtostock* does alter the state. The post-condition states that the state will be modified by adding to the number of products associated with *Product-name* the total number of products delivered. Now since the pre-condition for this operation states that the operation is only defined when the number of items associated with a particular product, plus the number of items delivered, are less than or equal to 1000, then this ensures that a product stored in the warehouse will never have more than 1000 items stocked.

An important point to make about the reasoning that we have gone through above is that it is informal. A high degree of validation was achieved without recourse to formal mathematical proof.

8.3 SUMMARY

This chapter has described the role of the data invariant in formal software development. A number of points have been discussed. First, the data invariant was defined as a predicate that must be true throughout the execution of a system. Second, data invariants tend to reflect real-world concerns. Third, as formal development proceeds the data invariant becomes more complicated.

9

SPECIFYING SYSTEMS

AIMS

- To describe how a high-level view of a system can be expressed as a data flow diagram.
- To describe how the sequencing of actions in a system can be described using a structure chart.
- To show the relationship between data flow diagrams and structure charts and specifications written in VDM.

9.1 INTRODUCTION

In the examples seen so far the problems have been reasonably small: it has been easy to identify the 'central core' of the program and to specify it. Issues such as input and output, and the order in which the operations should be performed have either been ignored or have not been relevant. However, most computer systems are not that simple, so how do formal methods scale up to larger problems, and how do they handle the issues of I/O and order? The remainder of this chapter attempts to answer this question. Since it is expository in nature no worked examples are included.

For large problems it is not always so clear how to even start to write a formal specification. For any problem the first step is usually to identify and define the state, i.e. the abstract data type, that represents the information that the system is manipulating, and then to define the operations on that state. However, for large systems there could be more than one logically disjoint 'chunk' of the real world that needs to be modelled. For these systems it is not always clear what the various components of the state are and what the operations on those components should be. A solution to this is to use the ideas of system specification and design which are already in use to develop large systems.

If many of the examples in the earlier chapters of this book are examined, it can be seen that the specification language has been used to describe what might be called abstract machines. The term *abstract machine* has been used to draw attention to the fact that a specification of a data type, together with the operations on that data type, is rather like a specification of a machine. These abstract machines are rather like real machines in that they have buttons and knobs which can be used to trigger internal state changes, and they have a way of displaying information about the internal state. The abstract machine's equivalent to the knobs, buttons and displays of a real machine are provided by functions and procedures together with results returned from them. An example of this is shown in Fig. 9.1. For both real and abstract machines, we should not be concerned with the exact details of how they work, but only with what functionality is provided by them.

Other development methods call these abstract machines abstract data types or objects. In the remainder of this book we will (mostly) use the more imaginative terminology of abstract machine, and readers can translate this either to abstract data types or objects according to their inclination.

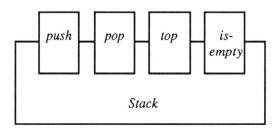

Figure 9.1   The *Stack* abstract machine.

The overall tactic of many successful development methods are the same: identify objects in the real world and model them with some sort of data representation and high-level operations on that data representation. This is the example that we will follow. The production of a large specification can, thus, be seen as identifying abstract machines and defining how these machines fit together and are controlled to provide the required functionality. To help with this problem of producing large specifications we shall use existing design tools that have a reasonable track record of success, namely, data flow diagrams and object-oriented design, to identify abstract machines and transformations on any data that needs to be done, and structure diagrams to sketch possible orders of operations.

When these abstract machines have been identified and specified, two other problems need to be solved. The first is how are these abstract machines used? How are they to be operated either by a user via some sort of interface or by another program? The second of the problems is how to implement, or build, the abstract machines in code (Fig. 9.2).

The implementation aspects will be considered in later chapters. In this chapter we will consider the specification of the mechanisms that surrounds the abstract machines and operate them which is related the problem of defining the order in which operations can be performed and specifying that order. To do this it is necessary to explain some additional VDM facilities which will allow the order of operations to be defined and some means of specifying how input/output works. The following chapters provide examples of many of the ideas described in this chapter in action.

9.2   THE COMMANDS OF VDM

Most procedural programming languages have 'glue' that sticks the basic components of the language together, and allows the programmer to specify the order and choice of the

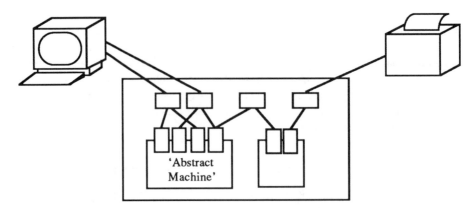

Figure 9.2 Operating abstract machines.

execution of these basic components. One example of this glue is the ';' which joins a component on its left with a component on its right. This operator (for that is what it is) describes the order in which the operations defined by the components should be done (the left operand first, followed by the right). Other examples are the conditional command (if ... then ... else ... end) that allows a choice to be specified, and the while loop command (while ... do ... end) which allows a command to be repeated zero or more times while some sort of condition is satisfied. Other constructs exist—but these are the most basic (and in fact any program can be written using just these three).

The glue of the VDM specification language will copy that of most procedural programming languages. The ';' will allow various operations to be joined together, and an 'if-then-else' construct and a 'while-do' construct will allow choice and iteration respectively. The meanings of each of these constructs is very close to their equivalent found in most programming languages—close enough that they can be directly translated; any differences are very subtle and of a technical nature, which (except for one) are beyond the scope of this book. This difference, which is both important and unimportant, is that a VDM specification does not 'execute' in the way that a program does. The meaning of a specification is static and requires no execution for it to be found. However, should a specification be read as a program, the resulting meaning will be correct 99.999 per cent of the time. (Executing an operation or function that is defined by pre- and post-conditions means, by some sort of magic, producing a (required) answer that satisfies the post condition—assuming that the 'input' to the operation or function satisfies the pre-condition.)

The technical difference between a static meaning and an execution meaning to a sequence of VDM-SL commands is roughly speaking the difference between how

$$f(g(x)) \quad \text{or equivalently} \quad f \circ g(x)$$

is understood. Does it mean apply the function g to x and then apply f to the result, or does it mean apply the function $f \circ g$ to x? The difference between an execution view of VDM-SL and a static view is just this, and in fact the ';' of VDM-SL and the 'o' operator are very closely related.

As has already been stated, the part of VDM-SL that defines the order of operations is very similar to a programming language, except for one or two interesting restrictions. These are that VDM does not allow expressions to have side effects and there are no pass-by-reference arguments (**var** parameters in Pascal or Modula-2 terms). The restriction that expressions cannot have side effects means that any functions used in expressions cannot have side effects—so an operation that is specified implicitly and has a reference to the state (signalled by ext wr in its definition) cannot be used in an expression!

First note the basic building blocks of what we will call sequential VDM-SL[1], a command can be defined as follows:

```
command  =   block statement
         |   bind statement
         |   assign command
         |   while loop command
         |   conditional command
         |   cases command
         |   operation call
         |   return command
         |   error command
         |   identity command
         |   input output command
         |   specification command ;
```

The '|' symbol should be read as *or*.

Most of the commands are similar to their programming language counterparts; the semantics of these commands are not too dissimilar from their equivalents in Pascal, Modula-2, ADA or C and will be discussed in turn.

```
block statement  =   '(', { declare statement }, command list, ')' ;

command list  =   command, { ';', command } ;
```

The curly brackets introduce zero or more occurrences of the object enclosed by the brackets. Items surrounded by the punctuation marks ' ' stand for themselves. A block statement consists of a declare statement which is zero or more 'declaration-like' statements that are the equivalent of the declaration statements of programming languages, followed a list of commands—a command is an 'executable statement'. A block statement allows us to specify a list of commands that are 'executed' in order—by 'execute' we mean that when the program is written that satisfies the specification the effect of the program would be equivalent to performing the commands in the order specified.

The declare statement allows the introduction of 'temporary variables'. By a variable we mean an addition to the state which only exists in the block statement that follows the declaration.

The declaration statement is just

```
declare statement  =   'dcl', dcl definition list, ';' ;

dcl definition list  =   dcl definition, { ',', dcl definition } ;

dcl definition  =   identifier list, ':', type ;

identifier list  =   identifier, { ',', identifier } ;
```

The semantics of a declaration preamble are very similar to those of programming languages. It allows the introduction of a variable whose value can be changed by an assignment—this variable is added to the state as a temporary component that is removed when the scope containing the declaration has disappeared. After the declaration

dcl x: **N**;

---

[1] See Appendix C for a full description of the VDM-SL syntax.

the state becomes

> state *Example* of
>
> $\qquad \cdots$
>
> $\qquad x \ : \ \mathsf{N}$
>
> end

where ... represent the original components of the state. The declaration preamble should not be used in specifications; it is there to be used when specifications are refined to designs. A declare statement can be refined in the obvious way.

The bind statement can be one of three variants:

> bind statement $=$ let statement
> $\qquad\qquad\qquad |$ let be statement
> $\qquad\qquad\qquad |$ definition statement ;

The two forms of the let statement introduces new identifiers that denote values; the scope of the identifiers is the command component. It should be noted that the value denoted by an identifier defined in this way cannot be changed in the command.

> let statement $=$ 'let', value definition list, 'in', command ;
>
> value definition list $=$ value definition, { ',', value definition } ;
>
> value definition $=$ pattern [':', type], '=', expression ;
>
> let be statement $=$ 'let', such that bind list, 'in', command ;
>
> such that bind list $=$ such that bind, { ',', such that bind } ;
>
> such that bind $=$ bind, ['be', 'st', expression] ;

The semantics of the two let statements are similar to those in the functional part of the language. In the first variant, the expression is evaluated and the result is pattern matched with the pattern component. In the second example the free identifiers in the pattern must be assigned values such that when the pattern is evaluated as an expression, the resulting value can be found in the set defined by the expression. If the optional be st followed by an expression is present, the result of that expression must be a Boolean value, and we are interested in binding the free identifiers of the pattern to values in such a way that the expression after the 'be such that' evaluates to true. In both cases the evaluation of the expression component must not have side effects; an operation that returns a value and changes (or accesses) the state cannot be used. Roughly speaking an operation that returns a value that has been defined using pre- and post-conditions cannot be used in an expression. (Such operations can, however, be used in assignment commands and in definition statements—see below.)

For example, with the following definitions:

> $A \ :: \ f \ : \ X$
> $\qquad\ \ s \ : \ Y$
>
> $B = A \,|\,\ldots$

and a set S which has been constructed such that S is a subset of B, then

> let *mk-A*$(a, b) \in S$ in
>
> $\qquad \cdots$

requires that the set S contains composite objects of type A, and the semantics are that an arbitrary element of S of type A is chosen and the first component is bound to the identifier a and the second component to b. This could also be written:

> let $x \in S$ be st $x \in A$ in
> let $a = x.f$ in
> let $b = x.s$ in
> . . .

The definition statement is similar to the let statement, in that it also allows identifiers that denote values to be introduced. The difference is that the evaluation of those values can have side effects—in the specification language expression evaluation is not allowed to change the state.

> definition statement = 'def', equals definition list, 'in', command ;
>
> equals definition list = equals definition, { ',', equals definition } ;
>
> equals definition = pattern bind, '=', expression
> | pattern bind, '=', operation call ;

In this context only, a right-hand side in the form of a call to an operation (that returns a value) is allowed to have side effects. The definition preamble is a flag to the effect that a side effect could occur when the right-hand side is evaluated. Also in this context, an identifier in the expression component can reference a state component.

The assignment command allows the value denoted by a component of the state to be changed. Usually that component is a temporary one which has been introduced by a declare preamble, but need not be. The syntax is as would be expected:

> assign command = state designator list, ':=', expression list
> | state designator, ':=', operation call ;
>
> state designator list = state designator, { ',', state designator } ;

Notice that if an operation that returns a value (i.e. a function that has a side effect) is used on the right-hand side of an assignment command, it cannot be part of an expression.

A state designator denotes a component of the state, if the component is a sequence it can be indexed and the indexed component modified, if it is a mapping it can be applied to an element of its domain and the corresponding range element modified and if it is a composite object a component can be selected and modified.

> state designator = identifier
> | field reference
> | map reference
> | sequence reference ;
>
> field reference = state designator, '.', identifier ;
>
> map reference = state designator, '(', expression, ')' ;
>
> sequence reference = state designator, '(', expression, ')' ;

Suppose the state for a system was

> state *Example* of
>   *value* : **N**
> end

and an operation to increment the only component of this state was defined:

> inc ()
>
> ext wr $value$: $\mathbb{N}$
>
> ————————
> post $value = \overleftarrow{value} + 1$

This operation could be defined using assignment:

> inc ()
> ($value$:= $value + 1$
>) $--$ inc

For more details on assignment see section 11.4.1 on page 191.

The other commands from the sequential part of the VDM-SL used are the conditional command:

> conditional command = 'if', expression ,
> 'then', command list,
> { elsif command },
> 'else', command list,
> 'end' ;
>
> elsif command = 'elseif', expression,
> 'then', command list ;

the while loop command:

> while loop command = 'while', expression, 'do', command list, 'end' ;

and the cases command:

> cases command = 'cases', expression, ':',
> cases choice list,
> [',', default command],
> 'end' ;
>
> cases choice list = cases choice, { ',', cases choice } ;
>
> cases choice = pattern list, '→', command ;
>
> default command = 'others', '→', command ;

The semantics of the 'conditional command', and the 'while loop command' are similar to their programming language equivalents. The 'cases command' is also similar, but has one or two useful extensions. The cases command explained in an operational sense is fairly straightforward. The expression component is evaluated and the resulting value is then compared with the patterns contained in the pattern list components of each of the cases choice list until a match occurs. If a pattern denotes or evaluates to a value then a match occurs if this value is equal to the value of the case expression. On the other hand, if the pattern contains some unbound identifiers then the value of the case expression must 'match' the pattern, this will be described after the syntax for patterns has been described.

The operation call allows an operation that has side effects to be 'activated', it cannot be part of an expression, but can only occur in a definition preamble and as the only component on the right-hand side of an assignment command:

    operation call = name, '(', [expression list], ')' ;

The return command allows a result to be returned from an operation:

    return command = 'return', expression ;

An error command is provided which allows us to state that something has gone wrong, but we leave it to the implementor to give a better diagnostic:

    error command = 'error' ;

The identity command allows us to do nothing:

    identity command = 'skip' ;

    It is useful in conditional commands as the VDM specification language does not allow an else component of a conditional command to be left out.

    specification command = [identifier], specification ;

    The specification command is discussed in more detail in Chapter 11 and input/output is discussed later in section 9.3.

9.2.1 Operations

So far we have only seen the implicit specification of operations using pre- and post-conditions, it is possible to specify them explicitly:

    operation definitions = 'operations', operation definition list ;

    operation definition list = operation definition, { [';'], operation definition } ;

    operation definition = operation heading, operation body ;

    operation heading = identifier, parameter types, [identifier type pair] ;

    parameter types = '(', [pattern type pair list], ')' ;

    pattern type pair list = pattern list, ':', type, { ',', pattern list,':', type } ;

    identifier type pair = identifier, ':', type ;

The body of an operation is either a specification or a command:

    operation body = specification | command ;

    specification = [frame],
                   ['pre', expression],
                   'post', expression ;

    frame = 'ext', var information, { var information } ;

    var information = mode, identifier list, [':', type] ;

    mode = 'rd' | 'wr' | 'lc' ;

As can be seen from the above an operation body can be defined using a command and this allows us to give a fairly low level specification or description of an operation. This means that we can write specifications without using pre- and post-conditions—a temptation that must be resisted! A specification should be thought of as a non-executable program—non-executable because it is a very abstract description. The development process is one of changing a specification into a design, and then a design into executable program code. The development process removes the non-executable restriction on specifications by replacing implicit specification and abstraction by detail which becomes (or is) executable code. The development process also supplies information about the order in which things are to be done and describes algorithms in more detail—such low-level detail should not be part of the specification.

9.2.2 Patterns and bindings

Patterns   The syntax for patterns produce constructs that look like expressions with some unbound identifiers—it is the values of these identifiers that are being defined.

$$\text{pattern list} \ = \ \text{pattern}, \{ \text{ ',', pattern } \} \ ;$$

$$
\begin{aligned}
\text{pattern} \ = \ & \text{pattern identifier} \\
\mid \ & \text{match value} \\
\mid \ & \text{set pattern} \\
\mid \ & \text{sequence pattern} \\
\mid \ & \text{tuple pattern} \\
\mid \ & \text{record pattern} \ ;
\end{aligned}
$$

$$\text{pattern identifier} \ = \ \text{identifier} \mid \text{'-'} \ ;$$

$$\text{match value} \ = \ \text{'(', expression, ')'} \mid \text{symbolic literal} \ ;$$

$$\text{set pattern} \ = \ \text{set enumeration pattern} \mid \text{set union pattern} \ ;$$

$$\text{set enumeration pattern} \ = \ \text{'\{', [pattern list], '\}'} \ ;$$

$$\text{set union pattern} \ = \ \text{pattern}, \text{'}\cup\text{'}, \text{pattern} \ ;$$

$$
\begin{aligned}
\text{sequence pattern} \ = \ & \text{sequence enumeration pattern} \\
\mid \ & \text{sequence catenation pattern} \ ;
\end{aligned}
$$

$$\text{sequence enumeration pattern} \ = \ \text{'[', pattern list, ']'} \ ;$$

$$\text{sequence catenation pattern} \ = \ \text{pattern}, \text{'}\frown\text{'}, \text{pattern} \ ;$$

$$\text{tuple pattern} \ = \ \text{'mk-'}, \text{'(', [pattern list], ')'} \ ;$$

$$\text{record pattern} \ = \ \text{identifier}, \text{'(', [pattern list], ')'} \ ;$$

Bindings   These restrict the value of the result of 'evaluating' a pattern (binding values to unbound identifiers) to be either a member of a set or to be of a particular type.

$$\text{pattern bind} \ = \ \text{pattern} \mid \text{bind} \ ;$$

$$\text{bind} \ = \ \text{set bind} \mid \text{type bind} \ ;$$

$$\text{set bind} \ = \ \text{pattern}, \text{'}\in\text{'}, \text{expression} \ ;$$

$$\text{type bind} \ = \ \text{pattern}, \text{':'}, \text{type} \ ;$$

Although the concrete syntax for patterns looks fairly complicated, the idea is straightforward. A pattern will consist of a series of identifiers and values. The identifiers that have no binding (i.e. no value) are being defined in terms of the value against which the pattern is to be matched.

The idea is that values are given to the defining occurrences of some of the identifiers in a pattern such that if the pattern (thought of as a restrictive sort of expression) is evaluated, the resulting value is equal to the value the pattern is to be matched against. The defining occurrences of identifiers are described in the concrete syntax by the production rule pattern identifier. For example,

$$\text{let } \{a\} \cup s = aset \text{ in}$$

$$\dots$$

is equivalent to

> let $a \in aset$ in
> let $s = aset - \{a\}$ in
> $\ldots$

and

> let $[a] \frown rest = alist$ in
> $\ldots$

is equivalent to

> let $a = \mathsf{hd}\ alist$ in
> let $rest = \mathsf{tl}\ alist$ in
> $\ldots$

The dash means 'don't care'; the dash is to be replaced by a value when doing the pattern matching but this value is not bound to any identifier. Used in a let preamble, a pattern allows a value to be taken apart, assuming it is a structured value, and various components of the value to be matched and bound to identifiers. It should be noted that there is a non-determinism here. For a particular identifier there could be several values which could be associated with that identifier—any value that works can be used for the binding.

Now we can explain what is meant by a value matching a pattern. A match occurs if there exists an assignment of values to the defining occurrences of the identifiers occurring in the pattern such that when the pattern, treated as an expression, is evaluated the resulting value of that expression is equal to the value being matched.

It is easy to see now what is meant by a match of a pattern occurring in a cases command with a value. If there is a match then the binding of identifiers with values occurred and the command corresponding to the case pattern is 'executed' with the identifier bindings as defined in the match.

The original syntax of VDM-SL was designed so that it looked like a programming language and if it was read as if it were a programming language and understood in that way the results of the specification would not be a surprise. The semantics of the sequential language are not defined in an executable manner, i.e. they are not defined in a way that says first do this and then do something else. The semantics are given in such a way that if the semantics are interpreted in an executable manner, the answer the reader would get would be the one intended by a writer who understood the full semantic definition of the equations that had been written down. To put it more simply, the sequential language or command language component of VDM-SL looks like a programming language and if interpreted in this way would give the right semantics.

9.3 INPUT AND OUTPUT

The next topic to be addressed is the problem of input/output. In this book we will take the liberty of extending VDM-SL in such a way that the pure language can be recovered if necessary. The approach taken with input/output is to include in the state a simple model of the file system, an abstract model of the component of the filing system of interest to the program that is being specified, and to use abbreviated read and write commands on those file components.

To do input/output, we first need a simple model of a filing system that can be added to the state

> state *Example* of
>
> $\qquad$ . . .
>
> $\qquad$ *file-system* : *Files*
>
> end

and the *Files* type can be modelled as

> $Files = File\text{-}name \xrightarrow{m} File$

We will assume that the mapping of a file name to a particular file is done for us by the operating system the final implementation uses; this can be abstracted out by using an abstract file name to refer to a particular file. The actual structure of a file depends on the system to be specified, and to some extent the environment in which the system will execute; e.g. a file might be

> $File = Sequential\text{-}file \mid Indexed\text{-}file \mid Text\text{-}file \mid \ldots$

where a sequential file can be described by a sequence of records

> $Sequential\text{-}file = Record^*$

and an indexed file as a mapping from a key to the record associated with that record:

> $Indexed\text{-}file = Key \xrightarrow{m} Record$

The exact form of a key and the exact form of a record would depend on the system being specified.

A text file could be modelled as

> $Text\text{-}file = Character^*$

or even

> $Text\text{-}file = Line^*$
>
> $Line = Character^*$

Which of these two possibilities is used, again depends on what is being specified.

9.3.1   Sequential files

As reading from and writing to a sequential file is so common when writing a specification for a system, or when designing the system, it is worth introducing a notation for this. First, for an input file we need some way of recording the current position as the file is traversed. The easiest way of doing this is to model an input file with a left component and a right component, each component being a sequence. The elements in the left component are those that have been read; those in the right component are those components about to be read, with the head of the right component being the next piece of input.

The input file is modelled as a sequence of values. The values are as complex as necessary and the sequence order defines the order in which these values are presented to the program. This technique will even be used for interactive input. The order of values in the sequence is defined by watching somebody use the implementation that satisfies the specification and writing down the order in which input is presented to the program.

This order, when tested against the specification, should define what the program will do.

The same approach can be used for output from a program. The execution of a program produces output in an order that matches the order in the specification. In fact this approach can be seen in an operating system such as UNIX or MS-DOS where the input or output, wherever it comes from or goes to, is always considered as a sequence of values.

As well as having operations to read from and write to a sequential file, it is useful to have operations that could be said to model the concept of opening a file for either input or output and closing a file. There is also a need for the equivalent of an end-of-file predicate.

With the above discussion in mind, the state when using input and output commands should always have a component of the form

> state *Example* of
> $$\ldots : \ldots$$
> *file* : *Files*
> end

> $$Files = File\text{-}name \xrightarrow{\ m\ } File$$

> $$File = X^*$$

In the following informal expansion, the *File* component should be replaced by

> $$File = Closed\text{-}file \mid Input\text{-}file \mid Output\text{-}file$$

> $$Closed\text{-}file :: file : X^*$$

> $$Input\text{-}file :: \quad left : X^*$$
> $$right : X^*$$

> $$Output\text{-}file :: file : X^*$$

Input Input into a program can be considered to be equivalent to assigning a value to a variable. This suggests a possible specification style for input:

> *read* (*id*: *File-name*) *r*: *X*
>
> ext wr *file* : *Files*
>
> pre true
>
> post *r* = next piece of input from file *id* $\land$
> some sort of change to the file associated with *id*

The post-condition of the *read* operation will be of the form that the result has something to do with the input channel, satisfies some condition and there is some change to the input channel. This operation could be used in a program:

> $$x := read(ch\text{-}id)$$

Rather than write this, we will adopt the style of many programming languages and introduce a read command:

> read command = state designator, 'from', identifier, ['st', expression] ;

A value whose type is the same as the component of the state designated by the state designator is read from some input medium identified by the identifier. The value must satisfy the expression (which has a Boolean result type). Each command of the form

x from id st $P(x)$

is understood to mean

> $read$ $(id: File\text{-}name)$
> ext wr $file$: $Files$
> x : X
> pre $file(id) \in Input\text{-}file \wedge$
> let $mk\text{-}Input\text{-}file(\text{-}, right) = file(id)$ in
> $right \neq [\,] \wedge P(\mathsf{hd}\ right)$
> post let $mk\text{-}Input\text{-}file(left, right) = \overleftarrow{file}(id)$ in
> $x = \mathsf{hd}\ right\ \wedge$
> $file = \overleftarrow{file} \dagger \{id \mapsto mk\text{-}Input\text{-}file(left \curvearrowright [\mathsf{hd}\ right], \mathsf{tl}\ right)\}$

It is assumed that the file has been opened, and that there is still input available to be read. All the above is saying in execution terms is: read the next piece of input. Note that a command of the form

x from id

is an abbreviation for

x from id st true

Output   For output the following abbreviation will be written:

output command = expression, 'to', identifier ;

and the informal expansion rule for an output command of the form

val to id

is

> $write$ $(val: X, id: File\text{-}name)$
> ext wr $file$: $Files$
> pre $file(id) \in Output\text{-}file$
> post let $mk\text{-}Output\text{-}file(data) = \overleftarrow{file}(id)$ in
> $file = \overleftarrow{file} \dagger \{id \mapsto mk\text{-}Output\text{-}file(data \curvearrowright [val])\}$

In execution terms, the value of the expression is written to the output file. As far as the rest of the state is concerned (i.e. the state not including the output file) the result of an output operation is equivalent to assigning a value to some implicit global variable.

Opening files   An open command is written

open command = 'open', expression, 'for', ('input' | 'output') ;

where the result of evaluating the expression is a file name (a value whose type is *File-name*). Therefore an open command of the form

open id for input

expands to

> *open-for-input* (*id*: *File-name*)
> **ext wr** *file* : *Files*
> **pre** *file*(*id*) ∈ *Closed-file*
> **post let** *mk-Closed-file*(*data*) = $\overleftarrow{file}$(*id*) **in**
>   *file* = $\overleftarrow{file}$ † {*id* ↦ *mk-Input-file*([], *data*)}

and

> **open** *id* **for output**

expands to

> *open-for-output* (*id*: *File-name*)
> **ext wr** *file* : *Files*
> **pre** *file*(*id*) ∈ *Closed-file*
> **post** *file* = $\overleftarrow{file}$ † {*id* ↦ *mk-Output-file*([])}

Closing files   The concrete syntax for a close command is

> close command = 'close', expression ;

where the result of evaluating the expression is a file name (a value whose type is *File-name*). Therefore a command of the form

> close *id*

expands to

> *close* (*id*: *File-name*)
> **ext wr** *file* : *Files*
> **pre** *file*(*id*) ∈ *Output-file* ∪ *Input-file*
> **post cases** *id* **of**
>   *mk-Input-file*(*left*, *right*) → *file* = $\overleftarrow{file}$ † {*id* ↦ *mk-Closed-file*(*left* ⌢ *right*)},
>   *mk-Output-file*(*out*) → *file* = $\overleftarrow{file}$ † {*id* ↦ *mk-Closed-file*(*out*)}
>   **end**

Testing for end of file   Finally the end-of-file prefix operator predicate is shown below, this is an additional operator that is globally available and its definition is just:

> input output expression = 'eof', expression ;

> *eof* (*id*: *File-name*) *r*: **B**
> **ext rd** *file* : *Files*
> **pre** *file*(*id*) ∈ *Input-file*
> **post let** *mk-Input-file*(-, *right*) = *file*(*id*) **in**
>   *r* ⇔ *right* = []

In those cases where it is important, or more information is necessary, we will build a model of the input/output mechanism necessary for the problem; otherwise we will use the above simple model and abbreviations.

9.4   THE DESIGN PROBLEM

The design problem is about structuring our specifications so it will lead to the development of a well-structured system. Using formal specifications does not guarantee a good architecture for a system, but it does help. It is possible to define operations in such a way that the resulting system will not have a good architecture and will be difficult to maintain. It is more difficult to do this using formal specifications, but it is possible.

In order to produce a good structure for our specification it will be useful to have some sort of sketching technique to allow us to identify the individual abstract machines, i.e. the operations and data types, of the system so the specification for these can be written.

There are two well-tried and relatively successful specification and development techniques, namely data flow design, and structured design. These, in various guises, have proved very successful ways of decomposing large systems, and they can be used as a sketching tool when applying formal methods. We will not use data flow diagrams or structure charts to the same level of detail as they would be used as a stand-alone technique, but they are a useful tool for sketching the top level of the system.

9.4.1   Data flow design

The data flow diagram   Data flow diagrams[2] pre-date computing by some 20 years; they were in fact invented in the 1920s to document the flow of information through an office. A data flow diagram models the components of a system (processes) and the interfaces (data flow) between them. It also shows the input (sources) and output (sinks) of the system and any file stores that hold information. It should be noted that a data flow diagram does not show flow of control, error handling or housekeeping functions. It is in fact an abstraction of the major functioning part of the system working with, in some sense, correct data.

Data flow diagrams were first used to reorganize an office full of clerks in a large quill-and-ink bureaucracy. Used in this way each clerk was represented by a circle and an arrow for each document type that passed between clerks. The components of a data flow diagram are shown in Fig. 9.3.

A data flow is a pipeline through which packets of information flow—data flows link processes. Each data flow, which is represented by a directed line segment, is labelled, and an abstract description of the data that flows along it can be written down. When sketching we might start by defining the data as being 'to be defined'; later more detail can be added using abstract syntax. The informal semantics of a data flow are that data cannot be changed or modified in any way; nor can data be created or destroyed in a data flow.

A process is a transformation of data or information between the input data flows and the output data flows: one or more input data streams are converted into one or

---

[2]Examples of the use of data flow diagrams can be found in later chapters.

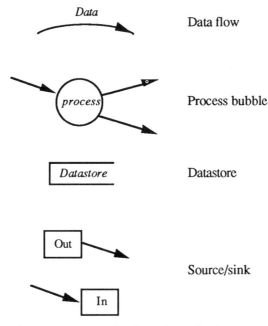

Figure 9.3   The main components of a data flow diagram.

more output data streams. A process is represented by a circle containing a name for the process and that name should describe what it does. As we sketch a design initially the label will be a very high level, abstract, description of what that process does. Later as more detail is added, a brief English description can be given, and finally the description of the process can be written formally using pre- and post-conditions.

Processes can change or transform data in either of two ways:

- Physically—the output is the result of doing some sort of processing on the input.
- Logically—the input and output are the same but are treated differently—one could say the output has more information content. This happens when a process checks the validity of the input data according to some rule. Typically we would be checking that some sort of invariant is satisfied, either an explicit one written down in the system or some implicit one given by the type rule. This sort of process will usually be reading input from a source and checking it for consistency before passing it on.

Processes can neither create nor destroy data, all output from a process must be derivable from the input and no data should just pass through a process. Either it is transformed or checked.

A data store is a buffer containing data for processing at a later time. In the twenties office model it would be equivalent to a filing cabinet or a folder containing information on somebody's desk. It is used to de-couple processes that work at a different rate.

A source/sink is a person, place or thing outside the system that will produce or consume the information processed by the system. The term source and sink are sometimes used interchangeably with the term 'terminator'. Sources and sinks are net suppliers or recipients of data, they represent objects that lie outside of the scope of the system and in fact define the boundary between the actual system itself and the outside world.

An informal semantics to a data flow diagram can be given: a process acts like a vacuum in that it 'draws' data towards itself through the data flows that input information into it, processes do not send or push data down output data flows. Processes effectively place their data at an exit port (a sort of 'out' tray) which another process can access by using a data flow pipeline. There may be some external trigger that will cause a particular process to extract data from those processes that are connected to it, and these are not usually shown on the data flow diagram (but there are notations that do show this control function). A process must stand between any information flowing from or going to a terminator or a data store.

In our use of data flow diagrams, as well as using data stores, a new piece of notation will be added to represent abstract machines; this is a modification of the Booch diagram. An abstract machine will usually replace a data store, but it could equally well replace a source or a sink if we wanted to hide the exact details of how the source or sink worked. Usually an abstract machine replaces a data store, and another good name for them would be an information store.

When considering an abstract machine, we will adhere to the following discipline when the operations of an abstract machine are defined (Fig. 9.4). We should think of an abstract machine as a black box and the operations as buttons on a control panel for that black box. We will restrict our operations to three classes: operations that create the abstract machine and initialize it, i.e. set up the internal state such that it satisfies a possible data invariant; operations that update the machine that will change the internal state, perhaps with data supplied from the outside world; and enquiry functions which will allow the internal state to be interrogated. We will make it a rule not to specify operations that both change the internal state and return a value. This discipline means that if we perform two enquiry operations one after the other we will get the same result, i.e. enquiry operations will not have side effects.

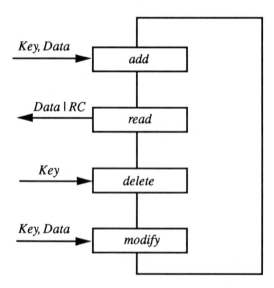

Figure 9.4   Example operations of an abstract machine.

Data may not flow directly from one abstract machine to another without an intervening process (we could remove this restriction and thus be in a position to implement information stores using objects in an object-oriented programming language but this is beyond the scope of this book). It is not a coincidence that rectangles which represent operations in an abstract machine have the same shaped symbol as those representing sources and sinks. With this use of the data flow notation they are performing a similar function: when we store data in an abstract machine it effectively leaves the system temporarily and comes back in via an operation that reads information from the data store. While it is in the data store, we are not interested in how that information is stored; it is effectively outside the system.

The context diagram   The context diagram gives an overview of the system. It shows all the main input and outputs of the system, i.e. all the main sources and sinks. Its purpose is to define the domain of the system. It usually consists of a single process bubble which represents the entire system.

Levelling   Levelling is a process where we add detail to a data flow diagram (Fig. 9.5). What happens is that a single process is treated as a 'mini context diagram' and this process is divided up into subprocesses linked together with data flows.

Levelling is a tool which enables a divide and conquer strategy to problem solving; we can take a data flow diagram and add more detail. With conventional data flow design, an interesting question which needs to be answered is: when is this levelling process finished? There is a simple answer to this—when there is an overwhelming urge to turn the data flow diagram into a flow chart or when there is an overwhelming urge to add low-level control. Just before this point is reached there is enough detail in the data flow diagram for it to act as the basis of a formal specification. In the use that this book makes of data flow design, we will stop levelling when each process can be described easily using pre- and post-conditions.

Building a data flow diagram for a system   Creating a data flow diagram for a system can be quite difficult. One particular approach is to start at the output end of the system, the sinks, and work back towards the input, the sources. The idea behind this approach is that the output is the most important part of the system so why not start there. (A system that produces no output is not very useful!)

Step 1.   Identify all the inputs and outputs used by the system. This implies that the first step for creating a data flow diagram for a system is to draw the context diagram, and this step should not be missed just because it seems too simple.

Step 2.   For each output data flow, starting with those that terminate in a sink, create a process that will produce this particular piece of output. The task of this new process will be to produce the data in the output data flow. Define the structure of the data carried in the output data flow using abstract syntax to describe it in detail—but not too much detail.

Step 3.   Identify the input information necessary to produce that output and create sufficient input data flows for the new process to produce the output of this process. Again, document the structure of these input data flows but again do not go into too much detail. Write a brief description of what this process does—sketch the pre- and post-conditions. These input data flows will now become output data flows for the next step.

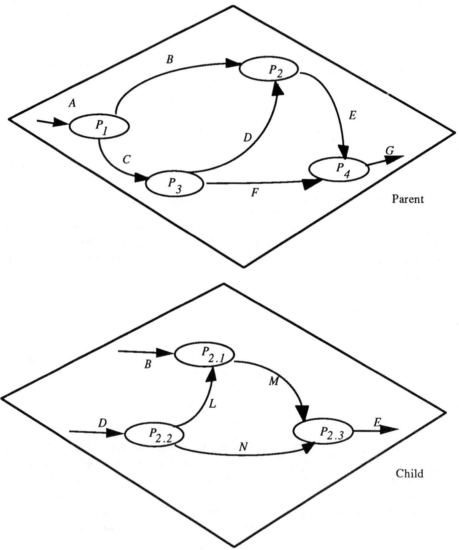

Figure 9.5 Levelling.

This process will start at each of the sinks and work backwards towards the sources, detail being filled in as we go along. The idea behind a data flow diagram is to produce a logical design—a design that is independent of any implementation. This can be used to our advantage. Why not pretend the system is to be implemented using clerks and pre-printed forms? A process will model the work of a clerk and the clerk's job description is the specification for that process. The data flows describe the information that needs to be communicated from one clerk to another on a pre-printed form. Abstract syntax notation allows us to record the information content of a pre-printed form—we are not too interested in the layout of any pre-printed forms, only in the information to be recorded on them. Sources become the in-trays for the department (system) and sinks become the out-trays. The question is: how do we organize the flow of information between clerks so that the job is done efficiently? Try to give each clerk only one job so it is much easier for them to do their job and for us to understand the organization.

We may find, of course, that a particular clerk's job, though easily described and looking like one job, could be divided and the single clerk be replaced by a group of clerks doing several jobs that contribute to the original job. This of course is the idea behind levelling. In this particular view, data stores represent filing cabinets or a stack of input/output trays.

If we continue with this view of the system, data stores (filing cabinets) with complex access should perhaps be better put in a separate room with a secretary managing their organization. The secretary will retrieve and store information on demand. Of course, we can then leave it up to the secretary as to how the information is actually stored in the filing cabinet. The secretary will interact with the clerks via some sort of high-level command interface. The secretary and the filing cabinets become an implementation of an abstract machine that manages information.

Perhaps only for simple data items should we allow the clerks to have direct access to the in/out trays or to the filing cabinets, and any complex access to information should be via an abstract machine, as shown in Fig. 9.6.

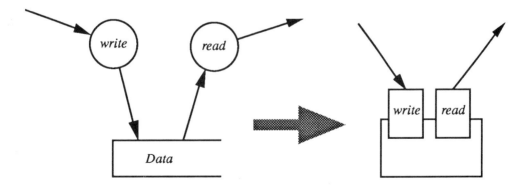

Figure 9.6   Transforming a data store to an abstract machine.

Whenever a data store occurs in a data flow diagram, try to work out what object(s) in the real world are being modelled by it. What is the abstraction it is representing? If an obvious one does not exist it could be that the design is wrong and it should be rethought. Any real-world object that is being modelled in the system should best be represented by an abstract machine (this is what object-oriented design is about).

Guidelines for drawing data flow diagrams

1. Identify all the inputs and outputs used by the system; do not skip drawing the context drawing just because it seems to be simple.
2. Determine the composition of each data flow, try to document the structure of the data flowing between each process, but do not go into too much detail at first—leave detail until later.
3. Determine the connections between the main inputs and outputs.
4. Label processes and write a brief statement of what they do; sketch the pre- and post-conditions.
5. Ignore control: initialization, setting up, wrapping up, etc.
6. Ignore error processing for the moment—this will be considered later.
7. Draw the next level as and when necessary.

Other hints

1. Name and document every flow, if a flow can not be named and documented, it may indicate an error.
2. Do not ignore the structure of a data flow by using general 'cover-all' names such as 'data' and 'info' and leave documentation of the detail—if you can't write an abstract description of the data moving along the data flow, then you do not understand the data.
3. Do not group flows that do not belong together; show them as separate flows. Conversely, do not show separate flows when they should be grouped. Using abstract syntax should help here—each piece of data should be a single atomic entity (which may have components, c.f. a date).
4. Datastores with complex access should be converted into abstract machines.

It may be necessary to have many attempts before obtaining a suitable set of data flow diagrams for the system.

9.5   THE ORDER OF OPERATIONS REVISITED

As has been described in the introduction to this chapter, one of the problems we have is identifying the abstract machines and specifying the order in which the buttons of those abstract machines are pressed.

Our notation for describing abstract machines and the data flow diagrams that contain these machines only deals with the processing/transformation of data that is required and the order in which these transformations are done. However, just giving the order is sometimes not enough; more control information may be necessary. Also the data flow diagram gives no structure for the overall control of the system—data flow diagrams do not show any control.

However, the structure chart design notation allows control information to be documented and thus can be used as a sketching tool when trying to develop a specification that describes the order and, thus, the structure of the whole system. Not only can it be used as a sketching tool it can also be a means by which the detailed VDM-SL can be introduced. One advantage of the structure chart notation is that it allows the expression of order without worrying about control—such things as the exact form of any Boolean tests can be ignored. In our use as a sketching tool we will not always annotate calls with parameters that are passed if these can be deduced from the corresponding data flow chart. When we are happy with the call hierarchy and control structure this can be translated into the formal VDM-SL sequential notation, which can then be used as the basis for the design. The notation is very straightforward and consists of the symbols shown in Fig. 9.7.

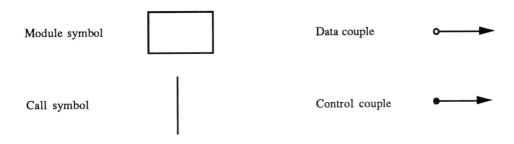

Figure 9.7 Structure chart symbols.

A structure chart shows the way in which a system is partitioned into modules (or procedures or operations) and the associated call hierarchy and organization of those components. It also shows the communication, i.e. the interface between the components, by showing what data and flags are passed to an operation when it is called and what data and flags are returned from that operation when it has completed its task.

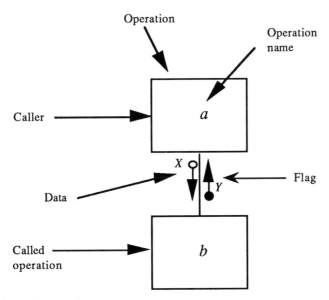

Figure 9.8 The call notation.

We can represent the fact that module a calls module b passing the data X and that b when complete returns the flag Y as shown in Fig. 9.8.

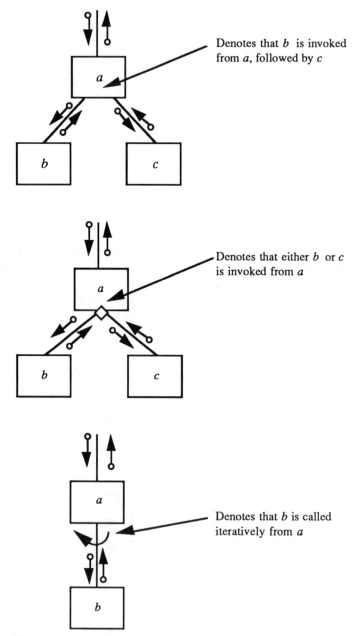

Figure 9.9 Showing order of operations, conditional choice and iteration.

Control information can be added to a structure chart as shown in Fig. 9.9. The first diagram illustrates how sequential control can be shown, module *a* will call module *b* followed by module *c*; when module *a* has completed it will return control to whichever module called it. The second diagram shows how conditional choice can be indicated, and the third shows iteration.

As has already been described, the normal semantics of a data flow diagram is that they are demand driven, i.e. when a sink requires information for output it 'reads' from the processes to which it is attached. These will then demand input from the processes which feed into it, produce the result and pass it through to the sink; that is data is effectively demand driven from the output side of the data flow, and each process must demand input from the processes it is attached to in order to carry out the transformation and produce results to pass on to the process that demanded output from it.

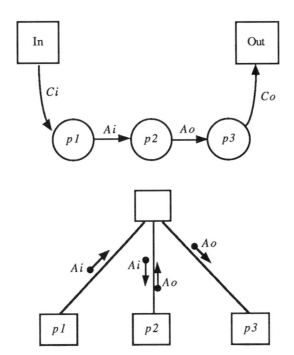

Figure 9.10   From data flow diagram to structure chart.

These semantics are fairly informal. The idea behind a structure chart is to produce a call hierarchy with a control module calling one or more processing modules, each processing module corresponding to a process in a data flow diagram. This is shown in Fig. 9.10. In this simple case the data flow diagram can be translated into a typical three-box 'input-process-output' structure chart.

9.6   SUMMARY

The purpose of this chapter is to briefly introduce the ideas of data flow design and structured design, and their corresponding notations, in order to show how they can be used with VDM as a way of developing an architectural specification for a computer system. These two tools can be used to decompose a large system into abstract machines and operations and processes to drive those abstract machines. The concept of an abstract machine is very much identical to that of an object in object-oriented design, therefore this approach can be used also. In either case we will use pre- and post-conditions to specify the abstract machine and the VDM-SL sequential language to show how the various functions supplied by the abstract machine are called and used. The next chapter will show some of the ideas described in this chapter in action.

LARGE SYSTEMS

AIMS

- To describe how formal techniques can be used to describe many of the aspects of a specification and high-level design of a system.
- To show how the graphical notations described in the previous chapter are applied in three case studies.
- To show how ordering can be incorporated into a formal specification by describing three case studies.

10.1 INTRODUCTION

One of the most difficult problems in writing formal specifications is the production of a formal description of a large system. The importance of getting the structure of a large specification correct cannot be emphasized too much. The whole of the development process is based on the specification and thus, in a sense, the specification will influence the overall architecture and development strategy for the system.

A further problem is the terseness of the notation; its power allows many complex ideas to be expressed in a reasonably simple and easy manner, and well-written specifications, even for large systems, tend to be quite small. Beware of the deduction that, because the specification is small the ensuing system should not take very long to develop—nothing could be further from the truth.

These points will be illustrated by looking at three large (by teaching standards) systems. Certain simplifications have been made to keep the size of the problems down to a reasonable level. The reader might like to consider what enhancements could be made to make the problems more realistic. The three examples described are a system for a small local library; a GREP-like pattern-matching program; and a stand-alone cash dispenser for a small bank. This chapter uses the concepts described in the previous chapter.

10.2 A LIBRARY SYSTEM

The first specification to be tackled is a computer system to keep track of books held in a local library. The system should be capable of recording who borrowed a book, and recording the return of a book. The system should also be capable of recording the addition of a new book to the library, and recording a book being removed from the library stock. It is also deemed to be useful to have some enquiry functions, such as an operation to enquire whether a book is available for a loan, the ability to list books by a particular author or to list books with a particular title. Finally, it might be useful to have an operation to list all books that are out on loan at the end of each week.

Before starting the specification for this problem we should examine the real world. The system will model books that are held in a library, i.e. books that are available for loan. Books are either on book-shelves, and are available immediately, or somebody has them out on loan and, on return, they can be re-issued. The library has users, and these need to be modelled.

How can books be modelled in the system? One possibility would be to use a book title, but this does not contain sufficient information: there could be two different books with the same title, for example *Easy Pascal*. Using both the title and the author's name might be a possible solution, but again this may not be sufficient—consider the second edition of *Easy Pascal*. The ISBN is unique for a particular book, but this does not solve the problem either; multiple copies of the same book might be held in the library, and each copy would have the same ISBN. The solution to the problem is to mirror what happens in a real library which uses a manual system: each book in the library has an individual number which is used to keep track of it. Thus a book can be modelled by its identifying number. The physical implementation of the book's identifier might be by a bar-code attached to the book which is read by a bar-code reader whenever the book is processed within the library.

How are users of the library to be modelled by the system? Is their name enough, or should both their name and address be used? There is an unlikely chance that people with the same name live at the same address, so the users are each given a unique identifying number, and that is used to model them. So that a user can be associated with a number, library users are issued with a card that identifies them; this card will included a unique identifying code, again encoded as a bar-code.

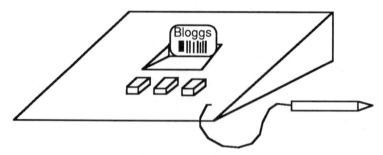

Figure 10.1   The library checkout station.

We first need to think about the various inputs for the system. The system will be driven by a terminal, and a special station for use by the librarians when checking books in and out. The operations to add and to delete a book, list books by title, list books by author and to find out if a book is available, will take their input and display their results on the terminal. The operations to record a book being borrowed and to record the return of a book will be carried out using the special station shown in Fig. 10.1. The station consists of a wand for reading bar-codes and three buttons: one to be pressed when the bar-code of a book that is to be borrowed is read, the second to be pressed when reading the bar-code on the library card and finally a third button to be pressed when reading the bar-code on a book that is being returned. The context diagram for the system is shown in Fig. 10.2.

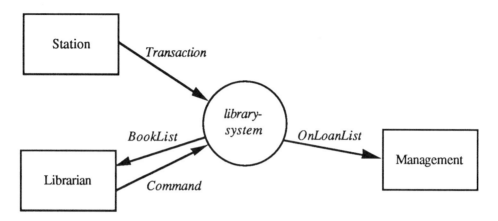

Figure 10.2   The context diagram for the library system.

The operations that are available to the librarian from the terminal can be documented as:

$$Command \quad = \quad AddBook$$
$$| \quad DeleteBook$$
$$| \quad ListByTitle$$
$$| \quad ListByAuthor$$
$$| \quad OnShelf$$
$$| \quad \text{LISTONLOAN}$$

$AddBook \ :: \ isbn \ : \ ISBN$

$DeleteBook \ :: \ book \ : \ Bookid$

$ListByTitle \ :: \ title \ : \ Title$

$ListByAuthor \ :: \ author \ : \ Name$

$OnShelf \ :: \ book \ : \ Bookid$

Notice how the abstract syntax for the type *Command* describes the (possible) information contents of each of the commands that can be issued by the users of the system. There has been no attempt to describe how the commands are to be issued—by menus or typing in text. The above is a first guess, it may need to be updated as the specification proceeds. The commands that can be issued from the station are:

$Transaction = BorrowBook \ | \ ReturnBook$

$BorrowBook \ :: \quad book \ : \ Bookid$
$$userid \ : \ User$$

$ReturnBook \ :: \ book \ : \ Bookid$

The exact format of a *Booklist* and an *OnLoanList* will be left for the moment:

$$BookList = \ldots$$

$$OnLoanList = \ldots$$

Notice how the input from the station has been made more abstract than is described in the specification of the station. The specification of the way the station works indicates that one of three buttons is pressed, and this is followed by the wand reading a number from a bar code. This could be documented by defining the information coming from the station as a signal; this is shown in Fig. 10.3 where a signal could be defined as

$$Signal = Code \mid Button\text{-}id$$

$$Code = \ldots$$

$$Button\text{-}id = \text{ONE} \mid \text{TWO} \mid \text{THREE}$$

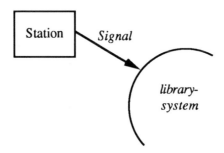

Figure 10.3   Reading from the checkout station.

The context diagram implies a more abstract representation of the input from the station than is described above. This is as it should be: implementation details should be hidden whenever possible, so rather than describing exactly what the signals from the station are, even if the signals are defined in an abstract manner, we will describe their information content.

The next step is to notice that there are three subsystems: one dealing with the checking in and checking out of books, another dealing with enquiries and management functions and a third producing a report of all the books that are on loan. Since this function only occurs weekly, it is considered separately from the other parts of the system, though it could be considered as part of the terminal enquiry component. Thus the expansion of the date flow diagram would look like that shown in Fig. 10.4, where the context diagram has been levelled by expanding its process bubble.

It can be seen that the overview data flow diagram is a reasonable model of the system and shows it divided into three components: those commands entered at the terminal, the transactions handled by the station and the management report function that lists all the books that are out on loan.

To keep things simple for the first example, we will assume that the terminal produces the commands in an abstract syntax form. Of course in real life the terminal will not do this; the user will type some sort of character string which must contain the information described by the abstract syntax for the commands, and the character string will need

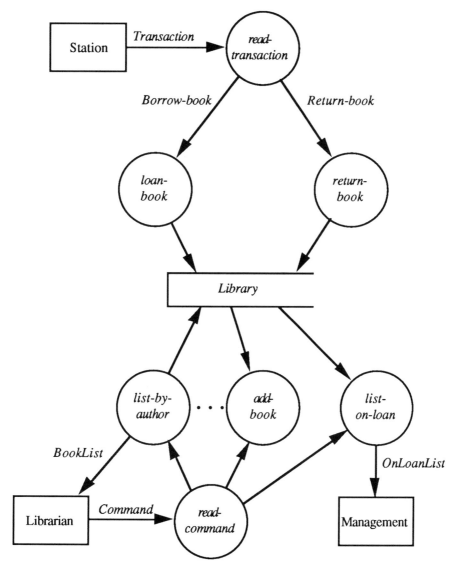

Figure 10.4 Overview data flow diagram.

to be decoded and translated into some internal form. This point will be addressed in a later chapter.

10.2.1 The state for the library

We have already decided that a book can be modelled by an identifying number. In the system, the details of a book, such as its author, title, and whether or not it is out on loan, could be associated with this identifier by a mapping. The users of the library will be modelled by a mapping that associates their name and address with the user identifying code. These considerations give the following first attempt at the state.

> **Worked example 10.1** Ignoring loans for the moment, write down an attempt at the state of the library.
>
> SOLUTION The state is shown below
>
> types
>
> $Book$ :: $author$: $Names$
> $title$: $Title$
>
> $Person$ :: $name$: $Name$
> $addr$: $Address$
>
> $Names = Name$-set
>
> $Bookid = \text{token}_1$
>
> $User = \text{token}_2$
>
> $Name = \ldots$
>
> state $Library$ of
> $books$: $Bookid \xrightarrow{m} Book$
> $users$: $User \xrightarrow{m} Person$
> end

$\blacksquare$

We will now consider the problems of loans; how will the books that are out on loan be modelled or, equivalently, how will the books that are on the library shelves be modelled—these two ideas are related since

> books on loan $\cup$ books on shelf $=$ all the books of the library

The books actually on the bookshelves at any one time can be modelled by using a set that contains all the identifiers of those books. As the system has inquiry functions about authors and titles of books, the system needs to have an author index and a title index. The author index could be modelled by

> $Name \xrightarrow{m} Bookid$-set

A set of book identifiers is necessary for the range of this mapping since an author could have written more than one book. The title index is modelled by

> $Title \xrightarrow{m} Bookid$-set

A set of book identifiers is again necessary, as there could be more than one book with the same title. The state now encapsulates the various components of the real-world library. There is also a rather complex invariant which states that the books on the shelves are a subset of the books in the library, and all the books in the author index are in the library and all the books in the title index are in the library:

> state *Library* of
>> $books \ : \ Bookid \xrightarrow{m} Book$
>> $users \ : \ User \xrightarrow{m} Person$
>> $shelves \ : \ Bookid\text{-set}$
>> $authors \ : \ Author \xrightarrow{m} Bookid\text{-set}$
>> $titles \ : \ Title \xrightarrow{m} Bookid\text{-set}$
>
> inv $mk\text{-}Library(books, -, shelves, authors, titles) \quad \triangleq$
>> $shelves \subseteq \text{dom } books \ \wedge$
>> $\bigcup \text{rng } authors = \text{dom } books \ \wedge$
>> $\bigcup \text{rng } titles = \text{dom } books$
>
> end

Worked example 10.2 Does this state adequately reflect the library?

SOLUTION No, there are several problems with this state. The books that are out on loan can be deduced from the domain of the books mapping and the shelves component of the state, but there is no information about who has a particular book out on loan! Also the last two components of the state, the author index and the title index, are not needed—the information held in them is contained in the original mapping from *Bookid* to details about a book (*Book*). ∎

The problem of who exactly has borrowed a book can be solved by adding an appropriate component to the information about the user that records what books he or she has out. With these changes the state can be altered to:

> **types**
>
> $Book \ :: \ author \ : \ Names$
> $\qquad\qquad\quad title \ : \ Title$
>
> $Person \ :: \ name \ : \ Names$
> $\qquad\qquad\quad addr \ : \ Address$
> $\qquad\qquad\quad books \ : \ Bookid\text{-set}$
>
> state *Library* of
>> $books \ : \ Bookid \xrightarrow{m} Book$
>> $users \ : \ User \xrightarrow{m} Person$
>> $\qquad \ldots$
>
> inv $mk\text{-}Library(books, users, \ldots) \quad \triangleq$
>> $on\text{-}loan(users) \subseteq \text{dom } books \ \wedge \ldots$
>
> end

The invariant for this state must record that the only books that can be out on loan are those that are in the library. This property models a real-world restriction—users of the library cannot borrow books that do not exist. We do not need to mark books as being out on loan in the books component—this is already recorded in the users component.

The auxiliary function *on-loan* defines those books that are not currently in the library, but are out on loan:

$$on\text{-}loan : (User \xrightarrow{m} Person) \rightarrow Book\text{-}id\text{-set}$$

$$on\text{-}loan(users) \quad \triangleq \quad \bigcup\{per.books \mid per \in rng\ users\}$$

The state given above can be improved even more. Why not separate out the concept of a book catalogue and the concept of the actual books that are in the library? This will enable the library to hold information on books it does not have in stock—the librarian will then be able to supply information about books that are not necessarily in the library. There is a further advantage with this approach, the catalogue could be supplied on a CD ROM disk that contains a listing of all books that have been or are currently published. With this approach, the ISBN can be used to retrieve the information about a particular book. Also the information about who has a particular book out on loan can be moved to a separate component of the state, and we can use the fact that a particular book can only be on loan to one person. This gives the final version of the state:

$$
\begin{aligned}
&\textbf{state}\ Library\ \textbf{of} \\
&\quad index\ :\ ISBN \xrightarrow{m} Book \\
&\quad\quad lib\ :\ Bookid \xrightarrow{m} ISBN \\
&\quad\quad out\ :\ Bookid \xrightarrow{m} User \\
&\quad\ users\ :\ User \xrightarrow{m} Person \\
&\textbf{inv}\ mk\text{-}Library(index, lib, out, users)\quad \triangleq \\
&\quad\quad \textbf{dom}\ out \subseteq \textbf{dom}\ lib\ \wedge \\
&\quad\quad \textbf{rng}\ out \subseteq \textbf{dom}\ users\ \wedge \\
&\quad\quad \textbf{rng}\ lib \subseteq \textbf{dom}\ index \\
&\textbf{end}
\end{aligned}
$$

The author index and the title index have been included, in the sense that the necessary information has been included, in the *index* component of the state. An implementation strategy might be to separate these out using separate indexes in an implementation for performance reasons, but this is an implementation decision.

The invariant records the fact that any book that is out on loan is from the library and on loan to a user, and that any book in the library is also in the index. Note that just because a book is in the index does not mean to say it is in the library—the index, as discussed above, could record all books published! All that remains is to specify the types and tidy up the definition of the state:

types

$$
\begin{aligned}
Book\ ::\quad &title\ :\ Title \\
&authors\ :\ Names
\end{aligned}
$$

$$Names = Name\text{-set}$$

$$
\begin{aligned}
Person\ ::\ &name\ :\ Name \\
&addr\ :\ Address
\end{aligned}
$$

$$Catalogue = ISBN \xrightarrow{m} Book$$

$$Books = Bookid \xrightarrow{m} ISBN$$

$$On\text{-}loan = Bookid \xrightarrow{m} User$$

$Customers = User \xrightarrow{m} Person$

$Bookid = \mathsf{token}_1$

$User = \mathsf{token}_2$

$Name = \ldots$

$Title = \ldots$

$ISBN = \ldots$

$Address = \ldots$

state *Library* of
      $index$: $Catalogue$
        lib : $Books$
       out : $On\text{-}loan$
    $users$: $Customers$
inv $mk\text{-}Library(index, lib, out, users)$ $\triangleq$
    dom $out \subseteq$ dom $lib \wedge$
    rng $out \subseteq$ dom $users \wedge$
    rng $lib \subseteq$ dom $index$
end

By considering the 'real world' we have managed to identify the state component of two abstract machines, one of which models books and the other users. When defining other systems, it might not be a bad idea to start with the data flow diagram and from that identify the objects or abstract machines that need to be specified. When trying to determine the structure of any large system, some sort of iteration technique is required, but at the end it should be possible to discern a paper model of what is happening in the real-world version of the system.

Worked example 10.3 The definition of the function *on-loan* given above needs to be changed to reflect the new structure of the state. Write a new definition for this function.

SOLUTION

    $on\text{-}loan : On\text{-}loan \rightarrow Bookid\text{-}\mathsf{set}$

    $on\text{-}loan(out)$ $\triangleq$ dom out

This function could be used to clarify the invariant.   ■

10.2.2 The operations

With this state it is now possible to proceed and specify each of the operations, one for each of the commands and transactions.

Worked example 10.4 Specify an operation *add-book* which adds a book to the library. Assume the book is already in the index, and that it is identified by its ISBN.

SOLUTION

> *add-book* (*isbn*: *ISBN*) *r*: *Bookid*
>
> **ext rd** *index* : *Catalogue*
> **wr** *lib*   : *Books*
>
> **pre** *isbn* ∈ dom *index*
>
> **post** *r* ∈ *Bookid* − (dom *lib*) ∧
>   *lib* = $\overleftarrow{lib}$ † {*r* ↦ *isbn*}

A new book is assigned an identifying number that is not currently in use by the system, and the details about the book are added to the library. The book number could be printed out in bar-code and character format on a sticky label that can be attached to the book.   ∎

The operation for removing a book is shown below, it assumes the book is left in the index:

> *delete-book* (*book*: *Bookid*)
>
> **ext wr** *lib* : *Books*
>   **rd** *out* : *On-loan*
>
> **pre** *book* ∈ dom *lib* ∧ *book* ∉ dom *out*
>
> **post** *lib* = {*book*} ◁ $\overleftarrow{lib}$

The operation assumes that the book is in the library, and not out on loan—a reasonable assumption as the librarian has the actual copy in front of him or her when this operation is carried out.

Worked example 10.5 Specify an operation *borrow-book* which records the borrowing of a book from the library.

SOLUTION

> *borrow-book* (*book*: *Bookid*, *userid*: *User*)
>
> **ext rd** *lib*   : *Books*
>   **wr** *out*   : *On-loan*
>   **rd** *users* : *Customers*
>
> **pre** *book* ∈ dom *lib* ∧
>   *book* ∉ dom *out* ∧
>   *userid* ∈ dom *users*
>
> **post** *out* = $\overleftarrow{out}$ † {*book* ↦ *userid*}

Again the operation assumes that the book is in the library and not out on loan— a reasonable assumption as the librarian has the actual copy in front of him or her in order that the bar-code on the book can be read.   ∎

The operation that records the return of a book is shown below:

return-book (*book*: *Bookid*)
ext rd *lib*   : *Books*
   wr *out* : *On-loan*
pre *book* $\in$ dom *lib* $\wedge$
   book $\in$ dom *out*

post *out* = {*book*} $\lhd\!\!\!\!-\ \overline{out}$

The book is checked in, and is thus available for loan.

To define the two operations that produce a report, it is necessary to define an auxiliary type:

   BookList = *Book*-set

The result of the operations *list-by-author*, and *list-by-title* will be of this type, and making it a set indicates that it is being left up to the implementation to decide in what order the books will be listed.

Note that we can fill in some of the detail that was left undefined in the description of the data in the context diagram:

   Response = *BookList* | *OnLoanList*

The operation to produce a list of books by a particular author is

   list-by-author (*author*: *Name*) *r*: *BookList*
   ext rd *index* : *Catalogue*
   post *r* = {*book* $\in$ rng *index* | *author* $\in$ *book.authors*}

and the operation to produce a list of books with a particular title is

   list-by-title (*title*: *Title*) *r*: *BookList*
   ext rd *index* : *Catalogue*
   post *r* = {*book* $\in$ rng *index* | *book.title* = *title*}

The operation to check whether a book is available is shown in the next example.

Worked example 10.6 Write down the specification of an operation that checks whether a book is available for loan.

SOLUTION

   is-on-shelf (*book*: *Bookid*) *r*: **B**
   ext rd *lib* : *Books*
     out : *On-loan*
   post *r* $\Leftrightarrow$ *book* $\in$ dom *lib* $\wedge$ *book* $\notin$ dom *out*

                                                                                ■

The final operation to specify is the one that produces a report that lists all of the books that are out on loan. On paper, the listing might look like the one shown in Fig. 7.2 on page 101.

However, we should not be interested in this; it is far too concrete and is about implementation. What we should be concerned with is what information is conveyed by the listing, and it is this which will be documented. The listing is made up of a collection of entries and if we were interested in the order of the entries this could be recorded:

$$OnLoanList = Entry^*$$

but if we are not interested in the order, we could write

$$OnLoanList = Entry\text{-set}$$

Now it is necessary to say what an *Entry* is; this is straightforward:

$$
\begin{array}{rll}
Entry :: & nm & : \; Name \\
         & addr & : \; Address \\
         & user & : \; User \\
         & bks & : \; Book\text{-}info\text{-set}
\end{array}
$$

$$
\begin{array}{rll}
Book\text{-}info :: & title & : \; Title \\
                    & authors & : \; Names \\
                    & copy & : \; Bookid
\end{array}
$$

These auxiliary types describe the information contained in the listing, leaving out all the implementation detail about titles, page numbers, etc. Having specified what the output from the operation is, we can now write the actual operation itself:

list-on-loan () *over: OnLoanList*

$$
\begin{array}{lll}
\text{ext rd } index & : \; Catalogue \\
\quad lib & : \; Books \\
\quad out & : \; On\text{-}loan \\
\quad users & : \; Customers
\end{array}
$$

post $over = \{mk\text{-}Entry(nm, addr, user, bks) \mid user \in \text{rng } out \land$
$$users(user).name = nm \land$$
$$users(user).addr = addr \land$$
$$\text{let } cpys = copies(user, out) \text{ in}$$
$$bks = book\text{-}info(cpys, lib, index)\}$$

The auxiliary function *copies* returns all the books that a user has out:

$$copies : User \times On\text{-}loan \rightarrow Bookid\text{-set}$$

$$copies(user, out) \quad \triangle \quad \{cpy \in \text{dom } out \mid out(cpy) = user\}$$

and the function *book-info* returns the information about a set of books.

$$book\text{-}info : Bookid\text{-set} \times Books \times Catalogue \rightarrow Book\text{-}info\text{-set}$$

$$book\text{-}info(cpys, lib, index) \quad \triangle$$
$$\{mk\text{-}Book\text{-}info(tle, auths, cpy) \mid cpy \in cpys \land$$
$$index(lib(cpy)).title = tle \land$$
$$index(lib(cpy)).authors = auths\}$$

This states that all of the books that are contained in the listing are exactly those books that are out on loan, and that the name and address associated with a book is the name and address of the user who has the book out on loan. It should be noted that no user occurs in the listing more than once.

This small example illustrates how the concept of objects or abstract machines and data flow can be used to derive a reasonable architecture for a simple system. It should be noted that the data flow diagrams were used to sketch the system and give an overview; for a real system we should iterate through the data flow diagrams and the specifications until they are consistent with each other.

Exercise 10.1

1. Add some operations to manage users of the library. There should be operations to enrol a new member, remove an existing member and change the details of a member.
2. Add some operations to manage the index of the library.
3. The library system specified above has no concept of time in it—books can be borrowed for any length of time. Change the state so the date on which a book is loaned can be recorded and respecify the issue and return operations. Assume that books can be lent out for a specified period only.
4. Add an operation to renew a book to the system; the operation should be able to work with a telephone renewal.
5. Add functions to the system to deal with overdue books, including a function to calculate the fine for a long-overdue book.
6. Add an operation to the system specified in question 5 that prints out reminder letters to those library users who have overdue books.
7. Books might be 'in the library' but not available for loan (they could be at the binders being repaired, or missing). Change the library state so that books may be tracked more closely, and respecify the operations as necessary. Add any additional operations that might be useful.
8. It is necessary to check that the invariant is preserved by each of the operations of the system. Do this.
9. Using the other versions of the state described above, specify the library operations and compare the results with the example above.

10.3   TEXT PATTERNS

The purpose of the program to be specified is to find certain patterns of characters in a text file. The program will scan its input file and produce a list of those text lines in the file that match a specified text pattern. The overall architecture of the program is reasonably straightforward and the context diagram can be quickly sketched to see the inputs and outputs that need to be considered. It is shown in Fig. 10.5.

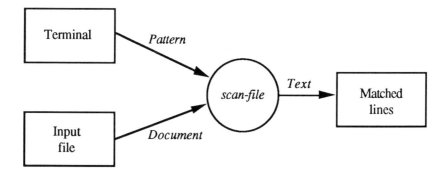

Figure 10.5   Context diagram for pattern matching program.

First we need to specify what a document is:

types

$Text = Line^*$

$Line = Char^*$

state $Document$ **of**
    doc : $Text$
end

We shall leave the exact form of a *Pattern* for the moment. The program can be specified using pre- and post-conditions:

scan-file $(p: Pattern)$ $r: Text$

ext rd doc : $Text$

post let $pats = eval\text{-}pattern(p)$ **in**
    $r = [doc(i) \mid 1 \le i \le \text{len } doc \land is\text{-}matched(pats, doc(i))]$

The operation *eval-pattern* produces a set of strings that can be derived from a pattern, if we define *String* as

$String = Char^*$

its signature can be written as

eval-pattern: $Pattern \rightarrow String$-set

The set of strings returned by this function is effectively those strings that exactly match a pattern; its definition will be given below after the definition of a pattern has been decided upon. The function *is-matched* checks if a string derived from a pattern occurs in a line:

is-matched : $String$-set $\times Line \rightarrow \mathbf{B}$

is-matched$(pats, line)$ $\triangleq$ $\exists pat \in pats \cdot pat$ **ins** $line$

The result of the **in** operator is true if the first argument is a subsequence of the second argument, otherwise it is false.

It can now be seen that the problem really reduces to defining exactly what a pattern is and what a match is. As soon as these two problems are solved, then the specification is complete.

10.3.1 The abstract syntax of patterns

The information about how a pattern is entered by the user is really part of the implementation. The usual approach taken by developers at this point is to write down the concrete syntax of a pattern, but if we are not careful this immediately leads us into consideration of 'how do you represent a tab?' and 'how should operators that combine patterns be distinguished from characters that make up the pattern?' This can be avoided by using the abstract syntax notation to describe the information content of a pattern—the concrete syntax can be designed later when it is known what information it must represent. So the first step is to write an abstract syntax for a pattern.

A pattern will obviously have more than one component, otherwise we will be restricted to looking for those lines that just contain a particular character. Thus the abstract syntax for a pattern could be started by stating that a pattern consists of a sequence of objects that are a 'unit of match'. We need a way of denoting a sequence type constructor that means one or more instances of an object—we use $^+$ for this purpose:

$$Pattern = Match\text{-}unit^+$$

Note that the abstract syntax does not allow a pattern to be an empty sequence (which would be found in any line and thus could be said to match every line in a document—not quite what we have in mind).

What candidates do we have for a 'unit of match'? An obvious candidate is a literal—a single character—and we are looking for an exact match. Another possibility is some sort of 'don't care'; anything matches this particular component of a pattern. Between these two extremes might be matching a range, or set, of characters, and this gives a third alternative. A pattern match can now be defined:

$$Match\text{-}unit = Character \mid Alternatives \mid \text{ANY}$$

$$Character :: ch : Char$$

$$Alternatives :: chs : Char\text{-set}$$

Another possible extension that could be considered is that instead of scanning the text for just one pattern we could scan the text for a set of alternative patterns; if any of the patterns that are listed occur in a line of text, then that line of text will be copied to the output file. This suggests that the syntax is extended with a definition for a set of patterns:

$$Patterns = Pattern\text{-set}$$

Are there any other extensions that could be made to the definition of a pattern? It should be noted that looking for the patterns

ABCA or ABDA

could be expressed as searching for the pattern

AB followed by either of CA or DA

(we have tried to avoid the exact concrete syntax for the moment). With this clue, could perhaps a set of patterns be added to the alternatives for a 'unit of match'?

$$Match\text{-}unit = Character \mid Alternatives \mid \text{ANY} \mid Patterns$$

We can do better than this, as the component that allows a set of characters to be specified can be replaced by the new component since it is a set of patterns, and a pattern can be a single character. This suggests the following modification to the abstract syntax:

$$Patterns = Pattern\text{-set}$$

$$Pattern = Match\text{-}unit^+$$

$$Match\text{-}unit = Character \mid Value \mid \text{ANY}$$

$$Character :: ch : Char$$

$$Value :: val : Patterns$$

We can get a better understanding of this abstract syntax by writing the body of the function which, when applied to a pattern, will return the set of strings that exactly match the pattern. The result of this function will be a set containing strings, where a string was defined as a sequence of characters:

$$eval\text{-}patterns : Patterns \rightarrow String\text{-set}$$

$$eval\text{-}patterns(pats) \quad \triangleq \quad \bigcup\{eval\text{-}pattern(pat) \mid pat \in pats\}$$

The function *eval-pattern* will return the set of strings that match a particular pattern and *eval-patterns* is defined in terms of this function in the obvious way. The function *eval-pattern* when applied to a single pattern will return a set containing all those strings that exactly match that pattern:

$$eval\text{-}pattern : Pattern \mapsto String\text{-set}$$

$eval\text{-}pattern(pat) \quad \triangleq$
    let $fset = $ cases hd pat of
               $mk\text{-}Character(ch) \rightarrow \{[ch]\},$
                  $mk\text{-}Value(p) \rightarrow eval\text{-}patterns(p),$
                      ANY $\rightarrow \{[ch] \mid ch \in Char\}$
           end
    in
    if tl $pat = []$
    then $fset$
    else let $bset = eval\text{-}pattern(\text{tl } pat)$ in
        $\{f \curvearrowright b \mid f \in fset \land b \in bset\}$

The operation *eval-pattern* will take a sequence of pattern matches apart, convert each component into the set of patterns that match it and join these back together again. Notice, also, how the structure of the function imitates the structure of the pattern as described in the abstract syntax, and how the recursion is based on the fact that a pattern can never be an empty sequence of pattern parts.

To improve the power of the pattern-matching program, an additional way of specifying patterns could be considered. We may wish to look for zero or more occurrences of a particular pattern character, e.g. we may wish to specify that we are looking for one of the following patterns in a file:

B, AB, AAB, AAAB, ...
zero or more occurrences of A followed by a B

This particular function would be useful, for example, if we were looking for all those lines in a document that contain an identifier. We would like to express that we are looking for any text string that begins with a letter followed by zero or more occurrences of a letter and/or digit. This operation of defining zero or more occurrences of something is called a closure, so we could add to our syntax for patterns:

$$Patterns = Pattern\text{-set}$$

$$Pattern = Match\text{-}unit^{+}$$

$$Match\text{-}unit = Closure \mid Pattern\text{-}expression$$

$$Closure :: cl : Pattern\text{-}expression$$

$Pattern\text{-}expression = Character \mid Value \mid \textsc{Any}$

$Character :: ch : Char$

$Value :: val : Patterns$

The *eval-patterns* function is unchanged; the *eval-pattern* operation will need to be extended to deal with the more complex abstract syntax for patterns:

$eval\text{-}pattern : Pattern \mapsto String\text{-}\mathsf{set}$

$eval\text{-}pattern(pat) \quad \underline{\triangle}$
  let $fset = $ cases hd pat of
       $mk\text{-}Closure(cl) \rightarrow$ let $fset = eval\text{-}pattern([cl])$ in
            $\{\mathsf{dconc}\ s \mid s \in fset^*\},$
      $mk\text{-}Character(ch) \rightarrow \{[ch]\},$
        $mk\text{-}Value(p) \rightarrow eval\text{-}patterns(p),$
          $\textsc{Any} \rightarrow \{[ch] \mid ch \in Char\}$
      end
  in
  if tl $pat = [\,]$
  then $fset$
  else let $bset = eval\text{-}pattern(\text{tl } pat)$ in
    $\{f \frown b \mid f \in fset \wedge b \in bset\}$

The definition of the *scan-file* function will need to be changed slightly:

$scan\text{-}file\ (p\text{:} Patterns)\ r\text{:} Text$

ext rd $doc\ :\ Text$

post let $pats = eval\text{-}patterns(p)$ in
  $r = [doc(i) \mid 1 \leq i \leq \mathsf{len}\ doc \wedge is\text{-}matched(pats, doc(i))]$

The definition of *scan-file* given above is very implicit and uses the property that the longest subsequence that contained at least one occurrence of the pattern was unique. A more algorithmic version could be written, which used recursion to scan the document line by line looking for a pattern match:

$scan\text{-}file\ (p\text{:} Patterns)\ r\text{:} Text$

ext rd $doc\ :\ Text$

post let $pats = eval\text{-}patterns(p)$ in
  $r = scan\text{-}text(pats, doc)$

$scan\text{-}text : Patterns \times Text \rightarrow Text$

$scan\text{-}text(pats, text) \quad \underline{\triangle}$
  if $text = [\,]$
  then $[\,]$
  elsif $is\text{-}matched(pats, \mathsf{hd}\ text)$
  then $[\mathsf{hd}\ text] \frown scan\text{-}text(pats, \mathsf{tl}\ text)$
  else $scan\text{-}text(pats, \mathsf{tl}\ text)$

Though this specification is more algorithmic, rather than implicit, it can still be seen to be correct. However, if we were implementing this specification it would still be necessary to translate the recursive version into an iterative one (unless we were programming in a functional language such as ML or LISP).

Looking ahead, we could continue the development and specify the top level of the solution to the pattern matching problem as a little iterative program. This would not be a specification, but would be a high-level design, and by inspection could be seen to be correct. We can sketch what operations need to be done and their order using the sequence language part of VDM, assuming that the name of the file to be processed is bound to the identifier STDIN, and that the value of the pattern is bound to *pattern*:

```
open STDIN for input;
open STDOUT for output;
while ¬ eof (STDIN) do
  line from STDIN;
  if match(line, pattern) then
    line to STDOUT
  else
    skip
  end
end;
close STDIN;
close STDOUT
```

Of course, the main part of the work to develop the program will be the refinement of the function *match*.

10.3.2 The concrete syntax for patterns

We have now reached the point where we ought to consider the concrete syntax for a pattern. A call to this program will be made by typing the command name followed by a set of patterns:

command = 'mp', patterns ;

where the syntax for patterns is shown in Fig. 10.6.

Notice how the concrete syntax mimics the abstract syntax—the abstract syntax is just concrete syntax with the punctuation removed. The punctuation is there to allow the code within the program to parse the command and remove the information content from it, i.e. to recover the abstract syntax. Also note that the concrete syntax supplies a way of specifying a range, the abstract syntax does not. This is because the specification of a range is a shorthand way of specifying a certain class of alternatives. An example of this syntax is:

mp ('a'..'z' | 'A'..'Z'), ('a'..'z' | 'A'..'Z' | '0'..'9')*

this would search for lines containing an identifier.

Formal techniques have been used in this example to explore the definition of a pattern-matching program. It was originally written as a specification of a GREP-like program as found in UNIX. Using formal notation produced a different style of program, especially the concrete syntax of the set of patterns to be matched. It is left as a (difficult) exercise to specify GREP and compare that specification with the one above.

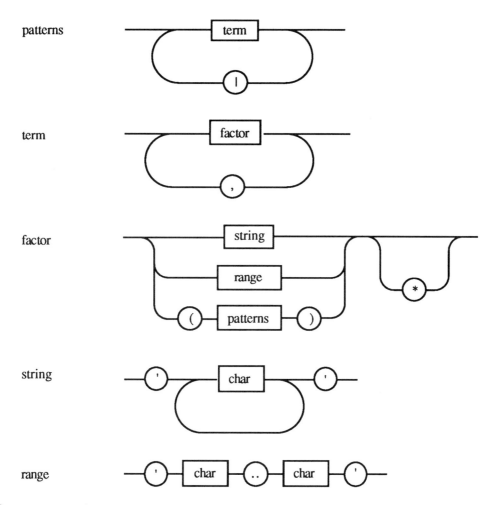

Figure 10.6 A concrete syntax for patterns.

Exercise 10.2

1. Add the ability to specify that a pattern is to be matched only if it is found at the start of a line or at the end of a line. Redo the abstract syntax, the specification and the concrete syntax to take account of the new functionality.

2. The example of the pattern-matching program described above is similar to the GREP program found on most UNIX systems. Find out how the UNIX GREP program works and specify a version of it with similar functions to the program described above:

   (a) Construct an abstract syntax for the commands.
   (b) Specify the program based on this abstract syntax.
   (c) Consider how you might implement it.
   (d) Compare your version of GREP with the one specified above.

10.4   CASH DISPENSER SYSTEM

This problem introduces a complication in that we need to describe the order in which operations are performed. The problem is as follows:

The Alloa-Alloa Software Company has been asked to develop a program to work in a microprocessor-controlled stand-alone cash dispenser. The cash dispenser will contain a file in which is recorded information about each customer who uses the dispenser. For each customer the system records the customer's name, PIN number and the cash limit per day for that customer. The customer's cash card includes a unique identifier encoded in a magnetic strip that will be read by the cash dispenser as part of the transaction. To use the cash dispenser the customer inserts his or her cash card; enters the PIN and then the amount of money they wish to withdraw. If the transaction is valid (correct card identifier, PIN and the daily cash limit for that customer has not been exceeded) a note is made of the transaction, the card is returned and then the cash is dispensed. If the PIN is invalid, the machine will keep the card.

The cash dispenser consists of a keypad with an enter key, two status keys labelled 'yes' and 'no', a slot for a cash card to be inserted and a slot for dispensing money. There is also a small display which can display a message of up to 20 characters. Inside the cash dispenser is a magazine holding the cash to be dispensed and a drawer that delivers money to the customer. The drawer is loaded with money from the magazine.

Attached to the system is a keyboard/screen that allows the bank staff to update the customer file. This system provides operations to add a customer (card), change the cash limit, change the PIN, delete a card and display customer information.

The manufacturers of the cash dispenser supply it with a software library that supports the following operations:

> *read-card*(): *Code*

This operation will wait for a card to be inserted; when it is, an identifier is read from the magnetic strip on the card.

> *read-keyboard*(): *Digits*

This operation will read the digits entered on the keypad; the number is terminated by the user pressing an 'enter' key.

> *read-status*(): **B**

This operation waits for one of the status keys to be pressed; the operation will return false if the 'no' key is pressed and true if the 'yes' key is pressed.

> *display*(*String*)

This operation will display a prompt of up to 20 characters.

> *return-card*(*return*: **B**)

This operation returns the card if the argument is true and keeps the card if the argument is false. Cards that are not returned are dropped into an internal box to be recovered by the bank staff when the machine is loaded with cash.

> *count-cash*(*amount*: **N**)

This operation counts the amount of cash given by the argument from the cash magazine into an internal drawer.

> *actual-amount*(): **N**

This operation returns the actual amount of cash in the internal drawer. If the money in the drawer has been delivered to the customer it will return 0, after *count-cash* it will return the actual amount counted into the drawer.

> *deliver-cash*()

This operation delivers the money in the internal drawer to the customer.

We need to write a specification on which a development could be based to produce a correct program for this system. There are some problems, however, that need to be addressed. For this problem, the order in which operations occur should really be part of the specification. If we ignore order for the moment the following operations suggest themselves (customers are modelled by the number on their cash card):

$is\text{-}valid\text{-}card(card\text{-}no\colon CardId)r\colon \mathbb{B}$

Check that a cashcard is valid.

$is\text{-}valid\text{-}pin(card\text{-}no\colon CardId, code\colon PIN)r\colon \mathbb{B}$

Check that an entered PIN is valid for the cashcard.

$is\text{-}valid\text{-}amount(card\text{-}no\colon CardId, amount\colon \mathbb{N})r\colon \mathbb{B}$

Check that the amount requested is valid.

$update\text{-}customer\text{-}file(card\text{-}no\colon CardId, amount\colon \mathbb{N})$

Update the information for a customer after he or she has withdrawn cash.

$add\text{-}card(code\colon PIN, name\colon Name, limit\colon \mathbb{N})r\colon CardId$

Add a new customer.

$change\text{-}pin(card\text{-}no\colon CardId, code\colon PIN)$

Change the PIN for a customer.

$delete\text{-}card(card\text{-}no\colon CardId)$

Remove a customer from the system.

It would be fairly easy to proceed and specify the state and these operations on the state. However, it is fairly obvious that the order in which things are done is important, e.g. nothing should be done unless a card and the PIN are valid, the card must be validated before the PIN is entered and the system should check that money is available for a particular customer before actually giving it. There must also be sufficient cash left in the cash dispenser to pay the customer before delivering the cash or updating the customer file. Therefore, if we are going to develop a system from this specification we need to worry about the order in which the operations are done, and this should be part of the specification.

10.4.1   The design problem

The design problem is about organizing a specification so that it will lead to the development of a well-structured system. Using formal specifications does not guarantee a good architecture for a system but it does help. It is possible to define operations in such a way that the resulting system will not have a good architecture and will be difficult to maintain; it is more difficult to do this using formal methods, but it is possible.

We will begin sketching a solution to this problem starting with a context diagram showing all the sources and sinks. This is shown in Fig. 10.7.

A brief description of the data is also useful at this point; remember it is not necessary to go into too much detail as at this stage, an overview is all that is required:

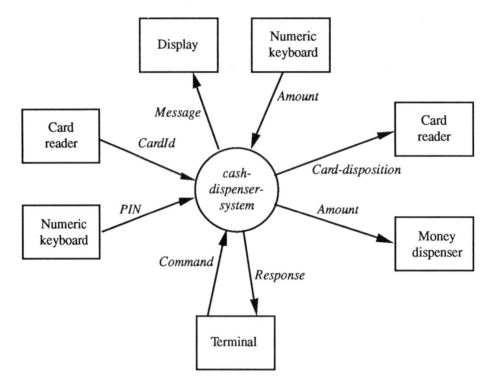

Figure 10.7   Context diagram for cash dispenser.

$$
\begin{array}{rcl}
Command & = & AddCard \\
& | & \textsc{Reset Limit} \\
& | & ChangePIN \\
& | & DeleteCard \\
& | & ShowDetails
\end{array}
$$

The types *Card-disposition*, *PIN*, *CardId*, *Response*, *Amount* and *Message* are left un-defined for the moment.

A careful reading of the specification indicates that this system can be constructed from two subsystems: one is concerned with dispensing cash, the other is concerned with managing customer details. We will also need an information store, an abstract machine, to record the details of customers. For the subsystem that dispenses cash, operations are needed to access a customer's PIN so that it can be validated, to access a customer's cash limit to validate the amount of money that has been requested, and to store the amount of money actually dispensed to the customer. The manage customer details operations will be needed to store customer details, to change the limit, to change the PIN, to delete a card and to examine details stored about a particular customer. We can now produce a second data flow diagram to record this, as shown in Fig. 10.8. This data flow diagram represents the levelling of the context diagram.

It should be noted that it looks as if this first decomposition of the problem was accomplished fairly quickly; a lot of experimentation could have gone on to reach this point. The graphical techniques of data flow diagrams allow the experimentation to be done simply and quickly with a pencil, paper and eraser until a satisfactory decomposition

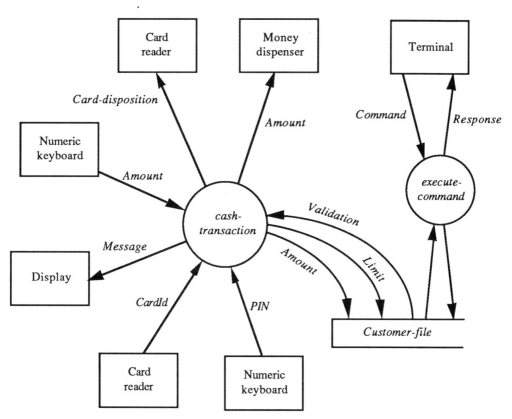

Figure 10.8   Overview data flow diagram.

of the original specification is found.

10.4.2 Dispensing cash

From the data flow diagram of Fig. 10.8 we can see that the complete system consists of two separate systems which share an information store, so each part can be specified separately. We will first look at the component that dispenses cash.

The specification of this component needs to incorporate the order in which things are done. There are other complications that occur during the implementation which should, perhaps, find their way into the specification in an abstract form. For example, each stage in the transaction should read the record that contains the information about a customer from disk, and write it back if the information in the record is changed. This is an integrity requirement: to read a customer record into store and leave it there until the end of a transaction would be unsafe if there was a system crash. Obviously it would not be necessary to keep reading a record at the start of each part of a transaction, just to write it back if it were changed. Therefore there is a need for some sort of flush/commit operation to write the updated record back at the end of the transaction. These sorts of problems should be reflected in the specification.

The approach the specification will take in an abstract manner is to read a customer record into store at the start of a transaction, an image of this record is shadowed on disk for integrity reasons, and a commit operation at the end of the transaction updates the customer record if necessary.

In order to do this, we need to read the magnetic stripe on the cash card, read the PIN from the keyboard, validate the card, read the amount of money requested from the keyboard and finally return the card and dispense the money. The various sources and sinks are known from the context diagram shown in Fig. 10.7. Some thought and a certain amount of experimentation might produce the data flow diagram shown in Fig. 10.9 (note that messages sent to the display have been omitted). The idea of shadowing the customer record in store is hidden in the operations, but they are ordered in such a way that the record can be read at the start of a transaction and the record can be written back if necessary as soon as the transaction completes—either successfully or not. We should also remember that we are being rigorous rather than formal, and initially some of the exact detail can be left so that the specification can initially concentrate on the essence of the system.

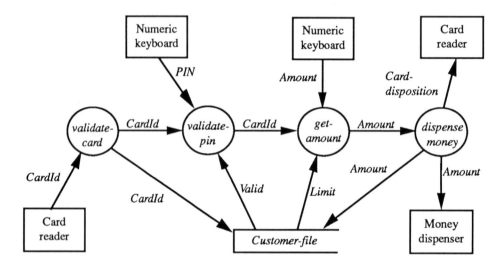

Figure 10.9   The cash transaction component.

The customer file will contain information about each customer. The best way of accessing the details of a particular customer will be to use the identifier recorded on the cash card. Thus, the main component of the state is a mapping which associates the details of a particular customer with the identifier held on his or her cash card. The system will also need to keep track of how much money it currently has available to dispense to customers—the system should not work if insufficient cash is available.

The specification should include operations to signal the start and end of a transaction, and to signal that a transaction should be aborted for some reason—for example an invalid PIN in entered or a customer asks for too much money. One way to do this would be to add a flag to the state to indicate that the transaction is valid. This flag can be used as a signal to commit/flush the customer buffer if necessary. An excellent candidate for this flag is the card identifier read from the cash card; if the card identifier is set, then we have a valid transaction underway with the customer identified by this identifier.

We will add the *CardId* as an additional component denoted by *cust* to the state and two operations to access this component: *validate-card* and *set-invalid-transaction*. A third operation to query the status is also necessary: *is-valid-transaction*. It is also a good idea to add another component *avail* which keeps track of whether there is enough money in the machine together with three operations to manage that component. These considerations would produce the following state:

values

$MAX : \mathbb{N}$

types

$Customers = CardId \xrightarrow{m} Customer$

$Amount = \mathbb{N}$

state *Customer-file* of
    file : *Customers*
    cust : [*CardId*]
    avail : *Amount*
inv *mk-Customer-file(file, cust, -)* $\triangleq$
    cust = nil $\lor$ *cust* $\in$ dom *file*
end

The value MAX denotes the maximum amount of money that each customer can get from the machine each day.

For each customer we need to store their PIN so that it can be checked, their name, the amount of money they have withdrawn today and the balance for the customer.

Customer ::   *pin* : *PIN*
      name : *Name*
      today : *Amount*
    balance : *Amount*

So far we have a reasonable decomposition of the system, but we still have not addressed the problem of defining the order in which operations occur, though a partial solution to this can be seen from examining the data-flow diagram. Unfortunately there are not enough semantics in data flow diagrams to totally fix the order, a more formal technique is necessary.

How can we specify the order in which operations occur in the card processing part of this system? We use the statement part of VDM-SL. First, we can sketch a solution using a structure chart, using it to show the order in which the operations occur, and the call hierarchy of the modules or subroutines that make up the system. For this particular example the structure chart is shown as Fig. 10.10; the three operations *validate-pin*, *get-amount* and *dispense-money* are only called if the transaction is valid.

This now does show the detail of the system and in what order the various operations are done, but unfortunately it still does not give enough detail, e.g. it does not say under what conditions the operations are performed. For a formal specification we need more information than is supplied by this picture.

By careful examination of the data flow diagram and structure chart we could sketch the following operation which defines the order in which things are done:

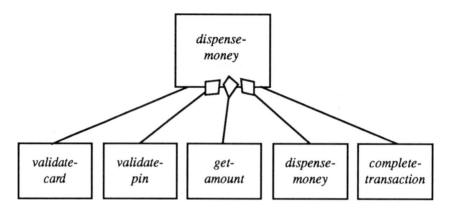

Figure 10.10 Structure chart for the dispenser.

cash-dispenser

(dcl *withdraw* : *Amount*;

validate-card();
if *is-valid-transaction*() then *validate-pin*() else skip end;
if *is-valid-transaction*() then *withdraw*:= *get-amount*() else skip end;
if *is-valid-transaction*() then *dispense-money*(*withdraw*) else skip end;
complete-transaction()
) $--$ *cash-dispenser*

An outline of the suboperations is given below:

is-valid-transaction () *r*: **B**

ext rd *cust* : [*CardId*]

post *r* $\Leftrightarrow$ *cust* $\neq$ nil

This operation checks that the *cust* component is set—indicating a valid transaction.

validate-card ()

ext rd *file*   : *Customers*
    wr *cust*   : [*CardId*]
    rd *card-no* : *CardId*

post let *valid* = (*card-no* $\in$ dom *file*) in
    (*valid* $\wedge$ *cust* = *card-no*) $\vee$ ($\neg$ *valid* $\wedge$ *cust* = nil)

This operation signals the start of a transaction. If the cash card is known to the system, then its identity is set in the state as a flag to subsequent operations. The card is known to the system if its identity is in the domain of the map that relates cards to the customer details. We have taken a slight liberty with the sequential VDM specification language by adding a temporary component to the state that holds the card identifier read from the cash card. The problem of reading the card identifier is not addressed in the specification of the operation; it assumes that the local component is set with the value read from the cash card by the hardware.

validate-pin ()

ext rd *file* : *Customers*
   wr *cust* : [*CardId*]
   rd *pin* : *PIN*

pre *cust* ∈ dom *file*

post let *valid* = (*pin* = *file*(*cust*).*pin*) in
    (*valid* ∧ *cust* = $\overleftarrow{cust}$) ∨ (¬ *valid* ∧ *cust* = nil)

This operation checks the PIN entered by the customer against the one held on record in the system. If there is a match the valid transaction flag is left set—the customer's cash card identification is left set. If the PIN is invalid then the valid transaction flag is cleared. Again the problem of I/O is not addressed; this operation assumes that the local state component *pin* is (somehow) set to the value entered on the keyboard by the customer.

get-amount () *r*: *Amount*

ext rd *file* : *Customers*
   wr *cust* : [*CardId*]
   rd *avail* : *Amount*
   request : *Amount*

pre *cust* ∈ dom *file*

post let *valid* = (*request* ≤ *file*(*cust*).*balance* ∧
              file(*cust*).*today* + *request* ≤ *MAX* ∧
              request ≤ *avail*)
  in
  valid ∧ *cust* = $\overleftarrow{cust}$ ∧ *r* = *request*
    ∨
  ¬ *valid* ∧ *cust* = nil ∧ *r* = 0

This operation checks that the amount of money requested by the customer is acceptable to the system. The customer has not exceeded the daily limit, and has money in the account. The operation assumes that the local state component *request* is set to the value entered by the customer.

Worked example 10.7 Sketch the specification of an operation that updates the customer's account details and updates the state component that keeps track of how much money has been dispensed.

SOLUTION

dispense-money (*request*: *Amount*)

ext wr *file* : *Customers*
   rd *cust* : [*CardId*]
   wr *avail* : *Amount*

pre *cust* ∈ dom *file* ∧
   request ≤ *file*(*cust*).*balance* ∧
   file(*cust*).*today* + *request* ≤ *MAX* ∧
   request ≤ *avail*

$$\text{post } avail = \overline{avail} - request \land$$

$$\text{let } newrec = \mu(\overline{file}(cust), balance \mapsto \overline{file}(cust).balance - request,$$

$$today \mapsto \overline{file}(cust).today + request)$$

in

$$file = \overline{file} \dagger \{cust \mapsto newrec\}$$

■

The following operation clears the valid transaction flag and also acts as a signal that the transaction has completed.

complete-transaction ()

ext wr *cust* : [*CardId*]

post *cust* = nil

We can go further with the specifications. We could specify some primitive operations that allow access to the actual state and implement the above operations in terms of those primitives. We are specifying an abstract machine which will need to supply the following operations to support a transaction. This is shown in Fig. 10.11.

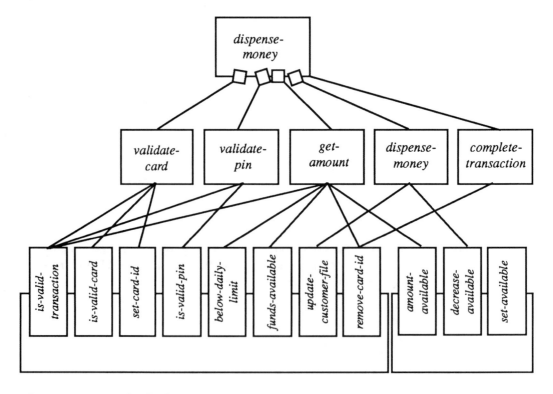

Figure 10.11   The final structure chart for the cash dispenser.

These can now be specified. Those operations that manage the customer transaction are as follows:

is-valid-card (*card-no*: *CardId*) *r*: **B**

ext rd *file* : *Customers*

post *r* ⇔ *card-no* ∈ dom *file*

This checks that the cash card is known to the system.

set-card-id (*card-no*: *CardId*)

ext rd *file* : *Customers*
    wr *cust* : [*CardId*]

pre *card-no* ∈ dom *file*

post *cust* = *card-no*

This sets the card identifier read from the cash card to signal the start of a valid transaction.

Worked example 10.8 Write down the specification of an operation which checks that a PIN is valid.

SOLUTION

is-valid-pin (*code*: *PIN*) *r*: **B**

ext rd *file* : *Customers*
    cust : [*CardId*]

pre *cust* ∈ dom *file*

post *r* ⇔ *file*(*cust*).*pin* = *code*

■

The remaining operations are shown below:

below-daily-limit (*request*: *Amount*) *r*: **B**

ext rd *file* : *Customers*
    cust : [*CardId*]

pre *cust* ∈ dom *file*

post *file*(*cust*).*today* + *request* ≤ *MAX*

Check that the daily limit has not been exceeded.

funds-available (*request*: *Amount*) *r*: **B**

ext rd *file* : *Customers*
    cust : [*CardId*]

pre *cust* ∈ dom *file*

post *request* ≤ *file*(*cust*).*balance*

Check that the customer has resources to allow cash to be withdrawn.

update-customer-file (*request*: *Amount*)

ext wr *file* : *Customers*
    rd *cust* : [*CardId*]

pre *cust* ∈ dom *file*

post let $newrec = \mu(\overleftarrow{file}(cust), balance \mapsto \overleftarrow{file}(cust).balance - request,$

$$today \mapsto \overleftarrow{file}(cust).today + request)$$

in

$$file = \overleftarrow{file} \dagger \{cust \mapsto newrec\}$$

Update the customer's account with the amount of money that has been withdrawn. Note that the above operations together are (roughly) equivalent to *dispense-money*.

$remove\text{-}card\text{-}id$ ()

ext wr $cust$: $[CardId]$

post $cust = $ nil

Remove the card identifier from the state to signal the end of a transaction.

Those operations that manage the record of how much cash there is in the cash drawer can now be specified.

Worked example 10.9 Write down specifications for a query operation that checks how much cash there is left in the cash drawer, an operation that records that cash has been dispensed, and an operation to set the initial amount of cash loaded into the machine.

SOLUTION The operation to check that the amount of cash requested is available in the machine:

$amount\text{-}available$ () r: $Amount$

ext rd $avail$: $Amount$

post $r = avail$

The operation to decrease the tally of how much cash there is left in the cash drawer:

$decrease\text{-}available$ ($amount$: $Amount$)

ext wr $avail$: $Amount$

pre $avail \geq amount$

post $avail = \overleftarrow{avail} - amount$

The operation to set the amount of money available in the cash drawer:

$set\text{-}available$ ($amount$: $Amount$)

ext wr $avail$: $Amount$

post $avail = amount$

This operation is used by the clerk when the cash dispenser is loaded with money at the start of the day (or whenever it is loaded with money). ∎

The following 'code' can be derived from the specifications using the techniques of Chapters 11 and 12. This code shows how the abstract machines defined above can be 'operated' by the various actions of the customer using the cash dispenser:

$validate\text{-}card$ ()

(**dcl** $card\text{-}no$: $CardId$;

```
    card-no: = to-CardId(read-card());
    if is-valid-card(card-no) then
      set-card-id(card-no)
    else
      remove-card-id()
    end
    ) -- validate-card
```

This operation signals the start of a transaction. It reads the cash card identifier from the card and, if it is known to the system, signals the start of a valid transaction by setting the identifier in the state. While this component is set to the card identifier, the transaction is valid.

Now that the problem of reading the card identifier has been addressed, a local state component is declared, and the operation supplied by the manufacturer of the cash dispenser is used to read the card. A type conversion function *to-CardId* has been introduced to convert the type of the result of the *read-card* operation to the appropriate type. This function is hiding implementation detail and will not be defined until the exact representation of the *CardId* type has been decided.

```
    validate-pin ()
    (dcl count : Amount;
         pin   : PIN;
    display('please enter your PIN');
    pin: = to-PIN(read-keyboard());
    count: = 1;
    while ¬ is-valid-pin(pin) ∧ count ≤ 3 do
      display('please enter your PIN');
      pin: = to-PIN(read-keyboard());
      count: = count + 1
    end;
    if ¬ is-valid-pin(pin) then
      return-card(false);
      remove-card-id();
      display('invalid PIN — card retained')
    else
      skip
    end
    ) -- validate-pin
```

This operation reads and validates the customer's PIN. The customer gets a fixed number of attempts, and if he or she does not enter it correctly their card is kept. The problem of reading the PIN from the keyboard has been addressed, a local state component is declared and the operation supplied by the manufacturer of the cash dispenser is used to read the keyboard. Again, a type conversion function has been introduced to avoid implementation issues.

```
    abort-get-amount (message: String) : Amount
```

```
(display(message);
 return-card(true);
 remove-card-id();
 return 0
) −− abort-get-amount
```

```
get-amount () : Amount
(dcl request : Amount;
 display('please enter amount');
 request:= to-Amount(read-keyboard());
 if amount-available() < request then
   abort-get-amount('machine empty')
 elsif ¬ funds-available(request) then
   abort-get-amount('insufficient funds available')
 elsif ¬ below-daily-limit(request) then
   abort-get-amount('above daily limit')
 else
   return request
 end
) −− get-amount
```

The operation prompts the user to enter the amount of cash required, reads the amount from the keyboard and checks that the amount requested is both valid and available. If it is not able to satisfy the request, an appropriate error message is shown to the user and the card is returned; the transaction is also ended. The problem of reading the amount of money required from the keyboard has been addressed, a local state component is declared and the operation supplied by the manufacturer of the cash dispenser is used to read the keyboard. Again note the use of a type conversion function to hide the representation of the input from the keyboard.

```
dispense-money (amount: Amount)
(count-cash(amount);
 decrease-available(amount);
 update-customer-file(amount);
 return-card(true);
 deliver-cash()
) −− dispense-money
```

This operation calls a hardware operation to count the required amount of cash into the cash drawer and records that the cash has been dispensed, updates the customer file, returns the customer's cash card and then delivers the cash.

```
complete-transaction ()
(remove-card-id()
) −− complete-transaction
```

This operation signals the end of a transaction by removing the cash card identifier from the state.

We can now put everything together and sketch the top-level control for the whole system. The program will loop while money is available to be dispensed to customers. We now have a formal specification and high-level design of the dispense money component of the cash dispenser.

cash-dispenser ()
(dcl *withdraw* : *Amount*;
 remove-card-id();
 while *amount-available*() $\neq$ 0 do
   validate-card();
   if *is-valid-transaction*() then *validate-pin*() else skip end;
   if *is-valid-transaction*() then *withdraw*: = *get-amount*() else skip end;
   if *is-valid-transaction*() then *dispense-money*(*withdraw*) else skip end;
   complete-transaction()
 end
) $--$ *cash-dispenser*

10.4.3   Managing the customer details

The next step is to specify the 'manage customer details' part of the problem. We will need processes to add a card, change the limits, change the PIN, delete a card and display details. The specification of the other component of the system identified an additional operation that was necessary: to set the amount of money available for dispensing to customers. We will also need a process that reads commands from the keyboard. The data flow diagram shown in Fig. 10.12 describes this.

The types for this part of the system are:

CardId = ...

PIN = ...

Amount = $\mathbb{N}$

Command = *AddCard*
              | RESETLIMIT
              | *ChangePIN*
              | *DeleteCard*
              | *ShowDetails*
              | *SetAvailable*

AddCard ::   *name* : *Name*
              limit : *Amount*
              code : *PIN*
            card-no : *CardId*

ChangePIN ::   *id* : *CardId*
                old : *PIN*
                new : *PIN*

DeleteCard :: *card-no* : *CardId*

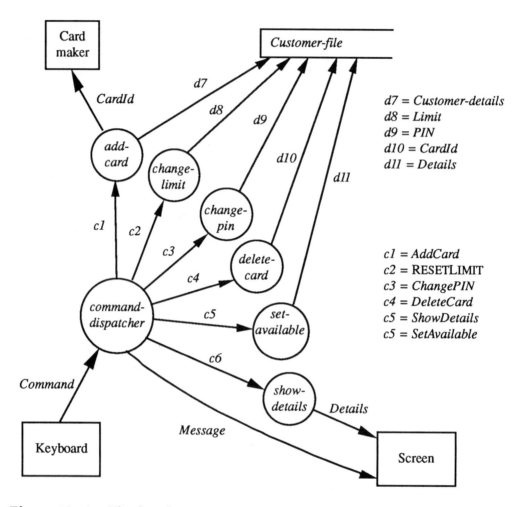

Figure 10.12 The data flow diagram for the command component.

$$ShowDetails :: card\text{-}no : CardId$$

$$SetAvailable :: amount : Amount$$

$$Message = \ldots$$

$$Customers = CardId \xrightarrow{m} Customer$$

$$Customer :: \quad pin : PIN$$
$$name : Name$$
$$today : Amount$$
$$balance : Amount$$

Each one of the processing bubbles describes a single operation which can be specified using pre- and post-conditions, except that perhaps the *read-command* operation may be a little difficult to do as it communicates with the outside world and will be discussed later. Each one of the commands defines an access function to our information file—the abstract machine that provides information about customers can be driven directly.

Deciding at what level the primitives should be is a creative activity. If it were not the whole process of producing a specification could be automated. A good guideline, though, is that the operations of an abstract machine should try to do just one thing.

A command can either add a card, change a limit, change the PIN, delete a card or display details. Any responses from the system will be left undefined for the present. The operations we require on the file store abstract machine for each of the commands are given below together with their specifications.

> add-$card$ ($name$: $Name$, $balance$: $Amount$, $code$: PIN, $card$: $CardId$)
>
> ext wr $file$: $Customers$
>
> pre $card \notin$ dom $file$
>
> post $file = \overleftarrow{file} \dagger \{card \mapsto mk\text{-}Customer(code, name, 0, balance)\}$

The add-$card$ command must contain all the information necessary to add a new customer/card.

> $reset$-$limit$ ()
>
> ext wr $file$: $Customers$
>
> post $file = \{cust \mapsto \mu(\overleftarrow{file}(cust), today \mapsto 0) \mid cust \in \text{dom} \overleftarrow{file}\}$

The $reset$-$limit$ command resets the count of how much money has been withdrawn in a particular day for all customers.

Worked example 10.10 Write down the specification of the operation that changes the PIN; it requires the old PIN, the new PIN and the card identifier.

SOLUTION

> $change$-pin (id: $CardId$, old, new: PIN)
>
> ext wr $file$: $Customers$
>
> pre $id \in$ dom $file$
>
> post $\overleftarrow{file}(id).pin = old \land file = \overleftarrow{file} \dagger \{id \mapsto \mu(\overleftarrow{file}(id), pin \mapsto new)\}$
>
> $\qquad \lor$
>
> $\overleftarrow{file}(id).pin \neq old \land file = \overleftarrow{file}$

∎

The $delete$-$card$ command just needs the card identifier as does $customer$-$details$:

> $delete$-$card$ (id: $CardId$)
>
> ext wr $file$: $Customers$
>
> $\quad$ rd $cust$: $[CardId]$
>
> pre $cust = $ nil
>
> post $file = \{id\} \triangleleft \overleftarrow{file}$

The information content of customer details is

> $Details$ :: $\quad name$: $Name$
>
> $\qquad\qquad today$: $Amount$
>
> $\qquad\qquad balance$: $Amount$

and is used to describe the output from the *show-details* operation. A temporary component *output* has been added to the state to represent some sort of output device:

> *show-details* (*id*: *CardId*)
>
> **ext rd** *file*   : *Customers*
>   **wr** *output* : *Details*
>
> **post let** *cust* = *file*(*id*) **in**
>   *output* = *mk-Details*(*cust.name*, *cust.today*, *cust.balance*)

The operation *set-available* was defined on page 172. The *command-dispatcher* can be specified as follows:

> *command-dispatcher*
> (**dcl** *cmmd* : *Command*;
> *cmmd*: = *read-command*();
> **cases** *cmmd* **of**
> *mk-AddCard*(*name*, *limit*, *pin*, *id*) → *add-card*(*name*, *limit*, *pin*, *id*),
>   RESETLIMIT → *reset-limit*(),
>   *mk-ChangePIN*(*id*, *old*, *new*) → *change-pin*(*id*, *old*, *new*),
>   *mk-DeleteCard*(*id*) → *delete-card*(*id*),
>   *mk-ShowDetails*(*id*) → *show-details*(*id*),
>   *mk-SetAvailable*(*amount*) → *set-available*(*amount*)
> **end**
>) -- *command-dispatcher*

The specification of the command dispatcher is straightforward. In some sense, once the system has obtained the required information from the user of the system and this information is described by the abstract syntax of the commands, the abstract machine that manages the customer file can be driven directly, and in these cases it is usual, when writing a specification using VDM, to leave such details out—the reader of the specification would just see the abstract syntax of the commands together with the specification of each of the operations that define the command. We have shown a specification of the command processor just to demonstrate how it could be done (see Fig. 10.13). We could, of course, go further and discuss how information is read in from the user.

If the system is to be command driven, with the commands typed in as character strings, the read command can be specified thus:

> *read-command* () *r*: *Command*
> **ext rd** *input* : *String*
> **post** *r* = *retr-command*(*input*)
>
> *retr-command* : *String* → *Command*
>
> *retr-command*(*str*) △ ...

It assumes that the local state component *input* contains the characters of the command typed in by the user. The retrieve function translates the external, concrete representation of a command into the internal, abstract syntax form. When written, this function will define the parsing of a command. The read command has buried within it details of how input is to be obtained, any error messages and the parsing technique used. All it

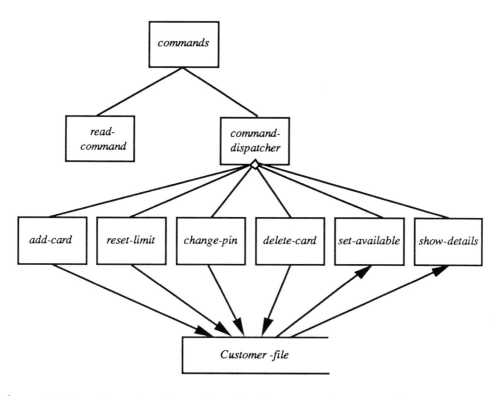

Figure 10.13 The order of operations for the command component.

has to deliver is an abstract representation of a command—the detailed design is to be done later.

Another way of obtaining information from the user would be to use menus. The abstract syntax describes what information is needed. We could proceed to define the menus that would be required. For example, a top-level menu and how the menu for the add customer command might look like is shown in Fig. 10.14.

Notice that the menus have been derived from the abstract syntax and that the command dispatcher defined above would not work in this case—it would need to be modified. The way that input is obtained from the user can be left until after the main part of the system has been specified, and can be made a separate concern. This problem will be addressed again in a later chapter.

10.4.4 Conclusions

The specification for a complete transaction is

$$get\text{-}money \; (id: CardId, pin: PIN, request: Amount)$$

ext wr *file* : *Customers*
    avail : *Amount*

```
Select function:

1. Add new customer
2. Change customer limit
3. Change customer PIN
4. Delete customer
5. Display customer details
5. Set Available money

Enter function number: __
```

```
              Add New Customer


  Name:              _____

  Card Number:        _____

  PIN:                _____
```

Figure 10.14   The top-level menu and one of the commands.

$$\text{post } \textit{is-valid-input}(\overleftarrow{\textit{file}}, \textit{id}, \textit{avail}, \textit{request}, \textit{pin}) \wedge$$

$$\quad \text{let } \textit{newrec} = \mu(\overleftarrow{\textit{file}}(\textit{id}), \textit{balance} \mapsto \overleftarrow{\textit{file}}(\textit{id}).\textit{balance} - \textit{request},$$

$$\qquad\qquad\qquad\qquad \textit{today} \mapsto \overleftarrow{\textit{file}}(\textit{id}).\textit{today} + \textit{request})$$

$$\quad \text{in}$$

$$\quad \textit{file} = \overleftarrow{\textit{file}} \dagger \{\textit{id} \mapsto \textit{newrec}\} \wedge$$

$$\quad \textit{avail} = \overleftarrow{\textit{avail}} - \textit{request}$$

$$\qquad \vee$$

$$\quad \neg\, \textit{is-valid-input}(\overleftarrow{\textit{file}}, \textit{id}, \textit{avail}, \textit{request}, \textit{pin}) \wedge$$

$$\quad \textit{file} = \overleftarrow{\textit{file}} \wedge$$

$$\quad \textit{avail} = \overleftarrow{\textit{avail}}$$

$$\textit{is-valid-input} : \textit{Customers} \times \textit{CardId} \times \textit{Amount} \times \textit{Amount} \times \textit{PIN} \rightarrow \mathbb{B}$$

$$\textit{is-valid-input}(\textit{file}, \textit{cust}, \textit{avail}, \textit{request}, \textit{pin}) \quad \triangle$$

$$\quad \textit{cust} \in \text{dom } \textit{file} \wedge$$

$$\quad \textit{request} \leq \textit{file}(\textit{cust}).\textit{balance} \wedge$$

$$\quad \textit{file}(\textit{cust}).\textit{today} + \textit{request} \leq \textit{MAX} \wedge$$

$$\quad \textit{request} \leq \textit{avail} \wedge$$

$$\quad \textit{file}(\textit{cust}).\textit{pin} = \textit{pin}$$

Notice that this specification does not define any order, but it does give a total description, which is a good point. It is fairly complicated and not a very intuitive solution, which is a bad point. Note that this example is a small one, so a larger example, which has some sort of inherent order that is hidden by writing a single operation, would probably be very complicated. A further problem is that this solution has not specified the requirements that the card must be kept if the PIN is invalid, that useful messages should be given to the user, that the card must be returned before the cash is released, that the PIN must be entered before the amount, etc. The approach taken in the solution to this problem showing order does provide an intuitive solution to the problem, and it is a good basis for development.

Exercise 10.3

1. The 'top-level' of the program that dispenses cash may not be very 'elegant' as it relies on the testing and setting of a flag; try to improve this.
2. Investigate the cash dispenser at your local bank (if it has one). Improve the model defined above by making it more realistic.

   (a) In the example above, there is no way of adding a new customer, only a way of providing a card for an existing customer. Remedy this.
   (b) Improve the customer/machine interface.
   (c) Some machines have a glass plate that is lowered to protect the machine. It is raised at the start of a transaction (if necessary) and lowered after a suitable time delay on the completion of a transaction. Add components to the system to control this piece of hardware. Note that the manufacturer of the system provides two additional functions to control the glass plate:

      raise-plate();
      lower-plate()

      Do not trap the customer's card in the machine!
   (d) Additional functions can be added so that, for example, the customer can query his or her account. Specify these.

3. This specification was for a stand-alone system. Try to write the requirements and specification for a networked system. Use some manufacturer supplied functions to hide the communication of the cash dispenser with the bank's central computer.
4. Specify a system for a bank for keeping customer records on a central computer. The system should allow for a variety of accounts—saving, deposit, current, etc. Customers should be allowed to have more than one account.
5. Question 3 above suggested that communications with the central bank system should be hidden behind certain functions. Question 4 above models a possible central system. Specify the communication functions using your system defined in question 3.

10.5   SUMMARY

This chapter has shown that it is possible to use formal techniques to describe many of the aspects of a specification and high-level design of a computer system. The approach has been to produce a very high-level design to deal with the problem of order, rather than just writing down a very abstract (and possibly unhelpful) specification that ignores order. At no point during this specification (or high-level design process) have bits or bytes or anything related to physical representation been discussed. When each of the operations are developed into code the interface between each of the operations should be kept at this abstract level. In the cash dispenser example we are always dealing with card identifiers, PINs and commands—never character strings or natural numbers. (However, cash amounts have been modelled by $\mathbb{N}$, but this is a very reasonable decision—banks have been using this model, or a variant, for years.) This high-level view of the system should be preserved as much as possible as the specification is turned into design, and finally into executable code.

Notice how data flow diagrams, structure charts and some sequential language have been used as sketching tools to understand the problem and produce an initial design (specification?) of the solution. When the problem is fully understood, using these techniques can produce a formal specification, preserving some of the sketches, suitably formalized. The development will be based on the resulting formal specification, not the data flow diagrams or structure charts, but these do supply a very good overview and sketch of the system. The specification could be thought of as the blueprint for a building and the DFDs and structure charts as sketches to show what the finished product will be like. Those readers who know the graphical techniques will also be aware that frequently some detail is left out (but not in the formal specifications).

What we have achieved is a way of decomposing the system into black boxes; the interface between those black boxes is at a very high-level and is described using abstract syntax, with this high-level interface being preserved during the complete development of the system. Some development strategies use the description 'logical design' to describe the first stage of the development instead of the term 'specification'. Logical design is defined as an implementation independent design, although it contains the architecture of the system, and is perhaps a better description of what a specification really is. A logical design also allows us to consider things such as order without feeling too guilty—a point that will be left for the reader to consider further. An interesting discussion to have is whether a specification should be independent of the final architecture of the system. For elegant specifications the answer is probably yes, for the practical application of formal specifications to real problems where the specification is to be used as the basis of the development the answer is probably no—there would not be time to do an elegant specification and a logical design.

These three examples illustrate that there is not one single approach that can be used to solve problems. The banking system and the library system are, at first hand, fairly similar, but each was tackled in a different way. The library system tried to identify the abstract machine first, and then built the operations around that. The banking system identified the operations, and then defined the abstract machine. In both cases a certain amount of iteration with the specification occurred and this is in fact what happens with larger, real-life examples.

In the other example, the 'GREP'-like program, the main concern is the representation of the commands. This was sketched using the abstract syntax to describe what information needs to be conveyed in the command and then the resulting abstract syntax used as a basis to derive the concrete syntax. The problem of translating the concrete syntax into abstract syntax was left, as any book on compiler design will describe various techniques that can be used to do this; also Chapter 17 tackles this for another example.

11

FROM SPECIFICATIONS TO CODE

AIMS

- To introduce the concept of proving the correctness of a program.
- Define and develop the idea of an equivalent specification.
- Define and develop the idea of a program satisfying a specification.
- To illustrate how a program and its proof or correctness can be developed in parallel.
- To describe and derive proof rules that aid in the development of correct programs.

11.1 INTRODUCTION

When writing specifications we have been concentrating on what a system does and trying to avoid, wherever possible, how. However, when the specification has been completed we are faced with the problem of implementing it. So what is the next step? Eventually a computer program has to be produced in which the execution matches the specification. We are faced with two tasks: implementing the abstract data structures of the specification in terms of data structures available in a favourite programming language and turning the specification of operations expressed as pre- and post-conditions into executable code that satisfies those specifications. A formal specification describes what a computer system should do. It is now time to look at the problem of how this function is to be supplied; how do we develop code that will satisfy the specification? At this point the reader is recommended to reread the preface which warns of the difficulty of formalism.

11.2 SATISFYING SPECIFICATIONS

If a program is written to satisfy a specification, the program will obviously attempt to supply the function described by the specification, but there is now an interesting question: what is meant by 'satisfying a specification'? An insight into this can be obtained from the normal course of events that occur after a program has been developed from a specification. One way of checking that the program matches the specification is to run some test cases. The specification defines valid input/output pairs, and these can be run through the program under test to see if it works correctly.

To test a program, valid input values are chosen, the program is run, and the output is checked to see if it is as described in the specification. This we can do for a variety of test cases chosen by some sort of criteria. The more test cases that are run and that work, the more we should be convinced that the program is correct. It is (theoretically) possible to guarantee the correctness of the program with respect to its specification by running all possible test cases, but for a significant problem this is impossible.

Is there an alternative approach? The answer to this question is 'yes'—take, for example, the following specification of division and a program that claims to satisfy the specification. How can we be sure that the program is correct, that it matches the specification?

div

ext rd a, b : **Z**

   wr q : **Z**

pre $0 \leq a \wedge 0 < b$

post $\exists r \in \mathbf{N} \cdot b \times q + r = a \wedge r < b$

The pre-condition states that the value in location a must be non-negative, and the value in location b must be positive. The post-condition states that q contains the result of dividing b into a. A program to achieve this is

```
--  0 ≤ a ∧ 0 < b
q: = 0;
r: = a;
while ¬ (r < b) do
   r: = r − b;
   q: = q + 1
end
--  b × q + r = a ∧ 0 ≤ r < b
```

The program has been annotated with comments that have been derived from the specification, and using these it is possible to construct a proof of correctness. If the more complex logical term is abbreviated to *inv*, the proof of correctness for this program against its specification can proceed as follows:

```
--  0 ≤ a ∧ 0 < b
q: = 0;
r: = a;
--  inv
while ¬ (r < b) do
   --  inv ∧ ¬ (r < b)
   r: = r − b;
   q: = q + 1
   --  inv
end
--  inv ∧ r < b
```

    where $inv \triangleq b \times q + r = a \wedge 0 \leq r$

First of all it is fairly easy to see that if *inv* is true just before the while loop command is entered, it will be true just before the body of the loop is executed for the first time—the execution of the while loop test, or guard, does not change any variables. It is easy to see that *inv* is preserved across the while loop body: all that happens is a value equal to the contents of location b is moved from one part of the term inv to another, leaving the value of the expression unchanged. Thus, if inv is true before the body of the loop is executed, then it is true on completion. Also, if it is true on completion of the loop body, it will be true just before the loop is executed again. Thus the body of the loop preserves the value of inv. The initialization that occurs before the while loop command establishes inv. Thus the following is true:

1. The term inv is initially true.
2. It is preserved across the loop body.
3. Thus on exit from the loop it is true.

In addition, completing the loop makes the Boolean expression $(r < b)$ true and therefore the program satisfies its specification. We should also show that if the input is valid, the program terminates. Notice that r is initialized to a positive value and decremented by a positive value, so at some point it must be true that the value of r is less than b and the loop must terminate. Notice that this assumes that the pre-condition is satisfied; if it is not, anything can happen and the program could even loop forever.

The above is a long, but fairly straightforward, 'proof of correctness'. For the doubters, this fairly informal proof can be made formal in the mathematical sense and machine checked. What has been done above is a symbolic execution of the program together with an inductive proof, and by this means all possible test cases have been run simultaneously. This proof strategy will work for any program, although it should be noted that the proofs become complicated for large programs. The lesson that can be gained from the above proof of correctness is that they are possible—that an argument of correctness can be recorded.

If a formal specification exists, what is required is a development methodology that allows the production of correct code which satisfies the specification. Ideally the proofs should be carried out alongside the code development; the proofs should be used to drive the development of code rather than developing the code and then proving it correct. It can be seen that developing code and then proving it correct is, even for the small example above, tedious. By developing the code and proof together, the final code will be correct by construction. If a development methodology is to be useful, it must encourage small development steps which are easily understood, and any development decisions documented.

It has been found that showing programmers it is possible to prove programs correct can have a radical effect on the way they approach programming. Bugs can no longer be 'blamed' on some outside interference—it is possible to develop correct programs. By carrying out a proof, the level of confidence in the correctness of the program has been increased, and formal methods in computing should be seen as doing just that. There is an increased confidence in the same sense that we have more confidence in those buildings put together by skilled engineers who have checked their designs mathematically than those designed on the back of an envelope by amateurs.

First let us formalize the concept of a program satisfying a specification:

- Denote the specification for a code fragment by OP.
- Denote a program fragment which satisfies the specification by p.
- Denote input, i.e. values of variables just before executing the code fragment, by i (i could stand for a vector (list) of values).

The meaning of satisfying the specification can be formalized by stating that if the input i to a program p satisfies the pre-condition of the specification then the result of executing the program p should satisfy the post-condition. It should be noted that this is exactly the criteria used for evaluating a test case when testing a program. Now a program is correct if it is correct for all valid input. If we denote the result of executing program p with given input i as $EXEC(p, i)$, then this can be written:

$$p \text{ sat } OP \quad \text{if} \quad \forall i \in State \cdot pre\text{-}OP(i) \ \Rightarrow \ post\text{-}OP(i, EXEC(p, i))$$

In words: p satisfies the specification OP, if, for any input that satisfies the pre-condition, then the execution of the program p with that input terminates and produces a result which, with the corresponding input values, satisfies the post-condition. The above equation, or proof rule as it is called, is a mathematical definition of the idea that an implementation satisfies its specification.

The function $EXEC$[1] is a mathematical model of program execution. Can the $EXEC$ function be realized? It is just the semantics of the programming language in which the program is written and would need to be specified formally; in fact, this function has been defined for many languages including PL/I, Pascal, Modula-2 and Ada. To use this particular approach we need (1) a formal definition of the programming language to be used, (2) to write the program and (3) to apply the $EXEC$ function to that program and check that the results satisfy the post-condition. This is exceptionally difficult and in fact the proof of *div* given above is an informal version of this.

Before we can continue, a more precise definition of $EXEC$ is required. $EXEC$ is a function from the set of all possible programs (or fragments of programs) and from the set of all possible values of variables—the *State*—into the set of all possible values of variables—the result of executing the program.

$$EXEC: Program \times State \rightarrow State$$

We will leave the definition of $EXEC$, which is beyond the scope of this book, and rely on our intuitive understanding of the semantics of programming languages.

11.3 STEPWISE REFINEMENT

To develop executable code from a specification, we will take an approach that breaks down the specification into smaller specifications, each defining an easier problem. These easier problems are solved, and the resulting code is put together to produce a program that satisfies the original specification. Each of the smaller specifications are tackled in an equivalent way; these will, in turn, be broken down into even smaller specifications until we eventually reach a point where the implementation of the code that satisfies a specification and the corresponding proofs of correctness are trivial. A further bonus will be that the techniques used to split specifications will provide the techniques to glue the code fragments together to give the final program (see Fig. 11.1).

What is the 'glue' that will be used to join everything together? The 'glue' will be the programming constructs found in nearly all programming languages; these are the semicolon, the conditional command (the if then else statement) and the while loop

---

[1] The $EXEC$ function is a specification of the programming language, and a compiler or interpreter for the language is a realization (implementation) of the specification.

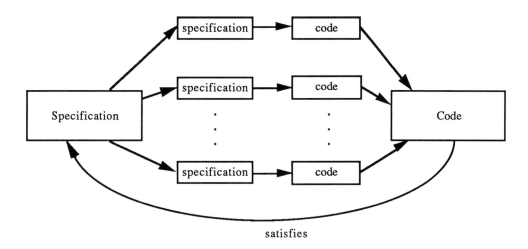

Figure 11.1   From specification to code.

command, and we will stop the decomposition of larger specifications into smaller specifications when we reach a situation where the specification can be easily satisfied by an assign command. At each step of this process we carry out a proof of correctness to show that any new decomposition, or 'refinement', of a specification does not effectively change anything. Also, we will make adjustments to pre- and post-conditions without fundamentally changing the problem. These ideas will allow us to break down a single large specification into a smaller set of specifications that can be translated into code.

Before tackling the problem of the programming language statements let us first look at the problem of defining an equivalent specification, i.e. what sort of adjustments could we make to pre- and post-conditions without really changing anything?

Supposing we have a specification OP, are there equivalent, i.e. equally satisfactory, specifications? Yes, a simple example would be to suppose OP had a non-trivial precondition. If OP was replaced by a specification OP' which had the trivial pre-condition true and a program was developed to satisfy OP', then that same program would also satisfy OP. In some sense it would do a better job in that it would deliver answers where the original specification OP did not care, but certainly any program that satisfied the specification OP' would also satisfy OP. In this example the new specification OP' is equivalent—equally acceptable—to the old specification OP. Can the idea of an equivalent specification be expanded? What sort of properties would we want of an equivalent specification?

We will take as our definition the following (informal) definition of equivalent: given a specification OP; another specification OP' is equivalent to OP if any program that satisfies OP' also satisfies OP. What we need to do is to remove the 'any program' part of this informal description, and to make it formal. First, from the program's point of view, any input that satisfies the pre-condition of OP must also satisfy the pre-condition of OP', for any program that satisfies OP' must also satisfy OP. Therefore it must certainly work under those conditions where the pre-condition of OP is true. Formally this means

$$\forall i \in State \cdot pre\text{-}OP(i) \implies pre\text{-}OP'(i)$$

Also the two specifications must agree on an answer for any input state values that satisfy the pre-condition for OP, i.e. the two specifications must agree on an answer for those states accepted by the pre-condition of OP. Remembering that the post-condition for a particular piece of input can specify a range of possible answers, any one of which would do, this means that the pairs of input/output values defined by OP', where the input value satisfies the pre-condition of OP, must be acceptable to the post-condition of OP. This can be written:

$$\forall i, o \in State \cdot pre\text{-}OP(i) \wedge post\text{-}OP'(i, o) \;\Rightarrow\; post\text{-}OP(i, o)$$

These two rules together give one definition of an equivalent specification—a definition that does not take implementability into account.

We will now expand the idea of a program satisfying a specification to that of a specification satisfying a specification. Here we can think in terms of a specification 'executing'—for any input that satisfies the pre-condition, by some 'magic', produce an output that satisfies the post-condition. It is the idea of a specification in some sense 'terminating' that needs to be added to the idea of an equivalent specification discussed above. This will allow the concept of a specification satisfying a specification to be defined. We already have a way of stating that a program p satisfies a specification OP:

$$p \text{ sat } OP \quad if \quad \forall i \in State \cdot pre\text{-}OP(i) \;\Rightarrow\; post\text{-}OP(i, EXEC(p, i))$$

This means that the program p satisfies the specification defined by the pre-condition and the post-condition. It assumes that the program *terminates* with an output value that, together with a valid input value, satisfies the post-condition.

The equivalent idea to termination for a specification is that it is implementable, and it is this concept that will be used:

$OP' \text{ sat } OP \text{ if}$
$\forall i \in State \cdot pre\text{-}OP(i) \;\Rightarrow\; pre\text{-}OP'(i)$
$\forall i, o \in State \cdot pre\text{-}OP(i) \wedge post\text{-}OP'(i, o) \;\Rightarrow\; post\text{-}OP(i, o)$
$\forall i \in State \cdot pre\text{-}OP'(i) \;\Rightarrow\; \exists o \in State \cdot post\text{-}OP'(i, o)$

The third equation is the specification version of the statement 'the program must terminate ...'. With this definition a program can be thought of as an executable specification, and, equivalently, a specification is a non-executable program.

The third equation prevents the possibility of replacing any specification by the following program (remember programs are specifications and specifications are programs):

miracle

pre true

post false

If the restriction about implementability was not present then the *miracle* program would satisfy any specification, and once an executable version of *miracle* had been written, all programming tasks would be solved! A moments consideration shows (luckily for those of us who earn our living by programming) that an executable version of *miracle* cannot be written. The *miracle* program must be willing to accept any input and produce no output—and a program that just loops would not do; such a program 'produces' an output of $\perp$, which is output. It can be shown that the implementability test prevents *miracle* being proposed as a solution to a specification.

We will not be too worried about proving that specifications are satisfiable—the production of a working program that satisfies the specification will be evidence that a specification is satisfiable. There is a problem, however—the *miracle* program can occur in disguise as an innocent specification, and there is the danger of introducing a disguised *miracle* while carrying out program refinement. If at some point *miracle* is introduced, it is impossible to remove and to return to an implementable specification. So if we do make a decision which accidentally introduces a miracle, it is impossible to remove. Thus the only danger with *miracle* is for it to be introduced in a disguised form and for the refinement to be continued. The only result will be wasted effort as a disguised miracle is slowly refined to the undisguised version. Experience will help in avoiding such development steps.

We will use a weaker form of satisfaction that allows the *miracle* program, calling this 'refinement', and denote it by the symbol $\sqsubseteq$ which is read as 'is refined by'. Notice that

$$A \text{ sat } B \;\Rightarrow\; B \sqsubseteq A$$

and

$$B \sqsubseteq A \wedge \text{'} A \text{ is implementable'} \;\Rightarrow\; A \text{ sat } B$$

With the concept of refinement, we will have a specification S and a series of refinements $R_1, R_2, \ldots, R_n$, and finally p where the final step is to produce an *executable* program p. The following will be true:

$$S \sqsubseteq R_1 \sqsubseteq R_2 \sqsubseteq \ldots \sqsubseteq R_n \sqsubseteq p \wedge p \text{ is executable} \;\Rightarrow\; p \text{ sat } S$$

Since the final step produces an executable program, the development is valid. If any of the steps produce either *miracle* or *miracle* in disguise, we are in trouble and we will not be able to produce an executable program. It turns out that this is not usually a problem.

We can abbreviate the first two rules by leaving out the quantification which is over the state (restricted to the frame—the ext identifiers), and knowing that the pre-condition is a function of the undecorated frame variables, and the post-condition a function of both decorated and undecorated frame variables.

With these conventions the first two rules of the above definition become:

$$\text{if } \left\{ \begin{array}{c} pre\text{-}OP \;\Rightarrow\; pre\text{-}OP' \\ pre\text{-}OP[x\backslash\overleftarrow{x}] \wedge post\text{-}OP' \;\Rightarrow\; post\text{-}OP \end{array} \right\} \text{ then } OP \sqsubseteq OP'$$

where the notation $E[x\backslash y]$ means replace all free[2] instances of the identifier x by y in the expression E. Another convention that will be used is that any code or specification (or even a mixture) that is written between a pre- and a post-condition should be a refinement of the specification defined by those predicates.

The two rules given above can be easily remembered from the diagram in Fig. 11.2. The convention used is as follows: an arrow from one predicate to another corresponds to an implication; if two paths join in forming an arrow, the predicates at the ends of the lines can be joined together with an *and* operator (e.g. Fig. 11.3) and if a line diverges the two predicates on the end of the lines can be joined with an *or* operator on the other side of an implication (Fig. 11.4).

To prove a particular predicate, just look at what arrows lead to it. Given the diagram in Fig. 11.2 we can quickly construct the proof rules. In order to prove *pre-OP'* we need *pre-OP* and in order to prove *post-OP* we need *post-OP'* and *pre-OP*. A further rule

---

[2]i.e. not bound by a quantifier.

pre *pre-OP*

pre *pre-OP'*
post *post-OP'*

post *post-OP*

Figure 11.2   Equivalent specification rule.

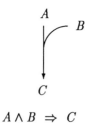

$$A \wedge B \implies C$$

Figure 11.3   A proof diagram for the *and* operator.

is necessary when two post-conditions are conjoined—it is necessary to introduce an intermediate state to join the two predicates together.

$$\exists m \in State \cdot \ldots post\text{-}OP(i, m) \wedge post\text{-}OP'(m, o) \ldots$$

11.3.1   Adding the pre-condition to the post-condition

Another way to produce an equivalent specification is to add the pre-condition to the post-condition. We are just reminding ourselves that the pre-condition must hold:

op (...) ...
ext wr *w*
  rd *r*
pre *P*
post *Q*

$$A \implies B \vee C$$

Figure 11.4   A proof diagram for the *or* operator.

is identical to the new specification:

op' $(\ldots)$ $\ldots$

   ext wr w

     rd r

   pre P

   post $(\exists w \cdot P) \wedge Q$

or equivalently

$$
\begin{array}{ccc}
\text{ext wr } w & & \text{ext wr } w \\
\quad \text{rd } r & & \quad \text{rd } r \\
\text{pre } P & \equiv & \text{pre } P \\
\text{post } Q & & \text{post } (\exists w \cdot P) \wedge Q
\end{array}
$$

where $A \equiv B$ means $A \sqsubseteq B$ and $B \sqsubseteq A$.

11.4   PROGRAM REFINEMENT

To illustrate the translation of an implicit specification into a program we will use the sequential part of the specification language. This language could easily be translated into Pascal, Modula-2 or C.

11.4.1   The assignment command

The specification language uses a variant of the assignment command—multiple assignment:

$$x_1, x_2, \ldots, x_n := E_1, E_2, \ldots, E_n$$

The semantics of this are straightforward: evaluate all of the expressions on the right-hand side and then assign the result to the variables on the left-hand side so that x_i is set to the value of expression E_i. These rules imply that all of the x_i are distinct and the evaluation of the right hand side expressions should have no side effects. In fact throughout all of this book expression evaluation is assumed to have no side effects.

As most programming languages do not have multiple assignment, care must be taken when translating parallel assignment into the familiar sequential form, i.e.

$$x, y := x + 1, y + x$$

is not equivalent to

$x := x + 1;$

$y := y + x$

but is equivalent to

$y := y + x;$

$x := x + 1$

Notice that we can write a multiple assignment command to swop two values

$$x, y := y, x$$

and that this is equivalent to neither

$$x := y;$$
$$y := x$$

nor

$$y := x;$$
$$x := y$$

The safest way of translating multiple assignment is to introduce an appropriate number of temporary variables t_1 through to t_n, and write

$$t_i := E_i$$

in any order, followed by

$$x_i := t_i$$

in any order. For swopping two variables, this gives

$$t_1 := x;$$
$$t_2 := y;$$
$$y := t_1;$$
$$x := t_2$$

A shorthand that may be used is

$$x_1, x_2, \ldots, x_n := E, E, \ldots, E$$

i.e. all the expressions are the same; this can be abbreviated to

$$x_1, x_2, \ldots, x_n := E$$

11.4.2   Setting variables

The basic building block of most programming languages is the assignment command; when can a specification be satisfied by assignment commands? Consider the following specification:

> *op*
>
> **ext wr** x
>   **rd** y
>
> **pre** *true*
>
> **post** $x = \overleftarrow{x} + y - 1$

This can obviously be satisfied by

$$x := x + y - 1$$

This seems to indicate that a specification of the form

> *op*
>
> **ext wr** x
>   **rd** other variables used in E
>
> **pre** true
>
> **post** $x = E$

where E involves $\overleftarrow{x}$, but does not involve x, can be realized by[3]

$$x := E$$

Using the convention that anything written between a pre- and post-condition is a refinement, we can write

> **ext wr** x
> **pre** $true$
>
> $$x := E$$
>
> **post** $x = E[x \backslash \overleftarrow{x}]$

It can also be shown that an assignment command of the form

$$x := E$$

can be 'refined' by the specification

> **ext wr** x
>   **rd** $\alpha(E) - \{x\}$
> **pre** true
> **post** $x = E[x \backslash \overleftarrow{x}]$

where $\alpha(E)$ denotes all the identifiers of E that represent variables, and thus $\alpha(E) - \{x\}$ denotes all the variables used in E other than x. This is using the idea that there is no real difference between a specification and a program; for example

$$x := x + y + 1$$

can be refined by

> **ext wr** x
>   **rd** y
> **post** $x = \overleftarrow{x} + y + 1$

Similarly

> **ext wr** x
>   **rd** $\alpha(E) - \{x\}$
> **post** $x = E$

can be refined by

$$x := E[\overleftarrow{x} \backslash x]$$

which is the law given above.

Now we can generalize the idea given at the start of this section; an assignment of the form

$$x, \ldots, y := E, \ldots, F$$

can be 'refined' by the specification

---

[3] We are assuming E only involves operators that are available in the target programming language; Chapter 13 covers the case when it does not.

ext wr $x, \ldots, y$
 rd $\alpha(E) - \{x, \ldots, y\}$
 $\ldots$
 rd $\alpha(F) - \{x, \ldots, y\}$
pre true
post $x = E[x\backslash\overleftarrow{x}, \ldots, y\backslash\overleftarrow{y}] \wedge$
 $\ldots \wedge$
 $y = E[x\backslash\overleftarrow{x}, \ldots, y\backslash\overleftarrow{y}]$

and vice versa.

These ideas can be developed to give a more general assignment rule. If we use the equivalent specification rule given above we might consider the proof diagram in Fig. 11.5. The resulting proof rule is

$$\text{if } \{pre\text{-}OP[x\backslash\overleftarrow{x}] \wedge x = E[x\backslash\overleftarrow{x}] \Rightarrow post\text{-}OP\} \text{ then } OP \sqsubseteq x := E$$

Note that x could denote a list of write variables and E a list of expressions.

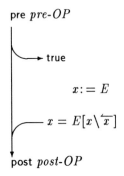

pre $pre\text{-}OP$

$\longrightarrow$ true

$x := E$

$x = E[x\backslash\overleftarrow{x}]$

post $post\text{-}OP$

Figure 11.5 The assignment rule.

11.4.3 Command sequences—divide and conquer

A well-known method of solving a large problem is to break it into smaller, subproblems, solve these subproblems and put the solutions back together to give a solution to the large problem. The glue for assembling the components of the solution is the semicolon and so the first way of dividing a large specification would be to break it into smaller specifications which are assembled using semicolons (Fig. 11.6).

Given a specification to implement, if we had a more restrictive, less general, stronger, pre-condition, it might be easier to establish the post-condition. We now have a subgoal, an intermediate step, to establish this more restrictive pre-condition. To do this we find a specification that defines the subgoal. An alternative approach would be to weaken the post-condition, i.e. establish part of it. Now we have two problems, the first is to establish the weaker post-condition and the second is to establish the full post-condition from this weaker one. Either of these two approaches gives us a way of decomposing one large specification into two smaller ones.

This can be thought of as first of all do something to start the solution, then do something else to complete it. So the solution to a big problem is the solution to one

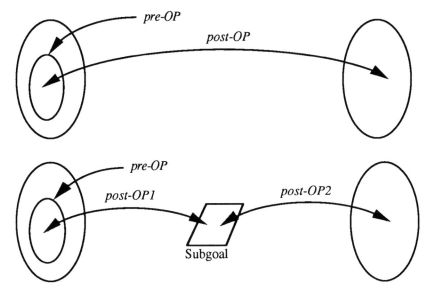

Figure 11.6 'Divide and conquer' used to establish a subgoal.

smaller problem followed by a solution to another smaller problem. We can express this in programming language terms as

$a; b$

We are trying to produce two subspecifications which, when put together with a semi-colon, are equivalent to the original specification. Suppose that we wish to refine a specification OP by this strategy. We need to find two (hopefully easier to refine) specifications OP_1 and OP_2 such that, if code p_1 is written to satisfy the specification OP_1 and code p_2 is written to satisfy the specification OP_2 then the result of executing the code p_1 followed by the code p_2 (i.e. executing p_1 ; p_2) should satisfy the original specification OP. Formally we are saying:

Given a specification OP find specifications OP_1 and OP_2 such that if

$OP_1 \sqsubseteq p_1$
$OP_2 \sqsubseteq p_2$

then

$OP \sqsubseteq p_1; p_2$

or equivalently

$OP \sqsubseteq OP_1; OP_2$

What sort of conditions should the two subspecifications OP_1 and OP_2 satisfy? The conditions are

$\forall s_0 \in State \cdot pre\text{-}OP(s_0) \Rightarrow pre\text{-}OP_1(s_0)$
$\forall s_0, s_1 \in State \cdot pre\text{-}OP(s_0) \wedge post\text{-}OP_1(s_0, s_1) \Rightarrow pre\text{-}OP_2(s_1)$
$\forall s_0, s \in State \cdot \exists s_m \in State \cdot pre\text{-}OP(s_0) \wedge post\text{-}OP_1(s_0, s_m) \wedge post\text{-}OP_2(s_m, s)$
$\Rightarrow post\text{-}OP(s_0, s)$

The rule can be easily remembered using the diagram in Fig. 11.7 and can be written using the abbreviated notation:

$$
\text{if} \left\{
\begin{array}{c}
pre\text{-}OP \;\Rightarrow\; pre\text{-}OP_1 \\
pre\text{-}OP[s\backslash\overleftarrow{s}] \wedge post\text{-}OP_1 \;\Rightarrow\; pre\text{-}OP_2 \\
\exists s_m \in State \cdot \;\; pre\text{-}OP[s\backslash\overleftarrow{s}] \wedge post\text{-}OP_1[s\backslash s_m] \wedge post\text{-}OP_2[\overleftarrow{s}\backslash s_m] \\
\Rightarrow\; post\text{-}OP
\end{array}
\right\} \quad \text{then}
$$

$$OP \sqsubseteq OP_1 \; ; \; OP_2$$

The rule can be generalized to three or more statements in the obvious way.

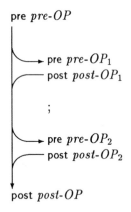

Figure 11.7   The semicolon refinement rule.

Care must be taken when applying the semicolon rule. Remember that a read component (for a variable x, say) in the frame is equivalent to $\overleftarrow{x} = x$ in the post-condition, and to apply the rule these terms should be added to the post-conditions. This means that the expressions that have to be proved sometimes look quite complicated, but usually some elementary housekeeping applied to the terms simplifies things. Frequently the proofs can be done by inspection, by mentally overlaying the picture used to describe the rule onto the code.

If this is not possible, then the (tedious) strategy shown in Fig. 11.8 will work. Use i subscripted identifiers to denote initial and intermediate state values—after the ith statement of the sequence has been executed the values of variables is denoted by their identifiers subscripted by i. The subscript 0 is used for the initial values and undecorated identifiers are used for the final values. Remembering to add the frame information, just write down all the pre- and post-conditions using the appropriate subscripts.

To illustrate this consider the following specification.

$swop$

ext x, y : $\mathbb{Z}$

post $x = \overleftarrow{y} \wedge y = \overleftarrow{x}$

The refinement is given by Fig. 11.9 and the proof is

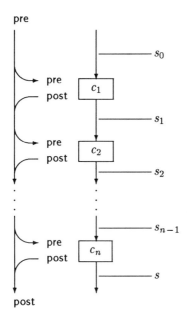

Figure 11.8   The proof diagram for a sequence of statements.

true $\wedge$	pre-condition
$t_1 = x_1 \wedge$	first post-condition
$x_0 = x_1 \wedge y_0 = y_1 \wedge$	rd in first frame
$x_2 = y_2 \wedge$	second post-condition
$t_1 = t_2 \wedge y_1 = y_2 \wedge$	rd in second frame
$y = t \wedge$	third post-condition
$x_2 = x \wedge t_2 = t$	rd in third frame
$\Rightarrow$	
$x = y_0 \wedge y = x_0$	post-condition

Housekeeping (removing the frame information) gives

$$\text{true} \wedge$$
$$t = x_0 \wedge$$
$$x = y_0 \wedge$$
$$y = t$$
$$\Rightarrow x = y_0 \wedge y = x_0$$

which is obviously true. Proving the pre-conditions is trivial.

11.4.4   The conditional command—case analysis

Another approach to reducing the size of the problem is to divide up the pre-conditions. (Fig. 11.10.) The pre-condition covers all possible eventualities, it may be possible to partition the possible inputs so that under certain assumptions, i.e. more restrictive pre-conditions, the problem can be solved.

What we need to do is to discover some restriction to the pre-condition such that under that restriction the problem can be solved, i.e. the post-condition can be established; and

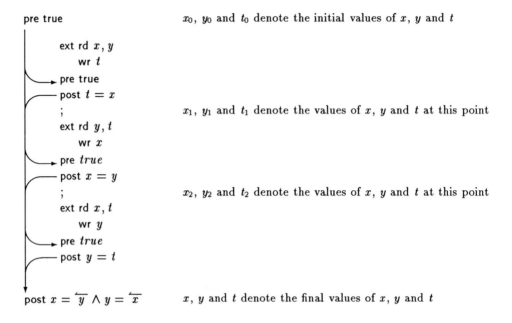

Figure 11.9   The proof diagram for swop.

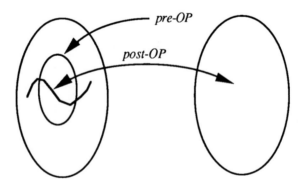

Figure 11.10   Case analysis.

under the remainder of the pre-condition the problem can be solved (another way). The glue for the solutions is the conditional command (if then else statement). This allows a particular problem to be broken up into two subproblems, one covered by the then-part the other covered by the else-part.

Given a specification OP, find a condition *cond* and specifications OP_t and OP_e, such that

$$OP_t \sqsubseteq p_t$$
$$OP_e \sqsubseteq p_e$$

then

$$OP \sqsubseteq \text{if } cond \text{ then } p_t \text{ else } p_e \text{ end}$$

or equivalently

$$OP \sqsubseteq \text{if } cond \text{ then } OP_t \text{ else } OP_e \text{ end}$$

The conditions that the subspecifications must satisfy are

$$\forall s_0 \in State \cdot pre\text{-}OP(s_0) \wedge cond(s_0) \Rightarrow pre\text{-}OP_t(s_0)$$
$$\forall s_0 \in State \cdot pre\text{-}OP(s_0) \wedge \neg cond(s_0) \Rightarrow pre\text{-}OP_e(s_0)$$
$$\forall s_0, s \in State \cdot pre\text{-}OP(s_0) \wedge cond(s_0) \wedge post\text{-}OP_t(s_0, s) \Rightarrow post\text{-}OP(s_0, s)$$
$$\forall s_0, s \in State \cdot pre\text{-}OP(s_0) \wedge \neg cond(s_0) \wedge post\text{-}OP_e(s_0, s) \Rightarrow post\text{-}OP(s_0, s)$$

Using our convention this rule can be written as:

$$\text{if } \left\{ \begin{array}{c} pre\text{-}OP \wedge cond \Rightarrow pre\text{-}OP_t \\ pre\text{-}OP \wedge \neg cond \Rightarrow pre\text{-}OP_e \\ pre\text{-}OP[s\backslash\overleftarrow{s}] \wedge cond[s\backslash\overleftarrow{s}] \wedge post\text{-}OP_t \Rightarrow post\text{-}OP \\ pre\text{-}OP[s\backslash\overleftarrow{s}] \wedge \neg cond[s\backslash\overleftarrow{s}] \wedge post\text{-}OP_e \Rightarrow post\text{-}OP \end{array} \right\} \text{ then}$$

$$OP \sqsubseteq \text{if } cond \text{ then } OP_t \text{ else } OP_e \text{ end}$$

Again the rule can be remembered using a diagram (Fig. 11.11). Notice that the following refinement rule is always true:

$$\begin{array}{ccl}
\begin{array}{l} \text{ext wr } w \\ \quad \text{rd } r \\ \text{pre } P \\ \text{post } Q \end{array} & \sqsubseteq &
\begin{array}{l}
\text{if } cond \text{ then} \\
\quad \text{ext wr } w \\
\qquad \text{rd } r \\
\quad \text{pre } P \wedge cond \\
\quad \text{post } Q \\
\text{else} \\
\quad \text{ext wr } w \\
\qquad \text{rd } r \\
\quad \text{pre } P \wedge \neg cond \\
\quad \text{post } Q \\
\text{end}
\end{array}
\end{array}$$

11.4.5 The while loop command—iteration

The idea behind this strategy is to keep applying a partial solution to a problem until it is solved. We will find a guard and a pre- and post-condition for the body of the loop so that when code is written that satisfies the specification for the body the resultant while loop command will satisfy the original specification.

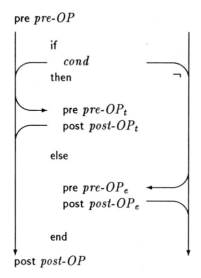

pre *pre-OP*

if

   cond

then

   pre *pre-OP$_t$*
   post *post-OP$_t$*

else

   pre *pre-OP$_e$*
   post *post-OP$_e$*

end

post *post-OP*

Figure 11.11 The conditional statement proof diagram.

Given a specification *OP*, find a condition *guard* and a specification *BODY* such that if

   BODY ⊑ *body*

then

   OP ⊑ while *guard* do *body* end

or equivalently

   OP ⊑ while *guard* do *BODY* end

However, this problem is better solved if we change it slightly—rather than look for a guard and a pre- and a post-conditions that specify the body of the loop, we will find three logical terms, a guard, an invariant and a variant. The invariant could be said to record what the loop body does not do and the variant what it does do. The specification of the body of the loop derived from these terms is, in some sense, the best: the specification demands the optimum amount of work that needs to be done—not too much and not too little.

The proof rule for the while loop command is shown below. As can be seen, it is complex—it is necessary to discover the invariant term *inv*, the variant term *var*, and loop guard *guard* such that

$$\forall s_0 \in State \cdot pre\text{-}OP(s_0) \;\Rightarrow\; inv(s_0)$$
$$\forall s_0, s \in State \cdot \neg\, guard(s_0) \wedge inv(s_0) \wedge (var(s_0, s) \vee I(s_0, s)) \;\Rightarrow\; post\text{-}OP(s_0, s)$$

where *I* is the identity relation—$I(x, x)$ is always true and if $x \neq y$, $I(x, y)$ is false. Then

   OP ⊑ while *guard* do
      pre *guard* ∧ *inv*
      post *inv* ∧ *var*
   end

The property *inv* is preserved by the body of the loop and because of this is called the loop invariant. The requirement on *guard* is that:

- it must be defined over the set (of states) defined by *inv*

and the requirements on *var* are that it must be:

- transitive, and
- well founded over the set defined by *inv*.

A set S is well founded if there is a relation R over S such that every non-empty subset of S has a minimal element:

> if $X \subseteq S$ and $a \in X$, then a is the minimal element of X if there is no $b \in X$ such that $R(b, a)$ and $b \neq a$.

The transitive property means

$$var(a, b) \wedge var(b, c) \implies var(a, c)$$

The well founded property is, roughly speaking, about there being no infinite chains in the relation. Infinite chains can occur in two ways: by having a loop in the relation $var(e, e)$ for some e is allowed and by having a chain, something like $0, -1, -2, \ldots$ for the integers. Note that with a transitive relation a loop can occur indirectly, it would be possible for

$$var(a, b), var(b, c), var(c, d), \ldots, var(e, a)$$

all to be true, which would give a loop because of the transitivity property. If every non-empty set has a minimal element, it is impossible to construct a loop, or an infinite chain.

These are very strong requirements on *var*. Can they be satisfied? Is it possible to find a relation with these properties? More relevant: how do we find a relation with these properties? The answer to the first question is always yes: for any loop, a relation, *var* with the appropriate properties can always be found—the initial values of the variables across the loop body that are changed by the loop body are related by a (suitable) relation to the final values across the loop body; the answer to the second question will have to wait until a later chapter.

Now what has all this to do with iteration? The *inv* predicate defines a subset of the state—the set of all values that satisfy the predicate. The *guard* must be defined over this set, and *var* must be well founded on the set. The existence of *var* is about the iteration terminating. Any iteration will produce a set of values, one value in the set for each iteration of the body of the while loop command. The requirements on *var* guarantee that this set of values has a minimal value, and the iteration must terminate on or before this minimal value is produced. If it did not, it would not be the minimal value—which is a contradiction! The full form of the rule is

$$\text{if} \left\{ \begin{array}{c} \text{pre-}OP \implies inv \\ \neg\, guard[x \backslash \overleftarrow{x}] \wedge inv[x \backslash \overleftarrow{x}] \wedge (var \vee I) \implies post\text{-}OP \\ var \text{ is transitive, and well founded over the set defined by } inv \end{array} \right\} \quad \text{then}$$

$$
\begin{array}{l}
OP \sqsubseteq \text{while } guard \text{ do} \\
\qquad \text{pre } guard \wedge inv \\
\qquad \text{post } inv \wedge var \\
\quad \text{end}
\end{array}
$$

and the diagram for this rule is given in Fig. 11.12.

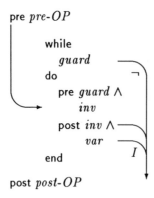

pre *pre-OP*

    while
      guard
    do
      pre *guard* ∧
        inv
      post *inv* ∧
        var
    end

post *post-OP*

Figure 11.12   The iteration proof rule.

11.5 INTEGER MULTIPLICATION

To illustrate the use of these rules, we will consider a simple problem (with a twist).

11.5.1 The problem

Consider the problem of providing a general integer multiplication routine to be implemented on a microcomputer that does not have a multiply instruction. The specification for the function is

$$mult\ (x, y : \mathbf{Z})\ r : \mathbf{Z}$$

post $r = x \times y$

As multiplication is just repeated addition, this specification could be satisfied by a loop that does repeated addition. A possible strategy is to count down in the first argument until zero is reached, adding the value of the second argument into a variable that keeps track of a running total.

11.5.2 Getting started

With this in mind, the first step is to introduce the framework for a function:

$$mult\ (x, y : \mathbf{Z}) : \mathbf{Z}$$

(dcl r : $\mathbf{Z}$;

 multbody

 ext wr $r, x, y : \mathbf{Z}$

 pre true

 post $r = \overleftarrow{x} \times \overleftarrow{y}$

 ;

 return r

) $--$ *mult*

However, what if the first argument is negative? Using it to count down to zero will produce an infinite loop as the value of the variable will (in theory[4]) never go through zero! Thus, before the suggested algorithm can be used, it will be necessary to guarantee that the counter is always non-negative; this suggests that the specification for *multbody* be broken down into two subspecifications: *makepos*, which will guarantee that the counter is non-negative, and *posmult*, which will do the multiplication of one non-negative number (to be used as the counter) by any other number.

Worked example 11.1 Decompose the specification of *mult* into the two subspecifications.

SOLUTION The decomposition is shown below:

> *multbody*
> ext wr r, x, y : $\mathbb{Z}$
> pre true
>
>> *makepos*
>> pre true
>> post $x \times y = \overleftarrow{x} \times \overleftarrow{y} \wedge 0 \leq x$
>> ;
>> *posmult*
>> pre $0 \leq x$
>> post $r = \overleftarrow{x} \times \overleftarrow{y}$
>
> post $r = \overleftarrow{x} \times \overleftarrow{y}$

∎

The specification *multbody* has been split into two subspecifications, *makepos* and *posmult*. Two pieces of code will be developed: one to satisfy the specification for *makepos* and the other to satisfy *posmult*. If the two pieces of code are combined with a 'semicolon', the resulting program fragment will satisfy the original specification *multbody*. There is a requirement to show that

> *makepos*; *posmult*

is equivalent to the original specification. This is done by showing that the semicolon proof rules are satisfied. For the multiply problem example, the two subspecifications could be substituted into the proof rules, but it is much easier to use the diagrammatic versions of the rules given in Fig. 11.13.

Most of the rules can be checked by inspection; the only difficult one is the last one, and the difficulty is really one of getting the notation right. Taking care with the intermediate values of variables and using the subscript rule given above, for this example we get:

> true $\wedge$
> $x_1 \times y_1 = x_0 \times y_0 \wedge 0 \leq x_1$
> $0 \leq x_1 \wedge r = x_1 \times y_1$
> $\Rightarrow r = x_0 \times y_0$

---

[4]ignoring the possibility of 'wrap-round'.

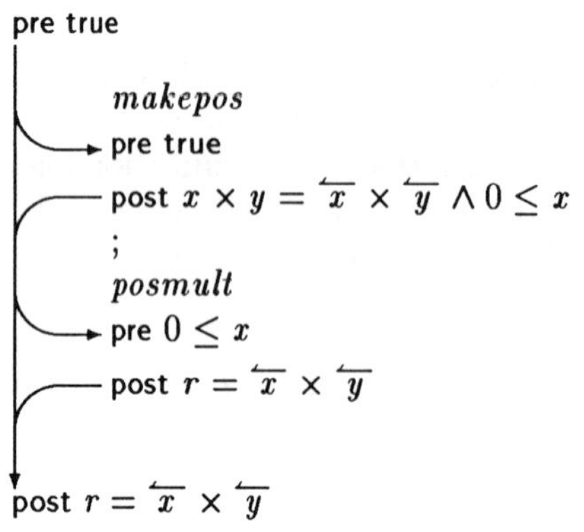

pre true

    makepos
    pre true
    post $x \times y = \overleftarrow{x} \times \overleftarrow{y} \wedge 0 \le x$
    ;
    posmult
    pre $0 \le x$
    post $r = \overleftarrow{x} \times \overleftarrow{y}$

post $r = \overleftarrow{x} \times \overleftarrow{y}$

Figure 11.13   The proof diagram for *multbody*.

which is obviously true. It has now been demonstrated that *makepos* followed by *posmult* is equivalent to *multbody*.

11.5.3   The refinement strategy continued

The next step is to decompose *makepos*. It is necessary to change the sign of x if it is negative, or leave it alone if it is not. The obvious glue in this case would be a conditional command. The operation to reverse the sign of x becomes the else part of the command; and a 'do nothing' operation becomes the then part.

Worked example 11.2 Decompose *makepos* into two subspecifications.

SOLUTION

   makepos
   ext wr x, y : **Z**
   pre true

       if $0 \le x$ then
       pos
       pre $0 \le x$
       post $x = \overleftarrow{x} \wedge y = \overleftarrow{y} \wedge 0 \le x$
       else
       neg
       pre $x < 0$
       post $x = -\overleftarrow{x} \wedge y = -\overleftarrow{y} \wedge 0 \le x$
       end
   post $x \times y = \overleftarrow{x} \times \overleftarrow{y} \wedge 0 \le x$

For the multiply example the proof diagram in Fig. 11.14 is obtained, and the proof is easy by inspection. The four rules derived from the proof diagram are

$$0 \leq x \;\Rightarrow\; 0 \leq x$$

$$0 \leq x \wedge x = \overleftarrow{x} \wedge y = \overleftarrow{y} \;\Rightarrow\; x \times y = \overleftarrow{x} \times \overleftarrow{y} \wedge 0 \leq x$$

$$\neg(0 \leq x) \;\Rightarrow\; x \leq 0$$

$$\neg(0 \leq x) \wedge x = -\overleftarrow{x} \wedge y = -\overleftarrow{y} \;\Rightarrow\; x \times y = \overleftarrow{x} \times \overleftarrow{y} \wedge 0 \leq x$$

The proofs are obvious.

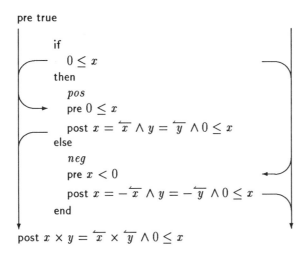

Figure 11.14   The proof diagram for *makepos*.

11.5.4   The final step

The decomposition of *posmult* is a little more difficult. The algorithm that is being developed requires a while loop command. The proposed algorithm is to add the second argument to a running total while keeping count in the first. The specification for this last part of the problem is

> *posmult*
>
> ext wr $r, x, y,\ :\ \mathbb{Z}$
>
> pre $0 \leq x$
>
> post $r = \overleftarrow{x} \times \overleftarrow{y}$

It is necessary to find a loop guard, an invariant and a variant relation that will define the loop.

Worked example 11.3   Write down the loop guard, the invariant and a well founded relation.

SOLUTION

guard $0 \neq x$
inv $0 \leq x$
var $r + x \times y = \overleftarrow{r} + \overleftarrow{x} \times \overleftarrow{y} \wedge x < \overleftarrow{x}$

■

The exact details of where the variant relation comes from are explained in the next chapter, but briefly, initially and after each iteration of the loop we have

$$r + x \times y = \text{'a constant value'}$$

This is a candidate for the loop invariant, except that the constant value it is equal to is the answer, which we do not have a way of denoting. Since the value of the expression $r + x \times y$ is constant at the end of each iteration, it is constant at the start of each iteration; therefore

$$r + x \times y = \overleftarrow{r} + \overleftarrow{x} \times \overleftarrow{y}$$

where the hooked version of the expression denotes the value of the term at the start of an iteration. This term is no longer suitable for use as an invariant (it contains hooked terms), however, it is transitive but is not well founded. Adding the extra term $x < \overleftarrow{x}$, which records the fact that we are counting down in x, makes the expression both transitive and well founded (as will be shown below), which are exactly the properties we require for it to be used as the variant expression.

This gives the following decomposition of the *posmult* operation:

posmult
ext wr r, x, y : $\mathbb{Z}$
pre $0 \leq x$

> $r := 0;$
> pre $0 \leq x$
>
>> while $0 \neq x$ do
>> pre $0 \neq x \wedge 0 \leq x$
>> post $0 \leq x \wedge r + x \times y = \overleftarrow{r} + \overleftarrow{x} \times \overleftarrow{y} \wedge x < \overleftarrow{x}$
>> end
>> post $0 \leq x \wedge r + x \times y = \overleftarrow{r} + \overleftarrow{x} \times \overleftarrow{y} \wedge x \leq \overleftarrow{x} \wedge x = 0$
>
> post $r = \overleftarrow{x} \times \overleftarrow{y}$

The post-condition for the loop as derived from the relation and invariant does not quite match the post-condition for *posmult*. Has something gone wrong? Remember that r is initialized to 0 and on completion of the loop x has the value 0. These facts are substituted into the post-condition for the loop to get

$$0 \leq 0 \wedge r + 0 \times y = 0 + \overleftarrow{x} \times \overleftarrow{y} \wedge 0 \leq \overleftarrow{x} \wedge 0 = 0$$

i.e.

$$r = \overleftarrow{x} \times \overleftarrow{y}$$

which is just what is required.

It is necessary to show that the variant relation *var* is both transitive and well founded; the relation *var* is given by

$$var(\overleftarrow{x}, \overleftarrow{y}, \overleftarrow{r}, x, y, r) \;\;\triangleq\;\; r + x \times y = \overleftarrow{r} + \overleftarrow{x} \times \overleftarrow{y} \wedge x < \overleftarrow{x}$$

Thus

$$var(x_0, y_0, r_0, x_1, y_1, r_1) = r_1 + x_1 \times y_1 = r_0 + x_0 \times y_0 \wedge x_1 < x_0$$

and

$$var(x_1, y_1, r_1, x_2, y_2, r_2) = r_2 + x_2 \times y_2 = r_1 + x_1 \times y_1 \wedge x_2 < x_1$$

so

$$var(x_0, y_0, r_0, x_1, y_1, r_1) \wedge var(x_1, y_1, r_1, x_2, y_2, r_2)$$
$$= \text{"definition of } var\text{"}$$
$$r_1 + x_1 \times y_1 = r_0 + x_0 \times y_0 \wedge x_1 < x_0 \wedge$$
$$r_2 + x_2 \times y_2 = r_1 + x_1 \times y_1 \wedge x_2 < x_1$$
$$= \text{"rules of arithmetic"}$$
$$r_2 + x_2 \times y_2 = r_0 + x_0 \times y_0 \wedge x_2 < x_0$$
$$= \text{"definition of } var\text{"}$$
$$var(x_0, y_0, r_0, x_2, y_2, r_2)$$

Thus *var* is transitive. That it is well founded over the set defined by the invariant can be deduced from the fact that x is non-negative and cannot be decreased indefinitely.

The specification of the loop body was derived from the guard and invariant and the variant relations:

ext wr r, x, y : $\mathbb{Z}$

pre $0 \neq x \wedge 0 \leq x$

post $0 \leq x \wedge r + x \times y = \overleftarrow{r} + \overleftarrow{x} \times \overleftarrow{y} \wedge x < \overleftarrow{x}$

which can be satisfied by the following code:

ext wr r, x, y : $\mathbb{Z}$
pre $0 \neq x \wedge 0 \leq x$

$$x, r := x - 1, r + y$$

post $0 \leq x \wedge r + x \times y = \overleftarrow{r} + \overleftarrow{x} \times \overleftarrow{y} \wedge x < \overleftarrow{x}$

The whole thing can now be 'back substituted' (or equivalently read backwards) to give the code for the *mult* function; some of the (easy) refinement steps have been left for the reader:

$mult\ (x\!:\mathbf{Z},y\!:\mathbf{Z}):\mathbf{Z}$
(dcl r : $\mathbf{Z}$;
  if $0 \leq x$ then
    skip
  else
    $x,y\!:=-x,-y$
  end;
  $r\!:=0$;
  while $0 \neq x$ do
    $x,r\!:=x-1,r+y$
  end;
  return r
) $--\ mult$

11.6   THE DIVISION PROBLEM REVISITED

We saw earlier in this chapter how it was possible to prove the correctness of a program, given the specification. In the example above the program and proof of correctness were derived together. We shall now briefly return to the division problem and derive the program directly from the specification. The specification was

div

ext rd a,b : $\mathbf{Z}$
   wr q : $\mathbf{Z}$

pre $0 \leq a \wedge 0 < b$

post $\exists r \in \mathbf{N} \cdot b \times q + r = a \wedge r < b$

The first task is to find the invariant expression.

Worked example 11.4 Write down the invariant expression.

SOLUTION If we examine the post-condition an obvious candidate is

$$b \times q + r = a \wedge 0 \leq r$$

■

The strategy we will follow is for some initialization code to establish the invariant and then a loop to establish the required post-condition. This approach produces the following decomposition; notice that we have introduced r as a (temporary) variable.

ext rd a, b : $\mathbb{Z}$
    wr r, q : $\mathbb{Z}$
pre $0 \leq a \wedge 0 < b$

        pre $0 \leq a \wedge 0 < b$
        post $b \times q + r = a \wedge 0 \leq r$
        ;
        pre $b \times q + r = a \wedge 0 \leq r$
        post $b \times q + r = a \wedge 0 \leq r < b$

post $b \times q + r = a \wedge 0 \leq r < b$

It can easily be seen by inspection that the sequence proof rules are satisfied. Though these proof rules are complicated their pictorial representation lends itself to proof by inspection most of the time. The first subspecification can easily be satisfied by

pre $0 \leq a \wedge 0 < b$

$$q, r := 0, a$$

post $b \times q + r = a \wedge 0 \leq r$

The second specification is to be implemented as a loop. We already have the invariant; it is now necessary to work out the guard and the variant relation. Inspection of the post-condition suggests that the guard is the term that requires r to be greater than the divisor:

guard $b \leq r$
inv $b \times q + r = a \wedge 0 \leq r$
var $r < \overleftarrow{r}$

The variant relation records the fact that r needs to be decreased. We now need to show that these values for the guard, invariant and variant terms satisfy the specification for the loop (Fig. 11.15). Again, it is easy to see by inspection that the rule is satisfied.

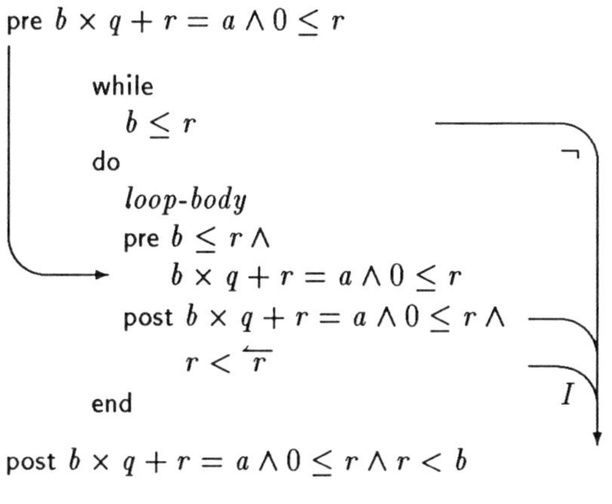

pre $b \times q + r = a \wedge 0 \leq r$

    while
      $b \leq r$
    do
      loop-body
      pre $b \leq r \wedge$
        $b \times q + r = a \wedge 0 \leq r$
      post $b \times q + r = a \wedge 0 \leq r \wedge$
        $r < \overleftarrow{r}$
    end I

post $b \times q + r = a \wedge 0 \leq r \wedge r < b$

Figure 11.15 The proof diagram for *div* problem.

The specification for the body of the loop is easily derived from the three terms given as the loop specification. The pre-condition is given by the guard and the invariant relation and the post-condition by the invariant and variant relations. The body of the loop is thus

pre $b \leq r \wedge b \times q + r = a \wedge 0 \leq r$

post $b \times q + r = a \wedge 0 \leq r \wedge r < \overleftarrow{r}$

Inspection of the invariant term suggests decreasing r by b:

$r := r - b$

and for the invariant to be preserved it will also be necessary to increase q:

$q := q + 1$

By inspection these two terms satisfy the specification for the body of the loop. Thus the final program is

```
q, r := 0, a;
while b ≤ r do
    q, r := q + 1, r - b
end
```

This little example shows how it is much easier to derive the proof and program together. In fact programming in the normal sense has been replaced by a goal-oriented activity where we look at the post-condition and try to establish parts of it. With this approach, traditional programming vanishes as an activity.

11.7   AN ALTERNATIVE APPROACH

If we compare the derivation of code from the *multp* specification with that of the *div* example, finding *inv* and *var* was much easier in the *div* problem. Why was this? It was because the initial values of a and b were effectively saved—these variables were read only, and therefore unchanged by the derived code and thus could be used in the *inv* expression. In the *posmult* example we wanted to talk about the answer when deriving the invariant, but could not since there was no way of referring to it using current or previous values of variables, except in the way it was done (remember the derivation of the variant term). This problem occurs in any example that overwrites its input values while calculating the result—in these cases we are forced to derive a term that is really an invariant and add it to the variant. However, there is a solution—returning to the specification of *posmult* on page 206:

> *posmult*
>
> ext wr r, x, y : $\mathbb{Z}$
>
> pre $0 \leq x$
>
> post $r = \overleftarrow{x} \times \overleftarrow{y}$

We will cheat by introducing an additional (temporary) variable c and initialize it:

$c := x \times y$

This really is cheating! However bear with us for the moment. A possible refinement of *posmult* is

posmult
pre $0 \leq x$

$c := x \times y$;
ext wr r, x, y
  rd c
pre $c = x \times y \wedge 0 \leq x$
post $r = c$

post $r = \overleftarrow{x} \times \overleftarrow{y}$

which can be seen to be valid. The second (specification) statement can be refined using a loop, and we can use the variable x (effectively treating it as a temporary variable) to rewrite the post-condition as

$$r + x \times y = c \wedge x = 0$$

This suggests the following guard, invariant and variant terms:

guard $x \neq 0$
inv $r + x \times y = c \wedge 0 \leq x$
var $x < \overleftarrow{x}$

and the following initialization

$r := 0$

so the derivation so far looks like

$c := x \times y$;
pre $c = x \times y \wedge 0 \leq x$

  $r := 0$;
  while $x \neq 0$ do
    posmult-body
    pre $x \neq 0 \wedge r + x \times y = c \wedge 0 \leq x$
    post $r + x \times y = c \wedge 0 \leq x \wedge x < \overleftarrow{x}$
  end
post $r = c$

and it is left as a simple exercise for the reader to show that the above is valid. The next step is to derive the body of the loop (again an easy exercise) to get the final program:

$c := x \times y$;
$r := 0$;
while $x \neq 0$ do
  $x, r := x - 1, r + y$
end

Notice that, having assigned a value to the variable c, it is only used in the derivation of the final code, and does not appear anywhere other than the initial assignment. Therefore that statement could be thrown away and we are left with the original solution, except that the derivation was a lot easier:

$r := 0;$
while $x \neq 0$ do
$\quad x, r := x - 1, r + y$
end

This trick can be used in any derivation of code from a specification that allows the initial values to be overwritten—a temporary variable is introduced and given a useful value (such as the answer), the code is derived using the techniques illustrated above, remembering not to use the temporary anywhere in the final code, and finally since the temporary is not used anywhere it can be deleted. This technique is so useful that we will introduce a notation for it[5]:

ext wr ...
$\quad$ rd ...
pre P

$\qquad c := E;$
$\qquad$ pre $P \wedge c = E$
$\qquad$ post Q

post Q

can be written as

ext wr ...
$\quad$ rd ...
$\quad$ lc ...
pre $P \wedge c = E$
post Q

The temporary 'variable' introduced is called a *logical constant*, and the semantics are that any logical constant that is introduced has a value such that the (new) pre-condition is satisfied. A more general rule can be derived. Since the expression $c = E$ in the pre-condition is equivalent to introducing a temporary variable and an assignment command of the form $c := E$ into the code that refines a specification, and since this statement can be deleted from the final code, it does not matter if it can not actually be implemented! In fact we could write something like

$\qquad c := $ let x be s.t. $P(x)$ in x

the only restriction is that the value 'assigned' to c must exist; this gives a more general rule:

---

[5] In fact it would be possible to redefine the ext convention. It is only really necessary to record those variables that can be changed in the frame: only those variables occurring in the ext can be altered—this would remove the need for the rd , wr and lc keywords, everything in the frame would automatically be wr , all other identifiers would be rd by convention.

if $\{\ P \ \Rightarrow\ \exists c \in C \cdot P'\ \}$ then

$$
\begin{array}{c}
\text{ext wr } \ w \\
\text{rd } \ r \\
\text{pre } P \\
\text{post } Q
\end{array}
\qquad \sqsubseteq \qquad
\begin{array}{c}
\text{ext wr } \ w \\
\text{rd } \ r \\
\text{lc } \ c : C \\
\text{pre } P' \\
\text{post } Q
\end{array}
$$

where c does not occur in w, P, or Q.

Beware of the following problem; at first sight the following command sequence cannot be implemented:

```
ext wr x  : N
    lc c  : N
pre c = x
post x > c
;
ext wr x  : N
    lc c  : N
pre c = x
post x > c
```

If we try to fix a value of c, it is impossible. What is required is some sort of scope convention which makes the second logical constant in the above example different from the first. The 'variable' c is really a constant within its scope, which is the specification that introduces it, and any refinements of that specification.

In order to make the above example work we could write:

```
(ext wr x  : N
     lc c  : N
pre c = x
post x > c
);
(ext wr x  : N
     lc c  : N
pre c = x
post x > c
)
```

and the two logical constants are distinct.

It should be noted that there is no way of declaring a logical constant, it can only occur in the frame of a specification. Therefore when we refine a specification that contains logical constants to executable code, they must all be removed—for otherwise we would have an identifier that is not declared[6]. In fact in most examples logical constants will mainly appear in proofs, sometimes in derived code, and never in the final executable code.

---

[6]VDM-SL insists that *all* identifiers are declared.

11.7.1   Some additional rules

Some of the rules discussed above have simple variants if logical constants are used, these can be found in Appendix E. Also, with logical constants the proof rule for loops can be simplified. If the post-condition of the operation to be refined by a loop does not contain any hooked variables, then

$$
\begin{array}{ccc}
\begin{array}{l}
\text{ext wr } w \\
\quad \text{rd } r \\
\text{pre } inv \\
\text{post } inv \wedge \neg\, guard
\end{array}
&
\sqsubseteq
&
\begin{array}{l}
\text{while } guard \text{ do} \\
\quad \text{ext wr } w \\
\quad\quad \text{rd } r \\
\quad \text{pre } guard \wedge inv \\
\quad \text{post } inv \wedge (0 \le E < \overleftarrow{E}) \\
\text{end}
\end{array}
\end{array}
$$

where E is some expression incorporating frame variables which has a result that is a non-negative integer, and $\overleftarrow{E}$ is $E[w\backslash\overleftarrow{w}]$. Rather than have a well-founded relation on the set of state values defined by the invariant, we will use this expression the value of which depends on the state. The value of this expression is always non-negative and is decreased by each loop iteration. Thus the expression can be used to prove that the loop must terminate. It should also be realized that feasibility is hidden in the rule, and may be lost. It is possible to derive an iterative loop whose body is infeasible—only *miracle* can satisfy it.

If the post-condition of the operation to be refined does contain hooked variables, these can always be removed by introducing logical constants!

$$
\begin{array}{ccc}
\begin{array}{l}
\text{ext wr } w \\
\quad \text{rd } r \\
\text{pre } P \\
\text{post } Q
\end{array}
&
\sqsubseteq
&
\begin{array}{l}
\text{ext wr } w \\
\quad \text{lc } c \\
\quad \text{rd } r \\
\text{pre } P \wedge w = c \\
\text{post } Q[\overleftarrow{w}\backslash c]
\end{array}
\end{array}
$$

Thus this simple rule can be applied when developing any loop. Examples of this are to be found in the next chapter. This rule together with one of the semicolon rules provides a simple refinement for initialized loops:

$$
\begin{array}{ccc}
\begin{array}{l}
\text{ext wr } w \\
\quad \text{rd } r \\
\text{pre } P \\
\text{post } inv \wedge \neg\, guard
\end{array}
&
\sqsubseteq
&
\begin{array}{l}
\text{ext wr } w \\
\quad \text{rd } r \\
\text{pre } P \\
\text{post } inv \\
; \\
\text{while } guard \text{ do} \\
\quad \text{ext wr } w \\
\quad\quad \text{rd } r \\
\quad \text{pre } guard \wedge inv \\
\quad \text{post } inv \wedge (0 \le E < \overleftarrow{E}) \\
\text{end}
\end{array}
\end{array}
$$

11.8   SUMMARY

This chapter has introduced the concept of program refinement and some proof rules and transformation rules that allow specifications to be translated into programs. The application of these rules has been illustrated using some simple examples, and although this looks complicated, with practice much of the work involved in any proofs that are necessary can be done by inspection. The next chapter will expand these ideas, and the remainder of the book will illustrate their application to software development.

12

PROGRAM DEVELOPMENT

AIMS

- To show that the techniques described in the previous chapter can be applied to the derivation of correct program code.
- To provide some examples of the formal derivation of program code from a mathematical specification.
- To provide some strategies for the formal development of loops.

12.1 THE FACTORIAL PROBLEM

We can gain some insight into how the guard, invariant, and variant relations can be discovered by looking at the fairly simple problem of calculating a factorial. The best approach to discovering these three terms is to initially ignore the variant relation and try to first find the invariant and then discover an appropriate guard. It must be remembered that the process of discovering these three terms cannot be mechanized (for if it could we would be able to automate the whole of programming!) and their discovery is effectively inventing the code for a loop, as should be realized from looking at the examples given in the previous chapter.

12.1.1 The first solution

The specification for the factorial problem is straightforward:

> *factorial*
> ext wr *fac* : $\mathbb{Z}$
>   rd *n* : $\mathbb{Z}$
> pre $n \geq 0$
> post $fac = n!$

An inspection of the proof rule for loops shows that it must be possible to derive the post-condition from the invariant and the negation of the guard, so one approach to finding these two terms would be to try to identify them in the post-condition. In the post-condition for the factorial there is only one term, and we need to find two, but if a temporary variable is introduced the post-condition can be reorganized so that it has two terms:

> post $fac = i! \wedge i = n$

The new specification is now

> $factorial$
>
> ext wr i, fac : **Z**
>   rd n : **Z**
>
> pre $n \geq 0$
> post $fac = i! \wedge i = n$

with two terms in the post-condition, the first of which is a possible candidate for the invariant and the other for the guard. The invariant can be established by setting $i = 0$ and $fac = 1$, and initialization for the loop solves part of the problem:

> $1 = 0!$

The second term is a good candidate for the guard, and the loop will be

> progress i towards n, keeping $fac = i!$

The guard indicates that the iteration will stop when i is equal to n and since i is initialized to 0, it is fairly obvious what the variant should be.

Worked example 12.1 Write down the initialization code, the guard, the invariant and the variant.

SOLUTION These are shown below:

> init $i = 0 \wedge fac = 1$
> guard $i \neq n$
> inv $fac = i!$
> var $0 \leq n - i < n - \overleftarrow{i}$

■

To derive the body of the loop we will increase i to establish the variant, and this will immediately break the invariant; thus the remainder of the code for the body should re-establish the invariant, which can be done by increasing the value of factorial. Putting this all together gives the first version of the factorial program:

```
i, fac: = 0, 1;
while i ≠ n do
    i: = i + 1;        -- break the invariant
    fac: = fac × i   -- re-establish invariant
od
```

The tactics used on this problem are fairly common for finding the terms from which the loop is developed:

1. Identify from the post-condition a suitable candidate for the invariant.
2. Find the guard; the guard can usually be deduced from the invariant and post-condition.
3. Find the variant; the variant can be found by finding an expression defined over the frame which evaluates to a natural number and is strictly decreasing.
4. Derive the initialization code that establishes the invariant.

5. The body of the loop can be discovered by first writing code that breaks the invariant, usually by establishing the variant, and then developing code that re-establishes the invariant.

12.1.2 A second solution

The first version of the factorial problem allowed the introduction of a temporary variable; in fact the specification was deliberately written to encourage this. What happens if the specification is altered to allow the value of the variable n to be changed and a temporary variable is not introduced?

> $factorial$
> **ext wr** fac, n : $\mathbb{Z}$
> **pre** $n \geq 0$
> **post** $fac = \overleftarrow{n}!$

Since the final value of n is not defined, there is a possibility of counting down in n and accumulating the result in fac. Given this, what is the invariant? This time we will not introduce a temporary variable, so there is a problem in identifying suitable terms in the post-condition to be the invariant and possibly the guard.

Now suppose the values of the two variables fac and n are changed by the body of the loop so that

$$fac \times n! = \text{constant}$$

This (invariant) expression is easily established by setting fac to 1, and if the body of the loop decreases n, then, when n has the value 0, fac has the same value as the constant. From this discussion we can deduce the value of the constant as $n!$—the answer. The next step is to introduce a logical constant to hold this value:

> $factorial$
> **ext wr** fac, n : $\mathbb{Z}$
>   **lc** c : $\mathbb{Z}$
> **pre** $n \geq 0 \wedge c = n!$
> **post** $fac = c$

The post-condition can be rewritten using the technique introduced in the previous development of fac:

> $factorial$
> **ext wr** fac, n : $\mathbb{Z}$
>   **lc** c : $\mathbb{Z}$
> **pre** $n \geq 0 \wedge c = n!$
> **post** $fac \times n! = c \wedge n = 0$

The body of the loop will decrease n, so the variant term is obvious. The initialization, guard, invariant and variant terms are thus

> **init** $fac = 1$
> **guard** $n \neq 0$
> **inv** $fac \times n! = c$
> **var** $0 \leq n < \overleftarrow{n}$

and the specification of the body of the loop is

> *loop-body*
> ext wr fac, n : $\mathbf{Z}$
>   lc c : $\mathbf{Z}$
> pre $n \neq 0 \wedge fac \times n! = c$
> post $fac \times n! = c \wedge 0 \leq n < \overleftarrow{n}$

The code of the body of the loop can now be developed. A possible first step is to break the invariant by decreasing n by 1:

> $n := n - 1$

We must now re-establish the invariant; the post-condition to do this can be found using the leading assignment rule (see Appendix C). We have also taken the liberty of strengthening the post-condition by adding the term $n = \overleftarrow{n}$. The refinement step for *loop-body* is thus:

> $n := n - 1;$
> ext wr fac, n : $\mathbf{Z}$
>   lc c : $\mathbf{Z}$
> pre $n + 1 \neq 0 \wedge$
> $fac \times (n + 1)! = c$
> post $fac \times n! = c \wedge 0 \leq n < \overleftarrow{n} + 1 \wedge n = \overleftarrow{n}$

Because c is constant

$$fac \times n! = c = \overleftarrow{fac} \times (\overleftarrow{n} + 1)!$$

From the post-condition we know that $n = \overleftarrow{n}$ and therefore

$$fac = \frac{\overleftarrow{fac} \times (n + 1)!}{n!} = \overleftarrow{fac} \times (n + 1)$$

from which the loop body can be derived:

> $n := n - 1;$
> $fac := fac \times (n + 1)$

Alternatively the assignment rule called 'following assignment' could be used

> $body \sqsubseteq$ pre $n \neq 0 \wedge fac \times n! = c$
>   post $fac \times (n - 1)! = c$
> $;$
> $n := n - 1$

The post-condition can be strengthened by adding $n = \overleftarrow{n}$ as before and a similar derivation to the one used with the leading assignment rule gives the following program:

> $fac := 1;$
> while $n \neq 0$ do
> $fac := fac \times n;$
> $n := n - 1$
> end

A final derivation: using the fact that c is a constant, the pre-condition is added to the post-condition, the original specification for the body of the loop can be rewriten as

> *body*
>
> ext wr fac, n : $\mathbb{Z}$
>
>   lc c : $\mathbb{Z}$
>
> pre $n \neq 0 \wedge fac \times n! = c$
>
> post $fac \times n! = \overleftarrow{fac} \times \overleftarrow{n}! \wedge 0 \leq n < \overleftarrow{n}$

and the assignment

> $fac, n := fac \times n, n - 1$

will satisfy the specification for *body*.

12.1.3 A third solution

A third approach to this problem is to refine the specification without using a logical constant. There are only two variables in the state; how are they related? From the above derivation we know

> $fac \times n! =$ constant

The constant value is, in fact, the answer. Unfortunately without the use of a logical constant this expression cannot be used as an invariant as it stands, but note that at the start (and end) of any iteration the equation given above is true. This means that

$$fac \times n! = \overleftarrow{fac} \times \overleftarrow{n}!$$

This term is certainly true at the start or finish of any loop iteration but is not suitable for use as an invariant as it contains the previous values of the two variables; however, this equation could be used for the variant relation except that nothing decreases. If we add the fact that n decreases across the body of the loop we have the following:

> var $fac \times n! = \overleftarrow{fac} \times \overleftarrow{n}! \wedge n < \overleftarrow{n}$

It is easy to see that this expression satisfies the requirements of the variant relation, but in this case now what is the invariant? It is the fact that n is never negative. The initialization and guard necessary for the loop can be found by inspecting the variant. Since the variant is transitive the following is true of the initial and final values for the loop:

> inv $n \geq 0$

By inspection we can see that a suitable guard is

> guard $n > 0$

and the initialization is

> init $fac = 1$

With this it is trivial to develop the loop

$fac := 1$;
while $n > 0$ do
  pre $n > 0 \wedge n \geq 0$

  post $n \geq 0 \wedge fac \times n! = \overleftarrow{fac} \times \overleftarrow{n}! \wedge n < \overleftarrow{n}$
end

The body of the loop can be developed, as before, to give the final program:

$fac := 1$;
while $n > 0$ do
  $fac := fac \times n$;
  $n := n - 1$
end

From this example it seems that logical constants and complicated relations are related (except that it is easier to do the development using logical constants). This point will be addressed in a postscript below.

12.2 FINDING GUARDS AND INVARIANTS

We have seen three separate solutions to the same problem. How do you choose which approach to take and thus how to find the invariant relation, the guard and the variant relation? In the problems seen so far, the guard and the invariant and variant relations are pulled out of the hat, so to speak. How were they discovered in the examples given in this and the previous chapter, and how can they be discovered for new problems? Loops are about building answers up from some initial value by repeating the execution of some operation, i.e. piece of code. Two main types of loop can be identified.

The first type of loop involves the introduction of temporary variables[1] to hold intermediate results that help with the construction of the answer. They contain, among other things, a record of how much work has been done. It is also probable that some part of the initial state is left undisturbed and can thus be used to check loop termination. This type of loop constructs the result with the temporaries keeping track of the work that has been done so far. We will call this type of loop an 'up' loop.

In the second type of loop, usually no new variables (temporaries) are introduced. Calculations are done *in situ* using the variables that are in the specification, i.e. that are in the state. This implies that the initial state is changed and therefore there is nothing to check completion against; therefore loop termination is checked by testing some value against some 'zero' value (0, an empty list, an empty set, etc.). The calculation is done by moving values around the variables of the state with some value decreasing; this value is the one to test for termination and measures how much work is left to do. This style of loop is called a 'down' loop.

The proof rule for loops is of the form:

$$inv \wedge \neg \, guard \ldots \; \Rightarrow \; post\text{-}condition$$

---

[1] By a temporary variable, we mean a value that does not exist before the loop, and is not needed on completion of the loop, i.e. a variable that is not part of the original specification but is introduced as part of the loop development—typically a counter.

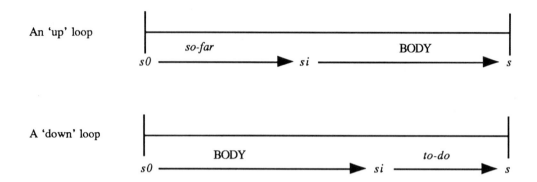

Figure 12.1 'Up' and 'down' loops.

An approach to finding the invariant, the guard and the variant relation is to identify expressions in the post-condition that could be candidates for the three terms we are looking for. It is usually best to leave the variant relation until last and just to look for terms in the post-condition that are possible candidates for the invariant and the guard. Again, more insight can be gained from concentrating on the invariant part first and then using that to deduce the guard and finally look for some term that decreases for the relation.

It may be possible to rewrite the post-condition by introducing a temporary variable:

> $\dots P(n)\dots$
> is transformed to
> $\dots P(i)\dots \wedge i = n$

The new term can be negated to give the guard. Alternatively, it may be possible to rewrite the post-condition by replacing a constant by a variable:

> $\dots k \dots$
> is transformed to
> $\dots i \dots \wedge i = k$

Again the new term can be negated to provide the guard. Both of these techniques work with the 'up' loop, the variable introduced being the temporary discussed above. If, in a specification, a variable is restricted to a range, a related strategy is to enlarge the range by replacing the constants that define the range by temporary variables:

> $\dots n \in \{lb, \dots, ub\} \dots$
> is transformed to
> $\dots n \in \{vlb, \dots, vub\} \dots \wedge vlb = lb \wedge vub = ub$

In this approach the body will, as part of its task, reduce the range of values defined by the temporary variables.

If temporaries are not to be introduced for one reason or another, we have the 'down' loop situation and it is a little trickier to find the three terms. A little insight is necessary to identify an invariant. In this case the invariant is usually some function of the variables and the result of the loop calculation. This means that some function of the (values of the) current state is equal to the result that the loop is trying to construct. The result must also be a function of the initial state. This can be expressed informally:

$$f(\text{current state}) = \text{constant} = g(\text{initial state})$$

where the function g calculates the answer.

There are two possibilities; one is to derive an invariant expression involving decorated and undecorated terms and use this together with a transitive relation to derive the variant relation, as in the third version of the factorial problem above, or to introduce a logical constant, which reduces the problem to an 'up' loop problem. The logical constant takes the part of a state variable that is not changed by the loop; one or more of the state variables act the part of the temporaries which are introduced in the 'down' loop situation, and the sort of techniques described above for finding the three terms can now be applied. Figure 12.2 attempts to show the difference between the two types of loop that are likely to occur.

	'up'	'down'
	Can the post-condition be weakened by introducing temporaries?	Is some function of the state constant? The function reflects fuctionality of loop
	Can 'next' values be based on 'current' values?	Does data-structure already exist? Loop will either 'add' structure or loop will preserve structure—we are using or establishing a data invariant
	Temporaries reflect story so far	Some state variables reflect work to do
	Each iteration contributes towards the answer	Each iteration eliminates work 'remaining'
Temporaries	Yes	No
Logical constants	No	Yes
Initialization	Results set to 'zero' Temporaries set to 'zero' (or an 'upperbound')	Logical constants reflects whole task
Initial state	Undisturbed	Changed
Invariant	Some function of temporaries and locals	Data invariant and/or some function of variables and logical constants
Variant	Temporaries increased (or decreased)	Some state variables approaching a limit value
Loop test	Test for temporary = some initial value (or temporary = 'zero')	Test for 'zero'

Figure 12.2 A comparison of 'up' and 'down' loops.

In general, the function of 'up' loops is to build up the answer in the variables of the state. The function of any temporaries that are introduced is to measure the work that has been done so far. Each execution of the loop adds information to that already constructed. Thus the strategy of 'up' loops is:

1. Build answer in steps.
2. Invariant is about the steps.
3. Variant relation is about steps being in right direction—towards the answer.

For 'up' loops the invariant can usually be found by reorganizing the post-condition and at the same time introducing temporary values. The guard can usually be deduced from any new terms introduced.

The body of a loop can be developed by writing code that initially 'breaks' the invariant and at the same time establishes the variant relation. The remainder of the loop body is about re-establishing the variant.

The initialization can be deduced from what values must be assigned to the temporaries, and perhaps other variables to establish the invariant.

The other form of loop, the 'down' loop, usually occurs when the data structure already exists, but information may be hidden, in the wrong place or not yet constructed, and the purpose of the loop is to find the information, move it to the right place or construct it. This means that the result of the loop is some function of the initial values, and the purpose of the loop is to calculate this function (this is true of 'up' loops, but we are talking about reorganization versus iteration). In this case the invariant is a data type invariant about the data of the loop. A logical constant is needed to record the fact that at any iteration the current values in the state are related to previous values, via the result of the loop, and the variant relation reflects the fact that progress is being made. With the 'down' loop it is sometimes necessary to introduce temporary values to measure the work to do. The initialization for this form of the loop is a little more difficult, but can be deduced from the result of the loop.

In either loop type, the approaches to finding invariants are:

1. Delete a conjunct and use the complement of that conjunct as a guard for the loop.
2. Replace a constant by a variable.
3. Enlarge the range of a variable.

The principle is to introduce a name to denote a value that is to be determined. If the invariant needs to refer to either initial or final values, introduce a logical constant.

12.2.1 Identifying the loop type incorrectly

Suppose we introduce a temporary variable and pretend that it is part of the state:

$factorial$
ext wr fac, i : $\mathbf{Z}$
    rd n : $\mathbf{Z}$
pre $n \geq 0$
post $fac = i! \land i = n$

The algorithm to be used will build the answer up in *fac*, so that it is the 'down' style that is being used. We need to find an expression that is constant across iterations; since we are building the answer in *fac*, with *i* keeping track of how far we have go, the following would be a good guess:

$$fac \times (i+1) \times (i+2) \times \ldots \times n = \text{ a constant} \qquad (= n!)$$

This can be rewritten as

$$\frac{fac \times n!}{i!} = \text{ a constant}$$

The specification can be rewritten:

> *factorial*
> **ext wr** *fac, i* : **Z**
>   **rd** *n*   : **Z**
>   **lc** *c*   : **Z**
> **pre** $n \geq 0 \wedge c = n!$
> **post** $c \times i! = fac \times n! \wedge i = n$

Each iteration of the loop should increase *i*, and this is the variant relation. The loop is then given by

> **guard** $i \neq n$
> **inv** $c \times i! = fac \times n!$
> **var** $0 < n - i \leq n - \overleftarrow{i}$

The initialization is a little more tricky. If *c* has the value *n*! then setting *fac* equal to 1 and *i* equal to 0 will do it. The loop terminates with *i* equal to *n*; thus the loop establishes

$$c \times n! = fac \times n! \quad \text{i.e. } fac = c$$

which is what is required. The program can now be easily derived:

```
i := 0;   -- establish the invariant
fac := 1;
while i ≠ n do
  i := i + 1;
  fac := fac × i
end
```

Thus, even if the wrong 'direction' for the loop is chosen, everything still works out in the end.

12.3   SOME REFINEMENT EXAMPLES

To illustrate the ideas of finding loop invariants, etc., we can consider some simple problems. In each case the derivation occurred (more or less) as presented here, the most difficult part being the reorganization of the post-condition to try to identify a suitable invariant relation.

12.3.1 A second approach to multiplication

As the algorithm depends on reducing the value of x to zero, a better solution might be obtained if we try to reduce x to zero as quickly as possible in the body of the loop. The second algorithm will use the fact that multiplication and division by 2 can be implemented as shift instructions on binary computers. If x is even, then it can be divided by 2 and y multiplied by 2 to keep the value of $x \times y$ constant. The specification for *posmult-body* from page 211 can be written:

> *posmult-body*
> ext wr r, x, y : $\mathbf{Z}$
>   lc c : $\mathbf{Z}$
> pre $x \neq 0 \wedge r + x \times y = c \wedge 0 \leq x$
> post $r + x \times y = c \wedge 0 \leq x < \overleftarrow{x}$

The division of x by 2 can only be done until x is odd, then the old algorithm must be used. This suggests the following refinement.

> *posmult-body*
> ext wr r, x, y : $\mathbf{Z}$
>   lc c : $\mathbf{Z}$
> pre $x \neq 0 \wedge r + x \times y = c \wedge 0 \leq x$
>
> > *mkodd*
> > ext lc d: $\mathbf{Z}$
> > pre $x \neq 0 \wedge d = x \times y$
> > post $d = x \times y \wedge 0 \leq x \leq \overleftarrow{x}$
> > ;
> > *mkeven*
> > pre $x \neq 0 \wedge r + x \times y = c \wedge 0 \leq x$
> > post $r + x \times y = c \wedge 0 \leq x < \overleftarrow{x}$
>
> post $r + x \times y = c \wedge 0 \leq x < \overleftarrow{x}$

By inspection this can be seen to be true.

Worked example 12.2 Write down the initialization, guard, invariant and variant for a loop that satisfies *mkodd*.

SOLUTION The specification for *mkodd* can be satisfied by a loop defined by

> init   true
> guard $is\text{-}even(x)$
> inv $d = x \times y$
> var $0 \leq x < \overleftarrow{x}$

                                                                           ■

The loop developed from these terms is

$$mkodd \sqsubseteq \text{while } is\text{-}even(x) \text{ do}$$
$$\text{pre } is\text{-}even(x) \wedge d = x \times y$$
$$\text{post } d = x \times y \wedge 0 \leq x < \overleftarrow{x}$$
$$\text{end}$$

and the body of the loop is given by

$$\text{pre } is\text{-}even(x) \wedge d = x \times y$$

$$x, y := x \div 2, y \times 2$$

$$\text{post } d = x \times y \wedge 0 \leq x < \overleftarrow{x}$$

and again the proof is fairly straightforward, but remember that as i is even, division by 2 is exact. The specification for *mkeven* is identical to the previous specification for *posmult-body* and can be satisfied by the code developed in the first version of this refinement (see page 211).

The various components can now be put together to give the final program:

```
mult (x, y: Z) : Z
(dcl r : Z;
if x ≥ 0 then
  skip
else
  x, y: = −x, −y
end;
r: = 0;
while x ≠ 0 do
  while is-even(x) do
    x, y: = x ÷ 2, y × 2
  end;
  x, r: = x − 1, r + y
end;
return r
) −− mult
```

12.3.2 Fast division

We now return to the division problem that was also tackled in the previous chapter. To provide some motivation for the problem the original specification stated that the computer on which this algorithm was to be implemented had no multiply or divide instructions. A further (unspoken) requirement might be that the algorithm should be as fast as possible. Is there any way in which we can improve the performance of the code to do division? The approaches to solving problems suggested so far have been to look at the post-condition for a problem and, if a loop is to be used, derive the invariant, guard and variant from this post-condition.

One possibility would be to follow the example of speeding up the multiplier problem which was to preserve the invariant of the loop body, but preserve it in a different way;

this approach is to be left as an exercise. Another way would be to rewrite the post-condition in an equivalent way, and from this derive a new invariant. This is what we shall do now. The original specification was

div

$\text{ext rd } a, b \; : \; \mathbf{Z}$
$\quad \text{wr } q \quad : \; \mathbf{Z}$
$\text{pre } 0 \le a \wedge 0 < b$
$\text{post } \exists r \in \mathbf{N} \cdot b \times q + r = a \wedge r < b$

From the post-condition, we can deduce that

$$b \times q \le a < b \times (q + 1)$$

One possibility for a reorganization of the post-condition is to use the above equation and to replace the $q + 1$ multiplier by a temporary variable u ('*upper bound*'). This gives the following:

$$b \times q \le a < b \times u \wedge u = q + 1$$

Worked example 12.3 Write down the guard and invariant for a loop to satisfy the specification for div.

SOLUTION

$\text{guard } u \ne q + 1$
$\text{inv} \quad b \times q \le a < b \times u$

■

Initial values will be given to q and u so that this invariant is trivially established, and the algorithm will squeeze q and u together until they finally differ by one. To establish the invariant all that is necessary is to set q to zero and u to $a + 1$. An initial guess for the initial value for u might be to set it to a, but it is not always true that

$$a < b \times a$$

For example, this is certainly not true if $b = 1$ but

$$a < b \times (a + 1)$$

is true provided $0 < b$, which it is. Squeezing q and u together suggests that the variant relation is

$$0 \le u - q < \overleftarrow{u} - \overleftarrow{q}$$

Putting this together suggests that the loop should be based on the following:

$\text{init} \quad q = 0 \wedge u = a + 1$
$\text{guard } u \ne q + 1$
$\text{inv} \quad b \times q \le a < b \times u$
$\text{var} \quad 0 \le u - q < \overleftarrow{u} - \overleftarrow{q}$

The body of the loop will squeeze the values of q and u together, and the quickest way of doing this will be to find the (approximate) mid-value, and set either q or u to this mid-value, depending on which of these assignments preserves the invariant. To find a value roughly halfway between q and u we can add q and u together and divide by 2 (by shifting right one place). Then we need to set q and u appropriately. An application of leading assignment and the conditional rules gives:

pre $u \neq q + 1 \wedge b \times q \leq a < b \times u$

```
    mid: = (q + u) ÷ 2;
    if b × mid ≤ a then
       q: = mid
    else
       u: = mid
    end
```

post $b \times q \leq a < b \times u \wedge 0 \leq u - q < \overleftarrow{u} - \overleftarrow{q}$

The final speeded-up code for this problem now looks like

```
q, u: = 0, a + 1;
while u ≠ q + 1 do
  mid: = (q + u) ÷ 2;
  if b × mid ≤ a then
    q: = mid
  else
    u: = mid
  end
end
```

Can this be improved on? Yes, further optimization can be achieved by using q and a displacement d from q instead of using q and u to bracket the value. Using this we get

$$d = u - q \quad \text{i.e.} \quad u = q + d$$

and the code to calculate the mid-point becomes

$$(q + u) \div 2 = \text{floor}\left(\frac{q + q + d}{2}\right) = q + d \div 2$$

With this substitution the new initialization, guard and invariant and variant relations are:

init $q = 0 \wedge d = a + 1$
guard $d \neq 1$
inv $b \times q \leq a < b \times (q + d)$
var $0 \leq d < \overleftarrow{d}$

The initialization code is fairly obvious, and the new body must arrange to preserve the invariant and establish the variant relation. With this change our new program is

```
q, d: = 0, a + 1
while d ≠ 1 do
  d: = d ÷ 2;
  if b × (q + d) ≤ a then
    q, d: = q + d, d + 1
  else
    skip
  end
end
```

By now the observant reader should notice that the multiplication operator has been used, which is an operation not allowed by the problem statement! Remember that there is a *mult* operation which was derived above, which worked using shift and addition. This could be used in place of the multiplication operation in the two versions of *div* given above. However, the multiplication is used in the test operation. Can the test be rewritten in such a way that the multiplication is unnecessary? Now the test can be written as

$$b \times q + b \times d \leq a$$

Two new temporary variables m and n will be introduced, defined as

$$m = b \times q$$
$$n = b \times d$$

The test is now just

$$m + n \leq a$$

and does not involve multiplication, but unfortunately all that has happened is that the multiplication has been moved to a different point in the program. Perhaps the temporary values m and n can be calculated as the algorithm proceeds, and this can be done without using any multiplication.

Since m and n are based on the current values of q and d, whenever these two variables are changed, m and n should be recalculated. The definitions of m and n can be added to the invariant:

$$\text{inv} \quad b \times q \leq a < b \times (q + d) \wedge m = b \times q \wedge n = b \times d$$

The changes that are necessary to m and n can be deduced by looking at the changes that are made to q and d. This can be done by replacing q and d in the definitions of m and n by their old values. It must always be true that

$$m = b \times q$$

therefore, when a change is made to q, a corresponding change must be made to m. The latest version of q is related to the previous, or old, value by

$$q = \overleftarrow{q} + d$$

Thus

$$m = (\overleftarrow{q} + d) \times b$$
$$= \overleftarrow{q} \times b + d \times b$$
$$= \overleftarrow{m} + n$$

So the new value of m is related to the old value of m and the new value of n, and already we have removed the multiplication from the expression that calculates the value of m. Thus if q changes, the new value of m is given by

$$m = \overleftarrow{m} + n$$

and if q does not change, then the value of m must remain unchanged:

$$m = \overleftarrow{m}$$

This derivation can be repeated for n:

$$n = b \times d$$
$$= b \times (\overleftarrow{d} \div 2)$$

In order to proceed further we must do something with the integer 'divide by 2' term. If the old value of $\overleftarrow{d}$ is even, the integer divide can be replaced by a normal divide:

$$
\begin{aligned}
b \times (\overleftarrow{d} \div 2) &= b \times \frac{\overleftarrow{d}}{2} \\
&= \frac{b \times \overleftarrow{d}}{2} \\
&= \frac{\overleftarrow{n}}{2} \\
&= \overleftarrow{n} \div 2
\end{aligned}
$$

The above uses the fact that if $\overleftarrow{d}$ is even, then so is $b \times \overleftarrow{d}$, which is equal to $\overleftarrow{n}$. If $\overleftarrow{d}$ is odd

$$
\begin{aligned}
b \times (\overleftarrow{d} \div 2) &= b \times \frac{\overleftarrow{d} - 1}{2} \\
&= \frac{b \times \overleftarrow{d} - b}{2} \\
&= \frac{\overleftarrow{n} - b}{2}
\end{aligned}
$$

Now $\overleftarrow{n} = b \times \overleftarrow{d}$ and remembering that $\overleftarrow{d}$ is assumed to be odd, then if b is odd, then $\overleftarrow{n}$ is odd and $\overleftarrow{n} - b$ is even; and if b is even, then $\overleftarrow{n}$ is even and $\overleftarrow{n} - b$ is even. Thus:

$$
\frac{\overleftarrow{n} - b}{2} = (\overleftarrow{n} - b) \div 2
$$

Thus

$$
n = \begin{cases}
\overleftarrow{n} \div 2, & \text{if } \overleftarrow{d} \text{ is even} \\
(\overleftarrow{n} - b) \div 2, & \text{if } \overleftarrow{d} \text{ is odd}
\end{cases}
$$

We have now expressed the new value of n in terms of the old value of n and the only operation used is a divide by 2, which can be implemented as a shift operation.

The original initialization to establish the invariant before the new terms were added was

$$
q, d := 0, a + 1
$$

So to establish the new invariant, it will be necessary to initialize n and m:

$$
q, d, m, n := 0, a + 1, 0, b \times (a + 1)
$$

There is still a multiplication to do but at least it is outside the loop. Can even this be replaced? The initialization is just required to set up the invariant; the multiplication is required to set up

$$
\dots \quad a < b \times (q + d) \wedge \quad \dots \quad \wedge n = b \times d
$$

so in fact any code that establishes this can be used. Since b is positive and as we set q to zero then we just need to set d so that $b \times d$ is greater than a. The multiplication can be replaced and the initialization changed to

$q, m := 0;$
$d, n := 1, b;$
while $n \leq a$ do $d, n := d \times 2, n \times 2$ end;

The initialization has a further advantage: the initial value of d is such that it is either 1 or it is even. Within the body of the loop d is always even, this fact can be used when calculating the new value of n. This now gives us our latest (and final) version of the program:

$q, m := 0;$
$d, n := 1, b;$
while $n \leq a$ do $d, n := d \times 2, n \times 2$ end;
while $d \neq 1$ do
  $d, n := d \div 2, n \div 2;$
  if $m + n \leq a$ then
    $q, m := q + d, m + n$
  else
    skip
  end
end

It is left for the reader to complete the derivation to obtain this result.

This problem is a subclass of the 'down' loop category, but perhaps it deserves a class of its own. If you look at the revised specification for this problem, what is happening is that a set is being searched for a value that satisfies a predicate. In the above example the set of integers is being searched for a value that is the result of dividing one number by another. The set that is to be searched is initially restricted by placing an upper and lower bound on it, and then reducing the size of the set to be searched as fast as possible, roughly halving the number of elements to be searched at each iteration. This approach can be used to solve many styles of problems, the trick being to identify the bounds and the set.

A further point—the sort of transformations that were carried out in this example are difficult to do if applied to code, but having a mathematical model available allows transformation experiments to be tried quickly and easily. It is usually much easier to reason in this way while the program is being written, rather than to try to do similar transformations on the final program.

12.3.3   A simple sort algorithm

Suppose a set S has an order defined on it by the relation '$<$', then a possible specification for *sort* is

sort

ext wr $t : S^*$

pre *true*

post $\forall i, j \in$ inds $t \cdot i \leq j \Rightarrow t(i) \leq t(j) \wedge \textit{is-perm}(\overleftarrow{t}, t)$

The function *is-perm* will not be defined, except that it does have the following properties:

- interchanging the *i*th and *j*th element gives a permutation:

  $is\text{-}perm(t, swop(t, i, j))$

- if *t* is a permutation of *s*, then *s* is a permutation of *t*:

  $is\text{-}perm(s, t) = is\text{-}perm(t, s)$

- if *t* is a permutation of *s*, and *u* is a permutation of *t*, then *u* is a permutation of *s*:

  $is\text{-}perm(s, t) \wedge is\text{-}perm(t, u) \Rightarrow is\text{-}perm(s, u)$

As the array will be sorted gradually, we are going to slowly add order to the structure. A predicate that allows a partly sorted array to be described might be useful:

> $is\text{-}ordered : S^* \times \mathbf{N} \times \mathbf{N} \rightarrow \mathbf{B}$
>
> $is\text{-}ordered(t, m, n) \quad \triangleq \quad \forall i, j \in \{m, \ldots, n\} \cdot i \leq j \Rightarrow t(i) \leq t(j)$
>
> pre $m, n \in$ inds t

and the specification can be rewritten in terms of this predicate, writing N for len t we get:

> *sort*
>
> ext wr t : S^*
>
> pre *true*
>
> post $is\text{-}ordered(t, 1, N) \wedge is\text{-}perm(\overleftarrow{t}, t)$

The first attempt Since we are introducing structure, a 'down' loop is indicated, and the recommended approach is to introduce a logical constant. There are at least two possibilities for the value of the logical constant—the initial value of the sequence to be sorted and the final value of the sequence after it has been sorted. Taking the first possibility we get

> *sort*
>
> ext wr t : S^*
>
>   lc c : S^*
>
> pre $c = t$
>
> post $is\text{-}ordered(t, 1, N) \wedge is\text{-}perm(c, t)$

A temporary variable can be introduced and the post-condition rewritten:

> $is\text{-}ordered(t, 1, p) \wedge p = N \wedge is\text{-}perm(c, t)$

This is a case where, even though we have a 'down' loop, a temporary variable is needed to keep track of how much more work there is still to do—the variable p such that everything to the left of p has been sorted (see Fig. 12.3).

> **Worked example 12.4** Derive the initialization, guard, invariant and variant for a loop that traverses the array.

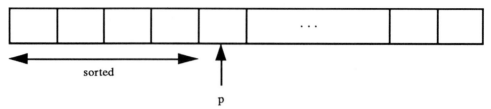

Figure 12.3 Sorting an array.

SOLUTION This is shown below:

   init $p = 1$
   guard $p \neq N$
   inv $\textit{is-ordered}(t, 1, p) \wedge \textit{is-perm}(c, t)$
   var $0 \leq N - p < N - \overleftarrow{p}$

                                                                                  ■

The first step for the derivation of the loop is

   $p := 1;$
   while $p \neq N$ do
     loop-body
     pre $p \neq N \wedge \textit{is-ordered}(t, 1, p) \wedge \textit{is-perm}(c, t)$
     post $\textit{is-ordered}(t, 1, p) \wedge \textit{is-perm}(c, t) \wedge 0 \leq N - p < N - \overleftarrow{p}$
   end

The loop body can be derived by first breaking the invariant to establish the variant relation; this can be done by increasing p by (at least) 1 and then re-establishing the invariant. Applying the forward assignment rule we get

   loop-body $\sqsubseteq$ $p := p + 1;$
              re-establish
             pre $p - 1 \neq N \wedge \textit{is-ordered}(t, 1, p - 1) \wedge \textit{is-perm}(c, t)$
             post $\textit{is-ordered}(t, 1, p) \wedge \textit{is-perm}(c, t) \wedge 0 \leq N - p < N - (\overleftarrow{p} - 1)$

After increasing p by 1, one of two things could happen: the new element indexed by p is in the right place with respect to the invariant and there is nothing to do, or the new element is not in the right place and there is some work to do to insert it into the correct place—this will need a loop. If *re-establish* does not change p we can see that the last term of the post-condition is established and the post-condition can be rewritten as

   post $\textit{is-ordered}(t, 1, p) \wedge \textit{is-perm}(c, t)$

The technique is as before: introduce a temporary and reorganize the post-condition to identify the invariant and guard. A first attempt at this is

   $\textit{is-ordered}(t, 1, q) \wedge \textit{is-ordered}(t, q, p) \wedge q = 1$

For this to work it is necessary to show that

   $\textit{is-ordered}(t, 1, q) \wedge \textit{is-ordered}(t, q, p) \Rightarrow \textit{is-ordered}(t, 1, p)$

which is fairly straightforward and is left as an exercise. Unfortunately it is difficult to do the intialization to establish the invariant—the initialization involves placing the element at p in its correct place, which is what we are trying to do. Another possible reorganization is

$$is\text{-}ordered(t, 1, q-1) \land is\text{-}ordered(t, q, p) \land (t(q-1) \leq t(q) \lor q = 1)$$

This will work as the invariant if the last two terms are deleted and (their negation) used as the guard. This invariant is easily established by setting $q = p$.

Worked example 12.5 Write down the initialization, guard, invariant and variant for the inner loop.

SOLUTION

```
init   q = p
guard  t(q − 1) > t(q) ∧ q ≠ 1
inv    is-ordered(t, 1, q − 1) ∧ is-ordered(t, q, p)
var    0 ≤ q < q⃖
```

∎

The code for the loop body can be derived using the usual strategy:

$q := q - 1$ $\quad -\!-$ break the invariant

Re-establish the invariant by swopping the qth and $(q + 1)$th element:

$swop(t, q, q + 1)$

This can be put together to give the final program:

```
p := 1;
while p < N do
  p := p + 1;
  q := p;
  while t(q − 1) > t(q) ∧ q ≠ 1 do
    q := q − 1;
    swop(t, q, q + 1)
  end
end
```

The other approach The second refinement of *sort* is obtained by setting the logical constant to the answer:

sort

ext wr t : S^*
    lc c : S^*

pre $is\text{-}ordered(c, 1, N) \land is\text{-}perm(c, t)$

post $c = t$

This can be rewritten by introducing a temporary variable as *sort*

ext wr t : S^*
i : $\mathbf{N}$
lc c : S^*

pre $is\text{-}ordered(c, 1, N) \wedge is\text{-}perm(c, t)$

post $c(1, \ldots, i) = t(1, \ldots, i) \wedge i = N$

and using the iteration rule this can be refined to

sort
ext wr t : S^*
i : $\mathbf{N}$
lc c : S^*
pre $c = is\text{-}ordered(c, 1, N) \wedge is\text{-}perm(c, t)$

    pre $c = is\text{-}ordered(c, 1, N) \wedge is\text{-}perm(c, t)$
    post $c(1, \ldots, i) = t(1, \ldots, i)$
    ;
    while $i \neq N$ **do**
      body
      pre $i \neq N \wedge c(1, \ldots, i) = t(1, \ldots, i)$
      post $c(1, \ldots, i) = t(1, \ldots, i) \wedge 0 \leq N - i < N - \overleftarrow{i}$
    end
post $c(1, \ldots, i) = t(1, \ldots, i) \wedge i = N$

which is easily shown to be correct. The next step is to refine the body of the loop; we will increase i by 1 to establish the variant and apply the initial assignment rule and strengthen the post-condition with $i = \overleftarrow{i}$ to produce

    body $\sqsubseteq$ $i := i + 1$;
      mini-sort
      ext wr t : S^*
        rd i : $\mathbf{N}$
        lc c : S^*
      pre $c(1, \ldots, i - 1) = t(1, \ldots, i - 1)$
      post $c(1, \ldots, i) = t(1, \ldots, i)$

The operation *mini-sort* can be refined using a semicolon rule to obtain

$mini\text{-}sort \sqsubseteq findmin$
     ext rd t : S^*
      i : $\mathbf{N}$
     wr j : $\mathbf{N}$
     lc c : S^*
     pre $c(1, \ldots, i-1) = t(1, \ldots, i-1)$
     post $\forall m \in \{i, \ldots, N\} \cdot t(j) \le t(m) \wedge c(1, \ldots, i-1) = t(1, \ldots, i-1)$
     ;
     $swop$
     ext wr t : S^*
      rd i, j : $\mathbf{N}$
      lc c : S^*
     pre $\forall m \in \{i, \ldots, N\} \cdot t(j) \le t(m) \wedge c(1, \ldots, i-1) = t(1, \ldots, i-1)$

      $swop(t, i, j)$

     post $c(1, \ldots, i) = t(1, \ldots, i)$

The post-condition of *findmin* can be rewritten as

$$\forall m \in \{i, \ldots, n\} \cdot t(j) \le t(m) \wedge n = N \wedge c(1, \ldots, i-1) = t(1, \ldots, i-1)$$

and the operation can be refined thus:

$findmin \sqsubseteq$
ext rd t : S^*
  i : $\mathbf{N}$
 wr j, n : $\mathbf{N}$
 lc c : S^*
pre $c(1, \ldots, i-1) = t(1, \ldots, i-1)$

   $n, j := i$

post $\forall m \in \{i, \ldots, n\} \cdot t(j) \le t(m) \wedge c(1, \ldots, i-1) = t(1, \ldots, i-1)$
;
while $n \ne N$ do
 findmin-body
 ext rd t : S^*
  i : $\mathbf{N}$
  wr j, n : $\mathbf{N}$
  lc c : S^*
 pre $n \ne N \wedge \forall m \in \{i, \ldots, n\} \cdot t(j) \le t(m) \wedge c(1, \ldots, i-1) = t(1, \ldots, i-1)$
 post $\forall m \in \{i, \ldots, n\} \cdot t(j) \le t(m) \wedge c(1, \ldots, i-1) = t(1, \ldots, i-1) \wedge$
  $0 \le N - n \le N - \overleftarrow{n}$
end

The next step is to refine *findmin-body* using the standard strategy of establishing the variant first and use the leading assignment rule to see what this suggests for the remainder of the body of the loop:

$findmin\text{-}body \sqsubseteq$
$n := n + 1;$
$choice$

ext rd n
   wr j
pre $\forall m \in \{i, \ldots, n - 1\} \cdot t(j) \leq t(m) \wedge c(1, \ldots, i - 1) = t(1, \ldots, i - 1)$
post $\forall m \in \{i, \ldots, n\} \cdot t(j) \leq t(m) \wedge c(1, \ldots, i - 1) = t(1, \ldots, i - 1)$

Use of the alternative rule solves *choice*:

$choice \sqsubseteq$
if $t(j) \leq t(n)$ then
   ext rd n
      wr j
   pre $\forall m \in \{i, \ldots, n - 1\} \cdot t(j) \leq t(m) \wedge c(1, \ldots, i - 1) = t(1, \ldots, i - 1) \wedge$
      $t(j) \leq t(n)$
   post $\forall m \in \{i, \ldots, n\} \cdot t(j) \leq t(m) \wedge c(1, \ldots, i - 1) = t(1, \ldots, i - 1)$
else
   ext rd n
      wr j
   pre $\forall m \in \{i, \ldots, n - 1\} \cdot t(j) \leq t(m) \wedge c(1, \ldots, i - 1) = t(1, \ldots, i - 1) \wedge$
      $t(j) > t(n)$
   post $\forall m \in \{i, \ldots, n\} \cdot t(j) \leq t(m) \wedge c(1, \ldots, i - 1) = t(1, \ldots, i - 1)$
end

The body of the two legs of the conditional command is obvious, and everything can be put together to give the final program:

$i := 0;$
while $i \neq N$ do
   $i := i + 1;$
   $n, j := i;$
   while $n \neq N$ do
      $n := n + 1;$
      if $t(j) \leq t(n)$ then
         skip
      else
         $j := n$
      end
   end;
   $swop(a, i, j)$
end

When the rules and techniques are understood, it is fairly easy to develop a style that makes the derivation of a program from a specification reasonably straightforward.

12.3.4   A search problem

Finally we will look at a standard problem, that of searching in a table for a value, and if the value is in the table then to return the position of the value in the table. First we need a model of a table:

$$Table = \{1, \ldots, N\} \xrightarrow{m} Data$$

inv t $\triangleq$ *is-ordered-table*$(t, 1, N)$

$$Data \; :: \; key \; : \; Keys$$
$$\ldots : \ldots$$

state *Search* of
      table : *Table*
end

The keys have an order defined on them, and the entries in the table are sorted according to this order. The specification of the problem is

find-entry (*target*: *Key*) m: $\mathbb{N}$

ext rd *table* : *Table*

post $m \in \{1, \ldots, N\} \wedge table(m).key = target \vee$
      $target \notin \{entry.key \mid entry \in$ elems $table\}$

The strategy to be used is the one outlined in the integer division problem. Since the keys are ordered, we will use a binary search algorithm to scan the table. We will also introduce a logical constant to help with the solution. (It should be noted that the approach described below was discovered after trying a development that did not use a logical constant—the logical constant was introduced to solve the problem of the last entry in the table.)

The first step is to introduce an operation with a body, and to also introduce the logical constant. This should, perhaps, be done in two steps, but with practice two or more small steps can be combined into one.

find-entry (*target*: *Key*) : $\mathbb{N}$

(dcl m : $\mathbb{N}$;

find-body
ext rd *table*: *Table*
    lc t: *Table*
pre $t = table \cup \{0 \mapsto mk\text{-}Data(-\infty, \ldots)\}$
             $\cup \{N + 1 \mapsto mk\text{-}Data(+\infty, \ldots)\}$
post $m \in \{1, \ldots, N\} \wedge t(m).key = target \vee$
     $target \notin \{entry.key \mid entry \in$ elems $t\}$
;
return m
) $--$ *find-entry*

where the types *Data* and *Key* have been extended in an obvious way.

The post-condition of *find-body* can be rewritten:

post $m, n \in \{0, \ldots, N + 1\} \wedge t(m).key \leq target < t(n).key \wedge m + 1 = n$

Worked example 12.6 Derive a loop from the specification directly above.

SOLUTION

$m, n := 0, N + 1;$
while $m + 1 \neq n$ do
  body
  ext wr m, n : $\mathbb{N}$
    rd *target* : *Key*
    lc t : *Table*
  pre $m + 1 \neq n \wedge t(m).key \leq target < t(n).key$
  post $t(m).key \leq target < t(n).key \wedge 0 \leq n - m < \overleftarrow{n} - \overleftarrow{m}$
end

■

In fact the answer to the worked example has established a stronger post-condition; the entry (if it is to be inserted) would go between m and n.

To refine the loop body the strategy will be to find a new value, *mid*, between m and n such that either

$$t(m).key \leq target < t(mid).key$$

or

$$t(mid).key \leq target < t(n).key$$

If the first case occurs then we will set n equal to *mid*, and in the second case m equal to *mid*—in either case the invariant will be preserved.

Worked example 12.7 Show how you would split the specification.

SOLUTION This is shown below

$body \sqsubseteq calc\text{-}mid$
    ext wr *mid* : $\mathbb{N}$
      rd m, n : $\mathbb{N}$
      target : *Key*
      lc t : *Table*
    pre $m + 1 \neq n \wedge t(m).key \leq target < t(n).key$
    post $m \leq mid \leq n \wedge t(m).key \leq target < t(n).key$
    ;
    update-limits
    ext rd *mid*   : $\mathbb{N}$
      wr m, n : $\mathbb{N}$
      rd *target* : *Key*
      lc t : *Table*
    pre $m \leq mid \leq n \wedge t(m).key \leq target < t(n).key$
    post $t(m).key \leq target < t(n).key \wedge 0 \leq n - m < \overleftarrow{n} - \overleftarrow{m}$

■

Note that the second operation can be refined using alternation:

$update\text{-}limits$ $\sqsubseteq$ if $t(mid).key \le target$ then
  ext rd mid
  wr m, n
  rd $target$
  lc t
  pre $t(mid).key \le target \land m \le mid \le n$
  post $t(m).key \le target < t(n).key \land 0 \le n - m < \overleftarrow{n} - \overleftarrow{m}$
else
  ext rd mid
  wr m, n
  rd $target$
  lc t
  pre $target < t(mid).key \land m \le mid \le n$
  post $t(m).key \le target < t(n).key \land 0 \le n - m < \overleftarrow{n} - \overleftarrow{m}$
end

$\sqsubseteq$ if $t(mid).key \le target$ then
  $m := mid$
else
  $n := mid$
end

A trivial check shows that these two refinement steps are correct. We now need to satisfy

$calc\text{-}mid$

ext wr mid : **N**
  rd m, n : **N**
  $target$: Key
  lc t : $Table$

pre $m + 1 \ne n \land t(m).key \le target < t(n).key$

post $m \le mid \le n \land t(m).key \le target < t(n).key$

A simple solution to this is to just choose the middle value between m and n, so

$calc\text{-}mid \sqsubseteq mid := (m + n) \div 2$

The final code is thus

$m, n := 0, N + 1$;
while $m + 1 \ne n$ do
  $mid := (m + n) \div 2$
  if $t(mid).key \le target$ then
    $m := mid$
  else
    $n := mid$
  end
end

which is correct except that it contains a logical constant! However, all is not lost. Now from the guard and the relation we can deduce that

$$
\begin{aligned}
m + 1 < n &\Rightarrow m < n - 1 \\
&\Rightarrow 2 \times m < m + n - 1 \\
&\Rightarrow m < (m + n - 1)/2 \le \text{floor}((m + n)/2) \\
&\Rightarrow m < (m + n) \div 2 \\
&\Rightarrow m < mid
\end{aligned}
$$

Similarly we can show

$$m < n \Rightarrow m + n < 2 \times n$$
$$\Rightarrow (m + n)/2 < n$$
$$\Rightarrow \text{floor}((m + n)/2) \leq (m + n)/2 < n$$
$$\Rightarrow (m + n) \div 2 < n$$
$$\Rightarrow mid < n$$

Now m is always increased and n is always decreased; thus

$$0 \leq m < mid < n \leq N + 1$$

and when the logical constant version of the table is indexed, it is aways mid that is used and the extra entries on the ends of the logical constant are never accessed. Thus we can replace the logical constant by the table everywhere in the program to get the final version:

```
find-entry (target: Key) : N
(dcl m, n : N;
  m, n := 0, N + 1;
  while m + 1 ≠ n do
    mid := (m + n) ÷ 2;
    if table(mid).key ≤ target then
      m := mid
    else
      n := mid
    end
  end;
  return m
) -- find-entry
```

and this completes the development and proof of search.

Exercise 12.1

1. Prove

$$is\text{-}ordered(t, 1, q) \wedge is\text{-}ordered(t, q, p) \Rightarrow is\text{-}ordered(t, 1, p)$$

2. Suppose $t \in \mathbb{Z}^+$ and $\text{len } t = N$. Develop a program to satisfy the following specification:

   $$sum()$$
   $$\text{ext rd } t : \mathbb{Z}^+$$
   $$\text{wr } s : \mathbb{Z}$$
   $$\text{post } s = \sum_{i=1}^{N} t(i)$$

3. Using the same sequence as in question 2 above, develop a program to satisfy the following specification of a function:

   $$max(t : \mathbb{Z}^+) r : \mathbb{N}$$
   $$\text{post } \forall i \in \{1, \ldots, N\} \cdot t(r) \geq t(i)$$

4. Derive a fast integer mod function (as in Pascal) that only uses addition, subtraction, shift left and shift right (multiplication and division by 2).

5. Specify and develop a program to find $\text{floor}(\sqrt{n})$ for $n \in \mathbb{N}$ with the same restrictions as question 4.

6. Make your solution to question 5 as fast as possible.
7. Specify and develop a fast function that finds the GCD (greatest common divisor) of two numbers.

12.4 POSTSCRIPT—AVOIDING LOGICAL CONSTANTS

If the invariant of a loop contains a logical constant, it can be removed. An invariant of the form

f(current state) $=$ logical constant ($=$ some function of the initial state)

To remove the logical constant, we proceed as follows. The result of the loop is constant for any particular iteration of the loop, and as the end value of a loop iteration is equal to the start value for the next iteration, we know that

f(state at start of loop body) $= f$(state at end of loop body)

Therefore

$$f(\overleftarrow{state}) = f(state)$$

The logical constant has now been eliminated, at the price of introducing a previous value of the state. This expression is no longer suitable for use as an invariant, but fortunately it is suitable for use as part of the variant. It should be noted that a predicate derived in this way is transitive:

$$f(state_0) = f(state_1) = \text{ a constant}$$
$$f(state_1) = f(state_2) = \text{ a constant}$$

Therefore

$$f(state_0) = f(state_2)$$

All that is necessary to do is to add a 'less than' term so that the relation that is produced is a well-formed order relation. The invariant term in this case is usually some sort of data invariant that defines the set that the guard and variant are defined over.

12.5 SUMMARY

The ideas behind decomposition are twofold. The first is to allow the separate development of the various components of a computer program. The second is to develop a proof of correctness hand in hand with the development of the code. Both of these requirements can be satisfied by a single development technique.

The most difficult refinement step is the introduction of a loop, but finding the four terms for deriving a loop is usually very straightforward. The two cases to look for are an 'up' loop, or a 'down' loop. In the first case the answer is to be built up in temporaries and in the second case either a data structure exists or is being built up. If it is a 'down' loop, then it is usually best to introduce a logical constant that contains either the answer or some initial configuration that can be used to measure progress. In both cases the strategy is to reorganize the post-condition and then look for terms that will serve as an invariant and a guard. The invariant will either summarize the work done ('up' loop) or the work to be done ('down' loop). In the latter case the answer is needed to measure the work to be done—hence the need for a logical constant that contains the answer. The initialization is usually obvious; finally it is necessary to find some integer expression over the state that is never negative and is strictly decreasing—this will show termination.

DATA REFINEMENT

AIMS

- To show how a specification can be developed into code.
- To show how design decisions can be made.
- To show the use of invariants in development.
- To illustrate how specifications using abstraction can be transformed.

13.1 INTRODUCTION

In the previous two chapters we have tackled the problem of converting specifications into code; in this chapter we will look at the other problem associated with developing executable programs—that of implementing the abstract data structures of the specification in terms of data structures available in a favourite programming language. This process is called *data refinement*.

13.2 THE CASH DISPENSER PROBLEM

13.2.1 The problem

To illustrate some of the ideas we will return to the cash dispenser problem considered earlier, but will simplify the implementation so as not to overwhelm the reader with detail. The specification will be changed slightly by adding an upper limit to the number of customers that can be handled by the system (denoted by N) and reducing the amount of information stored.

The upper limit to the number of customers may seem an artificial constraint, but consider a real-life implementation in a microcomputer. If the customer file is to be held in some local store, there will be an upper limit on the number of customers which is dictated by the size of the store, so in fact the restriction is a realistic one. The size of the local store can be thought of as a parameter that can be changed at system generation time to fit in with the amount of storage space available on the microcomputer.

The information stored about each customer is their PIN and the amount of money they have withdrawn today. The bank has a rule that no customer can withdraw more than MAX per day. A possible state for the system is values

$N, MAX : \mathbf{N}$

types

$Customers = CardId \xrightarrow{m} Customer$

$Customer ::$ pin : PIN
             $today$: $\mathbf{N}$

state *Customer-file* of
     $file$: $Customers$
     $cust$: $[CardId]$
inv $mk\text{-}Customer(file, cust)$ $\triangleq$
    card dom $file \leq N \wedge$
    $(cust = \text{nil} \vee cust \in \text{dom } file)$
end

The operations on the new system are an operation to check that the card is known:

$is\text{-}valid\text{-}card \ (card\text{-}no : CardId) \ r : \mathbf{B}$

ext rd *file* : $Customers$

post $r \Leftrightarrow card\text{-}no \in \text{dom } file$

Worked example 13.1 Write down the specification of an operation to set the card identifier for the current transaction.

SOLUTION This is shown below:

$set\text{-}card \ (card\text{-}no : CardId)$

ext rd *file*   : $Customers$
     wr *cust*   : $[CardId]$

pre $card\text{-}no \in \text{dom } file$

post $cust = card\text{-}no$

■

The operation to check that the PIN is valid is

$is\text{-}valid\text{-}pin \ (code : PIN) \ r : \mathbf{B}$

ext rd *file* : $Customers$
     cust   : $[CardId]$

pre $cust \in \text{dom } file$

post $r \Leftrightarrow file(cust).pin = code$

The operation to check that the customer has not exceeded the daily limit:

$is\text{-}valid\text{-}amount \ (amount : \mathbf{N}) \ r : \mathbf{B}$

ext rd *file* : $Customers$
     cust   : $[CardId]$

pre $cust \in \text{dom } file$

post $r \Leftrightarrow file(cust).today + amount \leq MAX$

The operation to update the customer file to record the transaction:

> $update\text{-}customer\text{-}file\ (amount: \mathbb{N})$
>
> **ext wr** $file$: $Customers$
> $\phantom{\text{ext }}$ **rd** $cust$: $[CardId]$
>
> **pre** $cust \in \mathsf{dom}\ file$
>
> **post** $file = \overleftarrow{file} \dagger \{cust \mapsto \mu(\overleftarrow{file}(cust), today \mapsto \overleftarrow{file}(cust).today + amount)\}$

Worked example 13.2 Write down the specification of an operation to add a new customer.

SOLUTION

> $add\text{-}card\ (card\text{-}no: CardId, code: PIN)$
>
> **ext wr** $file$: $Customers$
>
> **pre** $card\text{-}no \notin \mathsf{dom}\ file \wedge \mathsf{card}\ \mathsf{dom}\ file < N$
>
> **post** $file = \overleftarrow{file} \dagger \{card\text{-}no \mapsto mk\text{-}Customer(code, 0)\}$

■

The operation to remove a customer is

> $delete\text{-}card\ (card\text{-}no: CardId)$
>
> **ext wr** $file$: $Customers$
> $\phantom{\text{ext }}$ **rd** $cust$: $[CardId]$
>
> **pre** $cust = \mathsf{nil}$
>
> **post** $file = \{card\text{-}no\} \lhd \overleftarrow{file}$

We now have a specification for the customer file and the functions to access that customer file. How can we implement the abstract data, i.e. how can the file be represented using the data types of a programming language such as Pascal? A possible implementation would be a lookup table using the card identifier (read from the magnetic card stripe) as the key. Each entry in the table would record information about the card identifier number, the amount of money the customer has withdrawn today and the PIN, so that this could be checked when the customer types it in (see Fig. 13.1). Given this representation, the operations to support a particular transaction would be to first search the table using the card identifier to find the entry for that bank customer, and, as the transaction proceeded, the details for that customer could be checked and updated as necessary.

We have a formal definition for each of the operations. Can we rewrite these definitions so as to describe the operations on the new table representation? This will be done in two stages: the first stage is to define a new state in terms of the implementation data structures. We will still use the specification language to do this but will use data representations that are less abstract and in some sense more 'implementable' than those in the specification. Having done this, the operations will be redefined in terms of the new representation. It will be necessary to show that this new specification is in some sense equivalent to the old one. This will be done by showing that the new, less abstract, state contains at least as much information as the old one. The new state will probably contain more information than the original one, but this information is about implementation—it

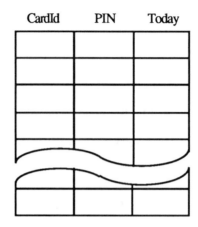

Figure 13.1 Table of customer information.

is extra information to aid performance and to enable an implementation to be built. Also the new operations should be related to the old—the new operations should change the information content of the state in the same way as the old ones.

The first step is to relate the new representation to the old. It is unlikely that a single state in the refinement represents two or more states in the specification, for if it did it means that two specification states would merge into one implementation state and it is highly probable that information would be lost. On the other hand, it is possible for two or more refinement states to represent the same specification state. In our cash dispenser given above, the mapping that records information about customers is represented by a table of customers. For a particular set of N customers, there would be $N!$ possible ways of storing the entries in the table, providing there were no duplicates.

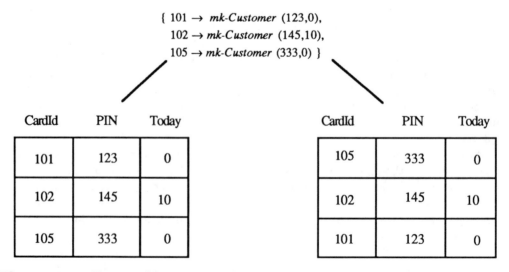

Figure 13.2 Two possible representations of a map.

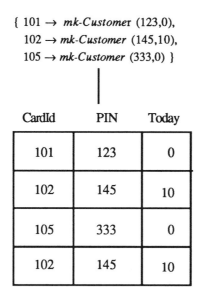

{ 101 → *mk-Customer* (123,0),
  102 → *mk-Customer* (145,10),
  105 → *mk-Customer* (333,0) }

CardId	PIN	Today
101	123	0
102	145	10
105	333	0
102	145	10

Figure 13.3   Another representation, with duplicates allowed.

But as repetition of elements is both allowed and meaningful in sequences (used to model tables), there is an infinite number of ways of storing information in a table that allows duplicate entries to represent a particular mapping—such a representation is rather generous. This freedom can be restricted by introducing a data invariant: the number of possible elements is restricted by requiring that the elements in a sequence are unique, for example there are only six possibilities for representing the mapping containing three elements (see Fig. 13.4). An alternative would be to ask that the names in the sequence be both unique and in an order dictated by the card identifiers. In this case there is only one representative sequence for each possible mapping.

{ 101 → *mk-Customer* (123,0),
  102 → *mk-Customer* (145,10),
  105 → *mk-Customer* (333,0) }

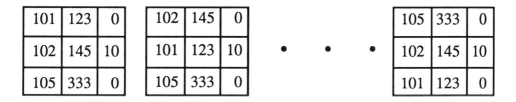

Figure 13.4   Modelling a map with no duplicates.

The next step is to relate the representation to the original abstract model. The fact that more than one implementation state can represent a single specification state suggests using a function to relate the two representations, since functions are allowed to be many to one. The function is called the retrieve function since it 'retrieves' one representation from another.

$$retr : Concrete\text{-}representation \rightarrow Abstract\text{-}representation$$

$$retr(cr) \quad \underline{\Delta} \quad \ldots$$

Having chosen a way of representing a mapping by a sequence, it is also necessary to show that the model is adequate, in the sense that every mapping that can occur in the original specification can be represented by a table (sequence) that satisfies the data invariant (Fig. 13.5).

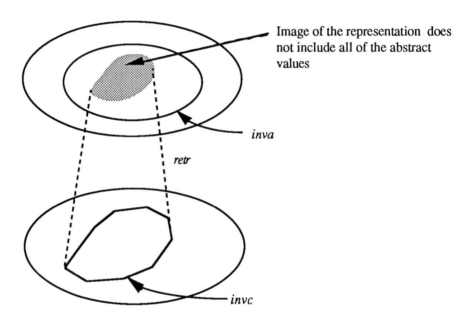

Figure 13.5   Adequacy—a problem in the domain of the retrieve function.

Having an adequate representation and a retrieve function is still not enough. There are other problems: the representation must not be too big ('too adequate'): it should not include values that do not occur in the specification (Fig. 13.6). For example, when representing a date, it is not necessary to be able to represent 30 February or the 32 December.

These two requirements can be satisfied if the retrieve function is a function from the representation onto the abstraction. This means that the retrieve function is total on the representation and the range of the function is everything in the original representation.

Stating that the retrieve function is total on the representation (restricted by the invariant) is just saying that it must really be a function defined over the representation. If the retrieve function is not total over the representation set, it means that there are extra elements in the representation that can be thrown out as they are not representing anything in the original specification.

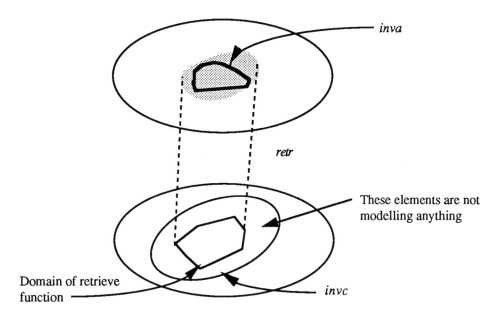

Figure 13.6   Totality—a problem in the domain of the retrieve function.

We also need to check that the range of the function is the original state including the invariant; otherwise we are again modelling things that are not allowed. If this restriction is satisfied then the representation is said to be adequate—every possible abstract state is modelled. What happens if we can not show adequacy? This could mean that our representation is too small; it can be made larger by loosening the invariant on the representation to include elements that might model abstract states that were left out. We can write down a proof rule, or logical statement, that describes adequacy:

$$\forall a \in Abs \cdot \exists s \in Con \cdot retr(s) = a$$

If the retrieve function is total and onto, we then know that all the values occurring in the representation are modelling values that could occur in the specification. The onto requirement means that every element in the abstraction has at least one element in the representation.

Returning to the example, the simplest concrete state and retrieve function is

    types

$Customers_1 = Customer_1^*$

$$Customer_1 :: \quad card \; : \; CardId$$
$$pin \; : \; PIN$$
$$today \; : \; \mathbf{N}$$

    state $Customer\text{-}file_1$ of
          $file \; : \; Customers_1$
          $cust \; : \; [\{1, \ldots, N\}]$
    inv ...
    end

We have left the invariant for the reader.

> **Worked example 13.3** Try to write down the retrieve function for the cash dipenser problem which relates the abstract customer file and the concrete customer file.

SOLUTION This is shown below:

$$retr\text{-}cust : Customer\text{-}file_1 \rightarrow Customer\text{-}file$$

$$retr\text{-}cust(mk\text{-}Customer\text{-}file_1(cf, cu)) \quad \triangleq$$
$$\quad \text{let } cust = \text{if } cu = \text{nil then nil else } cf(cu).card \text{ in}$$
$$\quad mk\text{-}Customer\text{-}file(\{c.card \mapsto mk\text{-}Customer\text{-}file(c.pin, c.today) \mid c \in \text{elems } cf\},$$
$$\quad\quad cust)$$

∎

Notice that the retrieve function throws away implementation detail, the implementation detail being the order in which the information is stored in the sequence.

This representation describes the fact that there is no ordering to the entries in the table and even repetitions are allowed. A customer could occur once, twice or even more times. An implementation based on this representation could have a particularly easy implementation for adding a new customer; it just puts the new entry representing the customer at the end of the list. This would present a problem of introducing inconsistencies, and it may be prudent to scan the whole table to check consistency before adding any new entry—which then suggests the question: why add it if it is already there (but we will ignore this for the moment)? With this implementation strategy the operations *is-valid-pin* and *delete-card* are both time consuming; this does not matter too much. This is not a particularly good implementation.

The first thing we could do to tighten things up is to improve the consistency of the file by disallowing duplicates. This would mean that the representation would be as follows:

$$\text{state } Customer\text{-}file_1 \text{ of}$$
$$\quad file \ : \ Customers_1$$
$$\quad cust \ : \ [\{1, \dots, N\}]$$
$$\text{inv } mk\text{-}Customer\text{-}file_1(file, cust) \quad \triangleq$$
$$\quad \text{len } file = \text{card } \{entry.card \mid entry \in \text{elems } file\} \land$$
$$\quad \text{len } file \leq N \land$$
$$\quad (cust = \text{nil} \lor cust \in \text{inds } file)$$
$$\text{end}$$

Now we have solved the consistency problem. The performance of the operation to add a new customer has decreased somewhat. We must check that a customer entry is not in the table before adding it and we have made some improvements to the operation to remove a customer—it need only find the first occurrence of a customer and delete that; it does not have to search the whole table to delete possible duplicate occurrences. Even in this simple example various trade-offs are appearing.

The third change is to demand that the entries in the sequence are held in order—preferably ordered by the card identifier. This would give the following representation:

state $Customer\text{-}file_1$ of
      $file$: $Customers_1$
      $cust$: $[\{1, \ldots, N\}]$
inv $mk\text{-}Customer\text{-}file_1(file, cust)$ $\triangleq$
    $is\text{-}ordered(file) \wedge$
    $\mathsf{len}\, file \leq N \wedge$
    $(cust = \mathsf{nil} \vee cust \in \mathsf{inds}\, file)$
end

$is\text{-}ordered : Customers_1 \rightarrow \mathbf{B}$

$is\text{-}ordered(file)$ $\triangleq$
    $\forall i, j \in \mathsf{inds}\, file \cdot i < j \ \Rightarrow \ file(i).card < file(j).card$

Now we have improved the performance of searching for a customer's entry and a binary search algorithm can be used so that on average it takes $N \log_2 N$ operations to look up a particular entry. The operations to add a new customer and delete a customer are more difficult, as in this implementation it will involve shuffling customer entries up and down in the table; however, this is a small price to pay since the *is-valid-pin* operation is probably the most important one.

The fourth possibility is to demand that the customer entries in the sequence are sorted, but to allow duplicates. This is a correct but rather strange implementation so it will not be discussed any further.

The implementation has in this example involved two things: choosing a representation and choosing an invariant on that representation. In most data refinements we will see this pattern emerging, choose a representation and choose an invariant on that representation, both together giving us the performance trade-offs we require to produce a good implementation of the original system. Implementing an abstract data representation involves adding extra information (such as order) which will aid the implementation. The retrieve function throws this extra information away when it relates the representation to the abstraction. The invariant on the representation makes the extra information consistent.

It should be noted that the first simple refinement of the customer file was to a sequence. The next step would be, perhaps, from a sequence to an array. The question is: why not go directly to an array? For this simple example there is probably no reason, but for a bigger system we do not want to add too much implementation detail at one time; in fact we are modelling the step-wise refinement aspects of developing a computer program, with a little bit of detail added at a time.

Data refinement is about implementation and implementation is about design, so before tackling a design for our cash dispenser we should know something about the environment. For the dispenser, suppose we are told the following: there is enough storage to keep a file of customers in active store, adding and deleting a card do not happen very often, accessing a file during a transaction should be fast. This information suggests that a good implementation would be to use an array representation for the table with the entities ordered by a card identifier, so some sort of fast lookup could be used. We will carry out a two stage development, this being the data equivalent of stepwise refinement—add detail, but not in one big chunk. The detail to be added is the implementation; this suggests that our state for the first data refinement is that the customer file should be a sequence of customer records, each customer record containing information about a customer including the card identifier.

We also need a pointer into this sequence which is modelling the current customer who is carrying out a transaction. This is so that we do not have to keep searching the array every time we want to do something to the customer details during a transaction. The invariant will contain information about our implementation decisions, the fact that the file is ordered, its length will be less than, or equal to, the total number of customers and whether the pointer is either empty or is a valid index into our sequence. The retrieve function must relate our representation to our original specification, and in fact the retrieve function will turn the sequence of customer records into a mapping in the obvious way. Before proceeding we must show that this retrieve function is total and it may be necessary to tighten the invariant on the representation to achieve this; the range must be the original state, i.e. the invariant should be satisfied; and, finally, there should be at least representation for each abstract object. That the first two are satisfied can be seen by inspection; we should prove that there is at least one representation for each abstract object:

values

$N, MAX : \mathbf{N}$

types

$Customers_1 = Customer_1^*$

$Customer_1 ::$ $card$: $CardId$
          pin : PIN
       $today$: $\mathbf{N}$

state $Customer\text{-}file_1$ of
    $file$: $Customers_1$
    $cust$: $[\{1, \ldots, N\}]$
inv $mk\text{-}Customer\text{-}file(file, cust)$ $\triangle$
    $is\text{-}ordered(file) \land$
    $\text{len } file \le N \land$
    $(cust = \text{nil} \lor cust \in \text{inds } file)$
end

$retr\text{-}cust : Customer\text{-}file_1 \to Customer\text{-}file$

$retr\text{-}cust(mk\text{-}Customer\text{-}file_1(cf, cu))$ $\triangle$
    let $cust = \text{if } cu = \text{nil then nil else } cf(cust).card$ in
    $mk\text{-}Customer\text{-}file(\{c.card \mapsto mk\text{-}Customer(c.pin, c.today) \mid c \in \text{elems } cf\},$
        $cust)$

To prove this, it is necessary to show

$$\forall a \in Abs \cdot \exists c \in Con \cdot retr(c) = a$$

and we shall do this by showing, given an a, how to construct a c. First, define a function that, given a member of the abstract state, will construct an element of the concrete state that represents it:

$con : Customers \rightarrow Customers_1$

$con(mk\text{-}Customer\text{-}file(file, cust)) \quad \triangleq$
    let $file_1 = to\text{-}seq(file)$ in
    let $cust_1 =$ if $cust =$ nil
                then nil
                else let $i \in$ inds $file_1$ be st $file_1(i).card = cust$ in i
        in
    $mk\text{-}Customerfile_1(file_1, cust_1)$

The auxiliary function *to-seq* needs to be defined:

$to\text{-}seq : Customer \rightarrow Customer_1$

$to\text{-}seq(s) \quad \triangleq$
    if $s = \{\,\}$
    then $[\,]$
    else let $id = mins(\text{dom } s)$ in
        $[mk\text{-}Customer_1(id, s(id).pin, s(id).today)] \frown to\text{-}seq(\{id\} \triangleleft s)$

The final step in the proof is to show

$retr\text{-}cust(con(s)) = s$

which solves the problem, for given any $s \in Customer\text{-}file$, we can apply the function *con* to give $con(s) \in Customer\text{-}file_1$ which is such that $retr\text{-}cust(con(s)) = s$. The proof of $retr\text{-}cust(con(s)) = s$ is fairly long, and will be left for the reader, but by construction can be seen to be correct. In fact this is the normal approach to proving adequacy. Show how to construct an element in the representation that corresponds to an element in the abstract specification.

The next step is to redefine the operations in terms of the new representation. Each of the operations are reasonably straightforward. The first checks that the card is known to the system:

$is\text{-}valid\text{-}card_1 \; (card\text{-}no: CardId) \; r: \mathbf{B}$

ext rd $file : Customers_1$

post $r \Leftrightarrow \exists! \, i \in$ inds $file \cdot file(i).card = card\text{-}no$

Worked example 13.4 Write down a specification for the operation that sets the card identifier for the transaction.

SOLUTION

$set\text{-}card_1 \; (card\text{-}no: CardId)$

ext rd $file \quad : Customers_1$
    wr $cust \; : \; [\{1, \ldots, N\}]$

pre $\exists! \, i \in$ inds $file \cdot file(i).card = card\text{-}no$

post $file(cust).card = card\text{-}no$

■

Check that the PIN is valid:

$is\text{-}valid\text{-}pin_1$ $(code\text{:}\,PIN)$ $r\text{:}\,\mathbf{B}$
ext rd $file$: $Customers_1$
    $cust$: $[\{1,\ldots,N\}]$
pre $cust \in$ inds $file$
post $r \Leftrightarrow file(cust).pin = code$

Check that the customer has not exceeded the daily limit:

$is\text{-}valid\text{-}amount_1$ $(amount\text{:}\,\mathbf{N})$ $r\text{:}\,\mathbf{B}$
ext rd $file$: $Customers_1$
    $cust$: $[\{1,\ldots,N\}]$
pre $cust \in$ inds $file$
post $r \Leftrightarrow file(cust).today + amount \leq MAX$

The customer file is updated to record the transaction:

$update\text{-}customer\text{-}file_1$ $(amount\text{:}\,\mathbf{N})$
ext wr $file$: $Customers_1$
   rd $cust$: $[\{1,\ldots,N\}]$
pre $cust \in$ inds $file$

post $file = front(\overleftarrow{file}, cust - 1) \frown$
        $[\mu(\overleftarrow{file}(cust), today \mapsto \overleftarrow{file}(cust).today + amount)] \frown$
        $rest(\overleftarrow{file}, cust + 1)$

Worked example 13.5 Write down the specification of the operation that adds a new customer to the system.

SOLUTION

$add\text{-}card_1$ $(card\text{-}no\text{:}\,CardId, code\text{:}\,PIN)$
ext wr $file$: $Customers_1$
pre $card\text{-}no \notin used(file) \wedge$ len $file < N$
post $is\text{-}ordered(file) \wedge$
    $\exists i \in$ inds $file \cdot$
        $del(file, i) = \overleftarrow{file} \wedge$
        $file(i) = mk\text{-}Customer_1(card\text{-}no, code, 0)$

$used : Customers_1 \to \mathbf{N}$
$used(file) \triangleq \{cu.card \mid cu \in$ elems $file\}$

$\blacksquare$

The next step is to show that the new specifications for each of the operations are the same as the original specification. First, we need to look at the domain for a particular operation (Fig. 13.7).

Consider a piece of input i that is accceptable to an abstract operation OPA. This means that it must satisfy the pre-condition for OPA, i.e. that $pre\text{-}OPA(i)$ is true. Suppose ci_a and ci_b are two values in the representation that are 'retrieved' to the input value i. If i is acceptable to the abstract operation, then the two representatives of this

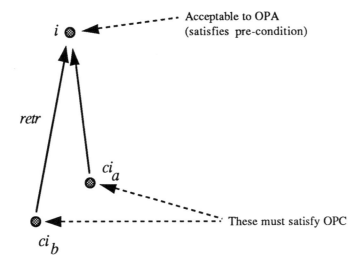

Figure 13.7   Modelling a pre-condition.

value should be acceptable for the new operation OPC. Formally this can be written as a predicate we will call the *domain rule*:

$$\forall s \in Con \cdot pre\text{-}OPA(retr(s)) \;\Rightarrow\; pre\text{-}OPC(s)$$

It should be remembered that both the concrete state and the abstract state are restricted by the appropriate invariants.

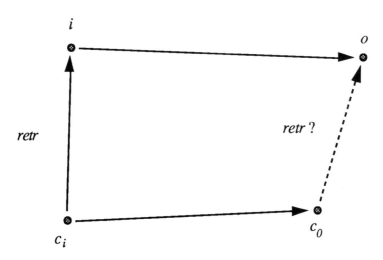

Figure 13.8   Modelling a post-condition.

For the actual operations themselves, things are a little bit more difficult. It is easier to consider a simpler example first, where each value in our abstract state is only represented by a single value in our representation state (Fig. 13.8). In this case, if i is related to o through a post-condition (this implies that i satisfies a precondition) then c_i ought to be related to c_o in the representation. This can be characterized by saying, that if the operation is carried out 'downstairs' in the concrete representation, this should be equivalent to going 'upstairs' to the abstract representation using the retrieve function, and executing the operation there.

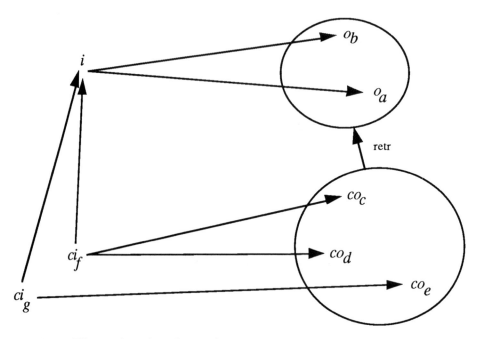

Figure 13.9   The retrieve function and operations.

In the more general case, life is not this easy. There could be more than one representation state which is mapped into the specification state by the retrieve function and more than one possible answer that satisfies the post-condition (Fig. 13.9). Now we would expect that whatever answer is obtained using a concrete operation, if the retrieve function is used to relate it to the abstract answer, the results ought to satisfy the post-condition for the abstract operation, this can written down formally as a predicate we will call the *range rule*:

$$\forall \overleftarrow{s}, s \in Con \cdot pre\text{-}OPA(retr(\overleftarrow{s})) \land post\text{-}OPC(\overleftarrow{s}, s)$$
$$\Rightarrow post\text{-}OPA(retr(\overleftarrow{s}), retr(s))$$

Again, the concrete state and the abstract state are restricted by the appropriate invariants.

To show these rules at work let us prove the operation *is-valid-card*:

> *is-valid-card*$_1$ (*card-no*: *CardId*) r: **B**
>
> **ext rd** *file* : *Customers*$_1$
>
> **post** $r \Leftrightarrow \exists! i \in \text{inds} \, file \cdot file(i).card = card\text{-}no$

For this particular operation there is no pre-condition, i.e. the pre-condition is true, so the domain equation is trivially satisfied. For the range equation, substitute the pre- and post-conditions for the various operation to get

$$\forall \overleftarrow{s}, s \in \textit{Customer-file}_1 \cdot \textit{pre-is-valid-card}(\textit{retr-cust}(\overleftarrow{s})) \land \textit{post-is-valid-card}_1(\overleftarrow{s}, s)$$
$$\Rightarrow \textit{post-is-valid-card}(\textit{retr-cust}(\overleftarrow{s}), \textit{retr-cust}(s))$$

If the definitions of each of the operations is substituted, we get the following:

$$\forall \textit{cardno} \in \textit{CardId}, r \in \mathbf{B}, \textit{file} \in \textit{Customers}_1 \cdot$$
$$\text{true} \land (r \iff \exists! \, i \in \text{inds} \, \textit{file} \cdot \textit{file}(i).\textit{card} = \textit{card-no})$$
$$\Rightarrow (r \iff \textit{card-no} \in \text{dom} \, \textit{retr-cust}(\textit{file}))$$

To show this holds the usual proof technique is used, which is to show that it holds for an arbitary set of values, i.e. we need to show

$$(r \iff \exists! \, i \in \text{inds} \, \textit{file} \cdot \textit{file}(i).\textit{card} = \textit{card-no})$$
$$\Rightarrow (r \iff \textit{card-no} \in \text{dom} \, \textit{retr-cust}(\textit{file}))$$

Substituting the retrieve function gives the following:

$$(r \iff \exists! \, i \in \text{inds} \, \textit{file} \cdot \textit{file}(i).\textit{card} = \textit{card-no})$$
$$\Rightarrow (r \iff \textit{card-no} \in \text{dom} \, \{\textit{cu.card} \mapsto \textit{mk-Customer}(\textit{cu.pin},$$
$$\textit{cu.today}) \mid \textit{cu} \in \text{elems} \, \textit{file}\})$$

The critical thing is the domain of the mapping constructed by the retrieve function. This can be written down as follows:

$$\text{dom} \, \{\textit{cu.card} \mapsto \textit{mk-Customer}(\textit{cu.pin}, \textit{cu.today}) \mid \textit{cu} \in \text{elems} \, \textit{file}\}$$

$$= \text{``definition of the dom operator''}$$
$$\{\textit{cu.card} \mid \textit{cu} \in \text{elems} \, \textit{file}\}$$

$$= \text{``definition of elems operator''}$$
$$\{\textit{file}(i).\textit{card} \mid i \in \text{inds} \, \textit{file}\}$$

Therefore, the right-hand side of the implication can now be written as

$$r \iff \textit{card-no} \in \{\textit{file}(i).\textit{card} \mid i \in \text{inds} \, \textit{file}\}$$

using the uniqueness part of the invariant, this is just

$$r \iff \exists! \, i \in \text{inds} \, \textit{file} \cdot \textit{file}(i).\textit{card} = \textit{card-no}$$

and the proof is complete. The *set-card* operation follows a similar pattern. The abstract specification is

$$\textit{set-card} \, (\textit{card-no}: \textit{CardId})$$
$$\text{ext rd } \textit{file} \quad : \textit{Customers}$$
$$\text{wr } \textit{cust} : [\textit{CardId}]$$
$$\text{pre } \textit{card-no} \in \text{dom} \, \textit{file}$$
$$\text{post } \textit{cust} = \textit{card-no}$$

and the corresponding refinement (concrete specification) is

$$\textit{set-card}_1 \, (\textit{card-no}: \textit{CardId})$$
$$\text{ext rd } \textit{file} \quad : \textit{Customers}_1$$
$$\text{wr } \textit{cust} : [\{1, \ldots, N\}]$$
$$\text{pre } \exists! \, i \in \text{inds} \, \textit{file} \cdot \textit{file}(i).\textit{card} = \textit{card-no}$$
$$\text{post } \textit{file}(\textit{cust}).\textit{card} = \textit{card-no}$$

For the domain we need to show:

$$\forall s \in Con \cdot pre\text{-}set\text{-}card(retr\text{-}cust(s)) \implies pre\text{-}set\text{-}card_1(s)$$

Substituting:

$$card\text{-}no \in \text{dom } retr\text{-}cust(file) \implies \exists! i \in \text{inds } file \cdot file(i).card = card\text{-}no$$

The left-hand side has already been expanded above, so we need to show:

$$card\text{-}no \in \{file(i).card \mid i \in \text{dom } file\} \implies \exists! i \in \text{inds } file \cdot file(i).card = card\text{-}no$$

which is true. The range rule expands to

$$card\text{-}no \in \text{dom } retr\text{-}cust(file) \land file(cust).card = card\text{-}no$$
$$\implies retr\text{-}cust(cust) = card\text{-}no$$

substituting for the retrieve function

$$card\text{-}no \in \{file(i).card \mid i \in \text{dom } file\} \land file(cust).card = card\text{-}no$$
$$\implies file(cust).card = card\text{-}no$$

which trivially holds.

If the proof of *add-card* is tackled, based on the two expressions below, it will be found that the *is-ordered* information is not used in the proof. This should not be surprising as this is about implementation details and one should not expect it to be used to prove that the implementation satisfies the specification. The *is-ordered* information will be used when deriving the code; it is the extra information that allows an efficient search of the array, and has nothing to do with the information stored in that array.

$$card\text{-}no \notin \text{dom } retr\text{-}cust(file) \land \text{card dom } file < N$$
$$\implies card\text{-}no \notin used(file) \land \text{len } file < N$$

$$card\text{-}no \notin \text{dom } file \land$$
$$is\text{-}ordered(file) \land$$
$$\exists i \in \text{inds } file \cdot$$
$$\qquad del(file, i) = \overleftarrow{file} \land$$
$$\qquad file(i) = mk\text{-}Customer_1(card\text{-}no, code, 0)$$
$$\implies retr\text{-}cust(file) = retr\text{-}cust(\overleftarrow{file}) \dagger \{card\text{-}no \mapsto mk\text{-}Customer(code, 0)\}$$

The actual proofs are left for the reader.

13.2.2   The next step

One view of an array is that it is a mapping, with restrictions on the domain, and usually that it is nothing more than a simple set—either integers or a set that can be put in correspondence with the integers. Thus a possible candidate to simulate an array in the executable part of the specification language is a mapping. Thus

$$\text{array } X \text{ to } Y \text{ will be simulated by } X \xrightarrow{m} Y$$

There is a problem with simulating an array with a mapping. What does the empty map represent? It simulates an uninitialized array; if a component of an array has not been set, it is (or at least should be) forbidden to index that component. Few compilers check this, and in fact any uninitialized array can be indexed and the result is whatever that particular location has been initialized to in store. Thus, there are two choices to model an uninitialized array. For compilers that check for uninitialized variables:

the empty mapping: $\{\}$

and for compilers that do not do any checking, an arbitrary mapping:

$$m \in Index \xrightarrow{m} Component$$

such that

$$\text{dom } m = Index$$

The arbitrary mapping that is chosen is supposed to reflect the random values that will be found in store.

If the program is correct, it does not matter which model is chosen, since the program will not be accessing uninitialized variables. Therefore in what follows, we will assume that the programs will be translated into a language that does check for initialized variables and we will use the simple mapping model for an array.

13.2.3 Now where?

The specification is now in terms of a data structure which can easily be translated into the implementation language. In the cash dispenser problem, as arrays are of a fixed size we need some means of modelling only those customers that occur. Therefore, the state will contain the array, the high water mark for the array (where everything to the left of that high water mark is a valid customer and space to the right of it is empty array space). The current customer will be modelled as an index into the array. This suggests the following state:

values

$N, MAX : \mathbf{N}$

types

$Customers_2 = \{1, \dots, N\} \xrightarrow{m} Customer_1$

$Customer_1 ::\quad card\ :\ CardId$
$\qquad\qquad\quad pin\ :\ PIN$
$\qquad\qquad\quad today\ :\ \mathbf{N}$

state $Customer\text{-}file_2$ of
$\qquad file\ :\ Customers_2$
$\qquad limit\ :\ \{0, \dots, N\}$
$\qquad cust\ :\ \{0, \dots, N\}$
inv $mk\text{-}Customer\text{-}file(file, limit, cust)\ \ \triangleq$
$\qquad is\text{-}ordered\text{-}array(file, limit)\ \wedge$
$\qquad \{1, \dots, limit\} \subseteq \text{dom } file\ \wedge$
$\qquad cust \in \{0, \dots, limit\}$
end

$is\text{-}ordered\text{-}array : Customers_2 \times \{0, \dots, N\} \to \mathbf{B}$

$is\text{-}ordered\text{-}array(file, limit)\ \ \triangleq$
$\qquad \forall i, j \in \{1, \dots, limit\} \cdot i < j\ \Rightarrow\ file(i).card < file(j).card$

The retrieve function documents that an empty customer array is modelled by the pointer having a value of zero and that the current customer pointer must either be zero or index an existing customer:

$$retr\text{-}cust_1 : Customer\text{-}file_2 \rightarrow Customer\text{-}file_1$$

$$retr\text{-}cust_1(mk\text{-}Customer\text{-}file_2(file, limit, cust)) \quad \triangleq$$
$$\text{let } ncust = \text{if } cust = 0 \text{ then nil else } cust \text{ in}$$
$$mk\text{-}Customer\text{-}file_1([file(i) \mid i \in \{1, \ldots, limit\}], ncust)$$

The retrieve function documents that an empty customer pointer is represented by 0; the invariant documents the property that the customer pointer must either be zero or point to an existing customer. By inspection, the retrieve function is total on the representation state (the invariant guarantees this), and the adequacy proof is left as an exercise. Informally it can be seen that the representation is adequate, for given any sequence it is easy to map that sequence onto an array, with the high water mark having the same value as the length of the sequence.

The operations can now be rewritten in terms of this representation:

$is\text{-}valid\text{-}card_2 \ (card\text{-}no: CardId) \ r: \mathbf{B}$
ext rd $file \ : \ Customers_2$
$\quad limit \ : \ \{0, \ldots, N\}$
post $r \ \Leftrightarrow \ \exists! \, i \in \{1, \ldots, limit\} \cdot file(i).card = card\text{-}no$

$set\text{-}card_2 \ (card\text{-}no: CardId)$
ext rd $file \quad : \ Customers_2$
$\quad limit \quad : \ \{0, \ldots, N\}$
$\quad$ wr $cust \ : \ \{0, \ldots, N\}$
pre $\exists! \, i \in \{1, \ldots, limit\} \cdot file(i).card = card\text{-}no$
post $file(cust).card = card\text{-}no$

$is\text{-}valid\text{-}pin_2 \ (code: PIN) \ r: \mathbf{B}$
ext rd $file \ : \ Customers_2$
$\quad limit \ : \ \{0, \ldots, N\}$
$\quad cust \ : \ \{0, \ldots, N\}$
pre $cust \in \{1, \ldots, limit\}$
post $r \ \Leftrightarrow \ file(cust).pin = code$

$is\text{-}valid\text{-}amount_2 \ (amount: \mathbf{N}) \ r: \mathbf{B}$
ext rd $file \ : \ Customers_2$
$\quad limit \ : \ \{0, \ldots, N\}$
$\quad cust \ : \ \{0, \ldots, N\}$
pre $cust \in \{1, \ldots, limit\}$
post $r \ \Leftrightarrow \ file(cust).today + amount \leq MAX$

$update\text{-}customer\text{-}file_2 \ (amount: \mathbf{N})$
ext wr $file \quad : \ Customers_2$
$\quad$ rd $limit \ : \ \{0, \ldots, N\}$
$\quad cust \quad : \ \{0, \ldots, N\}$
pre $cust \in \{1, \ldots, limit\}$

$$\text{post } file = \overleftarrow{file} \dagger \{cust \mapsto \mu(\overleftarrow{file}(cust), today \mapsto \overleftarrow{file}(cust).today + amount)\}$$

The next step, of course, is to derive the code for each of the operations using the techniques of Chapters 11 and 12—it will be necessary is to derive code that satisfies the pre- and post-conditions. It should be noted that the pre- and post-conditions have been rewritten in terms of the specification language operations, rather than in terms of operations on arrays available in, say, Pascal. It is in fact turning the specification language formulation of the operations into Pascal which will be most of the work in deriving code that satisfies the pre- and post-conditions of the specification.

Exercise 13.1

1. Define an operation on the sequence refinement to delete a card and show that it is correct with respect to the *delete-card* operation.
2. Prove the five operations defined above are correct with respect to their original specifications.
3. Complete the proof of adequacy above. First, show that it is true for the empty file and then complete the proof by induction over the structure of the mapping. It will be necessary to consider two sets of cases: the *cust* field being nil and the *cust* field being set to a card identifier.
4. Redo this refinement example, this time going straight from the original specification to a representation that uses arrays (as modelled above).

    (a) Define a retrieve function from *Customer-file$_2$* to *Customer-file*.
    (b) Show that the retrieve function is total and adequate.
    (c) Prove each of the operations defined on the state *Customer-file$_2$* are correct with respect to the original specification.

5. Refine each of the operations on page 262 and page 263.

13.3 A CHARACTER STACK

A stack together with its operations was specified in Chapter 6 on pages 86–88. We will concentrate on a simple finite stack of up to N characters and consider implementing this in two ways: as an array with a pointer and as a linked list.

The specification of the stack includes an operation to initialize the stack:

```
values

N : N

types

Stack = Char*

state Character-stack of
      st : Stack
inv mk-Character-stack(st)  △
      len st ≤ N
end
```

> *init* ()
>
> **ext wr** *st* : *Stack*
>
> **post** $st = [\,]$

Push a character onto the stack:

> *push* (*ch*: *Char*)
>
> **ext wr** *st* : *Stack*
>
> **pre len** $st < N$
>
> **post** $st = [ch] \curvearrowright \overleftarrow{st}$

Read the character on the top of the stack non-destructively:

> *top* () *r*: *Char*
>
> **ext rd** *st* : *Stack*
>
> **pre** $st \neq [\,]$
>
> **post** $r = \mathsf{hd}\, st$

Pop the stack; the character on the top is lost:

> *pop* ()
>
> **ext wr** *st* : *Stack*
>
> **pre** $st \neq [\,]$
>
> **post** $st = \mathsf{tl}\, \overleftarrow{st}$

Check whether the stack is empty or not:

> *is-empty* () *r*: **B**
>
> **ext rd** *st* : *Stack*
>
> **post** $r \Leftrightarrow st = [\,]$

Check whether the stack is full:

> *is-full* () *r*: **B**
>
> **ext rd** *st* : *Stack*
>
> **post** $r \Leftrightarrow \mathsf{len}\, st = N$

We have assumed that the stack is finite.

13.3.1   The stack as an array

Worked example 13.6 Write down a state which refines the stack as an array.

SOLUTION The stack can be represented by an array and a pointer into the array which indicates the current top of the stack. An array can be modelled by a mapping with a restricted domain:

types

$$Stacka = \{1, \ldots, N\} \xrightarrow{m} Char$$

$$Position = \{0, \ldots, N\}$$

state $Stack_1$ of
   st : $Stacka$
  pos : $Position$
end

■

The retrieve function is fairly straightforward:

$retr\text{-}stack : Stack_1 \rightarrow Stack$

$retr\text{-}stack(mk\text{-}Stack_1(st, pos)) \;\; \triangleq \;\; [st(pos - i + 1) \mid i \in \{1, \ldots, pos\}]$

Before doing any more work, it is necessary to show that the retrieve function is total and the representation is adequate. Adequacy is obvious, and a brief inspection seems to indicate that the retrieve function is total on $Stack_1$, but more care is needed. A valid element of the set $Stack_1$ is

$$mk\text{-}Stack_1(\{\,\}, N)$$

and the 'retrieve' of this element is undefined! The concrete state contains too many elements, and the solution is to remove some of them by introducing an invariant. The problem arises when the value of pos is not contained in the domain of the map st, so an invariant needs to be added to remove this possibility:

state $Stack_1$ of
   st : $Stacka$
  pos : $Position$
inv $mk\text{-}Stack_1(st, pos) \;\; \triangleq \;\; \{1, \ldots, pos\} \subseteq \text{dom } st$
end

Now the retrieve function is total. For adequacy it is necessary to show

$$\forall sta \in Stack \cdot \exists stc \in Stack_1 \cdot retr\text{-}stack(stc) = sta$$

and, by inspection, this can be seen to be true. Now that we know that the new representation is correct, the operations can be defined in terms of it:

$init_1$ ()
ext wr st : $Stacka$
   pos : $Position$
post $st = \{\,\} \land pos = 0$

Notice that the mapping is initialized to the empty map—we are assuming a clever compiler which checks for uninitialized array components.

$push_1 \ (ch: Char)$
ext wr $st \ : \ Stacka$
$\quad\quad pos \ : \ Position$
pre $pos < N$
post $pos = \overleftarrow{pos} + 1 \ \wedge$
$\quad\quad st = \overleftarrow{st} \ \dagger \ \{pos \mapsto ch\}$

The pre-condition reflects the fact that the stack is finite, the post-condition specifies that the top of stack position pointer should be incremented by one, and the new value copied into the array at the top-of-stack position.

$top_1 \ () \ r: Char$
ext rd $st \ : \ Stacka$
$\quad\quad pos \ : \ Position$
pre $pos \neq 0$
post $r = st(pos)$

The stack must not be empty, and the character on the top of the stack is returned.

$pop_1 \ ()$
ext wr $pos \ : \ Position$
pre $pos \neq 0$
post $pos = \overleftarrow{pos} - 1$

The stack must not be empty, and the top-of-stack pointer is decremented by one.

$is\text{-}empty_1 \ () \ r: \mathbf{B}$
ext rd $pos \ : \ Position$
post $r \ \Leftrightarrow \ pos = 0$

An empty stack is reflected by the position pointer having a value of zero.

$is\text{-}full_1 \ () \ r: \mathbf{B}$
ext rd $pos \ : \ Position$
post $r \ \Leftrightarrow \ pos = N$

A full stack is reflected by the position pointer having a value equal to the number of slots in the stack.

We shall just prove the *push* operation. For the pre-condition we need to show

$$\forall s \in Stack \cdot pre\text{-}push(retr\text{-}stack(s)) \ \Rightarrow \ pre\text{-}push_1(s)$$

For this example we need to show

$$\mathsf{len} \ retr\text{-}stack(st) < N \ \Rightarrow \ pos < N$$

now $\mathsf{len} \ retr\text{-}stack(st) = pos$ so the above is trivially true. For the post-condition we need to show

$$\forall \overleftarrow{s}, s \in Stack_1 \cdot pre\text{-}push(retr\text{-}stack(\overleftarrow{s})) \wedge post\text{-}push_1(\overleftarrow{s}, s)$$
$$\Rightarrow \ post\text{-}push(retr\text{-}stack(\overleftarrow{s}), retr\text{-}stack(s))$$

which is

$$\mathsf{len} \ retr\text{-}stack(\overleftarrow{st}) < N \wedge pos = \overleftarrow{pos} + 1 \wedge st = \overleftarrow{st} \ \dagger \ \{pos \mapsto ch\}$$
$$\Rightarrow \ retr\text{-}stack(st) = [ch] \ \frown \ retr\text{-}stack(\overleftarrow{st})$$

Now

$retr\text{-}stack(st)$

$=$ "definition of the retrieve function"

$[st(pos - i + 1) \mid i \in \{1, \ldots, pos\}]$

$=$ "hypothesis"

$[st(\overleftarrow{pos} + 1 - i + 1) \mid i \in \{1, \ldots, \overleftarrow{pos} + 1\}]$

$=$ "properties of sequences"

$[st(\overleftarrow{pos} + 1 - 1 + 1)] \curvearrowright [st(\overleftarrow{pos} + 1 - i + 1) \mid i \in \{2, \ldots, \overleftarrow{pos} + 1\}]$

$=$ "rules of arithmetic, properties of sequence construction"

$[st(\overleftarrow{pos} + 1)] \curvearrowright [st(\overleftarrow{pos} + 1 - i) \mid i \in \{1, \ldots, \overleftarrow{pos}\}]$

$=$ "hypothesis"

$[st(pos)] \curvearrowright [st(\overleftarrow{pos} + 1 - i) \mid i \in \{1, \ldots, \overleftarrow{pos}\}]$

$=$ "hypothesis"

$[ch] \curvearrowright [\overleftarrow{st}(\overleftarrow{pos} + 1 - i) \mid i \in \{1, \ldots, \overleftarrow{pos}\}]$

$=$ "definition of retrieve"

$[ch] \curvearrowright retr\text{-}stack(\overleftarrow{st})$

which completes the proof of the *push* operation.

13.3.2 The stack as a linked list

Another possible implementation of a stack is a linked list. To do this it is necessary to model pointers and storage allocation. This is done by modelling store as a mapping of a set of tokens to a set of elements. The token set is modelling storage locations and thus represent values that are modelling pointers. The set is modelling locations in store; the system knows what they are, but the user in Pascal or Modula-2 does not. The element set is nothing more than the value that a pointer references, so the state for the representation will be as follows:

types

$Store = Addr \xrightarrow{m} Element$

$Element :: value : Char$
$\qquad\qquad next : [Addr]$

$Addr =$ token

state $Stack_1$ of
$\qquad head : [Addr]$
$\qquad store : Store$
end

The set token is just an infinite set of tokens, their exact values does not matter. This refinement style happens frequently enough to be worth having its own notation. We will introduce two new type constructors:

$C =$ collection of T

This is a straightforward abbreviation for

$$C = \text{token} \xrightarrow{m} T$$

where token is as before, and

$$P = \text{pointer to } T$$

which is just an abbreviation for

$$P = [\text{token}]$$

We will also require (for readability only) a new constant empty which just denotes the empty map. Two additional operations are needed:

$$new \ (c\colon C) \ p\colon P$$

$$\text{post } p \in P - (\text{dom } c \cup \{\text{nil}\})$$

This operation models the allocation of a new piece of storage to hold a value of type T. If the specification is examined carefully, it can be seen that the operation *new* is modelling something like the *new* operation found in Pascal or Modula-2.

$$dispose \ (c\colon C, p\colon P) \ r\colon C$$

$$\text{pre } p \in \text{dom } c$$

$$\text{post } r = \{p\} \triangleleft c$$

This operation models the *dispose* operation of Pascal or Modula-2 and returns a piece of storage referenced by a pointer to the system. To use either of the two operations in a post-condition, remember that operation quotation must be used (see the definitions of *push* and *pop* below). The equivalent to dereferencing a pointer is to write $c(p)$.

The stack example can now be written:

types

$$ListEl = \text{pointer to } Element$$

$$Element \ ::\ value \ :\ Char$$
$$\qquad\qquad\quad next \ :\ ListEl$$

state $Stack_1$ **of**
$$\qquad head \ :\ ListEl$$
$$\qquad store \ :\ \text{collection of } Element$$
end

What does the retrieve function look like? The first guess is fairly straightforward. If the head has the value nil then this should represent an empty stack; if the head does not represent nil then we follow the pointer, i.e. use storage mapping to get to the first element of our linked list, extract the character from there and follow the link through using the next field. This gives us the following retrieve function:

$$retr\text{-}stack : Stack_1 \rightarrow Stack$$

$$retr\text{-}stack(mk\text{-}Stack_1(head, store)) \quad \triangleq$$
$$\qquad \text{if } head = \text{nil}$$
$$\qquad \text{then } mk\text{-}Stack([\,])$$
$$\qquad \text{else } mk\text{-}Stack([store(head).value] \frown retr\text{-}stack(mk\text{-}Stack_1(store(head).next, store)))$$

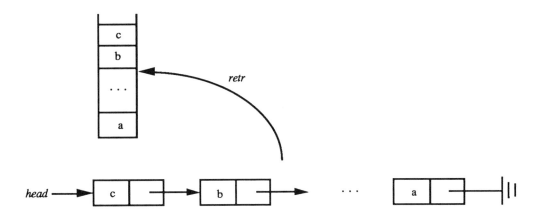

Figure 13.10 The retrieve function for the stack.

Adequacy is fairly easy to prove. Given any stack it is an easy exercise to produce a linked list that satisfies it (Fig. 13.10).

The danger is of course to assume that everything is all right and proceed, but we still need to check that the retrieve function matches its type clause (i.e. is total) and unfortunately it does not, e.g. the following representation is of a stack

$$mk\text{-}Stack_1(id_1, \{id_1 \mapsto mk\text{-}Element(\text{`a'}, id_1)\})$$

which corresponds to the situation shown in Fig. 13.11. This certainly is a member of the state $stack_1$, but is not actually retrieved to anything. What is needed is an invariant that says something along the line that there is always a nil to be found along a chain or equivalently there are no cycles and also that the $store$ contains no junk:

$inv\text{-}stack_1 : Stack_1 \rightarrow \mathbf{B}$

$inv\text{-}stack_1(mk\text{-}Stack_1(head, store)) \quad \triangle$
    dom $store \cup \{\text{nil}\} = collect\text{-}address(head, store, \{\ \})$

The $collect\text{-}address$ operation collects all the addresses in a chain; it needs to keep track of where it has been to avoid loops:

$collect\text{-}address : ListEl \times Store \times ListEl\text{-set} \rightarrow ListEl\text{-set}$

$collect\text{-}address(head, store, found) \quad \triangle$
    if $head = \text{nil}$
    then $\{\text{nil}\} \cup found$
    else if $head \in found$
        then $found$
        else let $mk\text{-}Element(value, next) = store(head)$ in
            $collect\text{-}address(next, store, \{next\} \cup found)$

This is a case where we need to add information—i.e. tighten up the invariant to disallow invalid stacks.

The next step is to respecify the operations. The $init$ operation initializes the stack:

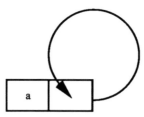

Figure 13.11 A problem with an 'infinite' stack.

$init_1$ ()
ext wr $head$: $ListEl$
    $store$: collection of $Element$
post $head = $ nil $\wedge$
    $store = $ empty

Perversely, an empty store as far as our specification is concerned denotes an unused (full) heap! The *push* operation allocates storage for the new element and adds it to the stack:

$push_1$ (ch: $Char$)
ext wr $head$: $ListEl$
    $store$: collection of $Element$
post $head \in$ token $-$ dom $store \wedge$
    $store = \overleftarrow{store} \dagger \{head \mapsto mk\text{-}Element(ch, \overleftarrow{head})\}$

We need a token (address) that has not been used so far and add this to our model of store; remember that *store* is those storage locations that have been allocated so far. Define *head* to be this new location and update our *store* mapping accordingly.

Now the result of the *new* function is a pointer value (i.e. a token) of the right type which is unused, so the operation *push* can be rewritten using this function:

$push_1$ (ch: $Char$)
ext wr $head$: $ListEl$
    $store$: collection of $Element$
post $head = new(\overleftarrow{store}) \wedge$
    $store = \overleftarrow{store} \dagger \{head \mapsto mk\text{-}Element(ch, \overleftarrow{head})\}$

The *top* operation is straightforward:

top_1 () r: $Char$
ext rd $head$: $ListEl$
    $store$: collection of $Element$
pre $head \neq$ nil
post $r = store(head).value$

it reads the character on the top of the stack non-destructively. The new *pop* operation is

pop_1 ()
ext wr $head$: $ListEl$
    $store$: collection of $Element$
pre $head \neq$ nil

$$\text{post } store = dispose(\overleftarrow{store}, \overleftarrow{head}) \wedge$$
$$head = \overleftarrow{store}(\overleftarrow{head}).next$$

and it just pops the stack; this is achieved by disposing of the storage referenced by the old head of the list, and updating the head of the list to reference the next element of the list (stack). The existential quantifier which occurs with a straightforward operation quotation of *dispose* has been removed.

$is\text{-}empty_1$ () r: **B**

ext rd *head* : *ListEl*

post $r \iff head = $ nil

This operation just checks whether the stack is empty or not; the stack is empty if the head of the list has the value nil.

$is\text{-}full_1$ () r: **B**

ext rd *head* : *ListEl*
       store   : collection of *Element*

post $r \iff size(head, store) = N$

This operation checks whether the stack is full; it does so by counting the number of elements in the stack. The definition of the function *size* is:

$size : ListEl \times$ collection of $Element \rightarrow$ **N**

$$size(p, e) \quad \triangleq \quad \text{if } p = \text{nil}$$
$$\text{then } 0$$
$$\text{else } 1 + size(e(p).next, e)$$

The proof of the data refinement of the operation *push* will be done; it is necessary to just prove the range rule:

$$head = new(\overleftarrow{store}) \wedge$$
$$store = \overleftarrow{store} \dagger \{head \mapsto mk\text{-}Element(ch, \overleftarrow{head})\}$$
$$\Rightarrow retr\text{-}stack(st) = [ch] \frown retr\text{-}stack(\overleftarrow{st})$$

Substituting for *new*:

$$head \in (\text{token} - \text{dom } \overleftarrow{store}) \wedge$$
$$store = \overleftarrow{store} \dagger \{head \mapsto mk\text{-}Element(ch, \overleftarrow{head})\}$$
$$\Rightarrow retr\text{-}stack(st) = [ch] \frown retr\text{-}stack(\overleftarrow{st})$$

Note that

$$store(head) = (\overleftarrow{store} \dagger \{head \mapsto mk\text{-}Element(ch, \overleftarrow{head})\})(head)$$
$$= mk\text{-}Element(ch, \overleftarrow{head})$$

and that *head* cannot have the value nil, we have

$retr\text{-}stack(st)$

   $= $ "expand the retrieve function"

$[store(head).value] \curvearrowright retr\text{-}stack(mk\text{-}Stack_1(store(head).next, store))$

   $= $ "apply the store mapping to head: $store(head).value = ch$"

$[ch] \curvearrowright retr\text{-}stack(mk\text{-}Stack_1(store(head).next, store))$

   $= $ "from the l.h.s. of the implication : $store(head).next = \overleftarrow{head}$"

$[ch] \curvearrowright retr\text{-}stack(mk\text{-}Stack_1(\overleftarrow{head}, store))$

   $= $ "$\{head\} \vartriangleleft store = \{head\} \vartriangleleft \overleftarrow{store}$ for the remainder of the stack"

$[ch] \curvearrowright retr\text{-}stack(mk\text{-}Stack_1(\overleftarrow{head}, \overleftarrow{store}))$

   $= $ "by definition of $\overleftarrow{st}$"

$[ch] \curvearrowright retr\text{-}stack(\overleftarrow{st})$

which completes the proof.

Exercise 13.2

1. Show that the invariant is preserved by the operations of the array implementation.
2. Prove the other operations correct for the array implementation of a stack.
3. Derive correct code for the array implementation of the stack.
4. Show that the invariant is preserved by the operations of the linked list implementation.
5. Prove the other operations correct for the linked list implementation of a stack.
6. Derive correct code for the linked list implementation of the stack.

13.4   MODELLING DATA

The specification language allows us to specify data using sets, lists and maps. The programming languages we use to implement these data structures contain arrays and pointers and scaler values. The process of data refinement involves taking the specification with sets, lists and maps and turning it into specifications using the data structures of our programming languages. We will not in this chapter attempt a full survey of this, this has already been done by many books on data structures. What we will do is to indicate some of the directions in which you could go.

13.4.1   Sets

Small sets with an upper bound to the number of elements could be represented by an array. If the specification is to be implemented in a programming language such as Pascal or Modula-2, for small sets the **SET OF** type could be used.

For a large set with an upper bound on size, possible implemenations might be an array, or a hash table, depending upon whether we might need to access the information in order or not, e.g. if we were trying to represent a set of names, if one of the operations was to print the names out in alphabetical order then an ordered array is an obvious implementation. If on the other hand we never needed to access the information in the table in an ordered fashion, a hash table would be equally good, if not better. For the large sets with no upper bounds, possible representations are binary trees, AVL-trees, B-trees, B^+-trees or extendable hashing. Each one of these representations have trade-offs of simplicity versus complications of implementation, performance aspects, etc.

13.4.2 Sequences

These could be represented by arrays, files or linked lists. In fact if you look at the definition of a file from Pascal you will see it is closely related to that of a sequence. Again the amount of data and the type of access required would dictate which of those representations would be used.

13.4.3 Mappings

If you consider a mapping as a set of pairs with the first element as a key, any representation of a set would also work for a mapping.

13.5 SUMMARY

The invariant is about design decisions and consistency of the representation. In fact, it can now be seen why we were so worried about invariants when writing specifications. The invariants we allowed were about real-life constraints rather than implementation constraints. This is because the specification is not about implementation; this has come later, as we have shown. The implementation aspect of a data type will introduce invariants which are about the representation. The invariants are in fact used to provide performance aspects or implementation aspects. We have already seen what is meant by this; our invariant for stacks said that the linked list did not contain any loops because if it did then it would be impossible to produce correct code. Refinement is about using a subset of the specification language—a subset that can be executed. If we had a full implementation of sets, lists and mappings in our programming language then we would have no need to do data refinement, but of course we would need to accept whatever implementation was given to us by the compiler writer. This does lead to the possibility of the compiler writer offering several implementations for sets, lists and maps and the user entering into a conversation with the compiler to choose the one best suited for the particular application. In fact one could envisage having ten or so implementations of each of the data types parameterized so that the best one could be chosen for a particular application.

14

A SIMPLE TEXT EDITOR

AIMS

- To specify a large system.
- To illustrate the use of formal methods as an aid to understanding a problem.
- To illustrate the use of abstract syntax to investigate syntax.
- To show how a specification can be checked for consistency.

14.1   INTRODUCTION

The purpose of this and subsequent chapters is to illustrate the development of a program from a specification to code; the program chosen is an (old-fashioned) text editor. The editor is to be interactive: reading commands from a keyboard, executing them and displaying any responses on a screen.

The editor can be used to edit an existing file from the filing system or create a new file. The editor will also enable text to be inserted, deleted and moved within a file. A file can be searched for a particular piece of text; these context searches are performed by an exact match of the string in the command with a string in a line of text. Text substitution can be done, and the operation is again a straightforward match and change. On completion of an editing session the file can be written back to the filing system.

To make the specification more difficult (and the implementation easier) there will be an assumption that there is a maximum length of 255 characters for any line of text in the file to be edited.

14.2   AN ARCHITECTURE FOR THE EDITOR

The overall structure of the editor is shown in the context diagram in Fig. 14.1. The context diagram can be expanded to show a possible overall architecture for the system. The editor will create and change files, taking input from the keyboard of a terminal and displaying results at the terminal screen. This is also shown in Fig. 14.1.

The file to be edited is copied from the file store into a buffer, and commands issued by the user may cause this image of the file in the buffer to be changed. On completion of an editing session with a particular document, it can be copied back into the file store. The editor will consist of two small components and one large component. The two small

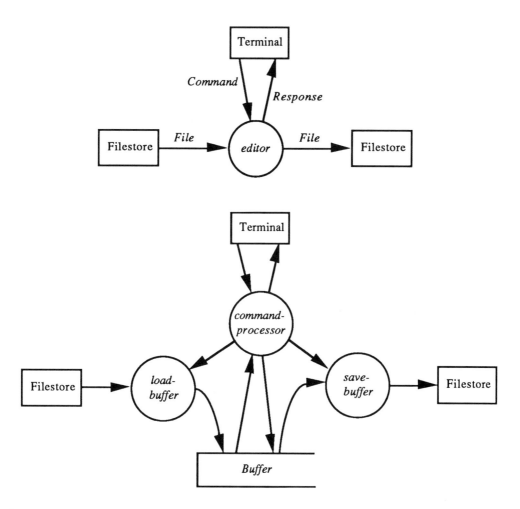

Figure 14.1   The context and overview data flow diagrams for the editor.

components are concerned with loading the file to be edited from the file store into the buffer and converting it into a suitable format, and for saving the buffer to the file store, converting it to the format required by the file store. The large component is a command interpreter together with command processors that perform the functions of the various editing commands. The two processes which carry out the loading and saving of the buffer will not be decomposed any more as they are reasonably straightforward, but the command processor can be levelled to produce the data flow diagram shown in Fig. 14.2.

The general architecture of the command interpreter is a procedure that will read a command from the terminal, analyse the command and issue error messages as necessary. If the command is correct it will then call an appropriate command processor to execute that command. Some of the commands will be associated with loading files into the buffer and writing them back into the file store again; this is how the two processes described above are actuated. The other commands are all associated with making changes to the image of the file in the buffer.

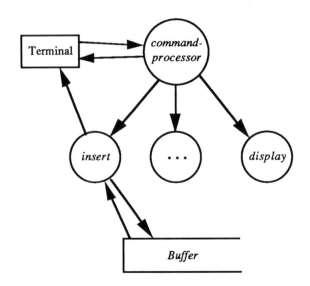

Figure 14.2   More detail.

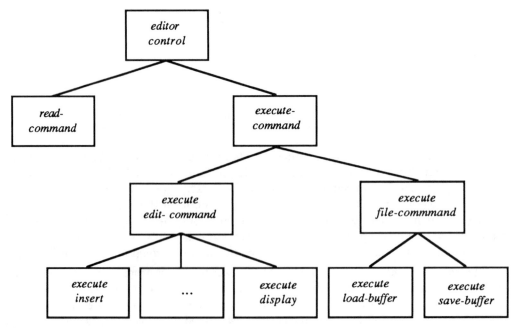

Figure 14.3   The overall control structure of the editor.

The data flow diagram can now be converted to a structure chart to show a possible control structure for the system. This is shown in Fig. 14.3. The aim behind this decomposition of the command processor is to: read a text string from the terminal, parse and check the correctness of the command encoded in the text string, construct an internal representation of the information supplied in the command and pass this internal representation to the appropriate command processor for execution.

When the editor is first activated, there is no file in store, and the first action will be to prompt the user for a command; the first command entered will determine what file is to be edited. If the user asks for a specific file to be loaded and the file exists, then it is copied into the buffer. If no file matching the request exists in the file store, then it is assumed a new file is to be created. If no file is requested, and some other command is entered, then a new (anonymous) file is created in the buffer. The actual details of this will be described by the formal specification.

As can be seen from the data flow diagram, the main component of the editor is the buffer, and for a better decomposition of the system into components, it would be prudent to hide operations on the buffer behind some access functions, i.e. turn the buffer into an abstract machine. The command processors would not need to know the format of the buffer, but are given access to it via the operations of the abstract machine. This means that the exact implementation of the buffer can be changed without impacting the command processor part of the editor too much—if at all—and the operations of the abstract machine provide a clean interface between the two major components.

At this point in the development, we could work out the various operations that will be needed to manage the buffer; based on the commands of the editor, knowledge of the problem would suggest operations to move text around, duplicate text and delete text, but until it is known exactly what the editor commands are, it is difficult to predict what operations will be necessary to support them. The best approach is to understand the buffer and the editor commands first.

14.3 THE BUFFER

The state component of the system will at least hold the name of the file currently being edited and a copy of the file in a buffer; it will also need to contain other house-keeping information. We should also be aware that the size of the buffer is finite, as we intend to implement it in computer store; therefore the specification should be written to allow for this, but in an abstract way, and the state will record that there is a size limit on the buffer. The file is organized as a sequence of lines numbered from 1, and if any lines of text are added or deleted, the lines are automatically renumbered. The first attempt at the state for the editor is

$$
\begin{array}{lll}
\textbf{state } \textit{Editor } \textbf{of} & & \\
\quad \textit{doc} & : \textit{Text} & \text{-- the copy of the file being edited} \\
\quad \textit{cline} & : \mathbf{N} & \text{-- the number of the current line} \\
\quad \textit{cfile} & : [\textit{File-name}] & \text{-- the name of the edit file} \\
\quad \textit{files} & : \textit{File-store} & \text{-- a model of the filing system} \\
\textbf{inv } \textit{mk-Editor}(\textit{doc}, -, -, -) & \triangleq \quad \textsf{len } \textit{doc} \leq D & \\
\textbf{end} & &
\end{array}
$$

The internal buffer of the editor can be represented as a sequence of lines and each line is a sequence of characters. Note that the definition of characters has been left and that any newline characters in a file have been interpreted.

$Text = Line^*$

$Line = Char^*$
inv l $\triangleq$ len $l \leq L$

$Char =$ set of (ASCII) characters not including newline

$File\text{-}store = \ldots$

14.4 THE EDITOR COMMANDS

The next step is to design the command language for the editor; the normal approach to this problem is to start writing down the concrete syntax, but, if we do this we are expressing how the commands are to be written, perhaps we should describe what the commands are? This is possible by documenting what information the commands contain, and leaving the design of how they contain that information to later.

14.4.1 The abstract syntax

To illustrate how the information content of the editor is to be written down, consider, for example, an *insert* command.

The insert command might consist of a line number specifying where some new text is to be inserted, the new text and some means of distinguishing the command from others; for example the concrete syntax might be

(*linenumber*) **insert**   insert text after the specified line (text follows)

The keyword 'insert' expresses the fact that it is an insert command. Following the command is the new text terminated by a line consisting of a full-stop as its only character. For example, to insert some text after line 10 the following would be written:

```
(10) insert
this is the text to be inserted
after line number 10
.
```

If all the details of punctuation are removed, the information needed for an insert command is a line number and a sequence of lines of text. This could be represented as

$Insert ::\ dest\ :\ Line\text{-}spec$
$\qquad\qquad text\ :\ Text$

The substitute command might consist of information on which lines are to be affected, the text to be searched for, and the new text which is to replace the old text:

```
(10,20) substitute old='cat' new='dog'
```

An abstract representation of this command would not be concerned with how all of this information is to be represented when the command is typed, but would specify the information that needs to be supplied with a substituted command. This consists of a line specification, the pattern to be searched for and the pattern that will replace it.

Worked example 14.1 Document the substitute command using abstract syntax.

Solution

$$Substitute :: \quad range : Block\text{-}spec$$
$$old : Pattern$$
$$new : Pattern$$

■

An interactive program should try to minimize the interactions between the user and itself without sacrificing any simplicity or ease of use. If we just wish to substitute one string for another in the current line with the substitute command as it stands, we would have to remember the current line number and use this to construct a range consisting of just that line. For example, to change 'cat' to 'dog' in the current line (assumed to be line 15) we would have to write:

```
(15,15) substitute old='cat' new='dog'
```

A better approach would use a default; for example:

```
substitute old='cat' new='dog'
```

With a careful (and consistent) choice of defaults, the user could be saved some typing. As well as specifying the information content of all the commands, we will also specify what information can be left off and define what the defaults are. Thus the abstract syntax for each of the commands will define the information content of each command. We will call this style of describing the information contents of commands the *external abstract syntax* of the commands.

From now on we will stick to the rules and only write down the abstract syntax for each command. Each command is represented as a composite object, the components of which describe the information that must be supplied in the concrete representation of the commands. We will assume that the component of the editor that deals with commands has access to the current line number and the length of the document, and that this component can construct and supply any defaults that might be necessary.

The commands will be divided into two classes to reflect the overall design decision; those to do with editing text and those to do with managing the files:

$$Editor\text{-}command = Edit\text{-}command \mid File\text{-}command$$

The edit commands can be split into those involving lines and those involving text within a line:

$$Edit\text{-}command = Line\text{-}command \mid Text\text{-}command$$

The commands that manipulate lines of text are a command to insert a block of text supplied by the user; commands to copy, delete and move a block of text within the file; and commands to change the current line, show the number of the current line and to display a block of text:

Line-command = Insert | Copy | Delete | Move | Current | SHOW *| Display*

The insert command specifies a line number and the text to be inserted; if no line is specified, the text is inserted after the current line.

Insert :: *dest* : *[Line-spec]*
text : *Text*

The copy command specifies the block of text to be copied and the destination of that block of text; as one possible default, we could allow the user to just specify a single line for the range, with the obvious meaning. If the destination line is left out then the block of text is copied after the current line.

Copy :: *range* : *[Block-spec]*
dest : *[Line-spec]*

The delete command specifies a block of text to be deleted; again, if only one line number is specified to define the range, only that line is affected. If no line or block is specified, then the current line is deleted.

Delete :: *range* : *[Block-spec]*

The move command specifies the block of text to be moved and the destination; the defaults for this command will be identical to the defaults for the copy command.

Move :: *range* : *[Block-spec]*
dest : *[Line-spec]*

The current command specifies a new current line; if no line is specified, the current line is left as it was.

Current :: *dest* : *[Line-spec]*

The show command displays the line number of the current line.

SHOW

The display command displays a block of text; if a single line is specified, then that line is displayed, and if nothing is written for the range, then the current line is displayed.

Display :: *range* : *[Block-spec]*

The text commands allow strings to be found and replaced:

Text-command = Find | Substitute

The find command finds an occurrence of a pattern within a specified block of text:

Find :: *range* : *[Block-spec]*
pat : *Pattern*

The substitute command changes all occurrences of a pattern, for another within a specified block of text:

Substitute :: *range* : *[Block-spec]*
old : *Pattern*
new : *Pattern*

In both of these commands, the usual default conventions hold.

A pattern is just a sequence of characters:

*Pattern = Char**

The definition of a *Line* and a *Char* have already been given.

As might have been guessed by now, a *Block-spec* specifies either a single line or the first and last line numbers of a block of text:

Block-spec = *Line-spec* | *Block*

Block :: *first* : *Line-spec*
last : *Line-spec*

A line is specified by an expression:

Line-spec = *Expression*

The expression used to specify a line number consists of a base and an optional positive or negative offset from that base:

Expression :: *base* : *Line-id*
offset : [**Z**]

A line can be identified by giving its actual line number in the document as a natural number, or by using one of three mnemonics standing for the zeroth line (which contains no text, and never can), the last line and the current line:

Line-id = **N** | FIRST | CURRENT | LAST

The file commands specify the file to be edited, the name of the file containing the document is to be given when it is saved, and a quit command:

File-command = *Edit* | *Write* | QUIT

The edit command specifies the file to be edited:

Edit :: *file* : [*File-name*]

If no file name is specified, a new file is created with an anonymous name.

Worked example 14.2 Specify the write command in the same style as the edit command.

SOLUTION

Write :: *file* : [*File-name*]

If no file name is specified, the old file is overwritten. ■

The quit command leaves the editor:

QUIT

This particular syntax has a denotation for line zero in order that text can be inserted or moved to a position before the first line by inserting it after line zero. If the denotation for line zero was removed, then it would be necessary to have pairs of commands; one for inserting or moving text before a particular line and one for inserting or appending after a particular line.

14.4.2 When are commands valid?

Just specifying the abstract syntax of the commands is not enough; there are also other details about the commands that must be documented. For example, the insert command allows a line to be specified as the destination of the inserted text, but it would certainly make sense to restrict the line number quoted to be in the document. This type of restriction can be expressed using truth valued functions that describe the 'well-formedness' of a command. The fact that a command is well formed can be expressed as follows:

$$wf\text{-}insert\text{-}command : Insert \times Env \to \mathbf{B}$$

$$wf\text{-}insert\text{-}command(mk\text{-}Insert(dest, text), env) \quad \triangle$$
the command is well formed if the destination of the inserted text is in
the document, there is room in the buffer for the text to be inserted and
the length of the lines of the inserted text is not too long

We will use the words *document* and *buffer* interchangeably. This can be expressed formally as

$$wf\text{-}insert\text{-}command : Insert \times Env \to \mathbf{B}$$

$$wf\text{-}insert\text{-}command(mk\text{-}Insert(dest, text), env) \quad \triangle$$
$$wf\text{-}line\text{-}spec(dest, env) \wedge$$
$$\mathsf{len}\ text + env.end \leq D \wedge$$
$$\forall l \in \mathsf{elems}\ text \cdot \mathsf{len}\ l \leq L$$

The identifier *env* denotes information about the current length of the document and the current line number. The function *eval*, described below, will use this information when it evaluates an expression:

$$Env :: \quad cline \ : \ \mathbf{N}$$
$$end \ : \ \mathbf{N}$$

as it is likely that any edit command is well formed if any *Line-spec* component is well formed and if any *Block-spec* component is well formed. Auxiliary functions have been introduced to do this checking—these components are well formed if they specify lines and blocks that are in the document.

$$wf\text{-}copy\text{-}command : Copy \times Env \to \mathbf{B}$$

$$wf\text{-}copy\text{-}command(mk\text{-}Copy(range, dest), env) \quad \triangle$$
$$wf\text{-}block\text{-}spec(range, env) \wedge$$
$$wf\text{-}line\text{-}spec(dest, env) \wedge$$
$$\mathsf{card}\ eval\text{-}block\text{-}spec(range, env) + env.end \leq D$$

A copy command is well formed if the specified line range for the text to be copied and destination line for the text are both in the document, and if there is room in the document to duplicate the text.

Worked example 14.3   Write down a specification that describes when the delete command is well formed.

SOLUTION

$$wf\text{-}delete\text{-}command : Delete \times Env \to \mathbf{B}$$

$$wf\text{-}delete\text{-}command(mk\text{-}Delete(range), env) \quad \triangle \quad wf\text{-}block\text{-}spec(range, env)$$

A delete command is well formed if the specified line range for the text to be deleted is in the document. ∎

$wf\text{-}move\text{-}command : Move \times Env \rightarrow \mathbf{B}$

$wf\text{-}move\text{-}command(mk\text{-}Move(range, dest), env) \quad \triangleq$
    $wf\text{-}block\text{-}spec(range, env) \wedge$
    $wf\text{-}line\text{-}spec(dest, env) \wedge$
    $dest \notin eval\text{-}block\text{-}spec(range, env)$

A move command is well formed if the specified line range for the text to be moved and destination line for the text are both in the document and there is no overlap.

Worked example 14.4 Write down a specification that describes when the current command is well formed.

SOLUTION

$wf\text{-}current\text{-}command : Current \times Env \rightarrow \mathbf{B}$

$wf\text{-}current\text{-}command(mk\text{-}Current(dest), env) \quad \triangleq$
    $wf\text{-}line\text{-}spec(dest, env) \wedge$
    $eval\text{-}line\text{-}spec(dest, env) \neq 0$

A current command is well formed if the specified line is in the document, (but is not the zeroth line!). ∎

$wf\text{-}show\text{-}command : \text{SHOW} \times Env \rightarrow \mathbf{B}$

$wf\text{-}show\text{-}command(\text{SHOW}, env) \quad \triangleq \quad \text{true}$

A show command is always well formed as it does not have any arguments to check for consistency.

$wf\text{-}display\text{-}command : Display \times Env \rightarrow \mathbf{B}$

$wf\text{-}display\text{-}command(mk\text{-}Display(range), env) \quad \triangleq \quad wf\text{-}block\text{-}spec(range, env)$

A display command is well formed if the specified line range is in the document. The well formed conditions for the two text commands are left as exercises and the file commands are always well formed; the abstract syntax contains all the semantic information.

At this point in the development we have specified the commands and described when they are valid. Checking that commands are well formed may be explicit in the final program—the code that does the necessary checks will be directly developed from the above definitions. Alternatively, the checking might be implicit—being done as necessary and when convenient as a command string is read in and processed. The second of these two approaches is more likely. The reason the well formed conditions are documented here is so that the form of the commands can be understood before implementation is started. In the case where the checking is implicit, the well formed conditions supply a checklist of what checking must be done.

The abstract syntax of the command given above illustrates how this technique can be used to describe the information content of the commands without having to say anything about their representation, i.e. their concrete syntax. It should also be noted that the syntax given above is a finished product.

During the design of the commands of a system, the author should sketch various alternatives using abstract syntax, the idea being to work out what we want to say first (develop the abstract syntax with their well formed conditions) and then work out how we are going to say it (develop the concrete syntax) only when the commands are fully understood.

The function to check the correctness of line and block specifications must also deal with the defaults. This will be done by introducing functions to evaluate an optional line specification and to evaluate an optional block specification.

$$wf\text{-}line\text{-}spec : [Line\text{-}spec] \times Env \rightarrow \mathbf{B}$$

$$wf\text{-}line\text{-}spec(ls, env) \quad \triangle$$
$$\quad \text{let } ln = \text{if } ls = \text{nil}$$
$$\quad\quad\quad \text{then } env.cline$$
$$\quad\quad\quad \text{else } eval\text{-}line\text{-}spec(ls, env) \text{ in}$$
$$\quad ln \in \{0, \ldots, env.end\}$$

A *Line-spec* is well formed if it consists of a single expression, and the line number that is denoted by the expression must either be zero or in the document. The expression that forms a line specification can be evaluated to give the corresponding line number:

$$eval\text{-}line\text{-}spec : Expression \times Env \rightarrow \mathbf{N}$$

$$eval\text{-}line\text{-}spec(mk\text{-}Expression(base, offset), env) \quad \triangle$$
$$\quad \text{let } eb = eval\text{-}base(base, env) \text{ in}$$
$$\quad \text{let } ef = \text{if } offset = \text{nil then } 0 \text{ else } offset \text{ in}$$
$$\quad eb + ef$$

The operation to evaluate the base component of an expression is

$$eval\text{-}base : Line\text{-}id \times Env \rightarrow \mathbf{N}$$

$$eval\text{-}base(lid, env) \quad \triangle$$
$$\quad \text{cases } lid \text{ of}$$
$$\quad\quad \text{FIRST} \rightarrow 0,$$
$$\quad\quad \text{CURRENT} \rightarrow env.cline,$$
$$\quad\quad\quad \text{LAST} \rightarrow env.end,$$
$$\quad \text{others } lid$$
$$\quad \text{end}$$

it replaces a denotation for a line with the actual line number.

$$wf\text{-}block\text{-}spec : [Block\text{-}spec] \times Env \rightarrow \mathbf{B}$$

$$wf\text{-}block\text{-}spec(bs, env) \quad \triangle$$
$$\quad \text{let } lr = \text{if } bs = \text{nil}$$
$$\quad\quad\quad \text{then } \{env.cline\}$$
$$\quad\quad\quad \text{else } eval\text{-}block\text{-}spec(bs, env) \text{ in}$$
$$\quad lr \neq \{\} \land lr \subseteq \{1, \ldots, env.end\}$$

A *Block-spec* is well formed if it is nil, if it consists of a single expression and the line number that is denoted by the expression is in the document, or if it consists of a pair of expressions, where both line numbers denoted by the expressions are in the document.

$eval\text{-}block\text{-}spec : Block\text{-}spec \times Env \rightarrow \mathbf{N}\text{-}set$

$eval\text{-}block\text{-}spec(bs, env) \quad \triangle$

    cases bs of

        $mk\text{-}Line\text{-}spec() \rightarrow$ let $ln = eval\text{-}line\text{-}spec(bs, env)$ in

                $\{ln\},$

       $mk\text{-}Block(first, last) \rightarrow$ let $fl = eval\text{-}line\text{-}spec(first, env)$ in

                let $ll = eval\text{-}line\text{-}spec(last, env)$ in

                $\{fl, \ldots, ll\}$

    end

The approach just taken has two advantages: first, we have specified what the defaults are formally and, second, because of the way the functions are used, the defaults for each of the commands are consistent—a useful feature for the user as he or she will have less to remember when trying to learn the editor.

At this point we have an abstract description of the external form of the commands and what the various defaults are. We have described checks on a correct command and, therefore, have a better understanding of the language we are trying to implement. The above is an abstract description of the user interface to the system. We have not yet specified how the information content of the commands will actually be supplied: it could be via menus or via a simple command language. This will be an implementation decision; nevertheless, we have described what information the user needs to supply and what information will be supplied for him should he choose to leave out parameters and take the defaults.

It is unlikely that the commands will be represented internally in this form but, as stated above, what is being described here is the external interface to the user—not an internal interface for the editor.

14.5   THE SPECIFICATION OF THE TEXT EDITOR

The next step is to specify the actual editing commands themselves. These commands produce a change on the buffer and can be described using the normal pre- and post-conditions. We will write down a second abstract syntax for correct commands which describes the commands after all the expressions have been evaluated and the defaults have been supplied so that when the function of each of the editor commands is described it need not concern itself with these issues. We will call this style of definition of the commands the *internal abstract syntax*.

$Command = EditCommand \mid FileCommand$

$EditCommand = LineCommand \mid TextCommand$

$LineCommand = InsertCommand$

          $\mid CopyCommand$

          $\mid DeleteCommand$

          $\mid MoveCommand$

          $\mid CurrentCommand$

          $\mid \textsc{Show Command}$

          $\mid DisplayCommand$

$InsertCommand \; :: \; dest \; : \; Line\text{-}num$
$\qquad\qquad\qquad\quad\; text \; : \; Text$

$CopyCommand \; :: \; range \; : \; Line\text{-}range$
$\qquad\qquad\qquad\quad\; dest \; : \; Line\text{-}num$

$DeleteCommand \; :: \; range \; : \; Line\text{-}range$

$MoveCommand \; :: \; range \; : \; Line\text{-}range$
$\qquad\qquad\qquad\quad\; dest \; : \; Line\text{-}num$

$CurrentCommand \; :: \; dest \; : \; Line\text{-}num$

$DisplayCommand \; :: \; range \; : \; Line\text{-}range$

$TextCommand = FindCommand \mid SubstituteCommand$

$FindCommand \; :: \; range \; : \; Line\text{-}range$
$\qquad\qquad\qquad\; pat \; : \; Pattern$

$SubstituteCommand \; :: \; range \; : \; Line\text{-}range$
$\qquad\qquad\qquad\qquad\; old \; : \; Pattern$
$\qquad\qquad\qquad\qquad\; new \; : \; Pattern$

$Pattern = Char^{*}$

$FileCommand = EditCommand \mid WriteCommand \mid \text{QUIT}\textsc{Command}$

$EditCommand \; :: \; file \; : \; [File\text{-}name]$

$WriteCommand \; :: \; file \; : \; [File\text{-}name]$

$Line\text{-}num = \mathbb{N}$

$Line\text{-}range \; :: \; first \; : \; \mathbb{N}$
$\qquad\qquad\qquad\; last \; : \; \mathbb{N}$

Some of the commands produce output to the terminal. To model this, an abstract description of all output from the editor must be defined—we could imagine the terminal echoing all output to the terminal on a separate printer; this output could then be described in an abstract manner. We will also treat the output as the file 'STDOUT' in the file system.

With this in mind, the output could be modelled as a sequence of items, an item being some representation of the real output. The editor will output either a line of text or the current line number:

$File\text{-}store = File\text{-}name \; \xrightarrow{\;m\;} \; File$

$File = \ldots \mid Output \mid \ldots$

$Output = Item^{*}$

$Item = Lnum\text{-}ecko \mid Line\text{-}ecko$

$Lnum\text{-}ecko \; :: \; line \; : \; \mathbb{N}$

$Line\text{-}ecko \; :: \; line \; : \; Line$

File-name = ...

Now we can proceed and describe the various operations, assuming the commands are correct.

14.5.1 The specification of the editing commands

The pre-conditions of all of the operations given below are satisfied by well formed editor commands. If a check is done on all commands before they are executed, then the pre-conditions will be satisfied.

The operations that perform the edits on the current file are

> *execute-insert* (*ln*: *Line-num*, *text*: *Text*)
>
> ext wr *doc* : *Text*
>   *cline* : $\mathbb{N}$
>
> pre *is-line-in-doc*(*ln*, *doc*) $\wedge$
>   len *text* + len *doc* $\leq$ *D* $\wedge$
> $\forall l \in$ elems *text* $\cdot$ len *l* $\leq$ *L*
>
> post *doc* = *front*($\overleftarrow{doc}$, *ln*) $\frown$ *text* $\frown$ *rest*($\overleftarrow{doc}$, *ln* + 1) $\wedge$
>   *cline* = *ln* + len *text*

The text to be inserted is placed after the line specified in the command and the current line pointer is set to point to the last line of the copied text. There is a possible choice of values to which the current line pointer could be set. These are:

1. The current line is left as it was.
2. The current line is updated to the line number parameter of the command.
3. The current line is updated to point to the last line of the inserted text.
4. The current line is updated to point to the line following the inserted text.

The above specification has chosen the penultimate option. This means that if the user does another insert operation using the default line number (which is the current line) the new text will be inserted after the previously inserted text, which probably will not be too much of a surprise to the user.

> *execute-copy* (*lr*: *Line-range*, *ln*: *Line-num*)
>
> ext wr *doc* : *Text*
>   *cline* : $\mathbb{N}$
>
> pre *is-range-in-doc*(*lr*, *doc*) $\wedge$
>   *is-line-in-doc*(*ln*, *doc*) $\wedge$
>   *size*(*lr*) + len *doc* $\leq$ *D*
>
> post *doc* = *front*($\overleftarrow{doc}$, *ln*) $\frown$ *sub-doc*($\overleftarrow{doc}$, *lr*) $\frown$ *rest*($\overleftarrow{doc}$, *ln* + 1) $\wedge$
>   *cline* = *ln* + *size*(*lr*)

The text to be copied is duplicated and inserted after the line specified in the command; this allows text to be copied into itself. Again, there are several possible choices for the new value of the current line number. These are:

1. The current line is left as it was.
2. The current line pointer is updated to the line number of the copy command.
3. The current line pointer is set to the first line of the copied text.

4. The current line is set to the last line of the copied text.

5. The current line is updated to the line following the copied text.

The above specification has chosen to be consistent with the insert command, thus, the current line is set to the last line of the copied text. Again the idea is not to surprise the user; if the user does multiple copies using the default line number, the text is placed after the last block of copied text.

Worked example 14.5 Write down a specification to describe the execution of the delete command.

SOLUTION

   execute-delete (*lr*: *Line-range*)

  ext wr *doc* : *Text*
      cline : $\mathbb{N}$

  pre *is-range-in-doc*(*lr*, *doc*)

  post $doc = front(\overleftarrow{doc}, lr.first - 1) \frown rest(\overleftarrow{doc}, lr.last + 1) \wedge$
      cline = *lr.first*

The text denoted by the line specification is deleted from the document.   ■

The answer to the previous worked example poses a problem: how should the current line pointer be set? This depends on the default arguments for the command—thinking in terms of the concrete syntax for the command for the moment, *delete* written with no parameters means delete the current line. Now will the user expect to move forward through the document or backwards through the document if they issue a series of delete commands with no parameters? Moving back through the document corresponds to setting the current line to point to the previous line, and moving forward means setting it to point to the line after the one deleted. How can we decide between these alternatives? Consider what happens if the current line is deleted (i.e. a delete with no parameters is executed) and then text is inserted after the current line (i.e. an insert with no parameters is executed)—this should be equivalent to replacing the current line. Thus after a 'delete' the new current line should be the one preceding the deleted text. This decision has an added advantage (or perhaps it is a disadvantage) that if the first line is deleted, the current line is set to line zero, and any operation other than adding text would be forbidden.

    execute-move (*lr*: *Line-range*, *ln*: *Line-num*)

  ext wr *doc* : *Text*
      cline : $\mathbb{N}$

  pre *is-range-in-doc*(*lr*, *doc*) $\wedge$
     is-line-in-doc(*ln*, *doc*) $\wedge$
     no-overlap(*ln*, *lr*)

post (let $mk\text{-}Line\text{-}range(s, f) = lr$ in
  let $moved = sub\text{-}doc(\overleftarrow{doc}, lr)$ in
  $ln < s \land$
  $doc = \overleftarrow{doc}(1, \ldots, ln) \frown moved \frown \overleftarrow{doc}(ln + 1, \ldots, s - 1) \frown rest(\overleftarrow{doc}, f + 1)$
  $\lor$
  $f \le ln \land$
  $doc = \overleftarrow{doc}(1, \ldots, s - 1) \frown \overleftarrow{doc}(f + 1, \ldots, ln) \frown moved \frown rest(\overleftarrow{doc}, ln + 1)) \land$
  $cline = ln + size(lr)$

The current line number is set to point to the last line of the text that is moved.

Worked example 14.6 Write down a specification that describes the execution of the current command.

SOLUTION

  $execute\text{-}current$ (ln: $Line\text{-}num$)
  ext rd doc : $Text$
    wr $cline$: $\mathbb{N}$
  pre $is\text{-}line\text{-}in\text{-}doc(ln, doc) \land ln \ne 0$
  post $cline = ln$

The current line is set to the new value.   ∎

  $execute\text{-}show$ ()
  ext rd $cline$: $\mathbb{N}$
    wr $files$: $File\text{-}store$
  pre $files(\text{STDOUT}) \in Output\text{-}file$

  post let $mk\text{-}Output\text{-}file(data) = \overleftarrow{files}(\text{STDOUT})$ in
    let $output = [mk\text{-}Lnum\text{-}ecko(cline)]$ in
    $files = \overleftarrow{files} \dagger \{\text{STDOUT} \mapsto mk\text{-}Output\text{-}file(data \frown output)\}$

The current line number is displayed at the terminal.

  $execute\text{-}display$ (lr: $Line\text{-}range$)
  ext rd doc : $Text$
    wr $cline$: $\mathbb{N}$
    $files$: $File\text{-}store$
  pre $files(\text{STDOUT}) \in Output\text{-}file \land$
    $is\text{-}range\text{-}in\text{-}doc(lr, doc)$

  post let $mk\text{-}Output\text{-}file(data) = \overleftarrow{files}(\text{STDOUT})$ in
    let $output = [mk\text{-}Line\text{-}ecko(doc(i)) \mid i \in \{lr.first, \ldots, lr.last\}]$ in
    $files = \overleftarrow{files} \dagger \{\text{STDOUT} \mapsto mk\text{-}Output\text{-}file(data \frown output)\} \land$
    $cline = lr.last$

The display command outputs the specified lines at the terminal. The current line pointer is set to point to the last line of text printed.

$execute\text{-}find$ $(lr\colon Line\text{-}range, pat\colon Pattern)$

ext rd doc : $Text$
    wr $cline$: $\mathbb{N}$

pre $is\text{-}range\text{-}in\text{-}doc(lr, doc)$

post pat ins $(sub\text{-}doc(doc, lr)(cline - lr.first + 1))$
$\vee$
$\neg \exists l \in$ elems $sub\text{-}doc(doc, lr) \cdot pat$ ins $l \wedge cline = \overleftarrow{cline}$

If the pattern is to be found somewhere in the lines specified, then the current line is set to a line that contains the pattern. If the pattern is not to be found, then the current line is left alone. Note that if the pattern occurs more than once, it is not specified which instances of the pattern are used to set the current line number.

Worked example 14.7 Write down a specification to describe the execution of the substitute command.

SOLUTION

$execute\text{-}substitute$ $(lr\colon Line\text{-}range, old\colon Pattern, new\colon Pattern)$

ext wr doc : $Text$
    $cline$: $\mathbb{N}$

pre $is\text{-}range\text{-}in\text{-}doc(lr, doc) \wedge$
    $\forall i \in$ inds $doc \cdot$ len $sub(old, new, doc(i)) \leq L$

post let $txt = subst(old, new, sub\text{-}doc(\overleftarrow{doc}, lr))$ in
    $doc = front(\overleftarrow{doc}, lr.first - 1) \,^\frown\, txt \,^\frown\, rest(\overleftarrow{doc}, lr.last + 1) \wedge$
    $cline = lr.last$

The pre-condition demands that if any substitution occurs, the line length of the new line is still less than or equal to the maximum line length for all of the lines of the document. All the lines that are in the range specified are scanned and any occurrences of the old pattern are replaced by the new pattern. ∎

Notice that the pre-conditions of each of these operations assumed that the commands were well formed, which is exactly the idea behind having a separate internal abstract syntax for the commands. This allowed us to concentrate on defining what needs to be implemented for each of the operations without worrying about any error situations that might have occurred. These should be dealt with much earlier on, and would certainly get in the way of the specification of the operations.

The auxiliary functions for this part of the specification are

$is\text{-}line\text{-}in\text{-}doc : Line\text{-}num \times Text \rightarrow \mathbb{B}$

$is\text{-}line\text{-}in\text{-}doc(l, doc)$ $\triangleq$ $l = 0 \vee l \in$ inds doc

Check that the line number describes a line that is part of the document.

$is\text{-}range\text{-}in\text{-}doc : Line\text{-}range \times Text \rightarrow \mathbb{B}$

$is\text{-}range\text{-}in\text{-}doc(lr, doc)$ $\triangleq$
    $lr.first \leq lr.last \wedge$
    $\{lr.first, \ldots, lr.last\} \subseteq$ inds doc

Check that a range of line numbers describe lines that are part of the document.

> **Worked example 14.8** Write down a specification for the auxiliary function *no-overlap* that checks that a particular line is not included in a range of lines.

SOLUTION

$$no\text{-}overlap : Line\text{-}num \times Line\text{-}range \rightarrow \mathbf{B}$$

$$no\text{-}overlap(ln, lr) \quad \triangleq \quad ln \notin \{lr.first, \ldots, lr.last\}$$

∎

Other functions that are needed is one to create a subdocument corresponding to a range of lines:

$$sub\text{-}doc : Text \times Line\text{-}range \rightarrow Text$$

$$sub\text{-}doc(doc, lr) \quad \triangleq \quad doc(lr.first, \ldots, lr.last)$$

one to calculate the number of lines in a range:

$$size : Line\text{-}range \rightarrow \mathbf{N}$$

$$size(lr) \quad \triangleq \quad lr.last - lr.first + 1$$

one to replace a text pattern in (part of) a document by another text pattern; substituting text in a sequence of lines is done by substitution on each of the lines in the sequence:

$$subst : Pattern \times Pattern \times Text \rightarrow Text$$

$$subst(old, new, txt) \quad \triangleq$$
$$\quad \text{if } txt = [\,]$$
$$\quad \text{then } [\,]$$
$$\quad \text{else } [sub(old, new, \text{hd } txt)] \frown subst(old, new, \text{tl } txt)$$

The above function needs a further function to deal with each line:

$$sub : Pattern \times Pattern \times Line \rightarrow Line$$

$$sub(old, new, line) \quad \triangleq$$
$$\quad \text{if } old \text{ ins } line$$
$$\quad \text{then let } i = index(old, line) \text{ in}$$
$$\quad\quad front(line, i - 1) \frown new \frown sub(old, new, rest(line, i + \text{len } old))$$
$$\quad \text{else } line$$

This defines how text substitution is to be done. All instances of the old pattern are to be replaced by the new one, with no rescanning of the line of text. Once an instance of the pattern has been replaced, scanning starts from a position immediately following the instance.

14.6   THE SPECIFICATION OF THE FILE COMMANDS

14.6.1   The file store

The filing system of the computer is complex and is not really part of the editor except that the editor needs to access the system to get a file for editing and to write the edited file back again at the end of the session. Details such as how the file name of a file is represented and how a file is even accessed can be hidden behind an abstraction. Most of the functions to do this are supplied by the operating system, but it is useful to specify exactly what needs to be provided.

A set *File-name* will be introduced which is the abstraction of all possible file names available on the system, and the actual filing system itself will be modelled by a mapping from *File-name* to *File*. Files will be modelled as a sequence of characters, with some sort of newline signal embedded in them:

$$File\text{-}store = File\text{-}name \xrightarrow{m} File$$

$$File = Document \mid Output \mid \ldots$$

$$Document = Achar^*$$

$$Achar = Char \mid \text{NEWLINE}$$

$$File\text{-}name = \text{token}$$

$$Untitled\text{-}names = \ldots$$

We require that *Untitled-names* $\subseteq$ *File-name*. The set *Untitled-names* is a set of tokens that represent file names including some values that denote (represent) names of the form 'untitled1', 'untitled2', ..., etc.

Any text supplied by the user will ultimately find its way into the text buffer; this is where it will be held while the user is typing the text in a line at a time. The low-level design is concerned with how the text is manipulated by the system; the original specification will need to be modified to reflect this. The approach taken to simulate the user typing text into the system will be to model a terminal. This can be done by adding a file to the file system which represents the lines of text which are read from the terminal—the name of this file will be STDIN.

This solution is similar to how output was handled: information sent to the terminal was simulated by having a sequence of lines appended to an output component of the state. Since input to the system is a sequence of lines of text which are either commands or input to the document, this is exactly how it will be modelled.

The file commands   The operations that access and change the file to be edited are specified below:

$$execute\text{-}edit \; (fn\text{:}[File\text{-}name])$$

ext wr *doc* : *Text*
    cline : **N**
    cfile : [*File-name*]
rd *files* : *File-store*

post $fn \notin \text{dom} \, files \land doc = [\,] \land cline = 0 \land cfile = fn$
    $\lor$
    $fn \in \text{dom} \, files \land files(fn) = [\,] \land doc = [\,] \land cline = 0 \land cfile = fn$
    $\lor$
    $fn \in \text{dom} \, files \land doc = file\text{-}to\text{-}buffer(files(fn)) \land cline = 1 \land cfile = fn$

If the file does not exist, or if one was not quoted, or it is empty, the buffer is initialized with the empty document. If the file exists in the filing system, then it is loaded into the buffer. The current file name is set if one was quoted; otherwise it is left empty.

$execute\text{-}write$ $(fn\colon [File\text{-}name])$

ext rd doc : $Text$
    $cfile$: $[File\text{-}name]$
    wr $files$: $File\text{-}store$

post let $afn =$ if $fn \neq$ nil
            then fn
            else if $cfile \neq$ nil
                then $cfile$
                else let $f \in (Untitled\text{-}names - \text{dom } files)$ in f
    in $files = \overleftarrow{files} \dagger \{afn \mapsto buffer\text{-}to\text{-}file(doc)\}$

The operation saves the file either under the supplied name or under the current file name if one exists; otherwise it saves it with a name of the form 'Untitled$n$', where n is one or more digits that represents a natural number. Care must be taken not to overwrite an existing 'Untitled$n$' file.

$execute\text{-}quit$

post true

The operation makes no changes to the state (except, perhaps, to throw it away). It may prompt the user to remind him or her to save the file if any changes have been made—but that has been left as an implementation decision.

Auxiliary definitions   The following auxiliary functions need to be defined.

$file\text{-}to\text{-}buffer$ $(f\colon Document)$ $r\colon Text$
post $buffer\text{-}to\text{-}file(r) = f$

This operation converts a file in the format of the filing system into the format used by the buffer.

$buffer\text{-}to\text{-}file : Text \rightarrow Document$

$buffer\text{-}to\text{-}file(t)$ $\triangleq$ if $t = [\,]$
                then $[\,]$
                else hd $t \frown$ [NEWLINE] $\frown buffer\text{-}to\text{-}file(\text{tl } t)$

This operation converts a file from the format used by the buffer into a format used by the filing system; it inserts a newline character after each line.

Exercise 14.1

1. Define well formed functions to check the two text commands. (Hint: they should 'check' the pre-conditions for the respective execute operations.)
2. Prove that each of the operations preserve the state data invariant.
3. It should be impossible to make the zeroth line the current line, check that this is true.

4. Define an exchange command that might have a concrete syntax as follows:

   ```
   (10,12) exchange
   this is the text to be inserted
   ```
   .

   The text specified in the range is replaced by the text supplied. How should the current line pointer be set? Write down an abstract syntax for the command and a specification of an *execute-xchange* command.

5. What other options exist for the current line number of the move operation? Decide on another consistent set of ways of setting the current line number, consistent with the phrase 'last affected line' in the specification. Note that any changes that affect the line numbers cause all the lines that follow the line(s) mentioned in the command to be affected; thus the last affected line is the current line. Change the specification to match your decision.

6. Modify the find command to use the ideas of the pattern matching program of Chapter 10 on pages 155–161.

7. In the definition of the *execute-find* operation, it was left undefined which occurrences of a pattern were to be used to set the current line number if the pattern occurred more than once. Respecify the operation so that it is the first occurrence of the pattern.

8. The current line is represented by a natural number, it could be defined as a value in the range $\{0, \ldots, D\}$. Make the appropriate changes in the specification to allow this representation.

14.6.2 A control structure for the editor

The specification given above provides no indication of the overall architecture of the editor. It does, however, specify how each of the operations work and how they interact with the buffer and the concept of the current line. This specification will be developed to be the 'guts' of an editor; the housekeeping functions and interaction with the terminal could be specified separately. The specification can be thought of as an abstract model of the editor; in fact, that is exactly what it is.

The structure chart gives the overall architecture of the editor and it is possible to see that the editor control component will read and execute an operation or command until the editor is terminated with the quit command. The structure chart can be translated into pseudo code to give the overall design for top-level control component of the editor.

```
state Editor of
    doc   :  Text          -- the text of the file being edited
    cline :  N             -- the current line
    cfile :  [File-name]   -- the name of the current file
    files :  File-store    -- a model of the filing system
  inv mk-Editor(doc, -, -, -)  ≜
    len doc ≤ D
    ∀l ∈ elems doc · len l ≤ L
  end
```

```
(dcl quit    : B;
     ccmd  : Char*;
     acmd  : Command | BADCOMMAND;
  initialize();
  quit: = false;
  while ¬ quit do
    ccmd: = read-command();
    acmd: = parse-command(ccmd);
    execute-command(acmd)
  end;
  terminate()
  )
```

The *read-command* operation will deal with reading a command from the terminal, the *parse-command* operation will translate the command into an abstract representation and check for correctness, and the *execute-command* operation will be concerned with the actual execution of the command.

The *read-command* will read a command from the terminal, the command will be represented as a sequence of characters. As discussed earlier, the specification assumes that input is represented as a sequence of *Lines*, each line containing either a command or a line of text to be inserted into the document. Experience (and looking ahead to the problem of parsing the text of the command) suggests that the sequence of characters be terminated by a carriage return.

$\quad$ *read-command* () *ccmd*: *Char**

$\quad$ ext wr *files* : *File-store*

$\quad$ pre *files*(STDIN) $\in$ *Input-file* $\land$
$\qquad$ let *mk-Input-file*(-, r) = *files*(STDIN) in
$\qquad$ $r \neq [\,]$

$\quad$ post let *mk-Input-file*(l, r) = $\overleftarrow{files}$(STDIN) in
$\qquad$ *ccmd* = hd r $^\frown$ [NEWLINE] $\land$
$\qquad$ *files* = $\overleftarrow{files}$ † {STDIN $\mapsto$ *mk-Input-file*(l $^\frown$ [hd r], tl r)}

The *parse-command* will translate the command, represented as a sequence of characters, into an abstract representation and check for correctness. The body of *wf-editor-command* is easy to write, it is just a case statement with a call to the appropriate well formed condition.

$\quad$ *parse-command* (*ccmd*: *Char**) r: (*Command* | BADCOMMAND)

$\quad$ ext rd *doc* : *Text*
$\qquad$ *cline* : N

$\quad$ post let *env* = *mk-Env*(*cline*, len *doc*) in
$\qquad$ let *ecmd* = *retr-editor-command*(*ccmd*) in
$\qquad$ *wf-editor-command*(*ecmd*, *env*) $\land$ r = *retr-command*(*ecmd*, *env*)
$\qquad\quad$ $\lor$
$\qquad$ ¬ *wf-editor-command*(*ecmd*, *env*) $\land$ r = BADCOMMAND

The operation is specified in terms of two retrieve functions, one of which relates the concrete representation to the external abstract syntax and the other relates the external abstract syntax to the internal abstract syntax. The use of the retrieve functions here is the best way of explaining what the operation *parse-command* must do; it must be possible to 'retrieve' the abstract representation, i.e. the information content, from the concrete representation of a command. The actual definition of the syntax of the commands and the definition of the syntax are independent and (now) isolated from the rest of the development and, therefore, can and will be left until last.

$$retr\text{-}editor\text{-}command : Char^* \to Editor\text{-}command$$

$$retr\text{-}editor\text{-}command(ccmd) \quad \triangleq \quad \ldots$$

$$retr\text{-}command : Editor\text{-}command \times Env \to Command$$

$$retr\text{-}command(ecmd) \quad \triangleq \quad \ldots$$

The *execute-command* operation deals with the problem of executing a command, if the command is valid, the appropriate operation (called a command processor) that deals with the command is invoked. Notice that the command will only be executed if it is 'well formed', i.e. if it is correct.

```
execute-command (acmd: Command | BadCommand)
(cases acmd of
                -- execute-line-command
        mk-InsertCommand(dest, text) → execute-insert(dest, text),
        mk-CopyCommand(range, dest) → execute-copy(range, dest),
        mk-DeleteCommand(range) → execute-delete(range),
        mk-MoveCommand(range, dest) → execute-move(range, dest),
        mk-CurrentCommand(line) → execute-current(line),
                ShowCommand → execute-show(),
        mk-DisplayCommand(range) → execute-display(range),
                -- execute-text-command
        mk-FindCommand(range, pat) → execute-find(range, pat),
        mk-SubstituteCommand(range, old, new) → execute-substitute(range, old, new),
                -- execute-file-command
        mk-EditCommand(fname) → execute-edit(fname),
        mk-WriteCommand(fname) → execute-write(fname),
                QuitCommand → quit: = true,
others write-error(acmd)
end

) -- execute-command
```

The final code for the editor will probably not look like this, but the sketch given above is a reasonable abstract model of the editor as it does describe the overall functionality. The final structure of the editor will ultimately depend on the concrete syntax of the commands, and exactly how they are entered, as the code necessary to read commands from the user will be a major part of the system and thus will, at least, have a major influence on the final structure.

The information content of a command is defined by the external abstract syntax on pages 279–281, and the well formed conditions on pages 281–285. The internal form of a command, with all the options completed, is the interface between the input side of the editor and the execution side (see Fig. 14.4). Notice that the first (external) abstract syntax of the commands describes the information content including defaults as seen by the user and that the second (internal) abstract syntax describes the information content, as seen by the system just before the command is executed, in this case the command is well formed and has been 'evaluated'.

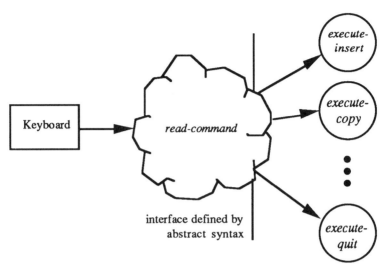

Figure 14.4   The internal interface.

The *read-command* and *parse-command* components could be implemented as a dialogue using menus, instead of as a straightforward parser translating a text command entered by the user after a prompt. In either case the result will be some sort of internal form, which should match the internal abstract syntax. Either form of the abstract syntax of a command may never be actually implemented, but both syntaxes describe what information must be contained in the command. When a concrete representation for a command is designed it must be possible to extract that information from the concrete representation.

The overall design of the top level of the editor is sufficiently simple to see that it works; it reads a command from the terminal, executes that command by making appropriate changes to the copy of the document held in the buffer, and continues to do this until the user has finished.

Finally, the *initialize* and *terminate* operations need to be defined:

initialize ()

ext wr *doc* : *Text*

    cline : $\mathbb{N}$

    cfile : [*File-name*]

    files : *File-store*

post *doc* = [ ] $\land$

    cline = 0 $\land$

    cfile = nil $\land$

    files will be set up by the operating system

terminate ()

ext wr *doc* : *Text*
  cline : **N**
  cfile : [*File-name*]
  files : *File-store*

post *doc* = [] ∧
  cline = 0 ∧
  cfile = nil ∧
  files will be returned to the operating system

14.7 SOME PROPERTIES OF THE SPECIFICATION

Before moving to the next stage of the development, it is well worth studying the specification in some detail. Properties of the specification can be written down and investigated. Some of the properties of the above specification are:

1. If the length of the document was n lines and m lines were added with the insert command, the new length of the document is $n + m$ lines.

2. If the length of the document was n lines and lines f through l are copied after line m, the new length of the document is $n + (l - f + 1)$ lines.

3. If the length of the document was n lines and lines f through l are deleted, the new length of the document is $n - (l - f + 1)$ lines.

4. If the length of the document was n lines and m lines were added with the insert command, the new length of the document is $n + m$ lines.

5. If an insert with no line number arguments is followed by a delete with no arguments, the result is no change.

The first property described above can be written as a theorem:

$$\forall \overleftarrow{doc}, doc, text \in Text \cdot$$
$$\forall cl, \overleftarrow{cl} \in \mathbf{N} \cdot$$
$$\forall ln \in \mathbf{N} \cdot$$
$$\text{len } \overleftarrow{doc} = n \wedge \text{len } text = m \wedge pre\text{-}execute\text{-}insert(ln, text, \overleftarrow{doc}, \overleftarrow{cl}) \wedge$$
$$post\text{-}execute\text{-}insert(ln, text, \overleftarrow{doc}, \overleftarrow{cl}, doc, cl)$$
$$\Rightarrow \text{ len } doc = n + m$$

Though the quantification looks complicated, it is just over all possible state and argument values. If the theorem can be proved then there is a greater sense of confidence that the insert command is more likely to be correct. The proof can be sketched as follows: first substitute the definitions of the pre- and post-conditions to get:

$$\text{len } \overleftarrow{doc} = n \wedge$$
$$\text{len } text = m \wedge$$
$$\textit{is-line-in-doc}(ln, \overleftarrow{doc}) \wedge$$
$$\text{len } text + \text{len } \overleftarrow{doc} \leq D \wedge$$
$$\forall l \in \text{elems } text \cdot \text{len } l \leq L \wedge$$
$$doc = front(\overleftarrow{doc}, ln) \frown text \frown rest(\overleftarrow{doc}, ln + 1) \wedge$$
$$cl = ln + \text{len } text$$
$$\Rightarrow \text{len } doc = n + m$$

Take the right-hand side of the implication, substituting the equalities as required to get the following:

$$
\begin{aligned}
\text{len } doc &= \text{len} \left(front(\overleftarrow{doc}, ln) \frown text \frown rest(\overleftarrow{doc}, ln + 1)\right)\\
&= \text{len} \left(front(\overleftarrow{doc}, ln)\right) + \text{len } text + \text{len } rest(\overleftarrow{doc}, ln + 1)\\
&= ln + m + (n - ln)\\
&= ln + m + n - ln\\
&= m + n
\end{aligned}
$$

The proof uses the property that

$$\text{len } (l \frown m) = \text{len } l + \text{len } m$$

Theorems about a specification and their proofs increase the confidence we have in the correctness of the specification. If a theorem cannot be shown to be correct, either the theorem is wrong or those parts of the specifications that are used by it are wrong. Careful examination of both should show which of the two is incorrect.

Other properties of the specification can be discussed. Some interesting ones are:

1. What happens if a block of text is moved to its current position?
2. What is the current line number set to if the whole document is deleted?
3. What is the current line number set to if text is appended at the end of the document.

The specification should be examined to see if the answer is what is expected.

Exercise 14.2

1. Property 2 on page 298 can be written down mathematically as

$$\forall \overleftarrow{doc}, doc, text \in \textit{Text} \cdot$$
$$\quad \forall cl, \overleftarrow{cl} \in \mathbf{N} \cdot$$
$$\qquad \text{len } \overleftarrow{doc} = n \wedge$$
$$\qquad \text{let } lr = \textit{mk-Line-range}(f, l) \text{ in}$$
$$\qquad \textit{pre-execute-copy}(lr, m, \overleftarrow{doc}, \overleftarrow{cl},) \wedge$$
$$\qquad \textit{post-execute-copy}(lr, m, \overleftarrow{doc}, \overleftarrow{cl}, doc, cl)$$
$$\qquad \Rightarrow \text{len } doc = n + (l - f + 1)$$

   Show that this theorem is true.
2. Write down the theorem for property 3 on page 298 and prove it correct.
3. Write down the theorem for property 4 on page 298 and prove it correct.
4. Write down a property, both in English and as a theorem, about the length of a document and the move command. Prove the theorem.

5. Write down formally and prove the following property of the exchange command of the exercises on page 294:

> If the length of the document was n lines and m lines are exchanged for lines f through l, the new length of the document is $n - (l - f + 1) + m$ lines.

6. Write down the theorem for property 5 on page 298 and prove it correct.

7. A delete followed by an insert should be equivalent to an exchange. Prove this.

14.8 SUMMARY

At this point of the development we have a specification of the functionality to be supplied by the editor. Various decisions have been documented, such as where the current line is set to point after an edit command has been executed. This is a particularly useful feature to get right at the start of the development, as the user would probably prefer a consistent rule which is what the specification describes. The danger with an English specification is that a feature such as this might get left for the implementor to decide on, as the English might not describe the rules accurately enough. The specification does contain some design decisions which may need to be changed, but the major part of it specifies what the editor does rather than how it works.

Some proofs of correctness have been carried out on the specification so we have some confidence in it. The specification also describes an overall implementation strategy for the control part of the editor, and this control structure can be used as the basis for the control component of the final product.

Project The editor described in this chapter is based on an old-fashioned line editor of a type similar to ED on UNIX or EDLIN on MSDOS. A more interesting specification is left for the reader—a specification for a modern style full-screen editor such as that found on the Apple Macintosh; base the specification on the following ideas.

The buffer for the editor should be character based rather than line based, and there should also be a 'clipboard' for use when moving text around. The state should be something like

```
state Editor of
        buffer  :  Char*
    clipboard  :  Char*
          . . .
end
```

Some of the commands to be implemented are:

$$Command = Cut \mid Copy \mid Clear \mid Paste \mid Find \mid Change \mid \ldots$$

Cut   Copy marked text from document to clipboard, and delete from the document.
Copy   Copy marked text from document to clipboard.
Clear   Delete marked text from the document.

These commands will mark text by giving the start and end positions by character numbers within the text. Note that the user will not need to do the counting, the computer will do this. The interface will allow the user to indicate the start and end positions by some means (probably a mouse, but that is an implementation decision).

Paste   Copy marked text from the clipboard into document. This command will indicate the position to which the text in the clipboard is to be copied by giving a character number.

Find   This command scans the selected text of the document, or the whole document if no text is selected, and finds the first occurrence of a character string.

Change   This command scans the selected text of the document, or the whole document if no text is selected, and changes all occurrences of the target character string for a replacement character string.

Before writing this specification, look at a mouse-based, full-screen editor on a Macintosh.

15

THE DEVELOPMENT OF THE EDITOR

AIMS

- To show the formal development of a large example using VDM.
- To outline the relationship that abstract machines have to the formal development process.

15.1   INTRODUCTION

The previous chapter suggested an architecture for a simple text editor, specified the state and the operations, and developed a possible structure for the overall control. The next step is to tackle the problem of the design of the editor; this will be solved by designing an abstract machine to hide the buffer and then specifying the commands so that they can be implemented in terms of the operations of the buffer abstract machine. The design will be concerned with how the abstract buffer machine is driven by the user, and what operations need to be provided by the machine.

The specification was written at a high-level of abstraction: those commands that added text to the document, such as insert, were supplied with the text to be added to the document as one of the parameters. This text is, somehow, obtained from the user and 'stored' somewhere before being passed as an argument to an operation to be inserted into the body of the document at the correct place. The specification and the high-level design did not concern itself where this chunk of text was held, between being entered and being inserted into the document. The final program will need to concern itself with this particular problem so, at some point during the development of the editor, the design must address this complication. As any text supplied by the user will ultimately find its way into the text buffer, this is a good place for it to be held while the user is typing the text in a line at a time—and it is this option that will be explored in detail.

15.2   THE HIGH-LEVEL DESIGN OF A TEXT EDITOR

The architecture for the text editor suggested that the buffer containing the document to be edited should be hidden by an abstract machine. The actual implementation of the buffer would not be known to the remainder of the system, and access to it would be granted through some basic operations.

302

The buffer could be implemented as an array of character strings, and a character string could be implemented as an array of characters. Changes to the document would be reflected by changing the elements of the array. In an abstract specification an array can be modelled by a sequence, and provided that we restrict the operations on the sequence to those that are easily implemented as operations on an array, the refinement step that replaces the sequence by an array will be straightforward (Fig 15.1).

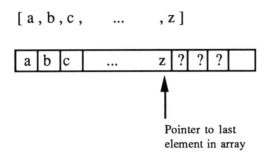

Figure 15.1   Simulating a sequence with an array.

Removing elements from, changing the elements of and adding elements to a sequence is simple as there are 'elegant' mathematical operations to do all the work for us. However, if a sequence is implemented as an array, it is obviously much easier to implement those operations that are restricted to do things at the far end of the sequence, which in the representation would correspond to operations on the right-hand end of an array. For example, removing elements from the right-hand end of a sequence would be modelled in an array refinement by changing a pointer.

Before progressing further with this design, it is necessary to look at the specifications in order to pick out what primitive operations on the buffer are needed, so that the functionality of the editor can be supported. Looking at the specifications it can be seen that the following operations are carried out on the text of the buffer; they are listed, together with a brief description of what changes to the buffer will be necessary to implement each of them.

insert   Text is to be inserted after the specified line; sufficient room has to be made in the buffer for the text, and the text moved into the space. The text can either be inserted in the correct place as it is typed (very inefficient) or collected somewhere, and moved when all the text to be inserted has been entered by the user.

copy   Make room in the buffer for the designated text and copy it into the space.

delete   Remove the designated text and close the gap that is caused by the deletion.

move   This operation is a combination of copy and delete.

The other commands just need access to the text in the buffer.

Although an array implementation is simple, by necessity there will be a lot of shuffling of the components of the array to implement any of the operations described above. Is there a possibility to devise one or two primitives that would enable these operations to be done reasonably efficiently? As the most difficult operation is probably *move*, this is a good place to start.

The approach is to define a *block-move* primitive; this operation would move a chunk of text from one part of the document to another, as efficiently as possible. Perhaps most of the other operations can be implemented in terms of this basic operation? There is also a need for a copy operation (*block-copy*) that copies text to the end of the buffer, and a simple delete operation (*delete-end*) that removes text from the end of the buffer (this is easily implemented by just changing a pointer).

With these three primitives and operations to add new text to the end of the buffer (which will be used by the command processor when it reads lines of texts from the terminal) and access text in the buffer, all of the basic edit operations can be implemented (see Fig. 15.2).

insert   The text which is input as part of the command is placed at the end of the buffer as it is typed in line by line. On completion of the command the new text is inserted in the correct place by using the *block-move* operation.

copy   The text is copied to the end of the buffer using the *block-copy* operation, and then *block-move* is used to move the text to the target position.

delete   The text to be deleted is moved to the end of the buffer using the *block-move* operation and then deleted with *delete-end*.

move   The *block-move* operation is used to move the text to the correct position.

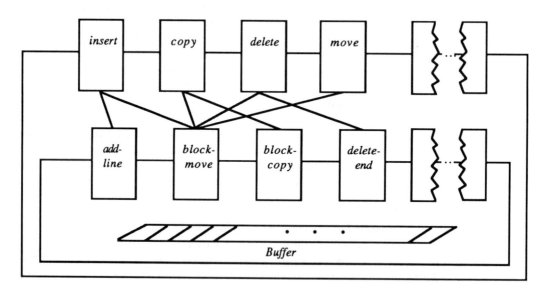

Figure 15.2   The buffer abstract machine.

The idea behind this approach is to implement the *block-move* operation as efficiently as possible. Instead of implementing the buffer as an array of character strings, a certain amount of efficiency could be gained by implementing the buffer storage as an array of pointers, each pointer referencing a chunk of text held elsewhere. Moving text around the buffer can now be replaced by shuffling pointers—instead of copying L characters per line it is now only necessary to copy a (four-byte) pointer.

The first step is to make certain we fully understand the primitives, and this is best done at an abstract level, ignoring the details of an implementation that uses pointers.

The buffer can be represented as a sequence of lines and each line is a sequence of characters. As has already been discussed, the intent is to implement a sequence as an array and an index which is the current length of the sequence. The specification assumes a maximum size of document that can be edited. This will be used to define the size of the array during the next refinement step. The operations can be defined as follows. The original state will be used as a basis for the definitions of the operations.

types

$Text = Line^*$

$Line = Char^*$

$Char =$ set of (ASCII) characters not including newline

$File\text{-}store = File\text{-}name \xrightarrow{m} File$

$File = Document \mid \ldots$

$Document = Line^*$

state $Editor$ of
$\quad\quad doc \;:\; Text$
$\quad\quad cline \;:\; \mathbb{N}$
$\quad\quad cfile \;:\; [File\text{-}name]$
$\quad\quad files \;:\; File\text{-}store$
inv $mk\text{-}Editor(doc, \text{-}, \text{-}, \text{-}) \;\;\triangleq$
$\quad$ len $doc \leq D \;\wedge$
$\quad\quad \forall l \in$ elems $doc \cdot$ len $l \leq L$
end

We will treat a text file as a sequence of $Lines$ in the remainder of this example and leave the refinement of the file commands as specified on pages 292–293 to the reader.

The primitive operations are

$block\text{-}copy \; (s, f : \mathbb{N})$
ext wr $doc \;:\; Text$
pre $s, f \in$ inds $doc \wedge s \leq f \wedge$ len $doc + (f - s + 1) \leq D$
post $doc = \overleftarrow{doc} \frown \overleftarrow{doc}(s, \ldots, f)$

The text between positions s and f inclusive is copied to the end of the document. There must be room in the buffer to duplicate the text.

Worked example 15.1 Write down the specification of the $delete\text{-}end$ operation which deletes the last n lines of a document

SOLUTION

$delete\text{-}end \; (n : \mathbb{N})$
ext wr $doc \;:\; Text$
pre $n \leq$ len doc
post $doc = \overleftarrow{doc}(1, \ldots, \text{len } \overleftarrow{doc} - n)$

The operation deletes the last n lines of the document. The value of the argument to this operation must not be greater than the number of lines currently in the document; i.e. it must not be greater than the current size of the edit buffer.

∎

The specification of the *block-move* operation is a little tricky. There is a restriction: text must not be moved into itself. The actual specification of the operation has to be considered in two parts, each part depending on whether the text to be copied is to be moved to a position in front of where it currently is or after. The complexity is caused by the fact that the text needs to be removed, as well as duplicated elsewhere.

$block$-$move$ $(p, s, f : \mathbb{N})$

ext wr doc : $Text$

pre $p, s, f \in$ inds $doc \land s \leq f \land p \notin \{s, \ldots, f\}$

post let $l = $ len $\overleftarrow{doc}$ in
$$p < s \land$$
$$doc = \overleftarrow{doc}(1, \ldots, p) \frown$$
$$\overleftarrow{doc}(s, \ldots, f) \frown$$
$$\overleftarrow{doc}(p + 1, \ldots, s - 1) \frown$$
$$\overleftarrow{doc}(f + 1, \ldots, l)$$
$$\lor$$
$$f \leq p \land$$
$$doc = \overleftarrow{doc}(1, \ldots, s - 1) \frown$$
$$\overleftarrow{doc}(f + 1, \ldots, p) \frown$$
$$\overleftarrow{doc}(s, \ldots, f) \frown$$
$$\overleftarrow{doc}(p + 1, \ldots, l)$$

The text between positions s and f inclusive is moved to be after line p. The length of the document does not change. The new position for the block of text cannot be inside the block of text that is being moved.

The whole of the correctness of the editor is going to be based on these four primitives; hence is it is well worth writing down some theorems that must hold. Some possibilities are:

- If n lines are deleted from the end of a document, its length must be reduced by that amount.
- If a line is added to the document, its length increases by one.
- If lines s through f are copied from a point within the document to the end, then the length of the document must increase by $f - s + 1$ lines.
- A *block-move* operation of the form $block$-$move(p, p+1, f)$ leaves the buffer unchanged.
- The *block-move* operation should not change the length of the document.

All but the last of these can easily be proved by inspection. The proof of the correctness of the block move property can be done by considering cases as follows:

Case 1. $p < s$

len $(\overleftarrow{doc}(1, \ldots, p) \frown \overleftarrow{doc}(s, \ldots, f) \frown \overleftarrow{doc}(p + 1, \ldots, s - 1) \frown \overleftarrow{doc}(f + 1, \ldots, l))$

$\quad = $ "property of length operator"

$\operatorname{len}\left(\overleftarrow{doc}(1,\ldots,p)\right) + \operatorname{len}\left(\overleftarrow{doc}(s,\ldots,f)\right) + \operatorname{len}\left(\overleftarrow{doc}(p+1,\ldots,s-1)\right) +$

$\quad \operatorname{len}\left(\overleftarrow{doc}(f+1,\ldots,l)\right)$

$\qquad = \text{``definition of length operator''}$

$(p-1+1) + (f-s+1) + (s-1-p-1+1) + (l-f-1+1)$

$\qquad = \text{``simplify''}$

$p + (f-s+1) + (s-1-p) + (l-f)$

$\qquad = \text{``simplify''}$

l

Case 2. $f \leq p$

$\operatorname{len}\left(\overleftarrow{doc}(1,\ldots,s-1) \smallfrown \overleftarrow{doc}(f+1,\ldots,p) \smallfrown \overleftarrow{doc}(s,\ldots,f) \smallfrown \overleftarrow{doc}(p+1,\ldots,l)\right)$

$\qquad = \text{``property of length operator''}$

$\operatorname{len}\left(\overleftarrow{doc}(1,\ldots,s-1)\right) + \operatorname{len}\left(\overleftarrow{doc}(f+1,\ldots,p)\right) + \operatorname{len}\left(\overleftarrow{doc}(s,\ldots,f)\right) +$

$\quad \operatorname{len}\left(\overleftarrow{doc}(p+1,\ldots,l)\right)$

$\qquad = \text{``definition of length operator''}$

$(s-1-1+1) + (p-f-1+1) + (f-s+1) + (l-p-1+1)$

$\qquad = \text{``simplify''}$

l

Rather than read in the text as part of the command and store it somewhere, and then move it to the end of the buffer, it would seem better to store the text in the buffer as it is read in. This suggests some additional primitive operations to the abstract machine. An operation to deal with the lines as they are typed in:

add-line (*ln*: *Line*)
ext wr *doc* : *Text*
pre len *doc* < $D \wedge$ len *ln* $\leq L$
post *doc* = $\overleftarrow{doc} \smallfrown [ln]$

The operation adds a line of text to the end of the buffer; there must be space in the buffer for the text.

Two more primitives are needed for the find and substitute commands; these are an operation to read a line of text and an operation to replace a line of text. They are not really necessary, since the buffer could be manipulated directly, but we will specify them so that the buffer need never be accessed directly, and thus all changes to the buffer can be done by using the abstract machine operations. With this approach, this part of the editor is now independent of the implementation of the buffer:

read-line (*n*:$\mathbb{N}$) *r*: *Line*
ext rd *doc* : *Text*
pre $n \in$ inds *doc*
post $r = doc(n)$

change-line (*n*:$\mathbb{N}$, *ln*: *Line*)
ext wr *doc* : *Text*
pre $n \in$ inds *doc* $\wedge$ len *ln* $\leq L$

$$\text{post } doc = front(\overleftarrow{doc}, n - 1) \mathbin{\frown} [ln] \mathbin{\frown} rest(\overleftarrow{doc}, n + 1)$$

Finally the *init-buffer* operation to clear the buffer:

init-buffer ()

ext wr *doc* : *Text*

post *doc* = [ ]

15.3   THE DEVELOPMENT OF THE EDITING COMMANDS

The next phase of the development is to develop a command processor for each of the edit commands that use the primitive operations on the buffer; these will be taken in the order in which they occur in the design of the editor control function.

15.3.1   The insert command

The operation *execute-insert* takes text as one of its arguments and, to make implementation easier, will have to be respecified so it reads text from the input stream as it executes. Thus the new version of this operation will not have the text as one of the arguments; the actual execution of the commands will read the text from the terminal a line at a time, placing it in the buffer as it goes along. For example, consider the following command to insert text after line 12, the user types:

```
(12) insert
The cat sat on the mat.
The quick brown fox jumps over the lazy dog.
The sky was blue.

.
```

The command can be implemented in terms of the primitive operations on the buffer and will be dealt with in two stages. The line consisting of the insert command alone will be read from the terminal by the *read-command* operation, decoded and control passed to the command processor for the remainder of the command. This command processor will read the remainder of the command (the text to be inserted) from the terminal and use the *add-line* operation to place the text into the buffer, until it reads a line consisting of just a '.'. The *block-move* operation can then be used to move this text to the insertion point. The current line pointer also needs to be reset.

   The *execute-insert* operation will need to be changed to reflect the decision to read the text component from the terminal line by line. The new specification is given below—we have skipped a step and specified the operation as a procedure and its body:

execute-insert (*ln*: *Line-num*)

$(execute\text{-}insert\text{-}body$

 ext rd $ln: \mathbb{N}$

  wr $doc: Text$

  $cline: \mathbb{N}$

  $files: File\text{-}store$

 pre $is\text{-}line\text{-}in\text{-}doc(ln, doc) \wedge$

  $files(\text{STDIN}) \in Input\text{-}file \wedge$

  let $mk\text{-}Input\text{-}file(\text{-}, r) = files(\text{STDIN})$ in

  $['.']$ ins $r \wedge$

  let $i = index(['.'], r)$ in

  let $t = front(r, i - 1)$ in

  $\forall l \in$ elems $t \cdot$ len $l \leq L \wedge$

  len $t +$ len $doc \leq D$

 post let $mk\text{-}Input\text{-}file(l, r) = \overleftarrow{files}(\text{STDIN})$ in

  let $i = index(['.'], r)$ in

  let $t = front(r, i - 1)$ in

  $doc = front(\overleftarrow{doc}, ln) \frown t \frown rest(\overleftarrow{doc}, ln + 1) \wedge$

  $cline = \overleftarrow{ln} +$ len $t \wedge$

  $files = \overleftarrow{files} \dagger \{\text{STDIN} \mapsto mk\text{-}Input\text{-}file(l \frown front(r, i), rest(r, i + 1))\}$

$) \; -- \; execute\text{-}insert$

Notice how the specification assumes that all the input is available—it models a complete session with the editor. The operation is guaranteed to always find a line consisting of a '.' character only, since the input stream STDIN is a representation of what is typed at the terminal, and the user of the editor must type a line consisting of a single full-stop to get out of input mode. It can be safely assumed that the user cannot type forever.

After the text has been read from the input stream it is appended after the line specified in the command, and the current line number is set to point to the last line of the appended text. There is a problem if the user types in more text than there is space in the buffer; one of the things that the implementation could do is to force the equivalent of a line consisting of just a period to be read if the text buffer becomes full, and issue a message warning that the buffer is full so that the user should save the buffer to disk. What the user would do next is not covered by this specification, and can not be.

The body of the operation can be split into two operations. The operation *read-and-mark-text* will place the new lines of text at the end of the buffer and record the position of the new text. The operation *move-text* will move it to the right place (the intention is to use the primitive *block-move* operation here).

A difficulty arises from the case when no text is appended, which happens if the user just types a line consisting of '.' as the body of the insert command. If the specification for *read-and-mark-text* is examined, the finish pointer certainly points to the last line of the document, but the value of *start* points to a position just off the end of the document, and its value does not designate a part of the document. Hence the pre-condition for *block-move* will not have been established by the *read-and-mark-text* operation. The problem can be solved by testing that some text has actually been entered, and this can be found by checking that the value of *start* is less than or equal to the value of *finish* before calling *block-move*, this decision has been reflected in the post-condition for *move-text*.

The pre-condition of *move-text* was obtained by knowing what pre-condition is required for *block-move* and making certain that the pre-condition of *move-text* sets things up correctly. Thus we have

$$ln \in \text{inds } doc \wedge ln < start$$

and have preserved the information that *ln* pointed to a line within the document before it was extended by the text that was read in from the user.

The refinement is shown in Fig. 15.3. To simplify the specification four logical constants have been introduced. Two are just to avoid the use of repeated let expressions, these are *i* to record the position of the '.' in the input stream and *t* to identify the text that is to be read in. The other two, *f* for the initial value of the file store and *d* for the initial value of the document, are used to remove hooked identifiers from the post-condition to prepare for the introduction of a loop. A reorganization of the post-condition that uses the fact that

$$l \frown front(r, i) = l \frown t \frown [\text{'.'}]$$

has also been carried out. Though the result looks rather complicated, the refinement can be seen to be correct by inspection.

The *read-and-mark-text* operation   This operation will read text from the terminal and insert it to the buffer. The operation can be refined into three suboperations: set the *start* pointer, read text from the user and place it in the buffer and then set the *finish* pointer.

$$
\begin{aligned}
&\textit{read-and-mark-text} \sqsubseteq \\
&\textit{start} := \text{len } doc + 1; \\
&; \\
&\textit{read-text} \\
&\textbf{ext wr } doc \qquad : \textit{Text} \\
&\qquad \textit{files} \qquad : \textit{File-store} \\
&\qquad \textbf{lc } i, d, t, f \\
&\textbf{pre } f(\text{STDIN}) \in \textit{Input-file} \wedge \\
&\qquad \text{len } t + \text{len } d \leq D \\
&\textbf{post let } mk\text{-}Input\text{-}file(l, r) = f(\text{STDIN}) \textbf{ in} \\
&\qquad doc = d \frown t \wedge \\
&\qquad files = f \dagger \{\text{STDIN} \mapsto mk\text{-}Input\text{-}file(l \frown t \frown [\text{'.'}], rest(r, i + 1)\} \\
&; \\
&\textit{finish} := \text{len } doc
\end{aligned}
$$

The refinement of *read-text* will obviously involve a loop that reads a line of text from the terminal and places it into the buffer. The post-condition for *read-text* can be rewritten using a temporary identifier *input* to denote the current input line

$$
\begin{aligned}
&\textbf{post let } mk\text{-}Input\text{-}file(l, r) = f(\text{STDIN}) \textbf{ in} \\
&\qquad input = \text{'.'} \wedge \\
&\qquad doc = d \frown t \wedge \\
&\qquad files = f \dagger \{\text{STDIN} \mapsto mk\text{-}Input\text{-}file(l \frown t \frown input, rest(r, i + 1)\}
\end{aligned}
$$

$execute\text{-}insert$ $(ln\!:Line\text{-}num)$

(dcl $start, finish$: $\mathbf{N}$;

  $execute\text{-}insert\text{-}body$

  ext rd $ln\!:\mathbf{N}$

      wr $doc\!:Text$

      $cline\!:\mathbf{N}$

      $files\!:File\text{-}store$

      lc $i\!:\mathbf{N}$ $d, t\!:Text$ $f\!:File\text{-}store$

  pre $d = doc \wedge f = files \wedge$

    $is\text{-}line\text{-}in\text{-}doc(ln, doc) \wedge$

    $files(\text{STDIN}) \in Input\text{-}file \wedge$

    let $mk\text{-}Input\text{-}file(\text{-}, r) = files(\text{STDIN})$ in

    $[\text{`.'}]$ ins $r \wedge$

    $i = index([\text{`.'}], r) \wedge$

    $t = front(r, i - 1) \wedge$

    $\forall l \in$ elems $t \cdot$ len $l \leq L \wedge$

    len $t +$ len $d \leq D$

        $read\text{-}and\text{-}mark\text{-}text$

        ext wr $doc, files$

          $start, finish\!:\mathbf{N}$

          lc i, d, t, f

        pre $f(\text{STDIN}) \in Input\text{-}File \wedge$

          len $t +$ len $d \leq D$

        post let $mk\text{-}Input\text{-}file(l, r) = f(\text{STDIN})$ in

            $doc = d \frown t \wedge$

            $files = f \dagger \{\text{STDIN} \mapsto mk\text{-}Input\text{-}file(l \frown t \frown [\text{`.'}], rest(r, i+1))\} \wedge$

            $start =$ len $d + 1 \wedge finish =$ len doc

        ;

        $move\text{-}text$

        ext wr $doc, cline$

          rd ln

          $start, finish\!:\mathbf{N}$

          lc d

        pre $ln \in$ inds $doc \wedge ln < start \wedge finish =$ len $doc \wedge start =$ len $d + 1$

        post $start \leq finish \wedge$

            $doc = d(1, \ldots, ln) \frown d(start, \ldots, finish) \frown d(ln+1, \ldots, start-1) \wedge$

            $cline = ln + finish - start + 1$

               $\vee$

            $start > finish \wedge$

            $doc = d \wedge$

            $cline = ln$

  post let $mk\text{-}Input\text{-}file(l, r) = f(\text{STDIN})$ in

    $doc = front(d, ln) \frown t \frown rest(d, ln+1) \wedge$

    $cline = ln +$ len $t \wedge$

    $files = f \dagger \{\text{STDIN} \mapsto mk\text{-}Input\text{-}file(l \frown front(r, i), rest(r, i+1))\}$

) $--$ $execute\text{-}insert$

Figure 15.3   The refinement of the operation $execute\text{-}insert$.

Now the standard technique of developing a loop by introducing a temporary variable will work.

Worked example 15.2 How should a temporary variable be introduced so that the loop can be developed to satisfy the specification for *read-text*?

SOLUTION If a temporary variable j is introduced of type $\mathbf{N}$ the post-condition can be rewritten as:

let $mk\text{-}Input\text{-}file(l, r) = f(\text{STDIN})$ in
$input = (t \frown [\text{'.'}])(j) \wedge$
$doc = d \frown t(1, \ldots, j-1) \wedge$
$files = f \dagger \{\text{STDIN} \mapsto mk\text{-}Input\text{-}file(l \frown t(1, \ldots, j-1) \frown input, rest(r, j+1))\} \wedge$
$j = i$

∎

The loop can now be derived from the new post-condition.

init $j := 1;$ *input* from STDIN
guard $j \neq i$
inv   let $mk\text{-}Input\text{-}file(l, r) = f(\text{STDIN})$ in
      $input = (t \frown [\text{'.'}])(j) \wedge$
      $doc = d \frown t(1, \ldots, j-1) \wedge$
      $files = f \dagger \{\text{STDIN} \mapsto mk\text{-}Input\text{-}file(l \frown t(1, \ldots, j-1) \frown input, rest(r, j+1))\}$
var $0 \leq i - j < i - \overleftarrow{j}$

We will increase j by one to establish the variant expression and then (re-)establish the invariant. The second term can be established by adding the new line to the buffer and the first term and third terms of the invariant can be established by reading the next line of text from the input stream. This gives the following code:

$j := 1;$
input from STDIN;
while $j \neq i$ do
$\quad j := j + 1;$
$\quad$ *add-line(input)*;
$\quad$ *input* from STDIN
end

which unfortunately contains the logical constant i. However, using the definitions of the logical constants, we can show that the test $j \neq i$ is equivalent to *input* $\neq$ '.' and can thus be replaced. We can also remove all references to j as well, therefore

$read\text{-}text \sqsubseteq$ *input* from STDIN;
$\qquad\qquad$ while *input* $\neq$ '.' do
$\qquad\qquad\quad$ *add-line(input)*;
$\qquad\qquad\quad$ *input* from STDIN
$\qquad\qquad$ end

The *move-text* operation The second operation in the refinement of *execute-insert-body* is one to move text from the end of the buffer to the correct place. This operation can be refined using alternation. If text has been entered, it is moved: in this case the insertion point for the text to be moved comes before the text to be moved, since the new text was placed at the end of the buffer and will be inserted somewhere in the middle of the existing text. If no text has been entered, there is no change to the buffer. If text does need to be moved, it can be moved by the *block-move* operation, which was the original intention. The refinement is shown in Fig. 15.4 and the proof of this can be done by inspection.

move-text
ext wr *doc*　　　　　　　: *Text*
　　　cline　　　　　: **N**
　　rd *ln, start, finish* : **N**
pre *ln* $\in$ inds *doc* $\wedge$ *ln* < *start* $\wedge$ *finish* = len *doc* $\wedge$ *start* = len *doc* + 1

$\qquad$ if *start* $\leq$ *finish* then
$\qquad\quad$ *move-input*

$\qquad\qquad$ pre *ln* $\in$ inds *doc* $\wedge$ *ln* < *start* $\wedge$ *start* = len $\overleftarrow{doc}$ + 1
$\qquad\qquad\quad$ *start* $\leq$ *finish* $\wedge$ *finish* = len *doc*
$\qquad\qquad$ post *doc* = *d*(1, ..., *ln*) $\frown$ *d*(*start*, ..., *finish*) $\frown$ *d*(*ln* + 1, ..., *start* − 1) $\wedge$
$\qquad\qquad\quad$ *cline* = *ln* + *finish* − *start* + 1
$\qquad$ else
$\qquad\quad$ *cline* := *ln*
$\qquad$ end
post *start* $\leq$ *finish* $\wedge$

$\qquad$ *doc* = *d*(1, ..., *ln*) $\frown$ *d*(*start*, ..., *finish*) $\frown$ *d*(*ln* + 1, ..., *start* − 1) $\wedge$
$\qquad$ *cline* = *ln* + *finish* − *start* + 1
$\qquad\qquad$ $\vee$
$\qquad$ *start* > *finish* $\wedge$
$\qquad$ *doc* = *d* $\wedge$
$\qquad$ *cline* = *ln*

move-input $\sqsubseteq$
pre *start* $\leq$ *finish* $\wedge$
$\qquad$ *ln* $\in$ inds *doc* $\wedge$ *ln* $\leq$ *finish* $\wedge$
$\qquad$ *start* = len $\overleftarrow{doc}$ + 1 $\wedge$ *finish* = len *doc*
post *doc* = *d*(1, ..., *ln*) $\frown$ *d*(*start*, ..., *finish*) $\frown$ *d*(*ln* + 1, ..., *start* − 1)
;
pre true
post *cline* = *ln* + *finish* − *start* + 1

Figure 15.4　A refinement of the operation *move-text*.

The code for the *execute-insert* **operation** This completes the correctness proof of the decomposition of *execute-insert*. Everything should be put together to produce the final code:

execute-insert (*ln*: *Line-num*)
(dcl *start*, *finish* : **N**;
  −− read-and-mark-text
  start: = len *doc* + 1;
  input from STDIN;
  while *input* ≠ '.' do
    add-line(*input*);
    input from STDIN
  end;
  finish: = len *doc*;
  −− move-text
  if *start* ≤ *finish* then
    block-move(*ln*, *start*, *finish*);
    cline: = *ln* + *finish* − *start* + 1
  else
    cline: = *ln*
  end
) −− *execute-insert*

15.3.2 The copy command

The *execute-copy* command had the following specification:

execute-copy (*lr*: *Line-range*, *ln*: *Line-num*)
ext wr *doc* : *Text*
  cline : **N**
pre *is-range-in-doc*(*lr*, *doc*) ∧
  is-line-in-doc(*ln*, *doc*) ∧
  size(*lr*) + len *doc* ≤ *D*
post *doc* = *front*($\overleftarrow{doc}$, *ln*) ⌢ *sub-doc*($\overleftarrow{doc}$, *lr*) ⌢ *rest*($\overleftarrow{doc}$, *ln* + 1) ∧
  cline = *ln* + *size*(*lr*)

The text to be copied is duplicated and the copy inserted after the line specified in the command. This can be implemented by replicating the text to be copied at the end of the buffer using the *block-copy* operation and then moving the text to the target position using *block-move*.

execute-copy (*lr*: *Line-range*, *ln*: *Line-num*)
(dcl *fin* : **N**;

    ext wr $doc\colon Text$

        $cline\colon \mathbb{N}$

    pre $is\text{-}range\text{-}in\text{-}doc(lr, doc) \wedge$

        $is\text{-}line\text{-}in\text{-}doc(ln, doc) \wedge$

        $size(lr) + \mathsf{len}\ doc \leq D$

            $fin\colon= \mathsf{len}\ doc;$

            $block\text{-}copy(lr.first, lr.last);$

            $block\text{-}move(ln, fin + 1, \mathsf{len}\ doc);$

            $cline\colon= ln + lr.last - lr.first + 1$

    post $doc = front(\overleftarrow{doc}, ln) \frown sub\text{-}doc(\overleftarrow{doc}, lr) \frown rest(\overleftarrow{doc}, ln + 1) \wedge$

        $cline = ln + size(lr)$

    $)\ -\!-\ execute\text{-}copy$

The proofs will be done informally for this operation. It is necessary to show that this sequence of four operations is a refinement of the specification for *execute-copy*. As usual, the proof is in two stages. The first stage is to show that the original pre-condition sets things up for the first operation of the refinement, and each of the operations in the sequence sets things up for the one that follows it—each operation establishes the pre-conditions for the next operation. The pre-conditions for *block-copy* and *block-move* are guaranteed by the pre-condition of *execute-copy*; the pre-conditions for the two assignments are true, so are trivially satisfied.

Second, that the post-condition for the sequence of four operations implies the post-condition for *execute-copy* can be seen by inspection.

The code for the operation is thus

    $execute\text{-}copy\ (lr\colon Line\text{-}range, ln\colon Line\text{-}num)$

    $(\mathsf{dcl}\ fin\ \colon\ \mathbb{N};$

    $fin\colon= \mathsf{len}\ doc;$

    $block\text{-}copy(lr.first, lr.last);$

    $block\text{-}move(ln, fin + 1, \mathsf{len}\ doc);$

    $cline\colon= ln + lr.last - lr.first + 1$

    $)\ -\!-\ execute\text{-}copy$

15.3.3 The delete command

The delete command was specified as follows:

    $execute\text{-}delete\ (lr\colon Line\text{-}range)$

    ext wr $doc\ \colon\ Text$

        $cline\ \ \colon\ \mathbb{N}$

    pre $is\text{-}range\text{-}in\text{-}doc(lr, doc)$

    post $doc = front(\overleftarrow{doc}, lr.first - 1) \frown rest(\overleftarrow{doc}, lr.last + 1) \wedge$

        $cline = lr.first$

The text specified by the line specification is removed from the document. In this command, the new current line is the one following the deleted text. The implementation of this in terms of the primitives will be to move the text to be deleted to the end of the buffer using the *block-move* operation, and then remove it by using the *delete-end* primitive, finally setting the current line.

$$execute\text{-}delete \ (lr: Line\text{-}range)$$

$$(execute\text{-}delete\text{-}body$$
$$\text{ext wr } doc: Text$$
$$cline: \mathbb{N}$$
$$\text{rd } lr: Line\text{-}range$$
$$\text{pre } is\text{-}range\text{-}in\text{-}doc(lr, doc)$$

$$block\text{-}move(\text{len } doc, lr.first, lr.last);$$
$$delete\text{-}end(lr.last - lr.first + 1);$$
$$cline := lr.first$$

$$\text{post } doc = front(\overleftarrow{doc}, lr.first - 1) \,^\frown rest(\overleftarrow{doc}, lr.last + 1) \land$$
$$cline = lr.first$$
$$) \ -- \ execute\text{-}delete$$

The pre-condition for the *execute-delete* operation, plus the fact that text is being moved to a target position which is within the document, namely the last line, guarantees the pre-condition for *block-move*. The pre-condition for *execute-delete* also guarantees the pre-condition for *delete-end* (remember that *block-move* does not change the line range). The last operation in the sequence has a pre-condition of true. Thus, all of the pre-conditions for the operations in the sequence are set up correctly.

The proof of the post-condition can be done by replacing each call by a suitable expansion of the pre- and post-conditions of the called operation. A sketch of the proof is show in Fig. 15.5.

15.3.4 The move command

The specification for this operation was

$$execute\text{-}move \ (lr: Line\text{-}range, ln: Line\text{-}num)$$

$$\text{ext wr } doc \ : \ Text$$
$$cline \ : \ \mathbb{N}$$

$$\text{pre } is\text{-}range\text{-}in\text{-}doc(lr, doc) \land$$
$$is\text{-}line\text{-}in\text{-}doc(ln, doc) \land$$
$$no\text{-}overlap(ln, lr)$$

$$\text{post } (\text{let } mk\text{-}Line\text{-}range(s, f) = lr \text{ in}$$
$$\text{let } moved = sub\text{-}doc(\overleftarrow{doc}, lr) \text{ in}$$
$$ln < s \land$$
$$doc = \overleftarrow{doc}(1, \ldots, ln) \,^\frown moved \,^\frown \overleftarrow{doc}(ln + 1, \ldots, s - 1) \,^\frown rest(\overleftarrow{doc}, f + 1)$$
$$\lor$$
$$f \leq ln \land$$
$$doc = \overleftarrow{doc}(1, \ldots, s - 1) \,^\frown \overleftarrow{doc}(f + 1, \ldots, ln) \,^\frown moved \,^\frown rest(\overleftarrow{doc}, ln + 1)) \land$$
$$cline = ln + size(lr)$$

Writing s for $lr.first$ and f for $lr.last$

$$\exists doc_1 \in Text \cdot \text{let } l = \text{len } doc_0 \text{ in}$$
$$(l < s \wedge \tag{2}$$
$$doc_1 = doc_0(1, \ldots, l)^\frown$$
$$doc_0(s, \ldots, f)^\frown$$
$$doc_0(l + 1, \ldots, s - 1)^\frown$$
$$doc_0(f + 1, \ldots, l)$$
$$\vee$$
$$f \leq l \wedge \tag{8}$$
$$doc_1 = doc_0(1, \ldots, s - 1)^\frown$$
$$doc_0(f + 1, \ldots, l)^\frown$$
$$doc_0(s, \ldots, f)^\frown$$
$$doc_0(l + 1, \ldots, l)$$
$$) \wedge$$
$$doc = doc_1(1, \ldots, l - (f - s + 1)) \wedge$$
$$cline = s \tag{15}$$
$$\Rightarrow \ doc = front(doc_0, s - 1) ^\frown rest(doc_0, f + 1) \wedge$$
$$cline = s$$

Now $f \leq l$, therefore

doc_1

$\quad = $ "line 9 of hypothesis"

$doc_0(1, \ldots, s - 1) ^\frown doc_0(f + 1, \ldots, l) ^\frown doc_0(s, \ldots, f) ^\frown doc_0(l + 1, \ldots, l)$

$\quad = $ "definition of indexing"

$doc_0(1, \ldots, s - 1) ^\frown doc_0(f + 1, \ldots, l) ^\frown doc_0(s, \ldots, f)$

and

doc

$\quad = $ "line 14 of hypothesis"

$doc_1(1, \ldots, l - (f - s + 1))$

$\quad = $ " substituting for doc_1"

$(doc_0(1, \ldots, s - 1) ^\frown doc_0(f + 1, \ldots, l) ^\frown doc_0(s, \ldots, f))(1, \ldots, l - (f - s + 1))$

$\quad = $ "the first $l - (f - s + 1)$ elements of doc_0"

$doc_0(1, \ldots, s - 1) ^\frown doc_0(f + 1, \ldots, l)$

$\quad = $ "definition of $front$ and $rest$"

$front(doc_0, s - 1) ^\frown rest(doc_0, f + 1)$

Figure 15.5 Sketch proof of *execute-delete*.

The current line number is set to the last line of the text that was moved.

> **Worked example 15.3** How can this specification be realized by using the *block-move* operation to move the text to the correct position? Write down a definition in the style of the previous definitions.

SOLUTION

$$execute\text{-}move\ (lr\colon Line\text{-}range, ln\colon Line\text{-}num)$$

$(execute\text{-}move\text{-}body$

ext wr $doc\colon Text$

$\qquad cline\colon\mathbb{N}$

pre $is\text{-}range\text{-}in\text{-}doc(ls, doc)\ \wedge$

$\qquad is\text{-}line\text{-}in\text{-}doc(ln, doc)\ \wedge$

$\qquad no\text{-}overlap(ln, lr)$

$$block\text{-}move(ln, lr.first, lr.last)$$

post (let $mk\text{-}Line\text{-}range(s, f) = lr$ in

$\qquad$ let $moved = sub\text{-}doc(\overleftarrow{doc}, lr)$ in

$\qquad ln < s\ \wedge$

$\qquad doc = \overleftarrow{doc}(1, \ldots, ln)\ \frown\ moved\ \frown\ \overleftarrow{doc}(ln+1, \ldots, s-1)\ \frown\ rest(\overleftarrow{doc}, f+1)$

$\qquad\qquad \vee$

$\qquad f \le ln\ \wedge$

$\qquad doc = \overleftarrow{doc}(1, \ldots, s-1)\ \frown\ \overleftarrow{doc}(f+1, \ldots, ln)\ \frown\ moved\ \frown\ rest(\overleftarrow{doc}, ln+1))\ \wedge$

$\qquad cline = ln + size(lr)$

$)\ --\ execute\text{-}move$

■

The proof of *execute-move-body* is straightforward as the pre- and post-conditions for *block-move* and *execute-move-body* are similar. The code is

$$execute\text{-}move\ (lr\colon Line\text{-}range, ln\colon Line\text{-}num)$$

$(block\text{-}move(ln, lr.first, lr.last)$

$)\ --\ execute\text{-}move$

15.3.5 The current-line command

The specification for this operation is

$$execute\text{-}current\ (ln\colon Line\text{-}num)$$

ext rd $doc\quad\colon Text$

$\quad$ wr $cline\ \colon\mathbb{N}$

pre $is\text{-}line\text{-}in\text{-}doc(ln, doc)\ \wedge\ ln \ne 0$

post $cline = ln$

The current line is set to the new value. This is trivially implemented as follows:

> *execute-current* (*ln*: **N**)
> (*cline*: = *ln*
>) -- *execute-current*

15.3.6 The show command

The show command displays the current line number at the terminal:

> *execute-show* ()
> ext rd *cline* : **N**
>   wr *files* : *File-store*
> pre *files*(STDOUT) ∈ *Output-file*
>
> post let *mk-Output-file*(*data*) = $\overleftarrow{files}$(STDOUT) in
>   let *output* = [*mk-Lnum-ecko*(*cline*)] in
>   *files* = $\overleftarrow{files}$ † {STDOUT ↦ *mk-Output-file*(*data* ⌢ *output*)}

The implementation of this is simple:

> *execute-show* ()
> (*mk-Lnum-ecko*(*cline*) to STDOUT
>) -- *execute-show*

15.3.7 The display command

The specification for this operation is

> *execute-display* (*lr*: *Line-range*)
> ext rd *doc* : *Text*
>   *cline* : **N**
>   wr *files* : *File-store*
> pre *files*(STDOUT) ∈ *Output-file* ∧
>   *is-range-in-doc*(*lr*, *doc*)
>
> post let *mk-Output-file*(*data*) = $\overleftarrow{files}$(STDOUT) in
>   let *output* = [*mk-Line-ecko*(*doc*(*i*)) | *i* ∈ {*lr.first*, ..., *lr.last*}] in
>   *files* = $\overleftarrow{files}$ † {STDOUT ↦ *mk-Output-file*(*data* ⌢ *output*)} ∧
>   *cline* = *lr.last*

The implementation is

> *execute-display* (*lr*: *Line-range*)
> (*cline*: = *lr.first*;
> while *cline* ≤ *lr.last* do
>   *mk-Text-echo*(*doc*(*cline*)) to STDOUT;
>   *cline*: = *cline* + 1
> end
>) -- *execute-display*

The output command puts the lines specified to the terminal. The current line number is set to the last line printed. The proof of *execute-display* is left as an exercise for the reader. A possible strategy is to write down the property that

$$cline - lr.first$$

counts the number of lines output, and that (roughly speaking)

$$\text{'text output so far'} \curvearrowright doc(cline, \ldots, lr.last)$$

is constant and equal to all the text that is to be displayed.

15.3.8   The find command

The specification for this command is

$$execute\text{-}find \; (lr: Line\text{-}range, pat: Pattern)$$

ext rd *doc*   : *Text*
  wr *cline* : $\mathbb{N}$

pre *is-range-in-doc*(*lr*, *doc*)

post *pat* ins $(sub\text{-}doc(doc, lr)(cline - lr.first + 1))$
  $\lor$
  $\neg \exists l \in$ elems $sub\text{-}doc(doc, lr) \cdot pat$ ins $l \land cline = \overleftarrow{cline}$

A possible method is to scan the buffer looking for a match. A loop can be constructed with an invariant which is about not finding a match so far, a relation which is about making progress and a guard which is about finding a match or not falling off the end of the buffer. These three predicates are

guard $i \leq lr.last \land \neg pat$ ins $read\text{-}line(i)$
inv $\neg \exists l \in$ elems $doc(lr.first, \ldots, i-1) \cdot pat$ ins l
var $0 \leq lr.last - i < lr.last - \overleftarrow{i}$

and it is left as an exercise to show that the following code is correct:

$$execute\text{-}find \; (lr: Line\text{-}range, pat: Pattern)$$
(dcl i : $\mathbb{N}$;
$i := lr.first$;
while $i \leq lr.last \land \neg pat$ ins $read\text{-}line(i)$ do
  $i := i + 1$
end;
if $i \leq lr.last$ then $cline := i$ else skip end
) $--$ *execute-find*

If the pattern is to be found somewhere in the lines specified, then the current line is set to a line that contains the pattern. If the pattern is not to be found, then the current line is left alone.

15.3.9   The substitute command

The specification for this command is

execute-substitute (*lr*: *Line-range*, *old*: *Pattern*, *new*: *Pattern*)
ext wr *doc* : *Text*
   cline : $\mathbb{N}$
pre *is-range-in-doc*(*lr*, *doc*) $\land$
   $\forall i \in$ **inds** *doc* $\cdot$ **len** *sub*(*old*, *new*, *doc*(*i*)) $\le L$
post let *txt* = *subst*(*old*, *new*, *sub-doc*($\overleftarrow{doc}$, *lr*)) **in**
   doc = *front*($\overleftarrow{doc}$, *lr.first* − 1) $^\frown$ *txt* $^\frown$ *rest*($\overleftarrow{doc}$, *lr.last* + 1) $\land$
   cline = *lr.last*

The definition of *subst* can be found on page 291.

The specification states that all the lines that are in range of the line specification are scanned, and any occurrences of the old pattern in the command are replaced by the new pattern. This sketch of an algorithm suggests that a loop to scan each of the lines is necessary, thus a guard, a relation and an invariant will need to be discovered. The relation for the loop must describe the relationship between two iterations of the loop; in this example, at any point during the scan of the buffer

front of the buffer $^\frown$ part of buffer still to be scanned $^\frown$ remainder

remains constant. An application of the function body rule, the following assignment rule and the introduction of logical constants will give

execute-substitute (*lr*: *Line-range*, *old*: *Pattern*, *new*: *Pattern*)
(*substitute-body*
  ext wr *doc*: *Text*
    lc *d*, *t*: *Text*
  pre *is-range-in-doc*(*lr*, *doc*) $\land$
    $\forall i \in$ **inds** *doc* $\cdot$ **len** *sub*(*old*, *new*, *doc*(*i*)) $\le L \land$
    d = *doc* $\land$ *t* = *subst*(*old*, *new*, *sub-doc*($\overleftarrow{doc}$, *lr*))
  post *doc* = *front*(*d*, *lr.first* − 1) $^\frown$ *t* $^\frown$ *rest*(*d*, *lr.last* + 1)
  ;
  cline:= *lr.last*
) −− *execute-substitute*

the post-condition of *substitute-body* can be rewritten as

doc = *front*(*d*, *lr.first* − 1) $^\frown$ *t*(1, . . . , *i*) $^\frown$ *rest*(*d*, *lr.first* + *i*) $\land$
i = *lr.last* − *lr.first* + 1

The guard, invariant and variant can now be easily derived, the specification for the loop is then given by

guard *i* $\ne$ *lr.last* − *lr.first* + 1
inv   *doc* = *front*(*d*, *lr.first* − 1) $^\frown$ *t*(1, . . . , *i*) $^\frown$ *rest*(*d*, *lr.first* + *i*)
var   0 $\le$ *lr.last* − *lr.first* + 1 − *i* < *lr.last* − *lr.first* + 1 − $\overleftarrow{i}$

The specification of the loop body is

loop-body
pre *i* $\ne$ *lr.last* − *lr.first* + 1 $\land$
    doc = *front*(*d*, *lr.first* − 1) $^\frown$ *t*(1, . . . , *i*) $^\frown$ *rest*(*d*, *lr.first* + *i*)

$$\text{post } doc = front(d, lr.first - 1) \frown t(1, \ldots, i) \frown rest(d, lr.first + i) \land$$
$$0 \le lr.last - lr.first + 1 - \overleftarrow{i} < lr.last - lr.first + 1 - i$$

It can be shown that

```
i:= 0;
line:= read-line(lr.first + i);
if old ins line then
   line:= sub(line, old, new);
   change-line(line, lr.first + i)
else
   skip
end;
i:= i + 1
```

satisfies the specification for the loop body. This is rather difficult and is done by unwinding the recursive definition of *subst*, and is left as an exercise for the reader, as is the refinement of the function *sub*. Putting this all together and replacing $lr.first + i$ by i gives:

```
execute-substitute (lr: Line-range, old: Pattern, new: Pattern)
(dcl i : N;
i:= lr.first;
while i ≤ lr.last do
   line:= read-line(i);
   if old ins line then
      line:= sub(line, old, new);
      change-line(line, i)
   else
      skip
   end;
   i:= i + 1;
end;
cline = lr.last
) -- execute-substitute
```

This is not the best possible refinement since there is likely to be a duplication of effort—the work done by the code to realize the test *old* ins *line* will be repeated by the *sub(line, old, new)* function.

Exercise 15.1

1. Replace the use of the ins operator by a function. Specify and refine your function.
2. Prove the refinement of the find command to be correct.
3. Prove the refinement of the operation *read-and-mark-text* into

```
start:= len doc + 1;
read-text;
finish:= len doc
```

4. Prove the refinement of the body of the operation *execute-copy* on page 315.

5. Prove the following refinement of the body of the operation *execute-display* on page 319.

6. Complete the development of *execute-substitute*. Can you improve on the final algorithm?

7. The text specified is replaced by the text supplied, and the current line is set to the line following the last line of the inserted text.

$$Xchange :: range : Line\text{-}spec$$
$$text : Line^*$$

A possible specification for the exchange command operation is

$execute\text{-}xchange\ (lr: Line\text{-}range)$

ext wr $doc\ :\ Text$
  $cline\quad :\ \mathbf{N}$
  $files\quad :\ File\text{-}store$

pre $is\text{-}range\text{-}in\text{-}doc(lr, doc)\ \wedge$
  let $mk\text{-}Input\text{-}file(\text{-}, r) = files(\text{STDIN})$ in
  $[\text{`.'}]$ ins $r\ \wedge$
  let $i = index([\text{`.'}], doc)$ in
  let $t = front(r, i - 1)$ in
  $\forall l \in$ elems $t \cdot$ len $l \leq L\ \wedge$
  len $doc +$ len $t \leq D$

post let $mk\text{-}Input\text{-}file(l, r) = \overleftarrow{files}(\text{STDIN})$ in
  let $i = index([\text{`.'}], r)$ in
  let $text = front(r, i - 1)$ in
  $doc = front(\overleftarrow{doc}, lr.first - 1) \frown text \frown rest(\overleftarrow{doc}, lr.last + 1)\ \wedge$
  $cline = lr.first +$ len $text\ \wedge$
  $files = \overleftarrow{files} \dagger \{\text{STDIN} \mapsto mk\text{-}Input\text{-}file(l \frown r(1, \ldots, i), rest(r, i + 1))\}$

The text specified is replaced by the text supplied, and the current line is set to the line following the last line of the inserted text. This can be implemented as follows: the text which is part of the command is placed at the end of the buffer; the text to be replaced is also moved to the end of the buffer using *block-move*. The new text is moved into its target position using the *block-move* command, and the text to be deleted can finally be removed from the end of the buffer using the *delete* operation. Develop and prove the correct the body of the following procedure.

$execute\text{-}xchange\ (lr: Line\text{-}range)$

$(\ldots$
$)\ -\!-\ execute\text{-}xchange$

15.4 THE DEVELOPMENT OF THE FILE COMMANDS

The operations that access and change the file to be edited are specified below.

15.4.1   The edit command

The buffer is initialized, the current line is set:

execute-edit (*fn*: [*File-name*])

ext wr *doc* : *Text*
    cline   : **N**
    cfile   : [*File-name*]
    rd *files* : *File-store*

post *fn* ∉ dom *files* ∧ *doc* = [ ] ∧ *cline* = 0 ∧ *cfile* = *fn*
    ∨
    fn ∈ dom *files* ∧ *files*(*fn*) = [ ] ∧ *doc* = [ ] ∧ *cline* = 0 ∧ *cfile* = *fn*
    ∨
    fn ∈ dom *files* ∧ *doc* = *files*(*fn*) ∧ *cline* = 1 ∧ *cfile* = *fn*

If the file does not exist, or if one was not quoted, or if the file is empty, the buffer is initialized with the empty document. If the file exists in the filing system, then it is loaded into the buffer. The current file name is set if one was quoted; otherwise it is left empty. The first refinement of this operation is to split the post-condition:

execute-edit (*fn*: [*File-name*])

(dcl *line* : *Line*;

  init-buffer();
  if *exists*(*fn*) then
    ext wr *doc*: *Text*
        cline: **N**
        cfile: [*File-name*]
        rd *files*: *File-store*
    pre *fn* ∈ dom *files*
    post *files*(*fn*) = [ ] ∧ *doc* = [ ] ∧ *cline* = 0
        ∨
        fn ∈ dom *files* ∧ *doc* = *files*(*fn*) ∧ *cline* = 1
  else
    skip
  end;
  cfile: = *fn*
) −− *execute-edit*

Each of the components of the if statement can be developed separately. The starting point for developing the loop is that at any time

text in buffer ⌢ text to be read from file = constant = original text of file

From this the loop can be developed to give the following refinement:

execute-edit (*fn*: [*File-name*])

(dcl *line* : *Line*;

```
    init-buffer();
    if exists(fn) then
       open fn for input;
       while ¬ eof(fn) do
          line from fn;
          add-line(line)
       end;
       close fn;
       cline: = if len doc > 0  then 1  else 0;
    else
       skip
    end;
    cfile: = fn
    ) −− execute-edit
```

This is a case where the code to be written is of a familiar style and where the proof of correctness can be done by inspection. As the problem is a familiar one, perhaps it would be worthwhile doing a proof of correctness just once, and this is left for the reader.

The auxiliary function *exists* is easily defined and implemented:

$exists$ $(fn\colon [\textit{File-name}])$ $r\colon \mathbf{B}$

ext rd $files$: $\textit{File-store}$

post $r \Leftrightarrow fn \in \mathrm{dom}\, files$

15.4.2   The write command

The specification of the *execute-write* command is:

$execute\text{-}write$ $(fn\colon [\textit{File-name}])$

ext rd doc : $\textit{Text}$
    $cfile$: $[\textit{File-name}]$
  wr $files$: $\textit{File-store}$

post let $afn =$ if $fn \neq$ nil
             then fn
             else if $cfile \neq$ nil
                then $cfile$
                else let f $\in$ ($\textit{Untitled-names} - \mathrm{dom}\, files$) in f
  in $files = \overline{files} \dagger \{afn \mapsto doc\}$

The operation saves the file under the current file name if one exists; otherwise it saves it with a name of the form 'Untitled$n$', where n is a natural number. Care must be taken not to overwrite an existing 'Untitled$n$' file.

execute-write (*fn*: [*File-name*])
(dcl *i* : **N**;
if *fn* ≠ nil then
    skip
elsif *cfile* ≠ nil then
    fn: = *cfile*
else
    fn: = *generate-temp-name*()
end;
open *fn* for output;
i: = 0;
while *i* ≠ len *doc* do
    i: = *i* + 1;
    read-line(*i*) to *fn*
end
) −− *execute-write*

The function *generate-temp-name* can be specified:

generate-temp-name () *r*: *File-name*
ext rd *files* : *File-store*
post *r* ∈ (*Untitled-names* − dom *files*)

The derivation of code and its proof of correctness is left as an exercise.

Exercise 15.2

1. Prove the refinement of the edit command to be correct.
2. Prove the refinement of the write command to be correct.
3. Rewrite the specification for the quit command so that it reminds the user to save the file if it has not already been saved. It may be necessary to keep track of any changes that have occurred since the last save—this might involve changes to the state and to some of the edit commands.

15.5   THE SPECIFICATION REVISITED

The specification of the top-level control function of the editor needs some minor changes to reflect the modifications made above, these are shown in Fig. 15.6. Still left unresolved is the exact form of the input—the concrete syntax of the commands—and how this should be dealt with. This will be covered by Chapter 17.

15.6   SUMMARY

At this point in the development a new abstract machine has been introduced which supplies the necessary functionality required of the original editing buffer. Each of the

execute-command (*acmd*: *Command* | BADCOMMAND)
(cases *acmd* of
  −− execute-line-command
    mk-InsertCommand(*dest*) → *execute-insert*(*dest*),
    mk-CopyCommand(*range*, *text*) → *execute-copy*(*range*, *dest*),
    mk-DeleteCommand(*range*) → *execute-delete*(*range*),
    mk-MoveCommand(*range*, *dest*) → *execute-move*(*range*, *dest*),
    mk-CurrentCommand(*line*) → *execute-current*(*line*),
    SHOWCOMMAND → *execute-show*(),
    mk-DisplayCommand(*range*) → *execute-display*(*range*),
  −− execute-text-command
    mk-FindCommand(*range*, *pat*) → *execute-find*(*range*, *pat*),
    mk-SubstituteCommand(*range*, *old*, *new*) → *execute-substitute*(*range*, *old*, *new*),
  −− execute-file-command
    mk-EditCommand(*fname*) → *execute-edit*(*fname*),
    mk-WriteCommand(*fname*) → *execute-write*(*fname*),
    QUITCOMMAND → *quit*: = true,
others *write-error*(*acmd*)
end
) −− *execute-command*

Figure 15.6 The control structure for *read-and-execute-command*.

editor commands has been replaced by a specification of the order in which more primitive operations must be done to drive the new abstract machine. Each of the refinement steps has been proved correct. The proofs in this chapter have supplied more detail than is perhaps necessary, but this has been done to illustrate the ideas. Now we have reduced the problem to implementing the buffer and the primitive operations on the buffer.

Project

1. Using the ideas of this chapter define a set of low-level operations on a buffer and a clipboard each of which consists of a sequence of characters, and refine each of the operations of the editor, defined in Chapter 14, in terms of these low-level operations.

buffer	free-space		clipboard

Hint: there is a need for an operation to copy from the end of the buffer into a clipboard and from the clipboard back to the end of the buffer.

2. A more advanced implementation of the buffer and clipboard is shown below. Define a state and low-level operations based on this implementation strategy as before.

buffer	clipboard	new text	free space

3. Suppose the computer on which you were implementing the editor had a very fast move character instruction which copied a block of text from one address to another.

To make the problem slightly easier, suppose access to this command was via a procedure call:

MVC(A, S, L, F, M)

where A is a single dimension array of characters, S and F are starting and finishing indexes, and L and M are lengths. If L is less than M then the array is padded with blanks; if L is bigger than M then the string of characters that are moved are truncated; and if L is equal to M we get a straightforward move. Write a specification of this instruction.

4. With the MVC procedure described above as the main primitive, together with other simple primitives, define a buffer abstract machine to implement the character editor described in Chapter 14.

THE BUFFER ABSTRACT MACHINE

AIMS

- To show data refinement in action on a large case study.
- To show, by using a large case study, how a large VDM specification would be implemented.

16.1 INTRODUCTION

At this point in the development we have a specification for the overall structure of the editor, specifications of each of the commands that provide the functions of the editor, a specification of the abstract buffer machine and a description of each of the commands in terms of the operations of the buffer machine. All the primitive operations of the abstract machine have been designed in such a way that any changes (except for *block-move*) are confined to one end of the buffer, and thus they should be easy to implement (see Fig 16.1).

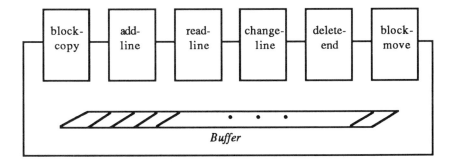

Figure 16.1   The buffer abstract machine.

The abstract machine has been designed so that it is unnecessary to consider how the operations are used; all that is necessary is to implement the operations of the abstract machine. The abstract machine provides access to the buffer and the data refinement of the buffer can be done with respect to the operations of the abstract machine only.

16.2 THE DATA REFINEMENT

The critical operation is *block-move* which involves shuffling the contents of the buffer. To speed things up, a way is needed to reduce the amount of text being copied around. Instead of copying strings of characters, it would make sense to move pointers instead and this suggests the style of implementation shown in Fig. 16.2.

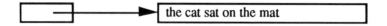

Figure 16.2   Lines represented by a pointer.

The pointers, each of which represent a line of text, will be stored in an array; so the document

```
The quick brown fox jumps over
the lazy
dog and
the cat sat on the mat.
```

would be represented as shown in Fig. 16.3.

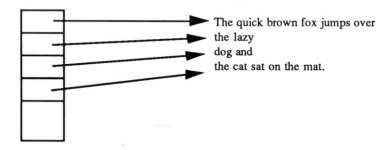

Figure 16.3   Representation of a document.

If Pascal, C or Modula-2 is assumed as the final implementation language, we have a useful ally in the heap facility as a way of managing storage for the lines of text. The text of the document can be placed in the heap area, with the pointers to each line of text being held in an array. Thus, the sequence of lines that make up the document will be implemented using an array and a pointer. However, at this point, not all possible design decisions have been made; there is still one more problem.

Consider the *block-copy* operation. This involves making copies of the pointers in the array. The pointer values will be duplicated at the end of the array buffer, but what about the text that is being referenced by these pointers? The situation shown in Fig. 16.4 could occur: more than one pointer could reference the same piece of text. One solution to is to duplicate the piece of text associated with a pointer whenever a pointer is duplicated (Fig. 16.5). If we take this route of duplicating text every time a line is copied, then any advantages gained from using pointers to represent lines of text, rather than the lines of text themselves, will be lost. However, if the version where text is shared is chosen, then any changes to a line of (shared) text must involve the construction of a copy of that line with any changes made reflected in it.

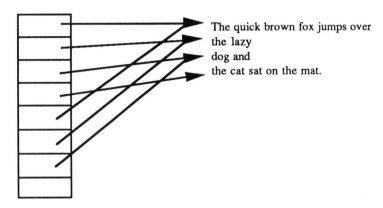

Figure 16.4   Text sharing.

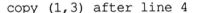

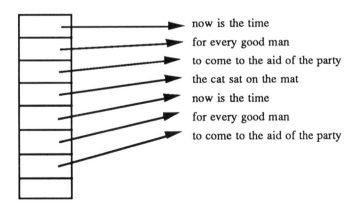

Figure 16.5   No text sharing.

Producing a new line every time the text of it is changed could produce lines of text that are not referenced by a pointer in the array buffer—these will be the old versions of the changed lines that are not shared by other pointers. This situation should never occur as the storage can only be recovered with difficulty. Now the only way to change a line of text is with the substitute command, so it is this operation that will need to deal with the problem of sharing. Just before we throw a line of text away the buffer needs to be scanned to see if anybody else has access to it. If they have we keep it; if not, it is disposed of. This is not the optimum solution but, providing it gives us a reasonable performance, there is no need to go to any more complexity.

There could also be both performance and space problems using the Pascal heap to allocate storage for the strings of text. If the standard versions of *new* and *dispose* are a problem these operations could be specified and then replaced by a private version. This can be left until we have actually implemented things and then it is possible to see whether performance is a problem or not.

It is just the *Text* component of the original specification that is to be refined, and we are only interested in the basic operations defined in the previous chapter—these were *block-copy*, *add-line*, *read-line*, *change-line*, *delete-end*, *block-move* and *init-buffer*. The new representation for the *Text* will be treated as a state and can be specified as follows:

types

$Linep$ = pointer to $Line$

$Store$ = collection of $Line$

$Buffer = \{1, \ldots, D\} \xrightarrow{m} Linep$

$Limit = \{0, \ldots, D\}$

state $Text_1$ **of**
    doc : $Buffer$
    $heap$: $Store$
    end : $Limit$
inv $mk\text{-}Text_1(doc, heap, end)$ $\triangleq$
    $\{1, \ldots, end\} \subseteq \text{dom } doc \wedge$
    $\forall ln \in \text{rng } heap \cdot$
        $\text{len } ln \leq L \wedge$
        $pointers\text{-}of(doc, end) = \text{dom } heap$
end

$pointers\text{-}of : Buffer \times Limit \rightarrow Linep\text{-set}$

$pointers\text{-}of(doc, end)$ $\triangleq$ $\text{rng } (\{1, \ldots, end\} \lhd doc)$

The data invariant demands that the heap only contains those lines of text that are in the document—those lines of text that have a pointer to them. The invariant contains part of the implementation decision that, when it can easily be decided that lines of text can be shared, they will be. The idea that text should be shared is hidden in (or defined in—depending on how you want to look at it) the mathematical properties of a mapping.

A possible model for a version where text is not shared is

state $Text'$ **of**
    doc : $\{1, \ldots, D\} \xrightarrow{m} Line$
    end : $Limit$
inv $mk\text{-}Buffer(doc, end)$ $\triangleq$
    $\{1, \ldots, end\} \subseteq \text{dom } doc \wedge$
    $\forall ln \in \text{elems } doc \cdot \text{len } ln \leq L$
end

$Line = Char^*$

Notice that since the design has decided to duplicate text when a line is copied, the advantages of using pointers vanishes, so the text is stored in the buffer directly.

Returning to the shared refinement, the retrieve function[1] is straightforward, the pointers are gathered up in order and mapped to the corresponding text held in the heap:

$$retr\text{-}txt : Text_1 \rightarrow Text$$

$$retr\text{-}txt(mk\text{-}Text_1(doc, heap, end)) \triangleq [heap(doc(i)) \mid i \in \{1, \ldots, end\}]$$

The new representation should be shown to be adequate. Given any document, i.e. given any sequence of lines of text, can an array of pointers and a heap mapping be constructed that are 'retrieved' correctly? It is obvious how this can be done, and will be left as an exercise for the reader. The operations can now be specified in terms of this new representation:

$block\text{-}copy_1\ (s, f : \mathbf{N})$

ext wr doc : $Buffer$
$\quad\quad end$: $Limit$

pre $s, f \in \{1, \ldots, end\} \wedge$
$\quad\quad s \leq f \wedge$
$\quad\quad end + (f - s + 1) \leq D$

post $doc = \overleftarrow{doc} \dagger \{\overleftarrow{end} + i \mapsto \overleftarrow{doc}(s + i - 1) \mid i \in \{1, \ldots, f - s + 1\}\} \wedge$
$\quad\quad end = \overleftarrow{end} + (f - s + 1)$

The pointers representing the text to be copied are duplicated at the end of the buffer.

$add\text{-}line_1\ (ln : Line)$

ext wr doc : $Buffer$
$\quad\quad heap$: $Store$
$\quad\quad end$: $Limit$

pre $end < D \wedge \operatorname{len} ln \leq L$

post let $p = new(\overleftarrow{heap})$ in
$\quad\quad doc = \overleftarrow{doc} \dagger \{end \mapsto p\} \wedge$
$\quad\quad heap = \overleftarrow{heap} \cup \{p \mapsto ln\} \wedge$
$\quad\quad end = \overleftarrow{end} + 1$

A line of text is added to the end of the buffer: a new pointer must be generated to point to the text which is added to the heap. The new pointer is added to the end of the buffer.

$read\text{-}line_1\ (i : \mathbf{N})\ r : Line$

ext rd doc : $Buffer$
$\quad\quad heap$: $Store$
$\quad\quad end$: $Limit$

pre $i \in \{1, \ldots, end\}$

post $r = heap(doc(i))$

---

[1]In the subsequent text we use the retrieve function without the $mk\text{-}Text_1$ pattern to simplify equations.

The new version of the *read-line* operation is straightforward: the text must be found in the heap.

$change\text{-}line_1\ (i\colon \mathbf{N}, ln\colon Line)$

ext wr doc : $Buffer$
    $heap$: $Store$
   rd end : $Limit$

pre $i \in \{1, \ldots, end\} \wedge \operatorname{len} ln \leq L$

post let $p = new(\overleftarrow{heap})$ in
    $doc = \overleftarrow{doc} \dagger \{i \mapsto p\}\ \wedge$
    $heap = pointers\text{-}of(doc, end) \lhd (\overleftarrow{heap} \dagger \{p \mapsto ln\})$

If a line in the buffer is changed, then the old version is replaced with the new version. The refinement of this operation must deal with the sharing problem.

Now you can see the advantages of having specified these two simple operations, rather than just allowing access to the buffer directly. The problem of sharing is hidden behind the *change-line* operation, and need not be a concern of the operations that use it.

$delete\text{-}end_1\ (n\colon \mathbf{N})$

ext rd doc : $Buffer$
   wr $heap$: $Store$
      end : $Limit$

pre $n \leq end$

post $heap = pointers\text{-}of(doc, end) \lhd \overleftarrow{heap}\ \wedge$
    $end = \overleftarrow{end} - n$

The pointers are removed from the end of the buffer by just decreasing the high-water-mark pointer; again there is the sharing problem and those pointers that are pointing to text that is not shared are freed.

$block\text{-}move_1\ (p, s, f\colon \mathbf{N})$

ext wr doc : $Buffer$
   rd end : $Limit$

pre $p, s, f \in \{1, \ldots, end\} \wedge s \leq f \wedge p \notin \{s, \ldots, f\}$

post $p < s\ \wedge$
    let $w = f - s + 1$ in
    $doc = \overleftarrow{doc} \dagger (\{p + i \mapsto \overleftarrow{doc}(s - 1 + i) \mid i \in \{1, \ldots, w\}\}\ \cup$
                $\{p + i \mapsto \overleftarrow{doc}(p + i - w) \mid i \in \{w + 1, \ldots, f - p\}\})$
    $\vee$
    $f \leq p\ \wedge$
    let $w = p - (f + 1) + 1$ in
    $doc = \overleftarrow{doc} \dagger (\{s - 1 + i \mapsto \overleftarrow{doc}(f + i) \mid i \in \{1, \ldots, w\}\}\ \cup$
                $\{s - 1 + i \mapsto \overleftarrow{doc}(s - 1 + i - w) \mid i \in \{w + 1, \ldots, p - s + 1\}\})$

The pointers are moved to represent the text being moved. There is no need to free or allocate any lines of text in the heap as no text is added or removed from the buffer.

Finally, to initialize the buffer:

$init\text{-}buffer_1$ ()

ext wr doc : $Buffer$
  $heap$: $Store$
  end : $Limit$

post $doc = \{\,\} \wedge$
  $heap = \mathsf{empty} \wedge$
  $end = 0$

The next step is to show that the operations preserve the invariant, this activity will be left for the reader.

Exercise 16.1

1. Prove adequacy both informally and formally.
2. Prove that all the refined operations preserve the data invariant.
3. Respecify each of the operations in terms of the non-sharing model using the state $Text'$ on page 332.
4. The state could be modified so that each line of text has a counter associated with it which counts how many pointers are pointing at it; thus the *block-copy* operation would bump this value by one and the *delete-end* operation would decrement it by one. A line of text with a counter that has a value of zero can be deleted from the heap or re-used. Construct the state for this model and respecify the primitive operations in terms of this representation.

16.3 THE PROOFS

As has already been stated, the correctness of these operations is fundamental to the correctness of the editor; thus to be reasonably certain of the correctness of the final editor the new operations should be proved to model the original ones.

16.3.1 The *block-copy* operation

To show that the refined version of the operation is correct, we need to use the domain and range rules to prove that the new operations are equivalent to the old.

The domain rule The domain rule is

$$\forall text_1 \cdot pre\text{-}block\text{-}copy(retr\text{-}txt(text_1)) \;\Rightarrow\; pre\text{-}block\text{-}copy_1(text_1)$$

The proofs will not show all the detail. Applying the retrieve functions to the state, pulling out the components we are interested in, and substituting the definitions of each of the functions, it is necessary to show for any 'document':

$$s, f \in \mathsf{inds}\,[heap(doc(i)) \mid i \in \{1, \ldots, end\}] \wedge$$
$$s \leq f \wedge$$
$$\mathsf{len}\,[heap(doc(i)) \mid i \in \{1, \ldots, end\}] + (f - s + 1) \leq D$$
$$\Rightarrow\; s, f \in \{1, \ldots, end\} \wedge s \leq f \wedge end + (f - s + 1) \leq D$$

which is straightforward since

$$\text{inds}\,[heap(doc(i)) \mid i \in \{1,\ldots,end\}] = \{1,\ldots,end\}$$

and

$$\text{len}\,[heap(doc(i)) \mid i \in \{1,\ldots,end\}] = end$$

The range rule   In terms of the *block-copy* operation, we need to show

$$\forall \overleftarrow{text_1}, text_1 \cdot pre\text{-}block\text{-}copy(retr\text{-}txt(\overleftarrow{text_1})) \wedge post\text{-}block\text{-}copy_1(\overleftarrow{text_1}, text_1)$$
$$\Rightarrow\ post\text{-}block\text{-}copy(retr\text{-}txt(\overleftarrow{text_1}), retr\text{-}txt(text_1))$$

Substitution and some simplification reduces this to

$$s, f \in \text{inds}\,[heap(\overleftarrow{doc}(i)) \mid i \in \{1,\ldots,\overleftarrow{end}\}] \wedge \tag{1}$$
$$s \leq f \wedge$$
$$\text{len}\,[heap(\overleftarrow{doc}(i)) \mid i \in \{1,\ldots,\overleftarrow{end}\}] + (f - s + 1) \leq D \wedge$$
$$doc = \overleftarrow{doc} \dagger \{\overleftarrow{end} + i \mapsto \overleftarrow{doc}(s + i - 1) \mid i \in \{1,\ldots,f - s + 1\}\} \wedge$$
$$end = \overleftarrow{end} + (f - s + 1) \tag{5}$$
$$\Rightarrow$$
$$retr\text{-}txt(doc, heap, end) = retr\text{-}txt(\overleftarrow{doc}, heap, \overleftarrow{end}) \curvearrowright$$
$$retr\text{-}txt(\overleftarrow{doc}, heap, \overleftarrow{end})(s,\ldots,f)$$

Using the usual strategy of using the left-hand side of the implication to prove the right-hand side, we can write

$$retr\text{-}txt(\overleftarrow{doc}, heap, \overleftarrow{end}) \curvearrowright retr\text{-}txt(\overleftarrow{doc}, heap, \overleftarrow{end})(s,\ldots,f)$$
$$= \text{“definition of the } retr\text{-}txt\text{”}$$

$$[heap(\overleftarrow{doc}(i)) \mid i \in \{1,\ldots,\overleftarrow{end}\}] \curvearrowright [heap(\overleftarrow{doc}(i)) \mid i \in \{1,\ldots,\overleftarrow{end}\}](s,\ldots,f)$$
$$= \text{“definition of sequence indexing and } s, f \in \{1,\ldots,\overleftarrow{end}\}\text{”}$$

$$[heap(\overleftarrow{doc}(i)) \mid i \in \{1,\ldots,\overleftarrow{end}\}] \curvearrowright [heap(\overleftarrow{doc}(i)) \mid i \in \{s,\ldots,f\}]$$
$$= \text{“hypothesis lines 1 and 4”}$$

$$[heap(doc(i)) \mid i \in \{1,\ldots,\overleftarrow{end}\}] \curvearrowright [heap(doc(i)) \mid i \in \{s,\ldots,f\}]$$
$$= \text{“hypothesis line 4”}$$

$$[heap(doc(i)) \mid i \in \{1,\ldots,\overleftarrow{end}\}] \curvearrowright [heap(doc(i)) \mid i \in \{\overleftarrow{end} + 1,\ldots,end\}]$$
$$= \text{“property of the sequence catenation operator”}$$
$$[heap(doc(i)) \mid i \in \{1,\ldots,end\}]$$
$$= \text{“definition of } retr\text{-}txt\text{”}$$
$$retr\text{-}txt(doc, heap, end)$$

Note that the hypothesis is never undefined, so that the above proof is valid. This completes the proof of the *block-copy* operation.

16.3.2   The *add-line* operation

The domain rule   The rule for this operation is

$$\forall text_1 \cdot pre\text{-}add\text{-}line(retr\text{-}txt(text_1)) \ \Rightarrow\ pre\text{-}add\text{-}line_1(text_1)$$

and after substitution and generalization we get

$$\text{len}\,[heap(doc(i)) \mid i \in \{1, \ldots, end\}] < D \wedge$$
$$\text{len}\,ln \le L$$
$$\Rightarrow end < D \wedge \text{len}\,ln \le L$$

which is trivial.

The range rule For this operation the rule is

$$\overleftarrow{text_1}, text_1 \cdot pre\text{-}add\text{-}line(retr\text{-}txt(\overleftarrow{text_1})) \wedge post\text{-}add\text{-}line_1(\overleftarrow{text_1}, text_1)$$
$$\Rightarrow post\text{-}add\text{-}line(retr\text{-}txt(\overleftarrow{text_1}), retr\text{-}txt(text_1))$$

After substitution and generalization, the rule becomes

$$\text{len}\,[heap(\overleftarrow{doc}(i)) \mid i \in \{1, \ldots, \overleftarrow{end}\}] < D \wedge \tag{1}$$
$$\text{len}\,ln \le L \wedge$$
$$\text{let }p = new(\overleftarrow{heap})\text{ in}$$
$$doc = \overleftarrow{doc} \dagger \{end \mapsto p\} \wedge$$
$$heap = \overleftarrow{heap} \cup \{p \mapsto ln\} \wedge \tag{5}$$
$$end = \overleftarrow{end} + 1$$
$$\Rightarrow retr\text{-}txt(doc, heap, end) = retr\text{-}txt(\overleftarrow{doc}, \overleftarrow{heap}, \overleftarrow{end}) \mathbin{\frown} [ln]$$

The usual strategy gives

$$retr\text{-}txt(doc, heap, end)$$
$$= \text{``definition of } retr\text{-}txt\text{''}$$
$$[heap(doc(i)) \mid i \in \{1, \ldots, end\}]$$
$$= \text{``property of the sequence catenation operator''}$$
$$[heap(doc(i)) \mid i \in \{1, \ldots, end - 1\}] \mathbin{\frown} [heap(doc(end))]$$
$$= \text{``hypothesis lines 4''}$$
$$[heap(doc(i)) \mid i \in \{1, \ldots, end - 1\}] \mathbin{\frown} [heap((\overleftarrow{doc} \dagger \{end \mapsto p\})(end))]$$
$$= \text{``definition of map application''}$$
$$[heap(doc(i)) \mid i \in \{1, \ldots, end - 1\}] \mathbin{\frown} [heap(p)]$$
$$= \text{``hypothesis line 4, 5 and 6 and the data invariant''}$$
$$[\overleftarrow{heap}(\overleftarrow{doc}(i)) \mid i \in \{1, \ldots, \overleftarrow{end}\}] \mathbin{\frown} [heap(p)]$$
$$= \text{``hypothesis line 4 and properties of map union operator''}$$
$$[\overleftarrow{heap}(\overleftarrow{doc}(i)) \mid i \in \{1, \ldots, \overleftarrow{end}\}] \mathbin{\frown} [ln]$$
$$= \text{``definition of } retr\text{-}txt\text{''}$$
$$retr\text{-}txt(\overleftarrow{doc}, \overleftarrow{heap}, \overleftarrow{end}) \mathbin{\frown} [ln]$$

As before, the hypothesis is always defined, and the proof is thus complete.

16.3.3 The *delete-end* operation

The domain rule

$$\forall text_1 \cdot pre\text{-}delete\text{-}end(retr\text{-}txt(text_1)) \;\Rightarrow\; pre\text{-}delete\text{-}end_1(text_1)$$

The proof of this is trivial.

The range rule

$$\forall \overleftarrow{text_1}, text_1 \cdot pre\text{-}delete\text{-}end(retr\text{-}txt(\overleftarrow{text_1})) \wedge$$
$$post\text{-}delete\text{-}end_1(\overleftarrow{text_1}, text_1)$$
$$\Rightarrow\; post\text{-}delete\text{-}end(retr\text{-}txt(\overleftarrow{text_1}), retr\text{-}txt(text_1))$$

After substitution and generalization, it is necessary to show

$$n \le \operatorname{len}[\overleftarrow{heap}(doc(i)) \mid i \in \{1,\dots,\overleftarrow{end}\}] \wedge \tag{1}$$
$$heap = pointers\text{-}of(doc, end) \lhd \overleftarrow{heap} \wedge$$
$$end = \overleftarrow{end} - n \tag{3}$$
$$\Rightarrow\; retr\text{-}txt(doc, heap, end) =$$
$$retr\text{-}txt(doc, \overleftarrow{heap}, \overleftarrow{end})(1,\dots,\operatorname{len} retr\text{-}txt(doc, \overleftarrow{heap}, \overleftarrow{end}) - n)$$

Now

$$retr\text{-}txt(doc, heap, end)$$
$$= \text{``definition of } retr\text{-}txt\text{''}$$
$$[heap(doc(i)) \mid i \in \{1,\dots,end\}]$$
$$= \text{``hypothesis line 2''}$$
$$[\overleftarrow{heap}(doc(i)) \mid i \in \{1,\dots,end\}]$$
$$= \text{``hypothesis line 3''}$$
$$[\overleftarrow{heap}(doc(i)) \mid i \in \{1,\dots,\overleftarrow{end} - n\}]$$
$$= \text{``property of indexing''}$$
$$[\overleftarrow{heap}(doc(i)) \mid i \in \{1,\dots,\overleftarrow{end}\}](1,\dots,\overleftarrow{end} - n)$$
$$= \text{``definition of } retr\text{-}txt\text{''}$$
$$retr\text{-}txt(doc, \overleftarrow{heap}, \overleftarrow{end})(1,\dots,\overleftarrow{end} - n)$$
$$= \text{``definition of } retr\text{-}txt\text{''}$$
$$retr\text{-}txt(doc, \overleftarrow{heap}, \overleftarrow{end})(1,\dots,\operatorname{len} retr\text{-}txt(doc, \overleftarrow{heap}, \overleftarrow{end}) - n)$$

Once more the hypothesis is always defined and the proof is complete.

16.3.4 The *block-move* operation

The domain rule It is necessary to show

$$\forall text_1 \cdot pre\text{-}block\text{-}move(retr\text{-}txt(text_1)) \;\Rightarrow\; pre\text{-}block\text{-}move_1(text_1)$$

After substitution and generalization, this becomes

$$p, s, f \in \operatorname{inds}[heap(doc(i)) \mid i \in \{1,\dots,end\}] \wedge s \le f \wedge p \notin \{s,\dots,f\}$$
$$\Rightarrow\; p, s, f \in \{1,\dots,end\} \wedge s \le f \wedge p \notin \{s,\dots,f\}$$

which is trivial.

The range rule It is necessary to show

$$\forall \overleftarrow{text_1}, text_1 \cdot$$

$$pre\text{-}block\text{-}move(retr\text{-}txt(\overleftarrow{text_1})) \wedge$$

$$post\text{-}block\text{-}move_1(\overleftarrow{text_1}, text_1)$$

$$\Rightarrow post\text{-}block\text{-}move(retr\text{-}txt(\overleftarrow{text_1}), retr\text{-}txt(text_1))$$

After substitution and generalization, this becomes

$$p, s, f \in \text{inds}\,[heap(\overleftarrow{doc}(i)) \mid i \in \{1, \dots, end\}] \wedge s \le f \wedge p \notin \{s, \dots, f\} \wedge \qquad (1)$$

$$(p < s \wedge$$

$$\text{let } w = f - s + 1 \text{ in}$$

$$doc = \overleftarrow{doc} \dagger (\{p + i \mapsto \overleftarrow{doc}(s - 1 + i) \mid i \in \{1, \dots, w\}\} \cup$$

$$\{p + i \mapsto \overleftarrow{doc}(p + i - w) \mid i \in \{w + 1, \dots, f - p\}\})$$

$$\vee \qquad\qquad (6)$$

$$f \le p \wedge$$

$$\text{let } w = p - (f + 1) + 1 \text{ in}$$

$$doc = \overleftarrow{doc} \dagger (\{s - 1 + i \mapsto \overleftarrow{doc}(f + i) \mid i \in \{1, \dots, w\}\} \cup$$

$$\{s - 1 + i \mapsto \overleftarrow{doc}(s - 1 + i - w) \mid i \in \{w + 1, \dots, p - s + 1\}\}))$$

$$\Rightarrow$$

$$\text{let } l = \text{len } retr\text{-}txt(\overleftarrow{doc}, heap, end) \text{ in}$$

$$p < s \wedge$$

$$retr\text{-}txt(doc, heap, end) = retr\text{-}txt(\overleftarrow{doc}, heap, end)(1, \dots, p) \,^\curvearrowright$$

$$retr\text{-}txt(\overleftarrow{doc}, heap, end)(s, \dots, f) \,^\curvearrowright$$

$$retr\text{-}txt(\overleftarrow{doc}, heap, end)(p + 1, \dots, s - 1) \,^\curvearrowright$$

$$retr\text{-}txt(\overleftarrow{doc}, heap, end)(f + 1, \dots, l)$$

$$\vee$$

$$f \le p \wedge$$

$$retr\text{-}txt(doc, heap, end) = retr\text{-}txt(\overleftarrow{doc}, heap, end)(1, \dots, s - 1) \,^\curvearrowright$$

$$retr\text{-}txt(\overleftarrow{doc}, heap, end)(f + 1, \dots, p) \,^\curvearrowright$$

$$retr\text{-}txt(\overleftarrow{doc}, heap, end)(s, \dots, f) \,^\curvearrowright$$

$$retr\text{-}txt(\overleftarrow{doc}, heap, end)(p + 1, \dots, l)$$

For any $a, b \in \{1, \dots, end\}$ we have

$$[heap(\overleftarrow{doc}(i)) \mid i \in \{1, \dots, end\}](a, \dots, b) = [heap(\overleftarrow{doc}(i)) \mid i \in \{a, \dots, b\}]$$

The proof is best done by cases.

Case 1. $p < s$
$$retr\text{-}txt(doc, heap, end)$$

$$= \text{``definition of } retr\text{-}txt\text{''}$$

$$[heap(doc(i)) \mid i \in \{1, \dots, l\}]$$

$$= \text{``property of the catenate operator for sequences''}$$

$$[heap(doc(i)) \mid i \in \{1, \ldots, p\}]\ ^\frown$$
$$[heap(doc(i)) \mid i \in \{p + 1, \ldots, p + w\}]\ ^\frown$$
$$[heap(doc(i)) \mid i \in \{p + w + 1, \ldots, f\}]\ ^\frown$$
$$[heap(doc(i)) \mid i \in \{f + 1, \ldots, l\}]$$

= "property of sequence definition"

$$[heap(doc(i)) \mid i \in \{1, \ldots, p\}]\ ^\frown$$
$$[heap(doc(p + i)) \mid i \in \{1, \ldots, w\}]\ ^\frown$$
$$[heap(doc(p + i)) \mid i \in \{w + 1, \ldots, f - p\}]\ ^\frown$$
$$[heap(doc(i)) \mid i \in \{f + 1, \ldots, l\}]$$

= "hypothesis line 4"

$$[heap(\overline{doc}(i)) \mid i \in \{1, \ldots, p\}]\ ^\frown$$
$$[heap(\overline{doc}(s - 1 + i)) \mid i \in \{1, \ldots, w\}]\ ^\frown$$
$$[heap(\overline{doc}(p + i - w)) \mid i \in \{w + 1, \ldots, f - p\}]\ ^\frown$$
$$[heap(\overline{doc}(i)) \mid i \in \{f + 1, \ldots, l\}]$$

= "property of sequence definition"

$$[heap(\overline{doc}(i)) \mid i \in \{1, \ldots, p\}]\ ^\frown$$
$$[heap(\overline{doc}(i)) \mid i \in \{s, \ldots, s - 1 + w\}]\ ^\frown$$
$$[heap(\overline{doc}(i)) \mid i \in \{p + 1, \ldots, f - w\}]\ ^\frown$$
$$[heap(\overline{doc}(i)) \mid i \in \{f + 1, \ldots, l\}]$$

= "property of sequence definition"

$$[heap(\overline{doc}(i)) \mid i \in \{1, \ldots, p\}]\ ^\frown$$
$$[heap(\overline{doc}(i)) \mid i \in \{s, \ldots, f\}]\ ^\frown$$
$$[heap(\overline{doc}(i)) \mid i \in \{p + 1, \ldots, s - 1\}]\ ^\frown$$
$$[heap(\overline{doc}(i)) \mid i \in \{f + 1, \ldots, l\}]$$

= "definition of retr-txt"

$$retr\text{-}txt(\overline{doc}, heap, end)(1, \ldots, p)\ ^\frown$$
$$retr\text{-}txt(\overline{doc}, heap, end)(s, \ldots, f)\ ^\frown$$
$$retr\text{-}txt(\overline{doc}, heap, end)(p + 1, \ldots, s - 1)\ ^\frown$$
$$retr\text{-}txt(\overline{doc}, heap, end)(f + 1, \ldots, l)$$

The second case is

$$\neg\, p < s \text{ or equivalently } p \geq s$$

but from the hypothesis line 1, we have

$$p \notin \{s, \ldots, f\}$$

Therefore $f < p$ the second case is equivalent to $f \leq p$ and is similar to case 1, and is left for the reader. The hypothesis is always defined; this completes the proof.

16.3.5   The *init-buffer* operation

The domain rule   There are no pre-conditions so there is nothing to prove.

The range rule   It is necessary to show

$$\forall \overline{text_1}, text_1 \cdot$$
$$\quad pre\text{-}init\text{-}buffer(retr\text{-}txt(\overline{text_1})) \land$$
$$\quad post\text{-}init\text{-}buffer_1(\overline{text_1}, text_1)$$
$$\Rightarrow post\text{-}init\text{-}buffer(retr\text{-}txt(\overline{text_1}), retr\text{-}txt(text_1))$$

after substitution and generalization, this becomes

$$doc = \{\,\} \land$$
$$heap = \mathsf{empty} \land$$
$$end = 0$$
$$\Rightarrow retr\text{-}txt(doc, heap, end) = [\,]$$

which is trivial.

Exercise 16.2

1. Prove that the refined version of *read-line* is correct.
2. Prove that the refined version of *change-line* is correct.
3. Two operations have been missed; one of these will load the buffer from the text file held on disk, and the other will write the buffer back to disk. Write specifications of these operations with respect to the buffer and with respect to the data refinement, and prove that the new specification matches the old.

16.4   IMPLEMENTING THE OPERATIONS

The next step in the development is to refine these basic abstract machine operations. The representation for the buffer is at a level where it could be translated directly into a programming language, but to complete the refinement, the operations that are specified in terms of pre- and post-conditions need to be refined into code. This will be the next step.

16.4.1   The proofs

As has already been stated, the correctness of these operations is fundamental to the correctness of the editor; thus to be reasonably certain of the correctness of the final editor the new operations should be proved to model the original ones.

The *block-copy* operation   The copy operation places a copy of part of the text buffer at the end of the buffer; the specification of the operation in terms of the data refinement is given below:

$block\text{-}copy_1\ (s, f : \mathbb{N})$
ext wr $doc\ :\ Buffer$
$\qquad end\quad :\ Limit$
pre $s, f \in \{1, \ldots, end\}\ \wedge$
$\qquad s \leq f\ \wedge$
$\qquad end + (f - s + 1) \leq D$
post $doc = \overleftarrow{doc}\ \dagger\ \{\overleftarrow{end} + i \mapsto \overleftarrow{doc}(s + i - 1) \mid i \in \{1, \ldots, f - s + 1\}\}\ \wedge$
$\qquad end = \overleftarrow{end} + (f - s + 1)$

The body of the operation can be refined, the following is equivalent to the above:

$block\text{-}copy_1\ (s, f : \mathbb{N})$
$(block\text{-}copy\text{-}body$
$\quad$**ext rd** $s, f : \mathbb{N}$
$\qquad$**wr** $doc: Buffer$
$\qquad end: Limit$
$\quad$**pre** $s, f \in \{1, \ldots, end\}\ \wedge$
$\qquad s \leq f\ \wedge$
$\qquad end + (f - s + 1) \leq D$
$\quad$**post** $doc = \overleftarrow{doc}\ \dagger\ \{i \mapsto \overleftarrow{doc}(s - \overleftarrow{end} - 1 + i) \mid i \in \{\overleftarrow{end} + 1, \ldots, \overleftarrow{end} + f - s + 1\}\}\ \wedge$
$\qquad end = \overleftarrow{end} + (f - s + 1)$
$)\ --\ block\text{-}copy_1$

The strategy to refine *block-copy-body* is to use a loop to copy the lines from the middle of the document to the end; since the buffer is to be changed, this loop will be of the 'up' type. To derive the loop invariant and loop variant, we will proceed as follows: since both *end* and *buffer* are to be changed, two logical constants will be introduced to contain the answer and another one to simplify the equations. It is easy to show that the following new specification of *block-copy-body* is equivalent to the one above.

$block\text{-}copy\text{-}body$
ext rd $s, f\ :\ \mathbb{N}$
$\qquad$**wr** $doc\ :\ Buffer$
$\qquad end\quad :\ Limit$
$\qquad$**lc** $d\quad :\ Buffer$
$\qquad e, l\quad :\ Limit$
pre $d = doc\ \wedge$
$\qquad e = end\ \wedge$
$\qquad l = f - s + 1\ \wedge$
$\qquad s, f \in \{1, \ldots, end\}\ \wedge$
$\qquad s \leq f\ \wedge$
$\qquad e + l \leq D$

post $doc = d\ \dagger\ \{i \mapsto d(s - e - 1 + i) \mid i \in \{e + 1, \ldots, end\}\}\ \wedge$
$\qquad end = e + l$

The intended algorithm suggests the following for the loop specification

> guard $end \neq e + l$
> inv $doc = d \dagger \{i \mapsto d(s - e - 1 + i) \mid i \in \{e + 1, \ldots, end\}\}$
> var $0 \leq e + l - end < e + l - \overleftarrow{end}$

The following code can be shown to satisfy the specification for the loop body.

> $end := end + 1;$
> $doc(end) := doc(s - e - 1 + end)$

The proof is based on the the fact that the second assignment statement is equivalent to a post-condition of the form

$$doc = \overleftarrow{doc} \dagger \{end \mapsto \overleftarrow{doc}(s - e - 1 + end)\}$$

Using the definition of the invariant, we get

> doc
>
> $\quad = $ "post-condition"
>
> $\overleftarrow{doc} \dagger \{end \mapsto \overleftarrow{doc}(s - e - 1 + end)\}$
>
> $\quad = $ "substitute the invariant for $\overleftarrow{doc}$"
>
> $(d \dagger \{i \mapsto d(s - e - 1 + i) \mid i \in \{e + 1, \ldots, \overleftarrow{end}\}\}) \dagger$
> $\quad \{end \mapsto \overleftarrow{doc}(s - e - 1 + end)\}$
>
> $\quad = $ "property of $\dagger$ operator"
>
> $d \dagger (\{i \mapsto d(s - e - 1 + i) \mid i \in \{e + 1, \ldots, \overleftarrow{end}\}\} \dagger$
> $\quad \{end \mapsto \overleftarrow{doc}(s - e - 1 + end)\})$
>
> $\quad = $ "$d = \overleftarrow{doc}$ and $end = \overleftarrow{end} + 1$"
>
> $d \dagger (\{i \mapsto d(s - e - 1 + i) \mid i \in \{e + 1, \ldots, end - 1\}\} \dagger$
> $\quad \{end \mapsto d(s - e - 1 + end)\})$
>
> $\quad = $ "property of $\dagger$ operator"
>
> $d \dagger \{i \mapsto d(s - e - 1 + i) \mid i \in \{e + 1, \ldots, end\}\}$

which shows the invariant is preserved. The first assignment establishes the variant. The code derived from the loop specification is

> while $end \neq e + l$ do
> $\quad end := end + 1;$
> $\quad doc(end) := doc(s - e - 1 + end)$
> end

The next step is to remove the logical constant which can be done by first introducing a variable i and adding the term $s - e - 1 + end = i$ to the invariant. A little work produces the following code:

$$i := s - 1;$$
$$\text{while } i \neq f \text{ do}$$
$$\quad end := end + 1;$$
$$\quad i := i + 1;$$
$$\quad doc(end) := doc(i)$$
$$\text{end}$$

The parameter variable s is not used in the code and can replace the variable i; this is done by adding $s = i + 1$ to the invariant and then removing i from the code. Putting it all together gives the operation $block\text{-}copy_1$

$$block\text{-}copy_1 \ (s, f : \mathbf{N})$$
$$(\text{while } s \neq f + 1 \text{ do}$$
$$\quad end := end + 1;$$
$$\quad doc(end) := doc(s);$$
$$\quad s := s + 1$$
$$\text{end}$$
$$) \ -- \ block\text{-}copy_1$$

The $add\text{-}line$ operation   The $add\text{-}line$ operation places a line of text passed as an argument at the end of the buffer. The specification is

$$add\text{-}line_1 \ (ln : Line)$$
$$\text{ext wr } doc \ : \ Buffer$$
$$\qquad heap \quad : \ Store$$
$$\qquad end \quad : \ Limit$$
$$\text{pre } end < D \wedge \text{len } ln \leq L$$

$$\text{post let } p = new(\overleftarrow{heap}) \text{ in}$$
$$\quad doc = \overleftarrow{doc} \dagger \{end \mapsto p\} \wedge$$
$$\quad heap = \overleftarrow{heap} \cup \{p \mapsto ln\} \wedge$$
$$\quad end = \overleftarrow{end} + 1$$

and the refinement is

$$add\text{-}line_1 \ (ln : Line)$$
$$(\text{dcl } p \ : \ Linep;$$
$$\quad p := new(heap);$$
$$\quad end := end + 1;$$
$$\quad doc(end) := p;$$
$$\quad heap(p) := ln$$
$$) \ -- \ add\text{-}line_1$$

The use of the new operation is equivalent to finding a pointer which is not already in use, i.e. is not already in the domain of the heap mapping. This can easily be proved correct using the sequence rule and the equivalence of the assigments to appropriate terms in the post-condition of $add\text{-}line$.

The *read-line* **operation**   This operation returns a line of text.

> $read\text{-}line_1$ $(i\colon\mathbf{N})$ $r\colon Line$
> **ext rd** doc : $Buffer$
> $heap$: $Store$
> end : $Limit$
> **pre** $i \in \{1, \ldots, end\}$
> **post** $r = heap(doc(i))$

The refinement of this is simple, as it just relies on the semantics of the programming language:

> $read\text{-}line_1$ (i) : $Line$
> (return $heap(doc(i))$
>) $--$ $read\text{-}line_1$

The *change-line* **operation**   This operation replaces a line of text with a new one:

> $change\text{-}line_1$ $(i\colon\mathbf{N}, ln\colon Line)$
> **ext wr** doc : $Buffer$
> $heap$: $Store$
>   **rd** end : $Limit$
> **pre** $i \in \{1, \ldots, end\} \wedge \mathsf{len}\, ln \leq L$
> **post let** $p = new(\overleftarrow{heap})$ **in**
> $doc = \overleftarrow{doc} \dagger \{i \mapsto p\} \wedge$
> $heap = pointers\text{-}of(doc, end) \lhd (\overleftarrow{heap} \dagger \{p \mapsto ln\})$

If the line of text being changed is shared, a copy must be made before it is changed. The new, changed, copy of the line is placed in the heap and its pointer placed in the document buffer. Any line of text that is no longer required is deleted from the heap. The *change-line* operation can be broken down into suboperations: allocating space in the heap for the new line, updating the heap with the new line, updating the document buffer and deleting the old copy of the line from the heap if it is not shared by another line of text. This last suboperation can be achieved by copying the old line to the end of the buffer and then deleting it using the operations of the abstract machine. This will automatically take care of the sharing problem. This suggests the following sketch of the algorithm:

> $change\text{-}line_1$ $(i\colon\mathbf{N}, ln\colon Line)$
> (dcl p : $Linep$;
> $block\text{-}copy(i, i)$;
> $p := new(heap)$;
> $doc(i), heap(p) := p, ln$;
> $delete\text{-}end(1)$
>) $--$ $change\text{-}line_1$

The proofs are left for the reader.

The *delete-end* **operation**   This operation is more difficult, and also more important, since the task of this operation is to free storage locations; there must be a careful check that the data invariant is not violated:

$delete\text{-}end_1$ $(n:\mathbf{N})$

ext rd *doc*   : *Buffer*
    wr *heap* : *Store*
      end   : *Limit*

pre $n \le end$

post $heap = pointers\text{-}of(doc, end) \lhd \overleftarrow{heap} \wedge$
    $end = \overleftarrow{end} - n$

A possible implementation of this specification is a loop that scans the buffer backwards, deleting a line of text in each iteration of the loop and making certain that the data invariant is preserved. This algorithm suggests that the data invariant for the buffer is used as the loop invariant and the loop variant will use the fact that the number of lines to be processed is decreased by one on each iteration. A variable is introduced which marks the start of the lines to be deleted in the pointer buffer; everything to the right of this marker is the text to be removed. The specification can be rewritten with this new variable introduced to give the first refinement step:

$delete\text{-}end_1$ $(n:\mathbf{N})$

$(n:= end - n;$
 delete-end-body
 ext rd *doc*: *Buffer*
     wr *heap*: *Store*
     end: *Limit*
     rd $n:\mathbf{N}$
     lc $h: Store$
 pre $h = heap \wedge$
     $0 \le n$
 post $heap = pointers\text{-}of(doc, end) \lhd h \wedge$
     $end = n$
$)$ $--$ $delete\text{-}end_1$

The code fragment *delete-end-body* will be refined by a loop, and the following specification can be deduced:

delete-end-body
init   true
guard $end \ne n$
inv $heap = pointers\text{-}of(doc, end) \lhd h$
var $0 \le end < \overleftarrow{end}$

The initialization for the loop will set things up as discussed above. The loop specification can be written in terms of pre- and post-conditions and shown to satisfy the operation *delete-end*; the proof is left as an exercise.

The specification of the loop gives the following code fragment:

$n := end - n;$
while $end \neq n$ do
  delete-one
  ext rd *doc*   : *Buffer*
    wr *heap* : *Store*
     end   : *Limit*
    lc *h*   : *Store*
  pre $end \neq n \wedge$
    $heap = pointers\text{-}of(doc, end) \lhd h$
  post $heap = pointers\text{-}of(doc, end) \lhd h \wedge$
     $0 \leq end < \overleftarrow{end}$
end

The body of the loop, the *delete-one* operation, will remove one line of text from the buffer. Before removing the actual line of text from the heap, it must be checked that it is not shared by another pointer; if it is, the line of text must not be removed from the heap. The buffer is scanned to check for any sharing by checking the pointer value for the line to be deleted with the other pointer values stored in the text buffer. If there is a match then sharing occurs, if there is no match, there is no sharing and it is possible to delete the line of text from the heap. The outline for the *delete-one* operation is thus

  scan-buffer;
  disposep

The *scan-buffer* operation will check for any shared lines; and *disposep* will remove those lines that are not shared.

The *scan-buffer* loop will be tackled first. A possible algorithm is to just scan the buffer looking for a match, which, if it exists, will mean that another pointer shares this line of text. If the buffer is searched left-to-right looking for a match, there is a guarantee of at least one: the pointer value must equal the line that is to be deleted. If it matches any other line, then sharing has occurred and the line of text in the heap cannot be removed.

The *scan-buffer* operation will return the first buffer location that matches the pointer that is to be deleted. This gives the following specification for the operation:

  scan-buffer
  ext rd *doc* : *Buffer*
     end   : *Limit*
    wr *i*   : **N**
  post $doc(end) \notin pointers\text{-}of(doc, i - 1) \wedge$
    $doc(i) = doc(end) \wedge$
    $i \leq end$

The *disposep* operation should only get rid of an unshared pointer. If *i* is equal to *end* then it is known that the corresponding line of text is not shared and so it can be deleted from the heap; if *i* is less than *end*, it is shared and thus the text cannot be deleted:

$disposep$
ext rd doc : $Buffer$
    wr $heap$: $Store$
      end : $Limit$
      rd i : $\mathbb{N}$
      lc h : $Store$
pre $i \leq end$
post $(i = \overleftarrow{end} \wedge heap = \{doc(\overleftarrow{end})\} \lhd \overleftarrow{heap}$
       $\vee$
    $i < \overleftarrow{end} \wedge heap = \overleftarrow{heap}) \wedge$
    $end = \overleftarrow{end} - 1$

The two operations can now be combined and shown to satisfy the original specification:

$delete\text{-}one$
ext rd doc : $Buffer$
    wr $heap$: $Store$
      end : $Limit$
      lc h : $Store$
pre $end \neq n \wedge$
    $heap = pointers\text{-}of(doc, end) \lhd h$

        $scan\text{-}buffer$
        ext rd doc, end
            wr $i : \mathbb{N}$
        post $doc(end) \notin pointers\text{-}of(doc, i - 1) \wedge$
            $doc(i) = doc(end) \wedge$
            $i \leq end$
        ;
        $disposep$
        ext rd doc
            $i : \mathbb{N}$
            wr $heap, end$
            lc h
        pre $i \leq end$
        post $(i = \overleftarrow{end} \wedge heap = \{doc(\overleftarrow{end})\} \lhd \overleftarrow{heap}$
               $\vee$
            $i < \overleftarrow{end} \wedge heap = \overleftarrow{heap}) \wedge$
            $end = \overleftarrow{end} - 1$
post $heap = pointers\text{-}of(doc, end) \lhd h \wedge$
    $0 \leq end < \overleftarrow{end}$

The check of the pre-conditions is left for the reader; the post-condition proof is (using the data invariant)

$$\exists heap_1, end_1, i_1 \cdot$$

$$end_0 \neq n \ \wedge$$
$$heap_0 = pointers\text{-}of(doc, end_0) \lhd h \ \wedge$$
$$heap_0 = heap_1 \ \wedge$$
$$end_0 = end_1 \ \wedge \tag{5}$$
$$doc(end_1) \notin pointers\text{-}of(doc, i_1 - 1) \ \wedge$$
$$doc(i_1) = doc(end_1) \ \wedge$$
$$i_1 \leq end_1 \ \wedge$$
$$i_1 = i \ \wedge$$
$$(i = end_1 \wedge heap = \{doc(end_1)\} \lhd heap_1 \tag{10}$$
$$\qquad \vee$$
$$i < end_1 \wedge heap = heap_1) \ \wedge$$
$$end = end_1 - 1$$
$$\Rightarrow \ heap = pointers\text{-}of(doc, end) \lhd h \wedge 0 \leq end < end_0$$

Lines 2 and 3 are from the pre-condition of *delete-one*; lines 4 and 5 are from the read identifiers of the frame of *scan-buffer*, and lines 6, 7 and 8 are from the post-condition. Line 9 is from the read identifiers of the frame of *dispose* and finally lines 10 through 13 are from the post-condition.

This can be shown to imply the overall requirement for the specification. Two cases need to be considered. The first is when the scanning pointer is equal to the entry in the buffer to be deleted; this means there is no shared storage. The second is where it is not equal to the entry to be deleted; there is shared text.

First assume $i = end_1$ then

$heap$

$\qquad =$ "hypothesis line 10"

$\{doc(end_1)\} \lhd heap_1$

$\qquad =$ "hypothesis lines 4 and 5"

$\{doc(end_0)\} \lhd heap_0$

$\qquad =$ "hypothesis line 3"

$\{doc(end_0)\} \lhd (pointers\text{-}of(doc, end_0) \lhd h)$

$\qquad =$ "property of mapping domain restrict and domain subtract operations"

$(pointers\text{-}of(doc, end_0) - \{doc(end_0)\}) \lhd h$

$\qquad =$ "assumption; hypothesis line 5"

$(pointers\text{-}of(doc, i) - \{doc(i)\}) \lhd h$

$\qquad =$ "definition of *pointers-of*"

$((pointers\text{-}of(doc, i - 1) \cup \{doc(i)\}) - \{doc(i)\}) \lhd h$

From the assumption and lines 6 and 9 of the hypothesis:

$$doc(i) \notin pointers\text{-}of(doc, i - 1)$$

Therefore

$$((\textit{pointers-of}(doc, i - 1) \cup \{doc(i)\}) - \{doc(i)\}) \lhd h$$
$$= \text{``properties of set operator''}$$
$$\textit{pointers-of}(doc, i - 1) \lhd h$$
$$= \text{``assumption; hypothesis line 13''}$$
$$\textit{pointers-of}(doc, end) \lhd h$$

Next assume $i < end_1$ then:

$$heap$$
$$= \text{``hypothesis lines 12, 4 and 3''}$$
$$\textit{pointers-of}(doc, end_0) \lhd h$$
$$= \text{``hypothesis lines 5 and 12''}$$
$$\textit{pointers-of}(doc, end + 1) \lhd h$$
$$= \text{``definition of } \textit{pointers-of}\text{''}$$
$$(\textit{pointers-of}(doc, end) \cup \{doc(end + 1)\}) \lhd h$$
$$= \text{``hypothesis line 12''}$$
$$(\textit{pointers-of}(doc, end) \cup \{doc(end_1)\}) \lhd h$$

Now $doc(i_1) = doc(end_1)$ and from the assumption we have $i < end_1$; therefore we know that $doc(end_1) \in \textit{pointers-of}(doc, end)$. Therefore

$$(\textit{pointers-of}(doc, end) \cup \{doc(end_1)\}) \lhd h$$
$$= \text{``}doc(end_1) \in \textit{pointers-of}(doc, end)\text{''}$$
$$\textit{pointers-of}(doc, end) \lhd h$$

It is easy to see that the value of end is decreased as required, and thus the proof is complete.

The loop *scan-buffer* can be defined as

```
init   i = 1
guard doc(i) ≠ doc(end)
inv    doc(end) ∉ pointers-of(doc, i − 1) ∧ i ≤ end
var    0 ≤ end − i < end − ⟵i
```

The loop invariant records that a match has yet to be found and the loop variant the fact that the scan pointer is increased. The guard records the fact that the scanning continues until a match is found. Searching algorithms frequently have a component in the invariant that records the fact that the target value is yet to be found. The completion of the proof is left as an exercise.

The specification for the body of the loop is

```
pre  doc(i) ≠ doc(end) ∧
     doc(end) ∉ pointers-of(doc, i − 1) ∧ i ≤ end
post doc(end) ∉ pointers-of(doc, i − 1) ∧ i ≤ end ∧
     0 ≤ end − i < end − ⟵i
```

The loop body can be satisfied by just increasing i by one. The various components of the decomposition can now be put together to produce the code for the *scan-buffer* operation:

$i := 1;$
while $doc(i) \neq doc(end)$ do
$\quad i := i + 1$
end

Now

$\quad disposep \sqsubseteq$ if $i = end$ then $\{doc(end)\} \lhd heap$ else skip end;
$\qquad\qquad end := end - 1$

The proof is left as an exercise. The operation

$\quad \{doc(end)\} \lhd heap$

is just *dispose* in disguise. Assembling all the code for the operation finally gives:

$delete\text{-}end_1\ (n:\mathbf{N})$
(dcl $i\ :\ \mathbf{N}$;
$\quad n := end - n;$
$\quad$ while $end \neq n$ do
$\quad\quad i := 1;$
$\quad\quad$ while $doc(i) \neq doc(end)$ do
$\quad\quad\quad i := i + 1$
$\quad\quad$ end;
$\quad\quad$ if $i = end$ then $dispose(doc(end))$ else skip end;
$\quad\quad end := end - 1$
$\quad$ end
) $--\ delete\text{-}end_1$

The *block-move* operation The representation of text allows pointers to be moved to model lines of text being moved. There is no need to free or allocate any storage in the heap, as no lines of text are added or removed from the document by this operation.

$block\text{-}move_1\ (p, s, f:\mathbf{N})$
ext wr $doc\ :\ Buffer$
$\quad$ rd $end\ :\ Limit$
pre $p, s, f \in \{1, \ldots, end\} \wedge s \leq f \wedge p \notin \{s, \ldots, f\}$
post $p < s\ \wedge$
$\quad$ let $w = f - s + 1$ in
$\quad doc = \overleftarrow{doc} \dagger (\{p + i \mapsto \overleftarrow{doc}(s - 1 + i) \mid i \in \{1, \ldots, w\}\} \cup$
$\qquad\qquad\qquad \{p + i \mapsto \overleftarrow{doc}(p + i - w) \mid i \in \{w + 1, \ldots, f - p\}\})$
$\qquad \vee$
$\quad f \leq p\ \wedge$
$\quad$ let $w = p - (f + 1) + 1$ in
$\quad doc = \overleftarrow{doc} \dagger (\{s - 1 + i \mapsto \overleftarrow{doc}(f + i) \mid i \in \{1, \ldots, w\}\} \cup$
$\qquad\qquad\qquad \{s - 1 + i \mapsto \overleftarrow{doc}(s - 1 + i - w) \mid i \in \{w + 1, \ldots, p - s + 1\}\})$

The form of the above specification suggests a decomposition using conditional commands, with a Boolean expression for each of the conditions in the post-condition; the *block-move* operation can be decomposed as follows:

$block\text{-}move_1$ $(p, s, f : \mathbb{N})$
(if $p < s$ then
  $block\text{-}move\text{-}left(p, s, f)$
else
  $block\text{-}move\text{-}right(p, s, f)$
end
) $--$ $block\text{-}move_1$

The *block-move-left* operation will move text to the left of its current position, and the *block-move-right* will move text to the right. The specifications are given below, and are simply the appropriate component of the *block-move* operation. There is an extra predicate in the pre-conditions of these two operations; that these are satisfied comes from the appropriate guard.

$block\text{-}move\text{-}left$ $(p, s, f : \mathbb{N})$
ext wr *doc* : *Buffer*
   rd *end* : *Limit*
pre $p < s \land p, s, f \in \{1, \ldots, end\} \land s \le f$
post let $w = f - s + 1$ in
$$doc = \overleftarrow{doc} \dagger (\{p + i \mapsto \overleftarrow{doc}(s - 1 + i) \mid i \in \{1, \ldots, w\}\} \cup$$
$$\{p + i \mapsto \overleftarrow{doc}(p + i - w) \mid i \in \{w + 1, \ldots, f - p\}\})$$

$block\text{-}move\text{-}right$ $(p, s, f : \mathbb{N})$
ext wr *doc* : *Buffer*
   rd *end* : *Limit*
pre $f \le p \land p, s, f \in \{1, \ldots, end\} \land s \le f$
post let $w = p - (f + 1) + 1$ in
$$doc = \overleftarrow{doc} \dagger (\{s - 1 + i \mapsto \overleftarrow{doc}(f + i) \mid i \in \{1, \ldots, w\}\} \cup$$
$$\{s - 1 + i \mapsto \overleftarrow{doc}(s - 1 + i - w) \mid i \in \{w + 1, \ldots, p - s + 1\}\})$$

The next step in the development is to decompose the *block-move-right* and *block-move-left* operations. A possible algorithm is to shuffle the text in the buffer to open a gap where the text will be moved to, copy the text into this gap and then delete it from its original position by shuffling the text again. This algorithm requires that the buffer is large enough to hold a copy of the text to be moved. In fact, the movement of text can be accomplished by three uses of one operation with no requirement for any extra storage. The operation needed to do this is one to reverse a section of text in the buffer:

$reverse$ $(m, n : \mathbb{N})$
ext wr *doc* : *Buffer*
   rd *end* : *Limit*
pre $m, n \in \{1, \ldots, end\}$
post $doc = \overleftarrow{doc} \dagger \{i \mapsto \overleftarrow{doc}(m + n - i) \mid i \in \{m, \ldots, n\}\}$

The operation takes two pointers into the buffer as arguments and reverses the sequence of pointers between these two values. The *block-move-left* operation is implemented by three uses of *reverse*. It is important that the use of the reverse operation in this way is proved correct, since *block-move* is a primitive operation and confidence in its correctness is required; additionally, its implementation is somewhat obscure. Running a few test cases is not a convincing proof of correctness.

The proof is done in the usual manner: the pre-conditions set things up correctly and the new post-condition is shown to be equivalent to the intended one. That the pre-conditions are correct can be seen by inspection:

> *block-move-left*
> ext wr *doc* : *Buffer*
>   rd *end* : *Limit*
> pre $p < s \wedge p, s, f \in \{1, \ldots, end\} \wedge s \leq f$
>
> $$reverse(p + 1, s - 1);$$
> $$reverse(s, f);$$
> $$reverse(p + 1, f)$$
>
> post let $w = f - s + 1$ in
> $$doc = \overleftarrow{doc} \dagger (\{p + i \mapsto \overleftarrow{doc}(s - 1 + i) \mid i \in \{1, \ldots, w\}\} \cup$$
> $$\{p + i \mapsto \overleftarrow{doc}(p + i - w) \mid i \in \{w + 1, \ldots, f - p\}\})$$

The proof of the post-condition of the sequence of statements is given by the usual rule. Substituting the various values for the post-conditions in the semicolon rule gives the following:

> $\exists doc_1, doc_2 \cdot$
> $$doc_1 = doc_0 \dagger \{i \mapsto doc_0((p + 1) + (s - 1) - i) \mid i \in \{p + 1, \ldots, s - 1\}\} \wedge$$
> $$doc_2 = doc_1 \dagger \{i \mapsto doc_1(s + f - i) \mid i \in \{s, \ldots, f\}\} \wedge$$
> $$doc = doc_2 \dagger \{i \mapsto doc_2((p + 1) + f - i) \mid i \in \{p + 1, \ldots, f\}\} \qquad (4)$$
> $\Rightarrow$
> let $w = f - s + 1$ in
> $$doc = doc_0 \dagger (\{p + i \mapsto doc_0(s - 1 + i) \mid i \in \{1, \ldots, w\}\} \cup$$
> $$\{p + i \mapsto doc_0(p + i - w) \mid i \in \{w + 1, \ldots, f - p\}\})$$

Now from line 3 of the hypothesis

> doc_2
>
>   = "hypothesis line 2"
> $$(doc_0 \dagger \{i \mapsto doc_0(p + s - i) \mid i \in \{p + 1, \ldots, s - 1\}\}) \dagger$$
> $$\{i \mapsto doc_1(s + f - i) \mid i \in \{s, \ldots, f\}\}$$
>   = "domains do not overlap"
> $$doc_0 \dagger (\{i \mapsto doc_0(p + s - i) \mid i \in \{p + 1, \ldots, s - 1\}\} \cup$$
> $$\{i \mapsto doc_0(s + f - i) \mid i \in \{s, \ldots, f\}\})$$

Now a possible strategy for the proof is to split the domain of the mapping that overwrites doc_2 in the hypothesis line 4:

$$doc = doc_2 \dagger \{i \mapsto doc_2((p+1)+f-i) \mid i \in \{p+1,\ldots,f\}\}$$
$$= doc_2 \dagger (\{i \mapsto doc_2(p+1+f-i) \mid i \in \{p+1,\ldots,s-1\}\} \cup$$
$$\{i \mapsto doc_2(p+1+f-i) \mid i \in \{s,\ldots,f\}\})$$

The next step is to reorganize the equation that defines doc_2 so that its value can be used in the equation for doc above.

$$doc_2 = doc_0 \dagger (\{p+1+f-i \mapsto doc_0(i-w) \mid i \in \{f-s+2+p,\ldots,f\}\} \cup$$
$$\{p+1+f-i \mapsto doc_0(s+i-1-p) \mid i \in \{1+p,\ldots,1+f-s+p\}\})$$

Thus we have

doc

$= $ "definition of doc_2 above"

$$doc_2 \dagger (\{i \mapsto doc_0(i-w) \mid i \in \{p+1,\ldots,s-1\}\} \cup$$
$$\{i \mapsto doc_0(s+i-1-p) \mid i \in \{s,\ldots,f\}\})$$

$= $ "change maplet ranges"

$$doc_2 \dagger (\{p+i \mapsto doc_0(i-w+p) \mid i \in \{1,\ldots,w\}\} \cup$$
$$\{p+i \mapsto doc_0(s+i-1) \mid i \in \{w+1,\ldots,f-p\}\})$$

The *block-move-right* operation can also be implemented using three reverses and should also be proved correct:

$block\text{-}move\text{-}right\ (p,s,f\colon \mathbf{N})$

$(\text{pre } f \leq p \wedge p,s,f \in \{1,\ldots,end\}$

$\quad reverse(s,f);$
$\quad reverse(f+1,p);$
$\quad reverse(s,p)$

$\text{post let } w = p - (f+1) + 1 \text{ in}$

$$doc = \overleftarrow{doc} \dagger (\{s-1+i \mapsto \overleftarrow{doc}(f+i) \mid i \in \{1,\ldots,w\}\} \cup$$
$$\{s-1+i \mapsto \overleftarrow{doc}(s-1+i-w) \mid i \in \{w+1,\ldots,p-s+1\}\})$$
$) \ -\!- \ block\text{-}move\text{-}right$

The proof is left as an exercise.

The next step is to refine *reverse*. The algorithm will exchange elements in the sequence starting from either end, working through the buffer exchanging pairs of pointers until the elements to be exchanged meet in the middle. This algorithm suggests a loop. At any point during this process, if we consider the answer and reverse those elements yet to be exchanged this will give the current situation of the algorithm. This suggests the introduction of a logical constant to give the following specification:

$reverse\ (m, n: \mathbf{N})$

$(reverse\text{-}body$

 ext wr $m, n: \mathbf{N}$

  $doc: Buffer$

  rd $end: Limit$

  lc $c: Buffer$

 pre $m, n \in \{1, \ldots, end\} \wedge$

  $c = doc \dagger \{i \mapsto doc(m + n - i) \mid i \in \{m, \ldots, n\}\}$

 post $doc = c \dagger \{i \mapsto c(m + n - i) \mid i \in \{m, \ldots, n\}\} \wedge m > n$

$)\ -\!-\ reverse$

The loop invariant has already been introduced, so the loop specification is

 init true

 guard $m \leq n$

 inv $c = doc \dagger \{i \mapsto doc(m + n - i) \mid i \in \{m, \ldots, n\}\}$

 var $0 \leq n - m < \overleftarrow{n} - \overleftarrow{m}$

Care must be taken with the guard; the obvious guard of m and n being equal will not work. (Consider the case where m is increased and n decreased in the body of the loop.) The specification for the body of the loop from the above is

$loop\text{-}body$

 ext wr $m, n\ : \mathbf{N}$

  doc $: Buffer$

  lc c $: Buffer$

 pre $m \leq n \wedge$

  $c = doc \dagger \{i \mapsto doc(m + n - i) \mid i \in \{m, \ldots, n\}\}$

 post $c = doc \dagger \{i \mapsto doc(m + n - i) \mid i \in \{m, \ldots, n\}\} \wedge$

  $0 \leq m - n < \overleftarrow{m} - \overleftarrow{n}$

The algorithm suggests that the ith and jth elements are exchanged, and then i increased and j decreased which will establish the variant. Following assignment can be used to give the following refinement of $loop\text{-}body$

$loop\text{-}body \sqsubseteq$

$swop$

 pre $m \leq n \wedge$

  $c = doc \dagger \{i \mapsto doc(m + n - i) \mid i \in \{m, \ldots, n\}\}$

 post $c = doc \dagger \{i \mapsto doc(m + n - i) \mid i \in \{m, \ldots, n\}\} \wedge$

  $0 \leq (n - 1) - (m + 1) < \overleftarrow{n} - \overleftarrow{m}$

 ;

$m, n := m + 1, n - 1$

The $swop$ operation can be refined by

$$swop \sqsubseteq doc(n), doc(m) := doc(m), doc(n)$$

Having completed all the refinements of the various components, the program can be recovered to give the final code for $block\text{-}move$ and $reverse$:

$reverse\ (m, n: \mathbf{N})$

(while $m \le n$ do
    $doc(n), doc(m) := doc(m), doc(n)$;
    $m, n := m + 1, n - 1$
end
) $--\ reverse$

$block\text{-}move_1\ (p, s, f: \mathbf{N})$

(if $p < s$ then
    $reverse(p + 1, s - 1)$;
    $reverse(s, f)$;
    $reverse(p + 1, f)$
else
    $reverse(s, f)$;
    $reverse(f + 1, p)$;
    $reverse(s, p)$
end
) $--\ block\text{-}move_1$

The *init-buffer* operation   The refinement and proof of this operation is left for the reader.

16.4.2   The final step

There is one refinement step left to do, that of choosing a data representation for a *Line* of text. There are two possibilities, one is to represent a line of text as an array of characters of size L together with the number of characters stored in the line:

$$Line_1\ ::\ nchar\ :\ \{0, \ldots, L\}$$
$$chars\ :\ \{1, \ldots, L\} \xrightarrow{m} Char$$
$$\text{inv } mk\text{-}Line_1\ \triangleq\ \{1, \ldots, nchar\} \subseteq \text{dom } chars$$

Alternatively a line could be represented as an array of characters of size $L + 1$, and with a terminating character (either a CR or a NULL) used to indicate the end of the line. This refinement is left to the reader as it is fairly straightforward.

Exercise 16.3

1. Prove the refinement of the *change-line* operation on page 345.
2. Complete the proof of the loop development given above.
3. Write a specification for the *execute-xchange* operation with respect to the data representation using an array of pointers and the heap.
4. Using a specification of *execute-xchange*, derive and prove correct a decomposition of the operation.
5. Derive and prove a refinement of *init-buffer*.

16.5 SUMMARY

The abstract machine has now been refined to a level where the specification can be translated into executable code. Notice how we were able to 'divide and conquer' to find a solution to the problem and concentrate on each aspect in isolation. The efficient implementation of the block-move operation was discovered and implemented. It should be noted that though the proofs look rather large and clumsy in print, most of the work can be done without writing down so much detail.

Project

1. Continue development of the character-based editor through to code in a style similar to that used for the line-based editor of this chapter.
2. The code was refined to a level where the Pascal (or Modula-2) *new* and *dispose* operations could be used. Suppose these were found to be inefficient. Using a (large) array of characters specify and develop code for *new* and *dispose* that could be used in place of the Pascal primitives.

17

THE USER INTERFACE

AIMS

- To demonstrate the low-level design of the editor case study.
- To demonstrate the relationship between concrete commands and abstract commands in the editor case study.

17.1 INTRODUCTION

In the previous chapters what might be called the 'editor engine' was specified and developed; to complete the program we need to develop the part of the editor program that interfaces with the user. This chapter will look at the specification and development of the code necessary to read a command from the user and call the appropriate command processor to execute that command. This could be approached in two or three development steps. The first would be to specify how to read a line of text from the user and translate this into the external abstract syntax; then to supply defaults, etc., and thus translate the external syntax representation of a command into the internal abstract syntax. Once we have the internal abstract syntax representation of a command, it is easy to pass this representation to the appropriate command processor for execution. This is more or less the approach that we will take, except that it is easier to do this in one step rather than two. However, before proceeding, we will consider the user's view of the system.

17.2 THE CONCRETE SYNTAX OF THE COMMANDS

17.2.1 A simple approach brings problems

We have now reached the point in the development where it would be useful to consider the concrete syntax for commands. An outline of a command might be:

    command = command name, command arguments ;

    command arguments = line specification | block specification | ... ;

The command arguments specify a line or a block of text and could be defined as

    line specification = expression ;

for a line specification, and

> block specification = expression, ',', expression ;

for a block specification. It would be useful to specify a line, for example, as

> .+1

where we could write '.' for the current line. This approach suggests that an expression used to specify a line could be a line number optionally followed by an offset

> expression = line number, [('+' | '−'), offset] ;

We will leave for the moment the exact form of a line number or an offset—except that they can be natural numbers.

This approach together with the default mechanism discussed in Chapter 14 would give problems. For example, consider

> move 5,8

Does it mean move line 5 after line 8, or does it mean move the block consisting of lines 5 through 8 after the current line? This ambiguity could be resolved by requiring that block specifications be written in brackets, so that

> move 5,8

would mean move line 5 after line 8. To move lines 5 through 8 after the current line would be written as

> move (5,8)

Though this removes some of the ambiguity problems, there are further complications when the find and substitute commands are considered. The problems can be resolved, but it is at the cost of increased complexity of the concrete syntax. An easier way of resolving these problems is to allow a line or block specification (depending on the command) to be typed before the command name; so the general form of the commands would be

> command = [line specification | block specification], command name, [arguments] ;

This approach has several advantages: the typing of each command involves few keystrokes and the ambiguity problem has been solved:

> (5,8) move   move lines 5 through 8 after the current line
> 5 move 8   move line 5 after line 8

There is a disadvantage: the command parser will have to deal with the line or block specification before we know what the command is. The well formed conditions define when a line specification is needed, when a block specification is needed and when they can be left out, and this knowledge can be used to define how each of the commands shall be processed. The concrete syntax that will be developed will be fairly generous and allow

> (4,7) quit

to be entered (it would be very difficult to forbid it), but the editor will offer an appropriate error message when the error is found, which will be as soon as the quit command has been recognized.

17.2.2   A first try

Before writing a formal specification for the concrete syntax, a rough sketch of the commands of the system that matches the abstract syntax will be written down to get a feel for the command language. The editing commands update the current file, and the file command changes the file that is being edited. The editing commands are:

i n	insert text after line n (text follows)
$[\,l\mid(s,f)\,]$ c n	copy the specified text after line n
$[\,l\mid(s,f)\,]$ d	delete the text of the specified lines
$[\,l\mid(s,f)\,]$ m n	move the specified text to after line n
n	make line n the current line
=	show the current line number
$[\,l\mid(s,f)\,]$ p	display the specified lines of the document
$[\,l\mid(s,f)\,]$ f/pat	find the first line in the range that contains pat
$[\,l\mid(s,f)\,]$ s/pat/new	substitute new for pat for the specified lines

where l stands for a line-number and (s,f) for a block specification, and text entered with an insert command is terminated by entering a line consisting of just a '.'. Commands may be preceded by no, one or two line numbers. If two line numbers are required by a command and only one is specified, it is used for both. If no line numbers are specified, a default rule is applied: usually the current line is used either to define a single line or a block of text just consisting of the current line.

Line numbers are formed from the following components:

n	a decimal number
@	the zeroth line (line 0)
.	the current line
$	the last line of the document

Components of a line number may be combined with '+' or '−' and a number, for example:

$.+1$	sum of '.' and 1: the line after the current line, the next line
$.-1$	the previous line
$\$-5$	five lines up from the bottom of the document

The file commands are:

e $file$	edit a file—the current document is discarded and the named file becomes the new document; at the start of an editing session there is an empty document to edit and it is called 'untitled...'
w $file$	write out the current document to file
q	quit the editor

The next step is to write out the concrete syntax in full using BNF. The input to the system is actually a sequence of characters that should represent a valid command. The formal description of the concrete syntax that BNF allows should match the requirements of the specification and thus match the information context as described by the (external) abstract syntax.

17.2.3   The concrete syntax

Before progressing, the informal sketch given above should be formalized. The actual concrete syntax of the sequence of characters that make up a command is given below in BNF. The BNF notation we will use conforms to the BSI Standard for syntax (see Appendix C, page 432). The syntax is divided into two, the first part describes the syntax down to the token level—tokens can be separated by zero or more spaces—and the second part addresses the problem of tokenization—terminals of those production rules must not be separated by spaces. The grammar for the top level of the syntax is

command = [line definition], command specification ;

line definition = line specification | block specification ;

line specification = expression ;

block specification = '(', expression, ',', expression, ')' ;

expression = line number, [sign, number] ;

line number = number | '@' | '.' | '$' ;

sign = '+' | '−' ;

command specification = insert
                      | copy
                      | delete
                      | move
                      | current
                      | show
                      | display
                      | find
                      | substitute
                      | edit
                      | write
                      | quit ;

insert = 'i', [line specification] ;

copy = 'c', [line specification] ;

delete = 'd' ;

move = 'm', [line specification] ;

current = ;

show = '=' ;

display = 'p' ;

find = 'f', string ;

substitute = 's', string ;

edit = 'e', [file name] ;

write = 'w', [file name] ;

quit = 'q' ;

The above grammar 'sees' the input as a sequence of tokens, with spaces removed. The tokenization will see the input as a sequence of characters, and must provide that sequence of tokens. The grammar for the token view of the input is

```
token  =   space
       |   separator
       |   number
       |   file name
       |   string ;

space  =   ' ' ;
separator  =   '('  | ')'  | '@'  | '.'  | '$'  | '+'  | '–'
           |   'i'  | 'c'  | 'd'  | 'm'  | '='  | 'p'  | 'f'  | 's'  | 'e'  | 'w'  | 'q' ;
number  =   digit, { digit } ;
file name  =   "'", fchar, { fchar }, "'" ;
string  =   delim, pat, [ delim, [ pattern ] ] ;
digit  =   '0'  | '1'  | '2'  | '3'  | '4'  | '5'  | '6'  | '7'  | '8'  | '9' ;
delim  =   char – ( ' ' ) ;
fchar  =   char – ( "'" ) ;
pattern  =   { char } ;
char  =   (* any ASCII character *) ;
```

This double view of the concrete syntax is fairly common; it allows the details of how spaces are to be treated to be pushed down to the bottom level and provides a description of the language which makes it obvious where spaces are allowed (between the objects that are at the bottom level of the first syntax).

There are different philosophies behind the concrete syntax and the abstract syntax. We have chosen to write the concrete syntax in a way that gives the overall structure of the commands and shows the similarities rather than their differences. The fact that the insert command must only have one expression in its line specification must be described in English somewhere. The abstract syntax shows the information content of the commands and is written in such a way as to minimize the need for 'well-formed-ness' functions (which are invariants!). Each has a particular job to do: the concrete syntax gives the syntax of the commands, while the abstract syntax will be used to give the 'information contents' of the commands so that the semantics can be defined.

17.2.4 A better representation

The concrete syntax defined using BNF is rather difficult to understand, a pictorial representation is much easier to visualize. Any BNF syntax description can be transformed into an equivalent graphical (pictorial) form. The translations for the various syntactic constructs is shown in Fig. 17.1. The graphs for the editor syntax are shown in Figs. 17.2 to 17.4. Obvious transformations have been made to cut down the number of components.

17.3 DERIVING THE CODE FOR THE COMMAND PROCESSOR

Now we have a formal description of the commands that the editor accepts. The next stage in the development is to derive the code that will translate a command into a call of the appropriate command processor.

A terminal symbol x

is represented by

A non-terminal symbol B

is represented by

$A = \tau_1 \mid \tau_2 \mid ... \mid \tau_n$;

is represented by

$A = \tau_1, \tau_2, ..., \tau_n$;

is represented by

$A = \{ \tau \}$;

is represented by

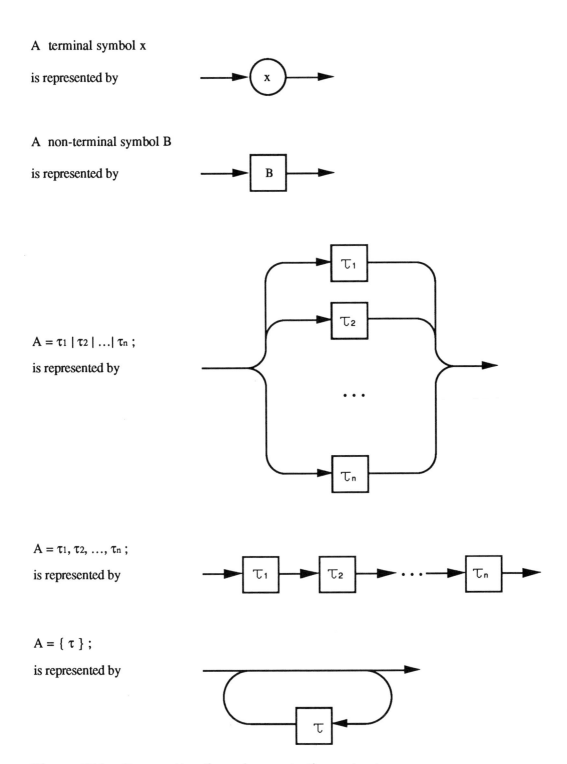

Figure 17.1 Representing the various syntactic constructs.

command

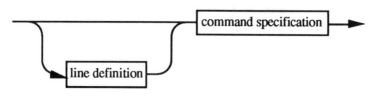

line definition

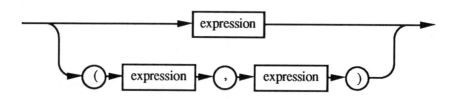

expression

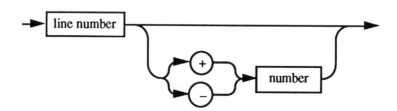

line number

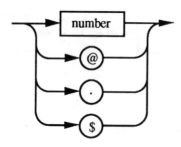

Figure 17.2 The command string.

command specification

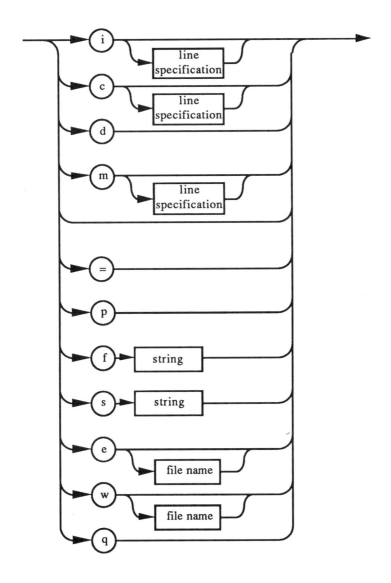

Figure 17.3 The commands.

number

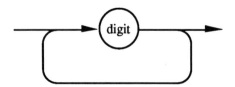

string

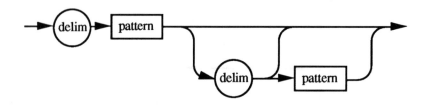

pattern

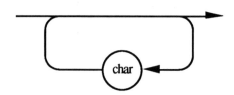

file name

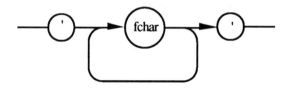

Figure 17.4　The tokens.

17.3.1 From graph to code

Since the description of the commands are formal, the description can be used as the basis from which the program that recognizes and processes commands can be developed. Each graph can be translated into a procedure that will recognize the language described by the graph. If the translation of the graph 'S' into a specification is denoted by $T(S)$, then the following procedure will translate a set of graphs that denote a concrete syntax into a program that will recognize that syntax.

Step 1. Reduce the set of graphs by appropriate substitutions. Try to keep a reasonable decomposition of the problem while doing this.

Step 2. Translate each graph into an operation using the rules defined below. (Since each graph usually becomes a procedure, the importance of trying to keep a reasonable decomposition in step 1 becomes obvious.)

Case 1. A graph element denoting a token (or terminal symbol) is translated into operations that process that token. Assuming that the variable *tok* contains the current token and the function *read-token* reads the next token from the text to be recognized, then Fig. 17.5 shows the translation from graph to code fragment.

Case 2. A graph element 'S' imbedded inside a graph is translated either into a call of a procedure that contains the translation of 'S' or it is translated directly. Fig. 17.5. shows this.

Case 3. A graph that contains a sequence of elements is translated into a sequence of operations (see Fig. 17.5).

Case 4. A graph that contains a choice of elements is translated into a choice of operations (see Fig. 17.6). The selection of a particular operation depends on which tokens start the corresponding production.

Case 5. A graph that contains a loop is translated into a while operation (see Fig. 17.6).

After processing (recognizing) a token the variable *tok* should be set to the next token in the input stream.

The *first* function used in cases 4 and 5 above defines the set of possible tokens that can start a production, and can be defined informally using recursion.

$$
\begin{aligned}
&\text{if } S = \text{a token} && \text{then } first(S) = \{\text{ATOKEN}\} \\
&\text{if } S = S_1, S_2, \ldots, S_n && \text{then } first(S) = \{first(S_1)\} \\
&\text{if } S = S_1 \mid S_2 \mid \ldots \mid S_n && \text{then } first(S) = \{first(S_1)\} \cup \{first(S_2)\} \cup \ldots \cup \{first(S_n)\} \\
&\text{if } S = \{P\} && \text{then } first(S) = first(P) \\
&\text{if } S = [P] && \text{then } first(S) = first(P)
\end{aligned}
$$

When dealing with the last two cases it may be necessary to look 'through' the production to find the *first* tokens of the production that follows.

Translation of a graph representing a terminal symbol.

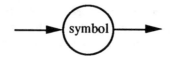

is translated into

> if *tok* = symbol then
>   -- symbol has been recognized
>   -- do any processing that needs to be associated
>   -- with this token and then read the next token
>   *tok:* = *read-token*()
> else
>   *error*
> end

Translation of a graph for a non-terminal.

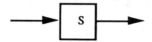

is translated into

$$T(S)$$

where $T(S)$ is either a translation of the appropriate graph component or a call to a procedure whose body is a translation of the appropriate graph component.

Translation of a graph for a sequence of non-terminals.

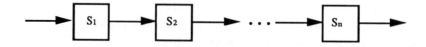

is translated into

$$T(S_1);$$
$$T(S_2);$$
$$\ldots$$
$$T(S_n)$$

Figure 17.5   Translating a syntax graph to code—part I.

Translating the graph for a choice of non-terminals.

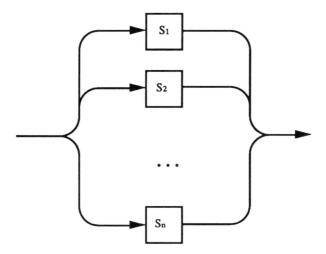

is translated into

> if $tok \in first(S_1)$ then
> $\quad T(S_1)$
> elsif $tok \in first(S_2)$ then
> $\quad T(S_2)$
> elsif ... then
> $\quad$ ...
> elsif $tok \in first(S_n)$ then
> $\quad T(S_n)$
> else
> $\quad error$
> end

where the function $first(S)$ defines all the possible initial tokens of the production S, its argument.

Translating the graph for an iteration of non-terminals.

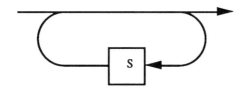

is translated into

> while $tok \in first(S)$ do
> $\quad T(S)$
> end

Figure 17.6 Translating a syntax graph to code—part II.

17.3.2 Translating the command syntax

The command will be typed in by the user and will be stored internally as a sequence of characters terminated by a carriage return symbol. To process this string two functions are assumed

> *read-token*()

this function returns the next token, and

> *get-ch*()

which returns the next character (this function is necessary to read in strings and file names correctly since, in those contexts, spaces are significant).

The code to recognize a command can be sketched using the rules given above, though care is necessary to deal with the case in which a block specification is missing. The overall syntax for a command is described by the syntax graph in Fig. 17.2, the code derived from it is shown below:

> *process-command* ()
>
> (if *tok* ∈ *first*(line definition) then
>   *line-definition*()
> elsif *tok* ∈ *first*(command specification) then
>   skip
> else
>   *error*('incorrect command syntax')
> end;
> *command-specification*()
>) −− *process-command*

The code has been wrapped up as an operation, so that it can be used later. However, it is necessary to do some processing as we go along. The concrete syntax assumes that a line definition starts each command (whether the semantics of a particular command demands it or not). Thus a line definition should be 'processed' to produce

- nothing—there was no line definition on this command to process.
- a line number—there was just one line expression.
- a line range—there were two line expressions.

Also an incorrect command can be picked up inside the operation *command-specification*. The code above can be modified to deal with these points:

> *process-command* ()
>
> (dcl *ld* : [*Line-range* | *Line-num*];
> if *tok* ∈ *first*(line definition) then
>   *ld*: = *line-definition*()
> else
>   *ld*: = nil
> end;
> *command-specification*(*ld*)
>) −− *process-command*

Notice how the new use of the operation *line-definition* assumes it to be a function that returns an abstract representation of what it found, and that the *command-specification* operation has been passed this information. Once a command has been recognized, then we can check if the semantics of that command require that a line definition should be present or not.

The operation *line-definition* together with the operations it will require should be tackled next. The syntax for a line definition was given on page 364 and the code derived from it is given in Fig. 17.7; this operation needs to recognize expressions. Note that the various denotations for a line definition have been translated into internal (abstract) representations. The syntax for an expression was given on page 364 and the code, with actions added, is shown in Fig. 17.8; this operation needs to check that the number it returns is non-negative, for otherwise it might return a negative value which would conflict with the type of the result. The syntax for a line number was given on page 364 and the corresponding code is shown in Fig. 17.9. These operations between them will deal with recognizing and dealing with a line definition.

```
line-definition () : [Line-range | Line-num]
(dcl f, l : N;
 if tok ∈ first(expression) then
   expression()
 elsif tok = '(' then
   tok: = read-token();
   f: = expression();
   if tok = ',' then
     tok: = read-token()
   else
     error('comma missing in block specification')
   end;
   l: = expression();
   if tok = ')' then
     tok: = read-token()
   else
     error('closing bracket missing')
   end;
   return mk-Line-range(f, l)
 else
   error('bad line specification or block specification')
 end
) -- line-definition
```

Figure 17.7   Recognizing a line definition.

```
expression () : N
(dcl l      : N,
     sign   : Separator,
     offset : Z;
 l: = line-number();
 if tok ∈ {'+', '−'} then
   sign: = tok;
   tok: = read-token();
   if tok ∈ N then
     if sign = '+' then
       offset: = tok
     else
       offset: = −tok
     end
   else
     error('offset is not a number')
   end
 else
   offset: = 0
 end;
 if 0 ≤ l + offset then
   return l + offset
 else
   error('line number specified is negative')
 end
) −− expression
```

Figure 17.8   Recognizing an expression.

```
line-number () : N
(dcl num : N;
 if tok ∈ N then
   num: = tok
 elsif tok = '@' then
   num: = 0
 elsif tok = '.' then
   num: = cline
 elsif tok = '$' then
   num: = end
 else
   error('incorrect line number')
 end;
 tok: = read-token();
 return num
) −− line-number
```

Figure 17.9   Recognizing a line number.

We now turn to the code that recognizes command specifications and deals with each of the commands. We will not develop the code to handle all of the commands, as the ideas used to develop the code should be fairly clear by now. However, we will tackle the delete, copy and insert commands, and (later) part of the find and replace commands, and leave the remainder as exercises.

The syntax diagram for a command specification was given on page 366 and the code that recognizes it is given in Fig. 17.10. We have replaced a conditional command by a case command and have also expanded the uses of the function *first*, for example

$$first(\text{insert command}) = \{\text{'i'}\}$$

and therefore

$$tok \in first(\text{insert command}) \iff tok \in \{\text{'i'}\} \iff tok = \text{'i'}$$

Once a command has been recognized, control can be passed to an appropriate command processor. The operations that process a command and call the appropriate operation to execute the command are responsible for checking the correctness of the arguments and completing any defaults—implicitly carrying out the well formed checks and translating from the external abstract representation of the commands to the internal form. Remember that the pre-conditions for each of the execute command operations assume that the commands are well formed and any defaults have been supplied.

The code for dealing with the delete, copy and insert commands is shown in Figs 17.11, 17.12 and 17.13 respectively. and finally we have linked up with the specification of *execute-delete*, *execute-copy* and *execute-insert*. The text that follows the insert command (the text that is to be inserted into the document) has already been dealt with in the specification and development of the insert command in Chapter 15.

```
command-specification (ld: [Line-range | Line-num])
(cases tok of
    'i' → process-insert-command(ld),
    'c' → process-copy-command(ld),
    'd' → process-delete-command(ld),
    'm' → process-move-command(ld),
    CR → process-current-command(ld),
    '=' → process-show-command(ld),
    'p' → process-display-command(ld),
    'f' → process-find-command(ld),
    's' → process-substitute-command(ld),
    'e' → process-edit-command(ld),
    'w' → process-write-command(ld),
    'q' → process-quit-command(ld),
    others error('command not recognized')
end

) -- command-specification
```

Figure 17.10   Recognizing a command specification.

```
process-delete-command (ld: [Line-range | Line-num])
(dcl lr : Line-range;
 tok: = read-tok();
 if tok = CR then
   lr: = supply-defaults(ld);
   if valid-line-range(lr) then
     execute-delete(lr)
   else
     error('incorrect line range')
   end
 else
   error('incorrect arguments to delete command')
 end
) -- process-delete-command
```

Figure 17.11   Dealing with a delete command.

```
process-copy-command (ld: [Line-range | Line-num])
(dcl dest : Line-num,
     lr   : Line-range;
 tok: = read-tok();
 if tok ∈ first(line specification) then
   dest: = expression()
 else
   dest: = cline
 end;
 if tok = CR then
   lr: = supply-defaults(ld);
   if valid-line-range(lr) ∧ valid-line(dest) then
     execute-copy(lr, dest)
   else
     error('incorrect line range or destination')
   end
 else
   error('incorrect arguments to copy command')
 end
) -- process-copy-command
```

Figure 17.12   Dealing with a copy command.

process-insert-command (*ld*: [*Line-range* | *Line-num*])
(dcl *dest* : *Line-num*;
  tok: = *read-tok*();
  if *tok* ∈ *first*(line specification) then
    dest: = *expression*()
  else
    dest: = *cline*
  end;
  if *ld* = nil ∧ *tok* = CR then
    if *valid-line*(*dest*) then
      execute-insert(*dest*)
    else
      error('incorrect destination')
    end
  else
    error('incorrect arguments to insert command')
  end
) −− *process-insert-command*

Figure 17.13 Dealing with an insert command.

supply-defaults (*ld*: [*Line-range* | *Line-num*) : *Line-range*
(if *ld* = nil then
    return *mk-Line-range*(*cline*, *cline*)
  elsif *ld* ∈ *Line-num* then
    return *mk-Line-range*(*ld*, *ld*)
  else
    return *ld*
  end
) −− *supply-defaults*

valid-line-range (*lr*: *Line-range*) : **B**
(return *lr*.*start* ≤ *lr*.*end* ∧ *lr*.*end* ≤ *end*
) −− *valid-line-range*

valid-line (*ln*: *Line-num*) : **B**
(return *ln* ≤ *end*
) −− *valid-line*

Figure 17.14 The *supply-defaults*, *valid-line-range* and *valid-line* operations.

17.3.3 Tokens

The final part of the problem is to break the line of text that represents the command into tokens. By now the reader should be quite good at seeing how the translation process works, so we shall take a few short-cuts with the string components. First, we must derive the top-level operation.

As has already been discussed, the input stream is a sequence of characters, and must be translated into a sequence of tokens. As well as providing this translation, the code must also provide tokens 'on demand' to be handled by the code already developed above. This problem can be tackled by considering the input as follows:

$$input \;=\; \{\; token \;\} \;;$$

where 'token' has already been defined on page 362. We will add a carriage return symbol to the definition of a token, to act as a guard to mark the end of the sequences of characters that make up a command.

We now write a recognizer for input, and dismember it so that it returns one token per call. We will not even translate the productions into a graph, but go direct from the syntax for a token to code:

```
input () : Token
(dcl sep : Separator;
  if ch = ' ' then
    ch: = get-ch();
    input()
  elsif ch ∈ first(separator) then
    separator()
  elsif ch ∈ first(number) then
    number()
  elsif ch ∈ first(file name) then
    filename()
  elsif ch ∈ first(string) then
    -- a problem here!
    string()
  elsif ch = CR then
    return CR
  else
    error('unknown character in command')
  end
) -- input
```

There is a problem with the above code. What exactly are the initial characters of a string? They are the delimiter used to start the pattern and can be any character. We could forbid the use of separators or a quote character, and this would solve the problem, but there is an easier solution. Strings can only occur after find and replace commands, so the context could be used to resolve any ambiguities and the first non-blank character that is found after the command name can be used as the delimiter. This means we need to obtain versions of the command that reads in a token, a general one, and one to be used after a find or replace command has been found. Taking this into account in the 'dismembering' we get:

```
read-token () : Token
(dcl sep : Separator;
  if ch = ' ' then
    ch := get-ch();
    read-token()
  elsif ch ∈ first(separator) then
    separator()
  elsif ch ∈ first(number) then
    number()
  elsif ch ∈ first(file name) then
    filename()
  elsif ch = CR then
    return CR
  else
    error('unknown character in command')
  end
) -- read-token
```

The specialized version of the command that reads a token after a find or replace command should skip over spaces to find the first non-blank character—this is the delimiter which it should return. The next call should return the sequence of characters that follow the delimiter (a pattern) up to, but not including, either the delimiter character or a carriage return. If the pattern was terminated by a carriage return we are (probably) done; if the pattern was terminated by a delimiter, then the next call should return the sequence of characters following the delimiter (another pattern). The code written for find or replace should use these tokens that are returned to construct their call to the appropriate command processor. However, using formal (or rigorous) methods should not blind us to shear native cunning. It would be better to do all of this analysis at this level which suggests the following function. This function will parse a sequence of characters and return one or two characters strings. It should (of course) be called by the *process-find* command or *process-replace* command in place of *read-token*.

When the 'cheating' operation needs to read a string component argument for a find or replace command, spaces are skipped and the first non-blank character is set up ready to be interpreted as the delimiter. The next piece of input should conform to the syntax for a string; this was given on page 366. The standard strategy can be applied, and the code to recognize and deal with a string is shown in Fig. 17.15. Dealing with the pattern components of a string is a little more difficult; assuming that the variable *delim* holds the delimiter; then we stop reading characters when we see either a carriage return character (CR) or the delimiter character. The syntax for a pattern was given on page 366 and this can be used to derive the code to recognize it. The pattern is read in one character at a time and assembled in a local variable *pat*. The code to do this is shown in Fig. 17.15.

The syntax diagram for a number was given on page 366 and the resulting code is given in Fig. 17.15. The number is read in one character at a time converted into binary and assembled in a local variable n. The function *to-Digit* converts an (ASCII) character value into its natural number (binary) representation.

number () :**N**
(dcl *num* : **N**;
 num: = *to-Digit*(*ch*);
 ch: = *get-ch*();
 while *ch* ∈ {'0', '1', '2', '3', '4', '5', '6', '7', '8', '9'} do
   num: = *num* × 10 + *to-Digit*(*ch*);
   ch: = *get-ch*()
 end;
 return *num*
) −− *number*

string () : [*Pattern* × *Pattern* | *Pattern*]
(dcl *delim*   : *Char*;
     pat₁, *pat₂* : *Pattern*;
 while *ch* = ' ' do
   ch: = *get-ch*()
 end;
 delim: = *ch*;
 pat₁: = *pattern*(*delim*);
 if *ch* = *delim* then
   pat₂: = *pattern*(*delim*);
   return *mk*-(*pat₁*, *pat₂*)
 else
   return *pat₁*
 end
) −− *string*

pattern (*delim*: *Char*) : *Pattern*
(dcl *pat* : *Char**;
 ch: = *get-ch*();
 pat: = [];
 while *ch* ∉ {*delim*, CR} do
   pat: = *pat* ⌢ [*ch*];
   ch: = *get-ch*()
 end;
 return *pat*
) −− *pattern*

Figure 17.15   Recognizing a number, a string and a pattern.

filename () : **N**
(dcl *name* : *Char**;
 name:= [];
 ch:= *get-ch*();
 while *ch* ≠ ''' do
  name:= *name* ⌢ [*ch*];
  ch:= *get-ch*()
 end;
 return *name*
) −− *filename*

separator () : *Separator*
(dcl *sep* : *Separator*;
 sep:= *ch*;
 ch:= *get-ch*();
 return *sep*
) −− *separator*

Figure 17.16   Recognizing a file name and a separator.

The *get-ch* function can be specified thus:

get-ch () *r*: *Char*
ext **wr** *ccmd* : *Char**
pre *ccmd* ≠ []
post *r* = hd $\overleftarrow{ccmd}$ ∧
  ccmd = tl $\overleftarrow{ccmd}$

and the derivation of the code is left as an exercise.

There is a similar problem with reading the file name argument from the commands that manipulate files—this is left as an exercise.

Finally the specification of the *read-command* needs to be modified to start the one character look ahead that the token operations require.

read-command ()

ext **wr** *files* : *File-store*
  ccmd   : *Char**
  ch   : *Char*

pre *files*(STDIN) ∈ *Input-file* ∧
  let *mk-Input-file*(-, *r*) = *files*(STDIN) in
  r ≠ []

$$\text{post let } \textit{mk-Input-file}(l, r) = \overleftarrow{\textit{files}}(\text{STDIN}) \text{ in}$$
$$\textit{ccmd} = \text{hd } r \frown [\text{CR}] \wedge$$
$$\textit{ch} = \text{hd } \underline{\textit{ccmd}} \wedge$$
$$\textit{files} = \overleftarrow{\textit{files}} \dagger \{\text{STDIN} \mapsto \textit{mk-Input-file}(l \frown [\text{hd } r], \text{tl } r)\}$$

Exercise 17.1

1. The syntax for a file name given in the syntax above was rather simplistic. Write a concrete syntax for the file names on your favourite operating system, and write a recognizer for it.
2. Develop the code to satisfy the *read-command*.
3. Write the code for the remainder of the operations of the editor.

17.4 THE CONTROL OF THE EDITOR

The original control structure for the editor was given in Chapter 14 on page 295. With the development of the parser for the editor commands given above, this will obviously need to be changed (but not too much, otherwise the development in the other chapters would be null and void). The case command of the original specification has been replaced by an alternative command buried in the code of the operation command. We could have kept to the original specification, but this would have meant constructing the abstract syntax for each command; the derivation above avoids this, but still sticks to the spirit of the original specification. The final control structure is shown in Fig 17.17, the operation *process-command* of this chapter is a combination of the *parse-command* and *execute-command* operations of Chapter 14.

Notice how the problem has been tackled using a divide and conquer technique. At each development step there has been one major problem to solve, and this problem can be solved in isolation. At each development step, design decisions have been made with a reasonable understanding of why that particular solution was chosen. Each component was isolated from the others, and performance considerations would be considered for a component, rather than in the usual *ad hoc* way. Having an external abstract syntax for commands allowed the concrete syntax to be developed. Having an internal abstract syntax for the commands allowed the command processor to be specified and developed without worrying too much about the user interface.

17.4.1 The final program

The translation of the VDM-SL into executable code in Pascal, Modula-2 or C should be fairly straightforward. Those compilers that do not allow structured values to be returned will need to have the function calls returning a value that is assigned to a variable replaced by a procedure call that has a 'var' (reference) parameter. Another problem would be the variables that have been declared in the form

$$x : [A \mid B]$$

values

$D : \mathbb{N}$

$L : \mathbb{N}$

types

$Linep$ = pointer to $Line$

$Store$ = collection of $Line$

$Buffer = \{1, ...D\} \xrightarrow{m} Linep$

$Limit = \{0, \dots, D\}$

$Line = Char^*$

$Char$ = set of (ASCII) characters not including newline

$File\text{-}store = File\text{-}name \xrightarrow{m} File$

$File = Document \mid Output \mid \dots$

state $Editor$ of
```
    doc   :  Buffer      -- text of the file being edited
    heap  :  Store       -- the heap
    end   :  Limit       -- high-water mark
    cline :  N           -- current line
    cfile :  [File-name] -- name of the current file
    files :  File-store  -- the file store
end
```

```
(dcl quit  : B;
     ccmd  : Char*;
     ch    : Char;
 initialize();
 quit: = false;
 while ¬ quit do
   -- get-command
   read-command();
   process-command()
 end;
 termination()
)
```

Figure 17.17   The final control structure of the Editor.

This can be simulated in Modula-2 and Pascal by variant records, and in C by unions. This approach is especially necessary for the *tok* value which is of type *Token*. In Pascal we could write:

```
type
  Token = record
            case tokenType :  (sepT, natT, fileT, strT) of
            natT : (setV : Char) ;
            sepT : (natV : Integer)
            fileT : (fileV : String) ;
            strT : (strV : String)
          end
```

and a test of the form

$$tok = \text{'('}$$

would have to be written as

```
tok.tokenType = sepT AND tok.sepV = '('
```

The command line has been represented as a sequence of characters, and taken apart using the head and tail operators. A data refinement is necessary here, perhaps representing a sequence as

$$Command\text{-}line \; :: \; string \; : \; Char^*$$
$$first \; : \; \mathbb{N}$$

with a retrieve function

$$retr\text{-}com : Command\text{-}line \rightarrow Char^*$$

$$retr\text{-}com(mk\text{-}Command\text{-}line(string, first)) \;\; \triangle \;\; string(first, \ldots, \operatorname{len} string)$$

The translation of the low-level design into the final program is (as usual) left to the reader.

17.5 BEHIND THE SCENES

A command will be typed at the keyboard and input as a sequence of characters

$$Command = Char^*$$

The concrete representation of commands can be related to the external abstract representation of commands with a retrieve function:

$$retr\text{-}external: Char^* \rightarrow (Editor\text{-}command \mid \text{ERROR})$$

It would then be possible with the information found in the state to write a further retrieve function that translated the external abstract syntax representation into the internal one

$$retr\text{-}internal: Editor\text{-}command \times Env \rightarrow EditCommand$$

The first retrieve function can be built up from a series of subfunctions derived from the concrete syntax; the possibility of the character sequence being an invalid command is dealt with by returning an error indication. Strictly speaking this retrieve function should be constructed; its derivation is fairly complex, but is technically straightforward although a rather lengthy process. The second retrieve function is straightforward, as its main function is to supply the defaults. The retrieve functions can then be translated into Pascal and are exactly the parsing routines we shall need to verify and translate the concrete representation of a command to its abstract equivalent.

This was not done since well-known techniques already exist for translating an abstract syntax straight into Pascal and it does not seem sensible to go via a functional language (for that is what we would be doing) and then translate this functional language into Pascal. We have also chosen to combine the two retrieve functions into one.

17.6 SUMMARY

This chapter established the link between the outside world of the user and the inside world of the command processors; it made the link between the concrete syntax and the internal form of the commands. The defaults defined in the specification chapter of the editor were supplied during the command recognition process, and the overall control of the editor was sketched. The final step is the translation of the executable VDM-SL into Pascal, C or Modula-2.

It is important to point out that we are not after absolute correctness—we are not willing to pay the price of doing all the proofs formally. We are after 'relative correctness'—the code is relatively error free. There is a rigorous argument of correctness for each step of the development. The problem has also been decomposed into small steps that can easily be understood. If during this process it is found that there is insufficient detail, a further decomposition step could be attempted before the translation process is completed. The result should be a small editor, the correctness of which we can be very confident about.

A low-level design has been developed, written in pseudo code for the complete editor, with the major components proved correct. The correctness of less important or simple components was not proved quite so rigorously; the proofs were done by inspection. At each stage there has been a convincing argument of the correctness of the code. If there is any possible doubt, it is only necessary to fill in more details for those proofs that were not done rigorously.

18

FURTHER DEVELOPMENT OF THE EDITOR

AIMS

- To add an additional feature to the editor.
- To complete the development of the editor case study.

18.1   AN ENHANCEMENT: THE UNDO COMMAND

The undo command allows the last editor command to be executed to be undone, thus if a mistake is made by using a command the user can revert back to the version of the document he had before the command was executed. It will only be possible to undo the result of the last editing command that was executed. This command is very easy to specify; all that is necessary is to preserve a copy of the document just before any command is executed. All the commands need to be respecified, but the changes to each of them are minor. As an example the delete command will be shown.

The new state is

types

$Text = Line^*$

$Line = Char^*$

$Char = $ set of (ASCII) characters not including newline

$Ostate :: \quad odoc : Text$
$\qquad\qquad ocline : \mathbf{N}$

state *Editor* **of**
$\quad doc \; : \; Text$ −− the text of the file being edited
$\quad cline \; : \; \mathbf{N}$ −− the current line
$\quad cfile \; : \; [File\text{-}name]$ −− the name of the current file
$\quad files \; : \; File\text{-}store$ −− a model of the filing system
$\quad prev \; : \; [Ostate]$ −− the last state of the buffer
inv ...
end

The new version of the delete command is

    execute-delete (*lr*: *Line-range*)

    ext wr *doc* : *Text*
        cline : $\mathbb{N}$
        prev : [*Ostate*]

    pre *is-range-in-doc*(*lr*, *doc*)

    post *doc* = *front*($\overleftarrow{doc}$, *lr.first* − 1) $\frown$ *rest*($\overleftarrow{doc}$, *lr.last* + 1) $\wedge$
        cline = *lr.first* $\wedge$
        prev = *mk-Ostate*($\overleftarrow{doc}$, $\overleftarrow{cline}$)

The undo command just makes the current buffer equal to the saved version and the saved version equal to the current buffer; repeated use of the undo command will just cycle through these two buffer copies. Care must be taken not to allow an undo command before any other command hase been carried out; this can be done by initializing the copy of the buffer to be the same as the buffer, or by setting the copy to nil and using the definition of the undo command given below:

    execute-undo

    ext wr *doc* : *Text*
        cline : $\mathbb{N}$
        prev : [*Ostate*]

    post $\overleftarrow{prev} \neq$ nil $\wedge$
        doc = $\overleftarrow{prev}$.*odoc* $\wedge$
        cline = $\overleftarrow{prev}$.*ocline* $\wedge$
        prev = *mk-Ostate*($\overleftarrow{doc}$, $\overleftarrow{cline}$)
          $\vee$
        $\overleftarrow{prev}$ = nil $\wedge$
        doc = $\overleftarrow{doc}$ $\wedge$ *cline* = $\overleftarrow{cline}$ $\wedge$ *prev* = $\overleftarrow{prev}$

To change the other operations, all that is necessary is to add

    . . . $\wedge$

    prev = *mk-Ostate*($\overleftarrow{doc}$, $\overleftarrow{cline}$)

to each of the post-conditions, and update the ext . . . component. The change information for the undo command must also be reset to nil if the current file being edited is changed to another one; i.e. if an edit command is executed.

18.2 IMPLEMENTING THE UNDO COMMAND

The advantage of this approach to the undo command is that it specifies exactly what undo does; the problem is that it would not (or should not) be implemented in this style. What approach should be taken for the implementation? A solution is to store the minimum amount of information that allows a command to be reversed. A data refinement can be undertaken that just tackles the representation needed to undo the last command, and leaves the remainder of the representation alone. Each of the operations can be respecified to save the information needed to reverse their last use, and the undo command can be specified to use this information to undo the effect of the last command.

If a retrieve function is defined and the new representation is shown to be adequate, then the new representation is equivalent to the old, but requires less storage to save the 'undo' information, as all that is stored is the 'undo-delta'—information about the changes that must be done to revert to the old version of the buffer. Before defining the retrieve function it is best to reverse the usual order of doing things and redefine each of the editing operations first so that we can work out exactly what information needs to be saved in order to reverse the effect of each operation. To show how this works, we will do it for the delete command.

To undo the effect of a delete command it is necessary to save the text that was deleted, where it was deleted from and the last current line number. The part of the state that retains enough information to reconstruct the last version of the document must now record what the last operation on the buffer was

$$Ostate = Insert\text{-}delta \mid Copy\text{-}delta \mid Delete\text{-}delta \mid \ldots$$

$$
\begin{aligned}
Delete\text{-}delta \; :: \; & ocline \; : \; \mathbf{N} \\
& cl \; : \; \mathbf{N} \\
& delta \; : \; Text
\end{aligned}
$$

The delete command must not only change the document to record the effect of the command; it must also remember the information necessary to undo the command:

> *execute-delete* (*lr: Line-range*)
>
> **ext wr** *doc* : *Text*
>   *cline*   : **N**
>   *prev*   : [*Ostate*]
>
> **pre** *is-range-in-doc*(*lr, doc*)
>
> **post** $doc = front(\overleftarrow{doc}, lr.first - 1) \curvearrowright rest(\overleftarrow{doc}, lr.last + 1) \wedge$
> $cline = lr.first \wedge$
> $prev = mk\text{-}Delete\text{-}delta(\overleftarrow{cline}, lr.first - 1, sub\text{-}doc(\overleftarrow{doc}, lr))$

The *undo-delete* operation just reverses the effect of the deletion; how? The specification is similar to *execute-insert*—the deleted text is just inserted after the line from which it was deleted. However, why not use the insert command to do the work for us? Intuitively, if the right information is saved, the insert command is the inverse of the delete command. Before executing the insert command, the information needs to be 'decoded':

> *undo-delete* ()
>
> **ext wr** *doc* : *Text*
>   *cline*   : **N**
>   *prev*   : [*Ostate*]
>
> **pre** *prev* ∈ *Delete-delta*
>
> **post** **let** $mk\text{-}Delete\text{-}delta(ocline, cl, delta) = \overleftarrow{prev}$ **in**
> $\exists cline' \in \mathbf{N} \cdot$
> $post\text{-}execute\text{-}insert(cl, delta, \overleftarrow{doc}, \overleftarrow{cline}, \overleftarrow{prev}, doc, cline', prev) \wedge$
> $cline = ocline$

The *execute-insert* command will construct the correct 'undo-delta' for itself. To reverse the insert command it is necessary to save the line number of the first piece of inserted text. The length of the inserted text can be worked out from this information and the current line number, which points to the last line of the inserted text. It is also necessary to save the old current line, as this could have been anywhere before the insert command is executed. Thus the 'undo delta' for the insert command is

$$Insert\text{-}delta :: \; ocline \; : \; \mathsf{N}$$
$$lr \; : \; Line\text{-}range$$

and the new specification of the insert command is

$execute\text{-}insert \; (ln\!:\mathsf{N}, text\!: Text)$

ext wr $doc \; : \; Text$
    $cline \quad : \; \mathsf{N}$
    $prev \quad : \; [Ostate]$

pre $is\text{-}line\text{-}in\text{-}doc(ln, doc) \wedge$
    len $text +$ len $doc \le D \wedge$
    $\forall l \in$ rng $text \cdot$ len $l \le L$

post $doc = front(\overleftarrow{doc}, ln) \frown text \frown rest(\overleftarrow{doc}, ln + 1) \wedge$
    $cline = ln +$ len $text \wedge$
    $prev = mk\text{-}Insert\text{-}delta(\overleftarrow{cline}, mk\text{-}Line\text{-}range(ln + 1, cline))$

Since the insert command is the 'inverse' of the delete command, the delete command is the inverse of the insert command. Thus the undo version of the insert command uses *execute-delete*:

$undo\text{-}insert \; ()$

ext wr $doc \; : \; Text$
    $cline \quad : \; \mathsf{N}$
    $prev \quad : \; [Ostate]$

pre $prev \in Insert\text{-}delta$

post let $mk\text{-}Insert\text{-}delta(ocline, lr) = prev$ in
    $\exists cline' \in \mathsf{N} \cdot post\text{-}execute\text{-}delete(lr, \overleftarrow{doc}, \overleftarrow{cline}, \overleftarrow{prev}, doc, cline', prev) \wedge$
    $cline = ocline$

Each operation will need its undo equivalent to be defined. When this has been done the definition of the new representation can be completed:

types

$Ostate = Insert\text{-}delta \mid Copy\text{-}delta \mid Delete\text{-}delta \mid \ldots$

$Insert\text{-}delta :: \; ocline \; : \; \mathsf{N}$
$\qquad\qquad\qquad lr \; : \; Line\text{-}range$

$Copy\text{-}delta :: \; ocline \; : \; \mathsf{N}$
$\qquad\qquad\qquad lr \; : \; Line\text{-}range$

$Delete\text{-}delta :: \; ocline \; : \; \mathsf{N}$
$\qquad\qquad\qquad\quad cl \; : \; \mathsf{N}$
$\qquad\qquad\qquad delta \; : \; Text$

```
state Editor of
      doc  : Text
     cline : N
     cfile : [File-name]
     files : File-store
     prev  : [Ostate]
inv ...
end
```

The other components of the state are defined as before.

18.3 PROVING THE UNDO COMMAND

The retrieve function will relate this representation to the original one.

$$retr\text{-}buf : Buffer_1 \rightarrow Buffer$$

$$retr\text{-}buf(buf) \quad \triangleq \quad ...$$

Unfortunately any attempt to construct this retrieve function and prove it adequate will be impossible. The reason is subtle. The abstract version of the buffer allows the copy of the document stored as the backup to be reinstalled when the undo command is executed—it allows any copy, not just one that was produced by the undo part of an edit command. The refinement will only allow versions of the document that differ from the buffer by the execution of an editing operation. What is missing in the abstract version of the state is an invariant to record the fact that the 'undo' version of the document only differs from the current version by the execution of an editing command.

The two states (the abstract version and the refined version) could be fixed to remove this difficulty, but it would add a major complication. A better approach would be to take the refinement as the specification, and convince ourselves that it is correct. To do this we could show that a command, together with its undo, is equivalent to doing nothing.

We will show that *execute-delete*, followed by *undo-delete*, will give the original document back. To do this it is first necessary to show that *execute-delete* sets things up for *undo-delete*—the pre-condition for *undo-delete* is satisfied—and that the result of the *execute-delete* operation if given as input to the *undo-delete* operation will produce final output that is identical to the original document before anything was deleted. The actual theorem that must be proved can be 'derived' as follows.

Given an initial state $\overleftarrow{s}$ that satisfies the pre-condition for *execute-delete*, there exists an output state s_1 that satisfies the post-condition for *execute-delete*. If s_1 satisfies the pre-condition for *undo-delete* then there exists a state s that satisfies the post-condition for *undo-delete*; if *execute-delete* followed by *undo-delete* is the identity transformation for the document, then $s.doc$ should be equal to $\overleftarrow{s}.doc$. This can be written more formally as:

$\exists s_1 \in Buffer \cdot$
  $pre\text{-}delete(\overleftarrow{s}) \wedge$
  $post\text{-}delete(\overleftarrow{s}, s_1) \wedge$
  $pre\text{-}undo\text{-}delete(s_1) \wedge$
  $post\text{-}undo\text{-}delete(s_1, s)$
$\Rightarrow \overleftarrow{s}.doc = s.doc \wedge \ldots$

Substituting in the above, we get

$\exists cline_1 \in \mathbf{N}, prev_1 \in Delete\text{-}delta, doc_1 \in Text \cdot$
  $is\text{-}range\text{-}in\text{-}doc(lr, doc) \wedge$
  $doc_1 = front(\overleftarrow{doc}, lr.first - 1) \frown rest(\overleftarrow{doc}, lr.last + 1) \wedge$
  $cline_1 = lr.first \wedge$
  $prev_1 = mk\text{-}Delete\text{-}delta(\overleftarrow{cline}, lr.first - 1, sub\text{-}doc(\overleftarrow{doc}, lr)) \wedge$ $\qquad$ (5)
  $\text{let } mk\text{-}Delete\text{-}delta(ocline, cl, delt) = prev_1 \text{ in}$
  $\exists cline' \in \mathbf{N} \cdot$
    $doc = front(doc_1, cl) \frown delt \frown rest(doc_1, cl + 1) \wedge$
    $cline' = cl + \mathsf{len}\, delt \wedge$
    $prev = mk\text{-}Insert\text{-}delta(cline_1, mk\text{-}Line\text{-}range(cl + 1, cline')) \wedge$ $\quad$ (10)
    $cline = ocline$
$\Rightarrow \overleftarrow{doc} = doc \wedge$
  $\overleftarrow{cline} = cline \wedge$
  $prev = mk\text{-}Insert\text{-}delta(lr.first, mk\text{-}Line\text{-}range(lr.first, lr.last))$

the *Insert-delta* reflect the fact that another (immediate) undo should redo the delete commmand. Combining lines (5) and (6) of the hypothesis gives

$\exists cline_1 \in \mathbf{N}, prev_1 \in Delete\text{-}delta, doc_1 \in Text \cdot$
  $is\text{-}range\text{-}in\text{-}doc(lr, doc) \wedge$
  $doc_1 = front(\overleftarrow{doc}, lr.first - 1) \frown rest(\overleftarrow{doc}, lr.last + 1) \wedge$
  $cline_1 = lr.first \wedge$
  $ocline = \overleftarrow{cline} \wedge$ $\qquad\qquad\qquad\qquad\qquad\qquad\qquad$ (5)
  $cl = lr.first - 1 \wedge$
  $delt = sub\text{-}doc(\overleftarrow{doc}, lr) \wedge$
  $\exists cline' \in \mathbf{N} \cdot$
    $doc = front(doc_1, cl) \frown delt \frown rest(doc_1, cl + 1) \wedge$
    $cline' = cl + \mathsf{len}\, delt \wedge$ $\qquad\qquad\qquad\qquad\qquad\qquad$ (10)
    $prev = mk\text{-}Insert\text{-}delta(cline_1, mk\text{-}Line\text{-}range(cl + 1, cline')) \wedge$
    $cline = ocline$
$\Rightarrow \overleftarrow{doc} = doc \wedge$
  $\overleftarrow{cline} = cline \wedge$
  $prev = mk\text{-}Insert\text{-}delta(lr.first, mk\text{-}Line\text{-}range(lr.first, lr.last))$

Assuming the above then the following equalities can be deduced:

cline

$= $ "line 12 of the hypothesis"

ocline

$= $ "line 5 of the hypothesis"

$\overline{cline}$

The final value of *doc* after performing *execute-insert* followed by *undo-insert* is given by:

$$doc = front(doc_1, cl) \frown delt \frown rest(doc_1, cl + 1)$$

Looking at each of the components on the right-hand side of the above equation:

$front(doc_1, cl)$

$= $ "line 3 of the hypothesis"

$front(front(\overline{doc}, lr.first - 1) \frown rest(\overline{doc}, lr.last + 1), cl)$

$= $ "line 6 of the hypothesis"

$front(\overline{doc}, lr.first - 1)$

from line 7 of the hypothesis:

$$delt = sub\text{-}doc(\overline{doc}, lr)$$

and

$rest(doc_1, cl + 1)$

$= $ "line 3 of the hypothesis"

$rest(front(\overline{doc}, lr.first - 1) \frown rest(\overline{doc}, lr.last + 1), cl + 1)$

$= $ "line 6 of the hypothesis and property of *rest* function"

$rest(\overline{doc}, lr.last + 1)$

Substituting in the above will give

doc

$= $ "line 9 of the hypothesis"

$front(doc_1, cl) \frown delt \frown rest(doc_1, cl + 1)$

$= $ "above"

$front(\overline{doc}, lr.first - 1) \frown sub\text{-}doc(\overline{doc}, lr) \frown rest(\overline{doc}, lr.last + 1)$

$= $ "definition of the catenate operator and the *front* and *rest* functions"

$\overline{doc}$

From this it can be seen that the document and current line number are reset. To complete the proof let us look at the information saved for another undo command:

prev

$= $ "line 11 of the hypothesis"

$mk\text{-}Insert\text{-}delta(cline_1, mk\text{-}Line\text{-}range(cl + 1, cline'))$

$= $ "lines 4, 6, and 10 of the hypothesis"

$mk\text{-}Insert\text{-}delta(lr.first, mk\text{-}Line\text{-}range(lr.first, cl + \text{len } delt))$

$= $ "lines 7 of the hypothesis and definition of the length operator"

$mk\text{-}Insert\text{-}delta(lr.first, mk\text{-}Line\text{-}range(lr.first, (lr.first-1)+(lr.last-lr.first+1)))$

$= $ "rules of arithmetic"

$mk\text{-}Insert\text{-}delta(lr.first, mk\text{-}Line\text{-}range(lr.first, lr.last))$

which is what we would expect.

Each of the operations of the editor together with their inverses can be defined and the above checks carried out. This is left as an exercise for the reader.

Exercise 18.1

1. Returning to the specification for a finite stack of characters in Chapter 13 on page 263, show that the *empty* operation followed by the *is-empty* operation returns true.

2. Remaining with the stack example, show that the *push* operation followed by an *is-empty* operation will return false.

3. Show *push* followed by *pop* will leave the stack unchanged.

4. Define a *length-of* operation for the finite stack, and show that if $length\text{-}of(stack) = N$ then *is-full* is true.

5. Change each of the operations defined in Chapter 14 so that they save the minimum amount of information for an undo function, then define an undo operation for each of the new definitions.

6. Prove your 'undo' operations are inverses of their corresponding 'do' operations.

7. The insert command used above was the original one that had the inserted text as part of its argument. Define a new insert command together with its inverse for the version that stored the inserted text at the end of the buffer.

8. Carry out a full development of the editor including the undo commands.

18.4 SUMMARY

The decomposition of each of the edit commands has now been completed and there exists a low-level design for the editor. During this development process it was necessary to go back and fix the specifications for some of the commands. A low level design has been developed, written in pseudo code for the complete editor, with the major components proved correct. The correctness of less important or simple components was not proved quite so rigorously; the proofs were done by inspection, though at each stage there has been a convincing argument of the correctness. If there is any possible doubt it is only necessary to fill in more detail for those proofs that were not rigorously demonstrated. It is a simple matter now to translate the code and the state into a suitable programming language such as Pascal. If during this process it is found that there is insufficient detail, a further decomposition step could be attempted before the translation process is completed. The result should be a small editor, the correctness of which we can be very confident about.

Project

1. Specify an undo for the character-based full-screen editor of the editor project of the various chapters.
2. How could the undo function be implemented?

19

POSTSCRIPT

19.1 INTRODUCTION

We have tried in this book to show that formal methods are applicable to real problems; the approach has been rigorous rather than formal and we have shown that formal methods are applicable even without doing formal, mathematical proofs.

Formal methods come in two parts. The first (and at present the most important) part is abstraction, and using a formal notation for expressing abstraction in the early phases of a software development. The specification ('blueprint') of a system can be expressed formally and abstractly—formal in the sense that a formal language is used, abstract in the sense that all implementation detail can be ignored. The specification expresses what the system should do and does not address how. (It should be noted that a programming language is formal—everything that is written down has an exact, unambiguous meaning. Unfortunately they are not very good at expressing abstraction; hence the need for a specification language.) The second part is about proving development steps and proving consistency. Doing proofs is an excellent intellectual exercise and mental discipline, and also gives much insight into program development. Once program refinement has been mastered, it has a profound effect on the way one tackles programming problems and writes programs, even if formal development methods are being ignored. (The authors know of nobody who formally develops shell scripts, but writing such things is program development.)

Proving theorems by hand is not to be recommended—there is too much scope for error (the authors would be very surprised if all the proofs in this book were correct, but we have confidence in the correctness of the final programs, more than we would have had they been developed by one of the conventional methods—hacking). What is needed is an 'easy to drive' theorem prover—proofs still await such a tool, but even this will not be the final answer—more on this point below.

What formal methods should do is change people's philosophy to programming and system development. Knowledge of formal methods and applying them judiciously should change the approach to developing systems. Formal methods encourage the development to remain at an abstract level for as long as possible. A computer system is a model of something in the 'real world' and it should be possible to examine the code of the computer system and indentify components of the 'real world' being modelled in the code. Thinking in terms of code sequences and bits and bytes means that the programmer loses sight of what he or she is doing. The concept of the abstract machine allows the 'real world' to be modelled in the code. The editor deals with documents made up of lines and lines made up from characters for as long as possible—we do not deal with **array of char** if it can possibly be avoided. We try to build a system from abstract machines that model things in the real world and hide implementation detail in the abstract machine, using the implementation language to hide detail for as long as possible. One of the major differences is that it encourages solutions in the problem domain (i.e. at a level of abstraction that can be related to the problem) rather than in the solution domain (how are the bits and bytes of the computer to be used?).

Program refinement is just a formalization of top-down structured programming. The gross algorithm is sketched (formally) and detail gradually added. This means that we can still think in terms of 'what' rather than 'how' while we are developing a solution to a (coding) problem. It should be noted that abstract machines are (almost) a formalization of the old 'bottom-up' software development strategy. Using a formal method approach to software development with few or no proofs will (should) still produce a better designed system with less bugs, and which will be easier to modify. It must be noted that formal methods are not a panacea—it is still possible to specify, design and implement a bad system. It does, however, provide developers with a powerful tool for handling complexity.

Returning to the problem of theorems and their proofs—the development of proofs still has a long way to go. Mechanical (why are they called mechanical rather than electronic?) thoerem provers are still in their infancy—most are difficult to use. Those who use them admit to hacking proofs out, and because of this an interesting problem has arisen. A piece of code together with its specification and proof of development is an ideal candidate for re-use. Before it is re-used it has been felt necessary to understand its proof of correctness. This has usually been done by 'hacking' out a proof using a mechanical theorem prover, and it is frequently easier to re-do the proof than try to understand the existing one. This aspect of formal methods still has some way to go before it is usable in an industrial development environment. It should be noted that current technology does allow proofs for systems to be done, and software in safety critical areas should be proved correct.

19.1.1 A calculus of correctness

It was long recognized that writing a program and then proving it correct is not the right approach. It is better to develop proof of correctness, alongside the development of the program. This process has now been simplified, and is the basis of the program refinement proofs used in this book. The work in this area, a 'theory of programming', has yet to work its way into programming languages. A rather elegant little theorem is

> If $F(P)$ is a program containing the program fragment P, and
> if for program fagment Q we have $P \sqsubseteq Q$, then
> $F(P) \sqsubseteq F(Q)$

This theorem is about code reusability—think of P as a specification imbedded in some code and Q as its realization; we can replace P by its implementation. Now consider two procedures P_1 and P_2 such that $P_1 \sqsubseteq P_2$. If we use variable parameters in the implementation of these procedures, then if we denote the use of the two procedures by P_1' and P_2' we do not necessarily have $P_1' \sqsubseteq P_2'$ because of the aliasing that can occur with variable parameters. All of this very roughly says 'if you want reusable code avoid variable parameters'.

The work in this book assumes no side effects in expressions—the code produced (the authors would claim) is still elegant and efficient. There are other programming style lessons that can be extracted from both formal methods and the programming calculus—it would be gratifying if programming language designers would absorb some of these ideas and lessons. Languages such as C seem to include and even encourage all that formal methods seem to indicate that is bad.

Do we continue hacking or start thinking about software development? The reader should by now have sufficient evidence to decide.

19.2 THE VDM-SL STANDARD

This book has not strictly followed the proposed Standard for VDM-SL. The authors have done this for two reasons: the BSI Proto Standard has frozen some aspects of the specification language, while other aspects are still under development. Appendix C describes extensions and restrictions that this book has adopted.

It should be noted that we have not adopted all ideas in current, 'frozen' VDM-SL. In this book the post-condition must explicitly establish the invariant; at present Standard VDM-SL allows the invariant to be established implicitly (see Appendix C). We have chosen the old approach as it keeps the invariant in the forefront, the other approach may allow it to be forgotten if we do not do all the proofs—especially the existence proofs. The philosophy we have taken is that if a working system is developed, an existence proof is unnecessary. The motivation behind this is that if developers are trying to build something, their experience is such that they are unlikely to specify or carry out a development step that is impossible to take further.

19.3 FURTHER READING

19.3.1 Logic, sets, map and sequences

There are many books on the abstract data modelling tools; unfortunately there is no agreement on notation, except for the operators on sets. Books that discuss modelling data using sets, sequences and maps—are Denvir, 1986, Ince, 1988, and Jones, 1986. Other good texts for other relevant mathematical notations and ideas are Stanat and McAllister, 1977, Polimeni and Straight, 1985, and Skvarcius and Robinson, 1986.

19.3.2 Specifying systems

Several books containing case studies of specifications using formal methods exist. A good overview of VDM can be found in Bjørner and Jones, 1982, and Jones and Shaw, 1990. There have been (to date) three conferences on VDM, the proceedings are Bjørner et al., 1987, Bloomfield et al., 1988, and Bjørner et al., 1990; all three books contain case studies and are worth perusing for ideas. If you can find a copy, the best introduction to the original VDM meta-language can be found in Bjørner and Jones, 1974. Various formal definitions of programming languages exist using VDM-SL, see Andrews and others, 1990, and Andrews and Henhapl, 1982.

19.3.3 Developing specifications

Two books on the specification, design and development of software systems using data flow design and structured design are Page-Jones, 1988, and Peters, 1988. The two books cover similar material, but with a different emphasis, and are worth looking at as an introduction to specification and design using graphical techniques; the books also cover some of the management aspects of software engineering.

Two books on specification and design using Ada are Booch, 1987a, and Booch, 1987b. The first book puts Ada firmly into a software engineering context and describes how it can be used as a functional specification and design medium. The second book concentrates on one aspect of Ada: its ability to package data structures in a way that leads to reusability. Booch examines a wide variety of data structures, including sets, queues, stacks and graphs and shows how they can be implemented in an elegant way using object-oriented design. These books can be raided for specification and design examples and ideas to which formal techniques can be applied.

An excellent introduction to software engineering is Bell *et al.*, 1987. This book describes a number of development techniques including: object-oriented design, functional decomposition, functional programming and data flow design, and is another book worth raiding for ideas. It is obvious from this book that it has been extensively class-tested.

19.3.4 From specifications to code

An early approach to obtaining code from a formal specification can be found in Jones, 1980; though out of print, it may still be available in libraries. A subsequent approach can be found in Jones, 1986, and Jones, 1990. Both books use a very formal approach to the development and proof of correctness of a program. Another approach to developing programs from specifications can be found in Naftalin, 1988. This is a particularly appealing approach using diagrams, which is well worth reading. The diagrams used to explain the proof rules used in this book were based on the ideas described in this paper.

Over the last seven or eight years J-R. Abrial, R-J. Back, C. C. Morgan and J. M. Morris have been working in the area of developing programs from specifications, any paper by these authors is probably worth investigating. The program refinement techniques of this book are based on the ideas of these authors.

The following books all use the weakest pre-condition approach to program correctness, but they are all worth investigating as many of the ideas can be easily transferred to the program refinement techniques taught in this book.

One of the first books on how to write correct programs is Dijkstra, 1976. In this book a series of problems are tackled and elegant, correct programs are developed to solve the problems using formal techniques.

A follow on from Dijkstra, 1976 is Dijkstra and Feijen, 1988. Rather mathematical for the general reader, but again making the point that good program development is about thinking, not hacking.

A more accessible account of a method of software development due to Edsgar Dijkstra is Gries, 1981. This method involves specifying what a program is to do using pre- and post-conditions, and then using the semantics of a programming language to develop the program code that meets this specification.

Yet another approach to program development is Hehner, 1984. This text uses logic as a basis and also weakest pre-conditions. The specifications are written using a logic notation and then developed into a logic based programming language—not of the PRO-LOG family, more of the Pascal form. Again, it illustrates that there are other ways of developing software apart from the usual technique of just sitting down and writing the code.

Finally, Reynolds, 1981 must be mentioned. The book covers the development of computer programs using formal methods. The author covers the correctness proofs for programs and then develops a logic and notation for proving a variety of programs correct. It is a little old fashioned in that the programming language used is Algol W but most, if not all, of the results would readily translate into Pascal and the techniques transferred to a program refinement framework.

19.3.5 Data refinement

Again papers by J-R. Abrial, R-J. Back, C. C. Morgan and J. M. Morris are worth investigating, as is Jones, 1990.

The texts given below describe the specification, design and development of programs using the abstract data type/object approach. They also describe implementations of all of the data representations mentioned in Appendix C.

The book Helman and Veroff, 1988 concentrates on abstract data types and encapsulation and the use of recursion as problem solving tools. It covers the use of abstraction as a way of simplifying problems and developing good solutions—a good introduction to this style of program development.

An introduction to the modern theory of data types is Stubbs, 1985. The book stresses data abstraction and the separation of the design and implementation of data structures. The programming language used is Pascal; hence, this book would make an excellent first text on programming. There is also a version of this book that uses Modula-2 as the programming language.

Wirth in Wirth, 1986 explains algorithm development and data structures using Modula-2. Some mathematical ideas are used to develop the programs—a good source of ideas.

19.3.6 Examples

The simple text editor is based on the one defined in Kernighan and Plauger, 1981. This text is an excellent source of examples to formally specify and develop programs from the specifications.

19.3.7 VDM

At the time of writing there are only two readily available descriptions of VDM and all of its meta-language, the are Bjørner and Jones, 1982, and Dawes, 1991; the first contains some interesting papers on the use of formal methods to define programming languages and computer systems and the second is a tutorial introduction to VDM-SL.

The first book on software development using VDM was Jones, 1980. It is definitely a good introduction to using formal methods to specify and develop computer programs, but it is now out of print.

Effectively a second edition to 'Software Development: a Rigorous Approach' is Jones, 1986. This takes a much more academic approach and is more difficult to read because of the emphasis on proofs rather than specification—the notation used is better than the original book; it is well-worth looking at.

19.3.8   Formal methods

A good overview of a variety of formal methods is Cohen *et al.*, 1986. The book is worth looking at as a first book on the subject before graduating to specialist books on Z or other techniques. Also the book Woodcock and Loomes, 1988, is a good introduction to the use of mathematics in the specification of software. The book also gives a good introduction to the Z method.

A collection of papers on the use of formal methods to describe computer systems is Hayes, 1986. The book introduces the notation and has a few simple examples. It illustrates how formal methods, i.e. mathematics, can be used to define computer systems in a readable way. It would be worth trying any of the examples in VDM-SL.

The book Meyers, 1988 shows how computer programs expressed in Modula-2 can be developed in a top-down fashion from a mathematical specification. It appears in the reading list because of the quality of the teaching.

19.4   BIBLIOGRAPHY

Aho, A. V., Hopcroft, J. E., and Ullman, J. E. (1974), *The Design and Analysis of Computer Algorithms*, Addison-Wesley.

Andrews, D. and Henhapl, W. (1982), 'Pascal', in *Formal Specifications and Software Development*, Bjørner, D. and Jones, C. B. (eds), pp. 175–251, Prentice-Hall.

Andrews, D. J. *et al.* (1990), *The Modula-2 Draft Standard*, BSI/ISO.

Back, R.-J. (1978), *On the correctness of refinement steps in program development*, Technical Report Report A-1978-4, University of Helsinki, Department of Computer Science.

Back, R.-J. (1980), *Correctness preserving program refinements: proof theory and applications.*, Technical Report Tract 131, Mathematisch Centrum, Amsterdam.

Back, R.-J. (1987), *A calculus of refinement for program derivations.*, Technical Report Report Ser.A 54, Swedish University of Åbo, Åbo, Finland.

Back, R.-J. (1987), *Procedural abstraction in the refinement calculus*, Technical Report Report Ser.A 55, Swedish University of Åbo, Åbo, Finland.

Bell, D., Morrey, I., and Pugh, J. (1987), *Software Engineering. A Programming Approach*, Prentice-Hall.

Bjørner, D. and Jones, C. B. (1974), *The Vienna Development Method: The Meta-Language*, volume 61 of *Lecture Notes in Computer Science*, Lecture Notes in Computer Science, Springer-Verlag.

Bjørner, D. and Jones, C. B. (1982), *Formal Specification and Software Development*, Prentice-Hall International.

Bjørner, D., Jones, C. B., Mac an Airchinnigh, M., and Neuhold, E. J. (eds) (1987), *VDM — A Formal Method at Work*, volume 252 of *Lecture Notes in Computer Science*, Lecture Notes in Computer Science, Springer-Verlag.

Bjørner, D., Hoare, C. A. R., and Langmaack, H. (eds) (1990), *VDM and Z — Formal Methods in Software Development*, volume 428 of *Lecture Notes in Computer Science*, Lecture Notes in Computer Science, Springer-Verlag.

Bloomfield, R., Jones, R. B., and Marshall, L. S. (eds) (1988), *VDM — The Way Ahead*, volume 328 of *Lecture Notes in Computer Science*, Lecture Notes in Computer Science, Springer-Verlag.

Booch, G. (1987), *Software Components with Ada*, Benjamin Cummings, Menlo Park, CA.

Booch, G. (1987), *Software Engineering with Ada*, Benjamin Cummings, Menlo Park, CA.

Cohen, B., Harwood, W. T., and Jackson, M. I. (1986), *The Specification of Complex Systems*, Addison-Wesley.

Dawes, J. (1991), *The VDM-SL Reference Guide*, Pitman.

Denvir, T. (1986), *Introduction to Discrete Mathematics for Software Engineering*, Macmillan.

Dijkstra, E. W. and Feijen, W. H. J. (1988), *A Method of Programming*, Addison-Wesley.

Dijkstra, E. W. (1976), *A Discipline of Programming*, Prentice-Hall.

Gries, D. (1981), *The Science of Programming*, Springer-Verlag.

Hayes, I. J. and Jones, C. B. (1989), 'Specifications are not (necessarily) executable', *Software Engineering Journal*, 4(6): 320–338.

Hayes, I. (1986), *Specification Case Studies*, Prentice-Hall International.

Hehner, E. C. R. (1984), *The Logic of Programming*, Prentice-Hall International.

Helman and Veroff (1988), *Intermediate Problem Solving and Data Structures*, Addison-Wesley.

Ince, D. (1988), *Introduction to Discrete Mathematics and Formal System Specification*, Oxford University Press.

Jones, C. B. and Shaw, R. C. F. (eds) (1990), *Case Studies in Systematic Software Development*, Prentice-Hall International.

Jones, C. B. (1980), *Software Development: a Rigorous Approach.*, Prentice-Hall International.

Jones, C. B. (1986), *Systematic Software Development using VDM*, Prentice-Hall International.

Jones, C. B. (1990), *Systematic Software Development Using VDM (2nd Edition)*, Prentice-Hall International.

Kernighan, B. and Plauger, P. (1981), *Software Tools in Pascal*, Addison-Wesley.

Meyers, T. J. (1988), *Equations, Models and Programs*, Prentice-Hall.

Morgan, C. C. and Gardiner, P. H. B. (1987), 'Specification statements and refinement', *IBM Journal of Research and Development*, **31**(5).

Morgan, C. C. (1988), 'Data refinement using miracles', *Information Processing Letters*, **26**(5): 243–246.

Morgan, C. C. (1988), 'Procedures, parameters, and abstractions: separate concerns', *Science of Computer Programming*, (11).

Morgan, C. C. (1988), 'The specification statement', *Transactions of Programming Languages and Systems*, **10**(3).

Morgan, C. C. (1990), *Programming from Specifications*, Prentice-Hall International.

Morris, J. M. (1987), 'A theoretical basis for stepwise refinement and the programming calculus', *Science of Computer Programming*, 9(3): 298–306.

Morris, J. M. (1990), 'A methodology for designing and refining specifications', in *Proceedings of the 3rd Workshop on Refinement* , Woodcock, J. (ed.), Springer-Verlag (BCS Workshop Series).

Morris, J. M. (1990), 'Piecewise data refinement', in *Formal Development of Programs and Proofs*, Addison-Wesley.

Morris, J. M. (1990), 'Programs from specifications', in *Formal Development of Programs and Proofs*, Dijkstra, E. W. (ed.), Addison-Wesley.

Naftalin, Maurice (1988), 'Correctness for beginners', in *VDM '88 VDM — The Way Ahead*, Bloomfield, R., Jones, R. B., and Marshall, L. S. (eds), Springer-Verlag.

Page-Jones, M. (1988), *Practical Guide to Structured Systems Design*, Prentice-Hall International.

Peters, Lawrence (1988), *Advanced Structured Analysis and Design*, Prentice-Hall International.

Polimeni, A. D. and Straight, H. J. (1985), *Foundations of Discrete Mathematics*, Brooks/Cole.

Reynolds, J. (1981), *The Craft of Programming*, Prentice-Hall International.

Skvarcius, R. and Robinson, W. B. (1986), *Discrete Mathematics with Computer Science Applications*, Benjamin-Cummings, Menlo Park, CA.

Stanat, D. F. and McAllister, D. F. (1977), *Discrete Mathematics in Computer Science*, Prentice-Hall International.

Stubbs, D. F. (1985), *Data Structures*, Brooks-Cole, Monterey, CA.

Wirth, N. (1986), *Algorithms and Data Structures*, Prentice-Hall International.

Woodcock, J. and Loomes, M. (1988), *Software Engineering Mathematics*, Pitman.

A

A SUMMARY OF NOTATION

TYPES

The basic types

The set of Boolean values is written as **B**

$$\mathbf{B} = \{\text{true}, \text{false}\}$$

The set of all natural numbers is written as **N**

$$\mathbf{N} = \{0, 1, 2, \ldots\}$$

The set of all positive natural numbers is written as $\mathbf{N}_1$

$$\mathbf{N}_1 = \{1, 2, \ldots\}$$
$$= \mathbf{N} - \{0\}$$

The set of all integers is written as **Z**

$$\mathbf{Z} = \{\ldots, -2, -1, 0, 1, 2, \ldots\}$$
$$= \{-n \mid n \in \mathbf{N}\} \cup \{n \mid n \in \mathbf{N}\}$$

The set of all rational numbers is written as **Q**, and the set of all real numbers is written as **R**. Note that

$$\mathbf{N}_1 \subset \mathbf{N} \subset \mathbf{Z} \subset \mathbf{Q} \subset \mathbf{R}$$

The set of all characters is written as char, and a set consisting of an infinite number of tokens is written token. If more than one such set is required, write token_i, $i = 0, 1, 2, \ldots$. The sets will be all mutually disjoint.

Type definitions

$A = B$ — Define another (new) name for the set of objects B. The two names are synonymous in the sense that the members of each set cannot be distinguished. A is a set of elements such that:

$$x \in A \iff x \in B$$

$A = \text{NAME}$ — Define a set consisting of the single object denoted by the constant NAME.

$$x \in A \iff x = \text{NAME}$$

$A = B$-set

The -set constructor produces the set of all finite subsets, so for a set B the B-set is the set of all possible subsets of B—thus an element of B-set is a subset of B.

$$x \in A \iff x \subseteq B$$

$A = B^*$

Given any set B, the * constructor builds the set of all sequences which have components from the set B. An element of the set B^* is a sequence whose elements come from the set A.

$$a \in A \implies \forall i \in \text{inds } a \cdot a(i) \in B$$

$A = B^+$

Given any set B, the $^+$ constructor builds the set of all none-empty sequences which have components from the set B.

$$a \in A \implies \forall i \in \text{inds } a \cdot a(i) \in B \wedge \text{len } a > 0$$

$M = D \xrightarrow{m} R$

Define M to be the set of possible mappings from the domain set D to the range set R.

$M = D \xleftarrow{m} R$

Define M to be the set of possible one-to-one mappings from the domain set D to the range set R.

$$m \in M$$
$$\implies \text{ dom } m \subseteq D \wedge \text{rng } m \subseteq R \wedge \text{card dom } m = \text{card rng } m$$

$P = S \times T$

Define P to be the product set consisting of all possible pairs of elements, with the first element of the pair drawn from the set S and the second element from the set T.

$$P = \{(s, t) \mid s \in S \wedge t \in T\}$$

$P = Q \mid R$

Define P to be the union of the two sets Q and R.

$$p \in P \iff p \in Q \vee p \in R$$

$A = [B]$

Define the elements of A to be either in B or 'missing'.

$$A = [B] \iff A = B \mid \text{nil}$$

$A = \text{compose } B \text{ of}$
$\quad sel_1 : Set_1$
$\quad sel_2 : Set_2$
$\quad\quad\quad Set_3$
end

Defines A to be a composite object, the name of the type of the composite object is B, the first component of which comes from the set Set_1, the second component from the set Set_2 and the third component from the set Set_3. The names sel_1 and sel_2 are selectors.

$$A = \{mk\text{-}B(x, y, z) \mid x \in Set_1 \wedge y \in Set_2 \wedge z \in Set_3\}$$

$$mk\text{-}B: Set_1 \times Set_2 \times Set_3 \to A$$

The following is also valid:

$B = \text{compose } B \text{ of}$
$\quad sel_1 : Set_1$
$\quad sel_2 : Set_2$
$\quad\quad\quad Set_3$
$\quad\text{end}$

and can be abbreviated to

$$B :: sel_1 : Set_1$$
$$sel_2 : Set_2$$
$$Set_3$$

...

The type has still to be defined; the choice has been postponed to a later step in the development.

LOGIC

Propositional operators

The propositional operators (in order of decreasing priority):

$\neg A$	Not A; the negation of the proposition A.
$A \wedge B$	A and B; the conjunction of the propositions A and B.
$A \vee B$	A or B; the disjunction of the propositions A and B.
$A \Rightarrow B$	Implication, A implies B; if A then B.
$A \Leftrightarrow B$	Equivalence of the two propositions A and B; A if and only if B.

Quantifiers

$\forall x \in X \cdot P(x)$	The universal quantifier; for all elements in the set X, the property P holds.
$\exists x \in X \cdot P(x)$	The existential quantifier; there exists one or more elements in the set X such that the property P holds.
$\exists! x \in X \cdot P(x)$	There exists exactly one element in the set X such that the property P holds.

Equivalent expressions

$$\exists i \in D \cdot P(i) \quad \neg(\forall i \in D \cdot \neg P(i))$$
$$\forall i \in D \cdot P(i) \quad \neg(\exists i \in D \cdot \neg P(i))$$

$a \wedge b$	$b \wedge a$	Commutativity
$a \vee b$	$b \vee a$	
$a \wedge (b \wedge c)$	$(a \wedge b) \wedge c$	Associativity
$a \vee (b \vee c)$	$(a \vee b) \vee c$	
$a \wedge (b \vee c)$	$(a \wedge b) \vee (a \wedge c)$	Distributivity
$a \vee (b \wedge c)$	$(a \vee b) \wedge (a \vee c)$	
$a \wedge \text{true}$	a	
$a \wedge \text{false}$	false	
$a \vee \text{false}$	a	
$a \vee \text{true}$	true	
$\neg (a \vee b)$	$\neg a \wedge \neg b$	de Morgan's Laws
$\neg (a \wedge b)$	$\neg a \vee \neg b$	
$\neg \neg a$	a	
$a \Rightarrow b$	$\neg a \vee b$	
$\text{true} \Rightarrow a$	a	
$\text{false} \Rightarrow a$	true	
$a \Leftrightarrow b$	$(a \Rightarrow b) \wedge (b \Rightarrow a)$	

SETS

Set expressions

$\{\}$

The empty set. The set with no members.

$\{x_1, x_2, \ldots, x_n\}$

Set enumeration. The explicit description of a set, the set with exactly the listed elements as members.

$\{e(x) \mid x \in S \cdot P(x)\}$

Set comprehension. The implicit description of a set, the set containing those elements $e(x)$ of the set S that satisfy the property (predicate) P.

$\{i, \ldots, j\}$

Set range expression. A subset of the integers, all the integers between i and j inclusive.

$$\{i, \ldots, j\} \triangleq \{n \in \mathbb{N} \mid i \leq n \wedge n \leq j\}$$

Set prefix operators

card S

The cardinality of a set. The number of elements in the set S.

$\mathcal{F}(S)$

The set of all finite subsets of the set S.

$$\mathcal{F}(x) \triangleq \{s \mid s \subseteq S \wedge \exists n \in \mathbb{N} \cdot \text{card } s < n\}$$

$\bigcup SS$

The distributed union operator. The union of all the sets contained in SS; SS must be a set of sets.

$$\bigcup SS \triangleq \{e \mid \exists s \in SS \cdot e \in s\}$$

$\bigcap SS$

The distributed intersection operator. The intersection of all the sets contained in SS; SS must be a set of sets.

$$\bigcap SS \triangleq \{e \mid \forall s \in SS \cdot e \in s\}$$

Set infix operators

$S_1 \cup S_2$

Set union. The set of elements, all of which are members of either S_1 or S_2 (or both).

$$S_1 \cup S_2 \;\triangleq\; \{e \mid e \in S_1 \vee e \in S_2\}$$

$S_1 \cap S_2$

Set intersection. The set of elements, all of which are members of both S_1 and S_2.

$$S_1 \cap S_2 \;\triangleq\; \{e \mid e \in S_1 \wedge e \in S_2\}$$

$S_1 - S_2$

Set difference. The set containing those elements of S_1 that are not in S_2.

$$S_1 - S_2 \;\triangleq\; \{e \mid e \in S_1 \wedge e \notin S_2\}$$

$S_1 \subseteq S_2$

The subset relation. All of the elements of S_1 are also elements of S_2.

$$S_1 \subseteq S_2 \;\triangleq\; \forall e \in S_1 \cdot e \in S_2$$

$S_1 \subset S_2$

The proper subset relation. The set S_1 is a subset of the set S_2 and S_2 contains at least one element that is not in S_1.

$$S_1 \subset S_2 \;\triangleq\; S_1 \subseteq S_2 \wedge S_1 \neq S_2$$

$e \in S$

Set membership. Tests if the element e is a member of the set S.

$e \notin S$

Negation of set membership. Tests if the element e is not a member of the set S.

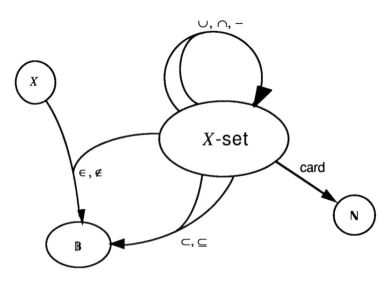

Figure A.1   The set operations.

SEQUENCES

Sequence expressions

[]	The empty sequence. The sequence with no elements.
$[e_1, e_2, \ldots, e_n]$	Sequence enumeration. An explicit sequence description (definition), the sequence with exactly the given elements in the order shown.
$[e(i) \mid i \in S \cdot P(i)]$	Sequence comprehension. The implicit description of a sequence, the sequence containing those elements indexed by the set S that satisfy the property (predicate) P. The set S must have an order defined on it.

$$
\begin{aligned}
&[e(i) \mid i \in S \cdot P(i)] \quad \triangleq \\
&\quad \text{if } S = \{\,\} \\
&\quad \text{then } [\,] \\
&\quad \text{else let } s = mins(S) \text{ in} \\
&\qquad \text{if } P(s) \\
&\qquad \text{then } [e(s)] \frown [e(i) \mid i \in (S - \{s\}) \cdot P(i)] \\
&\qquad \text{else } [e(i) \mid i \in (S - \{s\}) \cdot P(i)]
\end{aligned}
$$

$l(i, \ldots, j)$	Subsequence expression. The ith through jth element of the sequence l.

$$
l(i, \ldots, j) \quad \triangleq \quad [l(k) \mid k \in \{i, \ldots, j\}]
$$

Sequence prefix operators

hd l	The head of a sequence. The first element of the sequence l; the sequence must not be empty.
tl l	The tail of a sequence. The sequence obtained by removing the first element of l; the sequence must not be empty.
lt l	The last element of a sequence. The sequence must not be empty.
ft l	The front of a sequence. The sequence obtained by removing all but the last element of l. The sequence must not be empty.
len l	Length of a sequence. The number of elements in the sequence l.

$$
\begin{aligned}
\text{len } l \quad \triangleq \quad &\text{if } l = [\,] \\
&\text{then } 0 \\
&\text{else } 1 + \text{len tl } l
\end{aligned}
$$

inds l	The set of indices of a sequence. The set of integers that can be used as valid indices for the sequence l.

$$
\text{inds } l \quad \triangleq \quad \{1, \ldots, \text{len } l\}
$$

elems l	The set of elements that make up the sequence l.

$$
\text{elems } l \quad \triangleq \quad \{l(i) \mid 1 \leq i \wedge i \leq \text{len } l\}
$$

dconc l

The distributed concatenation operator. The elements of l, which must be sequences, are concatenated together.

$$\text{dconc } l \quad \triangleq \quad \begin{array}{l} \text{if } l = [] \\ \text{then } [] \\ \text{else hd } l \frown \text{dconc tl } l \end{array}$$

Sequence infix operators

$l_1 \frown l_2$

Sequence concatenation. The sequence containing the elements of l_1 followed by the elements of l_2.

s ins l

Sequence membership. Test if s is a subsequence of l.

$$s \text{ ins } l \quad \triangleq \quad \exists c, d \in X^* \cdot c \frown s \frown d = l$$

Sequence application

$l(i)$

Subscripting a sequence. The element of the sequence l with index i $(1 \leq i \leq \text{len } l)$.

$$l(i) \quad \triangleq \quad \begin{array}{l} \text{if } i = 1 \\ \text{then hd } l \\ \text{else tl } l(i - 1) \end{array}$$

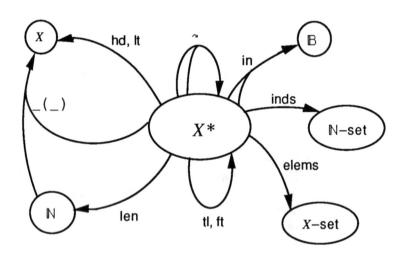

Figure A.2   The sequence operations.

MAPS

A map, m consists of pairs of elements from a set D and from a set R, and a rule that associates with each element of D a unique element of R.

Map expressions

$\{\,\}$	The empty map. The mapping with no pairs.
$\{d_1 \mapsto r_1, \ldots, d_n \mapsto r_n\}$	Map enumeration. Explicit map definition, the map with the given pairs—the order of the pairs is not important.
$\{d \mapsto f(d) \mid d \in D \cdot P(d)\}$	Map comprehension. Implicit mapping definition, the mapping whose pairs are such that their first elements satisfy P, and for each pair, the second element is derived from the first by applying f.

Map prefix and postfix operators

dom m The domain of a map m. The set of first elements of the pairs in the map m.

rng m The range of a map m. The set of second elements of the pairs in the map m.

$$\text{rng } m \ \triangleq \ \{m(d) \mid d \in \text{dom } m\}$$

merge M The merge of a set of maps M. The union of all the maps in the set M.

m^{-1} Map inversion. The inverse of the mapping m; the mapping must be one-to-one.

$$m^{-1}(x) \ \triangleq \ \text{let } y \text{ be st } m(y) = x \text{ in } y$$

Map infix operators

$m_1 \cup m_2$ Map union. A mapping with the information from the mapping m_1 and the information from m_2; the domains of the two maps must be disjoint.

$$m_1 \cup m_2 \ \triangleq \ \{d \mapsto r \mid \quad d \in \text{dom } m_1 \wedge r = m_1(d) \vee$$
$$d \in \text{dom } m_2 \wedge r = m_2(d)\}$$
$$\text{pre dom } m_1 \cap \text{dom } m_2 = \{\,\}$$

$m_1 \dagger m_2$ Map overwrite. A mapping with all of the information from the mapping m_1 and that information from m_2 which is not overwritten by m_2.

$$m_1 \dagger m_2 \ \triangleq \ \{d \mapsto r \mid d \in \text{dom } m_2 \wedge r = m_2(d) \vee$$
$$d \in (\text{dom } m_1 - \text{dom } m_2) \wedge r = m_1(d)\}$$

$S \vartriangleleft m$ Map domain restriction. A mapping with the pairs of mapping m whose first elements are also in the set S.

$$S \vartriangleleft m \ \triangleq \ \{d \mapsto m(d) \mid d \in (S \cap \text{dom } m)\}$$

$S \vartriangleleft\!\!\!- m$ Map domain substraction. The mapping which maps those domain elements of m that are not in the set S into the same range of elements as m.

$$S \vartriangleleft\!\!\!- m \ \triangleq \ \{d \mapsto m(d) \mid d \in (\text{dom } m - S)\}$$

$m \triangleright S$

Map range restriction. The mapping which maps those domain elements of m into the range of elements that are in the set S.

$$m \triangleright S \quad \triangleq \quad \{d \mapsto m(d) \mid m(d) \in (S \cap \text{rng } m)\}$$

$m \triangleright\!\!\!\!\!\!- S$

Map range subtraction. The mapping which maps those domain elements of m into the range of elements that are not in the set S.

$$m \triangleright\!\!\!\!\!\!- S \quad \triangleq \quad \{d \mapsto m(d) \mid m(d) \in (\text{rng } m - S)\}$$

m^i

Map iteration. The mapping obtained by applying m to its argument i times; the range of m must be contained in its domain.

$$m^i(x) \quad \triangleq \quad \begin{aligned} &\text{if } i = 0 \\ &\text{then } x \\ &\text{else } m^{(i-1)}(m(x)) \end{aligned}$$

$m \circ n$

Map composition. The mapping that is equivalent to first applying the map n and then applying m to the result. The range of n must be contained in the domain of m.

$$m \circ n(x) \quad \triangleq \quad m(n(x))$$

Map application

$m(d)$

Map application. The element of the range that corresponds to the element, d, of the domain.

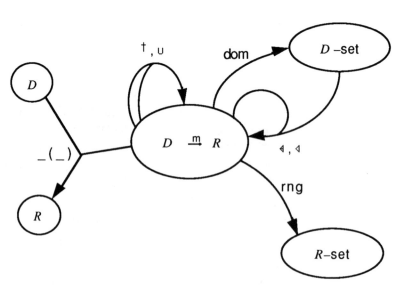

Figure A.3   The map operations.

RECORDS

Record expressions

Given the following composite object description:

$$B \;::\; sel_1 \;:\; Set_1$$
$$sel_2 \;:\; Set_2$$
$$Set_3$$

and if $s_1 \in Set_1$, $s_2 \in Set_2$ and $s_3 \in Set_3$ then the make function $mk\text{-}B$ is defined:

$$mk\text{-}B(s_1, s_2, s_3) \in B$$

where

$$mk\text{-}B \colon Set_1 \times Set_2 \times Set_3 \to B$$

if $x \in B$ and $s_1 \in Set_1$ then

$$\mu(x, sel_1 \mapsto s_1).sel_1 = s_1$$

and

$$\mu(x, sel_1 \mapsto s_1).sel_2 = x.s_2$$

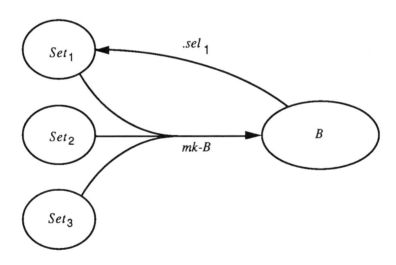

Figure A.4   The record operations.

B

SOME AUXILIARY FUNCTIONS

SETS

The *is-disj* truth-valued function checks to see if a family of sets are mutually disjoint:

$$is\text{-}disj : (X\text{-set})\text{-set} \rightarrow \textbf{B}$$

$$is\text{-}disj(SS) \quad \triangleq \quad \forall s, t \in SS \cdot s = t \lor s \cap t = \{\,\}$$

The *applys* function applies a function, which is one of its arguments, to every element of a set:

$$applys : (D \rightarrow R) \times D\text{-set} \rightarrow R\text{-set}$$

$$applys(f, S) \quad \triangleq \quad \{f(e) \mid e \in S\}$$

The *maxs* function finds the largest element of a set on which an order relation is defined:

$$maxs \ (s\text{:}X\text{-set}) \ r\text{:}X$$

pre $s \neq \{\,\}$

post $r \in s \land \forall j \in s \cdot r \geq j$

The *mins* function finds the smallest element of a set that has an order relation defined on it:

$$mins \ (s\text{:}X\text{-set}) \ r\text{:}X$$

pre $s \neq \{\,\}$

post $r \in s \land \forall j \in s \cdot r \leq j$

SEQUENCES

The *is-permutation* truth-valued function checks to see if one sequence is a permutation of another:

$$is\text{-}permutation : X^* \times X^* \rightarrow \textbf{B}$$

$$is\text{-}permutation(l_1, l_2) \quad \triangleq \quad items(l_1) = items(l_2)$$

The *items* function counts the number of occurrences of each element that occurs in a sequence:

$$items : X^* \rightarrow (X \xrightarrow{m} \textbf{N})$$

$$items(l) \quad \triangleq \quad \{x \mapsto \text{card}\,\{i \mid i \in \text{dom}\,l \land l(i) = x\} \mid x \in \text{elems}\,l\}$$

The *is-uniques* truth-valued function checks to see if all the elements occuring in a sequence are distinct:

$$is\text{-}uniques : X^* \to \mathbf{B}$$

$$is\text{-}uniques(l) \quad \triangleq \quad \forall i, j \in \text{inds } l \cdot i = j \vee l(i) \neq l(j)$$

The *rev* function reverses a sequence:

$$rev : X^* \to X^*$$

$$rev(l) \quad \triangleq \quad \text{if } l = []$$
$$\text{then } []$$
$$\text{else } rev(\text{tl } l) \frown [\text{hd } l]$$

If m is a map whose domain is an ordered set S, then the *squash* function returns a sequence derived from the elements of the range of the mapping in an (ascending) order derived from their corresponding domain value.

$$squash : (S \xrightarrow{m} X) \to X^*$$

$$squash(m) \quad \triangleq \quad \text{if } m = \{\}$$
$$\text{then } []$$
$$\text{else let } i \in mins(\text{dom } m) \text{ in}$$
$$[m(i)] \frown squash(\{i\} \lhd m)$$

Subsequences

The *front* function is a generalization of the ft (front) operator and returns a sequence consisting of the first n elements of a sequence:

$$front : X^* \times \mathbf{N} \to X^*$$

$$front(l, n) \quad \triangleq \quad l(1, \ldots, n)$$

The *last* function is a generalization of the lt (last) operator and returns the last n elements of a sequence:

$$last : X^* \times \mathbf{N} \to X^*$$

$$last(l, n) \quad \triangleq \quad l(\text{len } l - n + 1, \ldots, \text{len } l)$$

The *rest* function returns a sequence consisting of the ith through to the last element of a sequence:

$$rest : X^* \times \mathbf{N} \to X^*$$

$$rest(l, i) \quad \triangleq \quad l(i, \ldots, \text{len } l)$$

Locating elements in a sequence

The *locate* function returns the index of the start of the first occurrence of a (sub)sequence within a sequence; if the sequence is not present as a subsequence, the function returns 0:

$locate : X^* \times X^* \to \mathbf{N}$

$locate(s, l) \;\; \triangleq \;\;$ if s ins l
    then $mins(\{i \in$ inds $l \mid s = l(i, \ldots, i + $ len $s - 1)\})$
    else 0

The *allocs* function returns a set of indices that index all of the occurrences of an element in a sequence:

$allocs : X \times X^* \to \mathbf{N}_1\text{-set}$

$allocs(x, l) \;\; \triangleq \;\; \{i \in$ inds $l \mid x = l(i)\}$

The *firstocc* function returns the index of the first occurrence of an element within a sequence; if the element is not present in the sequence, the function returns 0:

$firstocc : X \times X^* \to \mathbf{N}$

$firstocc(x, l) \;\; \triangleq \;\;$ if $x \in$ elems l
    then $mins(\{i \in$ elems $l \mid x = l(i)\})$
    else 0

Operations for changing elements of a sequence

The *del* function removes the ith element of a sequence:

$del : X^* \times \mathbf{N} \to X^*$

$del(l, i) \;\; \triangleq \;\; l(1, \ldots, i - 1) \frown rest(l, i + 1)$

pre $i \in$ inds l

The *assign* function updates the ith element of a sequence:

$assign : X^* \times \mathbf{N} \times X \to X^*$

$assign(l, i, e) \;\; \triangleq \;\; front(l, i - 1) \frown [e] \frown rest(l, i + 1)$

pre $i \in$ inds l

Operations for constructing new sequences

The *subl* function uses a sequence of natural numbers to define a subsequence of a sequence:

$subl : X^* \times \mathbf{N}^* \to X^*$

$subl(l, xl) \;\; \triangleq \;\;$ if $xl = []$
    then $[]$
    else $[l($hd $xl)] \frown subl(l,$ tl $xl)$

pre elems $xl \subseteq$ inds l

Additional operators

The ins infix operator and the lt and fr prefix sequence operations have been introduced, and are defined as follows:

$$\_\text{ins}\_ : X^* \times X^* \to \mathbf{B}$$

$$x \text{ ins } y \quad \triangle \quad \exists c, d \in X^* \cdot c \frown x \frown d = y$$

$$\text{ft}\_ : X^* \to X^*$$

$$\text{ft } l \quad \triangle \quad l(1, \ldots, \text{len } l - 1)$$
$$\text{pre } l \neq []$$

$$\text{lt}\_ : X^* \to X^*$$

$$\text{lt } l \quad \triangle \quad l(\text{len } l)$$
$$\text{pre } l \neq []$$

C

AN OVERVIEW OF THE SPECIFICATION LANGUAGE

This appendix describes the syntax of the specification language used in this book. For differences between the proposed Standard for VDM-SL and this syntax see Section C below.

A SYNTAX FOR THE SPECIFICATION LANGUAGE

A specification document

   document = definition block, { [';'], definition block } ;

Definitions

   definition block = type definitions
         | state definition
         | value definitions
         | function definitions
         | operation definitions ;

Type definitions

   type definitions = 'types', type definition, { [';'], type definition } ;

   type definition = identifier, '=', type, [invariant]
         | identifier, '::', field list, [invariant] ;

   type = basic type
     | type name
     | quote type
     | set type
     | seq type
     | map type
     | product type
     | union type
     | optional type
     | composite type
     | bracketed type
     | pointer type
     | collection type ;

416

basic type = '**B**' | '**N**' | '**N**₁' | '**Z**' | '**Q**' | '**R**' | 'char' | 'token' ;

type name = identifier ;

quote type = quote literal ;

set type = type, '-set' ;

seq type = seq0 type
$\qquad$ | seq1 type ;

seq0 type = type, '*' ;

seq1 type = type, '+' ;

map type = general map type
$\qquad$ | injective map type ;

general map type = type, '$\xrightarrow{m}$', type ;

injective map type = type, '$\xleftrightarrow{m}$', type ;

product type = type, '×', type ;

union type = type, '|', type ;

optional type = '[', type, ']' ;

composite type = 'compose', identifier, 'of', field list, 'end' ;

field list = { field } ;

field = [identifier, ':'], type ;

bracketed type = '(', type, ')' ;

pointer type = 'pointer to', type ;

collection type = 'collection of', type ;

State definition

state definition = 'state', identifier, 'of',
$\qquad\qquad$ field list,
$\qquad\qquad$ [invariant],
$\qquad\qquad$ [initialization],
$\qquad\qquad$ 'end' ;

invariant = 'inv', pattern, '$\triangleq$', expression ;

initialization = 'init', pattern, '$\triangleq$', expression ;

Value definitions

value definitions = 'values', value definition, { [';'], value definition } ;

value definition = pattern, [':', type], '=', expression ;

Function definitions

function definitions = 'functions', function definition list ;

function definition list = function definition, { [';'], function definition } ;

function definition = function signature,
function parameters,
function body ;

function signature = identifier, ':', function type ;

function type = type, '→', type
| '()', '→', type ;

function parameters = identifier, parameter list ;

parameter list = parameters, { parameters } ;

parameters = '(', [pattern list], ')' ;

function body = '$\triangle$', expression, ['pre', expression] ;

Operation definitions

operation definitions = 'operations', operation definition list ;

operation definition list = operation definition, { [';'], operation definition } ;

operation definition = operation heading, operation body ;

operation heading = identifier, parameter types, [identifier type pair] ;

parameter types = '(', [pattern type pair list], ')' ;

pattern type pair list = pattern list, ':', type, { ',', pattern list, ':', type } ;

identifier type pair = identifier, ':', type ;

operation body = specification | command ;

specification = [frame],
['pre', expression],
'post', expression ;

frame = 'ext', var information, { var information } ;

var information = mode, identifier list, [':', type] ;

mode = 'rd' | 'wr' | 'lc' ;

Statements

command = block statement
| bind statement
| assign command
| while loop command
| conditional command
| cases command
| operation call
| return command
| error command
| identity command
| input output command
| specification command ;

```
block statement  =  '(', { declare statement }, command list, ')' ;

command list  =  command, { ';', command } ;

declare statement  =  'dcl', dcl definition list, ';' ;

dcl definition list  =  dcl definition, { ',', dcl definition } ;

dcl definition  =  identifier list, ':', type ;

bind statement  =  let statement
                |  let be statement
                |  definition statement ;

let statement  =  'let', value definition list, 'in', command ;

value definition list  =  value definition, { ',', value definition } ;

let be statement  =  'let', such that bind list, 'in', command ;

such that bind list  =  such that bind, { ',', such that bind } ;

such that bind  =  bind, [ 'be', 'st', expression ] ;

definition statement  =  'def', equals definition list, 'in', command ;

equals definition list  =  equals definition, { ';', equals definition } ;

equals definition  =  pattern bind, '=', expression
                   |  pattern bind, '=', operation call ;

assign command  =  state designator list, ':=', expression list
                |  state designator, ':=', operation call ;

state designator list  =  state designator, { ',', state designator } ;

while loop command  =  'while', expression, 'do', command list, 'end' ;

conditional command  =  'if', expression ,
                        'then', command list,
                        { elsif command },
                        'else', command list,
                        'end' ;

elsif command  =  'elseif', expression,
                  'then', command list ;

cases command  =  'cases', expression, ':',
                  cases choice list,
                  [ ',', default command ],
                  'end' ;

cases choice list  =  cases choice, { ',', cases choice } ;

cases choice  =  pattern list, '→', command ;

default command  =  'others', '→', command ;

operation call  =  identifier, '(', [ expression list ], ')' ;

return command  =  'return', expression ;

error command  =  'error' ;

identity command  =  'skip' ;
```

```
input output command  =  input command
                      |  output command
                      |  open command
                      |  close command ;

input command  =  state designator, 'from', identifier, 'st', expression ;

output command  =  expression, 'to', identifier ;

open command  =  'open', expression, 'for', ( 'input' | 'output' ) ;

close command  =  'close', expression ;

specification command  =  [ identifier ], specification ;
```

Expressions

```
expression list  =  expression, { ',', expression } ;

expression  =  bracketed expression
            |  expression preamble
            |  choice expression
            |  unary expression
            |  binary expression
            |  quantified expression
            |  iota expression
            |  set expression
            |  sequence expression
            |  map expression
            |  tuple expression
            |  record expression
            |  apply expression
            |  lambda expression
            |  is expression
            |  undefined expression
            |  symbolic literal
            |  name ;

bracketed expression  =  '(', expression, ')' ;
```

Expression preambles

```
expression preamble  =  let expression
                     |  let st expression ;

let expression  =  'let', pattern bind, '=', expression, 'in', expression ;

let st expression  =  'let', pattern bind, [ 'be', 'st', expression ], 'in', expression ;
```

Choice expressions

```
choice expression  =  conditional expression
                   |  cases expression ;

conditional expression  =  'if', expression,
                           'then', expression,
                           { elsif expression },
                           'else', expression ;
```

```
elsif expression  =  'elseif', expression,
                     'then', expression ;

cases expression  =  'cases', expression, ':',
                     cases expression alternatives,
                     [ ',', others expression ],
                     'end' ;

cases expression alternatives  =  cases expression alternative,
                                  { ',', cases expression alternative } ;

cases expression alternative  =  pattern list, '→',expression ;

others expression  =  'others', '→', expression ;
```

Unary expressions

```
unary expression  =  prefix expression | postfix expression ;

prefix expression  =  prefix operator, expression ;

prefix operator  =  arithmetic prefix operator
                 |  logical prefix operator
                 |  set prefix operator
                 |  sequence prefix operator
                 |  map prefix operator
                 |  file prefix operator ;

arithmetic prefix operator  =  '+' | '−' | 'abs' | 'floor' ;


logical prefix operator  =  '¬' ;


set prefix operator  =  'card' | '𝓕' | '⋃' | '⋂' ;


sequence prefix operator  =  'hd' | 'tl' | 'ft' | 'lt' | 'len'
                          |  'inds' | 'elems' | 'conc' ;


map prefix operator  =  'dom' | 'rng' | 'merge' ;


file prefix operator  =  'eof' ;

postfix expression  =  expression, postfix operator ;

postfix operator  =  map postfix operator ;

map postfix operator  =  '-1' ;
```

Binary expressions

binary expression = expression, infix operator, expression ;

infix operator = arithmetic infix operator
      | set infix operator
      | set relational operator
      | sequence infix operator
      | map infix operator
      | map infix combinator
      | logical infix operator
      | relational infix operator
      | function infix combinator ;

arithmetic infix operator = '+' | '−' | '×' | '/' | 'rem'
      | 'mod' | '÷' | '↑' ;

set infix operator = '∪' | '∩' | '−' ;

set relational operator = '⊆' | '⊂' | '∈' | '∉' ;

sequence infix operator = '⌢' | ' ins ' ;

map infix operator = '∪' | '†' | '◁' | '◁-' | '▷' | '▷-' ;

map infix combinator = '↑' | 'o' ;

logical infix operator = '∧' | '∨' | ' ⇒ ' | ' ⇔ ' ;

relational infix operator = '=' | '≠' | '<' | '≤' | '>' | '≥' ;

function infix combinator = '↑' | 'o' ;

Note: the $\uparrow$ infix operators can be replaced by a superscript: $m \uparrow n$ can be written as m^n.

Quantified expressions

quantified expression = universal quantified expression
      | existential quantified expression
      | unique quantified expression ;

universal quantified expression = '∀', bind list, '·', expression ;

existential quantified expression = '∃', bind list, '·', expression ;

bind list = bind, { ',', bind } ;

unique quantified expression = '∃!', bind, '·', expression ;

Iota expression

iota expression = 'ι', bind, '·', expression ;

Set expressions

```
set expression  =   empty set
                |   set enumeration
                |   set comprehension
                |   set range expression ;

empty set  =   '{ }' ;

set enumeration  =   '{', expression list, '}' ;

set comprehension  =   '{', expression, '|', bind list, [ '·', expression ], '}' ;

set range expression  =   '{', expression, ',', '...', ',', expression, '}' ;
```

Sequence expressions

```
sequence expression  =   empty sequence
                     |   sequence enumeration
                     |   sequence comprehension
                     |   subsequence expression ;

empty sequence  =   '[]' ;

sequence enumeration  =   '[', expression list, ']' ;

sequence comprehension  =   '[', expression, '|', set bind, [ '·', expression ], ']' ;

subsequence expression  =   expression, '(', expression, ',', '...', ',', expression, ')' ;
```

Map expressions

```
map expression  =   empty map
                |   map enumeration
                |   map comprehension ;

empty map  =   '{ }' ;

map enumeration  =   '{', maplet list, '}' ;

maplet list  =   maplet, { ',', maplet } ;

maplet  =   expression, '↦', expression ;

map comprehension  =   '{', maplet, '|', bind list, [ '·', expression ], '}' ;
```

Tuple expression

```
tuple expression  =   tuple constructor ;

tuple constructor  =   'mk-', '(', expression list, ')' ;
```

Record expressions

```
record expression  =   record constructor
                   |   record modifier ;

record constructor  =   identifier, '(', [ expression list ], ')' ;

record modifier  =   'μ', '(', expression, ',', record modification list, ')' ;

record modification list  =   record modification, { ',', record modification } ;

record modification  =   identifier, '↦', expression ;
```

Apply expressions

```
apply expression  =   function apply
                   |   sequence apply
                   |   map apply
                   |   field select ;

function apply  =   expression, '(', [ expression list ], ')' ;

sequence apply  =   expression, '(', expression, ')' ;

map apply  =   expression, '(', expression, ')' ;

field select  =   expression, '.', identifier ;
```

Lambda expressions

```
lambda expression  =   'λ', type bind list, '·', expression ;

type bind list  =   type bind, { ',', type bind } ;
```

Is expressions

```
is expression  =   identifier, '(', expression, ')'
               |   is basic type, '(', expression, ')' ;
```

Undefined expression

```
undefined expression  =   'undefined' ;
```

Names and identifiers

```
name  =   identifier | old identifier ;

old identifier  =   identifier, '  ‾  ' ;

identifier list  =   identifier, { ',', identifier } ;
```

Note: An old name such as *identifier*‾ can also be written as *identifier*‾.

State designators

```
state designator  =   identifier
                   |   field reference
                   |   map reference
                   |   sequence reference ;

field reference  =   state designator, '.', identifier ;

map reference  =   state designator, '(', expression, ')' ;

sequence reference  =   state designator, '(', expression, ')' ;
```

Patterns

    pattern list = pattern, { ',', pattern } ;

    pattern = pattern identifier
            | match value
            | set pattern
            | sequence pattern
            | tuple pattern
            | record pattern ;

    pattern identifier = identifier | '-' ;

    match value = '(', expression, ')' | symbolic literal ;

    set pattern = set enumeration pattern | set union pattern ;

    set enumeration pattern = '{', [pattern list], '}' ;

    set union pattern = pattern, '∪', pattern ;

    sequence pattern = sequence enumeration pattern
                    | sequence catenation pattern ;

    sequence enumeration pattern = '[', pattern list, ']' ;

    sequence catenation pattern = pattern, '⌢', pattern ;

    tuple pattern = 'mk-', '(', [pattern list], ')' ;

    record pattern = identifier, '(', [pattern list], ')' ;

Bindings

    pattern bind = pattern | bind ;

    bind = set bind | type bind ;

    set bind = pattern, '∈', expression ;

    type bind = pattern, ':', type ;

Lexical specification

General   The text of a specification in the mathematical concrete representation may be considered at three levels: as marks on paper, as a sequence of characters and as a sequence of symbols.

The character representation   When reading the concrete syntax, the usual English orthographic conventions for interpreting printed text are assumed (division into pages and lines, direction of reading, ignoring of page furniture such as headings and page numbers, identification of printed or written characters, and so on). Sequences of non-mathematical text may be interspersed with mathematical text using any convention of presentation that allows the mathematical text to be unambiguously identified.

    text of a specification = character, { character } ;

character = plain letter
| keyword letter
| distinguished letter
| Greek letter
| digit
| delimeter character
| other character
| separator ;

The character sets are shown below, with the forms of characters used in this syntax.

plain letters:

a	b	c	d	e	f	g	h	i	j	k	l	m
n	o	p	q	r	s	t	u	v	w	x	y	z
A	B	C	D	E	F	G	H	I	J	K	L	M
N	O	P	Q	R	S	T	U	V	W	X	Y	Z

keyword letters:

a b c d e f g h i j k l m
n o p q r s t u v w x y z

distinguished letters:

A B C D E F G H I J K L M
N O P Q R S T U V W X Y Z
A B C D E F G H I J K L M
N O P Q R S T U V W X Y Z

Greek letter:

α β γ δ ϵ ζ η θ ι κ λ μ
ν ξ o π ρ σ τ υ ϕ χ ψ ω
A B Γ Δ E Z H Θ I K Λ M
N Ξ O Π P Σ T Υ Φ X Ψ Ω

digits:

0 1 2 3 4 5 6 7 8 9

delimiter characters:

, : ; = ( ) | – [ ] { }
+ / < > $\leq$ $\geq$ $\neq$! $\forall$ $\exists$. *
+ $\overset{m}{\longleftrightarrow}$ $\overset{m}{\longrightarrow}$ $\longrightarrow$ $\overset{o}{\to}$ $\|$ $\Rightarrow$ $\Leftrightarrow$ $\in$ $\mapsto$ $\cap$
$\bigcup$ $^{-1}$ $\mathcal{F}$ $\triangleleft$ $\triangleright$ $\blacktriangleleft$ $\blacktriangleright$ ι λ μ $\cdot$ $\times$
$\overset{\triangle}{\lor}$ $\lnot$ $\cap$ $\cup$ $\uparrow$ $\subset$ $\subseteq$ $\notin$ $\frown$ $\dagger$ $\circ$ $\land$
$\lor$ **B** **N** **N₁** **Z** **Q** **R** ς

other characters:

– ' " @ $\longleftarrow$

separators:

These have no graphic form, but are a combination of white space and line break. There **are** two separators: without line break (white space) and with line break (newline).

The symbol representation The following kinds of symbols exist: keywords, delimiters, identifiers, symbolic literals, and comments. The transformation from characters to symbols is given by the following rules; these use the same notation as the syntax definition but differ in meaning in that no separators may appear between adjacent terminals. Where ambiguity is possible otherwise, two consecutive symbols must be separated by a separator.

$$\text{text of a specification} \; = \; \text{symbol}, \{ \, [\, \text{separator} \,], \text{symbol} \, \} \; ;$$

symbol = keyword
    | delimeter
    | identifer
    | symbolic literal
    | comment ;

keyword = 'as' | 'abs' | 'be' | 'card' | 'cases' | 'char' | 'compose'
    | 'conc' | 'dcl' | 'def' | 'div' | 'do' | 'dom'
    | 'elems' | 'else' | 'elseif' | 'empty' | 'end' | 'error' | 'ext' | 'false'
    | 'floor' | 'functions' | 'hd' | 'if' | 'in' | 'inds' | 'init'
    | 'inv' | 'is' | 'lc' | 'len' | 'let' | 'merge' | 'mod' | 'nil' | 'not'
    | 'of' | 'operations' | 'others' | 'parameters' | 'post' | 'pre'
    | 'rd' | 'rem' | 'return' | 'reverse' | 'rng' | 'skip' | 'st'
    | 'state' | 'then' | 'token' | 'tl' | 'to' | 'true' | 'types'
    | 'undefined' | 'values' | 'while' | 'wr' | ;

delimiter = delimiter character | compound delimiter ;

compound delimiter = '::' | ':=' | '...' | '∃!' | '−−' ;

identifier = first character, remaining characters ;

first character = plain letter | Greek letter ;

remaining characters = { (plain letter | Greek letter) | digit | " ' " | " ' " | '‿' } ;

Note: digits can be written as subscripts in identifiers.

is basic type = 'is-', ('$\mathbb{B}$' | '$\mathbb{N}$' | '$\mathbb{N}_1$' | '$\mathbb{Z}$' | '$\mathbb{Q}$' | '$\mathbb{R}$' | 'char' | 'token') ;

symbolic literal = numeric literal | Boolean literal
    | empty literal | nil literal
    | character literal | text literal | quote literal ;

numeral = digit, { digit } ;

numeric literal = numeral, ['.', digit, { digit }], [exponent] ;

exponent = '×10 ↑', ['+' | '−'], numeral ;

Note: $10 \uparrow n$ can be written 10^n.

Boolean literal = 'true' | 'false' ;

empty literal = 'empty' ;

nil literal = 'nil' ;

character literal = ' ' ', character − separator, ' ' ' ;

text literal = ' " ', { ' "" ' | character − (' " ' | separator) }, ' " ' ;

quote literal = distinguished letter, { '‿' | distinguished letter } ;

comment = '−−', { character − newline }, newline ;

Certain identifiers are reserved: the basic type names **token** and **char**, and all identifiers beginning with one of the reserved prefixes: *init-*, *inv-*, *is-*, *mk-*, *post-* and *pre-*.

Operator precedence

The precedence ordering for operators in the concrete syntax is defined using a two-level approach: operators are divided into families, and an upper-level precedence ordering, $>$, is given on the families, such that if families F_1 and F_2 satisfy

$$F_1 > F_2$$

then every operator in the family F_1 is of a higher precedence than every operator in the family F_2.

The relative precedences of the operators within families is determined by considering type information, and this is used to resolve ambiguity. The type constructors are treated separately, and are not placed in a precedence ordering with the other operators.

There are six families of operators, namely Combinators, Applicators, Evaluators, Relations, Connectives and Constructors.

Combinators: operations that allow functions and mappings to be combined.
Applicators: function application, field selection, sequence indexing, etc.
Evaluators: operators that are non-predicates.
Relations: operators that are relations.
Connectives: the logical connectives.
Constructors: operators that are used, implicitly or explicitly, in the construction of expressions; e.g. if-then-elsif-else-end, '$\mapsto$', '$\ldots$', etc.

The precedence ordering on the families is:

    combinators > applicators > evaluators > relations > connectives > constructors

The family of combinators   These combinators have the highest family priority.

    combinator = function infix combinator | map infix combinator ;

precedence level	combinator
1	$\circ$
2	$\uparrow$

The family of applicators   All applicators have equal precedence.

    applicator = subsequence expression
        | tuple constructor
        | apply expression
        | is expression ;

The family of evaluators   The family of evaluators is divided into nine groups, according to the type of expression they are used in.

    evaluator = arithmetic prefix operator
        | set prefix operator
        | sequence prefix operator
        | map prefix operator
        | file prefix operator
        | arithmetic infix operator
        | set infix operator
        | sequence infix operator
        | map infix operator ;

The precedence ordering follows a pattern of analogous operators. The family is defined in the following table.

precedence level	arithmetic	set	map	sequence	file
1	$+$ $-$	$\cup$ $-$	$\cup$ †	⌢	
2	$\times$ /	$\cap$		ins	
	rem				
	mod				
	$\div$				
3	↑				
4			◁ ◀		
			▷ ▶		
5	(unary) $+$	card	dom	inds	eof
	(unary) $-$	$\mathcal{F}$	rng	elems	
	abs	$\bigcap$	merge	hd tl	
	floor	$\bigcup$		ft lt	
				dconc	
				len	

The family of relations This family includes all the relational operators whose result is of type **B**.

>   relation = relational infix operator | set relational operator ;

precedence level	relation	
1	$\leq$	$<$
	$\geq$	$>$
	$=$	$\neq$
	$\subseteq$	$\subset$
	$\in$	$\notin$

All operators in the Relations family have equal precedence. Typing dictates that there is no meaningful way of using them adjacently.

The family of connectives This family includes all the logical operators whose result is of type **B**.

>   connectives = logical prefix operator | logical infix operator ;

precedence level	connective
1	$\Leftrightarrow$
2	$\Rightarrow$
3	$\lor$
4	$\land$
5	$\lnot$

The family of constructors This family includes all the operators used to construct a value. Their priority is given either by brackets, which are an implicit part of the operator, or by the syntax.

Grouping The grouping of operands of operators are as follows:

Combinators: right grouping.

Applicators: no grouping.

Connectives: the ' $\Rightarrow$ ' operator has right grouping. The other operators are associative and therefore right and left grouping are equivalent.

Evaluators: left grouping.

Relations: no grouping.

Constructors: no grouping.

The type operators

Type operators should have their own separate precedence ordering, as follows:

1. Function types: $\rightarrow \xleftarrow{m}, \xrightarrow{m}$ (right grouping).
2. Union type: | (no grouping).
3. Other binary type operators: × (no grouping).
4. Unary type operators: *, +, -set, pointer to, collection of.

DIFFERENCES FROM STANDARD VDM-SL

The following restrictions have been made to Standard VDM-SL.

1. The module facility has been removed.
2. The trap exit facilities have been removed.
3. The exceptions facility has been removed.
4. The syntax for operation definitions has been modified, the addition of the specification statement allows this part of the syntax to be simplified (see below).
5. The syntax for the explicit definition of an operation allows a style similar to that of most programming languages.
6. The syntax for function definitions has been modified. Functions can only be specified in a mathematical style, the ability to specify functions in a syntax which follows the form allowed by programming languages has been removed.
7. Declarations cannot be initialized.
8. The McCarthy command has been removed.
9. No expression syntax for list modification, an auxiliary function (*assign*) has been introduced to perform this function.
10. Semicolons are optional between components of definitions.

The restrictions made in 4, 5 and 6 have been made in this book to emphasize that operations are refined to code, and functions are used as aid to the readability of definitions.

The following extensions and changes have been made to Standard VDM-SL.

1. The syntax for the conditional command and the while command have been modified. Standard VDM-SL allows only a single statement as a component to a conditional command or a while command, the introduction of the end keyword to delimit the end of these syntactic structures allows sequences of commands as components.
2. The specification command has been introduced for refinement. Its informal semantics can be given by replacing the specification command by a operation call, and turning the specification command into an operation definition in the obvious way.
3. New commands for input/output have been introduced.
4. Some additional operators have been introduced (see Appendix B).
5. Collection and pointer types have been introduced for data refinement to programming language pointers and heaps.
6. The syntax has been extended with mathematical conventions where there is no ambiguity; for example in the notation used for set and map comprehension and the uses of sets and set operations where Standard VDM-SL uses types.

THE EXECUTABLE SPECIFICATION LANGUAGE

This section identifies an 'executable subset' of Standard VDM-SL which can be translated into programming languages such as Pascal, Modula-2, Ada or C. For code the following restrictions:

- No logical constant preambles.
- No specification statements.
- No implicit specifications of operations.
- No specifications of functions.

For data the following restrictions:

- No mapping except those with a domain that is a small, finite, simple set—those sets of values that the language allows as an index for an array.
- No types of the form S-set, except those with a base type that is a small finite simple set—those sets of values that are allowed as the base set of a SET OF type constructor in Pascal or Modula-2.
- No types of the form S^*, except sequences that are modelling sequenctial files. The operations on those files are restricted to those defined above for input and output.

The following refinements for more complex data types are suggested.

- Maps with finite scalar domains can be implemented by arrays.
- Sequences with restricted access can be modelled by sequential files.
- Composite objects can be modelled with records (structures).
- Small finite sets can be modelled with enumerated types.
- Token sets can be modelled with natural numbers, strings, characters, etc.
- Types of the form S-set can be modelled with SET OF S, providing the cardinal of the base set is not too large.

Large maps, sequences and sets must be refined to an appropriate collection of data structures. Maps and sets can be modelled by:

- hashing

- extendible hashing
- look-up tables, both ordered and unordered
- linked lists
- binary trees
- balanced search trees
- AVL trees
- 2-3 trees
- n-ary trees
- B-trees
- B^+-trees

Typically maps are modelled by keeping pairs of values in a data structure, the pairs being the maplet pairs that are in the mapping. Sets are modelled by just keeping the elements in a data structure.

Sequences can be modelled by:

- arrays
- linked-lists

Sequences can also be modelled as maps from **N** into the base set and therefore can be refined the same way as maps (and thus use any of the data structures that can be used to represent maps).

NOTATION

The concrete representation for the specification language used in this book is defined by a context-free grammar (see below) which conforms to the BSI standard for grammars. The grammar is described by means of a BNF notation which employs the following special symbols:

,	the concatenate symbol,
=	the define symbol.
|	the definition separator symbol.
[ ]	enclose optional syntactic items.
{ }	enclose syntactic items which may occur zero or more times.
' '	single quotes are used to enclose terminal symbols.
meta identifier	non-terminal symbols are written in lower-case letters (possibly including spaces).
;	terminator symbol to denote the end of a rule.
( )	used for grouping, e.g. a,(b | c) is equivalent to a, b | a, c.
−	denotes subtraction from a set of terminal symbols (e.g. 'character − ('+')' denotes all characters excepting the + character.)

The precedence of the metalanguage symbols is

Metalanguage symbol	Meaning
,	concatenate
|	or

D

PROOF OBLIGATIONS

SATISFIABILITY

$$\forall \overleftarrow{s} \in State \cdot pre\text{-}OP(\overleftarrow{s}) \;\Rightarrow\; \exists s \in State \cdot post\text{-}OP(\overleftarrow{s}, s)$$

Proving that a specification can be satisfied is often quite difficult, and frequently tedious. Usually we do not specify systems that cannot be implemented, but it is useful to check that data type invariants are preserved. The above proof obligation can be proved in two steps. First show that the specification can be satisfied on the general state:

$$\forall \overleftarrow{s} \in State^+ \cdot pre\text{-}OP(\overleftarrow{s}) \;\Rightarrow\; \exists s \in State^+ \cdot post\text{-}OP(\overleftarrow{s}, s)$$

and then show that an operation preserves the data invariant:

$$\forall \overleftarrow{s}, s \in State^+ \cdot pre\text{-}OP(\overleftarrow{s}) \wedge inv(\overleftarrow{s}) \wedge post\text{-}OP(\overleftarrow{s}, s) \;\Rightarrow\; inv(s)$$

where

$$State = \{s \in State^+ \mid inv(s)\}$$

Thus $State^+$ is the state ignoring the data type invariant.

Frequently the proof obligation that a specification can be satisfied can be left until last—exhibit the running program as the existence proof. The proof that operations preserve the invariant should be done if there is any doubt.

DATA REFINEMENT

1. Choose a new data representation.
2. Discover the retrieve function.

    $$retr\colon Rep \to Abs$$

3. The retrieve function must be defined everywhere on the data representation, and adequacy must be proved.

    $$\forall sa \in Abs \cdot \exists sr \in Rep \cdot sa = retr(sr)$$

4. Show that the new initial state is valid:

    $$retr(sr_0) = sa_0$$

5. Rewrite operations in terms of the new (concrete) data representation.
6. Show that the new operations are implementable (or at least show they preserve the data invariant).
7. Show that the new operations model those of the specification using the domain and range rules.

Domain rule

$$\forall sr \in Rep \cdot pre\text{-}OPA(retr(sr)) \implies pre\text{-}OPR(sr)$$

Range rule

$$\forall \overleftarrow{sr}, sr \in Rep \cdot pre\text{-}OPA(retr(\overleftarrow{sr})) \wedge post\text{-}OPR(\overleftarrow{sr}, sr)$$
$$\implies post\text{-}OPA(retr(\overleftarrow{sr}), retr(sr))$$

PROGRAM REFINEMENT RULES

In the following, identifiers occurring in a frame stand for a list of zero or more identifiers.

EQUIVALENT SPECIFICATION RULE

$$\text{if} \left\{ \begin{array}{c} P \Rightarrow P' \\ P[w \backslash \overleftarrow{w}] \wedge Q' \Rightarrow Q \end{array} \right\} \quad \text{then}$$

$$
\begin{array}{l}
\textbf{ext wr } w \\
\quad \textbf{rd } r \\
\textbf{pre } P \\
\textbf{post } Q
\end{array}
\quad \sqsubseteq \quad
\begin{array}{l}
\textbf{ext wr } w \\
\quad \textbf{rd } r \\
\textbf{pre } P' \\
\textbf{post } Q'
\end{array}
$$

THE CONSTANT INTRODUCTION RULE

$$\text{if} \left\{ P \Rightarrow \exists c \in C \cdot P' \right\} \quad \text{then}$$

$$
\begin{array}{l}
\textbf{ext wr } w \\
\quad \textbf{rd } r \\
\textbf{pre } P \\
\textbf{post } Q
\end{array}
\quad \sqsubseteq \quad
\begin{array}{l}
\textbf{ext wr } w \\
\quad \textbf{rd } r \\
\quad \textbf{lc } c : C \\
\textbf{pre } P' \\
\textbf{post } Q
\end{array}
$$

c does not occur in w, P, or Q. As specifications do not occur in the final (executable) code, there are no rules for removing logical constants.

ASSIGNMENT RULES

if $\left\{\ P[w\backslash\overleftarrow{w}] \wedge w = E[w\backslash\overleftarrow{w}] \ \Rightarrow \ Q \ \right\}$ then

$$
\begin{array}{ll}
\textbf{ext wr } w & \\
\quad \textbf{rd } r & \\
\textbf{pre } P & \sqsubseteq \quad w := E \\
\textbf{post } Q &
\end{array}
$$

$$
\begin{array}{ll}
\textbf{ext wr } w & \\
\quad \textbf{rd } r & \\
\textbf{pre true} & \equiv \quad w := E \\
\textbf{post } w = E[w\backslash\overleftarrow{w}] &
\end{array}
$$

THE SEMICOLON RULES

if $\left\{ \begin{array}{c} P \Rightarrow P_1 \\ P[w\backslash\overleftarrow{w}] \wedge Q_1 \Rightarrow P_2 \\ \exists i \in State \cdot P[w\backslash\overleftarrow{w}] \wedge Q_1[w\backslash i] \wedge Q_2[\overleftarrow{w}\backslash i] \Rightarrow Q \end{array} \right\}$ then

$$
\begin{array}{lll}
& & \textbf{ext wr } w \\
& & \quad \textbf{rd } r \\
& & \textbf{pre } P_1 \\
\textbf{ext wr } w & & \textbf{post } Q_1 \\
\quad \textbf{rd } r & \sqsubseteq & ; \\
\textbf{pre } P & & \textbf{ext wr } w \\
\textbf{post } Q & & \quad \textbf{rd } r \\
& & \textbf{pre } P_2 \\
& & \textbf{post } Q_2
\end{array}
$$

For any M that does not contain hooked identifiers other than $\overleftarrow{x}$, then

$$
\begin{array}{lll}
& & \textbf{ext wr } x \\
& & \quad \textbf{rd } r, w \\
& & \textbf{pre } P \\
\textbf{ext wr } w, x & & \textbf{post } M \\
\quad \textbf{rd } r & \sqsubseteq & ; \\
\textbf{pre } P & & \textbf{ext wr } w, x \\
\textbf{post } Q & & \quad \textbf{rd } r \\
& & \quad \textbf{lc } c \\
& & \textbf{pre } M[\overleftarrow{x}\backslash c] \\
& & \textbf{post } Q[\overleftarrow{x}\backslash c]
\end{array}
$$

Following assignment

$$
\begin{array}{l}
\text{ext wr } w, x \\
\quad \text{rd } r \\
\text{pre } P \\
\text{post } Q
\end{array}
\quad \sqsubseteq \quad
\begin{array}{l}
\text{ext wr } w, x \\
\quad \text{rd } r \\
\text{pre } P \\
\text{post } Q[x \backslash E] \\
; \\
x := E
\end{array}
$$

Leading assignment

$$
\begin{array}{l}
\text{ext wr } w, x \\
\quad \text{rd } r \\
\text{pre } P[x \backslash E] \\
\text{post } Q[\overleftarrow{x} \backslash \overleftarrow{E}]
\end{array}
\quad \sqsubseteq \quad
\begin{array}{l}
x := E \\
; \\
\text{ext wr } w, x \\
\quad \text{rd } r \\
\text{pre } P \\
\text{post } Q
\end{array}
$$

where $\overleftarrow{E}$ is equivalent to $E[w, x \backslash \overleftarrow{w}, \overleftarrow{x}]$

$$
\begin{array}{l}
\text{ext wr } w, x \\
\quad \text{rd} \\
\text{pre } P \\
\text{post } Q
\end{array}
\quad \sqsubseteq \quad
\begin{array}{l}
x := f(x) \\
; \\
\text{ext wr } w, x \\
\quad \text{rd } r \\
\text{pre } P[x \backslash f^{-1}(x)] \\
\text{post } Q
\end{array}
$$

SELECTION RULES

$$
\text{if} \left\{
\begin{array}{c}
P \wedge cond \;\Rightarrow\; P_t \\
P \wedge \neg\, cond \;\Rightarrow\; P_e \\
P[w \backslash \overleftarrow{w}] \wedge cond[w \backslash \overleftarrow{w}] \wedge Q_t \;\Rightarrow\; Q \\
P[w \backslash \overleftarrow{w}] \wedge \neg\, cond[w \backslash \overleftarrow{w}] \wedge Q_e \;\Rightarrow\; Q
\end{array}
\right\}
\text{ then}
$$

$$
\begin{array}{l}
\text{ext wr } w \\
\quad \text{rd } r \\
\text{pre } P \\
\text{post } Q
\end{array}
\quad \sqsubseteq \quad
\begin{array}{l}
\text{if } cond \text{ then} \\
\quad \text{ext wr } w \\
\qquad \text{rd } r \\
\quad \text{pre } P_t \\
\quad \text{post } Q_t \\
\text{else} \\
\quad \text{ext wr } w \\
\qquad \text{rd } r \\
\quad \text{pre } P_e \\
\quad \text{post } Q_e \\
\text{end}
\end{array}
$$

$$
\begin{array}{ccl}
& & \text{if } cond \text{ then} \\
& & \quad \text{ext wr } w \\
& & \qquad \text{rd } r \\
& & \quad \text{pre } P \land cond \\
\text{ext wr } w & & \quad \text{post } Q \\
\quad \text{rd } r & & \text{else} \\
\text{pre } P & \sqsubseteq & \quad \text{ext wr } w \\
\text{post } Q & & \qquad \text{rd } r \\
& & \quad \text{pre } P \land \neg\, cond \\
& & \quad \text{post } Q \\
& & \text{end}
\end{array}
$$

THE ITERATION RULE

$$
\text{if } \left\{
\begin{array}{c}
P \;\Rightarrow\; inv \\
\neg\, guard[w\backslash\overleftarrow{w}] \land inv \land (var \lor iden) \;\Rightarrow\; Q
\end{array}
\right\} \quad \text{then}
$$

$$
\begin{array}{ccl}
& & \text{while } guard \text{ do} \\
\text{ext wr } w & & \quad \text{ext wr } w \\
\quad \text{rd } r & & \qquad \text{rd } r \\
\text{pre } P & \sqsubseteq & \quad \text{pre } guard \land inv \\
\text{post } Q & & \quad \text{post } inv \land var \\
& & \text{end}
\end{array}
$$

iden is the identity relation.

The *inv* is preserved by the body. The *guard* must be defined over the set defined by *inv*. The *var* must be both transitive and well founded over the set defined by *inv*.

A set S is well founded if every non-empty subset of S has a minimal element. If $X \subseteq S$ and $a \in X$, then a is the minimal element of X if there is no $b \in X$ such that $R(b, a)$ and $b \neq a$.

$$
\begin{array}{ccl}
& & \text{ext wr } w \\
& & \qquad \text{rd } r \\
& & \text{pre } P \\
& & \text{post } inv \\
& & \;; \\
\text{ext wr } w & & \text{while } guard \text{ do} \\
\quad \text{rd } r & & \quad \text{ext wr } w \\
\text{pre } P & \sqsubseteq & \qquad \text{rd } r \\
\text{post } inv \land \neg\, guard & & \quad \text{pre } guard \land inv \\
& & \quad \text{post } inv \land (0 \le V < \overleftarrow{V}) \\
& & \text{end}
\end{array}
$$

where $\overleftarrow{V}$ is equivalent to $V[w\backslash\overleftarrow{w}]$.

V is a variant expression. It is an integer valued expression defined over the state.

THE FUNCTION BODY RULE

$fun(x : X)\ a : A$
ext wr $w : W$
  rd $r : R$
pre P
post Q

$\sqsubseteq$

$fun(\ x : X)\ a : A$
begin
  ext wr $w : W$
       $x : X$
       $a : A$
   rd $r : R$
 pre P
 post Q
end

THE ADD VARIABLE RULE

ext wr w
  rd r
pre P
post Q

$\sqsubseteq$

dcl $x : X$;
$\ldots$
ext wr w, x
  rd r
pre P
post Q

THE EXPAND FRAME RULE

ext wr w
  rd r
pre P
post Q

$\sqsubseteq$

ext wr w, x
  rd r
pre P
post $Q \wedge x = \overleftarrow{x}$

THE CONTRACT FRAME RULE

ext wr w, x
  rd r
pre P
post Q

$\sqsubseteq$

ext wr w
  rd r
pre P
post $Q[\overleftarrow{x} \setminus x]$

INDEX

∧, *see* and

dconc, *see* sequence distributed catenation

∃, *see* existential quantifier

∀, *see* universal quantifier

⇔ , *see* equivalence

⇒ , *see* implies

∩, *see* distributed intersection

¬, *see* not

∨, *see* or

∪, *see* distributed union

∃!, *see* unique existential quantifier

abs, *see* exponentiation

+, *see* addition

⊥, *see* bottom

card, *see* set cardinality

−, *see* set difference

÷, *see* integer division

dom, *see* map domain

◁, *see* map domain restriction

◀, *see* map domain subtraction

elems, *see* sequence elements

eof, *see* end of file

=, *see* equals

floor, *see* exponentiation

$\mathcal{F}$, *see* finite power set

ft, *see* sequence front

≥, *see* greater than or equals

>, *see* greater than

hd, *see* sequence head

∈, *see* set membership

inds, *see* sequence indices

ins , *see* sequence subsequence relation

∩, *see* set intersection

ι, *see* iota operation

len, *see* sequence length

≤, *see* less than or equal

lt, *see* sequence last

<, *see* less than

∘, *see* map composition

$^{-1}$, *see* map inversion

^{i}, *see* map iteration

↦, *see* maplet constructor

∪, *see* map union

merge, *see* map merge

−, *see* subtraction

mod, *see* modulus

≠, *see* not equals

∉, *see* set membership negation

†, *see* map overwrite

+, *see* prefix add

−, *see* negation

/, *see* division

rem, *see* remainder

rng, *see* map range

▷, *see* map range restriction

▶, *see* map range subtraction

⌢, *see* sequence catenation

⊂, *see* set proper subset relation

⊆, *see* set subset relation

tl, *see* sequence tail

∪, *see* set union

↑, *see* exponentiation

×, *see* multiplication

B, *see* Boolean values

Z, *see* Integer numbers

N, *see* Natural numbers

$\mathbf{N}_1$, *see* Positive natural numbers

Q, *see* Rational numbers

R, *see* Real numbers

{ }, *see* empty map

[], *see* empty sequence

{ }, *see* empty set

…, *see* to be defined

$\xrightarrow{m}$, *see* injective map type constructor

$\xrightarrow{m}$, *see* map type constructor

440

*, *see* sequence type constructor

+, *see* non-empty sequence type constructor

-set, *see* set type constructor

→, *see* function type constructor

|, *see* union type constructor

×, *see* product type constructor

abstract machine, 118, 119, 132, 134, 137, 138, 151, 154, 164, 170, 176, 178, 182, 327, 329, 357, 358

abstract syntax, 95, 156, 160, 182, 278, 279, 281, 283, 362, 371, 382, 402

abstract syntax, translation to, 277, 367, 370–380

abstraction, 146

acceptance testing, 3, 4

addition, 422, 429

adequate, 333

air-traffic control system, 82

algorithm, 7

analysis, 33, 34

and, 11, 13, 21, 26, 404, 422, 429

and-elimination rule, 19, 22

and-introduction rule, 20

array, 6, 253, 254, 260–265, 272, 273, 333, 356

assembler, 34

assignment command, 187, 191–193, 212

assignment rule, 194, 437

associative laws, 21, 22, 28, 430

axiom, 19

backing storage, 90

bags, 71–73
    bag-count, 72
    count, 72
    dec-bag, 73
    inc-bag, 73
    ins-bag, 73
    the state, 72

block statement, 121

BNF, 110, 362

Boolean values, 47, 48, 402, 417

bottom, 24, 25, 32

bound variable, 15

built-in functions
    allocs, 414
    applys, 412
    assign, 414
    del, 414
    dispose, 268
    firstocc, 414
    front, 413
    is-disj, 58, 412
    is-permutation, 412
    is-uniques, 413
    items, 412
    last, 413
    locate, 413
    maxs, 412
    mins, 412
    new, 268
    rest, 413
    rev, 413
    squash, 413
    subl, 414

C, 108

call notation, 139

cases command semantics, 124

cash dispenser, 143, 162–181
    abort-get-amount, 173
    add-card, 177
    amount-available, 172
    below-daily-limit, 171
    cash-dispenser, 167, 175
    change-pin, 177
    command-dispatcher, 178
    complete-transaction, 170, 174
    decrease-available, 172
    delete-card, 177
    dispense-money, 169, 174
    funds-available, 171
    get-amount, 169, 174
    get-money, 179
    is-valid-card, 170
    is-valid-input, 180
    is-valid-pin, 171
    is-valid-transaction, 168
    read-command, 178
    remove-card-id, 172
    reset-limit, 177
    set-available, 172

set-card-id, 171
show-details, 178
the state, 167
update-customer-file, 171
valdiate-pin, 168
validate-card, 168, *172*
validate-pin, *173*
char, 402
chemical reactor system, 53–58
add-react, 56, 57
check-react, 57
remove-react, 56, 57
the state, 54, 56
classical logic, 25, 30
close command semantics, 131
closing files, 131
command, 121
conditional, 186, 199
commutative laws, 28
composite objects, 95–97, 99, 100, 103, 108, 411
components, 95, 403
make function, 96, 100, 101, 126, 411
selecting components, 101
selectors, 96, 97, 99, 101
concrete data structure, 35
concrete syntax, 156, 160, 283, 296, 326, 358, 362, 367, 382
concrete syntax, translation from, 277, 296
conditional choice, 124, 140
conditional command, 120
conditional command semantics, 124
confidence in correctness, 185
constant value, 104, 402
constraint, 3
constructing composite objects, 96
constructors, 110
context diagram, 135, 145, 155, 163, 166, 274

data flow, 132
data flow design, 132, 141
data flow diagram, 118, 132, 135, 138, 146, 154, 164, 166, 167, 175, 182, 277
data flow diagram semantics, 134

data invariant, 6, 9, 38, 46, 54, 62, 66, 74, 86, 89, 111–117, 332
data refinement, 245, 329
data representation, 119
data store, 133, 137
data type, 118
De Morgan's laws, 21–23
defining order, 119, 121, 138, 167, 182, 294
design, 33
design problems, 132
detailed design, 2, 3
development methodology, 185
discrete mathematics, 9, 10
distributed intersection, 53, 62, 63, 405, 421, 429
distributed union, 53, 405, 421, 429
distributive laws, 21, 22
divide and conquer strategy, 46, 135
division, 422, 429
division problem, 184–185, 208–210, 227–232
div, 184, 208, *210*, 228
fast algorithm, 227
documentation, 4
domain, 68, 70
domain rule, 257, 434
down loop, 221–224, 232, 233, 243

editor, 274–392
add-line, 307, 333, *344*, 344
block-copy, 305, 333, 341, *344*
block-move, 306, 334, 351, *352*, *355*
block-move-left, 352
block-move-right, 352
buffer-to-file, 293
change-line, 307, 334, *345*, 345
command-specification, *373*
concrete syntax, 360, 361
delete-end, 305, 334, 346, *351*
Editor, 277, 294, 384, 387
eval-base, 284
eval-block-spec, 284
eval-line-spec, 284
execute-command, *296*, *327*
execute-copy, 287, 314, *315*
execute-current, 289, 318, *319*
execute-delete, 288, 315, 385, 386

execute-display, 289, *319*, 319
execute-edit, 292, 324, *324*
execute-find, 289, *320*, 320
execute-insert, 287, *314*, 387
execute-move, 288, 316, *318*
execute-quit, 293
execute-show, 289, *319*, 319
execute-substitute, 290, 320, *322*
execute-undo, 385
execute-write, 293, 325, *325*
expression, 372
file-to-buffer, 293
filename, 379
generate-temp-name, 326
get-ch, 379
init-buffer, 308, 335
initialize, 297
input, 376
is-line-in-doc, 290
is-range-in-doc, 290
line-definition, 371
line-number, 372
main control structure, 295, 381
no-overlap, 291
number, 378
parse-command, 295
pattern, 378
pointers-of, 332
process-command, 370
process-copy-command, 374
process-delete-command, 374
process-insert-command, 375
read-command, 295, 379
read-line, 307, 333, *345*, 345
read-token, 376
reverse, 352, *355*
separator, 379
size, 291
string, 378
sub, 291
sub-doc, 291
subst, 291
suppy-defaults, 375
terminate, 297
Text, 332
undo-delete, 386
undo-insert, 387
wf-block-spec, 284

wf-copy-command, 282
wf-display-command, 283
wf-insert-command, 282
wf-line-spec, 284
wf-move-command, 282
wf-show-command, 283
editor concrete syntax
    block specification, 361
    char, 362
    command, 361
    command specification, 361
    copy, 361
    current, 361
    delete, 361
    delim, 362
    digit, 362
    display, 361
    edit, 361
    expression, 361
    fchar, 362
    file name, 362
    find, 361
    input, 376
    insert, 361
    line definition, 361
    line number, 361
    line specification, 361
    move, 361
    number, 362
    pattern, 362
    quit, 361
    separator, 362
    show, 361
    sign, 361
    space, 362
    string, 362
    substitute, 361
    token, 362
    write, 361
empty map, 409, 423
empty sequence, 83, 84, 407, 423
empty set, 48, 49, 405, 423
empty stack, 87
end of file, 131, 429
enumerated type, 104
eof predicate semantics, 132
equals, 422, 429

equivalence, 12, 13, 20, 22, 27, 404, 422, 429

equivalence-introduction rule, 20

equivalence operator, 12, 13, 22

equivalence rule of inference, 22

equivalence-transitivity rule, 20

equivalent specifications, 187–190, 193

execution meaning of VDM-SL, 120

existential quantification, 9, 18

existential quantifier, 16, 18, 404, 422

exponentiation, 421, 422, 429

expression evaluation, 191

external abstract syntax, 279, 285, 296, 358, 360, 380

factorial problem, 216–221, 224–225

    factorial, 216, 218, 224, 225

file handler, 90–93

    bqadd, 92

    bqenough, 93

    bqinitialize, 93

    bqremove, 92

    the state, 91

file operations

    close, 131

    eof, 131

    open, 130, 131

    read, 129

    write, 130

finding loop invariants, 224

finite power set, 51, 405, 421, 429

first-in-first-out store, 86

flow charts, 3

following assignment rule, 219

formal proof, 32

forward Polish, 109

frame, 189, 196, 197, 203

function, 2, 72, 79

function type constructor, 430

functional specification, 34, 38, 115

graphical notation, 143

greater than, 422, 429

greater than or equals, 422, 429

heap, 330

high-level design, 143

high-level programming, 1

implementation strategies, 380

implication-elimination rule, 20, 22

implication operator, 12, 13

implication-transitivity rule, 20

implies, 12, 13, 20, 21, 27, 404, 422, 429

increase in confidence, 299

indexed files, 128

infinite set, 50

injective map type constructor, 417, 430

input, 127, 292

input files, 129

input/output, 127

input/output model, 129

integer division, 422, 429

Integer numbers, 47, 48, 402, 417

integration testing, 4

internal abstract syntax, 285, 290, 296, 358

iota operation, 422

iteration, 120, 124, 140, 201

law of contradiction, 21, 22

law of double negation, 20, 23

law of equality, 21

law of implication, 21

law of negation, 21, 22

law of the excluded middle, 21, 22

laws of *and* simplification, 21

laws of or simplification, 21

leading assignment rule, 219

less than, 422, 429

less than or equal, 422, 429

levelling, 135

library, 143–155

    add-book, 152

    book-info, 154

    borow-book, 152

    copies, 154

    delete-book, 152

    is-on-shelf, 153

    Library, 150

    list-by-author, 153

    list-by-title, 153

    list-on-loan, 154

    on-loan, 150

    return-book, 152

    the state, 150

linear search, 7

linked list, 6, 7, 108
logic, 10, 11
logic of partial functions, 20, 25, 32
logical constant, 212, 213, 243
logical operator, 404
loop development tactics, 217, 221
loop guard, 200, 221
loop invariant, 185, 200, 201, 206, 216–218, 221, 224, 342
loop tactics, 224, 244
loop termination, 185, 201
loop variant, 200, 201, 342
LPF
    see logic of partial functions, 20

make function, 39
map, 67, 69, 70, 72, 77
map composition, 410, 422, 428
map domain, 69, 409, 421, 429
map domain restriction, 70, 409, 422, 429
map domain subtraction, 70, 409, 422, 429
map inversion, 409
map iteration, 410, 422, 428
map merge, 409, 421, 429
map operator, 409
map overwrite, 70, 409, 422, 429
map range, 69, 409, 421, 429
map range restriction, 410, 422, 429
map range subtraction, 410, 422, 429
map type, 403
map type constructor, 417, 430
map union, 409, 422, 429
maplet, 68
maplet constructor, 68–70
maps, 103
mathematical proof, 25, 41
message queue, 88–90
    addq, 89
    inv-Numqueue, 90
    numinq, 89
    removeq, 89
    the state, 88, 89
message stack, 86–88
    inv-Message-stack, 87
    leng, 88
    pop, 87

    popn, 88
    push, 88
    the state, 86
Meta-IV, 36
miracle, 188
module, 3, 4
modulus, 422, 429
multiplication, 422, 429
multiply problem, 202–208, 210–212, 226–227
    mult, 202, 207
    posmult, 205, 210
    posmult-body, 211, 226

natural language, 4, 5, 57
Natural numbers, 14, 47, 48, 402, 417
natural numbers, 17, 48
negation, 421, 429
nil, 105, 403
non-empty sequence type constructor, 417, 430
non-executable program, 188
non-functional requirement, 7
not, 13, 21, 27, 404, 421, 429
not equals, 422, 429
null pointer, 108

object-oriented design, 1, 119, 137, 142
open command, 130
open command semantics, 131
opening files, 130
operating system, 1, 76, 82, 90, 111, 113
operations, 125
operator grouping, 430
operator precedence, 12, 13, 428
option brackets, 105, 108
optional type, 105
optional value, 108
or, 13, 20, 21, 26, 404, 422, 429
or-introduction rule, 20, 22
order of operations, 119, 121, 138–140
output, 127, 286
output command semantics, 130
output files, 130

parsing, 382
partial function, 43
Pascal, 74, 104, 108, 191, 263, 391

patern-matching, 155
pattern binding, 122
pattern identifier, 126
pattern matching, 100, 127
pattern-matching, 143
    eval-pattern, 158, 159
    eval-patterns, 158
    is-matched, 156
    scan-file, 156, 159
    scan-text, 159
    the state, 155
patterns, 126
pointers, 108, 267, 268, 272, 330
post-condition, 6, 7, 9, 36, 37, 45, 46, 56,
    65, 66, 73, 116, 120, 125
pre-condition, 6, 9, 36, 37, 45, 46, 55, 56,
    66, 116, 120, 125
precedence, *see* operator precedence, 11
predicate, 10
predicate calculus, 10
predicate calculus operators, 11
prefix add, 421, 429
procedure, 3, 4
process, 132, 133, 137
product type constructor, 417, 430
program correctness, 383
program design languages, 3
program execution, 186
program language definitions, 186
program proof, 184, 185
program refinement, 189, 191
program termination, 188
program testing, 183
programming, 2
programming language, 45
programs as specifications, 193
proof, 33
proof by induction, 28
proof obligation, 46
proper subset, 49
propositional operator, 404

quality assurance, 4, 35
quantified expression, 15, 16
queue, 88, 90, 111
quote type, 104

range, 68

range rule, 258, 434
Rational numbers, 47, 48, 402, 417
reactor management system, 38–43
    check-closed, 41
    close-down, 39
    close-down-all, 40
    no-shut-down, 40
    start-up, 40
read command semantics, 129, 130
Real numbers, 47, 48, 417
real-time system, 1, 82
record constructor, 97, 411
record library, 73–76
    borrow, 75
    return, 75
    the state, 74
record modifier, 102
recursive data types, 108
recursive definition, 45
recursive function, 80
refinement by assignment, 192, 193
refinement by semicolon, 194, 203
refinement by the conditional command,
    197
refinement by the while loop command,
    199, 205
relation, 36
remainder, 422, 429
representing an expression, 109
requirements analysis, 2
retrieve function, 296, 333, 382, 383, 386,
    388
rules of inference, 10, 19, 22, 29
rules of precedence, *see* operator prece-
    dence

safety-critical system, 28
satisfy, 183
satisfying a specification, 185, 186, 188,
    189
search problem, 238–242
    find-entry, 239, *242*
searching, 238, 242
semicolon, 120, 186, 194
semicolon combinator, 120
sequence, 82, 94, 140
sequence catenation, 84, 408, 422, 429

sequence distributed catenation, 408, 421, 429

sequence elements, 84, 407, 421, 429

sequence front, 407, 415, 421

sequence head, 83, 407, 421

sequence indices, 84, 407, 421, 429

sequence last, 407, 415, 421

sequence length, 83, 407, 421

sequence operator, 407

sequence rule, 196, 209

sequence subsequence relation, 408, 415, 422

sequence tail, 84, 407, 421

sequence type constructor, 83, 417, 430

sequences, 103

sequential files, 128

set, 6, 14, 47, 48, 50, 67, 110

set cardinality, 6, 53, 405, 421, 429

set comprehension, 36, 50–52

set difference, 52, 406, 422, 429

set inclusion, 49

set intersection, 52, 63, 406, 422, 429

set membership, 48, 406, 422, 429

set membership negation, 48, 406, 422, 429

set operator, 405

set proper subset relation, 49, 406, 422, 429

set subset relation, 49, 406, 422, 429

set type constructor, 417, 430

set union, 52, 56, 406, 422, 429

sets, 103

side effects, 191

simple banking system, 43–46
    credit, 44
    debit, 45
    newcustomer, 44
    sumof, 45
    the state, 43
    totalfunds, 45

simple filing subsystem, 76–81
    consistent-free-storage, 80
    count-files, 79
    create-file, 78
    delete-file, 78
    no-duplicate-names, 80
    no-shared-blocks, 80
    the state, 77
    user-owns, 80

simple library system, 58–60
    add-book, 60
    borrow-book, 58
    missing-book, 59
    no-of-borrowed, 59
    not-missing-book, 59
    return-book, 59
    the state, 58

simplified cash dispenser, 245–263
    add-card, 247, 256
    delete-card, 247
    is-ordered, 253
    is-ordered-array, 261
    is-valid-amount, 246, 256, 262
    is-valid-card, 246, 255, 258, 262
    is-valid-pin, 246, 255, 262
    set-card, 246, 255, 259, 262
    state, 245
    update-customer-file, 247, 256, 262
    used, 256

singleton set, 6, 48

sink, 133

software tools, 1

sort problem, 232–238
    sort, 232, 233, *235*, 235, *238*

sorting, 232, 233, 235, 238

source, 133

specification, 35
    miracle, 188
    reasoning about, 386
    swop, 196

specification language semantics, 127

specification notation, 5

specification, properties of, 298

specifications, reasoning about, 299, 300

stack, 86–88, 263–272
    collect-address, 269
    init, 263, 265, 269
    is-empty, 264, 266, 271
    is-full, 264, 266, 271
    pop, 264, 266, 270
    push, 264, 265, 270
    size, 271
    top, 264, 266, 270

state, 36, 37, 46, 61, 73, 77, 118

state designator, 123

statement of requirements, 2, 34, 54, 58, 61
static meaning of VDM-SL, 120
stepwise refinement, 186, 194, 197, 199, 210, 357, 380
stock control system, 5, 35
structure chart, 118, 138, 139, 182, 277
structure diagram, 119
structured design, 132, 141
subroutine, 3, 4, 35
subset, 68
substitution, 189
subtraction, 422, 429
symbol table, 6, 7, 34, 111, 114
system design, 1–5, 10
system specification, 2–5, 9, 10, 19, 34, 67
system specification notation, 9
system testing, 3, 4
systems analysis, 34

temporary variables, 221
text files, 128
theorem, 19, 23, 29, 33
thesaurus, 60–65
    add-word, 64
    count-word, 65
    find-word, 65
    remove-word, 64
    the state, 63
three-valued logic, 10
to be defined, 77
token, 103, 402
tokens, 361, 376
top-level specification, 7
transitive relation, 201, 206, 207
tree data structure, 108, 109
truth table, 11, 26, 27
type, 110
type aliasing, 106, 402
type constructors, 95, 110, 403
type invariant, 97
type name, 106
type renaming, 106, 402
type union operator, 104, 106, 403

union, 6
union operator, 6

union type constructor, 417, 430
unique existential quantifier, 404, 422
unit testing, 4
universal quantifier, 15–18, 404, 422
up loop, 221, 223, 224, 243
user requirements, 4

validation, 2, 3, 115, 116
validation activities, 3
VDM, 10, 23, 37, 41, 45, 46, 66, 79
VDM-SL concrete syntax
    applicator, 428
    apply expression, 424
    arithmetic infix operator, 422
    arithmetic prefix operator, 421
    assign command, 123, 419
    basic type, 402, 417
    binary expression, 422
    bind, 126, 425
    bind list, 422
    bind statement, 122, 419
    block statement, 121, 419
    Boolean literal, 427
    bracketed expression, 420
    bracketed type, 417
    cases choice, 124, 419
    cases choice list, 124, 419
    cases command, 124, 419
    cases expression, 421
    cases expression alternative, 421
    cases expression alternatives, 421
    character, 426
    character literal, 402, 427
    choice expression, 420
    close command, 131, 420
    collection type, 417
    combinator, 428
    command, 121, 418
    command list, 121, 419
    comment, 427
    composite type, 403, 417
    compound delimiter, 427
    conditional command, 124, 419
    conditional expression, 420
    connectives, 429
    dcl definition, 121, 419
    dcl definition list, 121, 419
    declare statement, 121, 419

default command, 124, 419
definition block, 416
definition statement, 123, 419
delimiter, 427
delimiter character, 426
digit, 426
distinguished letter, 426
document, 416
elsif command, 124, 419
elsif expression, 421
empty literal, 427
empty map , 423
empty sequence, 423
empty set, 423
equals definition, 123, 419
equals definition list, 123, 419
error command, 125, 419
evaluator, 428
existential quantified expression, 404, 422
exponent, 427
expression, 420
expression list, 420
expression preamble, 420
field, 417
field list, 417
field reference, 123, 424
field select, 411, 424
file prefix operator, 421
first character, 427
frame, 125, 418
function apply, 424
function body, 418
function definition, 418
function definition list, 418
function definitions, 418
function infix combinator, 422
function parameters, 418
function signature, 418
function type, 418
general map type, 403, 417
Greek letters, 426
identifier, 427
identifier list, 121, 424
identifier type pair, 125, 418
identity command, 125, 419
infix operator, 422
initialization, 417

injective map type, 403, 417
input command, 420
input output command, 420
input output expression, 131
invariant, 417
iota expression, 422
is basic type, 427
is expression, 424
keyword, 427
keyword letter, 426
lambda expression, 424
let be statement, 122, 419
let expression, 420
let st expression, 420
let statement, 122, 419
logical infix operator, 404, 422
logical prefix operator, 404, 421
map apply, 410, 424
map comprehension, 409, 423
map enumeration, 409, 423
map expression, 423
map infix combinator, 422
map infix operator, 422
map postfix operator, 421
map prefix operator, 421
map reference, 123, 424
map type, 417
maplet, 423
maplet list, 423
match value, 126, 425
mode, 125, 418
name, 424
newline, 426
nil literal, 427
numeral, 427
numeric literal, 427
old identifier, 424
open command, 130, 420
operation body, 125, 418
operation call, 125, 419
operation definition, 125, 418
operation definition list, 125, 418
operation definitions, 125, 418
operation heading, 125, 418
optional type, 403, 417
other characters, 426
others expression, 421
output command, 130, 420

parameter list, 418
parameter types, 125, 418
parameters, 418
pattern, 126, 425
pattern bind, 126, 425
pattern identifier, 126, 425
pattern list, 126, 425
pattern type pair list, 125, 418
plain letter, 426
pointer type, 417
postfix expression, 421
postfix operator, 421
prefix expression, 421
prefix operator, 421
product type, 403, 417
quantified expression, 422
quote literal, 427
quote type, 402, 417
read command, 129
record constructor, 423
record expression, 411, 423
record modification, 423
record modification list, 423
record modifier, 411, 423
record pattern, 126, 425
relation, 429
relational infix operator, 422
remaining characters, 427
return command, 125, 419
separator, 426
seq type, 403, 417
seq0 type, 403, 417
seq1 type, 403, 417
sequence apply, 408, 424
sequence catenation pattern, 126, 425
sequence comprehension, 407, 423
sequence enumeration, 407, 423
sequence enumeration pattern, 126, 425
sequence expression, 423
sequence infix operator, 408, 422
sequence pattern, 126, 425
sequence prefix operator, 407, 421
sequence reference, 123, 424
set bind, 126, 425
set comprehension, 405, 423
set enumeration, 405, 423
set enumeration pattern, 126, 425

set expression, 423
set infix operator, 406, 422
set pattern, 126, 425
set prefix operator, 405, 421
set range expression, 405, 423
set relational operator, 422
set type, 403, 417
set union pattern, 126, 425
specification, 125, 418
specification command, 125, 420
state definition, 417
state designator, 123, 424
state designator list, 123, 419
subsequence expression, 407, 423
such that bind, 122, 419
such that bind list, 122, 419
symbol, 427
symbolic literal, 427
text literal, 427
text of a specification, 425, 427
tuple constructor, 423
tuple expression, 423
tuple pattern, 126, 425
type, 416
type bind, 126, 425
type bind list, 424
type definition, 416
type definitions, 416
type name, 402, 417
unary expression, 421
undefined expression, 424
union type, 403, 417
unique quantified expression, 422
universal quantified expression, 404, 422
value definition, 122, 417
value definition list, 122, 419
value definitions, 417
var information, 125, 418
while loop command, 124, 419
white space, 426
verification, 2–4
Vienna Development Method, 36, 47

well formed conditions, 281, 296
well founded, 201, 207
while loop command, 120, 186
while loop command semantics, 124